MW00608753

The Gold House

"The Discovery"

by

John Clarence

~

With Tom Whittle

"...Man, proud man, dress'd in a little brief authority, most ignorant of
what he's most assur'd, his glassy essence, like an angry ape, plays such fantastic tricks
before high heaven, as make the angels weep..."
William Shakespeare – Measure for Measure

Disclaimer

Except where specifically noted or otherwise clearly indicated in context, the views, statements and opinions expressed in this book are solely those of the author and do not necessarily reflect those of the descendants of Ova and Doc Noss, their attorneys, agents or other representatives, or those of the Ova Noss Family Partnership, its affiliates or successors in interest, or its members, attorneys, agents or other representatives.

Soledad Publishing, Las Cruces, NM 88004
Soledad Publishing Company is a Limited Liability Corporation

First Soledad Publishing hardcover edition February 2013

Noss family photographs are provided by Terry Delonas.
Other photos used are in the public domain or otherwise credited.

FIRST EDITION

The Gold House—The Discovery
An Eco-Friendly Green Book
Printed in the United States of America by Thomson-Shore, Inc.

Book Design by Business Graphics
Cover by Greg Doramus

FIRST EDITION - Includes publication credits and Index

1 2 3 4 5 6 7 8 9 0 9 8 7 6 5 4 3 2 1

PUBLISHERS CATALOGING-IN-PUBLICATION DATA
Clarence, John.
The Gold House– The Discovery / by John Clarence. – 1st ed.
Las Cruces, NM: Soledad Publishing, c2011.
p. ; cm.
(*Gold House* trilogy; 1)
ISBN: 978-0-9834025 -0- 3 (hardcover)
Includes bibliographical references and index.
1. Treasure troves-- New Mexico-- Victorio Peak. 2. Treasure troves--New Mexico --White Sands Missile Range. 3. Victorio Peak
(N.M.)-- Gold discoveries. 4. Noss, Doc, d. 1949. 5. Noss, Babe, d. 1979. 6. Adventure and adventurers -- New Mexico-- Biography.
I. Title. II. Series.
F802.D6 C53 2011
978.9/ 66-dc22 1107

- Synopsis -
<u>The Gold House</u> Trilogy

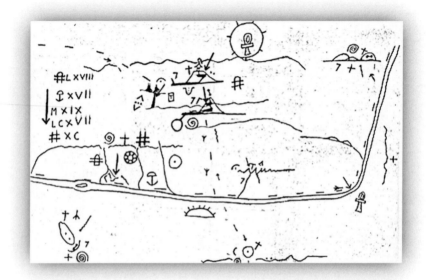

The three books of *The Gold House* tell the story of a hidden treasure, one of important historical significance and tremendous value. Its existence was first uncovered on November 7, 1937 within a rugged desert hill called Victorio Peak located on what is known today as White Sands Missile Range. With the onset of World War II, the Tularosa Basin, which lay directly east of the site, became a weapons testing area, which the military named White Sands Proving Ground. By the mid-1950s the area was renamed White Sands Missile Range and was expanded further westward beyond the San Andres Mountain Range, which included Victorio Peak. That's when the trouble began.

The first book of the trilogy, <u>*The Gold House, The Discovery*</u>, reveals the well-documented true story of Doc and Ova Noss, the discoverers and legal owners of a treasure they found inside Victorio Peak. Doc and Ova were extraordinary individuals; after finding the treasure, they endured a hostile environment most others could not have tolerated. In spite of being maligned and ridiculed by individuals in the military and the Treasury Department, they held fast to their position that they were the true owners of the treasure. Most of the ridicule was targeted at Doc, who had a propensity to drink, and did so heavily at times when he came under pressure with matters dealing with the treasure.

The treasure was discovered soon after Doc and Ova began camping for extended periods in Hembrillo Basin in a stone structure, perhaps a century or more old, which they called the *"rock house."* There they slept, hunted for wild game, cooked their meals, drew water from a nearby spring, and explored for treasure. The ancient map shown here eventually led Doc to the treasure site.

As primitive as the map is, the San Andres Mountains, the *"Bloody Hands"* site, Geronimo Peak, Victorio Peak, Hembrillo Basin, the western rim of the Basin, the Organ Mountain Range, the Caballo Mountain Range, and the Rio Grande are all clearly identifiable. The story of how Doc came upon the map is covered in book one of the trilogy. The landmarks described here all played their roles in the Victorio Peak saga, including accounts of a number of individuals who had also discovered Spanish treasure in the Caballo Mountains.

It was Doc and Ova Noss who time and history have recognized as the first and true discoverers of the Victorio Peak treasure, but time and history have not served them well. In the end, Doc's business partner, Charley Ryan, murdered him over a gold transaction gone wrong. The most-remembered photo of Doc shows his limp body slumped against the bumper of Ryan's truck. In Ryan's murder trial the presiding judge, William Scoggin, was a business partner in Doc's Cheyenne Mining Company. Another partner of Doc's in the same agreement was Benjamin Newell, who became Ryan's defense attorney. Gold was placed on the table and Ryan was acquitted.

Ova spent years trying to raise the treasure, but in 1955 she was forcibly removed from her claim by the military. Her story carries on into the beginning of the second book of the trilogy, *The Gold House, The Lies, The Thefts.* It was then that new names and new faces crept onto the scene; seven military people who maintained the gold belonged to them formed an association called the "Seven Heirs." On September 5, 1961, Leonard Fiege and Tom Berlett, two members of the group, were given polygraph examinations to determine if they had found the treasure. From the examiner's reports, in part:

> *Did you find [gold] bricks in a cave in the San Andres Mountains in November? Yes. Is your statement concerning the finding of the bricks completely true? Yes. Did Berlett also see these bricks in the cave? Yes.*

The polygraph examinations conducted on Fiege and Berlett proved they had seen part of the treasure Doc and Ova Noss had found decades earlier. Eventually, the commanding general at White Sands and one of his aides were caught lying to the Bureau of Land Management, denying the military was searching for the treasure. But they were, and they found it, and in 1961 individuals at White Sands Missile Range began to remove the gold.

The crimes committed by those involved during the 1960s were powder kegs waiting to explode. Fiege and Berlett set the stage when they rediscovered the Noss treasure. In spite of the public notoriety the treasure story was receiving, Leland Howard, Director of Silver & Gold Operations at the U.S. Mint, allowed Major General John Shinkle, commanding general at White Sands, to continue excavating the treasure site. Shinkle, drawn into the scandal because of his own devices, lied to New Mexico officials, denying the military had been excavating the site, claiming such rumors were a "myth."

In 1963 the military finally allowed an expedition to be conducted at the Noss treasure site. The expedition was permitted to forward the concept that the military had not excavated the site in the early 1960s, when a large amount of the Noss gold was removed. The 1963 excavation, a tightly controlled hard rock mining effort, was conducted under the sponsorship of the Museum of New Mexico with Gaddis Mining Company doing the excavation work. But there was more to the final outcome of the Gaddis expedition than was made public. Even before the operation began, the commanding general at White Sands, General Shinkle, had allegedly removed 700 gold bars from the site. According to a witness, William Gaddis had hired "a European investigative firm with access to numbered Swiss accounts." Gaddis was reportedly "satisfied" with the information that Shinkle had removed the 700 gold bars, but chose not to pursue the matter.

Nineteen months after the Gaddis/Museum search had ended, proof of wrongdoing came in an official report on the results of the exploration by Chester R. Johnson Jr., a credentialed Museum of New Mexico archeologist and cartographer; his report had been significantly altered to exclude all information that underscored the Army's past involvement in illegal operations at the Noss treasure site. This investigation shows that Colonel Richard E. Wade and others conspired to alter Johnson's report so that it would not accurately portray Shinkle's and the military's past activities at the treasure site. A letter dated November 8, 1963, from Robert K. Alexander, Curator of Salvage Archaeology, to Colonel Wade spelled out the arrangement. In part:

> *Dear Colonel Wade: Enclosed please find a manuscript of Mr. Johnson's report on the Gaddis Mining operation. We would appreciate your censoring this for any information that you would not like to have included. We would also appreciate the return of this manuscript, as soon as possible, since we are overdue in our obligations to the other agencies involved.*   —*Robert K. Alexander*

The letter told the story; a museum official conspired with White Sands military officials to alter a public document, one that was *not* paid for by the Army, a report voluntarily surrendered to the military on a *quid pro quo* arrangement, a pre-designed plot set up to cloak all prior military activity at the treasure site.

In 1973 operations were under way at the Pentagon and White Sands Missile Range to conduct yet another controlled search. The glowing embers of past-related issues and the throngs of individuals and groups who still claimed ownership to the gold inside Victorio Peak were intensifying, so much so that they, with the assistance of their attorneys, including F. Lee Bailey, mounted a formidable task force to pressure White Sands to allow another search. This time it was called Operation Goldfinder. It was targeted for 1977.

Before Operation Goldfinder began, however, another string of events unfolded at White Sands Missile Range that trumped any prior theft from the treasure, a theft that dispelled any past claim by the commanding generals at White Sands that there had never been any gold inside Victorio Peak, or niches of gold nearby, placed there by Doc Noss in the 1940s.

The events began during the first week of November 1973 when three Secret Service agents traveled to Arrey, New Mexico, and met with a man named Fred Drolte at a private residence to arrange a meeting with Richard Nixon. If the meeting between Drolte and Nixon took place, it apparently occurred on Sunday, November 18, 1973, at Biggs Army Airfield on Fort Bliss, Texas. Although his claim remains unverified, Drolte allegedly met with Nixon in a small jet and was given a key that opened a gate west of the treasure site.

Three days later, on Wednesday, November 21, 1973, the day before Thanksgiving, Drolte drove his military surplus 6x6 truck to Victorio Peak. When he left the site five days later on Sunday, November 25, 1973, 36.5 tons of gold had been removed. What followed was page after page of contracts, letters, warehouse receipts, bank letters, assay reports and a myriad of FBI reports and government documents—a trail of evidence detailing a theft of nearly $1.8 billion (at today's prices) in gold. The trail of evidence began to unravel the day after the theft operation ended. Letters and FBI documents show that on Monday morning, November 26, 1973, an attorney named David T. Austern, a "tipster," had called George Brazier at the Office of the Assistant Secretary of the Army to inform him that 37 tons of gold was taken from White Sands Missile Range over the holiday weekend. The names of the individuals involved were given to the FBI, but because they were "mere allegations" they were never interviewed. Austern today is president and general counsel of the Manville Trust, formed to settle personal injury claims stemming from exposure to asbestos products. When questioned about details of the November 1973 telephone call, Austern said he did not remember the call.

The trail of the gold theft began on December 3, 1973, when Lawrence Systems Inc., a warehousing company, issued five lots of warehouse receipts to Mark IV and Associates and International Smelting & Refining Company, both companies owned by Kenneth Meadows, a key figure in the Thanksgiving weekend gold theft and other dealings.

These five warehouse receipts, numbered 16077, 16078, 16080, 16081 and 16082, were the documented record of a number of steel drums that contained gold dory bars and artifacts removed to and stored at Lawrence's 421½ Hickox Street location in Santa Fe. The business office of Lawrence Systems was located in the same office building owned by the First National Bank of

Albuquerque, the bank that FBI reports indicate was involved in handling and moving the gold.

That same day, International Smelting & Refining Company turned around and issued warehouse receipt numbers 16080 and 16082 to Mark IV Associates. Mark IV Associates, also holding warehouse receipts numbers 16077, 16078 and 16081, issued by Lawrence Systems, turned all receipts over to the bank, which took physical possession of them.

By now, an FBI investigation was under way and three days later, on December 6, 1973, FBI Director Clarence Kelley was informed in an Albuquerque Airtel report that Lieutenant Colonel Raymond Armstrong had suspected that F. Lee Bailey had hired someone to "embarrass" the military at White Sands. The same day an Albuquerque FBI letterhead memorandum gave vague details of the holiday weekend theft in a report of little substance.

A week went by and on December 13, 1973, Director Kelley received a summary of activities in another FBI Albuquerque Airtel report that included a request for Brazier to identify the "tipster." Two weeks passed and on December 28, 1973, Kelley was given information that General Sweeney had learned David Austern had tipped off Brazier about the break-in.

By January 9, 1974, Las Cruces Resident FBI Agent Herb Greathouse wrote a letter that described trucks hauling 37 tons of gold "ingots" and "artifacts." The letter named: International Smelting & Refining Company, the First National Bank of Albuquerque and its bank officers "Mr. Morgan" and "Joseph Casey," Handy & Harmon, Paul Henson [alias alleged CIA asset Lloyd Tucker], David Austern and his clients Ed Atkins and William Shriver, and Gordon Hobbs at the Pentagon. That same day, the first of nine agreements involving Mark IV Associates, Pyramid Enterprises and the First National Bank of Albuquerque made reference to certain Lawrence System warehouse receipts: 16077, 16078, 16080, 16081 and 16082 which, according to the first agreement, were valued at $1,328,043. The agreement provided for a $300,000 loan to Kenneth Meadows from First National Bank of Albuquerque and a $1,000,000 letter of credit to collateralize the loan. It also stipulated that Meadows was to instruct Handy & Harmon to deliver the gold "bar stock" to Standard Safe Deposit Company in New York. Individuals party to the first agreement were: Kenneth D. Meadows as President of Mark IV Associates, Simon Ashley Smith as Authorized Representative of Pyramid Enterprises Inc., c/o Mellon Bank International, (Attention Barry Wohl, Executive Vice President), Joseph P. Casey as Vice President of First National Bank in Albuquerque, and J. J. Thompson as "Secretary" and Toni Thomas as Notary Public as attested to on February 13, 1974.

On January 10, 1974, certificates of insurance were issued to Pyramid Enterprises c/o Mellon Bank International by American National General Agencies. International Smelting & Refining Company was the "Assured" on the policies. The insurance companies were Lloyd's and Company, Yosemite Insurance, and Reserve Insurance Company.

Five days later, on January 15, 1974, the Washington Field Office provided FBI Director Kelley with more evidence that connected 37 tons of gold ingots, International Smelting & Refining Company, First National Bank of Albuquerque, certain bank officials, and Handy & Harmon, a California refinery. Then, one week later, on January 21, 1974, the second agreement was executed that amended the January 9, 1974 agreement, allowing Credit Suisse Bank, Chample Branch in Geneva, Switzerland, to become party to the first agreement. There were many other recitals in the agreement. Kenneth D. Meadows as President of Mark IV Associates, Simon Ashley Smith as Authorized Representative of Pyramid Enterprises Inc., Joseph P. Casey as Vice President for First National Bank in Albuquerque and J. J. Thompson as "Secretary," signed the second amendment. Notary Public Toni Thomas attested to the signatures on February 13, 1974.

The third agreement, executed on January 21, 1974, between Pyramid Enterprises, as Assignor, and Credit Suisse, a Swiss banking organization as Assignee, collateralized the $1,000,000.00 letter of credit called for in the first agreement. Credit Suisse held and acknowledged receipt of Lawrence Systems' warehouse receipts 16077, 16078, 16080, 16081 and 16082 in accordance with the terms and provisions of the January 9, 1974 amended agreement. These warehouse receipts were provided to Lawrence Systems by Mark IV Associates the same day, but prior to signing the agreement. Simon Ashley Smith signed for Pyramid Enterprises. A signature line was provided for Credit Suisse. Also on that day, and as a condition of the third agreement, First National Bank of Albuquerque provided Lawrence Systems with the original warehouse receipts dated December 3, 1973, which were stored at 421½ Hickox Street, Santa Fe. The bank, being the "receipt holder," directed Lawrence Systems to reissue certificates in the name of Pyramid Enterprises as "holder" and mail originals to Credit Suisse, Chample Branch, Geneva, Switzerland. That very day, January 21, 1974, FBI Director Kelley was told that the alleged gold theft was "nothing more than a play on a Spanish treasure story with little or no merit."

The following day, January 22, an Albuquerque FBI letterhead memorandum told of David Austern's role in telling the FBI Washington Field Office details of the story, information that had the effect of steering the investigation away from the Handy & Harmon refinery.

Just eight days later, on January 30, 1974, Austern provided Shriver with a list of companies holding export licenses to "sell gold abroad." Handy & Harmon was listed. Two weeks later, on February 14, 1974, Valley Agri-Services sent an assay to Credit Suisse Bank referencing Berkley/Pyramid Enterprises, Mark IV Associates, International Smelting & Refining Company, and "Code:" Lloyd Henson [an alias for Lloyd Tucker].

On March 5, 1974, a fraudulent Department of the Army inquiry was held at White Sands Missile Range by invitation only. On March 11, 1974, Bland West and Gordon Hobbs produced a misleading report on the March 5, 1974 inquiry. That same day the fourth agreement described the stolen gold as "sponge" gold, a gold-bearing emulsion formed by refining gold electronically, which was false. The next day, March 12, 1974, a fifth agreement, an amendment, was signed that furthered the money laundering process. Two days later, on March 14, 1974, FBI Director Kelley was given blatantly false information on an Albuquerque Letterhead Memorandum concerning the March 5, 1974, inquiry. On April 1, 1974, the sixth, seventh, and eighth agreements were signed; the eighth agreement "escrowed" the laundered money and "certain documents" at the Riggs National Bank in Washington, across the street from the Nixon White House.

Two days later, on April 3, 1974, William Shriver, the true owner of Pyramid Enterprises, signed the ninth agreement. Simon John Ashley Smith, a London-based gold dealer, also signed the agreement as "Authorized Signatory" for Berkley Enterprises. Ed Atkins, an oilman from Decatur, Illinois, and David Austern, witnessed the document. Three years later, on March 31, 1977, a reporter from the *El Paso Herald-Post* interviewed Atkins when he and Shriver visited Victorio Peak during Operation Goldfinder. From the article, in part:

> ..."*A Decatur, Illinois man, [Atkins] representing several people, says he had a bill of sale to prove the treasure being sought at Victorio Peak belongs to them...*"

Interviewed in 2012, David Austern said, "Ashley Smith, who was not a client of mine, had some kind of connection with Credit Suisse." He cited one deal where Ashley Smith was arranging for $1 million in 1978 or 1979 dollars which, Austern said, "I guess would be worth about $10 million today."

"Ashley Smith had access through Credit Suisse to some really heavy investors," Austern said. "He apparently had unfettered access to the Swiss." Austern recalled that Atkins and Shriver had a business relationship with Kenneth Meadows, but expressed surprise that his own name appeared on the series of agreements that dealt with the 37 tons of gold.

Betty Tucker claimed that her husband, Lloyd, and Simon John Ashley Smith, were lifelong friends and that Lloyd and Smith shared a joint interest in Berkley Enterprises. She also claimed that Lloyd was friendly with President Lyndon Johnson and that he was in some way connected to the Central Intelligent Agency. As book two shows, Shriver was murdered in 1982. Before he was murdered, Ed Atkins died. According to two sources, Lloyd Tucker, and an Atkins relative, Ed Atkins was also the victim of foul play. Kenneth Meadows was shot and killed by his wife, and William Gaddis, owner of Gaddis Mining Company, shot himself accidentally while cleaning a handgun, so it was said.

Austern said that in the late 1970s he was in New York City with Simon Ashley Smith, Bill Shriver, and Ed Atkins. They all headed to a restaurant for lunch, when suddenly Shriver and Atkins asked him to walk with them, but a block or so behind Smith, which they did. Austern, who merely thought his clients, Shriver and Atkins, wanted some private time with him, asked, "What is it that you wanted to discuss?"

They said, "We just wanted him to walk a block or two ahead."

I said, "Why is that?"

They said, "Well, his life has been threatened several times. If anything were to happen we don't want to be anywhere near him."

~

Documents presented in this book prove that Tucker was involved in the 1973 gold theft at the White Sands Missile Range. Tucker made the following comment during a recorded interview in 1993:

> *"...The government had the pictures. The government knows it, there're people in the government that know it. I can tell you one right now...Richard Nixon knows it as well as about anybody. His brother knows it better than most...there [were] some pretty powerful people in that deal. Lyndon Johnson [knew] it as well as Nixon..."*

Tucker's valid 1973 passport indicates he arrived in London, England, three weeks after the theft. Simon John Ashley Smith lived in London.

———

Book three, *The Gold House—Executive Order*, describes a modern replay of what the government did to Ova Noss during her years at Victorio Peak after Doc was murdered. The book begins in the 1990s when a more sophisticated sequence of tricks and deceitful behavior was played out against Terry Delonas, son of Dorothy Delonas, Ova's daughter. Lies and deceit, false and deliberate overbillings, and illegal changes to an agreed-upon license contract are cited. Coercion, intimidation and extortion were also some of the devices the United States Government used against ONFP (Ova Noss Family Partnership), during its search efforts at Victorio Peak.

- Acknowledgements -

Special gratitude is given to Betty Harrison, who supported the project from the very beginning. Without her input *The Gold House* trilogy might never have been published. Betty remains undeterred in her efforts to help make the project a success.

To Karen Cheatham for her tireless efforts in editing the final manuscripts, Alex Alonso for his constant input, Bob and Donna Bradley who contributed in so many ways, Tito and Hugo Gomez who supported and encouraged me throughout the years, the late Otis Embree and Dick Moyle for their important contributions, and to Tom Whittle for his encouragement and invaluable contribution to the work.

- For my children, Melanie and Alec -

—John Clarence

To Bill Shriver, a man of courage.
To Bill McGaw, a good journalist and even better friend.
To Jack Anderson, Jay Armes, F. Lee Bailey, Brent Bauer, Charles Berg, Tom Berlett, Odell Breeding, Howard Bryan, Ray Burns, John Carl, Terry Delonas, Lambert Dolphin, Jan Fiege, R.B. Gray, Letha Guthrie, Tony Jolley, Joan and Joe Newman, Pat Patterson, Lynn Porter, Marilyn Salas, Norman and Sam Scott, Sam Scott Jr., Jose Sedillo, Les Smith, Thayer Snipes, Harvey Snow, Chester Stout, Oren Swearingen and the many others who each in their own way helped to provide pieces of the puzzle.
To John Clarence, who persisted when so many others did not.
To my parents, Arthur and Jenny Whittle, without whose assistance my remains may have been planted in Texas in 1981.

—Tom Whittle

THEY SAID, "THERE'S NO GOLD IN THEM THAR HILLS."

...TURNS OUT THEY WERE DEAD WRONG.

"I was hooked, unable to close the pages of this unique treasure hunt story about homicides and the abuses of power. The fascinating details are in *The Gold House* trilogy, a monumental gathering of the facts and the presentation of those facts by John Clarence and Tom Whittle. America is greatly benefited by these two men."

—Barr McClellan, Attorney* and *New York Times* best selling author

—

"This is an amazingly detailed account of decades of material about one of the Old West's best treasure tales. The access a few people had to the gold in the middle of a desert mountain range is a real treasure tale worthy of a Hollywood movie."

—Jackson Polk, Documentary Filmmaker, "The El Paso History Show"

—

"They say America operates on the Golden Rule; those who have the gold, make the rules. Nowhere does this old bromide hold more true than in the book by John Clarence and Tom Whittle. This astounding and disturbing story moves the reader from a gold strike in the 1930s through a 1949 murder and on into the highest levels of the U.S. Government..."

—Jim Marrs, Journalist and *New York Times* best selling author

—

"The disturbing truth of *The Gold House* is that this story is not the product of a fanciful imagination. *The Gold House* is a jaw-dropping, mountainous achievement and treasure trove exposé that usurps all other conspiracy stories of our time."

—Colonel Gerald Schumacher, U.S. Army Special Forces, Retired
Author: *A Bloody Business*

---

*McClellan was attorney for LBJ and the Johnson interests from 1966 through 1977.

Contents

Introductory Note

The Gold House trilogy is a true story about a great treasure of untold wealth in ancient gold bullion and priceless antiquities, wrapped in a curious mixture of time and legend and deposited within a small, inconspicuous peak at a place known as the Hembrillo Basin in New Mexico. It is also a story of betrayal, conspiracy—and murder.

The extensive research required to write the three books of *The Gold House* was completed over a six-year period ending in 2010. The events described here are taken from the accounts of many eyewitnesses, affidavits, U.S. Army and government memorandums, letters and transcribed telephone conversations, private photographs and various documents found in the Noss family archives. The more incriminating records used in writing this story came from discovery documents (more than 80,000 items) turned over to the Ova Noss Family Partnership (ONFP) by the White Sands Missile Range as a result of a lawsuit against the United States Government filed on April 4, 1997 in the U.S. Court of Federal Claims. Among other things, the suit asserted improper handling of funds by the White Sands Missile Range accounting department and the Department of the Army related to monies turned over to the White Sands accounting office to pay for expenses incurred by the military during search efforts to recover the treasure. The ONFP filed the suit and its general partner, Terry Delonas, provided these important records and his immeasurable assistance in the development of this epic project.

Here is a factual account of events that took place on an isolated desert peak, a place the Native Indians of the American Southwest referred to as their *power mountain,* the command at White Sands Missile Range refers to as *Soledad* and the Central Intelligence Agency has code-named *Deep Space*. The Federal Bureau of Investigation referred to it in a top-secret "Letterhead Memorandum" as a "level four confidential" under classified "OPERATIONS number 62385-11." The White House refers to this place as case number WH 22036, but this notorious desert hill is widely known today as—***Victorio Peak***.

~

Victorio Peak, located east of the Jornada del Muerto, the ancient road known as the *journey of death,* lies at the center of an unbroken chain of events that has lasted for more than four hundred years. Indistinguishable as Victorio Peak is from other hills in the San Andres Mountain Range, so too are the outrageous string of occurrences that left their footprints on the doorstep of the Twentieth Century. Accounts of these happenings are a matter of public record, but the crimes that actually occurred there have for the most part escaped public scrutiny. As a consequence, the final chapter of American history as it relates to this obscure corner of the great American Southwest has never been told—until now.

It was at Victorio Peak that Doc and Ova Noss brought into modern awareness the existence of a massive treasure they had discovered in the Hembrillo Basin, a discovery unmatched in the northern hemisphere. For what they had accomplished, some revered them, yet others considered them to be con artists. How history will ultimately view Milton and Ova Noss is yet to be known, but the fury they ignited when they revealed their discovery and the subsequent string of crimes committed by a number of individuals at White Sands Missile Range when they stole from the Noss treasure is revealed here as a historical document. The thefts were followed by a stream of lies and international intrigue that stretched halfway around the world and back in time. One criminal act led to another and before the thefts ended, half of the Noss treasure trove had been stolen. Fortunately a seemingly endless source of documents marked the trail, which led to this investigation.

The Noss treasure was a windfall to select individuals who helped themselves to the gold. The subterranean storehouse of gold constituted a never-ending payday for those who plundered it. These illegal actions were sometimes cloaked under the devices of "Classified" or "Top-Secret" operations. Elaborate plans to loot the Noss treasure trove involved at least one CIA operative, shadowy individuals within the Treasury Department, a number of commanding generals at White Sands Missile Range and high-ranking subordinate officers—and at least two United States Presidents. The thefts were barely investigated; worse yet, when the Army was exposed, as it was during Nixon's presidency, the Federal Bureau of Investigation and the commanding general at White Sands Missile Range covered up the thefts in a phony military inquiry conducted in 1974.

Because of the secrecy that blanketed the thefts of gold from the Noss treasure at Victorio Peak, the criminal activity set in motion soon after WWII at White Sands has escaped close examination. With the approval and help of certain commanding generals at White Sands and the agencies that enabled them, a sinister cabal was formed and a fantastic conspiracy of wanton crimes was hatched. In addition to the many thefts from the Noss treasure by the military and the destruction of a large quantity of New Mexico's priceless antiquities is the strong possibility that a certain amount of gold and priceless art that once belonged to the people of Europe was also secreted somewhere on the White Sands Missile Range, a possibility that stems from the fact that a large cache of gold taken by Hitler's forces during WWII was secreted in the Bavarian Alps and other locations throughout Germany. Rumors persist to this day that much of this gold was covertly brought to the United States where it was hidden and that one of its hiding places was allegedly White Sands Missile Range, stored there for safekeeping. It is also rumored that some of the Nazi gold was stored in caves near or next to the ancient treasure trove found by Doc and Ova Noss—the perfect cover. The question whether or not Nazi gold was in fact brought to America and secreted at White Sands is for the reader to decide, but the existence of an ancient treasure discovered inside Victorio Peak by Doc and Ova Noss is irrefutable.

The questions raised about Nazi gold and White Sands Missile Range are but a small episode in the Victorio Peak treasure story, yet it is an important one from a historical perspective. It is difficult to believe that in the fog of war and by greed of men, Nazi gold hadn't found its way to White Sands Missile Range; too much innuendo and rumors abound that caused me to consider such a possibility. Not only is it a historical fact that American Army officers were dealing in black market items of gold coins and bullion after WWII had ended in Europe, but they also dealt in countless valuable personal effects stolen from Holocaust victims by Hitler. Local newspapers carried the story when it broke. One such report by the Associated Press came from the Albuquerque Tribune on Saturday, March 12, 2005. In part from the article:[1]

> MIAMI—*The federal government has reached a $25.5 million settlement with the families of Hungarian Holocaust victims and will acknowledge the U.S. Army's role in commandeering a trainload of the families' treasures during World War II.*

Here is a quote by Sam Dubbin, lawyer for the victims, which appeared in the article:

> *The case never really was about money alone. It was about having a reckoning with history.*

The article said that the settlement grew out of the commission President Clinton appointed in 1999, and that it was finally concluded that "high-ranking Army officers and troops plundered the train after it was intercepted on its way to Germany in May 1945 during the closing days of the war." More from the article:

> *The train carried gold, jewels, 1,200 paintings, silver, china, porcelain, 3,000 Oriental carpets and other heirlooms seized from Jewish families by the Nazis. The cargo would be worth $45 million to $90 million in today's dollars.*

~

It is also a fact that a great number of those items came to New York City where they disappeared into private collections. It is therefore imprudent to believe that the mentality *to the victor goes the spoils* was not a self-serving, misplaced credo that resulted in some of the Holocaust gold and art objects showing up in the United States after WWII had ended. Any denial that might arise from someone with brass stars on their shoulders would not dissuade one to believe that Nazi gold had not been brought to White Sands; there was too much treachery committed by the military at White Sands in dealing with the Noss treasure trove to think otherwise; too many documents containing too many lies exist. It was also difficult to be faithful to the honor and glory of high-ranking officers at White Sands who wrapped themselves in their rank and status to cloak the activities carried out against the Noss family or any civilian representing them. Therefore, any impulse to not bow to such people is strengthened by the facts of this case, and most importantly by the honor and loyalty displayed by every soldier, sailor and airman who fought, was wounded or died in the defense of our country.

Terry Delonas, Ova Noss' grandson spoke about the matter of Nazi gold during one of our recorded interviews. His remarks:

> *I'm just wondering how early in the timetable of events at Victorio Peak that Nazi gold became an issue with the Army, I mean as far as getting it out of Europe. I'm wondering if it was when the Army found the Nazi gold cache in the Merkers mines in 1945. And when was the decision made to bring it here; was it during Operation Paper Clip? I've always wondered about that, but I can't connect the dots. It seems logical to think that it was in 1945 when it was found at Merkers and that it was part of the military's overall mission to look for a place to stash the Nazi gold and other things over here in the United States.*
>
> *I'm also wondering when it was in Doc and Babe's early years at Victorio Peak that the military might have begun thinking about using the peak as a possible stash site. It's difficult to think that our government would do that, take gold that Hitler's SS stole from the banks in Europe; but then the Army wasn't shy about taking gold from Doc and my grandmother. So, like I say, it makes me wonder when the decision was made to connect Nazi gold and the Peak site as a possible hiding place at White Sands.*

~

The Noss family did not invent the question of Nazi gold existing somewhere on White Sands Missile Range, suspicions that have lingered in New Mexico since WWII ended. Call it local legend, or whatever one might wish to call it, but the fact remains that the question of Nazi gold *and* White Sands Missile Range still swirl around in the neighboring communities, as do the countless dust devils that can be seen traversing the Tularosa Basin where White Sands Missile Range is located. The criminal activity at White Sands was not limited to military personnel; others were involved. Regardless of who they were, the thefts are impossible to refute.

The three books of *The Gold House* tell the story of unchecked greed, theft and the unlawful military intercession and manipulation of civil matters, actions and activities that suppress the liberty, freedom and constitutional rights of every American. The numerous crimes that the Noss treasure trove set in motion were so blatant that it is difficult to believe that such events had ever taken place. But they did. Through the deliberate misuse of wealth and power in the hands of many conspirators, the course of American history was in fact altered. The crime scene was Victorio Peak, the victims include the Noss family members, but because of the constitutional issues and questions connected to the thefts, every citizen in the United States as well.

"We can have democracy or we can have great wealth concentrated in the hands of a few. We cannot have both."—Justice Louis Brandeis

The three books of the Gold House are nonfictional accounts of real events that occurred between the 1930s and the 1990s that deal primarily with the Noss treasure trove at Victorio Peak and a variety of other related issues. A concerted effort has been made to tell the story chronologically. In this effort, the largest percentage of the chronology is grounded upon letters, documents, affidavits, dated photos, newspaper articles, agreements, interviews, corporate notes and a wide variety of legal documents. A few events have been dramatized where gaps in time appear or because of the lack of physical records to support what might have happened during these events. In all other cases, transitional narratives are used to bridge these gaps whenever they appear. Oftentimes individuals will be presented or events will be introduced that are not in the strict chronological order of the story as it is told, however the context in which they are used is to simply introduce certain individuals and events early on to enhance reader understanding. National and international events, statewide and local issues are also added as a backdrop to the story, events that happened in real time or as a forecast of future matters to be presented.

Preface

Three hundred years before President Thomas Jefferson ordered the exploration of the American West, Spain had already claimed vast tracts of new territory in the same expanse. The historic voyage of Columbus to the West Indies was the first of many explorations of the New World by the Spanish Empire and for two centuries after Columbus' epic journey, reports of American Indian cities rich in gold filtered back to Spain. So compelling were the reports that in 1528 Spain sent explorer Cabeza de Vaca to find the gold and to claim more land in the Western Hemisphere.

De Vaca's journey from Florida to California lasted eight years. From his starting point near present-day Tampa, de Vaca headed west along the Florida panhandle, through Alabama, Mississippi and Louisiana forging westward across Texas. His journey took him northwest along the Pecos River to the Guadalupe Mountains just south of the Sacramento Range. During the expedition, native Indians talked of rich cities in the North confirming the reports that had already reached Spain. De Vaca crossed over the Tularosa Basin: the present-day site of the White Sands Missile Range, a thirty-mile wide, one-hundred-mile long flat, inhospitable desert. Running along the surface of this seemingly endless wasteland, large formations of volcanic rock called *The Malpais* streak diagonally across the basin where hot, barren alkali flats and pure white dunes glisten in the sun. From here, de Vaca journeyed westward toward the San Andres Mountains crossing over the range through the San Augustin Pass. Stretching northward was the Jornada del Muerto, a one-hundred-twenty-mile long, twenty-mile wide scorching desert that extended all the way to what would one day become Socorro, New Mexico. Along the eastern boundary of the Jornada del Muerto was the rugged San Andres Range. On the western boundary were the Fra Cristobal Range and Caballo Mountains and at the far reaches of their slopes, the Rio Grande meandered south. It was this parched stretch of land, the Jornada del Muerto, which became the hunting grounds for bands of marauders that raided caravans laden with gold, gold taken in lust by some, in anger and revenge by others; regardless of how and how often the gold changed hands, it was always covered in blood. In order to comprehend the vast amount of gold, silver and other treasure that entered the Jornada del Muerto but never reached its destination, it is helpful to know something about the region. The area along the Jornada del Muerto embodies the turbulence of history, life, and human survival as seen in the ever-changing cast of cultures within the eternal struggle for land, water, and gold. Before the Spanish Conquistadores arrived, large aboriginal civilizations flourished everywhere in the region, including Mexico, but more heavily there. Some of the civilizations, in the most recent order, were: Aztec, Toltec, Mixtec, Teotihuacan, Totonac, Maya and other cultures.

Although the exact chronology of these cultures changes from time to time with more unearthing of their civilizations, historians and anthropologists agree that the pinnacle of the Aztec culture was the most fascinating. The Aztecs, nomads that came to the Valley of Anahuac in 1325, took the region for their own and began building an empire. They worshiped their many gods, paid them respect and recognition through ritual killings and massive sacrifices, built their temples and pyramids and called their city Tenochtitlan, the final monument to early Mesoamerica culture, ritual, custom, and architecture. What the Aztecs had accomplished in less than two centuries is astonishing.

In 1519, the third expedition of King Charles V of Spain brought to the shores of Mexico's coastline explorer Hernan Cortez. Cortez sailed from Cuba and anchored in Cozumel and later in Tabasco claiming the land he saw in the name of Spain. From there he traveled north to Vera Cruz and headed inland. Aware of Cortez's arrival, Montezuma, the last emperor of the Aztecs, sent emissaries to greet him with gifts of gold. When Cortez reached Tenochtitlan (present day Mexico City), his arrival there was not unexpected; an ancient prophecy had predicted the arrival of a "bearded white man from the east." Cortez would later overthrow the Aztec empire and claim it as his own, fulfilling the prophecy of Quetzalcoatl, an ancient fable of the Aztecs' predecessor, the Toltec.

Cortez was shown temples with large rooms of gold and gems and after seeing these unbelievable treasures, his plan was to smelt the gold into bullion and ship it to Spain. After Cortez was shown the treasures, a series of events occurred that would three centuries later impact the Caballo and San Andres Mountain Ranges in the modern state of New Mexico. When Cortez saw the temple of Huitzilopochtli, the site of human sacrificial rituals, he ordered the destruction of the temple. A battle ensued and after inflicting terrible losses upon Cortez's men, the Aztecs drove the Spanish out of Tenochtitlan. His exhausted forces nearly spent, Cortez retreated to Tlaxcala, a distance of one hundred miles from Tenochtitlan. After great preparation, he regrouped and returned to Tenochtitlan to battle once more. Montezuma's nephew, Cuauhtemoc, led the Aztecs against the returning Spanish and after three months of warfare, and at great cost to both sides, Cortez prevailed, but most of the gold treasure he had seen earlier had vanished. While Cortez was regrouping in Tlaxcala, much of the treasure was carried off on the backs of thousands of Aztec natives and secreted in various places in the rugged mountain ranges to the north. Undaunted in the search for the "golden cities of the Cibola," Spain extended its rule north and west to the Pacific coastline.

In 1540, Spanish explorer Coronado came to the New World to expand Spain's rule into present day New Mexico and Arizona. This further expansion included the remainder of Mexico and Southwestern United States, but Coronado never found the "Seven Cities of Cibola" where legend told of great deposits of gold bullion, silver and gems; he found only adobe* villages[†] in western New Mexico. There he seized and destroyed nearly one hundred Indian pueblos and forced the native inhabitants into a system of slave labor, cruel punishment and butchery; only nineteen pueblos remain. New Mexico's northern region pueblos are: Nambe, Picuris, Pojoaque, San Ildefonso, San Juan, Santa Clara, Taos[‡] and Tesuqueblo. Pueblos near Albuquerque are: Sandia, Santo Domingo, San Felipe, Cochiti, Santa Ana, Jemez, Acoma and Isleta. New Mexico's Southern region pueblos are: Laguna and Zuni. Ultimately the Apache Indians, who were also victims of Spanish colonists, declared a state of war and staged spectacular raids on mines, caravans, and *ranchos* under Spanish control. Coronado's quest north in the unexplored lands of New Mexico and Arizona came at a great cost and in the end proved fruitless.

One figure who stands out during this turbulent time period was Pedro Navares, a man of Spanish decent and leader of a large number of Indian bandits whose camp was secluded deep in the Caballo Mountains along the Jornada del Muerto. Their raids on cargoes along this trail were as legendary as the enormous amount of loot they seized—caravans of gold and silver bullion and sacred church artifacts earmarked for Spanish missionaries throughout the Southwest. The amount of treasure Navares and his Indian raiders plundered was so great that the King of Spain dispatched soldiers to hunt him down. It wasn't long afterwards that Navares and many of his gang were captured and taken to Mexico City where they were tried, convicted, and sentenced to death.

Facing certain death, Pedro Navares asked for a priest and told "the pious one that he wanted to confess[1] his depredations along 'El Camino del Rey' and tell where he had stashed the loot." The El Camino del Rey is known today as the El Camino Real, an old travel route that stretches from Mexico City to Taos Pueblo, just north of Santa Fe.

A chart was made from Navares' confession[§] marking the location of a cave, the storehouse of all that he and his men robbed from the trail. Not only did Navares describe the location of gold and silver treasures hidden within the mountain ranges along Jornada del Muerto, he also described the contents of the treasures: *"Inside you will find arms, crockery, clothing and harnesses, and eighty mule trains[‖] of bars of silver. There should also be more than ten mule trains of finished silver and many other articles."* The estimated amount of silver bullion alone was about 135 tons.

~

---

* Structures built from bricks that were formed from earth and straw and then sun-dried

[†] These settlements were villages of various sizes, however the correct term for such a village is *pueblo*.

[‡] Taos Pueblo is the largest surviving multistoried Pueblo structure in America.

[§] The "Prediction [confession] of Pedro Navares, Convent of San Augustine, City of Mexico in November 1839"

[‖] A mule train consisted of at least ten mules, each mule carrying about 200 pounds.

After nearly a century and a half of cruelty, enslavement, and colonial rule, the Pueblo Indians in the territory united and a war was launched against the Spanish. The year was 1680—the great "Pueblo Revolt" had begun. Led by a charismatic shaman, Popè, from Taos Pueblo, the native tribes finally avenged the wrongdoings of the Spanish colonists. The success of Popè and his followers was attributed to an unprecedented number of warriors who attacked simultaneously, unexpectedly and swiftly. Those who were able to escape retreated south to Paseo del Norte, what is now El Paso, Texas. Spanish gold mines were sealed, ending an era of continuous gold mining. Twelve years later, after Popè died, Spanish soldiers under Diego de Vargas had reclaimed all of the territory that Popè and his people had rescued, but the hoards of gold and treasures that Popè had reclaimed from the Spanish were never found.

In spite of reversal of fortune, the Apache took up the fight against the Spanish. But with the different alliances the Spanish had utilized to make safe their journeys along the El Camino del Rey, the tides of war once again changed for the Apache. Comanches poured in from the plains, joining the Spanish in their battles against the Apache and the Pueblos. Skirmishes raged on and even more of the gold the Spanish coveted disappeared.

A person who played a significant role in the history of the Southwest was a French Jesuit priest named Felipe LaRue. He was also known as Padre LaRue or Father LaRue, a person whose presence in New Mexico, in fact his very existence, has long been a source of controversy; many of those who encounter his name in reading stories of the old Southwest hold to the belief that he was a fictional character, but he was quite real. With the permission of the church* and with a true desire to help spread the word of God, Father LaRue set out for "The New World"—Mexico. LaRue's destination was an area north of Chihuahua, Mexico, where a small settlement of poor, hardworking farmers made a sparse living from the crops they raised. Under his leadership, the little band of peasants built a small church and as time passed the spiritually renewed community began to prosper. One of the parishioners in the village, an old soldier who had survived the campaign days of "The Pueblo Revolt," became very ill and revealed to Father LaRue the existence of a fabulous gold mine far to the north.

Soon after the soldier's death drought struck the community and LaRue sent word of their plight to the Church in Mexico City. Disappointed by the Church's lack of response, LaRue revealed to his people what the old soldier had told him. Rather than face starvation, LaRue and his followers gathered their belongings and began a grueling journey to the north. Resting for a time at Paseo del Norte, they continued north along the Rio Grande, then soon

* Duc de Saint-Simon, Memoirs of Louis XIV "His Court and The Regency" (Globusz Publishing, New York)

headed east a short distance across the Jornada del Muerto, the ancient path the earliest inhabitants used to reach the Tularosa Basin. When they arrived there, they traveled north toward the seclusion of the San Andres Mountain Range. A few days later, Father LaRue and his band of settlers reached their destination. However, there is some uncertainty, actually a great deal of controversy, regarding the precise location where they finally settled; some claim that LaRue stopped and settled somewhere in the Franklin Mountain Range, immediately north of Paseo del Norte and went no further. Others support the claim that Padre LaRue's camp was in the Organ Mountains, which is located at the southernmost reach of the San Andres Mountain Range. Then there are some who believe his settlement was located in the Hembrillo Basin, deep within the San Andres Range. Regardless of the exact route they took, or where they had finally settled, along any of the trails that lead to any of the sites mentioned are spectacular mountain vistas and ancient petroglyphs and pictographs on canyon walls.

Eventually, LaRue's loyal followers discovered the source of the gold the old soldier had talked about and they began to mine and store the gold deep within a cave where the rich vein was found. Occasionally they used small amounts of gold to purchase provisions and tools from the distant settlements to which they traveled, an innocent form of commerce that would later prove to be fatal. When the reports of LaRue's exodus from Chihuahua and his subsequent successful gold mining efforts reached Mexico City, the Church hierarchy sent Maximo Milliano to find the priest, the rumored gold, and its source. LaRue and his parishioners were eventually captured and killed, but the secret hiding place of their rich storehouse of gold, and the location of the mine from which it came, remains a historical mystery.

The accumulation of gold and treasure within the general area did not end with LaRue's contributions. When Mexico's Emperor Maximilian Hapsburg, was executed during the Mexican Revolution in 1865, a large part of Mexico's royal treasury was stolen by Maximilian loyalists and removed from Mexico in a long wagon train that disappeared near Paseo del Norte. Pictographs on the rock canyon walls in the Hembrillo Basin are said to depict the wagon train and its capture by the Apache. It is here where our story begins when Doc and Ova Noss discovered not one, but two ancient treasures; the first treasure was located in the Caballo Mountains. Not long afterwards, early in 1937, they discovered a second treasure, a vast storehouse of gold bullion and ancient artifacts hidden inside Victorio Peak.

The Victorio Peak discovery was made known on November 7 that same year, however an ill-placed dynamite charge set off to remove a restriction inside the vertical entrance triggered a massive landslide that filled the entire shaft with debris, choking off the passageway to the main treasure rooms. Because of the technical difficulties involved in clearing the debris, regaining access to the passageway was continually delayed. In 1949, before the work was finished, Doc was murdered. For nearly three decades after Doc died, Ova tried valiantly to raise the treasure herself but she was thwarted in her efforts by officials at White Sands Missile Range *and* the White House and she was eventually removed from the claim site by the military in 1955. During the years that followed, a good deal of the treasure was stolen in a series of unlawful, covert activities conducted by various parties assisted by a number of Commanding Generals at White Sands Missile Range who had the technical and financial ability to clear the debris or bypass it.

Before Ova died, her grandson, Terry Delonas, spent most of his early life listening to the chronicle of events that took place in Doc and Ova's lives, augmented by countless other stories revealed to him in family meetings. A collection of photographs taken during the early years at Victorio Peak, and other places where Doc and Ova had lived, worked and explored for treasure, unveil the mood of those trying times and they are presented here. The summation of Terry's life experiences over the decades reflected nearly every aspect of Doc and Ova's time together, a tapestry of oral and written history of their adventures, especially their discovery of a great treasure hidden away inside Victorio Peak and the disastrous events that followed. So accurate were Terry's recollections that people often took his stories lightly or dismissed them entirely. But what he had learned and what he had seen for himself made him a believer. "Babe was a fighter," Terry said. Just before her death she handed the torch to Terry. "Terry will know what to do," she said to her two daughters, Letha and Dorothy in a weak and failing voice. Shortly afterwards, Ova died after unexpected surgery in 1979 while vacationing in the Bahamas. Two years later, Terry took up the fight to reclaim what had been stolen from his family and from the people of the State of New Mexico. But little did he know when he started his quest that such names as Fred Drolte, John Dean, John Ehrlichman, H.R. Haldeman, F. Lee Bailey, former Attorney General John Mitchell and Richard Nixon would all play a role in the Noss treasure story. Some of these people played small roles, while others were deeply involved—such as President Nixon.

In his efforts to recover what remained of the Noss treasure trove, Terry accomplished a great deal, but during the process many people around said that what he was trying to accomplish was impossible. They were right; in the end, military and civilian officials at White Sands Missile Range and individuals at the Pentagon, who had great influence at the White House level, betrayed him as they had betrayed his grandmother. Later in time, Terry came in contact with well-known individuals who knew many of the dark secrets the government held, secrets that were revealed to him. But the journey did not end with Terry in the 1990s when the U.S. Army stole from him and his financial supporters and the many volunteers who helped with the project; it continued on during the writing of *The Gold House* trilogy.

It has been difficult to write this book and escape the trappings of it becoming the work of conspiracy theorists. However, this investigation provides conclusive evidence of a string of great crimes by officials and agents of our own government against the citizenry. The many documents presented in the trilogy of *The Gold House* sustain the accusations made here and are presented as proof that serious crimes were committed. Once they are explained and shown for what they truly represent, it is for the reader to decide whether or not a great injustice was done.

———

The story of the Victorio Peak treasure discovery began in the 1930s when Ova and Doc first met, when they became a team, co-discoverers of a great treasure. This book not only tells the story of how the treasure was found, it also tells the story of Doc and Ova's time together, their stormy relationship—and Doc's murder. It also reveals information about the people who set the stage for this amazing story.

Prologue

Gus Delonas owned and operated the Busy Bee Café in Clovis, New Mexico, a popular eating place known for its tasty Greek cuisine, generous portions and friendly service. Back then, in the early 1940s, Clovis was a small, dusty town in the middle of the state of New Mexico just a few miles west of the Texas border. Prior to establishing the Clovis location, Gus owned and operated a restaurant by the same name in Hot Springs, New Mexico; Hot Springs was two hundred miles west and eighty miles south of Clovis, but it is known today as Truth or Consequence, locally referred to as—*T 'r C.*

Although Doc and Ova had no children of their own, Ova had four children from a previous marriage: Letha, Harold, Marvin, and Dorothy Beckwith. It was a result of the many times that Doc and Ova came to Gus' restaurant in Hot Springs that Dorothy eventually met Gus. Dorothy, a petite, spirited and charming young woman

eventually worked for Gus as a waitress. It wasn't long before they fell in love and were married. In time, Gus and Dorothy moved to Clovis where Terry and Jim, their only children, were born and grew up. It was Dorothy and Gus' children and Ova's children who knew the true story of Victorio Peak; they had either experienced a number of the episodes related to the Peak or they had heard many of the stories told to them during the course of their lives.

Letha and Dorothy were two ladies cut from the same piece of cloth: they were independent, smart and headstrong, and they had an unquenchable desire to spend as much time at Victorio Peak as circumstances allowed them. Dorothy is shown here sitting on the hood of her car at the Victorio Peak campsite; the photo was taken in 1941. Letha is sitting on the bumper of her car holding her son, Wesley; the photo was taken sometime between 1939 and 1940.

In 1952, after a costly and traumatic string of events that involved the Victorio Peak treasure and the murder of Doc, Ova Noss moved from Hot Springs to Clovis. Her decision to move there was not a retreat from the difficulties facing her at Victorio Peak, rather a necessity arising from events brought on by the U.S. Army at White Sands Proving Ground, the name given it prior to it becoming White Sands Missile Range.

For a short time, Ova moved in with Gus and Dorothy and her grandsons, Terry and Jim. But, being as independent as she was, she soon moved into her own home a block away where she could plan a strategy to return to Victorio Peak, a place she always referred to as *the mine*. After Ova had settled in, she started having family meetings concerning the Peak, meetings that invariably included Dorothy, Terry, Jim, and Letha and her children, all of whom had vivid memories and solid recollections of their days spent at the Victorio Peak campsite, a place they knew only as the Rock House. Although Terry didn't realize it at the time, Ova had set the stage for a transfer of information that would eventually impact greatly on his life, for the rest of his life.

Terry was about sixteen when his role and involvement at Victorio Peak began to come into focus. In my first interview with him, he recalled riding his bicycle down to Ova's home many times a week, often having breakfast with her. He recalled the constant stream of telephone calls Ova received from people who were inquiring about the Peak, or who gave her reports on matters they had learned during her absence from her claim site; newspaper reporters would often show up on her doorstep for a story. It was Terry's visits to his grand-mother's home that made him a witness to the stream of visitors who came to her door; some came to offer plans or ideas of how she could get back on the Peak, while others came to report that the military was stealing gold bullion from the Noss treasure. The witnesses to the thefts were reputable individuals, namely Magistrate and Municipal Judge Robert H. Bradley from Otero County, New Mexico, and noted Levelland, Texas, County Judge Hulon L. Moreland.

It was Terry's regular meetings with Ova where he sat at the kitchen table and listened to her retell the stories of her adventures with Doc that impressed him the most. It was because of the events that took place in Ova's kitchen, plus the many conversations with individual family members, aunts, uncles and cousins, who also encouraged Ova to return to Victorio Peak and regain access to the treasure caves, that Terry's knowledge grew. The information he absorbed from the time he was five years old until he was twenty-five gave him the rich and complete knowledge of the Victorio Peak story. His classroom was Ova's kitchen table; his mentors were his family members and the lessons he was taught usually began when Ova called him to come to her house. Whenever a visitor came to see her, she would call him and tell him that someone was coming over to talk about the Peak. He always responded promptly and dropped what he was doing so he could be with her. Terry explained it this way:

I don't know if she had me over there for her own protection, because she never knew many of the strangers who came to the house and it was comforting to have someone else with her, maybe for a little security or maybe it was because she was in her own sly way progressively indoctrinating me with the entire history of her experience at the Peak, planting more and more seeds in my mind: seeds of frustration, curiosity, and perhaps to instill a degree of zeal within me to later in my life see to it that justice was done and that the truth of Victorio Peak would eventually be told.

There were hundreds of these afternoon and evening sessions and occasionally there would be some sort of breakthrough and the whole family would convene, even come from out-of-town to be there. Old photos and maps would be pulled out of dusty suitcases and they would all gather around the table while my grandmother talked and explained where Doc had buried gold bars, routes he took to the Peak and the many adventures she and Doc had together.

~

From the time that Terry was eight until he was seventeen, and still in high school, he worked at the Clovis restaurant, then, after graduation, he took a second full-time job at the local bank as a teller and began working part-time in the bank's accounting department, but still remaining loyal to his father helping him keep the family restaurant business going. It was a close-knit family and what affected one member of the family affected the other, and that never changed. One of the hallmarks in Terry's life was the endearing relationship he had with his grandmother, a relationship that endured until her death. During one of the many interviews with Terry he said that his family referred to Ova as "Babe." He explained it this way:

That was what she insisted on being called. She never allowed any of us to call her grandmother; she used to say, 'It's nobody's business whether I'm old enough to be a grandmother or not. You just call me Babe.' So, that was the habit we got into. I guess she preferred that because that was Doc's name for her.

I was born on March 6, 1948 and Doc was killed on March 5, 1949, so I never met him, but he was as real to me as any person who was living in our home because I've seen so many pictures of Doc and heard so many colorful and hysterically funny stories about him. My picture of Doc Noss was a handsome, healthy, adventurer and I always thought of him being about forty years old, because that was his general age when most of the pictures of him were taken, at least the ones that I had seen. But, he had a great sense of humor; he was a practical joker and my grandmother delighted in telling the stories about jokes he played on her and just about everybody that came into his life. Doc had the trickster spirit in him.

The mental picture I always have of Doc, in addition to the photos I have seen, was a man caught between cultures, because according to my grandmother he was three-fourths Cheyenne Indian and he felt that he needed to, or was forced to live in the white man's world. Doc had his Indian ways and beliefs and possibly some superstitions mixed with his Native American spirituality, and at the same time he needed to succeed in business and make a living for his family. So, in my opinion, it was a difficulty that Doc had to deal with continually, not only personally, but also when he dealt with other people.

There has always been a lot of debate over whether or not Doc was a medical doctor, not in the family, but outside the family. I have never found evidence that Doc ever claimed he was a medical doctor, only a practitioner; even still, he was referred to as Doc Noss or Doctor Noss. I do know, though, that he had more than one chiropodist foot treatment* clinic; one was in Oklahoma and he had a business in Hot Springs. That was his business; he treated people's feet and people called him Doctor Noss. My impression always was that it was similar to the way people today refer to a chiropractor as a

doctor. Chiropractors, who do not have a medical degree, do not claim to be medical doctors and it seems to be the way it was with Doc and his practice. I never saw a medical license, but I did see boxes full of medical books, mainly books related to the feet and the bone structure. Many of those books were stored in our garage for a long time and as a kid I would open the boxes and go through them and noticed that on the front inside, blank pages

and also on the back ones, were these beautiful drawings, maps, treasure maps that Doc had sketched: mountains, ravines, streams and rivers, locations of springs, trees and many symbols and signs. In fact, all of the blank pages in these medical books contained these great drawings. I've always assumed these were Doc's treasure sites in the Caballos and San Andres Mountains or sites where he had buried gold bullion.

When I fully engaged myself in the project, which I began contemplating doing around 1982, I suddenly realized that we had to go back to the Peak to excavate for the treasure and hopefully find out what really happened to it. About that time, stories had begun to surface that revealed some of terrible things that had gone on at Victorio Peak during the 1960s that were not fully known to our family. We were not aware of it at the time, but other investigations underway that began appearing in various venues, woke us up to the fact that there was far more behind what we were told by the officials at White Sands Missile Range. An investigative reporter named Tom Whittle happened to be an Army lieutenant stationed at Fort Bliss in 1973 and 1974 and I learned he had very high clearance. At that time, General Sweeney was the Commander at White Sands

---

* The top photo of Doc in his foot care office was taken in Taloga, Oklahoma circa 1936. The lower photo was taken in Hot Springs, New Mexico.

and a large gold theft from Doc and Ova's treasure occurred in November 1973 while he was the commander. From what I understood later, when Mr. Whittle was no longer in the service, he began documenting what he had seen and experienced firsthand while he was still stationed at Fort Bliss. Eventually he became an investigative reporter with, I think it was Jack Anderson, and Mr. Whittle's account of what he had uncovered appeared in a magazine article; I believe it was Investigator magazine. But according to Mr. Whittle, Anderson for some reason or another edited his story heavily. As I understand it, Whittle later moved to California and wrote more about the corruption at Victorio Peak for Freedom magazine. Mr. Whittle still works there and I believe he's now the Senior Editor for the magazine.

So, after my grandmother died, and realizing now there was far more to the story, I was told she had chosen me to finish the work she started, because according to my Aunt Letha, my grandmother's last words to everybody in the family was to tell Terry to go forward; she said, 'He'll know what to do.' So, on the advice of attorneys, and just out of common sense, I asked the family to round up all of the Victorio Peak archival material, and they did. Then every family member signed legal affidavits turning custody and ownership of all the family archives over to me as the General Partner of the Ova Noss Family Partnership. I collected all of the material and most of it was kept in the ONFP project house in Las Cruces: artifacts, maps, papers, and many, many photographs. Everything was legally assigned to me as custodian. Later most everything was moved to California where my friend Alex Alonso lived, and still does. I lived there also, and I still do. So Alex and I began organizing all of this material for the purpose of documentation and we began interviewing everybody we could find that had some part of the story of Victorio Peak, or some version of it, and we videotaped everyone we could find.

Actually, prior to Alex's involvement, I had another friend, who was from the University of Arkansas, Scott Lunsford, doing the same thing, so we wound up with videotaped interviews of as many people as possible: my Aunt Letha, my mother, my uncles, Doc's lawyer, Melvin Rueckhaus and some other individuals.

What is so perplexing about the Victorio Peak story is that even though it was only seventy-five years ago we are still trying to unscramble what happened there. What is equally perplexing is that after investing thousands of hours and spending a couple million dollars, and having had limited access to the site, and having talked to so many people, studied dozens of geological reports and maps all in an effort to understand the true dynamics of the story, it seems that we are still at the same place that Babe was when she was removed from the site in the 1950s.

In fact, in April or May of 2004 when John Clarence began his independent investigation, we still hadn't figured out what really happened at Victorio Peak, things that were happening behind the scenes that had a fatal impact on our efforts to locate Doc's treasure rooms. In spite of all the time and the money ONFP spent, it seems now in looking back, that the evidence was staring us in the face; it was right there in front of us all the time. Our problem was that it was viewed through rose-colored glasses, "trusting filters" so to speak, not knowing that all along there was a systemic problem, something that involved our own government and to this day I still cannot believe what had been done to our organization, the ONFP, our entire family and those relentless and faithful volunteers who stayed with the project for years during the exploration.

My grandmother's version of the history of Victorio Peak that Doc and she had found an ancient treasure, possibly of Spanish origin, and that Victorio Peak had become a storehouse of treasures that accumulated over hundreds of years by the Apache tribes, maybe the Yaqui Indians, which might explain the conglomeration of materials Doc had found and had described. For instance, one of the things he reported finding, that didn't make any sense and didn't fit any history Babe knew from what Doc had told her over the years, were some bars that were nearly pure in content. When I started interviewing people and began going through many of the documents Babe had left behind, while trying to gain a historical view of what the source of the treasure was, I only thought in terms of ancient Spanish treasure, old treasure. I completely missed any references that Doc made to Babe that could have been references to Nazi gold. I had on this filter, as I said, that anything inside Victorio Peak had to be ancient. So when people came to us with stories that a certain Major, or a certain Colonel from White Sands had these 99.99 percent pure gold bars they took out of Victorio Peak in 1964, I thought to myself that those were not the kinds of bars Doc described, this is not pertinent to the Victorio Peak story. That's when I recalled what Ova had casually mentioned that Doc had removed bars that were nearly pure, but all along I had missed the possibility that Nazi gold could have been added to the ancient treasure.

The more I reflect on the whole story, the more aware I became of the things that I had missed, because as it turned out, I was trying to make the evidence fit the story, knowledge that I had pieced together in my mind, as opposed to something else being inside Victorio Peak, something in addition to any ancient treasure.

~

Even though there is much to consider when contemplating whether or not Nazi gold had been secreted somewhere on the White Sands Missile Range following WWII, the centerpiece of the story is about a vast storehouse of ancient gold and priceless artifacts discovered inside Victorio Peak. There is also an important story about the treasure's discoverers and what happened to them during the course of their lives. *The Gold House* is a true story about a catastrophic injustice committed by certain individuals and officials in the United States Government upon an American family, more accurately, an injustice committed by a group of people who had lost their way.

John Clarence:

In the beginning it was difficult to write negatively about American military personnel, but when the truth slowly unfolded it was not. The injustice that was committed by certain individuals had little to do with branch of service, rank, or badges, chevrons or uniforms, but it had everything to do with the men who wore them and how they hid behind their egos, their arrogance and their military status to justify their actions and in doing so they blatantly displayed their contempt for civilians. And if anyone is offended because they have loved ones or friends in the military service, I give no apology for what has been written here; what was done was done and what happened, happened. If this writer learned anything while researching this story it was that nonfiction is a demanding process that requires one to be true to the work.

~

When the books were in their final stages of editing, I struggled to find words that expressed how I felt about a few individuals who placed so many obstacles in my path. It was then that I recalled a quote Terry Delonas read to me over the telephone. I located the quote, copied it and read it again and again. It was written by William Hutchison Murray, a mountaineer who headed the Scottish Himalayan Expedition in 1951:

"Until one is committed there is hesitancy, the chance to draw back, always ineffectiveness.

Concerning all acts of initiative there is one elementary truth, the ignorance of which kills countless ideas and splendid plans: the moment one definitely commits oneself, then Providence moves too.

All sorts of things occur to help one that would otherwise never have occurred. A whole stream of events issues from the decision, raising in one's favor all manner of unforeseen incidents and meetings and material assistance, which no man could have dreamed would have come his way.

I have a deep respect for one of Goethe's* couplets: 'Whatever you can do, or dream you can—begin it. Boldness has genius, power and magic in it.'"   —W. H. Murray

~

It was true. Knowledge gained by committing oneself to begin a work and then follow it through to the end empowers one with a true sense of direction.

John Clarence:

The Providence Murray spoke of moved in my favor, as well; people I thought wouldn't talk to me—did. Documents came to me like a flood and productive opportunities appeared regularly. I was not born with genius, nor do I consider myself bold, but I experienced firsthand the power and magic Goethe referred to; it came with my persistence: persistence in not giving up and continually moving forward with the work, and persistence in learning to ignore my antagonists.

It was difficult to avoid writing myself into the book, but I tried not to. And I will not take all of the credit for what you are about to read; had it not been for Karen Cheatham, Bob and Donna Bradley, Betty Harrison and her family, Sherra and Jim Delonas, Dick Moyle, Alex Alonso, and certainly, Terry Delonas, the three books of The Gold House might not have been written. Pat Heydt—thank you for remaining loyal to the cause.

---

* Johann Wolfgang von Goethe is to Germany as William Shakespeare is to England.

Credit for editing book one of the trilogy is shared with Tom Whittle, who has maintained an ongoing interest in seeing that the full account of the Victorio Peak story was finally written. Tom and I first met in California when Terry Delonas took me to his office for a visit in 2005. From then on we moved forward bringing the necessary elements of the story together in a workable outline, sharing our investigations and documents, structuring the manuscripts, and finally completing the long editing process in each book of The Gold House.

Because I live at the epicenter of the story, at least where the events and activates occurred in the San Andres and Caballo Mountains, most of the latest fieldwork was done by me, fieldwork needed to complete or fill in segments of the story that were lacking in clarity or understanding. Tom had investigated a great deal of the Victorio Peak story while he was stationed at Fort Bliss, and later as an investigative reporter with Jack Anderson and one of his colleagues, Bill McGaw. It was Tom's early investigation that produced the articles in Investigator and Freedom magazines, poignant and straight forward reporting that pointed an accusing finger at President Johnson's involvement with stealing a large amount of Victorio Peak gold.

~

In this, the first book of the trilogy, you will read about the early times and the pain and betrayal that came with finding such a thing, a great treasure. Book Two is nearly unspeakable, and I'll leave it at that. Book Three is the unfinished episode of how the Noss family felt itself under the boot of the Pentagon *and* the White House.

At the White House level, George Herbert Walker Bush signed off on a new exploration of Victorio Peak by the Ova Noss Family Partnership (ONFP) and then turned his back on the project allowing certain commanders at White Sands Missile Range and their subordinates to continue with corrupt policies, lies, deceit and extortion. During the ONFP exploration of Victorio Peak, the White Sands' accounting office deliberately overbilled and falsely represented its costs, which finally depleted ONFP's operating funds. Although it is frightening to think it could happen, years earlier, in 1981 the Noss family was threatened with mortal consequences if they did not sign over the rights to the treasure to secret holding entities connected to the Central Intelligence Agency. As outrageous as it sounds—it happened. The true story of Victorio Peak begins here in Book One, *The Gold House—The Discovery.*

Ova and Doc Noss, circa 1945

Chapter 1
"Where gold goes, blood flows."

O va Noss was born Ova* Coultrup. She was reared in Saffordsville, Kansas. Doc Noss, whose real name was Milton E. Noss, was born and reared in Taloga, Oklahoma; Doc† was three-fourths Cheyenne Indian. Their lives were wrapped in mystery and adventure; in fact, *they* were legendary: the way

they lived, what they believed in and how they fought to keep what they had found together. No one in this world is perfect, and certainly they weren't, especially in Doc's case. Doc had a reputation in his own right; he liked to drink and that caused them more problems than either of them needed or could afford. Whether or not the criticisms mounted against Doc were deserved in every instance, no one will ever know.

The first time I met Terry Delonas was shortly after I came to Las Cruces when he came there to discuss the case with me; some days we talked for hours. It was through Terry that I began to understand how many of the characters interacted with each other and what roles they played in an astonishing and unbelievable true-life drama, a drama that involved the discovery of a fabulous treasure. I soon came to realize that the *true* story of Victorio Peak, which is the accounting of the

events and the people who came and went from there, was more valuable than the treasure Doc and Ova Noss had discovered.

To have a better grasp on the story of Victorio Peak treasure and the events that surrounded the discovery of the Noss treasure trove, it is helpful to know something about the dozens of colorful characters who worked and lived in the Caballo and San Andres Mountains and the events that took place when Doc and Ova Noss lived near the foot of Victorio Peak. Many of the people who came to the Caballo or San Andres Mountains were prospectors, thieves, murderers, the curious, and

*Ova Noss in her early twenties - taken in Saffordsville, Kansas
†Doc Noss thought to be in his late twenties. Taken in Taloga, Oklahoma

the well-intended. One other commonality they all shared, and as Ova Noss often was quoted saying, was that, "Where gold goes, blood flows." As in the case of many treasure hunters who had found gold, trouble followed close behind.

Although there were many characters who moved in and out of the area over the years, the key characters whose paths crossed in the Hembrillo Basin and in the Caballo Mountains from the 1930s to the late 1970s were: Willie Douthit, Buster Ward, and Fred Drolte. If Willie, Buster, Fred, Doc and Ova had anything in common, it was that they had all found ancient gold bars and valuable artifacts, especially Doc and Ova Noss who had found the mother of all treasures inside Victorio Peak.

To better appreciate the story of their discovery, one has to go back in time, back to the Great Depression when jobs were hard to find and earning a living was difficult. As was the case throughout the entire country, there weren't many

jobs in or around Las Cruces, New Mexico, even before the Depression, so it's not difficult to understand why there was always someone looking to find something of value that could be converted into cash. Although there were always people looking for gold, and there still are today, the incentive to find it was heightened because of bad times, when getting from one day to the next was the goal for the day and the hope for tomorrow.

It was during the Great Depression that the Victorio Peak treasure story began, at a time when Doc and Ova Noss started camping for long periods of time a short distance from the foot of Victorio Peak in the Hembrillo Basin. Their shelter was an ancient *rock house*, a primitive structure* that had stood for hundreds of years. There are a variety of stories about the origin of the building, but time has kept its secret of when it was built, for what reason, and by whom. When Doc and Ova first arrived in the Hembrillo Basin to explore for treasure, they needed a place to sleep, hunt for game, cook their meals and make

---

*Similar structures in the region are not uncommon; many are thought to be three centuries old.

their plans; the old house they had stumbled upon was perfect, and there was also a fresh supply of water gushing from a natural spring nearby. Although it needed some work: roof repairs, window coverings and eviction notices served on a few packrats and rattlesnakes that had taken up residence there, it wasn't long before they were ready to move in. As the years came and went, their new home-away-from-home was simply called—the Rock House.

During this time, but a few years earlier in the 1930's, a man named Willie Douthit also found a fortune in gold in a cave somewhere in the Caballo Mountains. Later Buster Ward found the same cave, or at least that's what Ward claimed. Some say that Willie took Buster in as a partner, but the accounts of their actual relationship, and there are plenty of them still floating around throughout the Southwest, remains somewhat of a mystery to this day. Willie Douthit, a man who was born poor and died wealthy, entered the world in 1908 in Midland, Texas. Although there were many variations of his last name, Willie's birth record lists his name as William Douthit; official records in California will bear that out. Before the saga ended, Douthit closed the entrance to his treasure cave with a charge of dynamite—the entrance has never been found. Buster Ward's real name was Robert Ward Jr., the second child of a homestead family that migrated from Texas to Palomas, New Mexico, where they settled on the east side of the Caballo Mountains. Later his father Robert and other members of Buster's family settled in Lordsburg, New Mexico, a well known Western town located about 110 miles west of present day Las Cruces.

As in most stories of the American Southwest, one can put a finger on a map and find the names of famous towns, cities, mountain ranges and rivers, landmarks that ring a tone of familiarity. But what made those places so familiar to us all were the people who lived in the region: the Native American Indians, the settlers, the explorers, the U.S. Cavalry, the ranchers, the cowboys and the outlaws as well. We will not list all of the characters, only a few, those whose lives significantly impacted the history of New Mexico as it relates to the Victorio Peak treasure discovery by Doc and Ova Noss.

The list of individuals who played a significant role in the formation of the American Southwest is a long one; but still, not unlike today, there were the good guys and there were the bad guys. Unfortunately, the bad guys usually got most of the attention. It was a turbulent time in this region, especially in the late 1700s, so a brief look at the history of this section of the United States during that time period will enhance the reader's insight and understanding of what is to come. We will trace events that made significant alterations in the historical fabric of the American Southwest, specifically New Mexico, and especially the lands along the Rio Grande from El Paso north to Santa Fe and the vast expanse of desert region known as the Jornada del Muerto, the Caballo and San Andres Mountain Ranges, and the Tularosa Basin where White Sands Missile Range is located.

One person who made a significant impact on the region was Padre LaRue; his footprints in this saga are an indelible part of the journey you are about to take. LaRue's fabled treasure story was one of the legends that lured many treasure hunters into the desert in the search for great wealth; Doc Noss was one of them. The search area stretched from El Paso north to the end of the San Andres Mountain Range, including the area west of the Caballo Mountains to the Rio Grande. LaRue's impact on the region started when he left France for the New World and ended in a cavern in New Mexico where he located a rich vein of gold, a vein that his loyal supporters worked and cast bars of gold into different sizes and shapes, crude ingots made from sotto stalks or sand molds, often referred to as dory* bars. The early miners would gather up clean sand and mix it with molasses or sugar water to hold the sand mold together. They would then make an impression in the sand and pack it tightly and pour the molten gold into it. During this process, the gold would often break through the crusted sand mold and form little "trees" or barbed-like protrusions that resembled a thorny cactus, which were cut off once the ingot cooled. The process did not produce the same clean bars produced today, but it was highly economical to refine then, as it is today.

The mining and transporting of gold through New Mexico was important to the commerce of the region, and up until 1880 trade and travel along the Santa Fe Trail sustained a steady growth. However, before the Santa Fe Trail's historic contribution to the general region's economy ended, a lot had happened that impacted greatly upon the lives of those who lived there. Much of the difficulties arose during periods of upheaval and unrest when the U.S. Army was at odds with the Native American Indians and when *they* were at odds with the settlers and the miners. One such Native American was Mangas Coloradas, a "huge man with a mane[†] of black hair" known also as Red Sleeves, who on one hand made alliances with many of the miners, yet in other areas of the region he raided other mine operations. Coloradas was the mentor to Cochise, Geronimo, and Victorio. Kathleen Chamberlain wrote[‡] in her book:

> *At times he* [Victorio] *was a war leader and a chief, but he was a sensitive man as well. He was both pragmatic and profoundly spiritual. Americans favored the more gregarious Cochise. Neither has Victorio generally appealed to Hollywood filmmakers, who consistently see Geronimo as the better story.*

~

* Dory ('y' is a long 'a' sound) is a term long-used by early prospectors. In the precious metal industry, Dory bars are also called *cactus* bars. For more clarification, a *dory* is a small, edible saltwater fish *golden* in color. Whether the term "dory bar" originated because of its resemblance to a Dory fish is unknown.
[†] J. Hook, *The Apaches* (Osprey Publishing, 1987)
[‡] K. Chamberlain, *Victorio, Apache Warrior and Chief,* (University of Oklahoma Press: Norman, 2007) p. (XV)

The centerpiece this story focuses on the many events connected to the Noss treasure discovered inside Victorio Peak, which was named after the legendary Warm Spring Apache warrior. Other tribes, such as the Chiricahua Apache paid respect and honored Victorio as their leader as they did Cochise and Geronimo.

November 1839

Another event that might have led to the discovery of the treasure trove inside Victorio Peak was the translation of the "Prediction of Pedro Navares." Before he was hanged, Navares confessed to his long history of raids and murderous ways, thus presenting a waybill, or narrative map where he had hidden much of the loot he had captured, treasures he and his bandits had stolen over the years. Those translations were made in the convent of San Augustine in Mexico City and then sometime between 1846 and 1849, they were translated into English. It was also common for treasure hunters such as Doc Noss to read Navares' confessions, supposedly true admissions made by Navares prior to him being hanged. During the investigation of the Noss treasure saga, this writer and three friends, Raul Garza, Tito Gomez and his brother, Hugo (Tito and Hugo are one-fourth Apache), explored the Caballo and San Andres Mountain Ranges together. In one such journey, we discovered signs* and markings that led us to the unmistakable conclusion that we had located one of Navares' mountain camps. Navares' confessions were commonplace in the region and were even reprinted in books and in newspaper over the years.

January 24, 1848

During this turbulent period, something else occurred that resurfaced the landscape of California, Arizona, Colorado, and New Mexico. On this date, James Marshall discovered gold at Sutter's Mill. The discovery triggered the California gold rush, but less fortunate prospectors and miners eventually drifted back to New Mexico and other locales from the California gold fields empty-handed, especially after the Civil War had ended. These new arrivals scarred the landscape with their mining operations and fenced off large areas for their livestock and were soon despised even more than the U.S. Cavalry Horse Soldiers by the native inhabitants. The miners and prospectors were among the thousands of "white eyes" who invaded the lands of Native American Indians and together with other settlers, they turned their hunting grounds into grazing land for their cattle. For nearly a half-century, beginning with the California Gold Rush of 1848, the population of Native Indians in the American Southwest was reduced eighty-nine percent; a loss of nearly 130,000 people is attributed to enslavement. Although the Gold Rush ended in 1859 with the discovery of silver in Nevada, the practice of genocide by enslavement for the purpose of

---

* Signs – a terminology used to refer to petroglyphs, pictographs and hand-placed rock formations that indicate a trail or path, an event, or the presences of valuable treasure or artifacts.

forced labor to mine gold and silver for the benefit of whites continued until about 1900.

As an enticement for the miners to leave their land, Mangas Coloradas, who had been captured during one of his raids, offered to show the miners "a hill of gold if they leave, forever." Instead of gaining his release, Coloradas was killed. In retaliation, the Apaches took to the warpath, killing miners and taking their gold. During this time Cochise, Juh, Nachee, Geronimo, and Victorio emerged as great warriors. Victorio, now considered a renegade by the U.S. Army, continued to wage war against the military, miners and settlers who had encroached upon their land. Chamberlain wrote:*

> *Thus, for most of winter 1879-80, Victorio stayed on the move, circling Warm Springs, moving to the Rio Grande and back, and generally keeping well ahead of the soldiers constantly tracking him. There were occasional clashes, but it was the Apache scouts that most worried Victorio.*

~

Chamberlain:[†]

> *By late March or early April, Victorio was still camped on the eastern side of the San Andres Mountains in a place called Hembrillo.*

~

One of the more celebrated battles between the U.S. Army and Victorio that earned him renegade status took place on May 28, 1880 near Victorio Peak in the Hembrillo Basin. By the end of May that year, Victorio was unbeaten, but reportedly demoralized. He headed south. Six months later, Nana and his Apache band took up the fight and attacked the small town of Chloride, New Mexico; then, on July 17, they ambushed a pack train of Lt. John F. Guilfoyle's 9th Cavalry. Guilfoyle pursued Nana and his warriors to the San Andres Mountains, but by July 25, Nana had escaped and throughout that summer his raids continued. One of those raids occurred on August 21, 1880, at Lake Valley, west of present day Hatch, New Mexico. Soon afterwards, he staged another attack on a wagon in Dog Canyon near Alamogordo and there joined with Victorio and his remaining braves, including Taza, the son of Cochise, who was chief of the Chiricahua before Geronimo.

By March 1883, Chato, chief of the Chiricahua Apache, and Geronimo continued raids and murdering near Silver City, New Mexico. Judge McComas and his wife were killed and his son was captured. B. Bramble Ownby, who later became associated with Doc and Ova Noss, was a Territorial Ranger at the time and rode with the posse that brought the bodies in from the Apache raids. But for Victorio and other Native American Indians who fought and died to preserve their way of life, the end would soon come.

Ibid, p. 180
[†] *Ibid*, p. 184

Eve Ball lived in the Ruidoso highlands close to the Mescalero Reservation, a close neighbor and friend of the Apache. Here are passages from her book* as told to her by James Kaywaykla, the nephew of Victorio and grandnephew of Nana; Kaywaykla was present when Victorio died at the Massacre of Tres Castillos. Eve Ball is speaking:

> *I was told that each Indian on the Mescalero Apache Reservation received a check each month from the government. People believed this to be true. It was not.*
>
> *I found it difficult to penetrate the wall of reserve behind which the Apache kept themselves. I met Ramona Chihuahua Daklugie, wife of Asa Daklugie, and through her sought an interview with her husband. It was four years before he decided to talk to me. He was very influential among his people, and induced several of them to talk to me also.*
>
> *When James Kaywaykla made his annual July visit to Mescalero for the 'Ceremonials for the Maiden', my Apache friends brought him to see me. Over a period of years following, he dictated to me the events of his childhood."*
>
> *James Kaywaykla is speaking: (XII)*
>
> *Until I was about ten years old I did not know that people died except by violence. This is because I am an Apache, a Warm Springs Apache, whose first vivid memories are of being driven from our reservation near Ojo Caliente with fire and sword.*
>
> *As I tell this story, I am the sole survivor of the Massacre of Tres Castillos in which our great leader, Chief Victorio, fired his last bullet before taking his own life, and in which his band of almost four hundred people was nearly exterminated. Among the seventeen who escaped death or slavery were my mother and myself..."*

~

Another account of how Victorio died appears in Chamberlain's book.[†] She wrote that according to Kaytennae, one of Victorio's warriors "arrived later and buried the bodies…" Kaytennae claimed he found Victorio with a knife "embedded in his heart."

In retaliation for Victorio's death, seventy year old Nana led what was left of Victorio's band of warriors in a series of dramatic raids where even more gold was seized.

James Kaywaykla is speaking: pages (XIII-XV)

> *Victorio had killed many people, but the count was small in comparison to the number of lives Nana exacted in retaliation for Victorio's death. This was conceded at one time by Geronimo and also by Juh, a Nednhi chief who terrorized southern Arizona for years.*
>
> *For twenty-seven years my people were prisoners of war. For several of these years I was a student at Carlisle Indian School in Pennsylvania. … I married Dorothy Naiche, and therefore was closely associated with this leader for years. … I hope, also,*

---

*E. Ball, *"In the Days of Victorio - Recollections of a Warm Springs Apache,"* (University of Arizona, 1970) p. IX, X.
[†] Chamberlain, **op. cit.**, p. 206

that this account may bring about a better understanding of the Apache among white Americans."   *—James Kaywaykla*

...James died in his sleep at Fort Sill Oklahoma, June 27, 1963.   *— Eve Ball*

~

More than half a century later, in 1916, Father Albert Braun was "assigned as a missionary of the Order of Franciscan Monks (O.F.M.) to the Mescalero Apaches." Before his arrival at the Mescalero Reservation, the Chiricahua, Warm Springs and Nednhi Apaches were also brought there. Father Braun wrote the foreword in Eve Ball's book. Here is an excerpt from his contribution:

> *Much has been written by the white man about the Apache: accounts have been written as military reports by young officers ambitious for promotion; reports have been compiled by Indian agents; by contemporary newspapers whose owners depended upon advertising paid for by merchants who lived by selling supplies to reservations; by pioneers who entered country occupied and claimed by the Apaches, especially following the Civil War. Some of those stories were written by men who wanted to take over Apache country, but because of heroic resistance on the part of the Apache were not immediately able to realize their objective. Seeking the support of public opinion, these intruders often pictured the Apache not only as warlike, but cruel and vicious—a people who should be driven from the mountains of the Southwest. At best, the truths in these portrayals were only partial. At worst, they were no truths at all.*   *—Father Albert Braun, O.F.M. (vii-viii)*

~

The lamp of truth shines brightly for those who choose to light it. Those who choose not to, stumble in the darkness forever. In writing the three books of *The Gold House*, I learned that little has changed since Father Braun wrote about his experiences with the different tribes of the Apache. Eve Ball's book points out the cause for these lies: a Chiricahua runner named Nicholas notes:

> *The White Eyes are superstitious about gold. Their lust for it is insatiable. They lie, steal, kill, die for it. If forced to choose between it and things many times exceeding it in value they unhesitatingly choose gold. Little do they care that they incur the wrath of the Mountain Gods. (32)*

~

It has been said that some things are true whether you believe them or not. Such is the case with the accumulated chain of broken promises, treachery, and the needless displacement of once peaceful American Indians by the U.S. Army whose actions set in motion a torrent of anger, revenge and slaughter. In its quest for domination over the original inhabitants of this country, the U.S. Army went about destroying the things most precious to the American Indians: their families, their land, their customs, and, most of all, their pride. As a result, thousands of Native Americans, settlers, and soldiers died needlessly.

The experiences and suffering of the Apache Indians of New Mexico, for that matter every other Native American Indian tribe in the United States, first came under the sword and guns of the United States Army, later from the politicians who imprisoned them and allowed them to die needlessly, railed them to prisons and detention centers in inhospitable territories, and finally corralled them in wilderness ghettos on their own land and called them *reservations*. The politicians of the time, who signed those treaties and agreements, broke every one of them. But it was not a simple issue of breaking a promise; it was a planned manipulation of a nation of people: promise them something of value, steal their land, enslave and imprison, commit genocide through forced confinement where it could control the surviving tribes. From Eve Ball's text:

> In 1870, Washington [D.C.]* promised Victorio that if his people would stay on a reservation they would be furnished with food, and would be given a thousand blankets. …The acceptance of the terms meant the relinquishment of a vast territory, which both chiefs knew they would eventually lose, but a small portion of their lands being assured to them. …Victorio was promised his reservation so long as the mountains should stand and the rivers exist. This promise was secured by a piece of paper called an Executive Order. …As Victorio feared, the word of the white Nantan† was worthless—as worthless as the paper which he had accepted. (49)
>
> ~

The breaking of a promise, specifically reconciliation by treaty, was a tactic carried out in the days of Victorio, carried out by the U.S. Government through its military resources at the time. The government made treaties, which were executed by the Army, and then deliberately violated them. The scheme was simple: create treaties with the Native American Indian tribal leaders, then cast aspersions upon their culture, degrade their worth and integrity, create fraudulent accounts of their true nature as a people to falsely justify breaking the treaty, which was done consistently. Similar tactics were used against the Noss family from the late 1930s through 2000 during the years in which the treasure trove issues were either developing or when the same issues were being largely scrutinized by the Ova Noss Family Partnership, namely its General Partner, Terry Delonas.

What the Chiricahua runner Nicholas said about gold and the white man's desperation for it was accurate—even prescient. The proof being that certain military leaders at the White Sands Missile Range were also guilty of such

---

* Inserted
† The Apache referred to General Crook as Nantan Lupan, often thought to mean Grey Wolf, which is incorrect. In a footnote on page 125 of the book, *Indeh, an Apache Odyssey*, written by Eve Ball, Nora Henn and Lynda Sanchez, Eugene Chihuahua stated, "You White Eyes think that Lupan means Gray Wolf, but it does not. They named the general that because of the color of the clothes he wore most of the time, and they were not gray; they were tan." Perhaps the term "white nantan" used by Victorio was a general reference to white soldiers and Washington politicians in general.

improper conduct concerning Victorio Peak during the seven decades mentioned; they did precisely what their military forebears had done to the Native American Indian. That is why Book Three of The Gold House is entitled, *The Gold House—Executive Order.*

May 17, 1885

A little more than two years later, and nine years before Milton Noss was born, Geronimo, Chihuahua, and Natchez were once again on the warpath and had ravaged the counties of Grant, Sierra, and Socorro in New Mexico, but by the end of the year, they had all surrendered to the U.S. Army. Geronimo was perhaps the most famous and revered Indian warrior, a great defender of his land, culture, and people. Faced with genocide, U.S. expansion, and the murder of his entire family, including his mother, Geronimo went to war against miners, settlers and the U.S. Army: three separate forces that had set out to destroy the Apache's way of life by stealing their land and making them surrender to the white man's laws. Under the promise of a truce, the U.S. Army murdered Mangas Coloradas, a great Apache leader who was loved by his people. The ruthless murder triggered yet another bloody war. Among others, Geronimo fought under Cochise and Victorio and became heralded for his cunning and survival as a warrior, a great war chief said to possess powers given to him by supernatural beings. His ability to elude the U.S. Army for more than a quarter century, gave rise to the legend he was able to walk in the desert sand and not leave footprints, and was able to see into the future. Geronimo was *the* Apache chief, a man of great wisdom, and a powerful and wise medicine man. His name became synonymous with bravery and cunning, but it was not enough to withstand the great pursuit and never-ending quest to drive the Apache from their homeland. Eventually Geronimo and his band of followers surrendered and by 1886 most Apache bands were beaten. It was in Skeleton Canyon, the site of the Monterrey treasure loot, where Geronimo, the last great chief, finally surrendered himself to U.S. forces.

In the early 1870s, the Apache faced extermination by starvation, but in spite of his surrender, Geronimo resisted the shredding of the Apache culture and way of life. In 1876, refusing to accept the Chiricahua's expulsion to the San Carlos Reservation, he fled with his new family and banded with other Apache survivors in Mexico. In an effort to cover their sins, settlers who grabbed the Apache's land, government officials and the U.S. Army who set out to exterminate them, labeled the Apache as murderers, savages who had to be imprisoned or killed, but if at all possible, the latter. To be used as an example, Geronimo was slated for elimination, but he survived many such attempts. Finally in 1880, tired of warring and killing, Geronimo returned to San Carlos. But when the U.S. Army tried to suppress a religious meeting attended by Geronimo himself, Geronimo led a fight against them and then fled San Carlos with many others from his tribe. By 1884 Geronimo and his band of followers, unable to sustain even a minimal existence, and to avoid starvation, were forced to return to San Carlos. Then, after a brief period and unable to endure the harsh treatment and the abolishment of Apache tradition, Geronimo and other prisoners of war who shared his discontent once again bolted from San Carlos. But the inevitability of defeat was once and for all at hand; Geronimo and a large contingency of Apache finally surrendered to General Nelson A. Miles in 1886.

Taking no chance of a repeat performance, Geronimo was immediately shipped to St. Augustine, Florida with hundreds of other Apaches in open boxcars. There, in St. Augustine, Geronimo and his Apache kinsmen became prisoners of war and were forced into hard labor where many died from malaria and tuberculosis and other diseases in the hot, humid Florida climate. After great suffering and hardship, in 1894 Geronimo and more than 300 prisoners of war were shipped to Fort Sill, Oklahoma where they were imprisoned. Their lifelong quest to be free and live in peace had vanished. In exchange for his release, Geronimo also offered to tell the soldiers the location of the massive gold hoard hidden in the Hembrillo Basin in New Mexico, but he was never released and there is no record of Geronimo revealing the information, except perhaps to one individual.

March 4, 1905

Permitted to travel with Pawnee Bill's Wild West Show for a short time, Geronimo wandered aimlessly in the white man's world and suffered the loss of his dignity. Then, on March 4, 1905, as a final insult, Teddy Roosevelt had Geronimo removed from where he was kept in the guard house at Fort Sill and shipped to Washington for his inauguration address; Geronimo was a human trophy who represented American military expansion policy: genocide, murder, and imprisonment. After the festivities, Geronimo was sent back to Fort Sill, Oklahoma where he was allowed to walk around freely. People would come to meet him and take his photograph. Four years later, on February 17, 1909, at the age of 83, Geronimo died, still a prisoner at Fort Sill. That same year, Milton Noss had turned fifteen.

Chapter 2

Doc, Ova and Others

People who knew Milton Noss, hereinafter referred to as *Doc*, said he was older than what he claimed to be; even Josie Belle Butler, a close childhood friend, said that he was older than he let on. Ova Noss had often told family members that her suspicions were that Doc, for some unknown reason, had hidden his true age. Josie said that he was not born on the date indicated on the 1913 School Census Record[3] in Taloga, Oklahoma, but rather on July 3, 1894. It was in Taloga that Doc was raised, schooled, and educated by the white man. Josie also said that his natural father was a man named Tom Starr. Starr's aunt was rumored to be the outlaw Belle Starr, but that issue has never been settled and most likely never will be. Terry Delonas talked about the issues concerning Doc's American Indian descent:

> *Doc was mostly Cheyenne Indian, and in the ancient custom and tradition there was someone in the tribe known as a "Peace Chief" who was more or less fated to go out and acquire things for the benefit of his people, but also in the same tradition, this individual could not keep any of these things for himself.*
>
> *Also as I understand it, most American Indian tribes seemed to have a prophecy or saying about the morning star and the person who would save their people would be the person who had the wisdom of the morning star. Interestingly, Chief Victorio's other name was Lucero, which means "Morning Star." It could well be that Doc, choosing to continue using the name Starr, made sort of a double-entendre, and by using this name it spoke to his larger mission, which might well have been to recover this source of value and use it for the benefit of his people.*

---

* The board shown in this photo was removed from inside Victorio Peak during excavations in the 1990s.

The fact that Doc left the T-star* board inside the top shaft might lend to that possibility. But too, it might be a simple coincidence. Also interesting is that the great grandchildren of Victorio live in Las Cruces.

~

During the 1990's expedition of Victorio Peak, site project manager Alex Alonso unearthed Doc's *"T☆ "* board, a tangible indication of the validity of his lifelong interest in the name. His connection to the name Tom Starr is also apparent from the burnt woodcarvings found on the Rock House door, a place he and Ova called home for two decades while they came and went from there to unearth the treasure inside Victorio Peak. Among the many other signs and treasure location symbols burned into the door with the narrow flame of a miner's lantern, is *"3/4 Cheyenne,"* a declaration of Doc's American-Indian heritage.

Tom Starr's father, James Starr, was a member of the Cherokee Nation and had signed the Removal Treaty of 1835. James was killed on November 9, 1845, leaving behind his wife Suke and eight children: Tom, Washington, Ellis, Bean, Buck, Creek, and two other children whose names are unknown. Buck was born crippled and died in 1845 at the age of fourteen. Bean was killed at an early age, but the cause of his death is not recorded. In vengeance for his father's death, Tom turned outlaw. He eventually settled in Briartown, Muskogee County, Oklahoma where he and his wife, Catherine, raised eight children: Sam, Ellis,

Cooper, Mosie, Tulsie, William, John (Jack), and Washington. When Julia Ann Noss, Doc's natural mother, remarried, Doc was left with a cruel and abusive stepfather. It wasn't long before he ran away from home. Alone and now on his own, Doc was taken in by a woman with a large family, but she was also a cruel person; after a short stay, he wandered home, defeated, tired, and hungry.

His return home was not welcomed; he was told he would have to sleep in the barn loft where his mother slipped him food and water. Doc's stepfather, whom he disliked, was now in charge of the large family and there was little his mother could do to raise her son in a caring and loving way. Having nowhere to go, he began working at a young age doing menial chores whenever he could find work. He had but one friend he could always count on to share a secret or to just pass the time of day, her name was Josie Belle; if anyone knew the real Doc Noss, it was Josie. When he grew older he worked on a nearby cattle ranch, but most of his days he lived among the Cheyenne and it brought him comfort. Doc's fate was on a course of its own; the years ahead would be difficult for the boy of mixed blood, but there is no question that Doc was proud to be an American Indian.

In 1895, Ova Coultrup came into this world, born of Wynona Lee Porter and John Coultrup of Saffordsville, Kansas. There were seven children in the Coultrup family: Will, Charlie, Orlie, Cecil, Amy, Ova and Irl. Ova, the second youngest in the family, recalled the days of her life at the homestead in Saffordville. Her father was a competent attorney and state circuit judge. Like the circuit judges of the old west, John Coultrup rode the Oklahoma circuit for years, an emissary of justice throughout the state. In time, fate would bring Doc and Ova together and they would eventually marry. Their lives together would embrace a saga that would leave an indelible mark on the landscape of American history.

~

Josie Belle Butler[4] (her full name was Josie Belle Ward Butler) claimed Doc had been confined to a detention area at Fort Sill, Oklahoma. Terry explained:

> *In an effort to go back to Doc's early life, his youth and childhood days, we came across a story told by a woman who claimed to have been a childhood friend of his. This woman lived in Albuquerque and her name was Josie Belle Butler. Josie wrote out an account of those times and passed it onto her nephew, who in turn shared it with us. We learned that when Doc was a young boy he stole a thoroughbred horse from an adjoining ranch and Josie claimed that he was taken to a retention center at Fort Sill, Oklahoma. At that time in his life, Doc lived near the fort, and it was because he was a half-breed Indian that the authorities decided to put him with other Indians, who were being held prisoner there, until they figured out what to do with him. Eventually, the owner of the horse came forward and vouched for Doc and he was soon released.*

~

Josie claimed Doc originally heard the story of Victorio Peak treasure from an Indian Chief who was being held at Fort Sill. According to Josie the Chief's name was Geronimo. She said that it was Geronimo who told Doc what was hidden in "a certain mountain," things that were so "valuable to the White Man." Geronimo claimed that it was his people who had taken many things there for hundreds of years, but the mountain had been sealed up. Even though Doc was a young boy, it was impressed upon him, that when he grew older he was to go out and find this place and use what was stored there for the betterment of his people and to make his search "his mission in life." Geronimo claimed that since Doc was part White and part Indian he would be free to live and prosper in the White Man's world, whereas "a full-blooded Indian could not." More of Terry's account:

> *What is so interesting about this whole account was Doc's age, as Josie claimed, only about eight, and for him to remember this unusual event so early in his life, and then to carry such a strong impression with him throughout the years, is somewhat extraordinary. Then to know that later in his adult life Doc found this amazing treasure inside Victorio Peak is even more extraordinary.*

~

The story of Doc's childhood encounter with Geronimo, a man who knew the secret of Victorio Peak, resonated with the Noss family from other treasure stories of the Southwest; it wasn't confined to what they knew about Doc's experiences when he was a young boy. It so happens that an Apache Indian Chief, Mangas Coloradas, attempted to bargain with the commander at the Fort Sill prison where he was also being held, that if he allowed his people to return safely to their land he would take him to a cave where the Indians had been storing yellow metal for hundreds of years. Coloradas remained a prisoner at Fort Sill, as did Geronimo, who died there as a prisoner of war.

The Noss family's connection to Geronimo, and specifically to Terry, did not end with Josie's account of Doc and Geronimo. Terry told a more modern version of the Geronimo connection:

> *Although I don't recall the purpose of the trip, when I was about thirteen years old I went on a trip with my grandmother down to Hatch from Clovis, but as I recall, it had nothing to do with Victorio Peak. But on the way back home to Clovis it was already night and when we were driving through Socorro. Babe said that she wanted to stop there because she wanted to introduce me to somebody. I thought it was kind of late to be visiting people, but she said, 'No, I want you to meet this person.' I asked her who it was and she said it was the grandson of Geronimo and as it turned out, Babe knew him through Doc.*
>
> *Babe wasn't shy; she went to a couple of houses, knocked on a few doors and asked where he lived. Finally someone pointed where to go. It had been some time that Babe had been there and it being dark, she had to drive around slowly looking for his place, but*

when we finally came to his house, she recognized it and we stopped and got out. The place where he lived was a small stucco apartment among a row of other buildings that looked just like it. When he came to the door, he immediately recognized my grandmother.

~

The man invited them inside and Ova introduced Terry to the aging Indian. Terry thought that he was in his seventies, describing him as a large man who was very wizened, "wrinkled, dry and rugged in appearance with a dark complexion" yet in contrast to his appearance he was shy and gentle with a "jovial, friendly gleam in his eyes." Being "hesitant with my presence the man was a little slow to speak." Eventually he told Terry that inside the Peak there were stacks of gold bars at least sixty-feet long and then, pointing to his kitchen, he said they "were that high." Terry continued:

> *Well, at the time, I didn't have any place to put his story in my mind in the larger scheme of things, other than my grandmother was certain there was a link to the treasure and Geronimo. But when he described what was there, he was a bit lacking in the narrative, so my grandmother had me ask him questions. It was probably my first Peak interview; I was still a young teenager.*
>
> *I asked him if he had actually seen gold bullion and he nodded and said, "Yes." And then I asked him if he had seen more than one stack and he said, "Oh, yes, many stacks and many bars" and there were coins and jewels there. He also talked about stone boxes, valuables in stone boxes. I really didn't know enough to ask better questions, but he also talked about how much dust there was in there.*

~

Terry believed that Ova's rationale for his meeting this man was so he could hear the story directly from an authoritative source and also to impress upon him that the history of Victorio Peak and its secrets were common knowledge among the Native Americans in the region, that the spiritual importance of Victorio Peak truly existed among the Native inhabitants throughout southern New Mexico, *and* that Geronimo told Doc about the treasure while he was with him at Fort Sill. Thereafter, having heard the story from the grandson of Geronimo, that Geronimo had told Doc about the treasure's existence, there was no longer any question in Terry's mind that the story was factual. Likewise, there was no question in his mind that Doc and Ova had found the ancient treasure. Terry finished his thoughts on his experience:

> *I knew then that it certainly wasn't my grandmother's intent to play up or highlight the Indian history of the Victorio Peak site to strengthen her legal claim on the treasure; she simply went out of her way to have Geronimo's grandson tell me the story for my benefit. When he began telling what was inside of the Peak, it was as though he had seen it himself. Then he told me he had seen it firsthand. Up until then, the only person that I had thought had been in there with Doc was Seraphin Sedillo and Benny Samaniego, men who had worked for Doc, and yet here was another elderly Native American*

who knew exactly what was inside Victorio Peak. The point of it all was that my grandmother wanted me to hear it firsthand, but more than just hearing it I was equally surprised that she had this relationship with someone who had a very famous relative such as Geronimo.

~

Geronimo was born in 1829 in western New Mexico at a time when the entire region was still Mexican territory. His homeland was in the Sierra Madres in Mexico where Geronimo's bloodlines and culture crossed three Apache divisions: the Bedonkohes, the Nednais, and the Chiricahuas. When he was young, the Apache called Geronimo, Goyathlay—"The One Who Yawns." He was taught to live off the land by his mother and how to survive in the inhospitable environment in the mountains and desert; it was his father who instructed him in the ways of a warrior. Early in his life, he settled at the headwaters of the Gila River where the Bedonkohes lived, the homeland of his wife, Alope, where she and Geronimo reared three children. But in Fort Sill, he was a prisoner. Under what circumstances Doc and Geronimo came to know each other and how long they were together, is not known, but his time with Geronimo was brief; that much is known, an encounter that was later verified by Josie Belle. What Geronimo had told Doc and the encouragement he gave him set him on a quest that ended in the Hembrillo Basin.

On June 8, 1906, President Theodore Roosevelt signed into law the Antiquities Act, officially entitled, *An Act for the Preservation of American Antiquities* (16 United States Code 431-433), thus making it a permanent law of the United States. The Act gave the President authority to curtail the use of federal lands passing on to the President power by Executive Order to circumvent any Congressional oversight. The thrust of the legislation was to protect historic Indian artifacts and tribal ruins deemed to be "antiquities" that were located on federal lands. Pre-existing treasure trove laws, which were on a state-by-state basis, were in some respects companions to the Antiquities Act. Rules concerning treasure troves were initially given genuine consideration in the Oregon Supreme Court in 1904, but the Court's ruling was flawed in that the finder was considered the owner, regardless of the landowner's claim, thus completely disenfranchising the true owner. Today, many states have enacted treasure trove laws. Simply stated, any treasure in question, primarily gold bullion, gold coins, and similar silver objects, had to be hidden; a requirement that favors the *finder*, even if found on property of another. Its issues embrace the fundamental adoption of "American majority rule with English common law roots" and remain in play to this day. Although numerous court cases have argued a variety of claims related to the doctrine, it still remains that under the current treasure trove laws in various states, the treasure belongs to the finder. The lure of gold remains incontestable and the clearly identifiable attraction to it among American Presidents and a number of high-ranking U.S. Army officers would endure.

In 1915, while World War I was raging in Europe, Ova Coultrup, now twenty-one, married Roy Beckwith. There were four children of the marriage: the oldest child, Letha was born in 1916, one year before America entered the war in Europe. Dorothy was born in 1919, right after the end of World War I. Two more children would follow, Marvin and Harold. Then, after twelve years of marriage Ova and Roy divorced. The four children of Ova Coultrup Beckwith would experience the unfolding of an American epic during a time of dire poverty—the Great Depression.

On November 11, 1918 World War I ended and soldiers were coming home from Europe, wounded, in caskets, or not at all; a bittersweet victory for the *American Doughboys.** In Europe it was much the same. Even though Germany had been defeated, victims of the war on both sides were climbing out of the rubble, scratching for food, shelter and their identity as human beings. At home, stateside, it was a time for peace, a time for quiet reflection, a time for healing. But in New Mexico, there was turmoil. Only six years had passed since New Mexico had become a state, and there was still much lawlessness: government and police corruption, murder, and robbery in a region still not in step with the rest of the country. The Great Depression was looming and organized crime had a grip on the big cities. America had growing pains, and at various times during the next half-century we were at war.

---

* The term Doughboy is thought to be the description of U.S. infantry forces during the Mexican-American War. While marching in the arid region of northern Mexico, their uniforms became covered with dust that gave the soldiers the appearance of unbaked dough.

Chapter 3

People of the Caballo Mountain Range

M any people, through their actions or involvement in one thing or another, have impacted on the history of New Mexico; some are more prominent than others. One such couple was Rebecca and Charlie Taggert. Rebecca was the niece of Porfirio Diaz, the dictator of Mexico until 1910 when he was executed by a firing squad. Before he met Rebecca, Charley Taggert lived in California; he was financially well off in his own right, in fact he owned a Rolls Royce and was known for his good looks and his tendency to be flamboyant. They fell in love, got married, and came to New Mexico in search of gold.

When Rebecca and Charlie arrived in Hatch, New Mexico, they hired a man named Milton Holden as a guide. Compared to their former, comfortable life styles, the Taggert's life of adventure and exploration in the Caballo Mountain Range is hard to visualize; their home was a scantly furnished cave situated high above Noah's Ark, a name given to the formidable rock outcropping by persons unknown. From there the rocky slopes of Granite Peak where Douthit's cave remains hidden can also be seen where the desert and the rugged surrounding terrain runs out to the Caballo Lake.

From their high perch, the Taggerts dug relentlessly to find the source of a rich vein of gold, reportedly seen by other prospectors. It wasn't long until the Taggerts contracted with Doc Noss to help with their mining operation at their claim site on Noah's Ark. The early years of their lives were spent hunting for treasure in the Caballo Range, and they claimed they had found skeletons entombed in a sealed cave. After Charlie died from a head injury sustained in their mine, Rebecca* remarried, and as of 1963 was living in El Paso, Texas, a two-hour drive from her former mountain cave-home east of Hatch, a small town along the Rio Grande seemingly undisturbed by time. Hatch, originally named Santa Barbara in 1851 was renamed Hatch in 1875 for Edward Hatch, an Indian fighter who later became the military commander of New Mexico.

---

* Details of Rebecca Taggert's business connection to Doc Noss are covered in Chapter 12.

21

John Clarence:

During one of the field investigations in the case, I stood beside Jerral Holden,* a man I had come to know while doing the research for The Gold House. From our position high on the slopes of the Caballo Mountain Range below Noah's Ark, Jerral pointed out the trails, arroyos and treacherous mountain roads prospectors, miners and murderers used to reach their secret caves, gold caches or the gravesites of fallen friends and enemies. It was not the first time I was there; I had been there many times before with Dick Moyle, a prospector who showed me where he watched as a man named Fred Drolte removed a fortune in gold bars from a deep shaft. But on this particular trip, I was with Jerral Holden, looking down at the hills where it all happened—rugged, untamed, as it was when Doc and Ova Noss, Douthit, Ward and the Taggerts were hunting for ancient buried treasure.

~

In little more than a decade a man named Leland Howard would begin his long career at the Treasury Department. There, he would serve as Chief of the Bureau of Domestic Gold & Silver Operations and at times as the Assistant Director of the Mint under Nellie Tayloe Ross. During his stay at the Treasury Howard would earn his political spurs; he would go to Germany after World War II, sort through tons of stolen gold bars and Nazi loot taken by Hitler's army and return to Washington to write what became known as the "Howard Report." He remained with the Treasury from 1934  to 1966, survived every president from Roosevelt to Johnson and moved about freely in the shadow of powerful individuals at the Pentagon. His tenure was similar to that of J. Edgar Hoover's long stay as director of the FBI. In Hoover's case, his place in government was assured because of his secret files on key individuals in Washington; Howard's long stay at the Treasury was assured because of what he knew about gold. Howard saw and *knew* things few civilians, politicians or military individuals ever experienced, specifically his direct involvement with the handling of Nazi gold and other valuable loot taken from the banks and museums of conquered European countries—and from Jews during WWII. He knew about the transportation of gold bullion and the treasures of Europe, down to the gold rim glasses and gold-filled teeth pulled from the mouths of Holocaust victims before they were cremated. Howard was

---

* The Holden family had lived in the area of the Caballo Mountains for decades. Jerral's mother had firsthand knowledge of the exploits of Willie Douthit and Buster Ward. I interviewed her in 2002.

dispatched to Germany where he made a report on what had been seen there; his official seven-page report became known as the "Howard Report." It was from his knowledge of and his involvement with the gold of conquered nations that his power grew and his position at the Treasury was assured until he voluntarily retired after more than four decades of government service.

Howard's knowledge of Nazi gold is a matter of history, yet his involvement with domestic gold is barely known. One such gold hoard, in which he was intimately and directly involved, was the Noss treasure trove, an involvement that would surface again and again. Howard's* strength and influence was apparent in the 1960s when he took control of a special matter involving a large cache of gold bullion that had been found inside Victorio Peak two years earlier; the two individuals who found the cache were both servicemen from Holloman Air Force Base. He would usurp the power and authority of the Pentagon and the Commanding General at White Sands Missile Range in 1961 and illegally and unlawfully order the excavation of the mountain where the treasure lay hidden.

Circa 1927

Then there was Anemone Margaret Perrone, daughter of English and French descent, born February 28, 1871, at Highland Park, Michigan. A bright and caring young woman, she entered the field of nursing and became a registered nurse. Shortly afterwards, Margaret attended the Northwestern School of Medicine and Surgery at Evanston, Illinois. She received her Doctor of Medicine, Surgery, and Obstetrics degree and served her internship at Lakeside Hospital in Chicago. Desirous to leave the congested area of Chicago, she left for the Southwest in 1927 and settled in Hot Springs, New Mexico (known today as Truth or Consequences) and operated a small hospital there. The hospital failed during the Depression, and Margaret went on to become a well-known midwife in Hot Springs and the surrounding area who spoke Spanish, English, French and the ancient Spanish dialect of Castilian. It was during these times that she came into contact with two men, Willie Douthit and Buster Ward. The Caballo Mountain Range, where Douthit and Ward were known to have frequented continually, was just east of town, an ominous outcropping of towering, rugged peaks and haunting canyons that run south as far as the eye could see, and is clearly visible from Hot Springs. She was one hundred-and-two years old when she died.[5]

~

It was Thursday, October 24, 1929, a day known in history as Black Thursday, a day when greed, corruption, fraud and the absence of government oversight in the commercial banking business caused the stock market to crash, an unstoppable event that triggered the Great Depression of the 1930s. The

---

* Howard's extensive involvement in the 1960s is covered in book two, *The Gold House—The Lies, the Thefts.*

failure of the commercial banking industry in the United States was followed by the passage of a bill in Congress that would greatly affect the activities of all banks, a bill that would mandate that investment banking and commercial banking were to be regarded as separate financial lending and investment institutions. It essentially prohibited commercial banks from making risky investments in the stock market with depositors' money, which was held to be the major cause of the stock market crash. It also established an independent agency called the Federal Deposit Insurance Corporation. The passage of the bill established the Banking Act of 1933, commonly known as the Glass-Steagall Act, named for its sponsors Carter Glass and Henry B. Steagall.

Glass, a conservative Lynchburg, Virginia Democrat, was elected to the U.S. House of Representatives in 1902, became the Chairman of the House Committee on Banking and Currency, and in 1918 was appointed Secretary of the Treasury. He was also the central figure in creating the Federal Reserve Banking System. Glass was appointed to the United States Senate in 1920 to fill a vacancy and he remained there until his death in 1946. Democrat Henry B. Steagall, who co-sponsored the bill, was elected to Congress in 1915 and thereafter, all succeeding Congresses until his death in 1943. In spite of the measures taken to prevent future

occurrences of such a catastrophic financial collapse, the fact remains that it was the absence of effective and honest government together with the systemic greed and fraud that permeated Washington politics that caused the crash, enabled by politicians who courted the Wall Street lobbyists and lined their pockets instead of protecting the interests of their constituents at home.

With the Glass-Steagall Act in place, no longer could commercial banks buy unsold securities with the massive cash reserves of depositors' money; now they were confined to fulfilling their intended role in the banking business by simply taking deposits and loaning money to qualified individuals and companies while investment banks, such as Goldman Sachs, Morgan Stanley and Lehman Brothers, were permitted to continue speculating in the wild world of stocks and bonds. The heyday of using the commercial bank's large cash reserves to make risky investments with the hope of earning huge profits for themselves was at an end; the banking scams that caused the Great Depression was quickly brought under tow. However, a little more than seven decades later, and under pressure by bank lobbyists, Washington politicians repealed the Glass-Steagall Act, setting off a second financial disaster in the United States that cost American taxpayers $1 trillion and greatly shook the financial industry worldwide.

November 6, 1929

Some people thought that Willie Douthit was a cowboy, but he wasn't, not in the true sense. Although he was wiry, lean, and tough, he never herded or branded cattle, rode fence, or participated in roundups. In fact, he could barely ride. He lived from hand to mouth on what little money he earned as a highway department flagman, a simple laborer with no other means of income who was otherwise penniless. At an early age he became a treasure hunter and soon developed a distrustful attitude that would make him a survivor. Then his life of poverty changed; Willie claimed that he had discovered a large amount of ancient gold bars secreted inside a cave on the slopes of the Caballo Mountain Range. He claimed that he discovered the treasure by following indications and signs of a treasure map he found in the walls of an old adobe house near Fort Selden, New Mexico, an old military fort not far from Hatch, a map that had been sealed up for ages, perhaps a century or longer, a map that Douthit claimed led him to a cave, an *accumulation room* for a large number of gold bars left there by unknown persons. He also claimed that his effort to learn the secrets of the map and his eventual success in finding the treasure cave didn't come easy. When he allegedly found the map, he was living with Milton and Jessie Holden on their small ranch in the valley just west of the Caballo Mountains* and claimed he took the map there and revealed it to the Holden family.

Milton and Jessie Holden could speak and read Spanish, but the waybill was written in Castilian† and they were unable to read it correctly. If Douthit was going to learn the secrets hidden in the old map, he had to find someone who could read the ancient Spanish writing. Eventually he arrived at the door of Margaret Perrone, who allegedly helped Willie decipher the odd symbols on the map. More of Douthit's good luck came when Perrone told him that if he was going to find the treasure he needed a sextant. Douthit claimed Perrone told him that two Swedish sailors were living in Hot Springs, so he sought them out. As not to reveal all of the secrets of the waybill, Willie wrote the strange numbers on a separate sheet of paper and showed them to the sailors, who confirmed the numbers were in fact navigational coordinates. He used their sextant to locate the treasure and claimed that a short time later, on Wednesday, November 6, 1929, he found the treasure. That was the sequence of events that Willie Douthit told over the years—that was Willie's side of the story.

---

* Today the Holden ranch lies deep beneath the Caballo Reservoir, officially called Caballo Lake State Park.

† *Castilian,* a Romantic dialect of Spanish, migrated from northern Spain to the Kingdom of *Castile* and became the official language of government and trade. *Castilian* followed Spain's colonization of the Americas beginning in the 15th Century.

Then there was Jack Reynolds, a boy who was directly associated with Perrone. Their relationship was simple: Jack was homeless, in his teens, very ill and Margaret Perrone took him in and nursed him back to good health and became his protector. After he recovered, he was riding his horse near Fort Selden when the weather turned bad, so he found shelter in the abandoned Fort Selden. While he was gathering scraps of wood to build a fire, he tore out an old windowsill and found the maps. He gathered them up and rode back to Hot Springs and showed them to Perrone. When she saw the maps, she couldn't believe what he had in his possession. She knew what the signs meant on the map and on a step-by-step basis she sent Jack out to confirm her findings and then return to explain what he had found. Soon the Reynolds boy found the cave and started removing a few of the gold bars and returned home with them. Somehow Douthit learned that Jack had found gold bars and followed him to the cave, went inside, killed Jack and left him there. Once Douthit got inside, he found other documents; that is how he came into possession of the maps he had claimed he found at Fort Selden. The last time Jack was seen was at Painted Pony Hill riding horseback near a place called the signature tree. Two days later, Jack's new, red, wool coat was found with two bullet holes in it and it was taken to Margaret Perrone, who had bought Jack the coat. There is more to the story, but it was Jack Reynolds who found the treasure cave, not Willie Douthit.

~

Unfortunately for Willie, he flaunted his good luck and showed one of his gold bars to some of the cowboys on the Holden ranch and Willie's luck turned sour; he was kidnapped at gunpoint and held in the Caballo Mountains where he was tortured. Douthit explained his kidnapping ordeal during a filming in 1989; he was in his late eighties when he allowed the following videotape interview: (indications in parenthesis are digital timing markers) (36:16)

> *Well, before my time there weren't a lot of treasure hunters in there [meaning in the Caballo Mountains]. But after that Argosy article came out, the treasure hunters came in there and they had rifles, and one guy had a .357 pistol…and shot his heel off. They came in with Army rifles and everything. It was dangerous. Women too, there were a lot of women who came in there.*
> *Well, I was very lucky, but the only thing is I did a stupid thing; I talked too much. I told these guys I was going to find a treasure. But they would laugh and they were out there around the corral, a half dozen of them I guess. Anyway, they were standing around there and I said, 'Alright, all of you bastards, you've been laughing at me, now laugh this off.' I just threw it [meaning a gold bar] on the ground, ya know. Boy they tasted it, and they drilled it and knocked chunks off and everything else.*

~

When this incident took place, the Holden family lived in the valley on Percha Creek on the Holden ranch. It wasn't until the late 1938s that the U.S.

Bureau of Reclamation created a reservoir on the Rio Grande and called it Caballo Lake. But just before the bragging incident at Holden's ranch took place, Willie had already been looking for a buyer for some of his gold. In researching Willie Douthit and his discovery, this writer learned that Willie had talked about going to Gallup, New Mexico, where he had intended to sell some of the gold, but the news of his good fortune had arrived in Gallup before he had. Arriving there with only a small sample of one of the gold bars, Willie completed his business on Saturday, November 9, and then returned to the Jornada Hotel in Hatch where he was staying. Willie's story continues about what had happened after he returned to the hotel where he had planned to meet his gold buyers the following day: *(40:15)*

> *So then, I got two of Holden's kids to take me to Hatch; their grandfather was a butcher [there]. Well, he looks it over and he bangs it up. Well, that night they came and got me. Ya' see like an idiot I talked too much. And they tried to make me tell them where it was. And the thing of it is there were five of them.*

~

Willie and the five men left the Jornada Hotel at gunpoint and he was driven to the Caballo Mountains. More from Douthit's interview: (40:53)

> *They kept me up there a couple days and it was snowing, and they wanted to go home and they left this one guy guarding me, see. The others went home. Well, I talked to him and said, 'I'll cut you in on this.' I convinced him, so he untied me and I took him down and I showed him the gold and he went crazy. He decided, well I'll just kill this guy then. But I got the best of him and got away.*

~

Willie reported the incident to the police and an investigation was conducted, but nothing developed. Here is the complete 1929 newspaper article[6] by Mrs. I. A. Cardwell:

> *- The El Paso Herald, Thursday Evening, November 19, 1929 -*
> *Claiming the discovery of an immense hidden treasure in gold bars in the Caballo Mountains and telling a story of having been kidnapped and held for several days as a prisoner at a remote point in the mountains, Willie Douthit has asked protection from the sheriff's office here against those he claims are watching him in an effort to learn the location of the treasure.*
> *Douthit claimed to Deputy Joe Lucero that he had been searching the Caballo Mountains for buried treasure for several weeks and that on November 6, he found it hidden in the crevasse of a cliff, and not a cave as formerly reported. He said there was a pile about twice as large as an ordinary office desk consisting of poured bars of pure gold varying in size. He said he took one bar from the cache and brought it to the Holden Ranch and later came to the Jornada Hotel, bringing the bar with him.*
> *At midnight, three armed men entered his room forcing him at the point of a drawn revolver to accompany them to where they had a car. Douthit claims he was bound,*

according to his story, and placed in the car. They then drove to Hot Springs, crossing the river at Elephant Butte dam by Engle to Cutter and into the Caballo Mountains from the east he said. Here they went into camp and were joined by three other men. They demanded that Douthit show them the location of the gold, but he told them he could not do so on account of not having his instruments.

"Held Several Days"

Douthit claims he was held at the camp in the Caballos for several days and finally they placed him in a car and together they drove him out again crossing the river and that near Socorro he succeeded at making his escape. He says that the report that the gold was carried away by the men in the car is erroneous but that he estimates the place where they were camped in the mountains is two or three miles from the cache.

Sheriff Felipe Lucero, who had been investigating the alleged kidnapping, says that several persons at Hatch and Caballo claim that they saw the bar, which Douthit claims he brought out with him. He also said the room at the Hatch hotel was left in disorder with Douthit's suitcase and belongings left in it.

Douthit claims that he found the gold cache with the aid of a chart, which he obtained from a monastery a short way north of Mexico City. He says the original chart he had was destroyed and that he will ask the monastery for another copy before again attempting to locate the treasure. He claims the men who kidnapped him are still watching him. Douthit was unable to describe the five men whom he claims held him a prisoner in the Caballos.

"Many Treasure Hunters"

The Caballo Mountains, adjacent to the Jornada del Muerto, have for years been a favorite hunting ground for buried treasure.

~

Willie finished his story:

Well, the main thing they did was they tied my finger to a spark plug on their car and started the engine. Don't think that didn't hurt like hell. And they thought they picked up some poor little country boy. They had their hands full. But I was lucky, I got mine [meaning a treasure trove] and I got out. But after all that excitement, I had a hard time settling down. I tried everything. I even tried the Army. That was pretty good duty. Well, I'm down to my last million and I'm going to have to start digging again, I guess. I've been living off the fat of the land ever since.

~

The event in November 1929 was not the only time that Douthit was kidnapped, there were others, but there was never a time when anyone attempted to kidnap Willie and Buster Ward together. On another occasion when Willie was kidnapped, Buster helped him escape. From the 1989 interview:

They'd catch us one apart. We were a little hard to handle and Buster was mean; it took about four men to handle him, and then some. I got a little bit mean, too. Yeah, they had me tied up down there in a canyon. They had me suspended and they were really giving me the business. Ol' Buster busted in and broke 'em up. When Buster got mean, he was mean.

He was a nice guy, actually, one of the nicest men I ever met. But people didn't like him because then, nobody had money and Buster had money to burn. That kind of makes people envious, but he didn't take crap off nobody.

~

Willie's kidnapping came as no surprise to those who knew him, including those who tracked his activities in the Caballo Mountain Range. The adventures of Douthit and Ward are told here in a chronicle of events that took place in the 1920s and 1930s related to large troves of gold bullion they had discovered. Willie Douthit and Buster Ward's discovery dismisses any doubt that ancient gold bars were hidden within the Caballo, San Andres, and Franklin Mountains to the south where the Rio Grande swings southeast dividing El Paso, Texas, and Ciudad Juarez, Mexico. In addition to Douthit, Doc Noss discovered another sizable treasure trove in the Caballo Mountains and it wasn't long afterwards that he discovered a second and much larger treasure at Victorio Peak located about 40 miles north of the White Sands Missile Range headquarters. The brief account given here concerning the trials of Willie Douthit, and later his partner Buster Ward, is a true story.

Circa May 6-8, 1930

Nearly six months after his first kidnapping, Willie took on Robert "Buster" Ward, as a partner; earlier in time, Ward's father* had ranched on the east side of the Caballo Mountains. Three years later, a lengthy family letter[7] explained how Buster learned about Willie's gold cave, a cave that Buster had also found. The letter gave a detailed account of the night of Saturday, May 6, 1930. Two days earlier, having made arrangements at a bank in Lordsburg to get a loan on the gold, Willie and Buster went into the hills to get the bars to take to the bank. They stopped at Hot Springs and unloaded a toolbox containing four gold bars from Willie's old car into a car provided by Judge Doan who lived in the town. When they finished transferring the gold, they headed to Lordsburg in Judge Doan's car with the gold. Judge Doan later testified that he actually saw Willie and Buster load the toolbox into his car. About a mile east of Deming, New Mexico, a car pulled across the road in front of them. Soon they were looking down a gun barrel and were immediately ordered into their car. The men opened the box, threw the gold bars and the two men in their car and headed for the suburbs of El Paso, Texas, where the outlaws stopped the car, removed the gold bars and disappeared. Willie and Buster, thinking they were

---

* Buster Ward's father wrote the original Ward letter. The original *carbon copy* of the letter was in the Noss files. Mr. Ward had retyped a letter that had been written by children in his family, which was signed, "your loving kids." The entire letter is located in the document catalog.

FREIGHT TRAIN GRINDS OFF N. M. MAN'S LEGS

ROBERT WARD HURT AS HE MISSES GRIP

Amputation of Both Limbs Below Knees Is Necessary

School Heads Testify In Court

PRINCIPAL SAYS PUPILS 'SHOOT CRAP'

Tells Why Students Not Permitted to Leave Austin Grounds

Clear Cemeteries For Storm Victims

WHOLESALE BURIALS IN TEXAS TORNADO AREAS; DEATH LIST IS STILL 70

Seriously Ill

Explosion Starts Costly Oil Blaze In Bayonne, N. J.

Kiddies Flock To 'Goliath'

Ysleta's Claim To Oldest Church In U.S. Still Good

DAYLIGHT BANDIT ROBS STORE; MAKES GETAWAY

Metropolitan Area

still in danger, darted from the car and made a run for a freight train that ran alongside the road. Tragically, Buster fell beneath the train and both his legs were cut off; he was then taken to the Masonic Hospital in El Paso. That night, Willie sent a telegram to Robert's family in Lordsburg that read: "Robert in Masonic hospital, both legs cut off. Bring Eunice." Later, while they were visiting Buster in the hospital, Willie talked of five skeletons in the cave and a *fresh one*. But Buster held up a warning finger. Soon after, Willie disappeared from the area, apparently to Phoenix, Arizona. Buster recovered, received artificial legs and continued riding in the Caballo Mountains. An article[8] in *The El Paso Herald* on May 8, 1930, tells of the event:

- ROBERT WARD HURT AS HE MISSES GRIP -
Amputation of Both Limbs Below Knees is Necessary

Buster Ward

Willie Douthit in the 1930s.

Robert Ward, 27, of Hot Springs, is in a critical condition at Masonic hospital, after having both legs cut off when he fell beneath a moving freight train to which he was attempting to swing* at Poplar and Mills street at 10:30 a.m.

Bones on both legs, just below the knees, were crushed. He was operated on at noon and both legs amputated.

Willie Douthit, 22, of Portales, N.M., Ward's companion, told police that he and Ward were "swinging a train out of town" after being brought to El Paso by two bandits who held them up near Deming, N.M. and robbed them of between $60,000 and $80,000 in gold bullion, which Douthit claims he found in the Caballo Mountains near Hot Springs.

Douthit last November told of being held up and robbed of $6,000 in gold bullion in a hotel in Hatch, N.M. Douthit claims he and Ward were on their way to Lordsburg, N.M. to cash the bullion when two men armed with shotguns, held them up, reloading 250 pounds of bullion into the bandit's car.

The bandits drove them to El Paso, Douthit said. The men abandoned the car and bullion somewhere in El Paso, leaving Douthit and Ward in the car. Douthit said he and Ward became frightened and ran off just before the accident.

---

* Swing is an old railyard term used to notate someone jumping onto a moving train, primarily an open boxcar. After a train has begun to move, the person hitching a ride will *swing* his arms upwards and jump at the same time. This movement increases the amount of upward force off the ground.

Police said they are skeptical of Douthit's story of the bullion, as New Mexico officers were equally skeptical of his story of the robbery last November.

~

A participant and eyewitness to everything that happened that day was Willie Douthit himself, and he had a little more to tell; more than what was printed in *The El Paso Herald* the day after the incident. Douthit gave a detailed account of what happened that night in May 1930. There was no mention of the large amount of money that Willie and Buster were carrying when they were kidnapped. From his 1989 video interview:

> *Buster and I sold a bunch of gold and we had our shirts full of money, see. We were goin' to catch a freight and go down to Brownsville or somewhere and enjoy life, and we*  *had to go over to Juarez and get a drink, according to Buster, and old Buster fell under the freight. I got on the freight first then I looked back at old Buster layin' there with his legs off. I thought, well, 'I'll leave.' Well, I couldn't do that, so I went back and put a tourniquet on his legs and somebody called the hospital. When they put him on the table they started opening his shirt and here was hundred dollar bills fallin' all over the place. They called the cops of course and the cops said to me, 'Don't leave this hospital.' They checked all the banks and everything else; they thought we had robbed a bank. But they could never find it, so then they gave Buster's money to his father, his father in the meantime came out there. Boy, he was there before you could turn around. And then they gave me mine back. I went on my way and Buster went on his way. But when he came back, he was good on those legs. He could get on a horse just like a monkey.*

~

December 1930

In December of that same year, after Buster had recovered and was moving around on his own, Willie tried another gold run. Unfortunately for Willie, he was kidnapped *again* and tortured, but once more he escaped with his life. It was the second time that Douthit had been kidnapped and tortured, but it was the last time. Taking his newest peril as the ultimate and final learning experience, he decided to leave the area. But he would eventually return in 1990 to tell a tale of murder.

Buster Ward was not the only person to find Willie Douthit's cave; Doc Noss had found it too. He told Willie time and time again that he had found it, but Willie didn't believe him. When Doc described the interior of the cave in perfect detail, and the size of the treasure and gave him a description of an old potbelly stove inside the cave, Willie finally believed him. During that recorded interview in the 1990s, Douthit also told the same story to members of the Noss family, confirming that Doc had described Willie's cave. Most of the gold Willie and Buster Ward discovered is still buried in the same cave where it was found, a cave which Douthit and Ward said had five skeletons and a *"fresh one."* But there were stories of other *fresher* human remains as well, people who had died at the hands of others, perhaps by Willie and Buster. Many rumors still float today that also point the finger at members of a group called the Guerrilla Gang. But are they more than rumors?

What Willie finally left behind in the form of a public accounting of his worth is but a small reflection of what he actually uncovered in the Caballo Mountains. Stories of vast treasures of gold stashed in the San Andres and Caballo Mountains go back for centuries, but until Willie Douthit brought out a bar of gold to attest to the validity of his find, there was no evidence that any of the rumors were valid. Those rumors came to an end with Willie's discovery.

November 7, 1931

With the legal assistance of attorney T.H. Lester, Seminole County, Oklahoma, Roy V. Beckwith was granted a divorce on grounds of desertion. Ova did not appear at the hearing, but the custody and education of her four children were granted to her. Under the terms of the divorce, lots 33 & 34 at 1029 SW 28th Street in Oklahoma City were also conveyed to her. The divorce decree was filed on November 7, 1931, but it did not become effective for 6 months. During that time, she worked as an elevator operator, a waitress, and a piano player for a dance hall, all in an effort to hold her family together. She eventually left Oklahoma City for Ponca City and then "moved around a little" with her children. Sometime in November 1931, she began playing the piano with a small band. Her band tour took her to Las Vegas for a short while, but, in an effort to lessen the strain on her children, Ova finally moved back to Oklahoma, sold her properties on SW 28th Street and moved into a small house on West 6th Street in the city. She continued to work hard supporting her family alone playing the piano and working as a waitress, but there were no more road trips. She remained at her residence on West 6th Street until 1933 when she met Doc Noss and began an on-and-off courtship with him.

January 10, 1932

An incident reported in various newspapers from Hot Springs to El Paso revealed Buster Ward's efforts to divulge the location of the entrance to the cave he and Willie Douthit had kept secret. For some unknown reason, Ward made plans to rent 10 trucks from a local lumberyard in Hot Springs at $100 each and move the rest of the gold out of the cave and turn it over to the authorities; the reason for this dramatic turn has never been clearly understood. Although Buster had gone to great lengths to set things in motion to remove the gold, at

the last minute when the trucks were approaching the area where the cave was located, Buster broke down and cried out that he couldn't go through with it. But there was even more drama attached to the moment.

According to accounts given by individuals who knew what happened that day, shortly after the convoy neared Granite Peak at a place close to where the gold was hidden, a flash of light reflected down on the men from a spot high on Granite Peak just above the truck caravan. Immediately, Buster assumed that it was Willie and let everyone know they were in danger, believing for certain that Douthit was sighting *him* with the business end of a rifle. Two Sheriff Deputies from Hatch and four Federal Marshals responded and rode out on horseback in the direction where the reflection had come from. However, it was most likely that the person they were chasing was *not* Willie Douthit; it was a well-known fact that Douthit couldn't ride a horse to save his life. When Willie saddled up, it was always a mule—not a horse. The man who rode away was spotted clearly by one of the Federal Marshals through his binoculars. He later reported that the person they were pursuing was an accomplished horseman who knew the terrain well, led the posse into a blind canyon, and then he seemed to disappear. The chase lasted for more than an hour. When the Marshals returned, their horses were exhausted. Whoever the authorities were chasing lost them in the mountains. Federal Marshals in the region were accomplished horsemen, to the man, so if they were in pursuit, the person they were tracking would have had to be cunning and a competent rider. It was surmised that the person they had chased was someone Willie had hired to scare Buster and stop him from leading the convoy to the gold. It was also believed at the time that the rider was a cowboy from a local ranch, someone Willie knew personally. When the incident occurred, Willie lived in a small stone cabin, a line shack, situated below Granite Peak in the Caballo Mountains. Johnny Gordon was the cattleman who owned the building and the large ranch that surrounded it. Then his son, John Gordon Jr., took ownership, and later *his* son-in-law, Bob Grantham, took over the property; the Gordons are deceased. Grantham died in 2009; the cabin shown here is the actual cabin and it exists to this day. Douthit claimed that he could see the entrance to the treasure cave from a window on the right side of the cabin. During the investigation of the case, this writer discovered a bent and rusted lid from an old tin can nailed to a board above the window on the right side of the cabin; it was intentionally placed there as a direction indicator. It points in an easterly direction and it is thought to be the general direction Willie would go to get to his treasure cave. People in the area, mostly prospectors who still work claims near the cabin, claim that Willie could leave and return in about a half an hour with a bar or two of gold from his secret treasure cave. The GoogleEarth image below shows the stone cabin and its location in relationship to Granite Peak and the rough terrain that engulfed it. An arrow in the image indicates the exact location (32°56′46.20″N 107°15′24.51″W) of the old Gordon cabin and rough terrain in the Caballo Mountains where the chase took place.

The small mountain peak seen below is referred to as Granite Peak, a

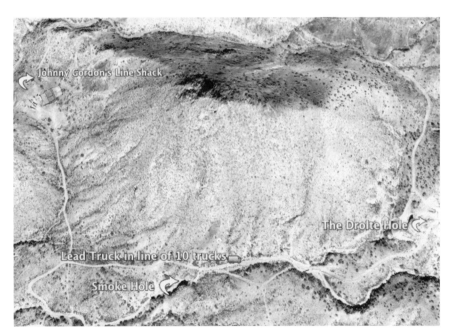

landmark widely known in the area. Gordon's line shack is located on the top-left of the photo, the "Drolte Hole"* is visible on the right, a cave known as the Smoke Hole is indicated near the bottom, and the "lead truck" seen in the photo is exactly where it had stopped ahead of the other nine trucks.

After it was over, Douthit did not take Buster Ward's actions lightly and according to Jerral Holden and others, Douthit threatened to kill Ward. Shortly afterwards Ward disappeared from the area and for more than a year he was seen drifting around the Southwest "like a man in a dream," as Holden described it. Over time, Douthit and Ward mended their fences and reestablished their friendship. Eventually, both men left the area and settled in California. With the exception of Douthit returning from time to time to scavenge a few gold bars from the cave, his departure to California was a permanent one, as was Ward's.

But it was Jerral Holden's mother, Madeline, who provided a concise account of her experiences with Buster Ward, claiming that she knew Ward personally.

John Clarence:
Knowing Jerral's mother had firsthand experiences with Douthit and Ward, it gave me an opportunity to verify some of the accounts I had learned about them. In October 2004 I called her and she granted me a telephone interview; then her name was Madeline Vivian Crockett and she lived in Veguita, New Mexico, a small village one hundred and seventy miles north of Las Cruces.

~

In 1941, Madeline married Jerral's father, Joe Buck Holden, and for a while they lived in Elephant Butte north of Hot Springs where Joe Buck worked for an electrical company. Joe Buck's father, Milton Holden, owned and operated a working cattle ranch on Percha Creek where they raised horses and "did a little farming." When they got married, Madeline and Joe Buck lived on the Holden ranch, but within a few months Joe Buck was drafted into the Army and Madeline moved into an apartment in Hot Springs; at that time, she was pregnant with Jerral, who was born in September 1942. Six weeks later, Madeline moved to Marianna, Florida, where her husband was stationed; she remained in Florida for about eighteen months. When Joe Buck was sent overseas she returned to the Holden ranch and shortly afterwards she moved to Long Beach, California, with Jerral where she stayed with her parents. She worked at the Lockheed factory there, but before the war ended Madeline moved back to Hot Springs. There was much more to the initial conversation, but I was soon convinced that she in fact had known Buster Ward personally as she had indicated earlier.

Her experiences with Ward began in 1941 before the United States was

---

* The Drolte Hole got its name in the late 1960s when a man named Fred Drolte filed a mining claim on the site. Drolte played a major role when he and others stole 36.5 tons of gold from Doc and Ova's treasure site at Victorio Peak in November 1973.

involved in World War II, at a time when she and Joe Buck were still living at the Holden Ranch before Jerral was born. Buster Ward described to her and the Milton family what was inside the treasure cave: (25:50)*

> *There was a bank of gold bars that was about three or four feet high and about six foot long against the wall of the cave. And then there was a chest over on one side with jewelry and necklaces; Mrs. Holden wore some earrings, they were rubies. One of those guys gave them to her, but I don't know if it was Willie or Ward that did, but she wore those earrings.*

~

Not long afterwards I called her back to learn how deep the stacks were, meaning how many bars from the front of the stack to the wall. Madeline told me that she thought he had said about four bars from the front to the back, which would roughly account for the 1,500 to 1,700 bars Douthit claimed were in the cave. She also verified the account of Buster Ward bringing people to the area near Granite Peak to open the cave. The following account of what Madeline heard took place at the Holden ranch:

> *I know that Ward was there and my brother-in-law, we called him Blondie. He had a semi-trailer and he brought it over there. Buster told everybody, 'Now look, if there's anybody with a gun, we won't open this thing at all.' So, there was a United States Marshal and a sheriff [there]. Those people were there, waiting for the time when they were going to see where all this gold was.*

~

Madeline made it clear that she was not present the day Ward was going to lead everyone to the cave, but she was present when the matter was discussed at the Holden ranch. (17:22)

> *On top of Granite Peak there was a man with a high-powered rifle. In the sunlight, when he was moving around he didn't think anyone could see him. But that Ward, he could see anything. Light flashed from the gun and he [Ward] stopped everything. He told Mr. Holden and he told the sheriff, there's a man on top of Granite Peak and I'm not going to open it up because there's going to be a killin'. So, everybody left.*

~

Madeline claimed she was certain that it was not Willie Douthit on Granite Peak. Other witnesses to the same event said the U.S. Marshals rode out after the man who was on Granite Peak, but I did not mention the other versions of the events to Madeline and wished only to have her unclouded recollection of what she knew and heard personally; at the time of the interview Madeline was eighty-three years old.

All of what Madeline told me she learned in 1941 came from what the

---

* Indicates minute and second indicator on digital recording

Holdens and Buster Ward told her about the different events. The actual events described by Ward had taken place around 1932. Then the matter concerning Margaret Perrone came up. Madeline mentioned it without being prompted and referred to Perrone as Mrs. Harris, which was her married name. Mrs. Harris will be referred to here as Perrone. Madeline said: (18:10)

> *I think that Ward was the one who killed Mrs. Perrone's son. The child followed somebody into this hole [the treasure cave]. Mr. Holden had thought that Ward had killed this little boy. He was sure the little boy was dead in the cave. The boy wasn't hers [Perrone's], she adopted him and he was about ten years old. Mr. Holden said that he was sure Ward went into the cave and the boy had gone into the cave to see what it was all about. Ward told Mr. Holden that he [Perrone's boy] was back in the cave and Ward told Mr. Holden, 'I didn't know what it was. I killed it.'*

~

In 1932, Franklin D. Roosevelt was elected President of the United States; his role in matters related to gold was about to change the face of a nation—and the value of money in America.

Chapter 4

Roosevelt and the Great Depression

William Cranch and William Marbury were known in their time as the "Midnight Judges." Cranch, who lived from 1769 to 1855, was the nephew of John Adams, who in 1801 appointed him judge of the District of Columbia circuit court. In the case of *Marbury v. Madison,* the Supreme Court had for the first time in U.S. history declared something unconstitutional, which led to the establishment of the concept of judicial review in the United States. The decision allowed courts to oversee and legally invalidate the actions of any branch of government, further defining the checks and balances of the American form of government.

- "All laws which are repugnant to the Constitution are null and void."* -

The history of the Noss treasure began in 1933 during a time of great despair in America, for that matter most of the world. One in four wage earners in the United States was out of work, banks were in crisis and prospects for a brighter tomorrow were not on the horizon for most Americans. Even though there was plenty of food, ironically, there was little to eat; it was a lean but eventful year: Franklin D. Roosevelt was sworn into office, Willie Douthit left New Mexico a very rich man and headed for California, and Doc Noss began searching for *his* treasure. With these events in motion, a dark cloud was forming and a string of connecting and disastrous events was slowly emerging. Noss would find his treasure and Douthit made unannounced visits to New Mexico to uncover more gold bars and take them back to California.

Early in 1934, Buster Ward went to Austin, Texas to sell some of the gold dory bars from his and Willie Douthit's treasure site. He went to the American National Bank there and rented a safety deposit box, placed his gold bars in it, and asked the bank president for a $10,000 loan offering the gold as collateral. The bank president wouldn't make the loan. He most likely refused because of a new law called the Gold Reserve Act (GRA) that made it unlawful to possess gold.[†]

Though nothing else is known about Ward's efforts at the American National Bank, the gold bars that he had presented to the bank were specifically excluded under the GRA, meaning that the new law did not apply to ancient dory bars because this specific type of gold had undeterminable and varying values. The new law made it a crime to possess gold bullion of determined value, gold coins

---

*Marbury v. Madison, 5 U.S. (2 Cranch) 137 (1803)
[†] The Gold Reserve Act of 1934

and gold certificates, but because of the specific exclusion in the GRA that applied to "gold prior to refining" it provided an opportunity for a handful of people who had found ancient "unrefined" dory bars to turn them over to the Treasury for cash—but there was a catch; the Treasury's position was "show us where you got it and we'll *consider* paying you." This attitude and the inherent distrust in the government forced treasure hunters to find other means to dispose of their gold. Even with the exclusion related to unrefined dory bars, and although the buyers in these transactions were protected by an assay that verified the percentage of gold in the bar, bankers and dealers in gold were generally fearful of handling dory bars regardless of the exclusion, thus forcing treasure hunters to sell their gold at a greatly reduced price. The bankers and gold dealers who did buy these kind of bars were usually sophisticated in turning the gold they received into cash in black-market fashion by smuggling it out of the country, usually to Mexico or Canada.

January 31, 1933

Roosevelt abandoned the dollar's relationship to gold on this date; you could no longer walk into a United States Mint and convert your paper money into gold bullion or gold coinage. The previous gold standard had historically set the value of the dollar since 1792 by public law, fixing the price of gold at $19.39 per troy ounce. From then on gold certificates (paper currency) were equal in value to US-minted gold coins in circulation. In this manner, paper gold certificates symbolized an actual gold coin. In 1837, forty-five years later, gold was again fixed slightly higher at $20.67. Having a precious metal backup, the true value and worth of a single dollar had endured for one hundred and forty-one years;

that is, until FDR was elected. Up until then the real and true value of a one-dollar gold certificate was set by law to equal 0.051656 troy ounces of gold. It meant that the fractional amount of each dollar bill was approximately 5% of the value of one troy ounce of gold, thus the 0.051656 equivalent. Expressing the relationship between a $10 gold coin and a $10 gold coin certificate in the following manner makes it easier to follow: *Gold was money and money was gold.* *
Gold certificates allowed those who dealt in millions of dollars to own gold

---

* Dr. P. Hein, "What President Roosevelt did to Gold," (White Paper Circa, 2005), p. 1.

without taking it into possession. It also applied to the common person who had much less.

Saturday, March 4, 1933

On this day, nearly twenty years after the establishment of the Federal Reserve, Franklin D. Roosevelt, now the 32nd President of the United States, faced the nation to deliver his inaugural address with a plate full of concerns about the economic state of the country. He pledged to "speak the truth, the whole truth, frankly and boldly." He talked about the "unscrupulous money changers that stand indicted in the court of public opinion." He talked of "outworn traditions" and "false leadership" and the call to restore that leadership. "The Nation asks for action, and action now," he said. Roosevelt called for immediate action in putting "America's national house in order and making income balance outgo." He pledged with his constitutional authority to "bring speedy adoption" of his plan to restore the nation. He would ask Congress for the "remaining instrument to meet the crisis—broad Executive power to wage the war against the emergency, as great a power that would be given to me if we were in fact invaded by a foreign foe."

Roosevelt had assured Americans during his inaugural address that they would endure and survive the bad state of the nation. He also reminded Americans that in "every dark hour," they had always been given the understanding and support to claim victory. Then he gave the nation the bad news, describing it as "our common difficulties." He said, "They concern, thank God, only material things." He talked about shrinking values, rising taxes and the falling ability of Americans to pay them, all of which had historically been controlled by Washington politicians. He used flowery words to describe things Americans already knew firsthand, identifying them as the "frozen currents of trade" and the "withered leaves of industrial enterprise." As if they were unaware, he reminded farmers that their produce had no market and that the "many years of savings in thousands [actually millions] of families" was now gone. He reminded the unemployed of the grim problem of their existence and stated that, "Only a foolish optimist can deny the dark realities of the moment." In his enthusiasm to stir hope in the hearts of every American, he painted a dim existence for the entire population if something weren't done to change the manner in which Washington handled the country's financial affairs and he promised a cure for America's financial ailments.

March 6-10, 1933

Even before Roosevelt became President the word was out among political insiders that he intended to come off the gold standard. His rationale to do so was based on the fear that many U.S. banks would fail if a sustained rush to redeem gold certificates arose; a condition that he felt would deplete the Treasury's gold reserves. To deal with the banking crisis caused by the Great Depression and to avoid a crippling run on banks, under Executive Order 6102

he closed the banks and declared a national bank holiday that began on March 6 and ended on March 9, thus preventing banks from paying out gold coins for gold certificates; for four days Americans could not exchange paper money for gold coins. The move effectively froze the availability of gold to investors, commerce in general, and individuals who held gold certificates. The initial months of Roosevelt's presidency came to be known as the "The Hundred Days" when new executive orders and laws poured from the floor of Congress; the economy was the battle cry of an ailing nation. During the declared holiday, on March 7, 1933, and only three days after he took the oath of office, Roosevelt set the wheels in motion to end the gold standard in America, which was the prelude to the Gold Reserve Act of 1934. Five days after he took office, he pushed an Emergency Banking Bill, H.R. 1491, through Congress. Its author was unknown. One copy was provided to the House. Debate on the bill was kept to twenty-minutes per party, there was no roll call, and it passed the Senate that same night. Roosevelt immediately signed it into law.

The new law retroactively covered the illegal bank holiday Roosevelt had declared on March 6, and it also gave him unprecedented powers during wartime *or* during any national emergency he declared, allowing him to regulate all financial transactions and all banks and confiscate gold. Americans living in the continental U.S. were required to deliver all gold coins, gold bullion* and gold certificates to a "Federal Reserve Bank or a branch or agency thereof, or to any member of the Federal Reserve System" and exchange it for paper money, a *greenback,* the Federal Reserve Note we know today, shown here. Exchanging gold coins was simple, but as of this writing there was no information available that explained *how* gold bullion was exchanged; hallmarked bullion might have been paid at its "stamped" value.

For the purposes of this book, the definition of gold bullion in the confiscation act is important since the law did not say that ancient unrefined dory bars were considered to be bullion.

April 5, 1933

Ignoring the free market, Roosevelt surged forward at a rapid pace and by April 5, only one month after he closed the banks, he made it *unlawful* for

---

* Gold bullion has an exact value by weight and percentage of pure gold, which is usually 9/10ths pure by refinement. This type of bullion is easily definable by a stamped hallmark determining its value.

UNDER EXECUTIVE ORDER OF THE PRESIDENT

issued April 5, 1933

all persons are required to deliver

ON OR BEFORE MAY 1, 1933

all GOLD COIN, GOLD BULLION, AND GOLD CERTIFICATES now owned by them to a Federal Reserve Bank, branch or agency, or to any member bank of the Federal Reserve System.

Executive Order

FORBIDDING THE HOARDING OF GOLD COIN, GOLD BULLION AND GOLD CERTIFICATES

By virtue of the authority vested in me by Section 5(b) of the Act of October 6, 1917, as amended by Section 2 of the Act of March 9, 1933, entitled "An Act to provide relief in the existing national emergency in banking, and for other purposes", in which amendatory Act Congress declared that a serious emergency exists, I, Franklin D. Roosevelt, President of the United States of America, do declare that said national emergency still continues to exist and pursuant to said section do hereby prohibit the hoarding of gold coin, gold bullion, and gold certificates within the continental United States by individuals, partnerships, associations and corporations and hereby prescribe the following regulations for carrying out the purposes of this order:

Section 1. For the purposes of this regulation, the term "hoarding" means the withdrawal and withholding of gold coin, gold bullion or gold certificates from the recognized and customary channels of trade. The term "person" means any individual, partnership, association or corporation.

Section 2. All persons are hereby required to deliver on or before May 1, 1933, to a Federal reserve bank or a branch or agency thereof or to any member bank of the Federal Reserve System all gold coin, gold bullion and gold certificates now owned by them or coming into their ownership on or before April 28, 1933, except the following:

(a) Such amount of gold as may be required for legitimate and customary use in industry, profession or art within a reasonable time, including gold prior to refining and stocks of gold in reasonable amounts for the usual trade requirements of owners mining and refining such gold.

(b) Gold coin and gold certificates in an amount not exceeding in the aggregate $100.00 belonging to any one person; and gold coins having a recognized special value to collectors of rare and unusual coins.

(c) Gold coin and bullion earmarked or held in trust for a recognized foreign government or foreign central bank or the Bank for International Settlements.

(d) Gold coin and bullion licensed for other proper transactions (not involving hoarding) including gold coin and bullion imported for reexport or held pending action on applications for export licenses.

Section 3. Until otherwise ordered any person becoming the owner of any gold coin, gold bullion, or gold certificate after April 28, 1933, shall, within three days after receipt thereof, deliver the same in the manner prescribed in Section 2; unless such gold coin, gold bullion or gold certificates are held for any of the purposes specified in paragraphs (a), (b) or (c) of Section 2; or unless such gold coin or gold bullion is held for purposes specified in paragraph (d) of Section 2 and the person holding it is, with respect to such gold coin or bullion, a licensee or applicant for license pending action thereon.

Section 4. Upon receipt of gold coin, gold bullion or gold certificates delivered to it in accordance with Sections 2 or 3, the Federal reserve bank or member bank will pay therefor an equivalent amount of any other form of coin or currency coined or issued under the laws of the United States.

Section 5. Member banks shall deliver all gold coin, gold bullion and gold certificates owned or received by them (other than as exempted under the provisions of Section 2) to the Federal reserve banks of their respective districts and receive credit or payment therefor.

Section 6. The Secretary of the Treasury, out of the sums made available to the President by Section 501 of the Act of March 9, 1933, will in all proper cases pay the reasonable costs of transportation of gold coin, gold bullion or gold certificates delivered to a member bank or Federal reserve bank in accordance with Sections 2, 3, or 5 hereof, including the cost of insurance, protection, and such other incidental costs as may be necessary, upon production of satisfactory evidence of such costs. Voucher forms for this purpose may be procured from Federal reserve banks.

Section 7. In cases where the delivery of gold coin, gold bullion or gold certificates by the owners thereof within the time set forth above will involve extraordinary hardship or difficulty, the Secretary of the Treasury may, in his discretion, extend the time within which such delivery must be made. Applications for such extensions must be made in writing under oath, addressed to the Secretary of the Treasury and filed with a Federal reserve bank. Each application must state the date to which the extension is desired, the amount and location of the gold coin, gold bullion and gold certificates in respect of which such application is made and the facts showing extension to be necessary to avoid extraordinary hardship or difficulty.

Section 8. The Secretary of the Treasury is hereby authorized and empowered to issue such further regulations as he may deem necessary to carry out the purposes of this order and to issue licenses thereunder, through such officers or agencies as he may designate, including licenses permitting the Federal reserve banks and member banks of the Federal Reserve System, in return for an equivalent amount of other coin, currency or credit, to deliver, earmark or hold in trust gold coin and bullion to or for persons showing the need for the same for any of the purposes specified in paragraphs (a), (c) and (d) of Section 2 of those regulations.

Section 9. Whoever willfully violates any provision of this Executive Order or of these regulations or of any rule, regulation or license issued thereunder may be fined not more than $10,000, or, if a natural person, may be imprisoned for not more than ten years, or both; and any officer, director, or agent of any corporation who knowingly participates in any such violation may be punished by a like fine, imprisonment, or both.

This order and these regulations may be modified or revoked at any time.

THE WHITE HOUSE   FRANKLIN D ROOSEVELT
April 5, 1933.

For Further Information Consult Your Local Bank

GOLD CERTIFICATES may be identified by the words "GOLD CERTIFICATE" appearing thereon. The serial number and the Treasury seal on the face of a **GOLD CERTIFICATE** are printed in YELLOW. Be careful not to confuse GOLD CERTIFICATES with other issues which are redeemable in gold but which are not GOLD CERTIFICATES. Federal Reserve Notes and United States Notes are "redeemable in gold" but are not "GOLD CERTIFICATES" and are not required to be surrendered

Special attention is directed to the exceptions allowed under Section 2 of the Executive Order

---

CRIMINAL PENALTIES FOR VIOLATION OF EXECUTIVE ORDER
$10,000 fine or 10 years imprisonment, or both, as provided in Section 9 of the order

Secretary of the Treasury.

Gold Reserve Act of 1934

American citizens to possess gold: gold bullion, gold coins, *and* gold certificates had to be turned over to Federal Reserve Banks on or before May 1, 1933 by Executive Order, which was referred to as the Gold Confiscation Act of April 5, 1933. To curtail cheating, Roosevelt put teeth in the confiscation program; anyone caught hoarding gold faced a fine of up to $10,000, imprisonment, or both. He also outlawed the export of gold; under the new law, exportation of gold from the United States required a license issued by the Treasury.

In spite of all the language in the Act that mandated surrender of all gold to the Treasury, there was an exception written into the new law that specifically excluded *dory bars*, the same kind of gold that Doc and Ova Noss had discovered. Section 2, of Roosevelt's Executive Order stated that: (underlining inserted)

> *All persons are hereby required to deliver on or before May 1, 1933, to a Federal Reserve bank or a branch or agency thereof or to any member bank of the Federal Reserve System, all gold coin, gold bullion, and gold certificates now owned by them or coming into their ownership on or before April 28, 1933, except the following:*
>
> *(a.) Such amount of gold as may be required for legitimate and customary use in industry, professional or art within a reasonable time, including gold prior to refining, and stocks of gold in reasonable amounts for the usual trade requirements of owners mining and refining such gold."*

~

There being such an exclusion in Executive Order 6102 Section 2.a., an exclusion that was also present in the Gold Reserve Act of 1934, by pure definition an argument can be made that neither Doc nor Ova Noss were in violation of the law by possessing dory bars.

In May that year, Nellie Tayloe Ross (1907-1991) began her twenty-year run as Director[9] of the U.S. Mint, President Roosevelt's handpicked appointment. Having served as the first woman governor in the country in Wyoming, Ross came to Washington with political savvy. She remained in the Roosevelt administration during his entire time in office and learned well the art of survival in the Washington political arena. After Roosevelt, she continued to hold her position at the Mint under President Truman and became the single longest and continuous Director of the Mint in U.S. history, also the first woman in U.S. history to run the Mint.

Frank Leland Howard, Roosevelt's mysterious gatekeeper in the Treasury Department, was a long-hauler in the political patronage arena, a man who made it through many administrations safely and untouched. He served at various times as the Acting Director of the Mint and as Director of the Bureau of Domestic Silver and Gold Operations and became an invaluable asset to every administration he served, especially after WWII when he was sent to Germany to evaluate a great treasure of vast proportions; gold bullion, coins, and currency looted from the banks of Europe, priceless art taken from museums and private collections, and the personal property of the Jewish Holocaust victims, who were enslaved and murdered by the millions under the Nazi domination of Europe. Some of the stolen loot was gold from rings, eyeglass frames and gold teeth fillings that had been collected by Hitler's S.S., much of which was melted down into ingots. Howard would assist in the accounting of the Nazi spoils of war. Some of the loot would be returned to the rightful owners, but a vast fortune slipped out of Europe and was taken to America, a historical fact.

When it came to gold, and while they served together, Nellie Ross and Leland Howard established the ground rules for evaluating GRA regulations as it specifically related to the Noss treasure trove, which in time led to deliberate distortions of official Treasury Department records. Those distortions consisted of letters, memorandums, directives and specific instructions that were intended to slip past the real legal issues related to the Noss treasure trove. In an effort to keep the genie in the bottle, Howard maintained a separate file concerning the Noss treasure trove, and the Nosses. In time, Howard secretly shared his *personal* files with elements of the military at White Sands Missile Range. The day eventually came when Howard, by misrepresenting his intentions in letters to the Secretary of the Army, set out to spearhead an illegal scheme to secure the Noss treasure trove for the United States Government.

But this was only 1933, and Leland Howard had only begun his service with the United States Mint in Washington. Eventually, Howard's path would lead to Victorio Peak and he would deal directly with the Noss treasure. A man of letters with a doctorate in international commerce would clash with a man who was three-fourths Cheyenne Indian, spoke five languages, and who held tightly to his homespun foot care practice to survive during the Great Depression, a condition neither Doc nor his ancestors created, but certainly a condition under which he, Ova, her children, and millions of other Americans suffered. You will soon read documented evidence that Howard had sent a verbal response to Ova Noss' request for information on the law as it related to gold, an oral message that took ninety days to reach her *third-hand*, a convoluted response to a straightforward question by Ova concerning questions regarding the GRA. You will also learn the reasons why Howard did not send her a pamphlet or proper letter on the correct workings and legal requirements of the new Act, an obvious attempt on Howard's part to bias the intent of the Gold Reserve Act, and more importantly to bolster his position in the Treasury by securing the Noss treasure for the government.

June 5, 1933

When the new GRA was in place and implemented, Americans could not transact with gold—but foreigners could. Any foreign tourist who found gold in the United States, or who had purchased contraband gold here, or who had acquired gold otherwise, could take it to the U.S. Mint and get $35 a troy ounce—but an American citizen could not.

Most Americans surrendered their sparse gold possessions, but there were many who did not. Those who were caught suffered heavy fines and jail sentences, a risk many were willing to take. Hoarding gold during the Great Depression was literally a statement of defiance and disagreement with the government taking one's personal property. Then there is the question as to whether or not wealthy people in America abided by the GRA. Some did, but most affluent people who had considerable amounts of gold coins and hallmarked gold ingots did not. The major banks of Europe, including Swiss banks, became the repositories of gold ingots and gold coins (mainly ten and twenty-dollar denominations) from the wealthiest Americans.

~

Toward the end of that summer in 1933, Douthit left for California and took a fortune in gold bullion with him. Because transporting any sizable amount of gold was difficult due to its weight, much of Douthit's treasure remained behind, buried. The other penalty for carrying more gold than was necessary for the purpose of conversion into cash was being caught and losing *all* of it; moving small portions at a time was a more prudent approach. Although there are many unanswered questions that surround Willie Douthit's life and his experiences with his treasure trove find in the Caballo Mountains, there is no question that he was kidnapped and tortured on two separate occasions and escaped each time. There is also no question that he moved to California with a good portion of his gold and in later years returned to Victorio Peak during the Operation Goldfinder Expedition in 1977 where he gave private video interviews to members of the Noss family describing accounts of his gold discovery and his relationship with Doc Noss.

When Willie Douthit died in 2001 at the age of eighty-three, he left an estate of over $3,500,000.00, not including the more than one million dollars a lady friend ran off with, nor the gold Willie buried and never recovered, nor what Buster Ward had taken with him to California. Neither did it include the gold bars that were taken from them by thieves, or perhaps even the Secret Service. Buster Ward was said to have finally settled in California with his small fortune where he purchased many properties and died an old man. As unbelievable as it may seem, a large amount of Willie Douthit's and Buster Ward's treasure is still hidden somewhere in the Caballo Mountains in New Mexico.

October 5, 1933

It was Thursday, October 5, 1933, when Doc sent a Western Union Telegram[10] to Ova's home on West 6th Street in Oklahoma City: "Rent a light apartment at once. Let me hear by mail." Two weeks later, on October 18, Ova Beckwith and Milton E. Noss were married[11] before Justice of the Peace G.C.

Pouri in Beckham County, Sayre, Oklahoma. From the 1975 deposition* of Ova Noss taken by her attorney, David Daar: (17) (18)

Q. Where was it that you married Doc Noss?
A. In Sayre, Oklahoma.
Q. Were you living in Sayre, at the time?
A. No. We were in a big hurry. We stopped there and got married.
Q. When you first came to New Mexico, where is it that you lived?
A. Las Vegas [Las Vegas, New Mexico].
Q. How long did you live in Las Vegas?
A. We stayed there until the spring of the next year.
Q. And after that, where did you move?
A. Hot Springs, New Mexico.

December 1933

By the end of 1933, Roosevelt set the value of gold at $35 per troy ounce. Gold certificates were out and the American greenback was in, a piece of paper that amounted to nothing more than an IOU from the U.S. Treasury.

When the word got out of an unprecedented payday looming on the horizon, many fortunate Americans purchased gold, either abroad or in the U.S. and then sat back and waited for Roosevelt's "Midas Touch" to kick in. The Gold Reserve Act of 1934 allowed for the purchase of gold by the Secretary of the Treasury in foreign countries. An American citizen could purchase gold in a foreign market, and then sell it abroad legally without violating the Act. Section 3700 of the GRA read: (underlining inserted)

With the approval of the President, the Secretary of the Treasury may purchase gold in any amounts, at home or <u>abroad</u>, with any direct obligations, coin, or currency of the United States, authorized by law, or with any funds in the Treasury not otherwise appropriated, at such rates and upon such term and conditions as he may deem most advantageous to the public interest.

~

When Roosevelt revalued the price of gold to $35, it was time to cash in; again, the rich got richer and the poor got poorer. The question could be asked whether or not the average American had access to gold, other than gold coins. Not only did millions of Americans possess gold, the average working American prior to the Great Depression had an inherent and invaluable asset few have today—thriftiness. There were no credit cards that dared one to leverage their

---

* Noss Deposition: "Ova M. Noss vs. David L. Norvell, Attorney General," (For District Court of Santa Fe County, NM March 24, 1975), pp. (as indicated) – Attorneys for Plaintiff: P.G. Bardacke, David Daar, Phil Koury. Attorneys for the Defense: F. Lee Bailey/George R. Harris Thomas L. Dunigan, Acting AG, State of New Mexico, Victor R. Ortega, U.S. Attorney, and others present.

good credit against frivolous expenditures; one merely walked into their local bank and signed for a loan on the strength of their name and good reputation and necessary collateral when required. Before the Great Depression, a large number of Americans held onto gold coins* and many had small nuggets of gold or small ingots of precise value hallmarked according to the gold's true value. Yes, a large amount of Americans had gold, not in any sizeable quantities, but the accumulated worth of the gold held by the average American citizen throughout the United States was considerable. Now they were holding the new greenback, not a gold certificate, but a dollar bill that no longer had a par value equal to one troy ounce of gold. After Roosevelt had completed his raid on American's assets, there wasn't a gold coin, a gold certificate or any gold bullion to be had in the American pantry—Roosevelt got it all.

In spite of the speed at which Roosevelt pushed his economic agenda, there were also mind-troubled politicians in Washington who found issue with the constitutionality of the GRA as it related to the Federal Reserve Banks. One year after the GRA became the law of the land, it was deemed *unconstitutional* to deposit gold issues in a Federal Reserve Bank; they were deemed *private quasi-public stock companies* and thus banned by the Constitution. Forced to alter the wording in the GRA to correct the situation, Congress passed a bill compelling surrender of gold to the Treasury instead.

January 30, 1934

By an Act of Congress, the Gold Reserve Act of 1934 was now the law of the land and it would play an important role in the manner in which the United States Government manipulated gold and the buying power of the dollar, an unparalleled transfer of power over coinage and currency given to the President by Congress, but it was limited: the value of the U.S. dollar could not be deflated by more than fifty percent, which meant that Roosevelt could not increase the price of one troy ounce of gold above $41.34, which was twice that of the $20.67 value per ounce. Resetting the value of gold had its desired effect, though; with the increased value per troy ounce, gold poured into the Treasury. The revaluation allowed the government to earn nearly $3 billion dollars in profit. But until the Gold Reserve Act was in place, Roosevelt had nothing to sell, short of depleting the Treasury's gold reserves. But after January 31, 1934, with gold coming in by the ton, the Treasury began purchasing gold at $34.9125, just below the newly set revaluation price and then turned around and sold gold to foreign monetary authorities and certain licensed gold users for $36.0875, making $1.18 on each ounce of gold the Treasury turned. The Federal Reserve simply printed the greenbacks to pay for the gold the Treasury was buying, in effect creating a low cost gold mining operation. For those more fortunate Americans who owned

---

* The convenience of gold certificates limited the amount of gold coins one would hold for day-to-day purchases.

hallmarked gold bullion or gold coins, it was a simple task of resmelting the gold, holding on to it until the Treasury started purchasing gold at $35, and then selling it to the Treasury for a 59% profit. Gold could be taken out of the U.S. and then brought back in and sold under a foreign identity. There was no limit; as long as you weren't an American citizen, anyone outside the country could ride the back of FDR's new cash cow by selling gold to the Mint, which produced more greenbacks, which bought more gold.

From 1935 to 1940, the value of the United States' gold stockpile at Fort Knox doubled—but it was Mr. and Mrs. America who picked up the tab. But by the end of 1940 the amount of gold bullion that flowed into the U.S. Treasury began to drop off and by the end of WWII the influx of gold into the Treasury had all but stopped; the margin between the $35 per troy ounce paid by the U.S. Treasury and the value of the dollar (the greenback) were nearly at par—the valuation differential was all but gone; the heyday for the more affluent in this country and foreigners came to an end. When the ban on possessing gold was repealed by President Ford in 1974, magically, tons of small gold ingots and huge amounts of gold coins reappeared in the U.S.; many coins thought to no longer exist came onto the market and were sold by coin dealers.

What did Roosevelt do to help Americans with their financial problems during the Depression? He put a lot of people back to work at a discounted labor rate of 40% creating the illusion of a recovery. But in looking back, legitimate questions can be raised whether or not there was something more behind Roosevelt's financial plans for the country. Had someone figured out that huge profits could be made if the more than century-old gold standard was abandoned in favor of Roosevelt's proposal? And had Roosevelt used the Great Depression as a rationale to abandon it? Did he use the trust he gained in his inauguration speech to accomplish this goal? Whether or not these questions at the time added strength to the argument that Roosevelt was involved in a massive financial scheme did little to curtail the end result; by the time Mr. and Mrs. America came out of the ether it was all over; the major financial surgery on their wallets was completed. Now, only *rich* Americans and foreigners could ride the golden cow Roosevelt had created.

Spring 1934

While all of the political wrangling was going on in Washington concerning the GRA, Doc and his new family arrived in Hot Springs in the spring of 1934. Money was hard to come by, but there were dollars to be made from people who needed comfort from aching feet. Doc opened a small office on Polk Street and continued working as a foot-care practitioner, earning a living; they were able to eat, pay the rent and stay warm and dry. Ova recalled those days in her deposition*:

---

* N. Deposition, ***op. cit.***, pp. 3, 19, 20

Q. How long was he there before the treasure situation came about in 1937?
A. He moved around in town there. He got a better place, kept moving.
Q. Did he have an established practice as a chiropodist?
A. Yes.
Q. Did he have a regular established clientele?
A. The town was full of bathhouses and people came in there crippled. They were hunting all kinds of doctors to treat this and that, and he had his share of people with foot trouble.

~

Doc and Ova had moved from place to place during their early life together, but before 1934, they moved to areas where they wanted to search for treasure. Another reason that they were so mobile was because of Doc's foot-care business. Doc made his living by making orthopedic devices to fit inside people's shoes. He made a decent living by setting up shops at various places where he would treat people's foot problems. However, because of the small population of some of the small towns he visited, within six months he would have done all the business there was to be done. In order to see more people they moved on to another town where he would run an ad in the local paper advertising his foot-care business. Doc would then make a deal with the owner of the general store in town where he would set up his bench and do his business in the corner of the store. In situations like that, he didn't need an office; he would just treat people as they came in. But when they arrived in Hot Springs, New Mexico, his foot-care business stabilized.

In 1934, Clyde Tingley was elected Governor of New Mexico; three years later, in May 1937, he dedicated a new hospital in Hot Springs and named it Carrie Tingley Hospital. The hospital served to aid children who were afflicted with polio. Ova's daughter, Letha, gave an account of what she knew about Doc's business:

> *Hot Springs was a small, poor town where Doc rented his office space; it wasn't big, but they had plenty of people coming in. There were a lot of people who said Doc had helped them tremendously. He did a lot of minor stuff like corns and bunions and Mama helped him out in the office. Doc gave a lot of free time to the kids at the children's hospital, too. Doc loved kids.*
>
> *A lot of people came in who were poor and if Doc saw their feet was in bad shape and he could help them, he did. I know for fact that he had lots of money out on the books that was owed. People even came to the house when the office was closed and Doc would fix their feet for them and all he got most of the time was thanks. Of course he had all of those things that he would put in their shoes and they had a place in the office where he'd wash the people's feet; Mama would usually do that, or he would if they weren't busy.*

November of 1934

Sometime in November of 1934, Doc Noss was in a beer parlor called Ann's Place on the edge of Roswell, New Mexico. He was arrested for waving his gun around. He claimed that he was "going to kill the first one that made a move." Doc displayed a deputy sheriff's and detective agency badge—he was also very drunk.

Chapter 5
Trouble in the Caballo Mountains

Another series of events began to unfold that would later impact Doc and Ova Noss. On May 19, 1935, Mr. and Mrs. George M. Lorius of East St. Louis, Illinois and friends Mr. Albert A. and Mrs. Tillie Heberer of Du Quoin, Illinois, left East St. Louis in Lorius' car. They drove from East St. Louis, Illinois and disappeared after leaving a hotel in Albuquerque. The hotel manager, Josie Belle Ward Butler, the childhood friend of Doc Noss mentioned earlier, told the city police that she remembered them. The following article[12] appeared in the *Albuquerque Tribune on* May 16, 1974, three days before the anniversary date of the tragic event.

-The Lorius Case or the Case of the Missing Tourists-

Mr. and Mrs. George M. Lorius of East St. Louis, Missouri and friends Mr. and Mrs. Albert A. Heberer of Du Quoin, Illinois vanished in New Mexico in May 1935 while on a leisurely motor trip to the West Coast. On May 19, 1935, the Loriuses and Heberers left East St. Louis in Lorius' car, a 1929 Nash sedan. They often traveled together, never picked up hitchhikers, never drove after dark, and spent nights in hotels. Lorius was a coal dealer and Heberer owned a barbershop. They were both Masons, members of various civic clubs, and solid citizens. They crossed the Missouri River the first day and spent the night of May 19 in Miami, Oklahoma, and the night of May 20 in Sayre, Oklahoma. Veering south on U.S. 60 at Amarillo, they entered New Mexico and spent the night of May 21 in a small motel at Vaughn. They left Vaughn for Albuquerque on May 22. Friends of Mrs. Heberer received a postcard from her mailed from Albuquerque on May 22, 1935. That was the last word anybody ever heard from them.

June 29, 1935

The *Albuquerque Tribune* article also said that on June 29, the charred remains of some luggage, a thermos bottle, and a medicine bottle were found on the edge of an arroyo on Albuquerque's east mesa located north of the present State Fairgrounds by two brothers, Wayland and Edward Fullingim. The burned items belonged to the Lorius party. Searches for the four missing tourists started in Vaughn, New Mexico, then along the highways west to Albuquerque and then south to Socorro, but no clues other than the burned luggage were ever found.

Then a break came in the investigation. The trail led to a small hotel in El Paso, Texas, where a person had registered there under the name of James Sullivan. Lorius' Shrine credentials were used as identification at the motel, suggesting that Sullivan was traveling with another person. Shortly afterwards, a U.S. Customs

Officer stopped Sullivan at the U.S.-Mexico border crossing at Fort Hancock, about 40 miles from El Paso where he was questioned and then waved through. Sullivan, or his companion, once again produced Lorius' Shrine credentials. The report seemed to indicate that Sullivan had entered Mexico and soon after returned to the U.S. He had also been spotted when passers-by helped him on two separate occasions after he had driven off the highway. The trail was pointing to Dallas, Texas.

On June 29, Lorius' car was found there, abandoned by a man who was described as having a heavily tattooed left arm and who had also left a string of forged travelers checks from El Paso to Dallas, checks that belonged to George M. Lorius. The clear trail of the mysterious young man, who signed his name as James Sullivan, came to an abrupt end in Dallas. The disappearances soon became an important case. Governor Clyde Tingley headed the search efforts and said in a public announcement, "Today we have found the baggage. Tomorrow we'll find the bodies." But the remains of the four individuals were never found and the case went unsolved.

After I read the cold case files provided to me by the New Mexico State Police, two individuals, who might have been directly connected in the crimes, surfaced, possible members of a group known as the "Guerrilla Gang," local characters who roamed the area, names I had recalled when I began looking into the Lorius-Heberer murder case in 2007. Later Merle Horzmann, who worked for Doc Noss and had served as secretary for Doc's mining* company, had identified Douthit and Ward in her writings as members of this pack of outlaws. She also mentioned a man named Robert Chenoweth as one of the gang members, a person who knew Doc well and had been to Victorio Peak frequently before Doc was murdered. Doc talked about the same gang on May 21, 1941, when he ordered that no one was to leave camp alone "because he had gold hidden out there and the old Guerrilla Gang had been around." But what was so strikingly unusual about Horzmann's relationship to Doc was the venomous manner in which she acted toward him and wrote about him. Horzmann's overwhelming dislike for Doc, and even Ova, was a compulsion that led her astray in her suspicion that Doc was in some way responsible for the Lorius-Heberer murders.

Curious about where the murder investigation had led, and knowing that Merle Horzmann had attempted on more than one occasion to link Doc Noss to the murders, I wondered if his name had surfaced sometime during the police investigation and resultantly appeared in the official police investigation file. To find out, I contacted the Du Quoin Police Department in St. Louis and talked to Police Chief Jim Booker. Chief Booker seemed interested in my call and advised me that Mr. Vallie West had been the Chief of Police in the 1950s and

---

* The Cheyenne Mining Company

that he was familiar with the Lorius-Heberer murder case. He gave me West's phone number and I made the call.

Harriet West, Vallie's wife, answered the phone; Mr. West was unable to come to the phone, but I learned that Harriet's parents were friends of one of the families who had disappeared, and that when she was a young girl, she recalled seeing a postcard mailed by one of the missing family members to her parents. The postcard arrived at her parents' home before suspicions grew strong that the couples had met with foul play. She also mentioned the name of the Du Quoin Police Chief at the time, "Butter" Pyle and that The Du Quoin Evening Call newspaper had carried the story, as there was much interest in the case. But soon the trail went cold and news about the couples' disappearance faded and took a backseat to current matters. There was little else Mrs. West knew about the Lorius-Heberer case.

May 26, 1935

From Horzmann's writings (referred to in later chapters as *Camp Notes*) and from what was learned from members of the Noss family, it became evident that Merle Horzmann hated Doc and did little in her writings to allay that interpretation. For more than six years after the couples disappeared, she persisted with erroneous and malicious attempts to connect Doc to the murders by writing letters to the New Mexico State Police describing endless and bizarre theories she felt linked Doc to the crimes. Times were turbulent then, especially at the site of Doc and Ova's camp at Victorio Peak; Horzmann didn't make life any easier for them. Horzmann never stopped in her efforts to link Doc to the missing tourists, which, in the end, she failed to do. Considering all the factors and knowing the contempt Horzmann had for Doc, the conclusion was not difficult to reach: Doc Noss had nothing to do with the Lorius-Heberer disappearances and whatever connection there might have been was born in Horzmann's mind.

John Clarence:

The strength of this conclusion is based on information I later secured directly from the New Mexico State Police. Sometime during August 2005, I called the headquarters in Santa Fe to find out if I could have access to the records (officially called the Lorius Case) in hopes of finding Horzmann's letters and other documents that might have legitimately linked Doc Noss to the murders. My call was redirected to the New Mexico State Police Las Cruces District Office, a short distance away. I spoke with Detective Norman Rhoads, who was polite and extremely helpful and told me that he had always been interested in the case. He listened intently. I asked if I could gain access to the case records, and he said that he would see what could be done. Three days later, he called and informed me that another Detective, Ron Taylor, stationed in Santa Fe, was able to secure the file and agreed to bring it to Las Cruces that weekend.

During the following week, I met with Detective Rhoads, and together we began paging through the case—a large one: letters, photos, investigation reports and suspects.

What was so strange, though, was that with the exception of a single letter Horzmann had sent to then-acting New Mexico State Police Chief Joseph P. Roach on March 20, 1951, there was no trace of any of the many letters Horzmann had sent to Chief Tom Summers or to Captain Roy Vermillion in Santa Fe; nor were there any of the letters from either person in response to her letters. The letter Horzmann had sent to Mr. Roach was received by him on March 21, 1951, and was stamped accordingly.

There was little information in the Noss family records that refers to the "gang" mentioned by Horzmann in her writings, only one she had mentioned and a reference to Doc having also mentioned the gang. The link to the Guer-rilla Gang, and other interesting facts, appeared in Horzmann's letter to Chief Roach; Horzmann was, by her own admission, closely associated with George Lorius on a business and personal basis, as was her husband, attorney Carl Horzmann, an association they obviously concealed during the time Merle Horzmann was secretary for Doc's mining business. It was during the time of Merle Horzmann's connection to Doc and Ova Noss, a connection that continued with Ova years after Doc was murdered, that drew my attention to Merle's specific behaviors. One issue was her efforts to convince New Mexico State Police Chief Tom Summers and Captain Roy Vermillion through infer-ence and innuendo that Doc had murdered the Illinois couples, an effort she took to the point of obsession.

The letter[13] was strange; Horzmann told Mr. Roach that she knew Mr. Lorius well, that she had "bought tons of coal from him." She wrote:

> ...The night before he (Mr. Lorius) left East St. Louis, he was in our home at 622 N. 32nd St., East St. Louis, Illinois, and took his final examination for Credits and Collections, which my husband was teaching at the time, and I served lunch after it was over, and he discussed his trip with us, which he was to begin the next day with the Heberers from Du Quoin, Ill.

~

The letter, which was written 16 years *after* the couples disappeared, was interesting to the extent that Merle gave a clear description of Mr. Lorius' features, his jewelry, and dental characteristics. She told Mr. Roach that a skull had been recently discovered in the Hembrillo Basin, and if it was the skull of George Lorius, she could easily identify it, even though all of the teeth were pulled and the skull was "discolored." She also mentioned in her letter that she contacted New Mexico State Police Chief Summers and Captain Roy Vermillion. Horzmann said that Vermillion came to see her with a Mr. Charles Eagleton of the New Mexico State Police District Office in Las Cruces. Mr. Roach answered her letter[14] on March 21, 1951:

> Received your letter and telegram with much interest. We have just recently run out some leads in the case, but to no avail. We most assuredly want to explore every angle

that is presented, and will in the near future, have an investigator call on you for further
details.   —*J. P. Roach, Acting Chief New Mexico State Police*

~

Horzmann told Roach she and her husband, Carl, had come to New Mexico May 8, 1940, and she even gave the *time*—2:30 a.m., which was odd in and of itself, namely that she had a record of the *exact* time and that she related that information to Roach. The oddity was her attention to specific details regarding her and her husband's interactions with Mr. Lorius four years short of two decades *after* the couples disappeared, as though she felt compelled to explain them. She also attached a business card to the letter that advertised herself as a public typist and notary public, and that her address was now 107 East Second Street, Lordsburg, New Mexico, obviously having sometime later moved from East St. Louis to Lordsburg, New Mexico. By her own admission, she and her husband had specific and detailed knowledge of Lorius' travel plans, his physical characteristics and the time of the couples' departure from Illinois for New Mexico. Considering that Doc and Ova arrived in Hot Springs in the spring of 1934, a year *before* the murders, and that Doc was operating a foot-care business on Polk Street there, her interest in weaving him into the scene of the crime 16 years after the fact, and her ability and willingness to resurrect such detailed information that long after the crime, is equally odd. As it stood, Merle Horzmann was the only individual at the Victorio Peak camp with a direct and personal connection to the Lorius and Heberer families.

John Clarence:
I was now determined to root out the facts of the case to discover Doc's involvement, if any. During my first visit to the Las Cruces District Office, Detective Taylor came into the small situation room. I stopped reading and began to explain my theory about the case. Based on what I knew from two sources, Horzmann's letters to Chief Summers and Captain Vermillion, and from a more recent conversation I had with someone who was familiar with the area of the Caballo Mountains, who told me that the Heberers and the Loriuses were lured into Willie Douthit and Buster Ward's treasure cave and murdered on the spot when a disagreement led to an argument, which resulted in murder. The gentleman who shared this information with me wishes to remain anonymous, so I'll call him Mr. North.

~

North said that his understanding concerning the murders was based on a firsthand conversation he had with a man who was either at or inside the cave while the bodies were still there. He did not give the name of his informant, who North claimed was now deceased. He also claimed that his informant told him that Doc Noss was implicated only to the extent that he was present in the cave sometime *after* three of the four St. Louis people were slain there and he emphasized that Noss was not responsible for the killings nor was he aware that it was going to happen when it did. North claimed that the murders were spontaneous and unprovoked killings by one of the people who accompanied the Loriuses and Heberers to Douthit and Ward's treasure cave. He also claimed that the person who killed them was a cripple. Doc Noss, although he had a history of displaying anger, which was amplified when he was drinking, was *not* a killer. Mr. North had nothing else to say about the matter.

Doc was not shy about tangling with others, going on drinking binges or drawing down on people when he was drunk; in fact, he held a New Mexico State policeman at gunpoint for stealing one of his gold bars and killing his tomcat. Even though such actions put him in jail time and time again, once for six months, many things were consistent about Doc's actions over his life-time: he did not trust government officials, he did not like the way the law was dispensed (although he had lawmen who were his friends), he was secretive and protective of Ova and her family, particularly as it related to the treasure, he used as many tricks against the Secret Service to keep from getting caught as they used to catch him, and he did not think twice about busting someone in the mouth if he felt they had it coming. Letha talked about Doc's drinking problems, in part:

> *Doc didn't have the ability to drink without gettin' drunk. What was behind it, they'd try to find out where the gold was because he had shown some people different pieces of gold. Doc didn't drink at first, but as time went by and the pressure got worse, his drinkin' got worse, too. Doc was the type of man that when he walked into a crowded place, like a bar, people would just come up to him. Doc got into a couple fights in his time, too. I don't know what every one of them was about because we weren't with him all the time. But of course we didn't like for him to get drunk. Mama didn't like it for sure, his drinkin', but she knew that people who wanted information from Doc were the ones that were behind it. Doc would go two or three days in a spurt then he'd go to town and get drunk. And then there would be months when he wouldn't have a drink, he wouldn't touch it.*

> *Most of the comments we heard about Doc was admiration, but the only thing that all of us resented very badly was the drinking. Doc would go down in town to have a cup of coffee and they'd say come on, let's go have a short beer. If you want to be truthful about it, Mama was quite tolerant, more tolerant than the rest of us was, but there were times when she was downright mad about it too, but I don't think it really bothered her as much as it did Dorothy and me.*

~

What was interesting about Horzmann's letter[15] to Captain Vermillion on September 8, 1941, which appears later in the chronology of events, was her description of something that she alleged happened "around May 26, 1935." In May of 1935, Ova and Doc were still living in Hot Springs, and, according to Horzmann regarding the above date, Ova had asked a man by the name of William (Bill) Loeffler, "to take her home (he supposedly drove her home) on the east side of town." In Horzmann's story, Ova "became panicky and screamed out about *Doc leaving those people out there in that hole.*" Not knowing what the exact conversation was in terms of how the matter came up, or what Loeffler told her, if he told her anything, or if Ova was told by someone else and then asked Loeffler to take her home, the inference was that Doc had seen more than one dead person in a hole somewhere, thus the comment by Ova "those people." What Ova's emotional state was *after* she was told about the incident could have been fear, anger or sympathy that evoked the response described by Horzman.

From what Horzmann claimed Ova had said about the matter, the inference was that Doc had seen bodies in a ground cave and did nothing except leave the scene and returned home to tell Ova what he saw. On the way to her home, Ova supposedly told Loeffler what Doc had told her. In Horzmann's own words, "This happened *after* they (Doc and the four people in the Lorius party) were seen together at the Sturges Hotel, and the four left following the N. car (Noss car) and were not seen after that." What is significant about Horzmann's version of what happened the night Loeffler drove Ova home on the east side of town, is that Horzmann's slant on the incident was based on Doc being in Albuquerque at the Sturges Hotel with the Lorius-Heberer couples and that someone saw them leaving together, and that "the four" were following the "N" car. In the next sentence, though, Horzmann said, "I could be all wrong, and so could they who told me, but it is one of the things that will have to be verified."

After an extensive review of the New Mexico State Police files, which included hundreds of interviews with people who wrote in about the case, dozens of suspects with criminal records who were analyzed thoroughly by local, state, and federal authorities, there is no mention of Doc Noss in the case at all, nothing, let alone Doc Noss having been a suspect. Most important to Horzmann's point is that Doc was at the Sturges Hotel in the company of the Lorius and Heberer couples. If there was any place in the investigation that got the most concentrated efforts of specific investigation, it was the place where the couples were last seen—the Sturges Hotel in Albuquerque. Noss' name *never* surfaced and was *never* connected to the hotel. The only connection to Noss at the Sturges Hotel was Josie Ward, who had known Doc very well since they were children. Had she talked about him, had she mentioned his name, had she referred the couples to Doc in Hot Springs, it never came up in the intensive police investigation. Could Josie have been covering for him? Possibly, yes, but considering the number of individuals involved in the case, and the intensive investigation by local and state police, and eventually the Federal Bureau of Investigation, it is unlikely.

What Horzmann had done by implicating Doc Noss sixteen years later merely wasted the time of investigators. The Lorius-Heberer couples' arrival and departure from the Sturges Hotel was put under a microscope, and had Doc, who had a criminal record and who had recently been released from the penitentiary in Santa Fe, been there, as Horzmann had led New Mexico State Police Chief Summers and Captain Roy Vermillion to believe, something surely would have surfaced that put the spotlight on him—but it never happened. The chance that Horzmann had lied about Doc being at the Sturges Hotel in Albuquerque, or she had embellished information given to her by someone, other than Loeffler, whom she did not reveal, is a much greater likelihood than Doc having been present when the Lorius party was at the hotel.

The disappearances of the Lorius-Heberer couples caused an avalanche of information: tips and letters from people with good intentions, every one of which claimed to know who had killed the couples, where their bodies could be found, and—equally interesting—their theories on why the couples disappeared. A great deal of time and effort was spent running these leads down, checking locations where the bodies might be found, digging by hand in suggested locations, using earthmoving equipment and even the use of suited divers in places where the bodies were to be found under water. There was so much information coming to the police from every direction imaginable that the workload taken from normal operations became exhausting and grueling, and it continued for years. No one gave up on the families, but their bodies were never located and no one was ever charged with the crimes.

One of the reports in the New Mexico State Police files stood out more than any, a report that was made on October 28, 1953, by Officer B. E. Lucas in Albuquerque. The report said that headquarters had received a letter from an informant named C.P. Newkirk from Hillsboro, New Mexico. Mr. Newkirk claimed he knew "who was responsible for the disappearance of victims" in the Lorius Case and offered a plan to snare the culprits. Officer Lucas' report[16] outlines Newkirk's meeting with Clarence Palmer:

> <u>Details:</u> (underlining inserted)
> This officer contacted Mr. Newkirk at his home on the evening of October 28, 1953 and obtained the following information: Mr. Newkirk states that he met a subject in 1944 by the name of Clarence* Arthur Palmer, about 47 years of age. He became close friends with Palmer and in the ensuing years obtained the following story: Clarence stated that he and his brother, Reece, who was paralyzed from the waist down, were operating a tourist [business] in Hot Springs, New Mexico.
>
> The Lorius, Heberer party spent the night there and inquired about the country in the vicinity of John Gordon's cabin, which is about six miles east of Caballo Lake. The Palmer brothers became suspicious since there is a belief that there is a large quantity of Old Spanish gold buried in that vicinity. The Palmer brothers arrived at the location ahead of the party and stationed themselves where they could observe the actions of the party.

---

*Clarence Arthur Palmer was commonly known in the area as Jack Palmer.

Palmer stated that the Lorius car was parked in some Hackberry trees, one lady stayed at the car, and the other three went about three quarters of a mile into the hills and entered a hole in the ground. The Palmer brothers then entered the hole, and according to Clarence, Reece* shot and killed the three of them. Clarence stated that the cave contained approximately a million dollars in gold bars. The three bodies were left in the cave. The other lady was killed in or near the car. The body was put in the car and Clarence drove the car to a point east of Albuquerque where he burned the luggage. He was afraid he might get caught in the mountains east of Albuquerque, so he headed back south on U.S. 85. Somewhere north of Hot Springs he wrecked the car slightly and drove on to El Paso and spent the night. Clarence stated he burned the body about nine miles from Van Horn, Texas, and then drove into Dallas and left the car. He then hitchhiked back to Hot Springs. Clarence stated to Newkirk that he had taken some gold from the cave, but was questioned too closely when he tried to dispose of it, so he returned it to the cave.

Mr. Newkirk states that Palmer has been under suspicion by the FBI on the case. He states that he and a subject by the name of Joe Rainey, of Artesia, were partners in trying to find some of the treasure. Rainey got mad at Palmer for giving him the run around on the location of the cave and turned him in to the FBI. Mr. Newkirk stated in his letter to headquarters that he had a plan, which would disclose the location of the bodies. His plan is as follows: Palmer should be arrested and taken to jail in Hot Springs. Mr. Newkirk is to then be arrested and allowed to talk to Palmer. He will tell Palmer that he has made up a fictitious confession by some unknown person concerning the Lorius Case. He states that he will extract a promise from Palmer to show him the location of the cave as soon as he is released and cleared on the strength of the dummy confession.

Mr. Newkirk let it be known that he was in no way interested in the criminal aspects of the case, but was interested only in the gold, which would be found with the bodies. Mr. Newkirk states that he believes that Palmer is now living in Portales.

This report is written just as Mr. Newkirk told it to me. There has been no effort made to check or verify any of the contents." Respectfully Submitted
—B.E. *Lucas, Officer New Mexico State Police, Albuquerque, New Mexico.*

~

According to Newkirk, the Palmer brothers said the couples "spent the night there" in Hot Springs and that the Palmers "were operating a tourist" business[†] in town, a rest or tourist camp that was owned by Jack and Reece Palmers' mother. Newkirk said the St. Louis party "inquired about the country in the vicinity of John Gordon's cabin."

---

* The degree of Reece Palmer's paralysis and his ambulatory ability is unknown. However, since he was able to mount and ride a mule, his ability to enter a cave and commit the murders Newkirk described to Officer Lucas cannot be ruled out; Buster Ward navigated the Caballo Mountains with artificial legs.

[†] Inserted

Josie Belle Ward-Butler, the desk clerk at the Sturges Hotel, was aware of many things: most of the facts surrounding the Douthit treasure, Doc's keen interest in treasure caves in the Caballo and San Andres Mountains, his connection to Willie Douthit, and that Doc knew the entrance location of Douthit and Ward's treasure cave. She also knew about the treasure Doc had also found in the Caballos, which was a separate and distinctly different treasure; the Douthit/Ward cave was lower on the western slopes of the Caballo range, most likely in an arroyo, while Doc's cave was much higher up on the face of the mountain, a steep climb to a difficult-to-find vertical entrance. There were a number of people who knew about Doc's Caballo treasure cave: Ova, Letha, a Yaqui Indian named Lino "Tony" Carriaga, and perhaps even Willie Douthit and Buster Ward; Doc did not find the Victorio Peak treasure until 1937.

Nowhere in the police record files is there any mention that anyone in the Lorius party had inquired about places to look for ancient gold bars. However, Josie Belle knew Doc was an expert on the Caballo Mountains and was well known in Hot Springs because of his foot care business on Polk Street. If the Lorius party had asked about gold, namely if there was any to be bought in or near the Caballo Mountains, Josie might very well have recommended they talk to Doc in Hot Springs when they arrived, all of which is pure conjecture. However, if the Lorius party had inquired about the area above "the John Gordon cabin," as Clarence Palmer told Newkirk they had, and had they gone there, they would have been in close proximity to the very cave where Willie Douthit and Buster Ward had found the ancient cache of gold bullion.

Newkirk claimed that the Palmer brothers went to the area ahead of the couples, waited for them to arrive, and then proceeded to commit murder; he said that Reece Palmer killed three of them in "the hole." It is not clear who killed the "woman at or near the car." Doc could have casually mentioned Douthit's treasure cave to someone in the party as mere conversation or one of the Palmer brothers could have mentioned it, again this is speculation. In a 1990s recorded video interview, Willie Douthit admitted he had found a treasure, and that Doc was able to describe the interior of Douthit's ground cave. In Douthit's video recording, he said that some people were snooping around his cave and they were killed, but they had "cleaned up" the cave, suggesting that there were bodies inside the treasure cave and were subsequently removed.

After reviewing that particular videotape, Terry was asked if he knew anything about Douthit's claim that the bodies were left inside this cave. Terry's remarks:

> *When Alex Alonso and I, and a few other people in our party, interviewed Willie Douthit, which was about 1989, we asked him if he would take us back to the site in the Caballos [Caballo Mountains] where he and Buster Ward had claimed they had found a treasure. We also knew that Doc had hung out with Willie from time to time.*

Willie said he wouldn't talk about it because he and Buster Ward had made a pact not to go back there. He was worried that he would be accused of being an accessory to the murder of those people from St. Louis, who had been killed at that site, actually inside his cave.

We asked him if there was anyway around that because it had been so many years ago. He said that if we could convince him that there was no legal jeopardy in talking about it, he would consider it. But Willie made it clear that he wasn't interested in fighting a legal battle at his age with his remaining years. We understood, but we asked him to describe the location of the cave. Then someone in our group said that he had an idea where it might be. Willie said, "Well tell me what you know and I'll tell you if you are close." Prior to talking to Douthit, we knew that the location of his cave was referred to as the "stove pipe" site.

There was a big investigation over the disappearance of these people and it wasn't long after they disappeared that Willie lit out for California.

~

The investigation into the disappearances of the St. Louis couples was becoming involved, but there was something about what Newkirk had told Officer Lucas that pointed to the possibility that the "stove pipe" cave and the Douthit/Ward treasure cave were one and the same cave.

Chapter 6

Gold in the Caballo Mountains and Bodies in a Cave

Dick Moyle was always candid about what he knew and he shared his knowledge freely during dozens of conversations and several recorded interviews. Dick said there were a number of caves in the Caballo Mountain Range where early Spanish settlers stored the gold bullion they had mined. Willie Douthit claimed he had found such a cave, and so had Doc and Tony Carriaga, a Yaqui Indian (shown at right). The cave they discovered in the Caballo Mountains held a large cache of Spanish gold bars, much larger than Douthit's discovery.

Doc took this photograph of the caves on the northern wall of the Burbank Canyon; Letha found his personal camera shortly after he was murdered in 1949 and had the film processed. When Doc snapped the picture, he was looking in the same general direction that was indicated by the metal marker fastened above the window at Johnny Gordon's cabin* where Willie Douthit had once lived. However, Doc and Carriaga's cave was high on the slopes of the canyon wall near "Bat Cave," a well-known site that is clearly visible in Doc's photo and can be seen for miles from the valley and the main highway, Rt. 25. Douthit's cave

was much lower in a ground cave near the Drolte Hole.

During one of Terry Delonas' recorded interviews, he talked about a six-month camping event in the Caballo Mountains in Burbank Canyon. It was interesting to hear him recall so many details of certain events. From time to time he talked about the same episode and most always the interviews were weeks, if not months apart. Not once was there a time when his accounts were contradictory. Instead, he provided additional information not previously mentioned in earlier or later interviews. Some of the information was repetitive

---

* Covered in Chapter 3

to some degree, but never was it inconsistent, which weighed heavily in favor of the credibility of his recollection of a wide variety of events, such as the six-month camping episode. Terry explained:

> In the 1970s, Babe, my Aunt Letha and my cousin Wesley took me to the foothills of a canyon in the Caballo Mountains to a natural spring where Doc and Babe had camped for six months. I learned that in 1938 my Aunt Letha had joined Doc and Babe there to help with the work, because they were trying to pump out a spring where Doc said that, according to one of the maps he found inside Victorio Peak, there were seventy mule loads of silver that had been buried there. So they were looking for that treasure, too.
>
> My Aunt Letha retold the story many times that when she first came to New Mexico, I think she was eighteen then, she had worked closely with Doc. I might add that her arrival in New Mexico came about because Babe wrote to her and told her that Doc had found a treasure and he promised her that he would use any money that came from the treasure to bring her whole family to New Mexico. So, Letha showed up with a two-year-old and a new baby. My cousins Danny and Jerry came, but cousin Wesley wasn't born yet.
>
> As it turned out, Doc liked Letha and he started trusting her. She told us that Doc would take her out with him in his truck and they'd drive up to a ridge [the plateau of Granite Peak] and he'd read to her from a word-map* the description of different areas they could actually see from where they were on this high ridge. She asked Doc what he was looking for because she knew that he had already found a treasure at Victorio Peak, so the question she asked him was why were they over in the Caballos still looking for one? Doc admitted, yes, he had found a treasure over at Victorio Peak, but he kept reading from this word-map and asked her, 'What does that sound like to you down there?' And Aunt Letha would still ask, 'I don't get it, why are we looking for more treasure?' Letha said he pointed down into the canyon and said there's another treasure down there in that spring. Then he told her that he had found not one, but two treasures in the Caballos, and one of them he said he could not go back to.

~

The treasure "he could not go back to" referred to Douthit's treasure cave, the reason being that the Lorius-Heberer bodies were inside the cave. Doc also told Letha that the waybills he had found inside Victorio Peak, he had to have translated because they were written in Old Spanish, most likely Castilian, which he had difficulty reading, and according to these documents, there was not one, but seven treasures. Doc's intent was to find all seven of them before he went public with the Victorio Peak treasure. He assured Letha that there was more than one large treasure in the Caballo Mountains and that he and the Yaqui Indian named Leno "Tony" Carriaga had already located one of

---

*A word-map is essentially a waybill where a location is described in writing, not in a drawn map.

them. Doc also told her that he fully intended to find the large silver treasure at or near the spring in the Burbank Canyon. Doc claimed he could dispose of silver easily and that they would use the money for whatever they needed. So far, Doc had found three of the seven treasures: the Victorio Peak treasure, the treasure he and Carriaga had found, and the treasure in Douthit's cave, which he "could not go back to."

~

But did the events as told by Newkirk to Officer Lucas on October 28, 1953 jibe with Mr. North's* story? If everything Newkirk told Lucas was truthful and accurate, why hadn't he mentioned Willie Douthit, Buster Ward and Doc Noss? Therefore, is Newkirk to be believed? Better yet, was his account of what he purported to know believable to *any* extent? If Newkirk *was* telling the truth, then there were mitigating circumstances why he omitted mentioning Douthit, Ward and Noss in his conversation with Officer Lucas. Was it because he wished only to indict the real murderer, which he said was Reece Palmer, and not implicate anyone else? Those questions remain. The New Mexico State Police followed up on Newkirk's story and sent men and equipment to the area to excavate suspected sites, but nothing was ever found.

Another question arises; did Doc enter the cave and see bodies there as he told Ova he had, and later his stepdaughter, Letha? Most likely, yes. In order for Doc to have seen bodies in Douthit's treasure cave he would have had to know the cave's location, which Douthit confirmed was the case in his 1989 video statement.

~

Since Douthit had established that Doc had found his cave is it not unreasonable to think that Doc had actually seen the bodies there. All questions raised and all matters considered, Ova was justifiably upset that Doc had walked away from the scene and left *"those people out there in that hole,"* the words Horzmann used to relate what Ova had said the evening Loeffler drove her home. It is also a casual next step to think that Ova's rant that night was nothing more than a genuine and human reaction to what she learned from Loeffler, and also an indication that Doc never told her that he had seen the bodies prior to her being told by Loeffler.

To simply take the position that Doc was *not* in the cave when the St. Louis couples were murdered, it is essential to know when these events took place in order to establish a foundation for such a position, such as the *year* when Loeffler drove Ova home. That occurred while Doc and Ova were living in Hot Springs and the six-month long camping trip was in 1938, but it is difficult to know if the event with Loeffler occurred *before, after* or *during* the time they were camping. It

---

*Mr. North was Clarence's confidential source. He claimed he had a conversation with someone that was either at or inside the cave while the bodies were still there, but were later removed and burned.

could well be that Ova came to Hot Springs to buy supplies needed at camp. Beside, there was more to the story; Terry mentioned something about the *Seven Cities of the Cibola* during a much earlier recording session.

> John Clarence:
> But when I reviewed the tape recording, I realized that his remarks amounted to a passing comment, so I called him to learn more, specifically that Doc had spent a considerable amount of his time in the Caballo Mountains because it was there that he and Carriaga had found a cave stacked with piles of gold bars.

> ~

The cave entrance was situated on the southern slope of the Burbank Canyon. Here is more of Terry's recollection of what Ova had told him about the Caballo treasure:

> Doc was sure he had stumbled onto two of the cities of gold, the Cibola, the Seven Cities of the Cibola, which Doc claimed all along were not cities, that they were actually caves filled with ancient Spanish gold bars and other artifacts.
> Letha told me that she had seen several bars that Doc had pulled out of that cave and confirmed that Carriaga was with him when he found the entrance. Babe told me that she knew Carriaga fairly well and after Doc was killed he would visit her and tell her about what was in the cave. Babe said that Carriaga was a Yaqui Indian and he really didn't care about the gold.

> ~

Again in the 1970s, Ova and Terry's Aunt Letha took him on a trip into the Caballo Mountains to a place known as the old Taggert claim. From the Taggert claim you can look down across the Burbank Canyon and see the entrance to the treasure cave Doc and Carriaga had found. According to what Letha told Terry, she was at the cave with Doc and had talked to him about it more than once and emphasized that Doc would not let her go inside claiming that it was too dangerous. Terry continued:

> Later on, Aunt Letha told Doc that she didn't understand why they were spending so much time looking for treasure when he had already found a treasure at Victorio Peak. She also asked him why he hadn't taken her to see the treasure cave he and Carriaga had found. She told me that Doc just laughed and said, "Well, youngun'... you were in one of them just the other day, one of the biggest ones." My Aunt Letha's frustration came because had she known it at the time, she would have insisted on going in with him and seeing the treasure for herself. She also said if she would have actually seen it, she would have never forgotten how to get back to it.

> ~

The Caballo treasure is discussed again in Chapter 7 where Carriaga wrote about the time when he and Doc had found it. Carriaga also described the treasure in detail.

Terry Delonas outlined the lasting issue over the Lorius-Heberer murders and how it impacted on Doc and Ova's treasure search efforts in the Caballo Mountains; the murders virtually ended treasure-hunting activities there after 1935. And there was also the issue that Ova was deeply bothered that Doc had seen the bodies of the St. Louis couples inside Douthit's cave. Terry discussed the event:

> It was something Babe talked about a lot, especially when she was upset about one thing or another. I guess I heard her mention this a half dozen times. These murders in the Caballo Mountains happened nearly two years after Doc got his foot-care business going in Hot Springs, but before he and Babe were living on a regular basis at the Rock House in the Hembrillo Basin and spent most of their time there with the Victorio Peak treasure.
>
> Babe was angry about the fact that Doc didn't bring the police in and show them where the bodies were. She told me that Doc was sure that he would be dragged into something he had nothing to do with, and he probably wasn't wrong because he had a record and he sure would have been tangled up in it. Babe finally admitted to that and as time went on she agreed with Doc's assessment, but she still didn't like the fact that the bodies were never brought out.
>
> So these murders, and that was a sad thing, put a curse on everything that was happening in the Caballos for quite a while. So Doc and Babe stopped going there and spent most or all of their time from then on in the Hembrillo Basin.
>
> But anyway, that's what I know, and if this Loeffler thing happened, and it probably did, Babe said that she was frightened when Doc told her, and something like that doesn't go away soon. She probably reacted to it every time it came up, and who knows what Horzmann might have said about Doc knowing those people were inside the cave, but Babe said he had nothing to do with it. Knowing my grandmother, if she thought for a second that Doc was somehow involved, she wouldn't have tolerated it and she would have left him.

~

The discovery of the Caballo treasure cave by Doc and Tony Carriaga and further efforts by Doc and Ova to uncover the loads of silver bars in or near the spring in Burbank Canyon, were separated by about three years because of the tragic event of the murders. When the murders occurred in 1935, Doc and Ova had already made the Victorio Peak treasure trove discovery, which was not announced until 1937. This discovery occurred while they were *allegedly* hunting deer at Victorio Peak. Terry described the event as the "authorized King James version" of when Doc and Ova first talked about finding the treasure there.

Eventually, when the impact of the murders had faded, they migrated back to the Caballo Mountains where they had abandoned the treasure cave discovered by Doc and Carriaga. Then, in 1938, Letha came to New Mexico and camped with Doc and Ova while they continued their search at the spring for the seventy mule loads of silver Doc suspected was buried at a spring in the Burbank Canyon. Then Terry added another chapter to the camping episode:

In the boredom of camp life and while they were busy digging at the spring, Doc would go off into the Caballo Mountains and after a while he would return after dark carrying gold bars. Eventually my Uncles Harold and Marvin came to join them at this particular campsite. Uncle Marvin, who was a teenager at the time, decided to follow Doc right up to a cave and watched him go inside. Then Marvin went up to the cave entrance and went inside a few feet. He discovered that Doc was bringing gold bars out to the entrance of the cave and piling them up there.

Well, Marvin took one of the bars and went back to camp and showed it to Babe and everybody there; of course they were excited that Harold knew where another one of Doc's gold sites was located. But when Doc came back to camp that evening he was really upset and told everyone to break camp because they were getting out of there because he said that he'd been followed. He said that somebody had followed him to a cave and had taken one of the gold bars he had removed from inside the cave. He said that somebody was watching them and it was dangerous for them to stay at the camp and they needed to get out of there immediately.

So then Marvin popped up and said it was he who followed him up there and took the bar and he handed it over. Well, Doc got real mad and he hit Marvin. Of course Babe and Doc got into a big fight over it. Anyway, they broke camp and went back to Hot Springs and Doc went on a drunk for a few days. As a result, Doc and Babe were at odds for a while.

~

Terry said that in looking back, he believed that Doc had found a total of three treasures, which included the Victorio Peak treasure, the one he and Carriaga had found, and of course Douthit's cave where the bodies were left.

Poor Aunt Letha was exasperated because six months of camping in the stark wilderness was rather arduous: pumping and hauling water, preparing meals, and who knows what else. Letha told Doc that he was working too hard, and then again she said, 'I don't get it. Why are we looking for treasure when you already found one?' Like I said, Doc's answer was that he wanted to find all seven of them before he went public. I got the impression from hearing the stories over the years that the treasure at Victorio Peak was the largest one, and that it was huge.

~

There was more to learn about the Palmer brothers' connection to the Lorius-Heberer couples. Dick Moyle said there was a man in Truth or Consequences who knew a lot about the murders and that he might have information that could possibly shed more light on the Palmers' connection and involvement with the St. Louis couples. A Sunday afternoon trip along the Rio Grande to Hot Springs was in order. Although the town of Hot Springs is now officially known as Truth or Consequences, its historic name is used through the course of this book.

John Clarence:

I drove there on a clear, breezy, Sunday afternoon with a good friend, Karen Cheatham, the wife of Jerry Cheatham, now deceased. Jerry was Letha's son and the grandson of Ova Noss.

We needed to find a man named Joe Edwards, a peculiar man Moyle warned. He lived at the Trail Motel in town, had a roadside buy-and-sell business, and he liked to tell stories about the Caballo Mountains—if the price was right. After Dick Moyle told me about Edwards, I found a document in the Noss files, a transcription of a conversation between several individuals who seemed to have a good amount of knowledge about the Caballo Mountains, Doc Noss, and a few people who were directly acquainted with the Lorius-Heberer couples after they left St. Louis. Joe Edwards was one of the people who participated in the conversation. I learned later that the transcript had made the rounds in the treasure hunter's circuit, an interesting account of the days immediately before the Lorius-Heberer couples were murdered.

Karen and I found him quickly, and I was not disappointed. I waited while he finished talking with a customer, and then I introduced myself. That's when it all began. I knew instantly that holding a normal conversation with him was impossible: there was no shortage of spontaneous exuberant flamboyance, excitement, words, body language and vehemence, all of which spewed from every pore of his body. He hit me with a salvo of questions, one presumption after another as to whom he thought I was, all of which I considered to be rude, ill-tempered, and unnecessary. Within minutes of meeting him, I found Edwards to be a rowdy, fire-and-brimstone, Bible-thumping roadside evangelist with his own twist on matters concerning the satanic meaning of every month of the year and every day of the week—and, of course, the Holy Bible, an initial encounter that served as a warning of things to come. An unpleasant and disjointed interview was underway, which turned out to be my first and only encounter with the man, one that I will never forget.

He rattled on with his long thinning, gray hair dancing in the wind and his wintry green eyes peering at us as if we were field mice waiting to be eaten by a hawk. Short, pot-bellied and looking like an old prospector, an old sourdough, a chuck wagon cook, or a self-proclaimed treasure hunter who professed to be an expert on the Caballo Mountains and the people who came and went from there was standing before us. Edwards was the culmination of every anxious moment I ever experienced in co-writing The Gold House trilogy. He was an accumulation of every person who shared a part of his personality and character, people who displayed avarice and contempt for anyone with a normal life, people whose eyes were blinded by their own failure to embrace what they coveted most—gold.

The last act of his performance, I assumed would be a portrayal of Walter Huston, who played "Howard" in the movie Treasure of the Sierra Madres, a little jig with his arms flailing about, some short well-rehearsed choreographed footwork to scare us away, but to our surprise it never came.

~

Edwards was a withered old man who claimed a piece of the history of the Caballo Mountains, a man who had looked for hidden treasures and lost, who "succumbed to the gnawing of greed," and who put a price on *everything*, even the truth of what they knew, a demand of an outlay of cash to loosen his tongue in recompense for treasures sought but never found. His demeanor became abrasive and at times nasty. He refused to answer questions, only to respond with unrelated counter questions of his own. But locked inside Edwards' head was information about two men he knew—the Palmer brothers.

John Clarence:
At the first opportunity, I stepped up to him and gave him a dose of his own medicine, I told him that I had interviewed many people in the course of writing The Gold House *books, but I found him to be the most ignorant, impolite, selfish person I had ever interviewed. It stopped him cold. If I was going to get anything out of him, now was the time. Edwards said, "If you want information from me, you're going to pay me." He claimed that Henry James* had approached him for a bit of information on some of his treasure stories. He said, "I'll tell you the same thing I told him. Put up or shut up." He also claimed that a Hollywood producer approached him and offered a quarter-million dollars for what he knew about the Caballo Mountains. My comment to Edwards was, "You never got a cent, did you?" He admitted that he hadn't. I let him know that he would never get a penny from me either and I told him that if he maintained his course of action, he would eventually die an old man with whatever information he had stored inside his head. It felt a bit strange to talk like that to him the way I did but one had to be there to fully understand the circumstances. I thought that I would never talk to anyone that way, but I did, and I must admit at the time it felt good, but later that day I wished that I had taken a different approach.*

He began to tremble, threw his hands above his head and said, "Praise the Lord," and then blurted out some distorted Bible verse, a passage he had invented. "Show me," I demanded of him. "I'll give you one thousand dollars if you show me that verse in the Bible." Edwards began frantically paging through his tattered book. Then I saw it; in front of me was page after page of alterations he had made to the scriptures: words he had crossed out and replaced with others claiming they were satanic. It was a cover-to-cover editing of the scriptures made to fit his interpretation of the way the Bible should have been written, the reason he gave for the editing job he had done.

I asked, "Is this the King James version?"

"Yes," he responded in anger. Then I looked down at the mangled text.

"It looks like the King Edwards version to me."

I turned to him and asked, "Who was Clarence A. Palmer?"

---

* Henry James authored "The Curse of the San Andres." In it he mentions Doc and Ova Noss and also gives reference to the "Letter of Seven" a manuscript by Holy Father LaRue from Rome, Italy 1797 and sealed to Father Rheuschone of Madrid, Spain in 1802. Doc found the manuscript inside Victorio Peak.

I told Edwards that I had brought along a transcript of a tape recording session, page after page; sixty-one pages in all that involved him as a participant. It was an interesting account of the days immediately before the Lorius-Heberer murders occurred, as you will soon read. Then I opened my folder and showed him my copy of the New Mexico State Police report that mentioned the Palmer brothers and C.P. Newkirk. Edwards took one glance and backed away and refused to look at either document. "I never knew a Clarence A. Palmer," he said in anger. "His name was Jack Palmer. His brother was Reece Palmer," he said.

~

After several minutes of confrontation, Edwards began talking. He said the Palmer brothers had a small service station and tourist camp in Hot Springs when the Loriuses and Heberers had disappeared, which correlated with Newkirk's story. He said that people came in there all the time. He said Reece was a cripple who spent most of his time living in a shack near Willie Douthit's cave. A hunchback, Reece could not walk normally and got around in the mountains riding a white mule. He also knew the location of Douthit's cave. Edward claimed that the Palmer brothers, Willie, and Buster had "pulled a lot of bars out of that cave." Edwards talked about bodies inside the cave but he wouldn't elaborate.

John Clarence:
I asked him if he knew who killed the St. Louis couples. He said, "Maybe they did it; the Palmers, or Reece, the hunchback, maybe Willie Douthit or maybe Buster Ward, or maybe Rainey did it." I knew immediately what he meant, and not wanting him to stop talking, I didn't pursue it. I knew that Reece was Reece Palmer; I knew that for certain, but I didn't know he was a hunchback; that was new material. And it was the first time that I had heard Clarence Arthur Palmer referred to as Jack Palmer. Then I thought...who was Rainey? Later, after studying the New Mexico State Police case file, I discovered that there were three Raineys in the case.

~

The first was an ophthalmologist, Dr. Clarence W. Rainey, M.D. from Evanston, Illinois, who wrote to New Mexico State Police Chief, Joseph Roach on April 14, 1958 with his theory on the case. His letter to Chief Roach was in the file. The other was Joe Rainey, of Artesia, who Newkirk described to New Mexico State Police Officer Lucas on October 28, 1953, which was mentioned above. The third person was Gus Rainey from Grants, New Mexico, purported to be a murderer who was also mentioned in the NMSP case file. From all indications Joe Rainey was the man Edwards was referring to; Newkirk claimed that Palmer and Joe Rainey were treasure-hunting partners, but Rainey had turned Palmer's name over to the FBI for not telling him the location of what was actually Willie Douthit's treasure cave.

John Clarence:
Edwards glared at me and then quickly fanned the pages of his Bible and in his haste he accidentally tore one of the pages. "Look what you made me do," he muttered rudely.

I eased up a bit, but I insisted that since he knew about the bodies, he had a moral duty to tell the truth. He began a torrent of jabbering and flung his hands in the air again and shouted, "Praise the Lord," and various incoherent incantations to steer me away from the core issue of our conversation.

It was time to back off and not take it any further, but since I was with Jerry's widow I asked him if he knew the Nosses. "Jerry Cheatham, Ova's grandson, did you know them?" He said he never met Jerry, but he knew the rest of them, Ova, Letha, and Letha's husband, E.M. Guthrie. He said Guthrie was a good friend of his, but the Nosses frightened him.

Whatever it was that drove him to act so bizarrely with someone he never met, I will never know. As it turned out, it was the ranting of Joe Edwards on that windy Sunday afternoon that convinced me of the validity of C.P. Newkirk's statement to New Mexico State Police Officer, B. E. Lucas on November 4, 1953.

~

Upon returning to Las Cruces, a review of the transcribed recording revealed that Howard Butler, Josie Belle's husband, and Howard's adopted daughter, Sue, and Edwards were all on the transcription. The date of the report by Officer Lucas and the date of the recording, circa June 1976, were separated in time by twenty-three years. Edwards had mentioned the name Doran Hunt and claimed that Hunt was rich and that he gave him money to travel to California to visit Willie Douthit and to explore for ancient treasure in the Caballo Mountains. A read of the transcript revealed that Newkirk's statement and some of what Edwards said that Sunday afternoon and sections of the recording transcription matched hand-in-glove. The last ten pages had a good deal of information about the Lorius-Heberer case that never hit the newspapers and did not appear in the New Mexico State Police file.

Why and under what circumstance the recording was made is unknown, but Howard Butler described what he knew to be the facts regarding the St. Louis couples. He claimed that just before the couples disappeared, he and Josie Belle were working the day they took rooms at the Sturges Hotel in Albuquerque and the New Mexico State Police files confirmed that was the case. But the Butlers were never summoned to appear at any criminal proceeding as material witnesses to the events leading up to the time when the couples disappeared, people who had first-hand knowledge of the Lorius-Heberer couples' movements and conversations just before they went missing.

Butler's and others in the transcript have been abridged, but careful attention was given to keep faith with the exact meaning as was intended by each person who spoke during the recording session; most of the transcript is word-for-word. What you will read is the end of the conversation among the participants. The conversation included a number of comments about Doc and Ova, Willie Douthit, Buster Ward and other individuals.

Narrative has been added to help explain the relevance of the conversation, provable information that was related to the Lorius-Heberer murders. Some words were missing, but the *obvious* missing word(s) have been inserted. From the transcript,[17] in part:

> *Butler: Palmer, up there; he won't tell you anything.*
> *Edwards: Willie Douthit, Doc and Reece and Jack Palmer…*
> *Hunt: Jack Palmer was associated with all of them.*
> *Butler: I'd leave that story alone, all together. Do you want me to lay off?*
> *Hunt: Why, why is that? (Laughter)*
> *Edwards: It's just not the right time of the day is it, Butler?*
> *Butler: Well, I might as well tell ya; Josie and me was running a hotel in Albuquerque, it was a second-class hotel, the Sturges Hotel on the corner of Fourth and Central.*
> *Hunt: Now this was at the same time you had your dealings with Doctor Noss? He was from Albuquerque?*
> *Butler: No.*
> *Edwards: Well, anyway, let him go ahead.*
> *Butler: This was two or three years, two years before…*
> *Hunt: Oh, I see, before Noss.*
> *Butler: We had a lot of tourists coming in and out there, you know. One morning, an old man and his wife and a young fella and his wife come in there dead-beat and wanting to park the car under the trees round back and they'd go in the alley and turn behind the hotel. The old man said, 'Take us up to our room and let me lie down and rest and get a shower. We've been driving day and night. This young couple behind us won't let us stop or rest hardly to eat. We're all in.'*

~

According to Howard Butler, the four tourists went up to their rooms. At five o'clock they had refreshed themselves, but they hadn't rested as long as they wanted, especially the older couple in the foursome. Josie Belle had taken them to their rooms immediately because the older couple was so distressed, 'all in' as Mr. Butler described their fatigue. Later, the four friends came down to the lobby; Howard Butler had just come down to work the nightshift. They asked if there was a good restaurant, and he sent them across the road to the Liberty Café. Butler explained what happened next:

> *When they had a good feed, they come back. And, the younger fella, he said, 'Where's your telephone?' I said there's a telephone booth in the corner of the lobby there. The younger* man went over and made a call and came back all excited and told the older couple, 'We got to go right away, right away. Hurry up and get your suitcase packed, we got to get out of here right away.' The old man said, 'Oh, hell no, I can't go. I'm tired. We can go tomorrow. I want to sleep all night.' 'No, no, we can't, we mustn't. We have*

---

*Lorius was 49. Heberer was 52.

to be there by ten o'clock tonight.' Well, with that the younger man went up and packed their suitcases for them, brought them down on the sidewalk and went round back and got the car and parked it at the curb. Josie helped them load the suitcases and things into the car and one of the women said, 'Open the back. There are two straps on the back of the car holding the lid down.' Josie lifted it up and looked in. She saw a jack and some tire tools. Josie said, 'I'll take them out and put them under your feet (meaning under the seat up front) because if you put your suitcases down on them, with the rattling on the road you'll knock holes in the suitcases.' That's what they did. They said they wanted to go to Gallup where they expected to make a big deal on a gold deal and they had a man waiting for them there in Gallup and if they didn't get there right away and make this deal that day they'd lose out on it. Now, he was a rich gold dealer from Ohio.

~

Whoever had transcribed the original audiotapes had typed in the word *coal*. Later someone crossed out *coal* and wrote *gold* above it. Since Lorius was a coal dealer in East St. Louis, the question is whether he intended to go to Gallup to buy coal or he intended to go there to deal in gold? Considering that the bituminous (soft) coalfield* near Gallup was mined primarily to supply the local demand for locomotive fuel, it is unlikely that Lorius would have been able to acquire coal at a good price so far away. Taking into consideration the distance involved in transporting coal to Illinois eliminates any notion that Lorius was intending to buy coal there. Lorius' home and coal business was located at the epicenter of the largest coalfields in the world: the U.S. Eastern, Western and the Appalachian Coal Regions; countless coalfields were near East St. Louis. Therefore, the editing marks were most likely justified.

Since the investigation of the missing couples began, a lot had been learned, but to put everything into perspective, it was necessary to stitch the pieces together, starting from the time the couples left East St. Louis May 19 in Lorius' car. They left home at 5:00 a.m. and crossed the Missouri River the first day, spent the night of May 19 in Miami, Oklahoma, the night of May 20 in Sayre, Oklahoma, the night of May 21 in a small motel at Vaughn. From the time they left East St. Louis until they arrived in Vaughn, New Mexico, they had traveled about 920 miles averaging about twenty-six miles per hour, which included stopping for meals, fuel and nights at motels along the way. Indications in the New Mexico State Police file show they arrived at the above stops and left early in the morning. Had they held to the same schedule and left the motel in Vaughn early and headed west toward Albuquerque, they would have a 106-mile drive to get there, which was about a two or three hour trip, depending if they stopped to eat and get gas, which would have put them in Albuquerque somewhere between 10:00 a.m. and noon. They did not arrive at the Sturges Hotel on the corner of Fourth and Central in Albuquerque until 4:00 p.m., leaving about six unaccounted hours.

---

* 1907 U.S. Geological Survey Bulletin 316, pp. 375-426

But they did not stay at the Sturges Hotel that night; they only *rested* until about 5 o'clock that evening, ate dinner "across the road" at the Liberty Café, returned to the hotel, repacked Lorius' car (with Josie's help) and drove off. According to what Butler said in the transcript, before the couples had supper at the café, the younger man in the party, Mr. Lorius, pushed to leave for Gallup where they had a transaction cooking with a *gold dealer* there. Whether the couples were buying or selling gold is unknown, but it was established that they did not stay the night at the Sturges Hotel. It was generally reported that it was the last time they were seen.

Since it was illegal then to have more than $100 in gold, and, if they were buying or selling gold in Gallup, the dealer there would hardly have stepped forward and reported to the police he had transacted gold business with them; one question would have led to another and the gold dealer would have been looking at large fines and imprisonment; this is perhaps the reason they were never reported being seen in Gallup. Doc Noss had disposed of his gold through a dealer in Gallup as well, and it might well have been the same dealer, but that is mere speculation.

The NMSP cold case file[18] read that on June 29 "ashes of an old fire were discovered approximately six miles east of Albuquerque by Wayland and Edward Fullingim not far from Albuquerque's East Mesa," which is north of the present-day State Fairgrounds. "In this fire were found personal articles belonging to members of this missing party." In the transcript Butler said that a cowboy "rode up to the Triangle Restaurant while FBI Agent Street and Josie were eating supper." The *official* report said both brothers found it, but only one of them came into the Triangle Restaurant. More from the transcript:[19]

> *The FBI and the police started inquiring; they was in and out of that hotel, searching it from top to bottom, looking for signs of a murder or struggle and I couldn't possibly give them any information, other than I'd seen when they took off from there that night.*

~

Butler said that one of the ladies in the party was sitting in the lobby and he walked up to her:

She was writing a lot of postcards, a few to Albuquerque, 'We're having a wonderful time, wish you were here,' you know, the usual stuff. She handed them to me and she said, 'Is there any way you can get these mailed so they'll be delivered in Ohio by tomorrow?' I said, maybe I can catch the mailman outside. Now those postcards

---

* The postcard shown here is one Tillie Heberer bought in Vaughn and mailed from the Sturges Hotel.

were the salvation of Josie and me. Those dad gummed detectives stayed at the hotel and there were questions and questions and they searched and searched.

The postcard was postmarked Albuquerque and reads:

…5-22- at 11a.m.…came through this place* this a.m. Everybody O.K. No Trouble of any kind. Going to Boulder Dam then to Los Cal. Get there Saturday. Tell all boys, hello. "   —*T. & A.*

Butler spotted the mailman in front of the hotel and went outside and handed him the postcards. He asked if they'd be delivered in Ohio by the next day. The postman told Howard, "They'll be put on the eight o'clock plane and they'll get through to Ohio, maybe a little late tomorrow, but they'll get through." Howard went back into the hotel and told her what the mailman said. The woman thanked him. The postcards were, in fact, delivered and were later taken as evidence by the New Mexico State Police and became part of their files. The NMSP case file confirmed what Harold Butler had said in the recording session; based on the postman having stopped at the mailbox, it established the exact day and the approximate time the Lorius party left the Sturges Hotel.

Butler continued with his account of what he had witnessed:

They disappeared off the face of the earth, the four of them. And the car, well, about a month afterwards the car was found deserted way down in Texas. It weren't wrecked; it was pulled up from the side of the road, the highway, near a bridge and it had been wiped clean of all fingerprints. The police didn't take much notice of it; they just pulled it into their garage and tried to trace it through the engine number and the tags. About 3 days after, they'd found out it was the Lorius' car, but the people had disappeared. Well, the mayor in Albuquerque was all against telling that the Loriuses and the Heberers ever came to Albuquerque. It was all bull; they'd been there. And it was a black eye to the town to even think that they'd been there.

The only thing they had to go on was if they'd been there and stayed at that hotel and registered. But Josie and I explained the circumstances of how come they didn't register. They paid for the room all right. Well, that big shot came down, Street, the head of the FBI in El Paso and he was very friendly talking to us a lot, you know, trying to get something. He asked if I could take the desk for Miss Josie. He said, 'I'll take her out to dinner tonight and talk this thing over.' So, I took over the desk and he went with Josie to the Triangle Restaurant and they had their dinner. This was about two months after the people disappeared. While they were eating their dinner a cowboy come riding up on a horse; he was working for the owner of the Triangle Restaurant. He said, 'I found the Lorius' luggage up in the middle of the mesa. It's been burned up.' So, Street naturally,

---

* The "place" was Starvation Peak, a well-known landmark along the Santa Fe Trail where settlers chose to die of *starvation*, rather than at the hands of Indian warriors; the same also noted on postcard.

and Josie, they jumped up and got in the car and followed the cowboy to where this fire was going and Street asked him, he said, 'Did you see anybody around this fire to start it?' The cowboy answered, 'No, but I saw a big black car drive away from there and it went down to Harris Canyon.'

~

The NMSP case file indicates there were two FBI agents involved in the case, Special Agent in Charge (SAIC or SAC) Street, who ran the El Paso Office, and SAIC A.R. Gere out of Albuquerque, but it seems that Gere was in charge. The NMSP case file also shows that the East St. Louis Police did not notify the NMSP until eighteen days after the couples went missing. The file shows that on August 27, 1937, over FBI Director J. Edgar Hoover's signature, on case number FBI-272793, the Bureau was involved in the case, but when that happened is not known; there were most likely a considerable number of FBI Agents involved in the investigation. The file also contained a report filed by NMSP detectives, H.C. Martin and Wooton*, that essentially validates a good deal of Butler's commentary as it relates to Josie and his presence at the Sturges Hotel. From the report:

> *- Mrs. Josephine Ward, Clerk at the Sturges Hotel, Albuquerque, New Mexico - On May 21ˢᵗ 1935, at about 4 P.M., the above-described couples came to the hotel and asked to see a room; they looked at rooms 18, 30 and 35. They did not take a room, but rented room 35 and took a bath, for which they paid Mrs. Ward $1.00 for same; she made an entry in her daybook. The above parties did not register, George M. Lorius paid her, they asked information about Gallup, El Paso, Elephant Butte dam, Hot Springs, and also stated that they were from Illinois, also asked about Juarez Mexico. She (Josie) gave Mr. Lorius her brother's address in Santa Monica, California, L.F. Morgan, M.D.*

~

Wherever the couples went after they left the Sturges Hotel in Albuquerque, whether it was to Gallup, New Mexico or somewhere else, was a mystery then and remains one to this day. A larger question is, what really happened to them, and where were they when they were murdered and by whom? That's what this writer tried to piece together during the investigation of this case because it involved a number of important issues and a number of people who played a significant role in the story of Victorio Peak.

After evaluating the material in the NMSP case file, it became clear that the couples disappeared in the same area of New Mexico where the events related to the Victorio Peak story took place, events that involved Doc and Ova Noss directly, and of course—gold. In an effort to find more pieces to the puzzle of a seemingly unsolvable murder mystery, more attention was given to a report written by two New Mexico State Police detectives, Martin and Wooton.

---

* First name or initials unknown

Their report confirmed Butler's statement that the couples were interested in Gallup and his description of the event concerning Mrs. Heberer signing postcards and that he had given them to the postman in front of the hotel. The report also mentioned that someone, probably Tillie Heberer, purchased 26 cents worth of postage stamps from Josie Ward; the rate for a single post-card in 1935 was 1¢, which supports Butler's statement that Tillie had written and mailed a number of postcards. The report also outlined the couples' travel plans to include not only Gallup, but also Elephant Butte Dam and Hot Springs in New Mexico and El Paso, Texas; they had also asked about Juarez, Mexico. When viewed as a whole, a close look at the couple's travel agenda and the places they were seen by eyewitnesses, combined with the list of "American Express Traveler's Checks" and the official statement given to New Mexico State Police Officer B.E. Lucas by C.P Newkirk, paint an interesting picture, if not a compelling one.

It is one hundred and forty-four miles from Albuquerque to Gallup, New Mexico, and in 1935, old Route 66, which was the route number then, was paved. If the couples drove to Gallup on the evening of May 21 and traveled at a safe speed, say 45-50 miles per hour, the trip in Lorius' six-year-old tan 1929 Nash Coach would have taken about three hours and ten minutes. They would have arrived in Gallup at about 9:15 P.M., on time for their 10:00 P.M. appointment. They could have taken a room somewhere in Gallup and gone to their appointment from there. The next day, Wednesday, May 22, they could have started out very early that morning, as they customarily had, say 6:00 a.m., and headed for El Paso. To get there, they would have passed through two of their points of interest, Elephant Butte Dam and Hot Springs. Juarez, Mexico, also on their agenda, abuts El Paso on the Rio Grande; they only needed to cross the border at El Paso to enter Juarez. However, there is no indication in the official statewide investigation that the couples went to Nevada or California, or for that matter Juarez.

Following the official 1935 New Mexico road map shown here, their path from Gallup to El Paso is easy to trace. On the return trip from Gallup, it would have made sense to bypass Albuquerque and stay on Route 66 to Los Lunas. From there, Socorro was only fifty-four miles south on Route 60-85 and San Antonio another eleven miles. In Martin and Wooton's report, a Mr. Maurice Chaves, the owner of a store and filling station in San Antonio said:

> ...A Nash car with 4 people in it, 2 men and 2 women, stopped at their filling station, bought 5 gallons of gasoline and offered to pay with the $10.00 Travelers Check. He identified Mr. Lorius as the man that bought the gas. According to Chaves, Lorius had asked about coal mining in that section of the country.

~

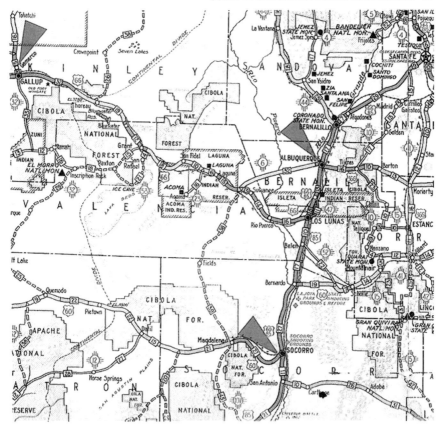

To get to the mining camp, Lorius had to turn east and drive ten miles to get to the Carthage-Tokay* coal mining camp. From the coal mining camp, the couples must have driven back to Socorro and took a motel for the night, because according to the detective's report, the owner of the Socorro Grill, a Mr. John N. Matthews, said:

> *Mr. George Lorius and party had dinner at his place of business between the hours of 9:00 and 10:00 P.M. Mr. Matthews positively identified Mr. Lorius as one of the party. Mrs. Matthews also identified Mr. Lorius and said that the two ladies had bandanas around their head, one blue, [and] the other red. She claimed that Mr. Lorius wore a gray suit, and the other man had a dark suit.*

That morning, Thursday, May 23, had they started out at about 6:00 a.m., or even 7:00 a.m., and drove from Socorro straight to El Paso, a two hundred

---

* The Carthage-Tokay mining site, known as the Government Mine, was the first coal mine worked in New Mexico. U.S. Army soldiers worked the mine in the 1860s for coal needed at Forts Selden, Bayard, and Stanton. In 1903, locals out of San Antonio reopened the mine. By 1907 the town had grown from 300 residents to more than a thousand. Little remains of the town today.

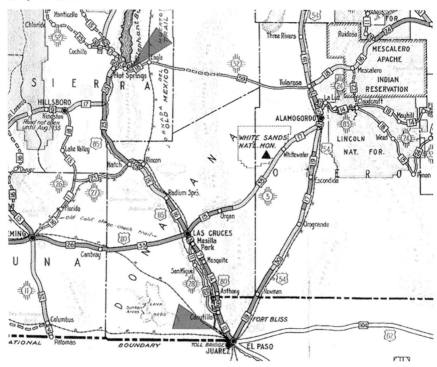

six mile, five hour drive, and stopping only for gas and meals, they could have easily arrived there that afternoon at about one o'clock. That day, two American Express Traveler's Checks were cashed in El Paso: one at Hugo's Service Station, and the other at U.S. Tire Service, an indication that Lorius' Nash car needed work done on the tires. It is this writer's belief that from El Paso, they traveled back to Hot Springs with hopes of buying gold. In the report by NMSP officer B.E. Lucas, Newkirk said (recap):

> *The Lorius, Heberer party spent the night there [Hot Springs] and inquired about the country in the vicinity of John Gordon's cabin, which is about six miles east of Caballo Lake. The Palmer brothers became suspicious since there is a belief that there is a large quantity of Old Spanish gold buried in that vicinity. The Palmer brothers arrived at the location [the Hackberry Grove] ahead of the party and stationed themselves where they could observe the actions of the party. Palmer states that the Lorius car parked in some Hackberry* trees, one lady stayed at the car, and the other three went about three quarters of a mile into the hills and entered a hole in the ground. The Palmer brothers then entered the hole, and according to Clarence, Reece shot and killed the three of them. Clarence stated that the cave contained approximately a million dollars in gold bars. The three bodies were left in the cave. The other lady was killed in or near the car. The body was put in the car,*

---

* The place where the couples had parked the 1929 Nash sedan was known as the Hackberry Grove.

and Clarence drove the car to a point east of Albuquerque where he burned the luggage. He was afraid he might get caught in the mountains east of Albuquerque, so he headed back south on US 85. Somewhere north of Hot Springs he wrecked the car slightly and drove on to El Paso and spent the night. He stated that he buried the body about nine miles from Van Horn, Texas and then drove into Dallas and left the car. He then hitchhiked back to Hot Springs. Clarence stated to Newkirk that he had taken some gold from the cave, but was questioned too closely when he tried to dispose of it, so he returned it to the cave.

Mr. Newkirk states that Palmer has been under suspicion by the FBI on this case. He states that he and a subject by the name of Joe Rainey, of Artesia, were partners in trying to find some of the treasure. Rainey got mad at Palmer for giving him the runaround on the location of the cave and turned him in to the FBI.

~

What is interesting about Newkirk's story is that some of the individuals and events were also described by Joe Edwards: 1) Jack Palmer, whom Newkirk referred to as *Clarence* Palmer, 2) Reece Palmer, Jack's brother, and 3) bodies inside Douthit's cave. Then there were the comments made by Willie Douthit himself during the 1989 video interview at Victorio Peak nearly six decades after the St. Louis couples disappeared:

Willie Douthit: Do you want to hear something off the record?
Alex Alonso: What's off the record mean?
Willie Douthit: It means you can't tell anybody. When I was over there lookin' around, why ah, when I first found that gold over there in the Caballos, why, ah, some people came and was messin' around with it. And for some reason or other, they got eliminated.
Alex Alonso: I think we know the story.
Willie Douthit: Of course it's cleaned up now.

~

Was Douthit admitting he played some role in the St. Louis couples' fate? From his comments he apparently knew of, sanctioned, or was in someway involved in the deaths of these people. In another interview, Douthit bragged about his involvement in an attempted murder of a person named Willie Stromm; an investigation into that event led John Clarence to a ground level cave at a place known as Hackberry Draw. Locals who are familiar with this area of the Caballo Mountains know the cave as Smoke Hole, a name given to it by treasure hunters who burned old tires inside of it hoping to see the smoke exit somewhere nearby where gold might be found. The man who knew about the site was very knowledgeable about the Caballo Mountains, and it was at this ground cave that Willie Douthit claimed he and Buster Ward plotted to murder Stromm. In Chapter 14, there is more written about the Willie Stromm episode, but it is here that the Lorius-Heberer murders are discussed.

Along the county road that winds through the foothills of the western slopes of the Caballo Mountains is a turnoff that leads due west. One hundred and fifty yards east of this particular turnoff there once stood a grove of hackberry trees where people used to come and picnic, camp, or get relief from the hot desert sun; the car seen in the top right of the photo is parked on the county road mentioned.

The barren draw in the center of the photo is the spot Newkirk described to Officer Lucas, but the grove of hackberry trees that once graced this spot is gone. It is common knowledge in the area that the grove was stripped clean by the three Sanders brothers who were searching for Douthit's gold. The remains of those trees were pushed across the county road. Three years prior to taking these photos, and knowing the significance of this site, this writer examined several of the destroyed hackberry trees and observed many strange markings, names and initials of individuals, including one heavy limb with the initials "DN-ON" carved on it—perhaps Doc Noss-Ova Noss. Heavy rains have since washed over the few remaining tree sections, burying them under the sandy floor of the draw.

The event involving the St. Louis couples began in Hot Springs where the Palmers' mother owned and operated a tourist motor camp and service station, a place that was frequently visited by travelers such as the Loriuses and Heberers. The couples spent the night there and according to Newkirk they had asked questions about the area near John Gordon's cabin; leaving little doubt they were looking to buy gold. Joe Edwards claimed that the Palmer brothers *knew* where the cave was located, contrary to Newkirk's account, as told to him by Jack Palmer, that the brothers *suspected* there was Spanish gold buried near

Gordon's cabin. Regardless, the Palmers drove to the area ahead of the couples. Then, from what Newkirk told Officer Lucas, the couples arrived there alone in their car, turned into Hackberry Draw and parked in Hackberry Grove; one of the women stayed with Lorius' car while the other three proceeded east up Hackberry Draw. Edwards also said that Reece was crippled and spent most of his time in a shack near Douthit's cave and that he rode around on a white mule. At no time in the accounts given by Edwards or Newkirk was Doc Noss' name mentioned in connection to the night before or the day of the murders.

The same person who took me to Smoke Hole also gave me the following account of that day. According to him, and what was also generally accepted as the string of events that took place that day, which was also similar to the accounts by Newkirk and Edwards, was that Jack and Reece Palmer reached the area *well* in advance of the couples and proceeded up Hackberry Draw. Jack was walking and Reece was riding his white mule, suggesting that the brothers stopped at Reece's shack near Douthit's place and picked up Reece's mule so that he could go along. They reached the site where Ward and Douthit's stash cave was located, watched the three people enter the cave, followed them inside where an argument began. The event, as told to this writer, was that Jack Palmer shot and killed the three people, but Reece, because he was in failing health, took the blame for the murders in the event they were ever arrested, tried, and found guilty of the killings.

This GoogleEarth image shows the location of Hackberry Grove west of the Smoke Hole. Smoke Hole is located .43 miles east of Hackberry Grove where

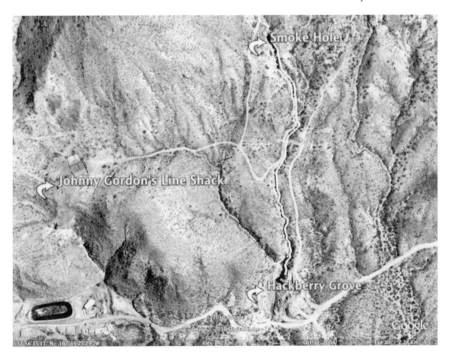

the Lorius' car was parked; this small cave is significant only to the extent that it was the cave where Douthit talked about shooting Willie Stromm. However, according to what Jack Palmer told Newkirk, the couples walked *"three quarters of a mile into the hills and entered a hole in the ground."* There is a discrepancy of more than .32 miles, which is significant, suggesting that three of the killings took place further up the draw. Regardless of what cave they were killed in, it was along this draw that the St. Louis couples died.

The exact place where three of the four St. Louis people were killed may never be found, nor is it likely that their bodies will ever be recovered, but the killings that took place in May of 1935 happened along Hackberry Draw in the Caballo Mountains. A closer examination of what happened at Smoke Hole is covered in Chapter 14.

~

Someone other than George Lorius cashed many of his American Express Traveler's Checks; the trail extending from El Paso, Texas to Dallas, Texas, and the sequence in which they turned up corresponded for the most part with the NMSP investigation. There is little question that the Lorius-Heberer couples were killed as a result of their interest in Willie Douthit's treasure trove, making it a near certainty that the junket they were on involved a scheme of buying and selling gold. The following is the continuation of Howard Butler's remarks in the transcript; it takes up where the Lorius-Heberer luggage was found on the East Mesa in Albuquerque:

Well, Josie began raking the burnt stuff around with a stick and eventually she found a piece of envelope with the Lorius' name written on it. So, they knew it was the Lorius' luggage. But somebody had taken and put it all in the middle of the mesa and set it all on fire, trying to prove that the Lorius' were in Albuquerque and had been killed there. So when they found the car, the Albuquerque cops come and looked at the car and asked Josie if she could recognize the car. She said, 'Yes, I believe I could.' They said, 'Well you'll have a chance to, we found the car, what we think is the car, and we got it mixed up with a lot of other cars down at the Owens' garage* and we want to see if you can recognize it.'

Well, they took her down and they drove her in and as soon as she got in there she said, 'Stop, that's the car over there.' And, they looked at each other. 'How do you know?' She said, 'Well there are certain things about it. I'm absolutely sure I know it. There're two straps on the back, one of them new and one of them old. I undid those straps to open up the end of that car.' Well, they said, 'that might be a coincidence. A new strap wouldn't prove anything.' 'Well,' she said, 'if one of you get out and rub your hand along the fender, the right hand side of the fender, you'll find a heart-shaped dent. While I was waiting for them to get in the car I leaned against that fender and felt that dent and I mentioned it to Lorius that he had a bad dent in his fender and he ought to

---

* Lorius' car was towed back to Owens' garage in Albuquerque.

get it straightened out.' Well, he said, 'I got it while I was driving yesterday. I bumped into a fire hydrant in town.'

Now, this fella that was in the car, he sent the other fella, the cop, out to feel the fender and he rubbed his hand on it and he says, 'Yup that's right.' So, she got out then and said, 'Let me have a look at the car now and see if there're any signs of foul play.' The one officer said, 'Oh it's not a good idea for you to do that, there's been more detectives and police looked at it, they've searched it.' She looked all over it. She looked at the cushions to see if they'd washed any bloodstains, and they hadn't. Then she walked to the back and undid the straps and lifted the lid and all that was there was just an old rag. And she looked in and said, 'Pull it out and let me see it.' So they pulled out a piece of an old, torn bedspread that had been lying across the bottom. At one end of it there was a big bloodstain. She looked at it and said, 'Great Heavens, that wasn't in the car when I put the suitcases in there.' The one police officer reacted and said, 'Oh yeah, it must have been put there so the suitcases wouldn't get dirty.' Josie said, 'No, no, no. I took out the jack and the tire tools and there was nothing in there. You better have that stain analyzed.' 'Oh,' they said, 'Let it be.' They didn't want to do that, you know, they didn't want to find anything.

But eventually one of the sergeants came down and they had it analyzed and in 10 minutes they found out it was a bloodstain. And, Josie turned around and said, 'I'm not a detective like you people are. You bring the car all the way from Texas and you're riding along with an absolute dead-set clue.'

Well, it turned out that the Loriuses and the Heberers had left Albuquerque and came to Hot Springs and somebody took them up in the mountains. They disappeared and they never found them. And since I been down here,* 'course all of this happened a long time ago, but what I heard from down here is this Palmer rest camp or tourist camp, that's where they disappeared. Now the theory is that they were going to buy his gold [Douthit's gold] and I don't know whether they fought over it or what, but they never come back alive, you know.

Hunt: *So this Jack Palmer, then, had a tourist camp here in Hot Springs?*

Butler: *His mother had the camp.*

Edwards: *His mother had it.*

Butler: *Now he had a brother who was a hunchback, see, and a regular devil, he knew where the hideout was, where the gold was, and from what little bit they've gathered since then, with Josie's help mostly, they [the Palmers] were entitled to that gold and they killed them. Now, the hunchback did the killing and Finch† died and the other two partners that the Palmers had with them, they're both dead. And, the FBI and the police have never got around to finding out the truth of the matter, what must have become of 'em.*

Edwards: *What'd that FBI man tell ya that came from Washington that time?*

---

* Howard Butler and Josie eventually moved to Hot Springs, but that was long after the disappearances.

† Finch's identity is unknown.

> *Butler: Now that night, oh brother, I was sitting in the house, in the front room and a big white car came riding up and a well-dressed fella walked up and said, 'Mrs. Butler and Mr. Butler live here?' Yes, sir, I said. He said, 'I'd like to come in and talk to you a while.'*

~

Butler allowed him to come in and invited the man to sit down and told him that he and Josie had "just about finished up for the night" and that he had been resting. It was then the man produced his credentials—he was an FBI agent from Washington and he was investigating the Lorius-Heberer disappearances. "I came down here to see if I could persuade you people and your friend, Doctor Noss, to make an agreeable deal with us. The only way we can deal with him is through you."

Josie said, "Well, what's the deal?"

The agent told them he had been sent there "to put it up to Noss to show" the FBI the cave. He also said they'd bring out all the gold and "weigh it right before his eyes and the whole thing would be up and aboveboard, and they'd give him every cent that was coming to him, and we'd keep the rest." He said, "Can you get in touch with him now?"

And Josie said, "Well, yes, I can."

He told Josie to ask Doc if he would take them up to his cave and they'd "get that gold out and get it out of the way and settled once and for all." Howard continued:

> *Josie said, 'Well, let me go to the phone.' Now, we didn't have a phone in the house, so she went out to the local store and called Noss. And, he said, 'Ask him how much I will receive out of the deal.' She came back and said, 'He wants to know how much he'll get out of the deal.' And this fella says, 'Well, we'll give him 19%, you see it's a treasure, he didn't have to mine the gold, he didn't have to work and sweat he just walked out there and found it. It's a treasure trove and the government will allow you 19%.' She said, 'I don't think he'll go for that.' 'Well, you ask him.' So, she went back to the phone and he said, 'Tell him to put it the other way around; they take 19% and I'll take 81%. Then I'll deal.' So she went back and told him. And he had his beautiful gun lying out on the table and I was struck with his drinking cocktails, and he said, 'Well, I don't think I can do that. It was a wild goose chase, they sent me all the way down from Washington down here to see you people and I suppose that's the end of my inquiry, I guess. We'll have to take a back seat.' And, I said you mean to say that you were only going to give him 19 dollars for every hundred dollars worth? 'Well,' he said, 'that's the law and we can't help it.' I said I don't see why you people in Washington are bothering your heads with what little gold we've got down here in New Mexico when you've got three quarters of the gold in the world up in Washington. That's a heck of a thing. 'Oh, look,' he said to me, 'that's not the point, Mr. Butler. The point is we want to get that stuff out of the way so nobody else will be killed over it, that's the point.' And that set me back on my haunches. And then with that he went [he left].*

~

Those remarks came at the end of the tape. There is little question that the Butler tapes and New Mexico State Police Officer Lucas' report of November 4, 1953, were linked, perhaps not in provable forensic evidence, but in substance, which even raises more questions than the tape and the report answer: Why was the FBI interested in Doc's* gold? Doc's Caballo Mountain treasure was hidden in a cave high on the ridge in Burbank Canyon. It was *not* a ground cave like the Douthit/Ward treasure cave, the place where three of the St. Louis people's bodies were allegedly hidden. And how did the FBI know the Lorius-Heberer disappearances had anything to do with gold?

John Clarence:
I didn't get exactly what I wanted from Edwards that Sunday afternoon, but I got enough to verify most of what was in the police report. After the grueling interview, I was totally convinced that Edwards knew far more about the Lorius-Heberer disappearances than he let on. Finally, I asked Edwards about Newkirk. He said that he knew him personally, that there was an incident where Newkirk pressed a loaded gun to his belly and then pushed it up under his nose and threatened his life, over what, or under what circumstances the event happened he did not say, nor did it matter; I was not the only one who found an immovable dislike for the man.

~

Doc Noss and Josie Butler were longtime friends, a friendship that went back to their childhood days. Josie was the last person who knew the location of Doc's gold cache in the Caballo Mountains. After Doc died, she gave Edwards a general description of the area where the cave was located, but not the specific location. As a result, Edwards began charging people money for the same information that Josie had given him. One person, a man named Guthrie, could not find the cave and went to Josie for more information. It turned out that Guthrie was E.M. Guthrie, Ova's son-in-law, husband to Letha, Ova's daughter. Josie knew them well, and liked them, but that was not the issue; Edwards had revealed that she was the source of the information that she had given to Edwards. Here is the letter[20] Josie sent to Edwards when she learned that he had betrayed her:

I feel awfully sorry for you. You know that at the time that we made our agreement that you were not to tell anybody about the cave in the Caballo Mountains. One month after I told you about it, a man from Las Cruces, N. Mex. came to my house and told me you had told him about it and told him where I lived. A man by the name of Guthrie also came to the house. Since my husband is blind and I am losing my eyesight, you have placed me in a very dangerous position.
That is the reason why you have not learned anymore about Dr. Noss' cave. You also called Mrs. Noss three times and she told you not to call anymore. So you see that you

---

* The reference to Doc's gold was not the treasure he and Ova had found at Victorio Peak.

have placed Mr. Butler and myself in serious danger. We have been contacted several times and people have tried to make us tell them about the cave. We have the names of all the ones that have contacted us if you want to see them.

You tried to borrow $40.00 from me at Christmas. I gave you $15.00. I am sorry I didn't fail you; you failed me and my husband. I am very sorry for you. Don't come to me for anything again. However, if Dorothy and the children need anything I will try to help them. Very truly   —Josie Butler

~

John Clarence:

It was the first and last time that I had such a verbal confrontation with anyone during the investigation of the case. In spite of my dislike for the man, I planned to pay him another visit the next time I went through Hot Springs. As it turned out, I never saw Edwards after that day.

Chapter 7

Imprisoned, Paroled, and Pardoned

D oc loved a good fight, whether he witnessed it happening at the end of his own knuckles or whether he heard it on the radio. It was the night of Thursday, June 13, 1935, when Jim Braddock beat Max Baer in fifteen rounds by unanimous decision in the Madison Square Garden Bowl in Long Island City, Queens, New York, winning the World Heavyweight title. Ova told Terry that Doc had hoped and prayed he wouldn't have to go to jail before the fight—he

didn't. Doc was finally sentenced[21] one month later on July 15, in Chaves County to serve a 6 to 9 month prison* term for the Ann's Place gun-waving gesture. At his sentencing hearing, and before he was sent to Santa Fe to begin serving his term, he had requested executive clemency from Governor Clyde Tingley. From the time the St. Louis families disappeared after leaving Albuquerque, until Doc was sentenced, nearly two months had gone by. He was received at the New Mexico State Penitentiary on July 17, and processed into the main population of the prison. He remained there for five months and twelve days.[†]

August 1935

On August 6, District Judge James B. McGhee of Roswell, New Mexico wrote[22] to Governor Clyde Tingley concerning the nature of Doc's crime, Doc's guilty plea, and his request for executive clemency. McGhee told Tingley that Doc had insulted people "while armed with a deadly weapon." The judge explained the mix-up[‡] happened at Ann's Place, a beer parlor at the edge of Roswell. While Doc was brandishing his side arm, he was quoted telling the patrons "he would kill the first one that made a move."

---

* Doc's mugshot when he was received at the New Mexico Penitentiary in Santa Fe on July 17, 1935 – Courtesy of New Mexico State Records Center and Archives
† Prison photo of Doc taken just prior to his parole
‡ Mix-up was a common term use during the time: i.e. fight, disagreement, altercation

A short letter[23] of acknowledgement from Governor Tingley to Judge McGhee was sent four days later on August 10, 1935. A little more than two weeks later, on August 23, 1935, Superintendent of New Mexico State Penitentiary John B. McManus, Santa Fe, New Mexico wrote[24] to Judge James B. McGhee requesting advice on Doc's clemency plea. McManus had to report back to the Board of Parole at their next meeting, which would occur by the middle of October. In his letter, McManus referred to the cause of Doc's sentencing, in Chaves County, namely, *"Insulting while Armed."* The New Mexico State Board of Parole met on August 21, 22; however, consideration on Doc Noss' case was postponed until the next parole meeting when District Judge McGhee had time to inform the board "what action" McGhee believed "the board should take." McGhee's answer came four days later, on Tuesday, August 27. McGhee expanded his position concerning the matter. He wrote,[25] and said:

> *I have your letter of August 23 in regard to the case of M.E. Noss. I think if you will talk with the Greek who runs the Plaza Hotel in Santa Fe, you will find that this man is a blackmailer. Deputy Sheriff Shortridge, former member of the Motor Patrol, says he is a bad egg.* —McGhee

~

October-November 1935/March 1936

In spite of the accusations, the New Mexico State Board of Parole granted Doc a conditional parole agreement on October 16, 1935. He was required to leave the State Penitentiary at Santa Fe on November 29, 1935 and to go to a halfway house at Pecos, San Miguel County, New Mexico and remain there for three months. Governor Tingley signed the Parole Agreement on November 22; Noss signed it on Friday, November 29, at which time he walked out of prison and headed for Pecos. On March 3, 1936, a little more than three months after the end of Doc's imprisonment, Governor Clyde Tingley issued an order of Executive Clemency and granted Doc Noss a complete and unconditional pardon.[26] In part:

> *Whereas said defendant has conducted himself in a law-abiding manner during his liberty and it appears that the ends of justice have been met and that he is entitled to executive clemency; Now, therefore, I, Clyde Tingley, Governor of the State of New Mexico, by virtue of the authority in me vested, do hereby grant to the said M.E. Noss a complete pardon from further service of said sentence and a restoration of his full rights of citizenship. The Superintendent of the Penitentiary upon receipt of this Executive Order properly signed and sealed will act accordingly.* —Tingley

~

Clyde K. Tingley was born on a farm near the small town of London, Ohio on January 5, 1882 where he attended public schools there. He moved to New Mexico in 1910 and served as alderman and a member of the City Commission in the Albuquerque district and two years as a district maintenance superintendent for the New Mexico State Highway Department. Tingley was chairman of the Albuquerque City Commission and was active in the New Mexico Democratic Party for twelve years and was a delegate to three Democratic National Conventions. He was elected Governor of New Mexico in 1936.

As far as the tragic fate of the Lorius-Heberer couples was concerned, Tingley all but hung his political hat on his promise to find their killers. It was a crime that plagued the Mayor of Albuquerque, the New Mexico State Police, county executive officers and Governor Clyde K. Tingley in Santa Fe. If there had been any suspicion that Doc Noss was directly or indirectly involved in the St. Louis couples' disappearance, it is unlikely he would have had an early release from prison, yet alone a complete pardon by Governor Tingley. Governor Tingley died in Albuquerque on December 24, 1960. He died shortly after his 78th birthday.

Was Governor Tingley aware of Doc's clinic in Hot Springs where he had treated children from the Carrie Tingley Hospital, which the Governor had dedicated as a tribute to his wife's lifelong efforts to aid crippled children? Letha said, *"Doc gave a lot of free time to the kids at the children's hospital, too. Doc loved kids."* Had Doc's efforts to help in that regard in someway influenced Governor Tingley to issue an order of Executive Clemency?

From the time that Doc went to prison for his antics at Ann's Place in Roswell, until he was paroled, he had served five months and twelve days of his sentence. More than five years later, after he and Ova had settled near Victorio Peak to concentrate on recovering the treasure they had found there, after he began his mining business, and after Doc had appointed Merle Horzmann secretary of his mining company, Horzmann began to accuse Doc of being involved in the disappearance of the Heberer-Lorius couples. She had also made a deal with someone at the state level and Secret Service agents at the federal level for her to infiltrate their camp at Victorio Peak and pass information along.

Except for the unexplained remarks by District Judge James McGhee to Superintendent McManus that the "Greek"* at the Plaza Hotel in Santa Fe thought of Doc as a "blackmailer" and that a former Motor Patrol member referred to him as a "bad egg," there is no evidence of Doc ever being convicted of any other serious crime, or standing out in the community as a hardened criminal. Beyond Doc's prison sentence were the problems he created for himself when he drank, which occurred sporadically throughout his life. When he drank, he usually got into a fight, which more often than not resulted in a small fine or a night in jail, or both. This pattern of behavior continued until the time of his death in 1949 when a business associate shot and killed him in Hatch, New Mexico.

---

*Nothing more ever surfaced concerning this person, other that the letter in which the comment was made.

Sunday – May 10, 1936

Shortly after he had completed his rehabilitation in Pecos, Doc renewed his treasure-hunting efforts. He returned to camp at the Rock House in the Hembrillo Basin and began his search for the treasure that Geronimo had once told him was hidden somewhere in a small mountain. Feeling sure that the treasure described to him by Geronimo was somewhere in the San Andres mountains, he concentrated his search efforts there. From his map, and from what he could recall from Geronimo's description of the area, Doc began an intense search of the hills and small mountains in and around the Hembrillo Basin. But he was also up to his old tricks—he left camp and showed up in Hobbs, New Mexico on Sunday, May 10, and got drunk. According to the FBI, he was fined $10 and let go; in spite of the five-hour drive from Hobbs, Doc returned to camp the same day. In her writings, Ova gave an account* of their activity when Doc returned to camp:

> *That day we found the skeleton of a soldier opposite the 'spring of the grapevines.' That spring, they say, is one the birds can drink out of and the animals can't. We used to get all our water from there when we lived in the Post House.*[†]

Midsummer 1936

That summer, Doc found signs and markers on a number of rock formations on the slopes of Victorio Peak. Checking the markings against his knowledge and the meaning of the symbols on his map, he found an entranceway that led to the interior of the small mountain. It was believed that he had also found another opening that also led to the treasure, which he kept secret from everybody, including Ova. Doc referred to his secret entrance the day before he was shot and killed in Hatch, but he took its exact location with him to the grave.

August 1936

The following month Doc expanded his foot-care business and rented a place in Gallup, New Mexico. He knew that it was not difficult to dispose of a few gold bars at a time in Gallup, a place where he had already developed some good contacts after his success in the Caballo Mountains when he found gold there. It was also the same town where Willie Douthit came to exchange gold for cash; and the same town that the Lorius-Heberer couples went to transact gold fourteen months earlier on Thursday, May 23, 1935. After Doc had made his discovery, his foot-care business in Gallup served as a means to go back and forth between there and Hot Springs without drawing attention to his activities. However, he maintained his foot-care business there for only one year, and during that period of time, Doc met a lawyer by the name of Melvin D. Rueckhaus, whom he confided in and came to know and trust.

---

*O. Noss, "The Writings of Ova Noss," p. 10.
[†]The Post House, its true origin and builders uncertain, was a reference to the Rock House.

Rueckhaus confirmed in a letter[27] dated July 7, 1976, that he "first met Doc Noss in Gallup, New Mexico in August of 1936." He also confirmed that Doc had a "small chiropodist shop in the rear of Otis Swinford's clothing store." Rueckhaus said they had several things in common: they each had an interest in mining and prospecting, Rueckhaus was a lawyer and Doc "was a fellow who had a propensity for all kinds of troubles." It was during a fishing trip to Blue Water, a town about 45 miles west of Grants, close to where Blue Water Lake is located, that Doc first told Rueckhaus about his gold discovery. While they were in Blue Water, Doc showed Rueckhaus a fluorspar* property they both agreed was "an attractive prospect." It was then that Doc told Rueckhaus that his gold could possibly be used "in exploiting the fluorspar property." Rueckhaus said, "At this time he described in generalities the find he had made and indicated that there were problems connected with it that he wasn't ready to go into with me." Rueckhaus had more dealings with Doc about one year later.

During this time period, Doc was prospecting in the Caballo Mountains searching for another gold cache and hoping to find other sites that he was sure were related to the Seven Cities of Gold, which were merely caves and very old, hard-to-find abandoned mines where much of the ancient treasures had been stored hundreds of years ago. Doc's first treasure discovery was in the Caballo Mountains where he and Tony Cariaga found a cave containing a large deposit of gold bars and a chest of artifacts with the cache.

Doc's second discovery was at Victorio Peak; it contained far more gold bars than were in the Caballo Mountain cave. Unlike the Caballo Mountain treasure, the Victorio Peak treasure contained a large amount of ancient artifacts. The Caballo Mountain treasure was on land owned by the State of New Mexico, land under the control of the Land Office in Santa Fe. The Victorio Peak treasure was also under the same jurisdiction, but it would eventually come under the control of the federal government, namely the Department of the Army, and become the White Sands Proving Ground and later the White Sands Missile Range. Those who knew of the Caballo Mountain discovery were Ova, Letha, her daughter, Willie Douthit, and Lino 'Tony' Carriaga.

October 16, 1936

According to the FBI, Doc was in Hatch on October 16, 1936, where he was once again charged with drunk and disorderly conduct. He was fined $9.50 and released. He was still active as a chiropodist in Hot Springs and Gallup when he was arrested.

---

* Fluorspar, also called fluorite, is halide mineral made up of calcium fluoride.

Chapter 8

Defying the Secret Service, the GRA, and the Second Discovery

S pringtime in 1937 was beautiful, as it usually is in the New Mexico desert, and traveling throughout the desert was never boring, but in the case of Doc Noss and those with whom he chose to acquaint himself, traveling with ancient gold bullion in hand was quite dangerous: a *cold war* of defiance by Doc and Ova Noss was about to begin.

Claiming it was safer to travel a good distance away from Hatch and Hot Springs to sell gold bars, Doc and his friend, B.D. Lampros, seen here together at

the Rock House, would often meet in Gallup and transact gold sales there; in fact, Lampros took a number of such trips with Doc over the years. Lampros had worked with him at the Peak and grubstaked him whenever it was necessary; even though Doc had gold at his fingertips, it was a common practice for him to start drinking and spend large sums of money foolishly and having little or nothing to show for it when he sobered up. As a result, Doc and Lampros would travel long distances to sell small pieces of high-grade gold and rich ore samples in order to finance the excavation work at Victorio Peak.

Lampros was not the only witness; according to other people, such as Willie Douthit, Doc had truly found and sold gold. Douthit confirmed this fact during one of his video interviews when he told the story about how he and Doc had palled around together in the early days at Victorio Peak *and* in the Caballo Mountain Range; Douthit chuckled when he told the story. Here is another excerpt from one of Douthit's interviews:

Doc and I were old friends. We used to drink grain alcohol and Coca-Cola and that kind of revs ya' up, ya' know. He says, 'I'll take you out* to show you somethin' that'll knock

---

*Out meant Victorio Peak. Doc and Willie were in the Caballo Mountains when the event took place.

your eyes out.' Ahh, Doc, you're crazy. 'No, I'm not either.' So, we got on our horses and we started out here* and we wound up right here, right in this little swale, just like it is. And again Doc says, 'I'm gonna show you somethin' that'll knock your eyes out.' So we went in, not too far in, and there was all kinds of goodies, boy, I'm tellin' ya'. Ol' Doc says, 'What'd I tell ya.' I said, Doc, you're right. And there's a bunch of rings there, I mean jewelry, and I says, Doc, can I have one of these here? 'Help yourself.' And I took one out. So, we had another shot and then we went out and rested our horses and went back home. That's the first time I was ever in here.

~

Although there were always a few locals who were willing to trade cash for gold, the risk of dealing in Hot Springs or Hatch was always high because Secret Service agents loomed nearby and they were keeping an eye on Doc Noss. Resultantly, Doc trusted few individuals and his distrust and dislike for Washington politicians outweighed his belief that the Treasury would allow him to keep his gold. His fear was that because he was part Indian, the government would steal it. Even though Congress amended the law because of constitutional issues, the exclusions were not changed in the revised Act, and since the type of bars Doc had discovered in the Caballo Mountains were cast centuries earlier under primitive conditions using primitive methods, it was difficult to determine the actual value of such a gold bar without having it properly refined. The gold bars Doc discovered were just that—crude, ancient castings. Additionally, there were few accounts of gold discoveries of this type, namely gold bars present in treasure trove discoveries. The GRA required gold coins[†] and refined gold bullion to be surrendered: gold free of impurities, alloys and sediment, gold processed through a refinery to a given standard of purity, in this case $9/10^{th}$ or .999 percent pure, stamped and weighed with a specific redeemable value. Doc's theory was that the gold bars from his treasure find were not reportable under the definitions of exclusions under the GRA.

Circa June or July 1937

According to Rueckhaus' 1976 letter, Doc went to Jack Levick, a reliable pawnshop owner in the 200 block of South First Street in Albuquerque to sell him a gold bar, but Levick was reluctant to deal with him. When Doc gave Levick Rueckhaus' name as a reference, Levick called him and soon afterwards Rueckhaus showed up at the pawnshop to witness the transaction. When Doc cut a slice off the bar, Levick used a karat tester. That particular sample was almost pure gold, but it still did not fit with the criteria of the GRA. Later, Doc sold the balance of the bar to one of Levick's customers—a Catholic priest. The sale price was $20,000.00. After the agreement, the priest delivered the money.

On another occasion, Doc had talked to the priest about selling him an ancient gold chalice. But the sale did not take place. Rueckhaus also wrote:

---

* Willie Douthit was at Victorio Peak when he gave the interview, thus the reference to "here."

† Executive Order 6102 exempt "rare and unusual coins."

Doc demurred about completing such a sale. Later I heard that the Bernalillo County Sheriff's Department had picked up a gold chalice. Noss asked me to check it for him and gave me a general description. I examined the gold chalice at the Sheriff's office and found it to somewhat answer the description given me by Noss. However, Noss then said he didn't want to pursue the matter any further.

~

The same day that Doc was at Jack Levick's pawnshop with Rueckhaus, he took him to his room at the King's Hotel on Central Street where he showed Rueckhaus six more bars similar to the one tested at the pawnshop. Noss told Rueckhaus that day he had also sold bars to Ruby Horowitz of Nogales. The price was $16,000.00, but Noss had settled for $8,000.00. According to Rueckhaus, Doc had five more bars, but expressed concern that he might have trouble since those bars were marked, indicating that Wells Fargo had "claimed title to the bars by virtue of a robbery* many years before." It wasn't long afterwards that Doc told Rueckhaus:

> *He had a mind to dispose of the marked bars by salting an old mine in either the Caballo Mountains or the San Andres. His efforts in this direction were somewhat hindered by his constant complaints of people following him, probably, in his mind, either the Wells Fargo people or government people.*

~

Rueckhaus said that after the sale to the priest, Noss went on a "spree of drinking and spending and depleted all of his cash within a period of about three weeks." Little is known of the fate of the Wells Fargo bars, but the contention is that most, if not all of them, remain inside the treasure rooms beneath Victorio Peak.

As the discovery of the treasure at Victorio Peak grew closer, the lines between which gold Doc was transporting, selling and hiding began to blur. People who worked for Doc during this time told of accounts that put Doc and Ova in the Hembrillo Basin at a campsite known as the Rock House. Doc had set up a camp in the Hembrillo Basin to search for the Victorio Peak treasure and was financing the operation with funds he received from selling gold from the Caballo Mountain treasure discovery.

Rueckhaus' letter[28] also referred to meeting a Dr. Miller of Clovis, New Mexico:

> *Noss had become acquainted with a Doctor Miller, the head of the Santa Fe Railroad Hospital in Clovis, New Mexico, where Doctor Miller lived. He had become very interested in the project, very intrigued by the remarkable description of gold stacked like cordwood and various relics and had invested some money and had recommended to several friends that they invest money.*

~

---

* There has never been any indication that Doc was ever involved in such a robbery. The gold inside Victorio Peak had many sources; some obviously included stagecoach robberies.

Dr. Miller's account was the same. His sworn statement[29] of November 1, 1952, tells of Doc's association with Dr. Miller:

> *I was personally acquainted with Mr. Milton E. Noss, known among his acquaintances as Doc Noss. He stated on his first and only trip into the cave he removed and brought out several bars of gold and silver bullion, of which he showed me two different bars, which looked and weighed like gold. He also stated there were hundreds of these bars in the cave, which contained gold and silver bullion, and other relics of value, since such exploration the opening in which he entered said cave caved in and he was seeking finances to remove the obstruction.*
>
> *...I would like very much to see the thing to a finish, and I understand sufficient financing is available if permission can be obtained from our Government, to enter the property.*   —*H. A. Miller, M.D.*

August 1937

During the summer of 1937, a young man named Joe Andregg took a summer job with Doc Noss helping him do a number of chores at Victorio Peak. Joe had turned fourteen on December 10th of the preceding year. His uncle owned and operated a cattle ranch about eight miles south of the Rock House. Joe would stand watch for Doc, ride with him, feed the animals, do the chores and "help with the assessment work on his mining claims." While he was working for Doc that first summer, Joe saw something—gold bars. He described what he had seen in his statement:[30]

> *The first summer I worked with him, we did a lot of riding. I was also helping out at my Uncle Frank's ranch. I came back to the mine about sunset, at suppertime. I went in. Doc was sitting at the end of the table. He told me to look under the blanket in the corner of the room. I raised the cover. There was a stack of 19 bars of what I believed to be gold. I left soon after that to go back to school.*

~

The Victorio Peak treasure discovery was months away. The bars seen by young Joe Andregg could only have come from Doc's other treasure find in the Caballo Mountains. Joe's experiences with Doc continued throughout his young life. Even during his adult life, Joe Andregg maintained an active interest in Victorio Peak and was a credible witness to what he had seen when he worked for Doc at Victorio Peak.

Winter 1937

Doc told family members he had found the location of the Victorio Peak treasure from an old map* given to him by an Indian, someone that Doc had treated for a foot ailment at his office in Hot Springs. The Indian had no money and Doc accepted the map as payment.

---

* Map that Doc was thought to have used to find the Victorio Peak treasure.

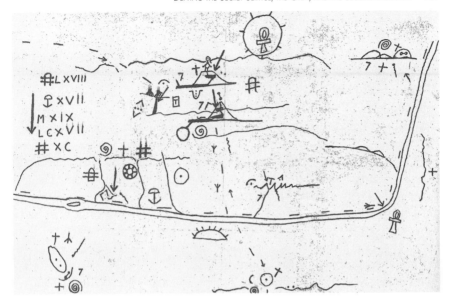

Doc was selling gold bars for at least two years before November 7, 1937, which was the discovery date of the Victorio Peak treasure. The difference in these time elements gives credence to the general contention that Doc had found a sizable treasure of gold bars in the Caballo Mountains, a find that clearly predates the Victorio Peak discovery. Then in the winter of 1937, Doc Noss stumbled upon an opening at the top of Victorio Peak in the Hembrillo Basin; an opening that he told Ova "needed investigation." Doc would soon find yet another treasure, one more of the seven treasure sites known as the "Seven *Cities of Gold," seven large treasures, most of which were located in the San Andres and Caballo Mountain Ranges, all of which have been mentioned in many historical references.

Letha knew that Doc was a skilled treasure hunter. She talked about it, in part:

> *When it came to finding places where there might be a treasure, Doc was good at it because he knew a lot of things and he had that quick eye and he'd see things the average person didn't see. He knew Indian signs and he'd explain them to us.*

~

The problems that besieged Doc and Ova Noss began when they casually let the word out about what they had found inside Victorio Peak. Reports of the discovery appeared in local newspapers and some radio broadcasts, and

---

* Also referred to as the Seven Cities of the Cibola. The Cibola National Forests begin just south of Gallup, New Mexico, and extends south to a point across from the Caballo Mountain Range. Further east they extend south and deep into the San Andres Mountain Range as well.

there were as many versions of the story as there were reports about it, as is the case in such stories. Regardless in what manner or how often Doc and Ova's discovery was reported, November 7, 1937, was the actual discovery date.

Doc had been searching vigorously for the treasure in the San Andres Mountains and had established the base camp at the Rock House in the Hembrillo Basin to be closer to the general search area. After a long and systematic exploration of the terrain, estimated to have been about two years, he came upon the entrance to the caverns that led to the great treasure—but quite by accident. Doc, Ova, and a few of their friends had been hunting in the Hembrillo Basin in search of deer; during the hunt, Doc had an old friend with him—his dog, Buster. They had separated from the rest of the hunting party and climbed a small mountain to get a better view of the terrain. From his position, he had a bird's-eye view of the basin, a perfect spot to see any deer that might be moving below him. Doc had been gone for some time and suspected that the rest of the hunting party was waiting for him at the Rock House. Below him, and slightly to the north was a long-lost battlefield of the 1800s where Victorio's band of followers had engaged their enemy—the U.S. Cavalry. It began to rain.

The deer-hunting trip is one of the single most important episodes in the entire time capsule of events that explain when and under what conditions Doc and Ova had actually made the discovery of the Victorio Peak treasure. Jim and Terry Delonas explained how they learned about it during their early lives in Clovis, New Mexico. Jim:

> *From what Terry and I have been told by our mother and my Aunt Letha, Doc was actively looking for the Victorio Peak treasure since 1934 or maybe even 1933. Doc and our grandmother, and our mother, had been living up in northern New Mexico looking for this treasure and going to every place in the state that had a hot springs, the Ojo Caliente [hot springs] connection, and a mountain with certain descriptions that was near a hot spring and also a fresh water spring nearby. The major portion of the 1937 deer-hunting story was factual, we're sure of that, and I really believe that it was at this point in time that Doc revealed to Babe that he thought he had found something important, and that's when and where he had actually discovered the location, while they were hunting deer at Victorio Peak. Remember, I heard this story all my life, and so did Terry, and every time I heard it I began to realize that Babe's version was reshaped a little bit, and then Terry and I realized that in 1961 that a big change in the story took place when Babe's attorney got involved; that was Phil Koury. I need to insert here that I was a young man and Terry was still a teenager, about fifteen or sixteen, when we first learned that a woman named Violet Yancey existed.*

> ~

Although the issues surrounding Violet Yancey are explained later in the book, the details of Jim and Terry's explanation concerning Ova's attempts to keep Violet Yancey out of the picture are presented here, but not in the proper chronology of the text. Terry:

Our grandmother had left her out of all of the Victorio Peak stories, including Doc's infidelity and his supposed marriage to Violet. Then, after we found out about the existence of Violet Yancey, and the fact that Doc had left Babe in 1945, and why he left her, we began to reflect back on the earlier versions of the story. We soon came to realize that my grandmother was leaving out certain things that were personally embarrassing to her, especially concerning Violet Yancey, because Yancey had a lot of Doc's things and Babe was afraid she might try to make a legal claim to the treasure.

Jim:

Then when Phil Koury came on board as Babe's attorney, he finally told her that she had to make a decision and asked her if she wanted to go into court and claim that she was also Doc's widow, or go into court as the co-discoverer. Koury was correct to explain to her that she was in a superior position to be the co-discoverer, which in fact she really was, if not the only remaining discoverer since Doc was dead.

Terry:

So the 1937 deer-hunting story suddenly became the authorized King James Version of the very first time that Doc talked to her about finding the site that they had been looking for since 1933 or 1934. Then when they returned to the same site several times together and they actually realized what they had found, Babe became the co-discoverer of the treasure the moment Doc brought up that bar and Babe realized that it was not pig iron, and it was gold. The reason they were hunting deer is because Doc and Babe were always hunting deer to provide meat for the table at camp, which was the Rock House, while they were out there looking for signs that led to the treasure.

~

Doc moved under a slight overhang to keep dry. Still hoping to spot a deer, he waited patiently. After a short while, he removed a hand-traced copy of his treasure map from his inside pocket and slowly unfolded it, a map that had been given to him by one of his patients, an Indian Doc had treated who had no money. He gazed around at the other small mountain to the east and suddenly realized that his surroundings not only matched the map he was holding, but it also prompted his recollection of the terrain described to him by Geronimo many years ago when he was a young boy. The map clearly showed an entrance to a cavern at the top of a small mountain, the one he was sitting on.

Then Doc noticed there was a draft coming up from below him. It held his attention. After sliding a slab of rock to the side, he noticed an opening large enough for someone to enter. Alone, and in wonderment, Doc stared down into an ancient ventilation shaft, a natural opening that led deep into the mountain. He must have checked his map a dozen times while he sat there. The illustration on the map clearly showed a vertical shaft that dropped downward into the mountain, which Doc immediately recognized as being exactly like the one below his feet. It also showed several horizontal dark lines, which Doc interpreted as caverns. He looked up from where he was standing and in the distance he saw a small mountain, Geronimo Peak, exactly as it appeared on his map. He was there, he was sure of it. Below in the dark, haunting abyss, the largest treasure ever found in America rested. Doc left the mountain and returned to camp to tell Ova about what he had seen.

It was during the March 24, 1975 deposition of Ova Noss that spelled out the actual sequence of events that established the order and the methods used to enter the top shaft that led to the treasure. Ova told her attorney David Daar that a group of them had gone deer hunting and that she and three or four other women stayed behind at camp; it was Sunday, November 7, 1937. Ova told Daar under oath, "Their husbands and Doc were out hunting deer. The men came in first and they were worried; they had lost Doc and they told me they were afraid that he had slipped and hurt himself. Well, then I worried."

While the others soon sat down to eat, Ova went outside and looked down the path and saw Doc walking toward her with his bulldog by his side. Ova told Daar that when Doc came up to the Rock House, one of the men said, "Doc, we lost you and we were afraid you were hurt." She explained that Doc walked by her and whispered, "Get your work done early and come to bed. I've got something to tell you."

"After the dishes were done, we went to bed under the tarpaulin." That was when Doc told Ova he had discovered something, something he believed was of great value and importance, and he described the site to be old workings. Ova explained that before they left camp that weekend, they were standing at a nearby waterhole; it was there that Doc said, "On top of that mountain right behind you is where I found something." From the deposition:*

> *Q. Did he tell anyone else that day?*
> *A. No, that was a family secret.*
> *Q. When was the first time you returned to that locale after that?*
> *A. It wasn't two weeks until we were back up there.*
> *Q. Who was it that returned?*
> *A. Him and I.*
> *Q. It was just the two of you?*
> *A. Just the two of us.*
> *Q. Did you go with him to that spot?*
> *A. I sure did.*

~

Letha gave her account of what she knew to be the truth about the discovery, how and when it was found, and how Doc and Ova kept it a secret. Letha:

> *That's the way it was, and that's the time when Doc found the treasure. He came over to her and told her to finish things up and then get to bed and then they made up a reason to go home so they would all get out of there. Later, Doc and Mama went back*

---

* N. Deposition, **op. cit.**, pp. 23, 24, 25.

out there by themselves. She went up there with him and after that, she was there with him one hundred percent of the time when he was investigating the cave. Down inside one of those spots he dropped a rock and it was a long time before it ever hit. Doc said he marked it off and he said if you see an "X" you weren't to go that way because it was very dangerous.

~

Ova explained that on or about November 18, 1937, they climbed up to the top of Victorio Peak and there were two levels at the top on Victorio Peak. "We were at the highest point." She told Daar, "There were four walls and there was an overhanging shelf off of this wall that hung over and kind of protected it." She said that since then the wall and the shelf were removed. "We slid in under and went down where we could see the paintings, evidence of somebody being there." On that particular day Ova claimed that Doc hadn't gone down any further than she had, but on the day Doc discovered the entrance he went down to only thirty-eight feet. From her deposition:*

Q. When you went down underneath this overhanging shelf, what is it that you saw?

~

Ova spoke of paintings on the walls and described it as "good looking stuff." She also described some of the figures: trees, a horse, and a man on a horse, an Indian, turtles, and snakes. She said the paintings were colored in red, green, blue and yellow, and that the walls were covered with a variety of paintings. Also on the south wall, thirty-eight feet down, they found a large rat's nest, which they raked away. Under the nest was a flat rock twenty-four inches wide and forty-two inches long, which had been "chiseled" to cover a hole on the floor of the small room where they were standing. Down inside the hole they saw a ladder about twenty-four feet long with niches carved into it and rungs (steps) lashed to the vertical posts with leather. Shining their carbide[†] lanterns (shown here) on the ladder, Doc slowly put his foot on the second rung and it broke away nearly causing him to fall into the opening. "We took a forty-five foot lariat rope and anchored it to a rock, and it left him very little [room] to go down through this hole where the ladder was." Ova said, "It was in March of 1938 before he got 'venturous enough [to go deeper]."

---

*N. Deposition, ***op. cit.***, pp. 26, 31.
† Carbide lamps and lanterns, as shown above, are an efficient beneath-ground lighting source, then and today. Carbide crystals are placed inside the lamp, water is added, acetylene gas is emitted and when lighted it produces an intense white light. Some of these lamps are among the Noss's private collection

Although it was a mild winter in the basin that year, there still was some light snowfall now and then, which created a serious problem. When it snowed, their tracks could easily lead some interloper directly to where they were working. So, they decided to stay out of the basin until spring came. They disguised the entrance hole at the top of the Peak, then broke camp and returned to Hot Springs where they would wait out the winter planning to return to the Peak when the weather was on their side. Letha told the story from her perspective when they would travel back and forth from Hot Springs to Victorio Peak, before they closed down their activities for the winter that year. In part:

> But from the time that Doc found the treasure he would only be open* two or three days a week where he and Mama could make a little money so they could run out to Victorio Peak. It took money to buy gas and groceries and it was fifty miles to get there. It wasn't that the food was so high, it was the car expenses; we tore up the car every time we went out there because there were no roads. We'd hit a gully and then we'd have to get out and push or move rocks; we had troubles all the time with the car.

February 28, 1938

It had been more than three months since Doc and Ova had left the Hembrillo Basin. Although it was tempting to return, they stayed in Hot Springs while Doc tended to his foot-care business on Polk Street. But once again, Doc strayed from the narrow path and got in trouble in El Paso. An El Paso newspaper reported that he had flashed some badge of authority and was jailed; it wasn't the first time Doc flashed a badge—and it wasn't the last. Then for some unknown reason, the impersonation charges were dropped. It happened quite often; the question is why. Were charges dropped because the Secret Service knew he had found a large cache of gold and opted to curtail Doc from being arrested in hopes they would find the source of the gold, or were certain law enforcement officials looking to get in on the action? The question remains. However, the general consensus has always been that Doc was generally handled with kid gloves by the government, especially the FBI, because they knew he had found gold.

March 11, 1938

Things calmed down and Doc got back on track. He continued working his popular foot-care business and kept a low profile for the rest of the winter. When the weather was on their side, they planned to temporarily close the doors at the clinic and secretly work the ventilation shaft at the Peak. They bided their time and stayed in Hot Springs.

The tales of Doc and Ova Noss seemed to have no end. The following is an abridged account from the writings[†] of Ova Noss of an incident that in-

---

*The reference to "open" meant Doc and Ova's foot-care clinic.
[†] O. Noss, **op. cit.**, pp. 7, 8.

volved Doc's money belt, his tomcat, a bag of spoiled groceries and the theft of one of Doc's gold bars by a New Mexico State Patrolman. It is solely a reflection of Ova's mental recollection of what took place, but the reason for his arrest was not made clear in Ova's account of the incident. She claimed that when he was arrested, and while State Patrolman Silas Salazar was questioning him, Doc had complained that his belt buckle was hurting him. He casually removed it and handed it to Ova; it was actually Doc's money belt, which was full of cash and disguised with a long zipper. Ova's account of what happened next is not that clear in terms of sequence, so let's stop here and look at Letha and Dorothy's account of the same incident, as told by them in the Guthrie/Delonas manuscript.

Here are the essential elements of Letha and Dorothy's account of what happened that day: Doc (and his tomcat) and Lino Carriaga were in Hatch selling a gold bar to buy groceries. Because there was gold in the car, Doc locked the car up and left it (and the cat) at Valley Auto for safekeeping while he and Lino went to one of the bars for a drink; that's when all the trouble began. They weren't at the bar long when Lino got into a fight, and, of course, Doc was on his side. The State Highway Patrol arrived and they were arrested, taken into custody and driven back to Las Cruces for a court hearing in the morning. Here is the story as told in the Guthrie/Delonas manuscript* starting on page 111, in part:

> *Along in 1938, a little incident took place, which the family will never forget, and not many of the ones who were involved. Doc and his helper, Lino Carriaga, had come into Hatch, and had a gold bar with them.*

> ~

If Lino and Doc were together in Hatch to sell gold, it was a gold bar from the treasure they had found in the Caballo Mountain cache. It was not until the next month in April that Doc brought out the first bar of gold from Victorio Peak. More from the Guthrie/Delonas manuscript:

> *They were in town to get a little money out of the gold and pick up a few supplies. The men were traveling in an old "Model A" Ford and had bought a box of groceries and put it in the trunk.*

> ~

It becomes apparent from the rest of the story that Doc drove his car to Hatch and Lino drove the "Model A" Ford, which was presumably Lino's personal vehicle. More:

> *Along about this time the officers were keeping a close tab on Doc, trying to get the deadwood on him about the gold he had found. The Noss family was living in the Rio*

---

* L. Guthrie, D. Delonas, "The Doc Noss Ill-Fated Gold at Victorio Peak," (Unpublished Manuscript Circa 1960) pp. 111-116.

Courts, on the highway, in Las Cruces. Mama had just stepped across the street from the courts to have herself a Coke and came back to the room; it was around seven o'clock in the evening. It was then that she noticed a state police car had pulled up to the room. The officer had Doc and Lino with him, under arrest. Mama went out and when she got there, Doc said, "Hello, Babe."

Mama responded with a friendly greeting, and inquired, "What's the matter?"

Doc then told her that Lino had been in a fight with a fellow while downtown, and the law had arrested them. Mama looked around and when she could not see Doc's car, she asked, "Where's the car?"

"It's locked up in the Valley Auto Garage in Hatch," he answered. "I'll get it tomorrow." A short pause ensued and a canny look came over Doc's face and he said, "Babe, go in and get me the belt off my other pants. This wide buckle is just cutting into me." Mama went inside and got the belt and brought it out to him. When she approached him and handed him the belt, he took her hand and squeezed it. She realized at once that Doc was trying to relay a message to her. Then Doc stooped forward to kiss her and whispered, "Babe, come to the courthouse in the morning and pay our fines. Look in the belt and get the money out."

Mama went inside after the cops had left with Lino and Doc and pulled the fastener open on the wide belt. She found $1,200. The next morning she went to the court and paid the fines for the two men, $45 for Lino Carriaga and $15 for Doc.

About ten o'clock in the morning, a strange situation commenced to develop. As soon as Doc was released, he called Mama to see if she was at the motel and told her that he and Lino were catching a ride back to Hatch to pick up the Ford they had stored in the garage, for security reasons.

As soon as Doc returned from Hatch he came to the motel and instructed Mama to call the police and tell them that Doc had arrived and was giving her lots of trouble, fussing and quarreling. She went across the street and used the telephone there. The cops soon rolled up, one in a car and the other on a motorcycle. Mama opened the door and told them to come in. Doc was standing behind the door. When they entered, Doc stepped from behind the door and drew down on them with a gun and ordered, "Throw up your hands!" He told them to pass over their guns to Mama and she laid them on the table. Doc then marched them out of the room to the outside, in the yard where Doc demanded, "Which one of you broke into my car in the Valley Auto Garage in Hatch?"

The cop who had come onto the scene in a car said that he had broken into the car. Then Doc further asked, "Which one of you shot the lock off my footlocker?" The same officer replied that he had. And Doc asked, "Now, I'm asking you one more question, and remember that I want no lying, or I'll put a hole through you one could drive a freight train through! Who took the gold bar from the footlocker?"

The men looked at each other, sheepish-like, and then the one who was riding the motorcycle replied, "I did. I took it home for a paperweight."

By this time people had commenced to gather around, curious as to what was going on. Doc pulled out his watch and looked at it. "How far do you live from here?" Without *waiting for a reply, Doc told the officer, "I'll give you just five minutes to go home and get back with that bar of gold!" With a motion of his gun, he told the man to pull out and said, "I'm holding your partner until you return."*

More people had gathered around. Doc continued to put questions to the officer. "Did you have a warrant to search the car?"

"No," the man retorted. By this time, the man who had gone for the gold bar returned and Doc shook him down to see if he had armed himself while away. The crowd had taken on proportions and jammed the street. Doc turned to Mama and said, "Babe, while these people are here, let them have a look at the gold bar, and let all of them who will, sign the old ledger* that they have seen it."

The people did and the names are attached to this account. Then Doc turned to the two officers and asked, "Which one of you killed my tomcat that was in the car and left him lying dead on my box of groceries and right on top of the slab of bacon?" The cop who was driving the auto spoke up and said he did as the cat offered to fight him when he broke into the car.

Doc then turned to Mama and told her to put the ledger in the hotel room and get into her car and follow him to Hatch. Mama went inside, picked up the officers' guns and put them into the car. She then turned to Doc and asked, "How do you intend to get to Hatch?"

He answered, "These dignified officers are insisting on helping me get there."

Doc rode in the car with the cops while Mama and I rode right along behind them. When we reached Doc's car, we found it in an awful mess. Blood from the slaughtered tomcat was everywhere and flies covered everything. Doc had the cat buried and the officers replaced the groceries in his car. This finished things up there, but Doc had no bacon sandwiches as he had planned. He was fond of this kind of sandwich. Anyway, the officers didn't bother Doc any more. Doc wanted to have a legal counsel, but his lawyer talked him into letting it drop."   —*Guthrie/Delonas manuscript*

~

On March 11, 1938, a lot of people saw Doc's gold. There were thirty-eight people from Las Cruces, two people from Rincon, and two people from Hatch, totaling 43 people who had witnessed[†] the event: L.B. French, Lula French, Gene Latimer, Bob Stratten, Mrs. Stratten, Hazel Bunch, Estes Salazar, Joe Barnes, Bob Barnes, Gene Wiatt, Laz Jones, Larry Ortiz, Jack Bruton (Hatch), Belle Davis, Joe Davis, Thelma Reemes, Doc Joe Harris, Nelda Johnson, Eva Johnson, J.B. Hall, L.B. Ruiz, Adams Drake, Adrian Guam, L.J. Guthrie, E.T. Barnes, Mrs. E.T. Barnes, Andy Pope, Larry Drake (Hatch), Mr. Marvin Pike (Los Angeles, California), Walt Henderson (Rincon), Joe Andregg (Rincon), Bill Hagen, Joe Hagen, Dat Hagan, J. Hazelwood, Martha Hazelwood, "Doc"

---

* From the handwriting on the *ledger,* it appears that someone wrote the names as people volunteered as witnesses, probably Letha Guthrie, who was present at the time; some might have signed their own name.

[†] L. Guthrie, D. Delonas, ***Ibid.,*** pp. 117, 118.

J.T. Tourney, Joe Wood, Jim Brown, Silas Salazar (one of the men on the State Highway Patrol), Martha Dune and Mr. Pane, the manager of the motel across the street from where it happened.

Letha included Ova on the ledger* as a witness too, as well as State Highway Patrolman Tiny Davis, the police officer who stole Doc's gold bar.

Lino Carriaga referred to the event in a letter[31] on April 25, 1966. Carriaga not only referenced the altercation; he also wrote about the treasure Doc had discovered in the Caballo Mountains and described it. Carriaga's entire letter:

> *I, Lino Carriaga, promise to show the entrance to the Dr. Noss cave, which he found. I was working for Doc when he found it. Ralph Westerdale promised to pay me $1,000.00 when I came to Truth or Consequences [to show him the cave]. He didn't fulfill his promise, but Mrs. Ova M. Noss is here now and promises to get me the $800.00 balance upon my arrival in Truth or Consequences and I promise to go within 15 ft. of the entrance. The gold is [stacked] 10 ft. high and 50 ft. long, also [there is] a chest 3x6 full of money and artifacts.*   —*Lino Carriaga*
>
> *25% for me and 75% for the Noss group.*
> *Witnessed by E. M. Guthrie & Letha Guthrie*
> *P.S. He [Doc] was a year and two days in finding it. We tried to declare it to the government and Carlos Lucero and Tiny Davis arrested us and took our bar of gold [which was] 99.90 fine. They [Lucero and Davis] were State Policemen.*

~

It was getting warmer and there was little chance of any snowfall, so Doc and Ova set their plan into action and packed up everything they thought they would need. The last thing they did before they left was to hang an "out of town" sign on the office door. Together they headed for the Hembrillo Basin. When they reached the Rock House, they did a quick check—everything was as they had left it. Together they unpacked their gear from the car and carried it into the Rock House, brought water in from the spring and started a campfire. While Ova packed their lunch, Doc boiled water and made the coffee for the thermos bottles they would take with them. Soon they were on their way up the slope to the top of Victorio Peak. When they got to the entrance shaft, they

---

* Only the first page of the ledger is shown here.

made a brief check of the surroundings; they were in luck: no one had disturbed the site. Little did either of them know what they were about to find.

This time they came prepared and brought along a good flashlight and extra batteries. "We had one that would shoot a 1,500-watt beam," Ova said. They also brought along a Lufkin tapeline and a Brunton compass. She told Mr. Daar that Doc tied a knot in the lariat rope every two feet. In this way, Doc had a grip so he wouldn't slip and fall and he could also brace himself against the wall. They started at the thirty-eight foot level. Doc dropped eight feet and landed on a ledge and went through a bottleneck. His back was to the south wall. Ova said, "Directly to his left, there were five boulders that went down into a path, a tunnel. But directly on his north was a huge hole."

Ova said that sickly fumes came up from the hole. "We didn't know what the fumes were, but he would break out around the top of his socks." Because of the fumes, Doc did not venture down the huge hole; instead he went down the spiral-like tunnel or path on his left. From her deposition:*

> *Q. What's the furthest that you personally ever went into that hole?*
> *A. 113 or 118 feet. I think 118.*
> *Q. You indicated that over a period of time Doc went deeper into this cave system.*
> *A. Yes.*
> *Q. Were you with him every time he went into the cave?*
> *A. Every time.*
> *Q. On the occasions when Doc would go down into the hole, what did you do?*
> *A. I was guard.*
>
> ~

Ova said, "When he went down in that spiral, I lost sight of him, except that his flashlight would flash up and I could see the reflections." From her deposition:†

> *Q. How long was it before something of value came out?*
> *A. In March or April of '38.*
> *Q. When he brought something out was anyone there with you?*
> *A. No. Just us. It was a family secret.*
>
> ~

It was *not* in March of 1938 that Doc brought up anything of value, it was in April, which is clarified later in the deposition. Ova said that she was with him when the first articles of the treasure came up. "I even helped him to lug them over the boulder, the big ledge." She described Doc bringing up a lot of paper money in *morrales*.‡ She told her attorney, "And these were full of money, but

---

* N. Deposition, **op. cit.**, pp. 34, 35.
† N. Deposition, **op. cit.**, pp. 36.
‡ Morrales is a Spanish term for feedbags, leather nosebags that are strapped around the head of a mule or horse.

they were rotten. He went to lift them up and the bottom fell out and money
went everywhere. Doc had his pockets full, and a bank sack that he took down
with him." When asked to describe what the money looked like, Ova gave the
following description: "All of it was old foreign money, very little American
money. I saw one that attracted my attention and I still have it. It was an English
half crown." From her deposition*:

> *Q. And you say that was among the things he brought out?*
> *A. Yes. It said 1803.*

~

Then Ova began to give a broader account of the variety of things that
Doc described. "He said there were *lots* of crowns. Doc found one crown that
weighed about seven and a half pounds and it had two hundred and forty-three
diamonds and one pigeon-blood ruby. There were trunks and clothing, lots of
chains with crosses on them, and lots of jewels. He told me that there must
have been the biggest market the world ever seen for pig iron. He said he never
seen such ricks. He told me how many steps long he thought they were, and
double ricks, and that made two ricks. On our next trip he brought out jewels,
not many because they were valuable, he knew." From her deposition†:

> *A. I kept begging him to see some of that pig iron.*
> *Q. Did he bring some out?*
> *A. He brought one out.*
> *Q. After how many trips did he bring out some of the iron?*
> *A. That was close to April.*
> *Q. April of '38?*
> *A. April of '38.*
> *Q. When he brought that out, who was present?*
> *A. It was just Doc and I.*

~

"He was down there four hours and twenty minutes and I was worried
because there had been no tug on the rope. Then he hollered, 'I'm coming up.'"
She gave more details to her attorney. From her deposition‡

> *Q. When he came up on that occasion what did he bring with him?*
> *A. He pulled this out and threw it out across the rock floor and it just kind of
> skidded.*
> *Q. What was it?*
> *A. He said 'that's the last one of these things I'll ever bring out.'*

~

Ova gave an account of that particular event. She said that Doc had "pretty
near thrown it down two or three times because it was so heavy." Doc said he

---

*N. Deposition, ***op. cit.,*** pp. 41
†N. Deposition, ***op. cit.,*** pp. 45.
‡N. Deposition, ***op. cit.,*** pp. 45, 46.

brought it up for me. She described the metal bar as being tarnished.* "I looked at it. It didn't interest me, and we ate. Finally I went over there, after we got through eating, and I started to pick it up. Doc said, 'Pick it up, Babe; pick it up.' And he laughed. You couldn't. He handed me his knife and I put it under the metal and rolled it over, but when I did, why, it had scuffed on them pebbles and it was shiny. And I said, 'Look here Doc, that's yellow.' And he came over on his legs a shaking and trembling from straining coming out. He took his knife and he scraped it. 'Well,' he said, 'If this is gold, we can call John D. Rockefeller a tramp.'" Ova described the bar as being about "fifteen to eighteen inches long, four or five inches wide, and about two inches thick."

Terry Delonas confirmed the Rockefeller comment, and from what was learned from reading the family records, Doc had a sensible rationale to keep what he knew to himself. Ova told Terry, "Doc told us that if someone came and took me or Letha away to find out where this gold† was coming from, it was best for us to know as little as possible. He said what we didn't know we couldn't tell 'em. Not knowing how to get to the gold might be the very thing that saves our lives."

But a larger question arises about Doc's mention of *pig iron*. It was difficult to believe that the second Doc had seen those ricks, that he didn't immediately investigate what they were, meaning a quick check by scraping them with his knife to see if it was gold. If there was one thing Doc knew about, it was the color of gold, and according to him, he was describing a cavern filled with treasure. It would have been a casual connection that those ricks were something more valuable than pig iron. Terry agreed and laughed. He said that Ova finally squeezed it out of Doc. She told Terry, "After I was sure it was gold we were looking at, I said to Doc, 'Don't you tell me Doc Noss that you didn't know that was gold you were looking at down there.' Doc laughed and said he couldn't count the times he wanted to tell me, but he wanted me to discover what they were to make me happy. I couldn't have kept my mouth shut even if the good Lord showed up at our back door and told me it was a good idea." Terry said there were many things that Ova could do, but keeping a secret wasn't one of them. "If she was thinking it, she was saying it. It's no wonder Doc wouldn't tell her anything," he said laughing.

Ova said there were times when Doc had to take his food down there with him because he knew he was going to be down there for a long time. "He took canned sardines and tomatoes, because he said that would give him water. The tomatoes were liquid, and gave him strength to work on."

---

* Pure gold is not affected by oxidation (tarnishing). However, impure gold will most likely tarnish over time. The tarnish appears as a dark film on the surface.
† The gold came from deep under Victorio Peak. Later, Doc found an easier 'secret' entrance that also led to the main caverns where the large caches were hidden. The 'secret' entrance is discussed later in the book.

He finally came out of the shaft and when he got to the top, he handed Ova a letter he had carried up with him. He told Ova to put it in her purse, which she did, and said to her, "I've got my identification on an envelope under a bar." Ova asked Doc how many bars there were. Together they figured it up and it came to 16,112 bars. And there was another rick of 3,000, while another rick was estimated to have 9,056 bars. In describing a rick Doc said it was stacked like cordwood. More from the deposition*:

> *Q. How many bars were taken out of the hole in your presence?*
> *A. I saw twenty-three he brought in and laid on the kitchen table.*
> *Q. Were there any others that he might have taken out?*
> *A. Yes.*
> *Q. How many might he have taken out?*
> *A. Several hundred.*
> *Q. How do you know to say several hundred?*
> *A. He worked every night and all day.*
> *Q. Did he always work in your presence?*
> *A. Yes, except at night, and then I would go up there and sleep in a bedroll while he was down there working.*
> *Q. Was there a time when he went down there without you?*
> *A. Yes, he did. I would always know when he was up there. He would work at night and come in the next morning and sweat would be all around his khaki clothes, and he would sleep practically all day. He was so tired.*

~

They all saw and held some of the bars, and to share in the thrill of having gold in their hands, Doc allowed Letha and Dorothy to keep a bar overnight with them in bed. Letha described being too excited and worried to sleep. Not wanting to give the bar up, she kept it for a few days and moved it from one hiding place to another; the four children worked at the Peak at various times. Doc rehid his bars a few at a time: buried by a telephone pole, in a cattle tank, or under a bush with a rock on top of them. Once Doc sold a small statue, a picture of which was given to the Land Office as proof of his find. Another time, he had a solid gold chalice stolen from him. More than once he arranged to sell a bar or two, only to have the purchaser depart without making the agreed payment.

Being mostly Cheyenne Indian, Doc had a deep distrust of the government, especially the Army. Considering this and his never-ending fear of the government, he felt there was a good chance that something would prevent him from gaining legal title to the treasure inside Victorio Peak. To prevent losing all of the treasure to the government, he worked hard to secure the treasure in safer places, a prophetic move that history would bear out. Doc decided to remove

---

*N. Deposition, **op. cit.**, pp. 53, 54.

as much of the Victorio Peak treasure as possible to other locations, such as small difficult-to-enter caves within the mountain itself, and in canyons, ravines, and arroyo walls—secret places that only he knew about. In one removal period during the year, they brought out eighty-six bars and took twenty-three of them to camp. Ova said they brought out "several hundred" bars during that month; some were shaped like cigars, while others resembled Hershey bars: 12" x 3-3/4" x 2" with rounded corners. The crude bars had pieces of charcoal embedded in them. Doc had an assay made on one of the bars. More: (61)

> *Q. You saw yellow, but how did you find it to be gold?*
> *A. We had it assayed in El Paso.*
> *Q. Where was it assayed?*
> *A. ...At Jimmy Gantz's place.*
> *Q. Do you know where in El Paso he is?*
> *A. Close to the Hilton Hotel. It's up on the second floor.*
> *Q. Okay. And was there a written assay report?*
> *A. Yes.*

~

Doc and Ova hired Seraphin Sedillo [known as *Jose* Sedillo], to help carry out the bars for 4 or 5 weeks. Then for some reason, but over time, as Sedillo continued to work with Doc in the caverns, he gradually seemed "dangerous" to Doc and Ova, and they were suspicious of him. Later on they told him he was no longer needed. (65)

> *Q. Was Seraphin a paid employee?*
> *A. He was a paid employee.*
> *Q. Did he go down into the earth with Doc?*
> *A. Yes.*
> *Q. Did he go down further into the earth than you had ever gone?*
> *A. Oh, yes. He went to help carry it out.*
> *Q. How long did Sedillo work there?*
> *A. Not over a month or five weeks. He became dangerous.*
> *Q. In what way was that?*
> *A. His eyes were a-roving at the gold and we became suspicious of him. We all did. Doc did too, more than me.*
> *Q. Did there come a time when he was no longer present at the site?*
> *A. Yes*

Ova recalled the early days. From her writings:*

> *There was hardly a road, he took a team and a Fresno and began his road. We used to carry the groceries down on our shoulders. Doc would take the bag of potatoes and I'd take the rest of the stuff.*

---

*O. Noss, **op. cit.**, pp. 8, 9.

The two different style Fresno scrapers seen here are the actual equipment Doc and Ova used to clear the roads to Victorio Peak. Fresones are small plow-like scrapers pulled by mules or horses. More from Ova's writings:

> *Doc brought in barrels of honey that he found in the rocks. Of course it had a few bees in it, but I took them out. We camped in the old Post House.* We made a cave in the cliff by the old riverbed and hung our meats there. We put a heavy screen across it to keep the animals out. It was nice and cool in there. Doc and I put a new roof on and put in those windows and a door. There was no door between the two rooms.*
>
> ~

When they needed money, they sold bars cheaply on the Texas-Mexico border for $20 an ounce. Most of the time, Doc created nuggets from the bars and they used them to buy food and supplies.

The course Doc and Ova followed and the string of events connected to the treasure discovery at Victorio Peak would come to a tragic end. While Doc and Ova were together, there were moments of joy and happiness, anger, betrayal, divorce, and then murder. Ova would be left alone and the years ahead for her would be turbulent ones. The greed of others to take from her what she and Doc had discovered during their early-married life would eventually come to visit and show its dark, ugly face.

---

* Another reference to the Rock House

Chapter 9
Gold...and the Problems that Came with It

Victorio Peak,* the "Power Mountain" of the Apache, had been breached, and it was Milton "Doc" Noss who had risked his life to locate the treasure that lay deep beneath the mountain; as a result, Doc and Ova became the treasure's co-discoverers. From the time Doc located the top entrance shaft and went inside and brought items to the surface covered a span of more than a year.

Circa April 1938

After the initial discovery, and at great personal risk, Doc began to explore the underground labyrinth of passageways and caverns. But ancient gold ingots were not all that he had seen: he saw rings, knives with jeweled handles, swords, and many trunks containing velvet and lace clothing, a gold medallion and metal boxes full of letters mailed from Europe. There were wooden trunks filled with personal items, chests marked *sealed silver,* church garments, statues of religious figures, two bull-hide bellows, and piles of mountain mahogany† used as fuel for the crude smelting operation. He also told of the remains of numerous skeletons.

April 11, 1938

The rumor mill never stopped grinding. Hubert Heath, the editor of *The Herald* newspaper in Hot Springs claimed that the Chief of the New Mexico State Police had seized some of Doc's gold and that a friend of his, Heath's, alleged that the gold had come from a buried treasure. His friend said the gold was being used to support Juarez's revolutionaries in Mexico. After receiving the information, on April 11, 1938 he wrote[32] to the U.S. Treasury Intelligence Division in Washington, D.C. Heath's letter:

> *Gentlemen, on the evening of March 29, word was relayed into my office that 1,000 ounces of gold had been seized here by E.J. House, Chief of the New Mexico State Police.*

---

* Doc and Ova Noss at the top of Victorio Peak shortly after the discovery
† Mountain Mahogany is a small tree found in some New Mexico ranges above 1,200 meters.

The report is that the gold was taken from a fellow known locally as Dr. M.E. Noss. In the past he has used the name Knoss, Nos and Moss, the latter is said to be the name under which he did time in Oklahoma according to a man who knew him there.

Noss, or Moss, is affiliated with the Fat Hoy-Leo Smith gang. His wife told a friend of mine that the gold came from buried treasure he had found. Another man who is in our shop went to Juarez and interviewed revolutionaries and was told the gold was sent across to pay for guns for the Gold Shirts,* or at least for revolutionaries.

Very little has leaked out about the matter, but he was told that great quantities of guns were being crossed, greater than at any time in the past and that the guns were being paid for in gold dust.   —*Hubert H. Heath*

~

Stories abound about the life and times of Doc Noss, but Heath's letter was the kind of thing that whetted the appetite of the Treasury Department. In all of the information released by the Treasury, the FBI, and the Secret Service, there has never been any record uncovered of Doc Noss ever being involved in such matters suggested by Hubert H. Heath, including any information concerning the Fat Hoy-Leo Smith gang. Before the ink was dry on Heath's letter, it would be proven that he had shot himself in the foot by not confirming the information he had received third-hand.

April 18, 1938

One week later, Heath's letter reached the desk of Frank J. Wilson, Chief of the Secret Service at the Treasury in Washington. Wilson wrote[33] to Heath in response to his letter:

Your letter of April 11, 1938, addressed to the Intelligence Division, Treasury Department, Washington, D.C., has by proper reference reached this office for attention.

The matter is being given due consideration and we appreciate the motive that prompted you to send the information to the Department.   —*Frank J. Wilson*

~

The same day, Wilson wrote[34] to the Treasury's General Counsel:

We would appreciate the benefit of any information or advice you may be able to furnish us with respect to any possible gold violations on the part of Dr. M.E. Noss, alias Knoss, Nos and Moss, as alleged in the attached copy of letter from Hubert H. Heath, Editor, The Herald, Hot Springs, New Mexico.

We have already acknowledged receipt of this letter.   —*Frank Wilson*

~

April 22, 1938

Four days later Wilson received a letter[35] from the Administrative Assistant to the Secretary of the Treasury:

---

*General Nicolás Rodríguez Carrasco founded the Gold Shirts in 1933. Carrasco named the group after the *Dorados*, Pancho Villa's "golden" group of elite soldiers. The Gold Shirts were visible and violent, demanding the deportation of Jews and Chinese from Mexico.

Reference is made to your memorandum of April 18, 1938 with respect to possible gold violations referred to in a letter from Mr. Hubert H. Heath, Editor, The Herald, Hot Springs, New Mexico.

Please have this matter investigated in order to ascertain whether the gold laws, orders, and regulations are being violated. A copy of Hubert H. Heath's letter is being sent to the Customs Bureau and the State Department will be notified thereof.

—[Carbon copy, no signature]

~

May 31, 1938

Proof of Wilson's request for an investigation came on May 31, 1938 in a "Initial and Final" report[36] written by Supervising Agent Rowland K. Goddard, which referenced the April 28 request by Wilson:

This report is submitted in answer to Chief's memorandum dated April 28, 1938, enclosing memorandum of the Administrative Assistant dated April 28, 1938, requesting that investigation be made in connection with an alleged gold violation of the part of one Dr. M.E. Noss. This is the controlling District.

~

The exact date the actual Secret Service investigation began is uncertain; however, agent Rowland K. Goddard wrote to Wilson on May 31 advising him that agent Emmet B. Hargett of the Albuquerque Division responded to Heath's letter. In turn, agent Hargett contacted E.J. House, Chief of the New Mexico State Police "who denied having made any seizure of gold." House gave yet another story that an "unnamed" person suspected that Doc Noss was handling "narcotics." Hargett's report also outlined the charges stemming from Doc's gun waving stunt at Ann's Place in Roswell that landed him the Santa Fe Penitentiary. The report also mentioned that Governor Tingley had pardoned Doc after serving part of his six to nine month term. More of Hargett's report, in part:

In no instance has such information proved to be of any definite value, and evidently prompted by the fact that the Hot Springs Herald was very much opposed to the administration of the Mayor in Hot Springs. Agent Hargett states that his investigation indicates that in his opinion Editor Hubert H. Heath had been misinformed in connection with the alleged gold violation apparently, and that the information he submitted is not based on fact. Accordingly, the file is being retained and the case closed in this District.   *— Agent Rowland K. Goddard*

~

Doc Noss had been falsely accused by Hubert Heath, and in view of Hargett's report to Frank Wilson, Doc was cleared of any wrongdoing by the Secret Service from charges made by Hubert Heath. But it was not over; more of Doc's blood would be spilled when Leland Howard got hold of Goddard's report over a year later.

June 1938

It was early June and young Joe Andregg was out of school until fall. The long-awaited summer vacation had just begun and he returned to his uncle's ranch in the Hembrillo Basin. "Doc came over to get me again," Joe said in his sworn statement.[37] That summer, Joe would have a chance to actually go down inside the top entrance to the treasure cave, a dark and dangerous journey:

> *That summer Doc took me to the top of Victorio Peak. Both of us went down to the first level. He told me to wait for him. He was gone about an hour. When he came up he had some coins in a leather bag that he took with him.*

~

Joe Andregg's next summer vacation would prove to be a disastrous one:

> *The next time I worked for him was the time the shaft was blown up.*

~

July 23, 1938

Doc stayed at the Rock House continually while he worked hard to remove the treasure. That year, Ova's sons, Harold and Marvin Beckwith, came to stay and help out at the Peak, but only during school vacations. While Marvin was with Doc in the caverns, he claimed that he took a photo of one of the gold ricks and then made a hole in each bar with a pin across the top of the rick, up the side and from the front to the back. Then he did the math. He said the rick contained about 15,000 bars. In the early 1950s, while Marvin was a college student in Stillwater, Oklahoma, he met a freelance writer named R.C. Casper; Casper wrote Westerns and some of his stories were published in *Life* and *Look* magazines, as well as in *Metropolitan Magazine*. Marvin claimed he gave the photos to Casper with hopes that a book would be written about Doc's discovery. Soon afterward, Marvin joined the Marines and lost contact with Casper. Years later, he went back to Stillwater to try and find him and learned that Casper had moved to Sheridan, Wyoming. He was never able to find him; Casper would be in his eighties today.

Claude Fincher also worked for Doc, but Claude was rather old then and was unable to climb in and out of the ventilation shaft to do the required work; instead, he did most of the cooking for the camp.

July 23, 1938

Three weeks after Joe Andregg arrived at the Victorio Peak campsite, Doc drove to Las Cruces and was arrested for DWI, but he was released at the request of the FBI: they were still tailing him. It was during this time period that threats against the family began.

August 1, 1938

In August that year, Ova's daughter, Letha, came to live with them. Attached to a memorandum[38] by the Washington office of the Secret Service to the Bureau of Customs dated August 1, 1938, was a copy of a report from the

Albuquerque office dated May 27, but no information was uncovered regarding that report. Customs was also given a report made by the Denver, Colorado office dated May 31, 1938, but no information was uncovered. Apparently the investigation triggered by Heath had run its course.

Late August 1938

In spite of the distance saved by traveling from Las Cruces to the Peak, living full time in Hot Springs and commuting every day to work the caverns was no longer an option. From Ova's 1975 deposition*:

> *Q. When was the first time that any of your children came to the scene?*
> *A. Letha came in August 1938.*
> *Q. Do you recall whether or not Doc had closed down his practice?*
> *A. Yes, he had closed it down.*
> *Q. So by then, Letha had come.*
> *A. Yes.*
> *Q. How old was she at the time?*
> *A. About twenty-one, I think.*
> *Q. Where were you living at the time?*
> *A. I lived in Las Cruces in a motel, because it was a shorter route to the mine.*
>
> ~

The move to Las Cruces not only saved them a lot of travel time, but it also eliminated a certain amount of worriment. According to Ova's deposition, she said that while they were living in Hot Springs they were getting a lot of *"jabs in the ribs."* (56)

> *Q. What do you mean by jabs in the ribs?*
> *A. Followers and people were knocking on our doors. Curious people who wanted to get a foot in and help us. Word had got out that we had got it.*
>
> ~

It was then that serious problems began to surface—big ones. Ova never knew the exact number of bars Doc had taken from the caverns, but he knew the wealth that lay inside the caverns and he worked day and night bringing gold bars to the surface. But having access to a treasure came at a price; in August and September of 1938, family members were threatened with kidnapping, not an uncommon event when lawless people struck with gold fever coveted the good fortune of others. The threat of kidnapping was real. Terry explained what happened to Doc:

> *It's easy to understand what made Doc so mean at times and what made him drink the way he did. My grandmother told a very poignant story about Doc being kidnapped one time by people trying to force him to lead them to gold he had buried. She said that he had limped back to their house in Hot Springs and that the bottoms of his feet had*

---

*N. Deposition, ***op. cit.***, pp. 54, 55.

been badly burned and that he had been kidnapped and tortured. Babe said that it was a cruel blow to Doc, and that she spread lard all over his feet and wrapped them in strips of flour sacks to keep the flesh soft. She told us that Doc was crippled up for months after that and it changed him, he was not quite the same guy afterwards. What happened to him hyped his paranoia.

~

Much had happened since Douthit's discovery, but Doc and Ova attributed the attention they were receiving to a gold buyer located somewhere between Las Cruces and Hot Springs with a gold bar Doc had taken from inside Victorio Peak to trade for cash, which turned out to be a mistake. The buyer looked at Doc's gold bar and said, "My gosh, where, where did you get that?" Ova quoted Doc as saying, "Never mind. How rich is it?" Without responding to his question, the buyer said, "That's what they've been hunting for in the Caballo Mountains; that's where you found it, didn't you?"

Doc's answer was a clever one. "How'd you guess?" he said, and allowed the buyer to think he had hit the mark. Then, detecting Doc's concern, the man assured them he wasn't going to tell anybody about the bar. They were paid for the gold and left. According to Ova, she and Doc weren't aware that people were searching for Willie Douthit's cave in the Caballo Mountains; they were too busy at Victorio Peak and had temporarily moved from Hot Springs to Las Cruces so they could be closer to the campsite at the Rock House.

Nevertheless, as a result of their encounter with the gold buyer, and fearing that they might be followed when they returned to Victorio Peak, they kept driving and headed for Hot Springs to their small apartment over Doc's business office. But their return to Hot Springs did not go unnoticed; soon people were knocking on their door at the business and asking thinly-veiled and roundabout questions, and if they had gotten *lucky* in the Caballos. It became necessary to make it look like Doc was back at it, selling corrective shoes and fixing sore feet, but it was only for a few days; it was simply a front, a stall to get the attention away from them—and Victorio Peak.

The following Monday morning, they left Hot Springs and headed back to Victorio Peak. On the way there, they stopped along the road across from the Caballo Mountains and got out of the car. Doc looked up with his binoculars and then handed them to Ova. "It looked like Chinatown—tents were everywhere. They were thick," Ova said. "I would say there were fifty tents up there, and people still a-comin'."

What they had seen on the mountainside caused them to take an unwanted break in further exploration and moving gold from Victorio Peak, but only as a precaution. For now, they knew they had to make a presence in the search area near where Douthit's treasure was thought to be located. "We had to show up at the Caballos," Ova said, "or they would know where we were going. So, it was a 'hunt the button' sort of thing for a while. I'm telling you, it was quite the game."

When Doc and Ova were at the Caballo Mountains, faking it, people seemed to let them alone. There were questions at first, but those who were on the hunt were more interested in finding Douthit's cave than in talking to Doc and Ova. Doc even went to an area where he had been years before and pointed to the ground and told the cluster of people around him that it was there he had found a gold bar years ago, but just one bar and that he had given up on finding any more since then. It was a good diversion, albeit a bogus one, but the gold stampede in the Caballos Mountains went on for weeks. Doc watched while people tore up the area where he said he had found the bar. To further embellish their ploy, they set up a small day campsite on the slopes of the mountain, still playing out their charade. Later, thinking it was safer to be closer to the actual cave site, Doc and Ova decided to move to a spot were Doc could actually see the general entrance area where the Douthit/Ward gold cave was located, thinking the treasure hunters would think Doc and Ova would not camp close to the actual cave entrance.

While they were there, a man named Bob Coker came to their camp, which was located close to Johnny Gordon's[39] line shack at Cleto Springs. Although their connection or relationship is unknown or why they were together that day, Doc and Coker went looking for *signs* near the spring: ancient sculptures, pictographs, and petroglyphs that often pointed to a treasure site. On the east side of the spring they had found several such indications, but because they realized that they were being watched constantly, they did not pursue them and only marked their location for future exploration.

While at their campsite, Lino "Tony" Carriaga and Doc took Ova and Letha to another treasure cave that Lino and Doc had discovered while they were exploring the slopes of Burbank Canyon, but on the way, Buster Ward saw them and began shooting at them, not to actually hit them, but to run them off. Fearing that Buster *would* hit them, they returned to camp. It wasn't the first time that Doc had encountered Buster Ward; several times when Lino and Doc were moving a few gold bars out of the Burbank Canyon cave, Ward sat in seclusion and watched them. Although Ward had his own gold discovery with Willie Douthit, according to Doc, Ward was constantly paranoid that someone would take the gold out; and Doc was no exception. Douthit knew that Doc had been inside their cave, but there were never any problems between them. However, Buster Ward was not as cordial about the matter.

While Doc and Ova moved back and forth daily between Hot Springs and the Caballo Mountains, Letha and Ova kept busy reading Doc's map; it was the first time Letha had seen it, and she was impressed, gaining insight into how Doc was able to find the entrance that led to the treasure at Victorio Peak. It was during that time period that Doc had the scrolls he had found inside Victorio Peak translated into English, old writings on brittle velum, known today as the Seven Letters.

Chapter 10

Having Things Became a Problem

Doc and Ova's charade of searching for gold bars in the Caballo Mountains was not producing the desired results; people who were told they had found gold in the immediate area maintained a constant vigil, keeping an eye on them, watching their every move. Becoming desperate to locate the source of their find, a plan was hatched to take a more serious approach and apply direct pressure to the Noss family. While they were in the Caballos during the day, the pestering was minimal, but not when they returned to Hot Springs for the night—that's when the pressure came.

The fact was that Doc and Ova had *things*; personal belongings the average person didn't have in those days when a buck was difficult to come by. Doc's foot care business was in many ways a deflection, a way of explaining some of the material things they had, which over time became apparent to outsiders. Doc had closed the business and was not in Hot Springs for long stretches at a time, but now he and Ova were back and people became suspicious.

Ova said in her deposition, "Oh, yes, we had pressure." But it wasn't just pressure from people who openly asked them questions about what they had found in the Caballo Mountains—it grew worse. "They put a kidnapping note on our door." In August or September, a jeweler from town came by one night to

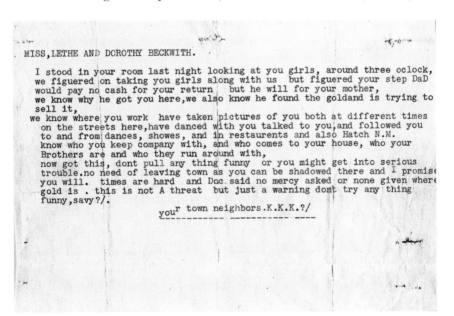

```
MISS,LETHE AND DOROTHY BECKWITH.

   I stood in your room last night looking at you girls, around three oclock,
   we figured on taking you girls along with us  but figured your step DaD
   would pay no cash for your return  but he will for your mother,
   we know why he got you here,we also know he found the goldand is trying to
   sell it,
   we know where you work  have taken pictures of you both at different times
   on the streets here,have danced with you talked to you,and followed you
   to and from dances, showes, and in restaurents and also Hatch N.M.
   know who you keep company with, and who comes to your house, who your
   Brothers are and who they run around with,
   now got this, dont pull any thing funny  or you might get into serious
   trouble.no need of leaving town as you can be shadowed there and I promise
   you will.  times are hard  and Doc said no mercy asked or none given where
   gold is . this is not A threat  but just a warning dont try any thing
   funny,savy?/.
              your town neighbors .K.K.K.?/
```

the back door of Doc's office. "The jeweler said that they were running over each other out there a-looking for the treasure. You better get out of town. They're going to kidnap you," Ova said. The warning galvanized the family into action; they immediately moved to Gallup, New Mexico, where Doc received help from friends in town. Soon after they arrived, Doc frequently slipped back into the Hembrillo Basin to Victorio Peak while Ova and Letha stayed in Gallup.

Ova told her attorney what it was like. From her March 4, 1975 deposition*:

Q. So, you folks were in fear?
A. Always, constantly, we had to watch what we said and who we talked to.
Q. Beyond these kidnap threats, were there any other incidents of personal violence to you and Doc or your family, around the Caballo Mountains?
A. I don't recall if there was any that stood out more than the other.
Q. What did Doc do with the gold he brought out those first few times?
A. He hid it. He hid it in various spots, because he knew that eventually that White Sands was coming in there, and he had to get it off the property.
Q. Around the time that you first found these bars and the word got out that you had some, at that time, what was Doc doing with those bars?
A. Getting them out and burying them in different various spots.
Q. Did you personally hide any of these bars?
A. I went with him when he hid twenty-six, and I believe they're undisturbed today. I think I'm the only one who knows where to go.

~

On that occasion, they drove there in separate cars. Ova covered his back and watched from her car as Doc drove away to hide them. "I could see him going over a rise and the next one coming up, and then disappearing. He didn't come up on the third, so I know pretty well where he was when he hid them." Eventually, Ova and Letha returned to the motel in Las Cruces.

August 1938

In August, a gold paperweight was stolen from the motel; Doc had also met with a priest in Albuquerque to discuss selling him more gold. Also during the month Doc sold a small statue of the Virgin Mary to a banker in El Paso; the small amount of money he received was used to pay for costs and expenses at the Victorio Peak worksite. Then Doc attempted to convert gold bars into cash with someone he had dealt with before, a Mr. Goldstein in Phoenix, Arizona. Goldstein was a jewelry buyer, and he was also a dealer in old gold bars. His office was situated across from the Adams Hotel in downtown Phoenix. Ova said, "We took two bars out there and he bought them. Letha and I were in the car. Doc came back and showed us a check for $32,000. He called the bank and confirmed that his check was good." In 1938, the Adams Hotel and the bank in question took up the entire block. Across the street from the bank and

*N. Deposition, ***op. cit.***, pp. 59, 60.

the hotel was a jewelry store, but according to official city records, the owner was not someone named Goldstein; perhaps Goldstein worked for the jewelry store's proprietor.

They walked directly to the bank, but, when they arrived there, Doc went to the counter and showed the teller the check and told him he wanted to cash it. The teller knew Doc, but according to Ova, the teller said, "I'm sorry, Doc, but Goldstein called in and called payment down on that, because Doc forgot to put his cattle brand* on it." Whether or not Goldstein had merely called the bank and asked the teller not to honor the check is unknown, but Doc had left his gold bars in Goldstein's office on good faith; now suspicious and fearing that he had been duped, he headed straight for Goldstein's office to collect his gold bars. When he arrived minutes later, Goldstein had locked his door and was gone; the transaction was never converted into cash and Doc had to sell his typewriter for gas money to get them back to Las Cruces. Ova said in her deposition, "We couldn't do anything about it. He had called payment down on it."

Letha was there when the matter concerning Goldstein took place and she gave her account of it. Although the amount of money in the transaction is a bit off, the account of the event is essentially the same. Another issue mentioned in Letha's account of the incident was the question related to the absence of a hallmark on the bars. Her statement suggests that there was a discussion about there being no hallmark on the bars when Doc negotiated the price with Goldstein. From Letha's recorded interview, in part:

> *There was this man named Goldstein that beat Doc out of some gold bars he brought to him. Doc lost some $30,000 because Goldstein claimed since the bars had no hallmark on them they weren't worth nothin', but he kept the gold. We had to get out of there; Goldstein not only beat Doc out of the money, he threatened to have Doc put in jail. We were very disappointed that time and Doc had to pawn his typewriter so we could get back to Hot Springs. I remembered that we stayed in a little motel, but then we drove straight through.*

~

Ova told a similar story to Terry about another incident where Doc was tricked. According to his comments during one of our interviews he said that Doc got paid in cash for a large gold bar he had sold to a banker at a low price. Before he left the bank, a friend of Doc's, who was working as a teller there and who had cashed the check for him, warned him that he should not spend the money, as it was marked and that he was being set up. Terry gave the details on the transaction:

---

*The cattle brand might have been a reference to there not being a hallmark of Doc's gold bars.

Part of the family history was that Doc had sold so much bullion before his death that he had as much as one hundred thousand dollars in cash stashed away in a large trunk or footlocker. Although he died with two dollars and sixteen cents in his pocket and he was bouncing checks, people in our family reported they'd seen this cash. My mother said that she sat out in the car at a plaza in front of the a bank in Santa Fe while Doc went in and sold several gold bars and returned to the car with a satchel full of cash. Later, Doc became paranoid and was afraid to spend it.

Babe told the story about that particular day many times. She said that this same banker had bought some gold bars from Doc before, but for whatever reason, this time the banker became nervous and was worried that Doc might go on a spending spree, which he was notorious for, and he would draw attention to himself and this money would eventually be traced back to the banker. So, as Babe told it, in an effort to keep Doc from going on a spending spree, the banker sent a warning to Doc to not spend any of the money he had given him. Doc was already paranoid about being discovered, and being told this by the banker probably sent him over the top and consequently he was afraid to spend any of the money.

That story didn't end there. Years later, I was up in Santa Fe trying to get the help of a local congressman. I was sitting in his office waiting while his chief aide was talking to me prior to meeting the congressman. He told me that he knew why I was there, namely to get help with the Army over some billing problems. Then he said that he didn't want me to waste my breath trying to convince him, or the congressman, that Doc had gold, because they knew he did. He went on to say that his family was a long-time historic New Mexico family and that their family's best friends were the people who owned the First National Bank in Santa Fe. He also told me that his job as a teenager was to kind of be this bank owner's caretaker and driver. He claimed that he used to take him on errands all over the state and that he was told that if anyone ever hears the story about Victorio Peak and Doc Noss and ever wonders if it was true or not, you can believe it. According to the aide, the banker bought gold bars from Doc and that in fact he had bought a lot of gold from him and gave him a lot of cash for it. I don't recall the name of the banker, but it is a matter of record; they were a well-known family in Santa Fe.

So, it's ironic that Doc could have had that much cash and yet need money all the time. But one of the stories often told by Babe was that one of the reasons Doc and her had a big breakup was that she got into the cash and removed twenty or thirty dollars to buy groceries. When Doc found out, he got all over her and screamed at her and began to distrust her. He told her that the money was probably marked and if they spent it, it would trace back to him. The disposition of the cash was supposed to be inside that trunk, or footlocker along with some of the old codices from the Peak and a number of the purified bars of gold and a jewel-studded crown and other items of importance from the Peak. Supposedly the one hundred thousand dollars in cash was inside that trunk and to keep Babe from getting at it again, Doc buried it somewhere in the desert.

~

Ova told Terry the same story, but the trunk has never been found. Terry continued:

At this late date, I'm confused about the boxes and trunks and footlockers, but Joe Andregg often talked about a wooden footlocker-size box that weighed about four hundred pounds or more. Joe could never figure out how Doc got it out of the pickup without his help, but he came back to where Joe was waiting for him and he didn't have the trunk. I know that the other metal footlocker that had the cash and the crown in it was a separate box, a different trunk.

~

Many documents have been found among the Noss family papers, but few of them are in Doc's handwriting. But in 1939, he was interested enough about a certain event that he wrote[40] about it. Doc was not alone when the event took place; Lino "Tony" Carriaga, the Yaqui Indian, who had explored with Doc in the Caballo Mountains, was with him. In Doc's words:

In 1939, after making several trips in and out of these crevices, the Yaqui and myself came out to have lunch. We were carrying out some of the things we found deep inside this cave. While eating our lunch, not over ten minutes after we came out, there was a loud rumble and the earth quivered below us.

~

Doc had no idea what the noise meant, where it came from, or if there had been any damage to the passageways into the caverns beneath Victorio Peak. Another person who witnessed the same event with Doc was Ernest Gatlin. Gatlin was from Muleshoe, Texas, only twenty-five miles from Ova's home in Clovis, New Mexico. Terry Delonas relates the story:

One of the people we were able to track down during the 1990s was a man named Ernest Gatlin, a contemporary of Doc's who worked with him at Victorio Peak. Gatlin, who was in his eighties when he came out to the Peak during the ONFP excavation, told us that he and Doc were working together on the side of the Peak facing Bloody Hands, which is located in a northeasterly direction from the Peak. He said that right after they had done some light blasting work they heard a rumbling noise that sounded like something rolling under the ground. He turned to Doc and said, 'What's that?' Doc said to him that the dynamite must have knocked something loose. Then Gatlin told us that this rumbling sound continued away from the Peak and that Doc said to him that it was going in the direction of one of the entrances and they started running to follow it.

When Mr. Gatlin took us to the very spot where he and Doc were sitting when this event took place, we ran a trajectory based on the direction Gatlin showed us and it pointed in the same general direction where the Bloody Hands site is located in Hembrillo Canyon. We didn't know what the significance of the sound was or what it represented, but what was significant was that Doc had admitted to Mr. Gatlin that the Bloody Hands site was one of the entrances that led to the treasure rooms. We also learned from Babe and my mother and my Aunt Letha that Doc's long-held story was that the maps he found *inside the Peak revealed there were seven treasures, but there were seven entrances that led to a number of caves inside the Peak and also to the large caverns where the main treasure rooms were deep under the ground. Doc always talked about a 2,700-foot long cavern beneath Victorio Peak big enough for a train locomotive to fit inside of it. As it turns out, you* discovered that Bloody Hands was the place where 37 tons of gold was removed in late 1973. So I guess that Doc was right, and he knew what he was talking about, because he had seen it.*

That wasn't the first time Doc heard the same rumbling sound in the same place. Much earlier, I recall that it was years earlier, he and Tony Carriaga, who Doc referred to as "the Yaqui," were working in the very same place when he heard it the first time and Carriaga and Doc reacted pretty much in the same way when the rumbling happened then.

~

There was also another rumbling noise on the earth, and it wasn't in the Hembrillo Basin—World War II had erupted in Europe, a global conflict that began on September 1, 1939 when Germany invaded Poland and France. When it ended, more than seventy million people, mostly civilians, were dead. When the United States entered the war, and after it had ended in 1945, it had a direct effect on what happened and didn't happen in the Hembrillo Basin.

---

*Mr. Delonas' reference was to this writer, who was taking the interview.

Chapter 11

The Man from Santa Monica and Other Characters

T he full context of the man from Santa Monica will be discussed later, but since the events involving him began in February of 1939, it is best to introduce him here. Doc had sold a gold bar to a man named Charles E. Ussher of Santa Monica, California, but Doc never dealt directly with him; he dealt through Ussher's associate, a Mr. Grogan, who received the gold from Doc and then turned it over to Ussher. Grogan thought that Doc's source of the bars was at a place eighteen miles west of Engle along old highway 85, which leads to Las Cruces, ten miles east of the Caballo Mountains.

Less than a year later, Ussher gave Grogan $200 with instructions to return to New Mexico to find the source of Doc's gold bars. Once the location was determined, Grogan was to use the $200 to buy the ground where the bars were hidden. Over the years, the story of Charles E. Ussher played a significant role at the Treasury by portraying Doc as a swindler, a game played out by the Director of the Mint, Nellie Tayloe Ross and at times by Acting Director of the Mint, Leland Howard. The Ussher story was bantered about by Doc's adversaries at the Mint and at White Sands Missile Range up into the 1990s, a

ASSAYERS CHEMISTS		**HAWLEY & HAWLEY**					*Litho Cantrell*	SHIPPERS REPRESENTATIVES BULLION BUYERS ORE BUYERS	
EL PASO, TEXAS Box 4		W. E. HAWLEY, Manager DOUGLAS, ARIZONA 537 TWELFTH STREET Box 1060							
WE HEREBY CERTIFY THAT THE FOLLOWING RESULTS WERE OBTAINED FROM SAMPLES OF						Dr. M. E. Noss, by B. D. Lampros			

OFFICE NO.	MARKED	GOLD OZS.	SILVER OZS.	LEAD PER CENT	COPPER PER CENT	ZINC PER CENT	IRON PER CENT		
		Ozs per ton							
141034	Sampled received and assayed 2/4/1939	146.18	87.3		71.18				
	C O P Y								

METAL QUOTATIONS:				
GOLD $35.00 PER OZ. COPPER ____ C PER LB. CHARGES: $_____				HAWLEY & HAWLEY
$ ___ IR ____ PER OZ. ____ PER LB. DATE **12/13/1952** _____		PER _____ ASSAYER.		

story this writer has titled "Poor Ussher." Ussher was one of many characters in the Noss treasure story. We pause in the Ussher story and continue with the chronology of events.

February 4, 1939

On February 4, 1939, Doc and B.D. Lampros drove to Douglas, Arizona, to Hawley & Hawley, assayers and chemists, to sell gold, which William Hawley assayed and then provided him with the assay report.[41] The firm purchased the crude bars and the ore that they brought in, which Doc sold at a greatly discounted price to move it quickly. Being that gold was banned and the Depression was in full swing, it was not uncommon for Doc to transact in this manner. He had been removing gold from Victorio Peak for more than a year now, and what was taken to Hawley & Hawley on February 4, 1939, assayed at 146.18 ounces of gold per ton, which at $34.912 per ounce totaled $5,103.14 per ton. The silver was assayed at $72.45 per ton and the copper at $344.36 per ton.

February 18, 1939

Doc and Lampros returned to Hawley & Hawley two weeks later with more gold. The February 18, 1939, assay[42] was slightly less: 140.00 ounces of gold per ton, which at $34.912 per ounce totaled $4,887.40 per ton. The silver was 91.40 ounces per ton, which produced $75.86 per ton; the copper produced $330.33 a ton. William E. Hawley provided signed original duplicates of these assay reports to Ova Noss on December 13, 1952, when she drove to Arizona to secure them.

OFFICE NO.	MARKED	GOLD OZS.	SILVER OZS.	LEAD PER CENT	COPPER PER CENT	ZINC PER CENT	IRON PER CENT		
		Ozs per ton							
141190	Sample received and assayed 2/18/1939.	140.00	91.4		68.26				

ASSAYERS CHEMISTS — EL PASO, TEXAS Box 4

HAWLEY & HAWLEY — W. E. HAWLEY, Manager — DOUGLAS, ARIZONA — 537 TWELFTH STREET — Box 1060

SHIPPERS REPRESENTATIVES BULLION BUYERS ORE BUYERS

WE HEREBY CERTIFY THAT THE FOLLOWING RESULTS WERE OBTAINED FROM SAMPLES OF Dr. M. E. Noss

COPY

METAL QUOTATIONS: GOLD $35.00 PER OZ. COPPER ___ C PER LB. CHARGES: $ ___ SILVER ___ PER OZ. ___ PER LB. DATE 12/13/1952

HAWLEY & HAWLEY PER ___ ASSAYER.

May 29, 1939

Much of the discovery and the filings of claims related to Victorio Peak were recorded at the State Land Office in Santa Fe, or other regional offices such as Las Cruces and in Socorro County. On May 29, 1939, Doc and J. F. Thomas located the "Cheyenne Mine"; S. Birchfield and George W. Manning witnessed the discovery. The location was "one mile east of Old Collins Spring" in the Hembrillo Canyon. The claim was filed on June 7, 1939, in Book 120, pg. 192, Socorro County. Conversations with Terry Delonas revealed that the Secret Service was told to investigate the filings, however the details as to why the Service investigated the filings are unknown.

Doc also sold gold in Telluride, Colorado. Evidence of this was recorded in writing on the back of the photograph, which read:

> *Right-hand drive Cadillac with overload springs. We took 56 bars to Telluride, Colo. to have refined. 23 lbs. of 16 oz. resulted of pure gold…1939 Joe Aberto*
>
> ~

The front of the photo was a snapshot of a Cadillac owned by a man named L. L. Leroy. According to what is written on the photo, Doc was selling gold in Telluride, Colorado; Terry Delonas speculated that Doc had been going to Telluride to avoid the Secret Service in New Mexico. The front of the photo shows a rare look at a vintage right-hand drive 1930s V-8 Cadillac.*

Telluride, Colorado (seen here) enjoyed the "gold boom" that began shortly after the silver crash in the late 1800s. During the early 1900s, Telluride was a growing boomtown and it was pretty much the same when Leroy and Doc went there in 1939. However, the refinery business dropped off after the Gold

Main Street

Reserve Act of 1934 and by then the Bank of Telluride had already closed its doors. Gone were the bordellos and the dance-halls, but the lure of profits from smelting someone's gold bullion persisted; there was always someone who would refine gold for the right price. The front of the next photograph reads:

L. L. Leroy, Manning and others 1939…

---

*This particular car, "the Madam X" named after a painting of the same name, was available with a V-16 engine.

The person (cut off) on the left side of the *second* Cadillac photo is George Manning; Manning worked for Doc at Victorio Peak before and after the top shaft collapsed. The reference to *others* refers to L.L. Leroy and Doc, from left to right in the photo; *others* in the photos were cropped out of the picture.

In order to move gold quickly, discounts were always available because of the newly enacted laws related to gold in the GRA, so if the gold refined out to twenty-three pounds of sixteen-ounce pure gold, the *Troy* ounce equivalent would be about 394 ounces, establishing a gross price-value of about $13,800.00 based on $35 per Troy ounce. The profit to the refiner could have easily been $3,800.00, leaving the balance to be settled between Doc and Leroy, whatever that might have been.

The above photograph appears to have been taken in the Caballo Mountains, but whether Doc was taking the gold from his Caballo treasure or the Victorio Peak treasure is unknown. Regardless of where the gold came from, money was needed to do the work to construct a suitable and safe shaft to access the treasure rooms from the top of Victorio Peak. Doc and Ova were sitting on a king's ransom, but money remained a problem.

Doc was not above having some spirited fun; even though he had an immeasurable amount of distain for local law enforcement, politicians, and the government in general, he held an equal amount of love for his country. Here, Claude Fincher and Doc are seen in Hot Springs with fireworks they had purchased to celebrate the 4th of July.

Chapter 12

Ova vs. the Mint, Disaster at the Peak, More on Ussher, the First Camp Notes

The Great Depression, which began in 1929, started in the United States and spread worldwide. It ended at various stages beginning in the 1930s and through the early years of 1940. It was heralded by the stock market crash of October 29, 1929, referred to as Black Tuesday. The Great Depression set the stage for World War II in Europe, and it was also a time when severe poverty drove Americans out of their homes onto the streets or into tents. Countless photographs were taken in those years depicting the abject conditions people were forced to endure to survive. In March 1936, Dorothea Lange took this famous photograph of Florence Owens Thompson, a destitute pea picker from Nipomo, California.

~

Although unsubstantiated, that year Ova claimed she had sent a piece of a gold bar to the Treasury Department in Washington to be analyzed. However, there is no question that she in fact wrote to the U.S. Mint in Washington from the Hotel Baker in Deming, New Mexico seeking information about "U.S. law" on a find of gold bars. Her letter was undated, but the Mint received it on July 17, 1939, putting an approximate date of July 10, 1939 when Ova most likely sent the letter:[43] (underlining inserted)

> *Dear Sir: I am seeking some information that you alone can give me. We are residents of New Mexico and find lots of stories about buried treasures, such as bars of gold and silver, also Mexican money.*
>
> *Now we have in our possession an old map that tells a story of rich gold bars and Mexican money. Now we are searching in the vicinity of where it's liable to be and <u>what I want to know is what the U.S. law is on a find of that kind.</u> Can we take it to the United States Mint and sell it, or will the government claim the treasure?*
>
> *<u>Please answer this letter at your earliest convenience.</u> Denver, Colorado isn't far from here and if we can take bars of gold to the mint and get paid for it, I sure want to know about it. <u>If you have the law on that please let me know just how to go about disposing of gold in the form of bars. Write me at Hot Springs, New Mexico</u>*
>
> *—Mrs. M.E. Noss*

~

In her undated letter, Ova was clear about what she wanted to know; simply—what was the "U.S. law" regarding the disposition of gold bars found in a treasure trove? She asked that a response come to her in *writing*. Leland Howard's answer eventually arrived, but not on a timely basis, nor in writing as requested by Ova. Apparently, Howard had Ova's letter retyped, but only the second page of the retyped letter[44] was ever found. It was most likely retyped for the purpose of clarity and was used as an attachment to a formal directive by Leland Howard requesting action on Ova's request.

On July 26, 1939, Leland Howard, instructed[45] the Chief of the Secret Service, Frank J. Wilson to "have an agent contact Mrs. Noss, advising her *orally* that the finding of any gold in this country by any person *should* be reported promptly to the Treasury Department together with a statement as to the circumstances under which it was found, in order that specific instructions may be given." No other information or instructions were given to Wilson, just Howard's bizarre order to provide only an oral response. Howard had signed the directive as the Acting Director of the Mint.

Nine days had passed since Howard had received and read Ova's letter and wrote to Frank J. Wilson. However, the *first* thing Howard mentioned in his directive to Wilson was not Ova's letter of inquiry, he referred to the May 31, 1938 report by Albuquerque's Secret Service Supervising Agent, Roland K. Goddard, who had previously written to Wilson about Agent Hargett's investigation into the accusations made by Hubert Heath, Editor of the Herald Newspaper in Hot Springs. Finding no connection to Noss and the allegations made by Heath *and* New Mexico State Police Chief J. House, the District office in Albuquerque closed their files. As indicated earlier, Hargett claimed that Heath's accusations were politically motivated. The case had been closed for nearly fourteen months, yet Howard stirred the information into his letter to Frank Wilson. He first reminded Wilson of the Heath matter, then instructed him to give an *oral* message to Ova Noss on her request for information. He ended his letter to Wilson by saying that if "further investigation of this matter [the Heath/Noss allegations] is warranted, it will be appreciated if you will instigate such an investigation [in reality a reinvestigation]." Howard appeared to be more interested in what Hubert Heath had to say about the charges he levied against Doc—not Ova's letter. Wilson's investigation would show that Heath's accusations were unfounded. The fact is, that from the time Howard knew of Ova's request for information concerning matters involving gold, until she finally got word from the Treasury, 110 days would elapse.

August 1939

From his teens to his early twenties, Benny Samaniego earned a living as a clerk at Duarte's Grocery Store, nestled between Gutierrez's Drug Store and the old Hotel Herndon on Main Street in Las Cruces. Next to the hotel was the Main Street Café where locals came to eat and sip a few drinks while they

Benny Samaniego with Spanish armor

discussed current events. Benny was known to be kind and soft-spoken, as was his wife, Marguerite, who was a schoolteacher in town. Together, they shared a happy and caring life.

One day, while Benny was working at the grocery store, Doc came in to purchase some food for the camp at the Peak. Benny was finishing up the last few minutes of his workday when Doc placed his groceries on the counter. A conversation struck up and it wasn't long afterwards, sometime in August of 1939, that Doc hired Benny to work at his treasure site. It was a much better paying job and Benny was a good worker.

According to what Ova told Terry, Benny was alone much of the time when he worked at Victorio Peak. Doc left him there to keep the torches lit and various other tasks, which included inventorying the treasure. Ova told Terry that Benny did a lot of things while he worked for them, but the climb down was too hard and dangerous for her to manage; therefore, she never was able to go down to the main rooms where the bulk of the treasure was hidden. Ova told Terry that she always wished she could have gone down. She told him, "But I was usually with him when he talked about the treasure. He would describe everything to me and tell me about the things he was unable to bring to the surface. I used to listen like a schoolchild and I would enjoy the stories almost as much as if I were down there with him."

One of the pieces in the treasure Benny always admired was a complete suit of ancient Spanish armor. Doc liked him a great deal and allowed him to remove it from the treasure; it included an Old Spanish helmet and an armored breastplate, each clad with chainmaille (Fr.), all shown here. Ova said that Benny wore it many times in while riding horseback in parades in the area. His younger brother believes that Benny sold the armor to a museum in Denver, Colorado. Another photo of him posing with the armor appeared in *The New Mexico Sentinel* on December 22, 1939. The article[46] read that Samaniego found it "the other day* in a cave in the Caballo Mountains, 50 miles north and east of Las Cruces." Ova told Terry, "That was the story Doc and Benny agreed on. We didn't want anyone to know that the armor came from Victorio Peak. We didn't want to draw any more attention to what we had found. We were having enough problems as it was after word got out about the treasure." Two years had passed between the time of the discovery and when the article appeared in the *Sentinel*. Ova told Terry that Benny worked on the armored suit for a long

---

*Underlined inserted

time until he showed it off. "There was a lot of repair work done to it. Benny put on a new helmet strap and the leather that held everything together was rotted away." Ova's account made sense; it is unlikely that the centuries-old armor would have been in such perfect condition as the article claimed.

All that summer Doc and Benny kept working, moving up and down the ventilation shaft and bringing out many items. All the while he and Benny moved in and out of the shaft, Doc struggled to make an easier passageway in from the top. The other entrances, which also took him to the treasure rooms, were to remain his secret. By August, Doc decided to remove a large rock that obstructed the downward pathway inside the shaft, a problem that had concerned him from the very day he descended to explore the depths of the cave and the caverns far below, an obstacle that made it difficult to navigate through the narrow shaft opening. To make it easier to come up and down the shaft, the obstruction would have to be removed. It was a formidable task and Doc realized he needed the help of a mining engineer, someone who could assess the work and recommend a solution to the problem. Doc wrote:[47]

> *Then I came in contact with S.E. Montgomery* [aka "Monty" Montgomery] in Hot Springs in August of 1939. He told me that he was a Mining Engineer and understood mining, excavating, and that he would have this financed with very reliable people for an interest or percentage. He brought his people down there, and we made the trade.*

~

Ova also spoke more about Montgomery during her March 24, 1975 deposition. However, more detailed account appears in her personal writings:[†]

> *In the fall of 1939, a dynamite explosion closed up the cave. S.E. Montgomery put off the shot. The boys worked from the fall of 1939 until the spring of 1941 trying to get the dirt out. A rock obstruction in the shaft was the reason for the explosion. The shaft by which Doc went in and out was like a spiral, and this rock formed a bottleneck that you could not get around easily. Doc had told him not to let any rock as big as your fist fall down that shaft. Shutting that off like that stopped up the crack with a good 60 feet of dirt, and he was never able to get into that from the time Montgomery shot it off. Charley Ryan killed Doc before he ever got the dirt out.* —Ova Noss

~

---

*Photo of S.E. "Monty" Montgomery was taken at Hog's Water Ranch in Arizona circa 1939

†O. Noss, ***op. cit.***, p. 2..

School would soon be starting and Joe Andregg, now living near Las Cruces, had to get back home so he could attend classes. Doc said he'd take him home, but first there were a few stops along the way, including a last stop in El Paso to get some cash. His first stop though was in Alamogordo, more than an hour drive from Victorio Peak to the east. By the end of summer 1939, Joe Andregg had grown taller, stronger, and better tuned to what was expected of him at the Peak. It was his third summer on the job, and it was *not* an uneventful one. It was also Joe's senior year in high school; after graduation, Joe enlisted. From Joe Andregg's December 10, 1987 statement:[48]

> *The next time I worked for him was the time the shaft was blown up. He decided to shut the mine down. It was late in the summer. He decided to take me home by the way of El Paso. We got in the pick-up and drove down the canyon about a half-mile. He backed up to a bank. We uncovered a heavy box about the size of a footlocker and we rolled it in the back of the pickup on some fence post. It was too heavy to carry on. I believe it weighed in the excess of 300 lbs. We drove into Alamogordo, stayed overnight at a motel. He left by foot late that night. He came back about 3 P.M. the next day. He had just enough money to pay the motel and fill the tank with gas.*
>
> *We started to El Paso, he turned off on an old wagon road and we drove in about 3 or 4 miles. He stopped [and] gave me his rifle. He told me to watch over [the] back trail and to shoot 3 times if I saw anyone following us. I watched him go out of sight. He was gone 2 hours. We went on to El Paso [and] checked into a hotel. He told me to stay in the room. He had to go sell some stuff. He came back the next morning. He had $2,500 dollars in travel checks. He took me to Las Cruces. That was the last time I saw him until I got out of the service.*   —*Joe Andregg*

~

Doc had made up his mind, and thought the best thing to do for the time being was to close down the mine operation until he could work things out, and that meant getting enough funds together to do a proper job of clearing the debris from the shaft.

August 25, 1939

The cave was accidentally sealed on or about August 25, 1939, shutting off the serpentine access route to the treasure. The whole idea was to improve the passageway to the caverns, but Montgomery's decision to place the sticks where he did, and in such an excessive amount, was a disaster; an avalanche of debris shot downward, filling the top entrance to the caverns—a blast that would eventually be heard around the world. From the deposition* of Ova Noss on March 24, 1975:

> *Q. Did there come a time when Mr. Montgomery came to the scene?*
> *A. He was a mining engineer. He claimed he got his degree from Cisco, California.*

---

*N. Deposition, ***op. cit.***, pp. 68-72.

Q. What was the purpose for bringing him to Victorio Peak?

A. We had a rock obstruction in the shaft.

Q. How long was Montgomery on the scene?

A. His trip was short. Doc fired him right then.

Q. Would you describe what you saw?

A. I heard the boom and I started to run. I didn't do much looking around, but I did see a rock falling down, and dirt hundreds of feet high in the air.

Q. Did you go up to the top of the Peak?

A. The rest did. It was thin ice up there [meaning it was dangerous at all times].

Q. What did the entrance to the cave look like after the explosion?

A. It was a mess. I don't know how to tell you. Everything had to be done over, a hole put in and a shaft.

Q. This large room where the paintings were, did that still exist?

A. No. It shattered the walls.

~

The shaft* had to be cleaned out, and that would take cash, a good deal of it. Doc began converting some of the old coins and money from the treasure rooms into cash. For those items he dealt mostly with coin collectors out of the area: Albuquerque, El Paso, and Alamogordo. Coin dealers usually took advantage of him; what little he received helped, but it didn't last long and there were too many questions asked about where he was getting all the unusual coins and paper money. Some of the ancient jewels brought good prices too, but they were hard to sell and there were always a lot of questions. On top of that, Doc really had no idea of their true value. So, he stuck with what he knew best—the gold bars.

On September 8, 1939, only two weeks after the collapse of the top entrance shaft at Victorio Peak, Vences "Benny" Samaniego purchased four lots[49] and a home in Las Cruces, New Mexico from J. Austin and Sigrid E. Gustafson, husband and wife. The value of the property on Warranty Deed No. 19289 stated a consideration of only $10.00—an obvious attempt to conceal the true amount of the transaction and allay concerns over how he was able to afford

---

*Photo of debris-filled shaft were taken shortly after Montgomery set off the dynamite charge.

such a large purchase. The fact was that Benny had been salting away some of the treasure he was able to remove when Doc was not present. David Chandler wrote in his book* that, "within two weeks of the cave-in, the previously penniless Samaniego bought a home and lots at 937 South Melendres Street in Las Cruces." The value was $16,000. When Benny died his estate† was worth $73,672.

Times were tough in America in 1939 and having enough money to pay cash for real estate was uncommon. The Noss family believes that Benny had removed gold bars from the Peak while he worked for Doc and that he used Doc's gold to purchase the lots and the house. Before Benny died in February 1971, he gave two checks to a friend, a local businessman and historical archivist, Evan Davies. Benny had instructed him to deliver the checks to certain churches in Las Cruces; each check was for $10,000.00. Doc didn't care if Benny had profited from the gold, Ova told Terry and knowing Doc's true nature, he was happy that someone had enjoyed some benefits from the treasure; it was the crooked politicians and government officials that Doc detested. "He remembered the old days," Ova told Terry, "when the American Indian was mere cannon fodder or a target for the Army. He remembered what happened to Geronimo and talked about it to me when he was down and feelin' bad, which was quite often after the cave-in."

It was during the final summer with Doc that Joe Andregg recalled helping him cut a bar of gold in half. From Andregg's December 10, 1987, statement:[50]

> *He left the cabin that morning. He was gone about an hour and a half and brought a bar back to the cabin. Doc got a hacksaw from the pickup. I held the bar while he sawed. Doc wanted to know how pure the gold was. When we finished, he took the half bar back out in the hills. He took the other half to Socorro to the assay office. I never did learn the results of the assay, and I have never had any reason to believe that it was anything other than gold.*

~

Doc continued to work at the Peak and kept a minimum of three men working daily. With his back against the wall, he decided the best thing to do was to make an official claim on the treasure site and sought the advice of the State Land Office authorities. So he took photos of the stacks of gold bars and filed them at the Land Office in Santa Fe. Land Office personnel advised him to enlarge the opening and make it safe for inspection; he could then proceed with a mining operation to not only uncover the treasure, but to gain access to the large gold vein, which Doc claimed he had discovered deep underground.

---

*D. L. Chandler, *One Hundred Tons of Gold*, (Doubleday & Company, New York, 1975), p. 118
†The Last Will and Testament of Marguerite G. Samaniego as filed in Doña Ana County on May 13, 1974

It was the best advice he could come up with. Even though Doc and Ova maintained a healthy workforce at the Peak, the problem was always getting money to finance the work: timbers and tools had to be purchased and workers had to be paid. It was too much work for Doc and Ova to do on their own, so they hired laborers. The average workforce included about ten men doing the excavation work. The women, mainly their wives, helped Ova at the Rock House

setting up and moving tents, preparing meals, cleaning clothes and attending to minor wounds incurred by the men.

But now, more than ever, Doc was being watched and it was becoming increasingly difficult to exchange the large amount of gold he had stashed away for cash.

September 11, 1939

Finally, and in response to Leland Howard's July 26 request, Secret Service Agent Emmett Hargett wrote[51] and advised Secret Service Chief Francis J. Wilson on September 11, 1939, that: (underline by author)

> *Endeavor was made to locate Mrs. Noss, through the post office and individuals in Hot Springs, but without avail. They are known to be in the section, but their exact whereabouts is not known. The Postmaster promised to have information concerning the whereabouts of Mrs. Noss and family upon my next visit to Hot Springs. At that time the* <u>*message*</u> *will be delivered.*   —Hargett

~

Late Fall 1939

Attorney Rueckhaus had recommended that Doc take a few gold bars to the Mint in Denver and exchange them for cash. He and Ova talked it over and decided to take Rueckhaus' advice and chance taking five bars to the Mint to properly handle the disposition of the gold and get badly needed cash for the excavation work. In a letter[52] dated July 7, 1976, Rueckhaus wrote, "He agreed to attempt this and told me that he had. I did not handle any part of this endeavor."

But when Doc, Ova, Claude Fincher and Letha drove to Denver to deliver the gold, their plans of getting much needed working capital collapsed; the Mint took Doc's gold bars and the only thing he got in return was a receipt for $97,000 and a lot of questions about the gold and where the caverns were located. Ova referred to the receipt as a *hold certificate*. Doc was told he would receive actual payment when he showed the Treasury where the treasure trove site was located, and after he proved his ownership, they would then consider paying him the money. Leland Howard and the Director of the Mint were one step ahead of Doc and Ova; they were not going to be allowed to make a treasure trove claim, not if they could help it.

During the 1975 Deposition* of Ova Noss, attorney Daar asked Ova if she and Doc had gone to the Denver Mint with gold bars. She said they had gone there, but she was not quite certain about the exact year:

> *Q. Were there other times when you sold gold?*
> *A. We took five[†] bars to the Denver Mint. He thought if he couldn't deal with men, he could go to the government.*
> *Q. There was a time when you actually went to the Denver Mint with gold bars?*
> *A. Yes.*
> *Q. When was that?*
> *A. It was in 1941 or '42. Now, I don't know the exact date,[‡] but it was in that period of time.*
> *Q. Did you personally go there?*
> *A. I was in the car. Claude Fincher and Doc carried it in the Mint.*
> *Q. Did you ever see a receipt from the mint?*
> *A. I sure did.*
> *Q. When was that?*

> ~

She told Attorney Daar that when Doc and Claude Fincher came back to the car, Doc said, "They were going to confiscate the gold. They said it was old gold." Ova added that Doc also said the people inside "admitted that it *was* gold, but they accused him of stealing it in Old Mexico." According to Ova, Doc responded and said, "Then, you're going to steal it from me?" One can assume that a lot more was said when Doc and Fincher returned to the car. The *confiscation* word was no secret, and I'm sure that it was tossed about when they drove away from the Mint.

---

* N. Deposition, *op. cit.*, pp. 104, 105.
† There has always been some contention whether it was four bars or five. Ova always maintained it was five.
‡ The trip to the Denver Mint occurred during late autumn of 1939.

Then, for some reason, Eleanor Roosevelt's name came up in the confab, but it is difficult to determine from the deposition whether Doc had mentioned her name inside the Mint or when he got back to the car. Later, it was learned that Doc had made arrangements to fly to Washington to meet with President Roosevelt concerning the matter. He might have been dealing directly with Eleanor Roosevelt, and there was some degree of speculation in that regard, but it would not be the last time that a U.S. President became involved; there were others after Roosevelt. In fact, Ova Noss told Terry on many occasions that a Secret Service agent by the name of *Wells* was present at Doc's funeral asking questions quietly of people who attended the funeral; and that there were other Secret Service agents present, as well as several FBI agents. According to Terry, Letha also mentioned a Secret Service agent by the same name, and referred to him as being one of the agents assigned to protect Eleanor Roosevelt. Terry's belief that a high-level Secret Service agent was directly involved in Doc's activities was expressed during one of our interviews:

> *I've always felt that the connection to Doc and Babe's discovery of the Victorio Peak treasure and the historical importance of Roosevelt's 1934 Gold Reserve Act was an uncanny coincidence in timing. Because of the Act's language regarding the restrictions in owning gold, it turned out that during the last couple of years before Doc was killed, a Secret Service agent was sent to New Mexico from Washington to shadow him and find out where he was getting his gold. As we understand it, this agent's previous assignment had been the security for Eleanor Roosevelt. I don't recall his exact name, though Walsh or Wells comes to mind, but I'm not sure. Then a few days after Doc was killed this same agent came forward and interviewed several people, including Charley Ryan, and revealed that he had been following Doc. Prior to that, Babe told us that Doc knew he was being watched all the time. The surveillance took place off and on after FDR died, but during the same time period this agent was still guarding Mrs. Eleanor Roosevelt. That's our understanding, and that's what we feel is the true case.*

~

From a letter[53] by Doc's friend and attorney, Melvin Rueckhaus dated July 7, 1976:

> *After Doc's death I was approached by a Civil [Secret] Service man by the name of Wells who exhibited to me a bar which did not resemble the bars that I had examined earlier, and which appeared to, and was told to me by Mr. Wells, not to contain gold. I do not recall at present whether Mr. Wells told me the source of this bar or not.*
> —*Melvin Rueckhaus*

~

Ova explained in her deposition* that instead of confiscating the gold, the individuals at the Mint gave Doc a *hold certificate:*

---

*N. Deposition, ***op. cit.,*** pp. 105, 106.

Q. He had a hold certificate?

A. Yes, a hold certificate.

Q. It was from the Denver mint?

A. Yes.

Q. You were with them on the day they went to the Mint?

A. Yes, but I wasn't inside.

Q. Okay. But you know that they went there --

A. Yes.

Q. They went there with gold bars?

A. Yes.

Q. And you know it was gold bars?

A. Yes, it came to $97,000.

~

Letha and Dorothy's perspective on some of the accounts presented in *The Gold House* books were taken directly from a manuscript[54] written by them entitled *The Doc Noss Ill-fated Gold at Victorio Peak.* However, the title page of the manuscript reads, "As Told by Kit Carson." *The* Kit Carson was an American frontiersman who was known for the many books he wrote during his lifetime. He was most noted for being John C. Fremont's guide in the American West. He also became well-known in California at the time of the 1846 Mexican-American War. Carson died on May 23, 1868 at the age of 58.

Kit Carson, who was identified in *The Doc Noss Ill-fated Gold at Victorio Peak* manuscript, was in fact Xanthus "Kit" Carson from Albuquerque, New Mexico, obviously not the noted frontiersman. On May 1, 1973, Xanthus' name came up when he wrote[55] to Norman Scott* concerning the Noss treasure and a bill[56] for $234 sent to him by Attorney Leonard L. Pickering of Albuquerque for legal fees regarding Victorio Peak and the Doc Noss story; the fee included a "review of manuscript" and other related matters. On August 2, 1973, Carson wrote[57] to Scott again and enclosed Pickering's invoice for payment and spoke of an agreement Carson presumably had with Scott that stemmed from a meeting at the Albuquerque Hilton Inn that June. On August 6, 1973, Scott wrote[58] to Carson saying, "We had no agreement at all," and adding, "I also bring to your attention that you used copyrighted pictures of ours without permission in a recent article in Treasure Magazine."

Several sections of the Guthrie-Delonas manuscript will be referred to in this book, but it is unknown what role Carson played in compiling it or if some of the events described were fictionalized or embellished by him. Attempts to locate Carson have been unsuccessful. What *is* certain though is that the manuscript

---

*Norman Scott headed Expeditions Unlimited, Inc., a worldwide exploration firm, which conducted an extensive effort to uncover the treasure. His name appears throughout book two of *The Gold House—The Lies, The Thefts.*

indicates that Letha Cantrell Guthrie *"in Conjunction With Dorothy Delonas"* are the true authors in their own right, both daughters of Ova Noss. The sisters lived and experienced firsthand the events portrayed in their manuscript. If Xanthus Carson in some degree co-authored the manuscript and is entitled to receive an acknowledgement, such acknowledgement for those sections quoted from the manuscript and used periodically in *The Gold House* book(s) is noted.

Letha and Dorothy wrote about the Denver trip in the manuscript:*

> *At one time, he carried four[†] gold bars to the Denver Mint, where he thought he could surely sell them for what they were worth on the legal market. Here he met with more trouble than he had ever dreamed of. He stirred the acting superintendent, a fellow by the name of Howard, who stuck a finger in the pie and kept it there at Victorio Peak until the lawyers ran him off. We needed money very badly at this time, as the incident was often told. When Doc returned from the Denver Mint, he was actually frightened. He said the people at the Mint had demanded to know where he got the bars, and when he refused to tell them and asked for the return of the gold, they only gave him a receipt and told him they would give him the money if and when he could prove that he was the legal owner. Other people were interested in these particular bars, and they had correspondence later with the institutions, and were directed to take up correspondence with the Mint, Washington, 25, D.C.*
>
> *Leland Howard, Acting Director of the Mint, said, 'We have no record showing the receipt of gold from the depositor mentioned therein.'*

~

On December 13, 1952, Carl W. Horzmann also made a reference to the Denver Mint incident in an affidavit he signed on that date. The last two paragraphs of Horzmann's affidavit were presented in the Letha Guthrie/Dorothy Delonas *Peak* manuscript[59] entitled *The Doc Noss Ill-Fated Gold at Victorio*. However, here is Carl Horzmann's *entire* affidavit:[‡60]

> *I, Carl W. Horzmann, of the City of Lordsburg, County of Hidalgo, State of New Mexico, do hereby make the following statement of facts regarding my association with Dr. M.E. Noss, now deceased, but at that time living at Hot Springs, N.M.*
>
> *I became acquainted with Dr. Noss personally in 1941 at the office of Attorney Newell in Las Cruces, N.M., where I helped organize the now defunct Cheyenne Mining Co.*
>
> *I did not see him personally again until 1945, when he stopped several times at my office in Lordsburg, at which time we discussed the treasure Dr. Noss claimed to have found in the San Andres Mountains. I was rather skeptical until he showed me a bar of gold, which he claimed came out of the treasure cave. This bar is supposed to assay 900 fine.*
>
> *In 1946, he came to the office late one evening, rather upset. Said he was ready to lift the main treasure but was afraid of the government. He claimed to have deposited with*

---

*L. Guthrie, D. Delonas, **op. cit.**, pp. 105
[†] In a separate statement, Letha corrected the number of bars to "four or five."
[‡] L. Guthrie, D. Delonas, **op. cit.**, pp. 106

the U.S. Mint in Denver, Colo., four bars of gold bullion and that he got a receipt for over $97,000 but no money, the mint telling him he would get paid as soon as he turned over the rest of the gold. That was in the fall of 1939. He said he had the receipt with him, but I did not ask to see it.

Dr. Noss wanted me to represent him in all future dealings with the government since he claimed I was the only honest man he had run across in years. We finally came to an understanding and he took me out to the ranch where I still live. That was the last time I saw him.   *—Carl W. Horzmann*

~

Horzmann's December 13, 1952 affidavit confirmed Doc's claim and his early affiliation with him. Although one of the equally significant points of Horzmann's affidavit was his mention of being involved with Attorney Newell in forming the Cheyenne Mining Company. District Attorney William T. Scoggin Jr., was also involved in setting up the company for Doc. Newell and Scoggin each had a percentage of the company. Ten years would pass, Doc would be murdered and J. Benson Newell would represent Doc's killer, Charley Ryan. The judge in the murder trial was William T. Scoggin Jr.; Doc's killer would go free.

There was more information about the $97,000 Mint receipt: B.D. Lampros and Letha signed a joint statement that they had seen the receipt from the Denver Mint "in the fall of 1939." Their *To Whom It May Concern* statement[61] read, in full:

We, the undersigned, do hereby state that we personally saw a receipt in the possession of Dr. M.E. Noss, now deceased, according to which he had turned over four or five bars of Gold Bullion to the U. S. Mint at Denver, Colorado, in the fall of 1939, and that the value of said bullion was in excess of $97,000. Dr. Noss stated at that time the mint did not pay for the gold, saying they would hold up payment pending the delivery of other bars Dr. Noss had in his possession.

—B.D. Lampros, Letha Beckwith Berato*

~

The issue over whether Doc had taken samples of the gold to the Denver Mint had persisted for many years and by 1961, it had obviously become a sensitive one. On August 14, 1961, a woman by the name of Ella Binion from Safford, Arizona, wrote to the Superintendent of the U.S. Mint at Denver and requested information on the gold that Doc had left there. Mrs. Binion's letter was not found in the Noss papers; however, it is believed that she was a friend of the Noss family and she had written on Ova's behalf. When the Denver Mint

---

*Letha Cantrell was now Letha Berato. Her fifth and last husband, E.M. Guthrie, was kidnapped in California and beaten to death. He had fled, unsuccessfully, from people trying to gain access to the treasure, all of which is covered in book two. Letha married five times before she died of natural causes.

responded, Fern V. Miller, Superintendent, sent the following letter[62] to Mrs. Binion on August 17, 1961. Miller's complete letter:

We have your inquiry of August 14, 1961 regarding Dr. M.E. Noss deceased. For information on this subject, we suggest that you write to the Director of the Mint, Washington, 25 D.C. as this office can give you no information on the subject.

—Fern V. Miller

~

Why was the Superintendent of the Denver Mint unable to give Ova information to answer such a simple request on his own? It could be argued that the Mint no longer had the information, but why was it necessary for Binion to write to Leland Howard? Miller was in charge of the Denver Mint; he *should* have been able to respond, but he refused. Was the Noss file at the Denver Mint tagged as a hot potato? Binion wrote to Leland Howard on August 25, 1961. Howard answered four days later on August 29, 1961. Howard's complete letter:[63]

In reply to your letter of August 25, 1961, we have no record showing the receipt of gold from the depositor mentioned therein.   *—Leland Howard*

~

After leaving the Denver Mint, Doc and Ova returned to the Hembrillo Basin fearing the worst now that the Mint knew for certain they were sitting on a pile of gold. When they attempted to play by the rules set down by the Treasury, they were turned away and not paid for the gold. Doc Noss contended that the Government of the United States could never be trusted to do what was proper, *especially* the military and the Treasury Department; it turned out that he was right. The times ahead would be difficult for them, especially for Doc, who became a main attraction for the Secret Service. They would follow him and investigate his activities; what eventually unfolded in Doc and Ova's efforts to bring out the treasure were like scenes from the *Treasure of the Sierra Madre* where distrust, greed, murder, and bandits pursued those who had gold. But in the case of Ova and Doc, the bandits were not a pack of seedy *banditos* armed with rifles, handguns and bandoleers slung across their chests; they were federal agents.

Now, having only a receipt for their efforts, Doc and Ova hired attorney Benson Newell to draw up organization papers for a mining company. With the assistance of Rueckhaus, Newell set up the Cheyenne Mining Company. With a proper company structure recorded with the state of New Mexico, Doc and Ova could legitimately raise funds to cover excavation costs; it was a step in the right direction. They spent the next ten years working hard to reopen the caverns, but sorrow, betrayal, and death camped with them in the Hembrillo Basin.

October 8, 1939

Doc was drunk *again* and caused some trouble in Las Cruces. He was charged with impersonating a federal law enforcement officer for the second time since his pardon on March 3, 1936, three years and seven months earlier. According to the FBI he was only arrested for drunk and disorderly conduct and was released after paying a $15 fine. Ova said that Doc had no use for the FBI in general or the guys behind their badges. Ova claimed that Doc would often mock them by impersonating them when he got drunk.

Three weeks later, while in Douglas, Arizona, Doc made the acquaintance of Grogan, Charles E. Ussher's associate from Santa Monica, California. Doc had given gold to Grogan, who was acting as Ussher's agent. The episode involving Doc, Grogan, Ussher, Nellie Tayloe Ross, the Director of the Mint, and Leland Howard, Ross' protégé, was about to unwind. Ova said that in October, Doc had also filed mining and prospecting claims in Socorro County. Doc was in constant motion, moving from one adventure to the next, and from one project to the next. But now, his main objective since the Denver Mint scare was to keep a low profile, which he did, for a while.

October 21, 1939

During the month of October 1939, Doc and Rebecca Taggart signed a cooperative mining agreement.[64] The Taggerts had decided to lease a mining operation to Doc in the Caballo Mountains for a percentage of any gold found. The life of Rebecca Taggert, her husband, and their mining site high on a mountaintop known as Noah's Ark, is yet another colorful account of hidden treasure in the Caballo Mountain region. Her story is outlined in a small book written by her, a blood relative to the deposed Mexican dictator, Porfirio Diaz, a story that tells of her life and that of her husband, Charlie.

Rebecca lived in Mexico City during the time of the Mexican Revolution, and as a child, she played with many of the children whose parents worked in the American Embassy there. Porfirio Diaz, a brutal opportunist and dictator for thirty-five years, had sold off Mexico's land at next-to-nothing prices to his friends, pressed millions of peasants into slavery, and therefore was destined to fall. He had three powerful enemies: Pancho Villa, whose real name was José Doroteo Arango Arámbula, a cattle thief and revolutionary who had won the hearts of patriots throughout Mexico, Emiliano Zapata who led forces against Diaz's government, and Venustiano Carranza who helped implement a new constitution for Mexico. In 1911, Diaz, at the age of 81, was executed by a firing squad. Before the execution, and when Americans were leaving Mexico, Rebecca, then about eight years old, was taken to live in San Francisco where she was educated and grew up.

It was in San Francisco that she met a rich, handsome man by the name of Charlie Taggert. He had heard of an intelligent young Mexican woman who could read and speak Spanish and who was reported to be lively and quite beautiful. Taggert's mission was a simple one, find her and make her acquaintance, but his intentions also contained a hidden agenda: Taggert had come into possession of a treasure map written in Spanish—Rebecca was going to be his translator. They met, fell in love, and were married. The location where Charlie and Rebecca had staked their claim was a place high on the Caballo Mountain Range known to the Apaches as "The Nose," or more commonly known today as Noah's Ark, a lookout site where the Apaches tracked the comings and goings of the cavalry. Charlie's Rolls Royce was of little use in the mountains, so he and Rebecca rented horses from Milton Holden for the long and dangerous trip to the top of the mountain. As a point of historical interest, Rebecca and Charlie had befriended an elderly man who had taken the name of Silva. Silva told her that when he was a young man, he rode with Cochise against the cavalry. Soon after they met, Silva died of natural causes in Hatch, New Mexico.

For years, Rebecca and Charlie Taggert searched for gold on the mining claim and labored long and hard, but whether they recovered any gold is not known. During their quest, Rebecca was said to have found a cave with skeletons inside and sealed it up, similar to that of Doc's account of skeletons found inside Victorio Peak. Charlie passed away from a serious head injury. Rebecca retired to El Paso. One of her friends was Doc Noss who had agreed to work her claim site after Charlie died. The agreement was struck on October 20, 1939. The claim remains active to this date and the cave where Rebecca and Charlie once lived is still there. Later in life, she wrote *Phantom of the Caballos*, a haunting story of her life and times with her husband Charlie in the Caballo Mountains. Rebecca remained in El Paso until her death.

November 1940

Handling and transporting gold from the treasure was tricky business; the Secret Service was constantly on Doc's trail, as was the Federal Bureau of Investigation, trying to catch him with the gold. Ova claimed that on several occasions Doc had been relieved of his gold bars by individuals claiming to be Secret Service agents or federal agents, even Texas Rangers along the routes he had traveled on the Texas and New Mexico border, and from unsavory characters in Old Mexico where Doc had once done a lot of trading, but these accounts are impossible to substantiate.

November 3, 1939

Finally, on November 3, 1939, Secret Service Agent Emmet B. Hargett submitted a supplemental report to his boss, Frank Wilson. Two days earlier, on November 1, he had fulfilled his assignment, and it was the final report,[65] in part: (underlining inserted)

> *Per the request of Mr. Leland Howard, Acting Director of the Mint, I delivered the following oral message to Harold Beckwith, son of Mrs. M.E. Noss, that he might deliver same to his mother, in view of the absence of his mother from her home 'that finding of any gold in this country by any person <u>should</u> be reported promptly to the Treasury Department, together with a statement as to the circumstances under which it was found.'* —Hargett

~

Ova didn't receive the information firsthand; Harold had to pass it on to her. The net result of Howard needing information "in order that specific instructions may be given" had lost its meaning; where and how were the Nosses going to get the specific instructions? They had already gone to the Denver Mint, and Ova had written to the Treasury in Washington. When Howard's charade ended, nothing was accomplished; the oral message was delivered and the case was closed. The fact is that Doc took the gold to the Mint; *they* stole it from him and then accused *him* of stealing it "in Old Mexico."

It would have been far more binding if Hargett had delivered a bona fide letter from Leland Howard that addressed the exact requirements under which an American citizen was compelled by order of law, the Gold Reserve Act of 1934, in matters related to the questions raised by Ova Noss in her letter—but that was not done. Although ignorance of the law is no excuse, neither is there any excuse to deliberately conceal or blur the intent or meaning of the law as Howard obviously had done. A 3¢ stamp, a 1¢ envelope, and a simple letter would have done wonders, and it would have taken only a few days. Instead, Hargett spent at least two days on the road, had traveled at least 600 miles, spent money for meals, motels and gasoline to deliver a worthless oral message that even Hargett seemed to resent—and it took more than three months to complete the mission. Leland Howard's actions were an example of a wastrel, a poor guardian of taxpayer money, an insensitive, overbearing bureaucrat with nothing better to do. But there was something more sinister at play, as facts will prove to be the case.

In order to help finance the excavation operation, Doc and Ova made individual agreements over the years with certain people who had the ability to invest. When gold was in the wind, those with money to spare found the trail that led to Victorio Peak and it was never difficult to attract investors; Doc would demonstrate the existence of the treasure by showing interested individuals gold bars as proof. Most of the investors were permitted to take a sample of the gold to be assayed, and in every case the assays were high in gold content. In exchange for their investments they were given a share of the return when the treasure was brought up, title established in a court of law under the treasure trove laws, valued, converted to cash and then paid out as agreed. All of the agreements entered into by Doc and Ova, and more so after Doc's murder, had provisions that if the investor's efforts and timely deposits were not strictly adhered to, the investor forfeited any amount of return specified in the agreement; everyone had a shot at it, so to speak. Many of the larger investors over the years sold Doc and Ova on *their* ability to move in, excavate, and get the gold out, but they all failed.

Agreements were structured in various ways, but largely on a performance basis where the investor agreed to complete the work in a certain time frame, under certain conditions or until the investment capital was spent, a common practice to this day by modern treasure hunters and their investors. In most cases where an investor put up money under the terms of such an agreement, the investor rarely did the work; the physical labor and equipment required was usually subbed out to others. It was usually the case that individuals came to Doc and Ova with their money and their bragging rights to sell them on their ability to bring up the treasure. Most were discouraged: their intentions were not honorable, they appeared to be shifty or it was known that it was the last of their money and therefore Ova would not allow them to invest. There were many cases like that, but there were a few complainers; mostly people who put a few hundred dollars on the table and thought they owned the treasure, people who wrote hate letters or contacted government officials and complained. Money that the *serious* investors put up was used to pay for labor, materials, and equipment expenses. Those investors took their licks and retreated after they failed to perform as agreed. Doc and Ova usually worked through an attorney when they entered into any arrangement with people who were willing to finance the excavation work completely. Only a few arrangements appear to be made without the involvement of an attorney. Even though Doc and Ova had signed away a portion of the treasure, it was so vast that the net balance of their remaining shares was so large that it mattered little to them.

After the collapse of the top entrance shaft, attempts to reach the treasure was a formidable challenge, more than anyone could have ever imagined. Moving gold bars they had taken out to secure places had been a problem, as was selling small amounts of the treasure for cash, but they were not the only problems Doc and Ova faced—Merle Horzmann, the wife of attorney Carl Horzmann, was a problem as well. The woman turned out to be a mean-spirited person who worked relentlessly to remove Doc from the picture, a manipulator and schemer who had Doc in her sights all during the time she was employed by him and involved at Victorio Peak. Her traits of disloyalty and unkind treatment of Ova and Doc were numerous and were often logged with many other accounts of the daily camp life at Victorio Peak. The recording of events was her assigned responsibility when she was at camp, an assignment given to her by Doc. Horzmann's records provide an important window into the past, an opportunity to look back in time and learn much about life at Victorio Peak.

Horzmann was not at Victorio Peak for her physical ability, strength or endurance, but she *was* recognized for her organizational skills and her willingness to take the bull by the horns. In the process, Ova and Doc tolerated most of her antics—to a point; therefore, she was kept on during the crucial years that preceded Doc's murder until shortly afterwards when she was killed in an automobile accident. Although some records are directly attributed to Doc, the rest of the information regarding their lives, apart from what Horzmann had recorded, is given by Ova and her children in letters, notes they had written, and the oral accounts of events as they recalled them, especially information given to Terry Delonas, Ova's grandson.

But it was the periodic log Merle Horzmann kept that gives a historical glimpse of life at a desert camp in the Hembrillo Basin near Victorio Peak, a place the American Indian called Soledad. It is from this perspective the story can better be told. These entries will be expressed as *Camp Notes* with date references. Unless otherwise indicated, Merle Horzmann is the author of all such notes; however, Doc and Ova Noss were the rightful and legal owners of camp log entries.

Horzmann sometimes wrote in the third person, but that has been changed, abridged, or expressed in narrative form for ease of reading. These notes serve as a porthole view of events as they happened. Letters that come to her are usually not listed as camp log entries. However, when she responded to any letter that dealt with the operation at Victorio Peak, those letters and correspondence were considered to be camp notes.

Beginning of Camp Notes

The first use of Horzmann's camp notes started in January 1940. Throughout the years, these records chronicled many of the events in the Hembrillo Basin, snapshots of life in the desert at Victorio Peak and the Rock House; a hard life, one of tribulation, great struggle—and betrayal.

Camp Notes — January 1940 [66]

> *[The men] attempted to reenter the cave, but due to closing of the entrance by falling debris, it was necessary to raise money. B.D. Lampros furnished some financing as a grubstake, B.B. Ownby furnished some too, and O.G. Turner came in on it through Ownby and the engineer, Montgomery. Ownby had a waybill describing such a cave but it was written in Spanish. This was translated and thought to compare with the description Dr. Noss gave of the caves. Each entry into the cave was made only when someone else was there.*
> —Merle Horzmann

~

The same day that Horzmann entered her account of Lampros, Turner, and Ownby, the man from Santa Monica, Charles Ussher, was taking action on another matter; a matter that involved his interaction with the Treasury Department was taking shape. The United States Treasury Department was about to deal Doc Noss a dirty hand. The end of the thread in the Treasury's shabby attempt to cast Doc Noss as a villain, thief, con man and criminal began in late October 1939 when Doc met Mr. Grogan.

January 25, 1940

Charles E. Ussher's letter of January 25, 1940, to Nellie Tayloe Ross, the off-and-on Director of the Mint, was a weapon used against Doc and Ova, and later in the 1990s. Leland Howard carried the incident forward concerning Ussher, Grogan and Ross throughout the years, especially when Ross was replaced after WWII ended and Eisenhower was elected President. When it came to the Noss family and Victorio Peak, Howard had no shame using whatever instrument he could to cast an element of doubt on the Noss treasure trove claim; the Ussher matter was one of Howard's favorite weapons. The case was only one of the weapons contained in Leland Howard's files, copies of which were later distributed among certain individuals and high ranking officers at White Sands Missile Range to promote the military's criminal agenda concerning the Noss treasure. In the 1990s Terry became the General Partner of ONFP, which was organized to excavate Victorio Peak a half-century after Charles E. Ussher wrote the following January 25, 1940 letter:[67]

> *Dear Mrs. Ross: Your letter of January 10th duly received. The piece or lump of metal you refer to is not all gold. It is supposed to have been an end of a lump given to me by a Mr. Grogan of Los Angeles and he told me he knew of many more of them hidden away in New Mexico.*
>
> *I turned it over to Mr. Carl Eliason U.S. Secret Service P.O. Box 567 Federal Bldg., Los Angeles. He made an investigation for me and the department found I had been gypped and was out $200.00, which I gave to Mr. Grogan. The story of these bars was told [to] me in April of 1939 and on the 18th of April I wrote to the Director of the Mint in San Francisco to know what could be done with these bars if they were found, for at that time I believed the story and gave Grogan the money to go to New Mexico and see if he could buy the land where these bars were supposed to be. I do not know where this lump came from or what kind of gold went into it. An assay showed 220.20 Oz. of silver and 139.92 Oz. of gold per ton. Assay made April 14th 1939 by Lewis & Walker, 214 West 11th St., Los Angeles. Mr. Carl Eliason had the piece in his office. I would appreciate it if you will write him to give it back to me for I would like to keep it for a paperweight on my desk.   —Charles E. Ussher*

~

A handwritten notation on Ross' copy of Ussher's letter read:

> *Note that Mrs. Noss wrote to Mint in July 1939, that they had a map & were searching in vicinity. But the story is that Noss made his discovery in 1937 with his wife. And she asked Denver Mint re: deposits made between Nov. 1939 & March 1940. Ans. 12/3/40.*

~

Ussher sent Grogan to New Mexico to buy the "land where these bars were supposed to be." The two hundred dollars he gave to Grogan was certainly not enough money to cover Grogan's traveling expenses and to buy land. Ussher referred to the piece he received from Grogan as a "lump of metal" and as "an end of a lump" that Grogan eventually turned over to him. It was Grogan who told Ussher that "he knew of many more of them hid away in New Mexico." Ussher pointed to the idea that the "lump" was part of a gold bar, but if Ussher's assay on April 14, 1939 by Lewis & Walker of Los Angeles was correct, then he had nothing to complain about. Only two months earlier, Hawley & Hawley of Douglas, Arizona, assayed Doc's samples setting silver at .83 and gold at 34.91 ounces per ton respectively. Using those values, Ussher's silver assayed at $182.77 a ton (.83x220.20) and the gold assayed at $4,884.61 a ton (34.91x139.92). Although Ussher didn't appear to be the bad guy here, his own assays indicated that he stood to make a sizable profit. He then expected to buy the land where the gold came from for only two hundred dollars, to which one could say—*Poor Ussher*. But the Mint had taken an opposite, misleading and adversarial position on the Ussher matter; the war was on.

Summer 1940

In June Doc was arrested *again* for drunk and disorderly conduct in Hot Springs—the FBI supplied the information to Ova; it was becoming obvious that FBI agents had tethered themselves to Doc, even when he drank. But when Doc was at the treasure site, he focused on getting back into the caverns. Throughout the summer, he kept up the assessment work with the Land Office and continued to explore the Peak area.

The blockage of the entrance to the caverns hit Doc hard; the work required to reopen it was difficult and dangerous, but it was also a deterrent to those who sought the treasure. Then Doc worked out a plan to resolve the issue that concerned him and others—the GRA; he sought to settle the matter at the White House. If that failed he contemplated taking the treasure out through his secret entrance. Dwelling on the matter, he took a month or two to himself and dropped out of sight. He returned to the Peak in mid-October 1940 to finish the work he had left behind. In Doc's handwriting:[68]

> *I then moved back into the mountains to finish where we had left off two years previous.* After three months spent doing the assessment work, attempting to clean out the cave, and working short-handed and short of food rations, on October 15, 1940, the day before the Selective Service Registration was being called, all of the camp seemed to be in an uproar. Not knowing, myself, that they had obtained my plats, maps, locations of the mine, they drifted out one at a time until finally all that was left in camp was my very good friend, Mr. C.C. Fincher of Hot Springs and [S.E.] Monty Montgomery.*
>
> *We stayed there about a month, until about November 15, 1940, the beginning of deer season. The mountains were full of deer hunters from various places and we felt ourselves in danger that we might have trouble with hunters that were also treasure seekers.*
>
> *On leaving camp, Mr. Montgomery, Mr. Hugh Hunter, Mr. Harry Loffler, and Jack Howard went up to the cave where we had been working. They placed in there some thirteen sticks of 80% dynamite and shot it off. I saw with my own eyes a rock weighing about 250 pounds that went away 250' into the air. After the shot, tons and tons of rock, sandstone and soapstone tumbled in.*

~

---

*It was in March or April of 1938 that Doc and Ova began bringing up small amounts of the treasure. Doc's reference *"to finish where we had left off two years previous"* was a reference to that time.

The cave Doc had described, where they used thirteen sticks of 80% dynamite to close it, was not the main shaft at the top of Victorio Peak, but another entrance Doc knew led to the caverns. Another "Monty" Montgomery would soon surface, L.C. "Monty" Montgomery, who claimed to be a mining engineer. His poor judgment in the use of too much dynamite collapsed the entrance to the top shaft on Victorio Peak.

January 30, 1941

Doc and Tony Carriaga believed they found an ancient mine that was once operated by Spanish miners. On January 30, 1941, Doc, Ova, Claude Fincher and S.E. Montgomery signed an agreement[69] that related to the discovery of the lost mine. Its location is not identified here for obvious reasons. However, the contents of the mine as shown on the agreement is as follows, in part:

> *They found a large amount of partially smelted bullion, and other valuable ores together with minted coins, metal ornaments, and other materials of value. It is represented by Dr. Noss and some of his associates that after the opening of said mine, there will be available bullion and other materials of value that can be used to produce funds to carry on any future development of the properties.*

Most likely the mine was reopened, but there is nothing in the Noss files to validate that anything else was performed beyond the Agreement document shown here.

January 1941

Per the FBI, Doc was in El Paso, drunk, *again.*

In February, when Doc returned to the Peak to close down the operation, he met a man named Roscoe Parr at the work site waiting for him. Doc and Parr seemed to hit it off and continued a long relationship in working to raise the treasure from within the caverns.

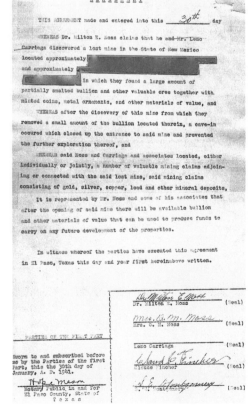

Chapter 13

Horzmann's Big Payday, Mr. Montoya, and the Spy Sent in by Federal Marshals

On December 12, 1952, Ted Farnsworth signed an affidavit claiming that he was "very closely acquainted" with Doc and had known Doc and Ova from 1938 to 1943; Farnsworth was a permanent resident at the Hotel McCoy* in El Paso, Texas. In 1941 he had made a number of visits to the Victorio Peak camp at which time Doc showed him several bars of metal that Farnsworth was certain to be gold. Farnsworth's affidavit:[70]

I knew Dr. M.E. Noss as of 1938 and became very closely acquainted with him in the years to follow up to 1943. In 1941, I made several visits to his camp in Hembrillo Basin, San Andres Mountains at which time Dr. Noss showed me several bars of metal of which I am convinced was gold. But to further my conviction, Mr. Noss gave me a small piece, which Dr. Noss and I sawed off of one corner of one of four bars he had in his possession at that time. I took this to Los Angeles and had an assay run on it at Captain Zimmerman's laboratory. I do not remember the exact figures on the assay, but I recall it ran very high and about 900 fine. It was a very good grade of gold.

The several bars I saw I estimated them to weigh about 20 lbs. each. I testify that Dr. M.E. Noss had these bars in his possession and they had to come from somewhere. They were of ancient moldings and I am positive that Dr. M.E. Noss was telling the truth when he said there were more where he got the one he had.

Dr. Noss in a sense gave his life trying to uncover the treasure that he had found. In my opinion, Dr. M.E. Noss was at times almost or very near to a nervous breakdown not knowing what to do with the vast fortune he claimed to have found for fear of losing it or his life, which ended in him losing his life.

I would sincerely like to see Mrs. Ova Noss obtain whatever necessary help either from the state or the U.S. government to continue the search for this vast fortune, which I sincerely believe in, and sincerely believe Mrs. Noss is entitled to any cooperation that the government or officials might be able to give her.   —Ted Farnsworth

~

---

* In the 1930s the hotel was one of several in the Alberts Hotel chain; the stationary reads: *McCoy Hotel.*

In 1941, Doc filed more claims and formed a company with minimum financing to remove the debris, but he was faced with a multitude of problems: difficulty in gaining access to the Peak, lack of manpower because of World War II and threats and harassment. These problems combined prevented any hope of a successful completion.

Camp Notes —January 1941

Horzmann wrote a synopsis[71] of the entire year 1941:

> *Considerably excited and worried over the closing of the only entrance, brought about concerted activity to get help, and a group was formed consisting of more than 20 people. Later, more financing was raised, and the shaft was opened up, timbered, and other exploration work was done from the 12th day of May 1941 through July 12, 1941.*
>
> *A contract had been let to a pair of investors, Barman & Robinson, who failed to reopen the cavern and forfeited their contract. Doc claimed the tunnel leading to the rooms containing the valuables was 2,750 feet long. Many attempts were made to convict Doc of fraud, but there was never any evidence to prove such. His freedom was worth more than his conviction. He claimed to have been a secret investigator, and had various cards to show he was connected with the sheriff's office.*

April 2, 1941

In contrast to the January 1941 synopsis, much can be drawn from Horzmann's writings only three months later on April 2, 1941, that she and her husband, Carl, had a plan of action aimed at putting Doc in jail and a jingle in their own pockets. The inference made by her writings was that Governor John E. Miles was somehow playing a role behind-the-scenes in their scheme, but it is most likely not true. Although the real truth and depth of Horzmann's secret activities were never discovered during the time that she had worked at Victorio Peak, Ova, Letha, and Doc had long *suspected* that she and Carl were acting as agents or collaborators for individuals at the local and/or federal level. Merle had been successful at establishing herself in the middle of Doc's camp at Victorio Peak, and judging from the letters and camp notes written by her over the years, the Noss family's uncertainties about Horzmann's loyalties were well founded. Horzmann ate their food, was paid cash for her efforts and she was given a 1% interest in the treasure by Doc and Ova for her services as secretary of the soon-to-be-formed Cheyenne Mining Company, yet she chose to scheme against them, especially against Doc. A letter written by Merle to her husband on April 2, 1941, supports the Noss family's suspicions that Merle maintained an undercover status on behalf of different law enforcement agencies. From her letter:[72] (underlining inserted)

Camp notes —April 2, 1941

Just a few lines this morning; I had a talk with Ownby last night and if it is known that this thing [the Victorio Peak treasure] is being unearthed, we will all be cut out of the deal, so keep mum...

But it is entirely too big a thing to let go by without doing all we can to help the old folks out, and ultimately ourselves. Whatever it is, will be reverted back to the Mexican Government, I think, but if you will get "Coronado's Children" from the library, I think it will contain the story of the deposed ruler, Maximilian. I am enclosing a paper I want you to keep under tight cover, so you will have it when the time comes. The next one [a paper or letter] involves $225,000,000, but if too much gets out about this one, they will be unable to go after the other. But when the time comes, I have access now to N.Y. Times, L.A. Times, Life, Curtis, etc. [I] will probably take a 'con' letter [confirming letter] shortly. You see, Mr. O's [Ownby's] part will be close to $2--- ---- [$2 million dollars], and my share will be somewhere about 1/8 or more, provided I can do my part ($32.5 million in 1941). I am afraid to do anything that might complicate matters in any way. My status is entirely different here from what it was before, so you can understand a lot now.

By the end of the week many things will look different, as Ownby is looking for a letter concerning everything there. It is probable I wouldn't be allowed in on it, but that can be managed, too, and especially if Mr. Martin* comes with his plane.

I know this all sounds like big talk, and it is just a lot better if we don't say anything, but unless you understood just how it all is, and which I can't explain now, you would see why. Tell A.M. he can read this paper, but you keep it yourself. It was taken from the original copy. I have one that nobody knows about, and I am sending you the carbon. <u>You better not tell anybody there I am in on Government Affairs</u>, or it may make it hard for me in case I should fail to obey the rules. This is information for you and Herman [Merle and Carl's son] and me, and that is what I referred to about him a few months ago.

This job with Holt is in order that all of this can be worked out, because he [Holt] is a personal friend of Governor Miles, even if I don't get a salary, so that is still another angle nobody else knows about. He is a personal friend of Governor Miles and Mrs. Miles, and they visit back and forth.   —Merle

P.S. ---I hate to deprive you of the car, but it may be the means of our getting on top now, so just get ready, just in case. Will see how I can manage by the end of this week.

~

Merle Horzmann might have never known it, but Commissioner Miles and Doc had a few things in common: they were both from Oklahoma, they had moved from there to New Mexico, Doc was a descendant from the Cheyenne Nation and Miles was a descendant from the Cherokee Nation, and Miles' wife, Susie, was a descendant of the Choctaw Nation. Miles full name was John Easten Miles, born on July 28, 1884, in Murfreesboro, Tennessee. Doc left home at the age of ten; Miles set out on his own when he was seventeen, but when it came to politics, they went in opposite directions; Doc disliked politics and most politicians, especially at the federal level. Not so for John Miles, drawn

---

* The reference to a Mr. Martin and his plane is unknown.

by his desire to seek a position in government, he became active in politics, which began in the 1920s: Quay County Assessor, New Mexico State Tax Commission and by 1935, Democratic State Central Committee Secretary and finally a dark horse in the race for Governor in 1938. His success in politics was attributed to his keen understanding of the principles of government and an unquenchable thirst to serve in public office, but he was forced to keep his Native American ancestry under a bushel basket, otherwise racism in New Mexico politics would have dealt him out of contention. When he completed his term of office as governor, Miles became Chairman of the Public Service Commission and served in that position from 1943 to 1948. He also served as the Commissioner of Public Lands from 1944 to 1948 and one term as Congressman. John Miles died in October 1971.

Camp Notes —May 2, 1941

Horzmann became more involved in Doc and Ova's exploration activities, but not yet as secretary for their mining company. According to Horzmann, O.G. Turner had called Ownby from Las Cruces to see if he was still interested in the Victorio Peak operation; J.W. Parr, the father of Roscoe Parr, took Horzmann and Colonel Holt to Lordsburg. Either she or Ownby introduced Colonel Holt to J.W. Parr. Holt invested in the recovery operation.

Camp Notes —May 7, 1941

On May 7, Horzmann wrote two letters[73] to Carl, but it is not certain which one was drafted first. The more polite letter is shown here: Horzmann wrote:

> Dr. Noss and Mr. Parr were here this afternoon; much to our surprise, and at the same time the letter came. They had trouble getting Mr. Holt's check cashed and drove all the way from Las Cruces to get it here.
>
> Mr. Holt and Mr. Ownby and probably I, will go to Alamogordo next Sunday if they have the cave opened enough for us to see it, and begin compiling our data for publicity.
>
> I thought for a while Holt was going to hold up payment of the check and he deliberated a long time before he finally went to the bank and got it, but I was not the one to say do or don't. But it is only $500, and Holt gets the publicity rights. I guess I will have the work to do. But I can do it if they let me go along and see whatever there is to see, but if they try to keep me out of it, I think I shall kick up about it—maybe.
>
> Anyway, if you do get the hundred, will have to have some expense money to run around with, and will write my own copy for whatever my angle of the story would be for something that would not interfere with theirs, or his [meaning Doc]. Dr. Noss was offered $10,000 for the publicity rights from the El Paso Times and $20,000 from the L.A. Times, but he is turning it over to us---Holt.

Well, probably I can squeeze in some groove with it, but just where, I don't know yet, until I get certain other information. I think they are planning to let us in the cave to take pictures and get advance material. But Holt is so old and slow, I'm just afraid he will not be able to handle it all. Just wish we could get hold of a movie camera. Will have to get flashes, and what not. Was just hoping that Hahn would come on down with his. It isn't everybody I would give out information to, but I think he would be all right.

You could write about me and my part in this thing from what you know about things I have done out here and wind up with my final story of the search for the golden keys. Or probably Elizabeth would like to do that. Anyway, if it does break, there will be no time to do it after it starts, because every paper in the country and all the magazines will be after it.

Just talked to an aviator about flying over it and getting overhead pictures, and he thinks he can do it if he has a little time to prepare for time from the students. So things are developing fast. So I am wondering if I can have time to visit when you do come down.

I told Dr. Noss a while ago that I had written you to come on down with a good strong man and some good six-shooters to help haul the bullion. He said that was just fine, to come right along. They seem to like me real well.

Well, won't write more tonight, as it is time to get out another story from the aviator. Will write more as things progress.

Thanks for the check. It comes in darned handy. Was wondering how to stretch things, but hope it won't have to be this way much longer.   —*Merle*

~

Horzmann's second letter[74] to her husband that day was disingenuous; her reference to Doc seemed to be a deliberate ethnic slur, which she extended to Ova, naming her as the chief's wife. Her second letter, in part: (underlining inserted)

Just got your letter with the enclosure, and just as I started to answer it Mr. Holt got in from Las Cruces, and tells me I don't need the money. But I think I am going to get a definite statement from Ownby that I am to come in on his [meaning that her interest in the treasure would come from B. B. Ownby's interest], in order that I may be protected. He said the engineers came in with $5,000.00 and promised to do their part, but they are to get 1/3. <u>The chief [Doc] and his wife</u> are to have 1/3, and Ownby, Turner and Parr are to have the other 1/3. Then Mr. Holt is to be protected out of <u>the chief's part</u>, and I am to be protected out of Ownby's and Parr and Turner's sons are to be protected out of theirs. This is the way I understand it, but there is one other I can't quite get straight, who comes in on a grubstake to the <u>Indian</u> [a reference to Doc]?

Now, don't expect that we will get anything out of this thing right away, but the Gov't will have to identify it, accept it, etc., and then make their deductions, and all the other details come in on it, but they are trying to keep it as simple as possible.

They are to start operating no later than Monday, and expect it to be all over within 30 days. That may be while you are here, and it may be later, but I am not leaving until it all clears up, so don't bother to bring anything with you except little things like I will tell you about later, to get along with while you are here. They [Barman & Robinson] were given six months, however, to do the work in.

~

There were other matters discussed in the second letter, such as Carl's $10.00 grocery bill, a $23.00 gasoline bill and a $6.33 gas and water bill, however, the focus of her letter was based on what she and Carl expected to gain once the treasure was uncovered and the government had taken its share. Whatever Merle and Carl's connection was to the government was not evident in these letters, and the division of each one's interest was somewhat convoluted. But one thing was clear, even though Doc, according to Horzmann, had been offered $10,000 for the "publicity rights" to the story from the El Paso Times and $20,000 from the L. A. Times, he chose to turn that income over to the others, meaning Horzmann and Colonel Holt. The contrast between how she referenced Doc and Ova in the first letter as *Dr. Noss* and in the second as the *chief and his wife* and the *Indian* is consistent with other demeaning remarks linked to her ongoing efforts to corral Doc with the Lorius-Heberer murders. Four months later, on September 12, while Horzmann was highly involved with Chief Summers and Captain Vermillion, she wrote, "We are about to see the end of an Indian's pipe dream, I think."

Camp Notes —May 14, 1941

After her visits to the Hembrillo basin it was common for Merle to confer with her husband about the goings on there; a week later, she wrote to Carl providing him with information about recent activity. From her letter of May 14, 1941:

This thing is in a sort of a mess. He [Doc] showed me all about the places they had dug, according to the signs, and they have all checked up as represented. But so far, [I] have not seen anything taken out, other than what I told you in my last letter. Will be there at least 20 days, if not thirty, but [I] am all right. It is a hard place to get to and you would never find it alone.

~

According to Horzmann, Doc had contracted with Barman & Robinson to do the needed excavation work, but they did not fulfill his contract, at least up to this date. But Doc had received a call from Robinson indicating that they would be out to the Peak. More from her letter:

The main thing about the thing is, that as I see it, there was a cave-in,* or slide, which prevented them from getting into it without an engineer, and the one they had contracted with has not fulfilled his contract up to this time, but there was a phone call from him

---

* The cave-in was a reference to the collapse of the top entrance on November 15, 1940, six months earlier.

when we got in saying he would be out. So that there should be plenty doing right away. They have 20 days to carry it out.

~

It was Doc's actions and Horzmann's interpretation of events that set the tempo of her letters and accusations against him. Doc was certainly a pistol, but there is rarely a time in her writings, perhaps only once, when Horzmann exhibited a sense of understanding about the conditions and the stress generated by the presence of the treasure and what it took in terms of organization and effort to maintain a reasonable recovery effort. Horzmann never rested when it came to portraying Doc negatively, even when Doc was apparently being a jokester, and she rarely failed to insert her opinion and influence in all matters and was equally diligent in making Doc appear to be the quintessential madman of the Hembrillo Basin. More:

Believe me, I certainly miss hearing from you, but there is something doing all the time out there. But Monday night [the 12th] he threatened a killing before morning and everyone was on their toes. It was really funny, but it turned out all right by morning. He got drunk, and when he gets a little it is a little too dangerous to cross him in any way, and if he thought anybody was double-crossing him, it would be just too bad.

~

Horzmann did not stay at the Rock House full-time; all indications were that she roomed in town with another interested party, perhaps Holt and his wife. When she wasn't staying at the Rock House, or the Henderson bunkhouse, she and the others who were there to do the needed work pitched their tents and set up their lean-tos near the Rock House and parked the cars and trucks wherever a spot could be found. There was always someone there to do the cooking and there was a spring nearby where water could be fetched for drinking, cooking and bathing. Letha and Dorothy would come to Victorio Peak often to take part in the excitement associated with the treasure. Seen here with their friend, Kay Milner, the trio rarely missed a chance to

be together at camp, which always included Buster. Even in the colder spring months, the girls often climbed to the top of the Peak to view the collapsed shaft. Letha, Dorothy, Kay and Ova are seen here with an engineer (name unknown) surveying the possibilities of rebuilding the top shaft shoring that was damaged and buried in the collapse.

When Letha was not with her friends, she would cherish the times she rode the Hembrillo Basin on her horse, Gallup,*and viewed the sights and searched for ancient petroglyphs and Spanish treasure signs that were in great number in the basin. Her favorite spot was the Hembrillo Canyon, the site of Bloody Hands, a sacred place that three decades later would be the source of great wealth for a few criminals who came there to plunder part of the Noss treasure, tons of gold bullion that Doc had hidden there over a ten-year period.

The campsite at Victorio Peak was rugged, demanding, and yet beautiful to those who enjoyed being in a desert wilderness. Horzmann commented on the challenge it presented. From her letter: [75]

> *Believe me, life out there should toughen me a little both spiritually and physically, and I believe it will. The only thing is, that it is fifty-miles from any place and over flats and mountains. Will be out to meet you when you come down, unless the fireworks are on, and in that case, you had better go on to Lordsburg, but I just can't plan a thing yet.*

> ~

Apart from the common issues she discussed in her letters with Carl, there was the other side of the coin: the agenda that she and Carl kept hidden from everyone—their betrayal of Doc and Ova.

> *Well, all the officers are waiting for me to let them know what I have found out, and [I] have several letters to write before 5. Am at the C. of C.† office now taking advantage of their hospitality, and Mr. Holt's introduction...*   —*Yours, Merle*

> ~

The impression that can be drawn from this letter is Horzmann's own estimate of her capabilities as a spy or a criminal investigator for law enforcement officials. In the end, she produced nothing of substance concerning Doc's activities. Instead, she intentionally misdirected the police by making broad accusations and unfounded claims promoted by her disloyal, divisive and hostile mindset.

---

* After the town, Gallup, in New Mexico where Doc traded gold for cash
† "C of C" was the Lordsburg, New Mexico Chamber of Commerce; Colonel Willard E. Holt was its Secretary. He was also supposed to have been a faculty member of a local school or college.

With all of the difficulties that arose at the Rock House, and apart from Horzmann's personal agenda that festered in the background, there was always the chance of Doc, or someone in the camp, being kidnapped and tortured to learn where the gold was located. And there was the ever-increasing risk of Doc getting picked up by the Secret Service for possessing gold bars, or being shot by someone who knew he had them. But greater than any problem that came with finding and having a claim on an outrageously large treasure trove was the aftermath *and* the real-time consequences that stemmed from Doc's drinking habits and his wild spending habits when he was drunk. No matter how much money Doc had after he sold some of the gold bars, he chose to celebrate and consequently the cash went through his hands like water through a sieve. Another serious problem he had was his general unawareness that someone working for him was also working *against* him in the shadows for personal gain.

Camp Notes — May 15, 1941

She wrote another letter to Carl the following day. It began with a brief story describing how she and others were driving back to camp and had to turn around and go back to Las Cruces because the car was overheating. Merle Horzmann's letters were written from a variety of venues: among them, was a letter she wrote from Lordsburg's Chamber of Commerce office where Colonel Willard E. Holt worked as the Chamber's Secretary. It was in 1927 that Charles Lindbergh stopped at Lordsburg's newly constructed airfield during his transcontinental "Spirit of Saint Louis" flight. During the early expansion days of the old west, Lordsburg was the quintessential *cowboy town* depicted in many western films.

But Lordsburg had a dark history as well. It was there during World War II that 1,500 American citizens were held captive in a Japanese-American internment camp; the U.S. Army oversaw its operation. The camp also held captured Italian and German soldiers. It wasn't long after it opened that an Army sentry, Private First Class Clarence Burleson, shot and killed two Japanese-American prisoners there. However, a military court-martial found that Burleson had acted within the law when he killed the prisoners.

Lordsburg was also the birthplace of New Mexico's official state song, *O Fair New Mexico*. It was written by one of its residents, a blind woman who was the daughter of Sheriff Pat Garrett. Elizabeth Garrett's father lived in Las Cruces and was murdered there while he was the town's sheriff. The opening verses of Elizabeth's song:

> *Under a sky of azure,*
> *Where balmy breezes blow,*
> *Kissed by the golden sunshine,*
> *is Nuevo Mejico.*
> *Land of the Montezuma,*
> *With fiery hearts aglow,*
> *Land of the deeds historic,*
> *is Nuevo Mejico.*
> *~*

Horzmann often wrote her letters from the Hotel Herndon in Las Cruces or from one of the outbuildings situated at the Henderson ranch where people who were working at the Noss claim site on Victorio Peak often stayed. Merle Horzmann's May 15th letter:[76]

> *Just got your letter this morning. …As far as I know, there had been no contact with any other paper on the publicity rights. Mr. Holt and I have the contract to get the publicity, and to sell it to who ever we want to.*
>
> *So far, I have put in very little, but as I believe I explained in one of my recent letters to you, my share will come through Holt and Ownby without much investment on my part, but things are so touchy that one can never tell which way the wind is going to blow. Noss and his wife don't pull together, and she does little things sometime that just put a crimp in what he does, and it makes him hard to get along with, but I can't blame him much. He has things figured out to a fine point, and if he could get the cooperation from the people he is dealing with without her, he could get it done and it would be all right, or she could get it done without him. But he drinks, and they said last night that the next time he came in and got drunk they would slap him in jail and hold him until we could get it opened up, and then we could come and get him and have him check it [the treasure] all over. It might be one safe way to do [it], but he has also said that if he couldn't enjoy it nobody could. But anyway, if it is still there as he said, it is worth working for.*
>
> *Mr. Holt came up last night, and two of the men came in and met him, and took him out to look it over, and it is a good thing they took him instead of me. But we have all the groceries in this car, and they were out of some of the things. But*  *they will be in again today, so if I can't get back out, they can take them on out with them. The Hup* is too low to get it over these roads, and the body is too long, but a Ford or Chevrolet or the older model is all right.*
>
> *Noss told me yesterday that if I could stay on the job he knew he could get things done, because I understand how to do things from a business standpoint, and he just wished he had known me when he first found it. But at that time, of course, I wouldn't have had the experience and knowledge I have now, either.*
>
> *Did I tell you that I had gotten a Deputy's Commission for Otero County? That is in order to be able to qualify to witness the removal and check on it according to Law. I might reveal to you now, too, that I have become Secret Service Operator, 3549-G. This is my first assignment, and they have welcomed my effort. No one has been able to get up to the place before—that is the investigators. So, one more score, and if I come out on this one, I have it from still another angle.*

~

* *Hup* is a *Hupmobile*, as seen in this 1934 (417-W) 4-Dr. Sedan. Source: Lars-Göran Lindgren, Sweden

Here is a case where Horzmann boasts about the confidence Doc has in her and her abilities, then, on the other hand she boasts about her connections to the U.S. Secret Service and how she will fare in her efforts because of her work and association with the government. More from her letter:

Things are now pivoted around whatever I say, and up to a certain point are carried out pretty much the same way. Went in to the bank here, and Mr. Spence, the President, cashed my check right now without any red tape I have to go through in Lordsburg. He is one of the men I met at the convention. The people here are so friendly and nice, and everybody I have met so far have just offered to do anything they could to help me in whatever I might need. But then the letter from Mr. Holt has been the trick that did it. But now, I have access to the best people here. Mr. Spence asked me what I was doing here, and I told him I was investigating a case, but right now he's all smiles. So I believe if I wanted a job I could get it doing that right here. It pays around $125.00 a month, so as soon as I know where this other thing [the Noss treasure trove issue] is or isn't, will get some recommendations and start traveling towards home, or whatever direction I can make it with assurance that I could get into things if I wanted to. Won't get a salary on this case, but will share some of the find.

However, this is confidential, just between you and me, and may not turn out just that way, but I believe if I prove this case [blaming the Lorius-Heberer murders on Doc Noss] it will put me tops with even the FBI who have tried to get into it and couldn't. The only thing they have been able to do was to get his fingerprints, but they have never been on the property. There have been two planes flying over it [Victorio Peak], though, since I have been out there. Whether that is them or not, I wouldn't know just yet.

...They are digging the new shaft, and then the engineer who started on it before called yesterday [Barman & Robinson] and said he would be there in a few days with a crew to work on it, so nobody knows just what to do.

I thought the news part of the story would have come out first. Just as soon as there is something to write about, and we have the official check-up on it, will start the ball rolling. But will know more when I have a chance to talk to Mr. Holt. Had just a few minutes last night, and the rest seemed to be afraid I would talk about something they [a possible reference to people with the FBI or the Secret Service] didn't want me to, so his [Holt's] time was taken up with them and I didn't get a chance to say a word. Though if they got back today, would be able to.

The people [a possible reference to the Secret Service] here have been of the opinion that this bar was smuggled in. But I don't know about that. His [Doc's] story is too logical, and his proof so far has checked up with the copy I sent, so far as I can tell.

——*Merle*

~

In the years to come (during the mid-60s to the mid-70s), the shibboleth of the Army at White Sands Proving Ground (later in the 50s it was re-named White Sands Missile Range) was that if there *was* gold inside Victorio Peak someone smuggled it in.

May 19, 1941

The military conflicts with the Native tribes in the American Southwest began around 1846 and continued beyond the Civil War that ended in 1865; many Civil War veterans fought in the Indian Wars that ended in 1895. The conflict with the tribes, or bands living in the Southwest, which included nearly every non-Pueblo tribe, raged off and on between periods of fighting and trading for hundreds of years, long before the United States annexed the same geographical region from Mexico in 1848.

It was in March of 1883 that Territorial Ranger Brad Bramble Ownby rode from Lordsburg with a posse to Silver City forty-four miles to the north. They returned with the bodies of Judge McComas and his wife, who were killed by Geronimo and Chato, the Chief of the Chiricahua Apache. Ownby was well known and played a significant role in the process of law in Lordsburg; not only was he a retired Indian War veteran, but he was also a National Judge-Advocate. Ownby wrote[77] to Horzmann on May 19th. His letter:

> Your letter also the card received. Was glad to hear from you and to know that you are well pleased with the outlook. I let Holt [Colonel Holt] and Bradley* read the letter and they both seemed to be very well pleased. Everything is going along over here about as usual and as I hear anything of importance to write about I will.
>
> —B. B. Ownby

~

Ownby's connection to Victorio Peak might have begun with a personal relationship he had with Doc Noss. However, Horzmann and Ownby lived in Lordsburg, a more likely cause of his being involved with the Noss treasure, but that is conjecture.

Camp Notes — May 21 - 28, 1941

The problems at Victorio Peak went beyond the difficulties experienced in gaining access to the treasure. Marauders were also a problem. Horzmann wrote about it:

> Three of the "Old Guerrilla Gang" had been around. Doc made a rule that no one was to leave camp alone because he had gold hidden out there. Funds are getting low. Many times Doc made the remark that he would make every pale face he could suffer for the wrongs done to his family, Starr [a reference to outlaws Tom and Belle Starr], and his tribe and the Indians in general. Doc grew very bitter at times over it, and this seemed to be his way of getting vengeance.[78]
>
> Ben Galloway, Chapman, Duncan, friends of Turner and Parr, arrived, also Jack Bruton, landowner, looking for some of his cattle. Doc came back. No release. He was supposed to get approval from Washington on a permit for removal of bullion, but did not get it. All he did was to have the attorney write Washington for instructions for

---

* B. B. Ownby's middle name was Brad. Bradley was likely his son.

removing the bullion. Doc had $16 left of $120/155; spent money for a quart of wine, fine of $9.80, $20 for horse straps, cooking gas, hotel bills, $28 for telephone call to Washington, in which he was to have promised President Roosevelt to be there Monday morning. The call was supposedly made from Bill Goodman's office in El Paso. Doc was also to have made arrangements to fly to Washington in Goodman's plane. They were also supposed to go to the Smithsonian Institute with the crown, the crucifix, a gold bar, and other items. Holt was to go with them.   *—Merle Horzmann*[79]

~

After supper on the 28th, Ova gave an account* of that night. Doc said,

> *One night after supper at the camp, Doc said, 'You boys come back when the table is cleared off, I want to talk to you.' They came in, and Doc laid down his paper and said, 'Boys, people are the most peculiar things on this earth. Animals don't hurt the animals. They just eat when they want. A little bird told me that we have a Judas in our midst. To think a son-of-a-bitch would eat my food, sleep in my bed, while I pay him wages.' They said one after another, and said it to Doc, 'It isn't me.'*
>
> *Doc realized there was a stool pigeon in the crowd. Coming in one night (on their way to Hot Springs) he stopped the car when we came to a bridge, and went under the bridge. Eppie Montoya was the stool pigeon. Doc always pulls his gloves on when he's ready to start a scrap. When they came into town they stopped at a drugstore and Eppie used the phone to call the sheriff, who brought his man and searched the baggage and Doc insisted that they repack the bags. They said they didn't have time. Doc said he didn't have the time either. They finally repacked the bags. On the way back, Doc stopped at the bridge and retrieved the bar of gold, and they teased him about having to stop so often. They all took pictures of the bullion.*   *—Babe*

~

These were the things that pushed Doc to the edge, but his accusations that Montoya was a spy eventually came to light. In May 1941, Eppie Montoya, who was from Santa Fe, went to work for Doc at Victorio Peak; Doc had met Montoya earlier in the year in Alamogordo. Little did anyone know at the time, but when Montoya showed up for work, he had been deputized by a U.S. Marshal, and if he was ever found out, Montoya was to give the story that he had been hired to protect Doc's claim when and if Doc began moving the gold from the main cavern. Soon afterwards, and it is not clear how it came about, but Doc had been given the heads up on Montoya. Years later, on October 19, 1952, Montoya signed the following affidavit:[80]

> *On this 19ᵗʰ day of October, A.D. 1952, I, Eppie Montoya, a resident of 622 Alto St., Santa Fe, New Mexico, telephone 38472 was employed by B.D. Lampros. In May 1941, I was deputized by U.S. Marshals to go to work for (Doc) M.E. Noss at the El Hembrillo Basin in the San Andres Mountains, New Mexico, Socorro County, (at*

---

* O. Noss, *op. cit.*, pp. 6-8

old ranch house) to excavate for a treasure of Doc M.E. Noss, which he is supposed to have found. During my stay there, I had the opportunity and privilege to see some bars supposed to be gold, and yellow in color which he had taken out of this cave in Victorio Peak, one of which I held and examined. It was brick form, larger at bottom than at top, slanting up on all sides, and weighing approximately twenty to twenty-five pounds. Doc told me that there was a great many more in the cave that had caved in. Dirt and rubbish had to be removed to get to the room. At the time that I discovered this bar there were four or five people present. —Eppie Montoya

~

Montoya had been working for Lampros in Santa Fe. What type of work he did for him is unknown, but when help was needed at Victorio Peak, Lampros encouraged him to come and help with the excavation work. Considering that Doc and Lampros were close friends, it is most likely that Lampros was unaware of Montoya's arrangements with the U.S. Marshal's office. What information Montoya might have given to the federal agents, if any, is also unknown.

Camp Notes —May 31, 1941

Merle was counting her chickens before they hatched, again. In her May 31 letter[81] to Carl she heightened the suspense by encouraging him to do the math on their share from the future sale of the treasure. At first the numbers meant little. In part from her letter:

…I can't tell you about things now, but just set tight. Don't plan anything right now, other than to just take care of things there. It may take two more weeks here and it may take 6 months, but just know that I'm not going to do any planning, either until it is all over and I know what to do and how. One false move right now would spoil everything. No one is permitted to leave camp, and no one permitted to enter without heavy guard, so you will have to draw your own conclusions until I can tell you all about it when the time is right. But one thing I can tell you is to take these figures and work them out. 152 x 53 x 2 x 10,000 - 1 % ratio of 120 =? But don't tell anyone about it. It may figure much different by the time it is over with, as no one knows just what it is. Am not even permitted to write Mr. Holt, and if I leave camp, can't get back in again.

Must quit now as someone will be going in soon now and I can send this in. Am also sending the lease back to Mr. Long. Told him to send it on back to Santa Fe and let them send it to Mr. Hahn. …Thanks for the blue slip. You should see me riding the horse and carrying my 6-shooter. —Merle

~

Hahn remains a mystery, as does Mr. Long.

Camp Notes —June 6, 1941

More notes from Horzmann:

Money is needed for the trip to Washington, D.C., which had been planned. Parr and Roscoe went to town. —Merle Horzmann

~

The same day:

Doc planned to break for his Washington trip from 8th to 22nd so he could make rounds for final preliminaries. He took pictures of the peak and padlocked shaft.

—Merle Horzmann[82]

Camp Notes —June 6, 1941

Carl wrote to Merle the same day with the financials he calculated from the figures she sent him a week earlier, illustrating their potential return on the sale of Doc and Ova's gold. From Carl's letter:[83]

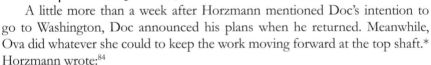

...The total of the figures you sent me was $165,120,000.00 and 1% of the amount would be $1,651,200.00 or a return of over 100,000 per dollar invested. Just hope that it will all come out the way it looks now, because then all of our dreams could come true.

—CWH

~

The actual amount would have been $161,120,000.00.

Camp Notes —June 7, 1941

A little more than a week after Horzmann mentioned Doc's intention to go to Washington, Doc announced his plans when he returned. Meanwhile, Ova did whatever she could to keep the work moving forward at the top shaft.*
Horzmann wrote:[84]

A meeting was called in the rock house at 11:30 by the president, Dr. M.E. Noss, and he discussed his plans informally for the opening of the cave around June 22, if all goes well [in Washington] and his preparations in the meantime. The shaft was padlocked. Instructions were given that all were to return to camp on that date provided there were no accidents or other valid reasons. Camp broke temporarily at twelve o'clock noon.

—Merle Horzmann

Camp Notes —June 7, 1941[85]

As good as his intentions were, Doc never made it out of Socorro County. Ova wrote:

Most all of the crew left camp. Doc was arrested and put in jail. He apparently had entered Ritch's Townhouse and picked a fuss. Merle Horzmann and Doc each thought the other were to blame. Parr not back yet. We were told to go to Hot Springs. The charges against Doc were made from Socorro County. Doc held in Otero County.   —Babe

~

---

* Hugh Hunter, Ova Noss, Merle Horzmann and Claude Fincher are seen here preparing to work in the top shaft.

The account mentioned in Ova's letter referred to another brawl Doc had been involved in at Ritch's Townhouse in Hot Springs. Apparently, Watson Ritch Jr. was the owner of the business where Doc got involved. It is not clear what happened, but whatever it was, it landed Doc in jail—*again*. Apparently, Doc, Ova and Horzmann were together when things got out of control. Since Doc landed in jail, it is unlikely that it was simply a shouting match—he was probably the first one to throw. Doc always packed his six-shooter and that must have presented a problem for the sheriff *and* Doc. It seemed to be a needless replay of the event that took place at Ann's Place in Roswell, New Mexico, nearly seven years earlier in November 1934.

Camp Notes —June 9-13, 1941[86]

Colonel Holt signed Doc's bond in Alamo* Courthouse. Doc's trial was set for Saturday in Socorro. He had a meeting and the Washington D.C. trip plan was knocked in the head. Doc showed Attorney Newell the sword and a gold bar but Newell remained neutral on the matter. Doc promised to pay Merle Horzmann $25 expense money. The big dinner we had probably had been paid for by Ben Galloway. Merle Horzmann checked with the attorney in Las Cruces. He said he wasn't going to represent Doc in the case. No confidence in the case. But finances were arranged and he then agreed to represent Doc. The money apparently came from Parr. Newell went to Socorro—childish charges. A $300 bond was set. Case set for fall term. —Babe

~

There was a conference today for drawing up agreements for percentages.

—Merle [87]

Camp Notes —June 14, 1941

The meeting on June 14, 1941 was the first meeting[88] of the Cheyenne Mining Company held in Las Cruces at the office of J. Benson Newell; the agreements were drafted at that meeting. Present were: Doc, Ova, Claude Fincher, Letha (Guthrie) Beckwith, O.G. Turner, J.W. Parr, Roy Chapman, G.R. Duncan, George Turner, Don Callaway, Mack Turner, Ernest Gatlin, Roscoe Parr, B.D. Lampros, Carl W. Horzmann, Benson Newell, William Scoggin, Colonel Willard Holt, Don and Mrs. Breech, and C.D. Patterson. Company members were Doc, Ova, Roscoe Parr, Lampros, Fincher, Willard Holt, Don Breech, C.D. Patterson, and twelve others; the largest shareholders were Fred Barman and Lester L. Robinson of Los Angeles, who were brought into the group by someone other than Doc, possibly Roscoe Parr. The other highest interest holders were Ova, Doc, and Jack Bruton.

Doc was made President, Ova, Vice President, Claude Fincher, Treasurer, and Merle Horzmann, Secretary. The agreement stated that the failure of

---

* Alamo is located on the Alamo Bend Navajo Indian Reservation about 100 miles from Victorio Peak.

anyone to perform for thirty days after the work was required to begin constituted a forfeiture of their rights and interest in benefits, except forfeiture was
not applicable to vested interest by work done.

The officers of the company were to conduct business and obtain supplies. A contract between Doc and Elzo Smith was recognized. Smith was an
engineer and had exclusive control of operations on the shaft work and work
had to be done to comply with the contract between Doc and Jack Bruton, who
held the state lease* on the land where the shaft was located. Company officers
were to provide boarding facilities for the crew and charge only non-workers
for boarding. Prevailing wages were to be figured by the officers, who were not
charged for subsistence at camp. Any injury or Selective Service draft would
not cost one's interest.

Percentages of interest were as follows: Don Breech of Portales 1%, Jack
Bruton of Rincon 5.22%, Ova 18.78%, Claude Fincher of Hot Springs 3%,
Merle Horzmann of Lordsburg 1%, Letha (Guthrie) Beckwith of Hot Springs
1%, O.G. Turner of Friona, Texas 3%, J.W. Parr of Muleshoe, Texas 3%, Roy
Chapman of Cimarron, New Mexico 3%, G.R. Duncan of Texico, New Mexico
3%, George Turner of Friona 1%, Ben Galloway of Friona 3%, Mack Turner
of Friona 1%, B.B. Ownby of Lordsburg 1%, Ernest Gatlin of Muleshoe, Texas
1%, Roscoe W. Parr of Clovis 3%, Ermile Smith of Long Beach, California
1%, B.D. Lampros of Nogales, Arizona 3%, Barman and Robinson of Los
Angeles, California, 33.3%, and Doc of Alamogordo 10.67%; Doc and Ova
held Barman and Robinson's 33.3% voting rights. Six people at the meeting
agreed to dispose of ½ of 1% of their share to raise working capital. Lampros
agreed to put up $100 when all others deposited a like sum: Turner, J.W. Parr,
Roy Chapman, Duncan, Ben Galloway, Roscoe Parr, Fred Barman and Lester
L. Robinson, and W. Parr. The officers were to notify authorities in case of a
find and comply with the law. The secretary was to file the agreement in Socorro
County and have it notarized.

The following day, Sunday, July 15, 1941, those named therein signed and
executed the agreement. More from the minutes of the meeting, in part: (underlining inserted)

> *Elzo Smith's 3%, Jack Bruton's 5.22% and Newell and Scoggin, Attorneys 3% may
> all be first deducted from proceeds of any development of this enterprise, and then the
> balance remaining shall be distributed according to the interests set-forth in said contract,
> or according to any change of interest as it may show on the records of the group when
> such distribution may be made. Newell & Scoggin are to attend to any and all legal
> matters for the group as a whole from this date on so long as the group may continue
> operations under said contract.*

~

---

* Bruton had a cattle-grazing lease only..

Under the terms of the agreement made on Friday, June 13, 1941, Scoggin and Newell stood to profit from the venture. Attorneys William Scoggin Jr. and J. Benson Newell had engaged themselves in legal and financial transactions with Doc's newly formed company, the Cheyenne Mining Company; Newell and Scoggin took a 3% professional fee from the top before other interests were distributed, as did Smith and Bruton.

In the years to come, Scoggin would be elected Las Cruces District Attorney and later Judge in Doña Ana County. Newell became counsel for the defense in a celebrated murder trial; the State of New Mexico vs. Charley Ryan of Alice, Texas—the murder victim was Doc Noss. At the time of his murder, Doc controlled nearly 63% of the voting rights of the Cheyenne Mining Company jointly with Ova.

~

In criminal case No. 4794 under charges of "insulting another while armed with a deadly weapon contrary to Section 35-3406 New Mexico statute" stemming from Doc's brawl at Ritch's Townhouse in Hot Springs, Doc went before District Attorney Claren M. Waggoner on September 11, 1941; the case was filed the next day. Then, on Tuesday, October 14, a jury trial[89] commenced. This time, unlike the incident at Ann's Place in Roswell, Doc was found not guilty:

> *We, the Jury, find the defendant, M.E. Noss, not guilty under instructions of the*
> *Court.   —Manuel Torrez, Foreman*

~

In May 1944, Winnie Ritch, Watson Ritch's wife, was accused of breaking into the Rock House and removing "sundry" items and mining equipment belonging to the "Cheyenne Mining Company" valued at $1,500.00. The case was filed in Socorro County, a protracted one that hung in legal limbo and not pursued by Doc on a timely basis. The case was also tangled in a string of legal procedural questions that were never brought to a conclusion. Doc probably lost interest. The case was eventually dismissed.

Chapter 14

More Camp Notes, Murder, Bodies, and Who Done It

L ife in the Hembrillo Basin was demanding; living in a parched desert presented many personal challenges and sacrifices, and, when gold was the centerpiece on the dinner table at the Rock House, distrust, betrayal and even death followed close behind. Ova Noss was often quoted saying, "Where gold goes, blood flows." Just off the footpath of the Jornada del Muerto, Victorio Peak stands today, a monument to an unbroken chain of events that spanned more than four hundred years of crimes and violence that have left their footprints on the doorstep of the 21st Century.

Camp Notes —June 25, 1941

Owing to unforeseen circumstances, a special meeting was held in the office of J. Benson Newell, Las Cruces, in which Elzo B. Smith submitted the following notice from Fred Barman and Lester L. Robinson of Los Angeles, California. —Merle Horzmann

~

The next matter in question at the June 25 meeting was a letter sent to Doc, Ova, Claude Fincher and S.E. Montgomery. The Robinson-Barman letter and the call for the special meeting, as stated above, was typed on a separate memorandum along with other notations:

All parties claiming any interest in the property covered by this notice, you are hereby notified, that the terms of that certain agreement dated on or about January 30, 1941, entered into by yourselves and the undersigned have been fulfilled and that the work called for thereunder has been completed and the entrance to the mine has been timbered and is ready for inspection and all further development and protection of the project is to be provided for as stipulated in said agreement, and the disposition of the treasure is to be made as therein provided. You will therefore take notice that after inspection of the mine and its underground workings, if the bullion and other treasures are found therein as represented by Dr. M.E. Noss, a meeting of all of the parties in interest will be immediately called, for the purpose of organizing an association to which each of us will convey our respective titles for which we will receive evidences of ownership in properties to our various interests and at such meeting, officers will be elected and such [action] taken as may be necessary to safeguard the rights of all parties in interest. Said agreement stipulates that the disposition of the assets and the future policy governing the further development of the project is to be first agreed to by 70% of all the vested interests as you will therefore govern yourselves accordingly.

—*Lester L. Robinson, Fred Barman*

Camp Notes —June 28, 1941[90]

All assembled at camp again on June 28, 1941. Work continued diligently until July 12 when it was temporarily suspended.

~

Barman and Robinson claimed that the construction work and shoring in the mine was complete and was ready for inspection. The notice also reminded them that should entrance to the treasure be gained as a result of the work completed, the division of shares was to proceed as called for in accordance with prior signed agreements of January 30, 1941. Reference to development and protection of the project was stipulated, and disposition of treasures to be made was provided. After the find, a meeting of all shareholders was to be called and the organization and division was to be made. The agreement was to stipulate that no disposition of assets or policy change could be made unless 70 percent agreed. But there was one problem: Barman and Robinson's money ran out and the timbered shoring went down no further than their money had, which did not provide access to the tunnel system that led to the treasure and there are no documents that indicate any suit was filed against Doc or Ova. When the Cheyenne Mining Company was formed, Barman and Robinson's percentage of interest in the treasure was indicated; however they did not have any voting rights, only a percentage of the treasure if they fulfilled their agreement of January 30. It also seems that Doc had found Horzmann's notes; whether he simply stumbled onto them or he knew where she kept them, is unknown. Regardless, the fact remains that he saw them and read them. Ova wrote about it.

Camp Notes —June 26, 1941[91]

Merle Horzmann gave notes to Bill Scoggin to put in his safe. Horzmann did not want the notes in camp. When checking her notes with Elzo Smith, Doc burst [out] in anger. His words made her think he had read her outgoing mail, so there were arguments. Doc, Breech and Frank (the cook) returned to camp. A day or so later Doc saw the letter from Holt in which he said things that Merle Horzmann knew were being conveyed to the California people (Fred Barman and Lester L. Robinson). Doc thought he should be the one to give out that information.   —Babe

Camp Notes —June 27 & 30, 1941[92]

Everyone else went to camp, including Patterson. I got Mrs. Fincher to go with me. Mrs. Fincher apparently told Doc that I had given my diary to attorney Scoggin. I went to the sheriff's office intending to talk to Tony Trujillo. Only Parker was there. My card* had expired and he tore it up, saying he would get me a new one from Tony. Doc was angry that night.   —Merle Horzmann

Doc went to town to the lawyer's office. Before he left, he gave Joe Andregg orders to take a letter over to Jack Bruton. I went along with Joe. It was about 7 miles to Paul Feydt's

---

* The card was a courtesy deputy sheriff's identification card.

place and then another 5 miles to Jack Bruton's ranch. The papers Joe delivered made
Bruton a little testy regarding the finances. He is expected to be at the coming meeting.
Jack didn't believe anything they were selling and wanted possession. Joe Andregg told
Bruton that he helped Doc hide 86 bars in a nearby canyon. Jack Bruton told Joe there
could possibly be trouble over having knowledge of it. We got lost on the return trip.

—*Merle Horzmann*[93]

~

Ova spent a great deal of time gathering corroborating testimony from individuals who claimed the discovery was genuine. Her efforts produced a sizeable number of testimonies from people who knew Doc personally, who had been to and stayed at Victorio Peak for various periods of time, and who had personally seen and held some of the bars from the treasure. Although her efforts to gather credible witnesses continued throughout her life, in 1952 she had obtained affidavits from a core of individuals who knew and trusted Doc and understood the complexities of claiming such a monumental discovery.

In July, Doc invited C.D. Patterson and Don Breech back to Victorio Peak; it was their second of several visits. They were from Portales, New Mexico. Patterson was the Mayor of Portales. The following is Patterson's affidavit[94] concerning his relationship with Doc and his knowledge of seeing gold that came from the treasure rooms. In part:

I believe I know "Doc" M.E. Noss as well as any person living today. I have had
several heart to heart talks with "Doc" and I feel he spoke the truth as to his find in the

said Victoria [Victorio] Peak. He was more
or less seeking help as to how to get the dirt out
of the cave, which was hindering his getting into
it. He offered to show me what he had taken
out before it caved in and said he had taken out
almost one hundred. When I visited Hembrillo
Basin in Socorro County in July 1941, there
were a lot of people out there helping him and
I took the opportunity to walk with "Doc." We
didn't walk far when he went over to a bush
and pulled out a bar from underneath. I was
amazed at what I saw. This one was sawed* in
two and looked like gold all the way through,
beautiful yellow, and golden. It was longer than it
was wide, and was about (3) three inches thick,
and weighed around (20) twenty pounds. Each
would have been about (40) forty pounds before

---

* Some of the gold bars were not cut completely in half, such as the one Ova Noss is holding; photo taken in the summer of 1941.

it was cut in half. Knowing how people go wild and crazy when they see gold, we never talked about our conversation when we returned to the house.*

Outsiders hindered the work being done. Not just would-be doubters, but greedy, troublemakers. Any kind of charge that could be framed against him seemed to be the trick always grabbed at. "Doc" won out in each and all courts he was hauled into, then the ones, which caused the trouble, would come crawling back to him for work.

That man went through many trials and tribulations and then was killed before he ever got to finish opening the cave he said he has found, and of which I am sure he found.

—C.D. Patterson

~

Don Breech had visited Doc at Victorio Peak for several days; he contributed to the cost of buying food for the camp to keep the work going forward. They were good friends. Here is Breech's sworn affidavit.[95] In part:

At the time I visited Doc M.E. Noss at El Humbrillo [sic] Basin in July 1941, I owned the Ford agency in Portales, New Mexico. I, along with Mr. C.D. Patterson and Mr. E.F. Foreman, all of this town, visited there for several days. Doc needed a truck of some kind to haul supplies out to the camp, so I loaned him one of mine. He kept it for several months, but after his help left, the truck was returned. I had so much confidence in the possibilities of Doc's adventure that I contributed several dollars to be used for the purchase of groceries.

While I was visiting there, I heard Doc tell the story of his find, which later, he confirmed as proof. I was shown a sword, napkin ring, old money, and a fan, which I had never seen one like before. And last, but not least, several bars, which looked like gold. Some of these had holes drilled in them, and showed the same contents as deep as the drill hole went.

In my estimation, Doc had found just what he said he had. He wasn't a blowhard and all his mind was ever on was to figure a way to remove the dirt, which had blocked his getting into where his vast wealth was.

The Second World War was declared and that stopped his getting the cave open. Few people ever had the chance to see the contents in brick form, and a treasure that had been buried many, many years.

I for one, would like to see the cave reopened, but regret very much that the finder never lived to reap his reward here on earth.   —Don Breech

~

Edgar Foreman, also from Portales, submitted a sworn statement.[96] In part:

…I was a close friend of "Doc" M.E. Noss. I visited the Humbrillo [sic] Basin in Socorro County in July 1944, and found "Doc" and his helpers at work trying to remove dirt, which had closed the entrance to the cave. An engineer named Montgomery had caused a slide in. At the time of my visit, I had the opportunity to see some of the

---

* The reference was to the Rock House.

relics and some of the bars of gold, which "Doc" said he had taken from the cave. He talked with all sincerity about the great amount still in the cave and I saw one large bar, which weighed about 40 lbs. "Doc" never at any time gave me the impression that he was out to secure money from suckers. He was very likeable, and agreeable at all times, and I know he spent all of his time and money on that mountain known as Victorio Peak. I would like to add that I am sure the bar, which "Doc" showed me, and I held in my hands, was the real stuff. I was privileged to shave off some for an assay. I do not know how pure it was, but I did see assays, which ran high in gold. Some of the men drilled holes in it and it was very pretty.

I give this statement of my own free will, and I for one, sure would like to see this treasure story of "Doc's" proven once and for all.   —Edgar F. Foreman

~

Leo D. O'Connell met Doc in Flagstaff, Arizona in 1942 and decided to quit his work and help him open the shaft. O'Connell's signed affidavit,[97] in part:

…Doc M.E. Noss told me of his find in the Hembrillo Basin so I decided to quit my work and help him open it. I immediately went to the basin and started work and he showed me gold bricks out of the mine, and his enthusiasm and what he showed me was evidence enough to convince me. Due to the fact that we ran short of finances I had to quit work, but my enthusiasm remains the same and I am ready to start work any time I can. I saw four gold bricks and tested them with acid, which convinced me that it was gold and not copper. There were several people present when the acid test was made. Doc M.E. Noss and myself worked hand in hand on Victorio Peak for a period of time approximately five and one-half months and that is where Doc said it was. Doc said there were several hundred more in there. As Doc was a personal friend of mine, and living with the man for two years, I truly believe that Doc M.E. Noss is on the right track and I am with him one hundred percent.

Of course, Doc M.E. Noss is not with us anymore and I am still ready to help finish the work that he never got finished in his lifetime.   —Leo D. O'Connell

~

B.D. Lampros met Doc in 1937 at Gallup New Mexico. When they met, Doc had already found the treasure. Lampros was one of many who submitted an affidavit after Doc had been murdered. Lampros' affidavit:[98]

I, B.D. Lampros, El Fidel Hotel, Santa Fe, New Mexico, met (Doc) M.E. Noss in Gallup, New Mexico, in the year 1937 who had recently discovered a cave at the El Humbrillo [sp] Basin, Victorio Peak, with hundreds of gold bars in a cave and later Dr. M.E. Noss and S.E. Montgomery, engineer, went over to the peak and put some dynamite sticks to make the entrance from the top larger so that they could go down into the cave easier, and unfortunately the entrance was caved in and ever since that time, up to this date, big efforts were made to open up the entrance in order to go down to the cave. Many thousands of dollars were spent in this effort. In 1939, I took one bar of gold to Douglas, Arizona, and had Hawley & Hawley assay it and it was found

that this roughly volcanic formation bar to run over five thousand dollars in gold per ton. In 1941, we were with a group of associates in the month of June that were up in the Victorio Peak where Elzo D. Smith, engineer,* who was working to open up the cave. There, we had made many pictures, I B.D. Lampros and Col. Willard E. Holt, of Lordsburg, New Mexico, were holding one-half bar each as the bar was sawed in two. The bar was a regular Wells Fargo gold bar. I saw quite a few other bars of the same type. I have financed in many occasions Dr. M.E. Noss and helped him to make his complete excavations to the entrance to the cave, and up to this date sincerely I am in hope to see the complete excavation of this cave and the great treasure to come to reality.   —*B.D. Lampros*

~

Doc was never short on engineers; besides S.E. Montgomery, the man responsible for the collapse of the shaft, who *claimed* to be a mining engineer, there was Frank Wicks, who *was* a mining engineer, who represented Barman and Robinson's interests. Elzo Smith, a regular inhabitant at the Victorio Peak site, was also an engineer, but what kind of engineer is unknown. But getting good advice from a competent engineer was not Doc's only problem; Horzmann's loyalty to the Cheyenne Mining Company was under close scrutiny.

Camp Notes —July 1-2, 1941

Babe, Letha, and Dorothy went to Alamogordo. The Breeches, Finchers, Doc, Frank and I stayed at camp. Joe and Bill Boone Davis went for lumber. Then a stranger appeared. He said he was doing assessment work on some claims Doc had filed on. Doc showed him his proof of labor. Later, the stranger left.   —*Merle Horzmann*

Doc and Don worked on my car. Later, Doc and Babe met with Prince[†] Hilliard, U.S. Commissioner,[‡] and Letha went in Farnsworth's car. I tried to get the papers from Judge Scoggin, and then I went to Lordsburg and checked to see how Doc got his information about me, especially with the "oil well" people. In one letter I wrote these things had been discussed with Mr. Ownby.   —*Merle Horzmann*

~

---

* 1941 Photo of Frank Wicks (mining engineer for Barman and Robinson) and Elzo Smith

† Prince Hilliard's role in the events at Victorio Peak was never made clear: at one time he seemed to be an investor, Doc's bodyguard, and perhaps an attorney as well.

‡ Hilliard's designation as a *U.S. Commissioner* is never explained, clarified, nor understood.

Long before Doc's murder, Horzmann was interacting with Scoggin, who by now was a County Judge. If Horzmann's connection with Scoggin was on an information-sharing basis, it probably concerned matters that involved the contract Doc had with Barman and Robinson. It seems strange that a sitting judge would be involved in legal issues regarding the Cheyenne Mining Company, a company he and Newell represented.

Seven weeks earlier, Barman and Robinson claimed that, pending an official state inspection of the shoring work they had done, they had completed the required work that would allow reentrance into the treasure rooms. By letter, Barman and Robinson claimed, *"that the terms of that certain agreement dated on or about January 30, 1941"* that Doc had entered into with them had *"been fulfilled and that the work called for thereunder has been completed."* Scoggins and Newell had attended the meeting where Robinson and Barman's interest percentages were recognized; now there was a legal issue over whether or not Robinson and Barman had performed as agreed.

On June 26, Doc was concerned that Horzmann was not keeping him advised on interactions with Barman and Robinson, a concern, which was understandable and proper. As secretary of the Cheyenne Mining Company, Horzmann should have been more concerned with providing Doc proper information about company business than she was in trying to find out how Doc discovered she was secretly conveying company information to Fred Barman and Lester L. Robinson in California. As Ova said in her June 26 letter, "Doc thought he should be the one to give out that information." The exact reason for Horzmann's direct involvement with Scoggin is unknown.

Such intrigue at the Victorio Peak campsite never ceased.

Camp Notes —July 5, 1941[99]

> I wrote to Judge Scoggin. Everyone had seen my papers. We headed out to camp the next day. It was the last day that Turner and Parr had to put up their $3,500 to complete their part of opening the shaft. Barman and Robinson had until Monday night to get it finished. Otherwise Doc and the boys were to take over.   —Merle Horzmann

Camp Notes —July 6, 1941[100]

> I photographed the Petroglyphs in the canyon Doc called the 'Bloody Hands' area or 'Aha de Ojo,' 'water under the rocks.' Parts of the drawings were paintings he called 'Alarenanda.' Another area he called 'Big Spring.' He called another area 'Ojo de Plata,' meaning 'Silver Spring.' Doc was mad today. He accused me of talking to the Turners who got the state cops and the FBI after him. Judge Scoggin and a Mr. Johnston and another man arrived today. I told them about Asa* Daklugie. She was a Chihuahua Indian living on the San Carlos reservation.   —Merle Horzmann

---

* Asa Daklugie was the husband of Ramona Chihuahua Daklugie, who Eve Ball wrote about in her book, *In the Days of Victorio.*

Camp Notes —July 7, 1941[101]

Joe Andregg was to go to his Uncle Frank's ranch but we found a Mexican in camp and he couldn't get to it. I am curious about the Mexican, Lino 'Tony' Carriaga.

—Merle Horzmann.

~

Apparently, Horzmann was not aware of Carriaga's relationship with Doc; with her ability to gather and disseminate information, it is surprising that she did not know Carriaga, or at least his long-time relationship with Doc and with the gold cache discovery in the Caballo Mountains.

Camp Notes —July 8, 10, 1941[102]

Bill Boone Davis saw a stranger ride through the Hembrillo Canyon on a black horse. A few days later, another stranger rode through on a gray horse.

—Merle Horzmann

~

One of the few times that Merle Horzmann ever showed an ounce of concern or compassion toward Doc surfaced on Thursday, July 10, 1941. It was mid-summer and the desert, as always, was oppressive. Doc was working hard in the shaft attempting to clear it. Horzmann wrote:[103]

Jack Bruton, Mr. Thompson, and Mr. Henderson, the new ranch owner, came to camp. I observed Doc as a 'pathetic' figure, who worried so much that he lost weight and he is not really himself. They went into the hole at 1:40 and at 5:20 they broke through it. When Babe came in, they told her the hole was open but nothing any of us could say would soften the hurt, whatever it was. She started to cry and said she was not even interested. She cried for a long time.

In one of the cars was her youngest son, Harold Dean Beckwith. Doc was in conversation with the Finchers about Babe and Letha. Doc had been drinking and when he approached Harold, he hit Doc with a rock. Doc struck him with the butt of his revolver. Babe fired three wild shots in the air and split wide open with profanity. Bill Lampros tried to calm things down, but he was told to back away. I thought the cause of the fuss was Doc's fault; 'Doc said he was going to get a divorce and that Letha and Harold were to get out of his life.' Fincher, Elzo Smith and his wife left the camp. Babe, Letha and Harold also left, but Doc and Turner raced after them. Babe had the key to the shaft. Doc begged them to come back. Babe came back. Later Smith came back with Letha and the others. Ted went back to Mexico. Prince Hilliard was in Alamo as sort of a personal bodyguard for Doc.   *—Merle Horzmann*

~

If there were ever a time when a crack appeared in the egg it was during July of 1941—Doc was coming apart; he was drained with the emotional stress of having a vast treasure, but unable to bring it out to show the world what he and Ova had accomplished. While he labored, he also struggled to keep it safe from marauders, but mostly from the government, always maintaining that the government wanted the treasure for its own purposes. In his world of anger, disappointment and fear of losing the entire treasure, and perhaps even their lives, he struck out at the ones he loved most. He had threatened Ova with a divorce and told Letha and Harold to get out of his life, three people whom he loved dearly. Tension and tempers must have been running in high gear that day; but relationships and feelings were now on a slow downward spiral with Ova and her children. It would come to an end, soon.

Camp Notes —July 12, 1941[104]

Work was temporarily suspended today. Elzo Smith had called Robinson for money for a transit and compass. Barman and Robinson had agreed by June 14 to furnish finances to complete the job; if the money was not received by then, the Turner-Parr group was to do so. If they failed to come up with the money, Doc was to take over. Doc raised $250 today. Also, $1,570 was agreed to be paid to Prince Hilliard as Doc's personal representative, and then later repaid to Doc by the Turner group, but no later than June 30. On June 28, Hilliard came to camp. He had a telegram from Roscoe Parr telling him they would not see him until the following week. So the deadline passed for Barman and Robinson and an extension was given to the Turner and Parr group. Doc had given Elzo Smith a blank check in the event that Barman and Robinson failed. Smith used $90 of it.

Doc took whiskey, shoes and flashlights and went into the shaft about 10:40 and remained there for 2 hours and 40 minutes. He came out drunk. 'Well folks,' he said. 'It's just like I left it. Nothing has been disturbed and nobody has been down there to touch a thing.'

Doc went back down to bring up the chest of jewels and we lowered him on the windlass. Doc called to be pulled up when rocks and dirt were being pushed in on him. When he came up he wanted Elzo Smith to go down with him, but Elzo refused to go further than the lower level, which was 54 feet deep. The timbers extended down 27 feet to an opening. It is 54 feet to the opening and it is 30 feet to the bottom and 2700 feet back to the bullion. All of the money raised was not used to sink the shaft. If $500 was spent on that, it was a lot.

Doc went down again. Smith held the light so he could watch. He brought up two items in his pockets, saying he had two bars, but they were two wooden wedges; 2 x 4s ten inches long, tapered to 1 inch on the one end. He went back down. Wind and rain began. The men wanted to leave Doc down there until he sobered up, but they stayed out of loyalty to him. We had a bad trip back to camp. Doc was all bloody and he kept falling. He was in miserable pain, both mental and physical. He continued to verbally abuse Letha and Babe. Turner and Lampros went to town to get Deputy U.S. Marshal and the sheriff. That night Doc said, 'Babe, I'll take two years in the pen. I've got $32,000 and $1,250 in traveler's checks. Think you can live for a while on that?'

—Merle Horzmann

~

This is one of the more interesting and puzzling notes concerning the collapsed entrance at the top of Victorio Peak. From all indications, there has never been a time when anyone had ever mentioned that Doc had broken through the debris in the collapsed shaft. All other information suggests that the top entrance had never been opened; however, in Horzmann's account of that day, she clearly indicated that Doc had been down to the cavern to retrieve a chest of jewels. Horzmann was not working for Doc and Ova when the top entrance *was* open, or when Doc was bringing out gold bars and some of the other treasures. There are two possible explanations: one, either Doc had been able to open the shaft and get to the treasure rooms, or he had lied about being able to finally regain access to the treasure. More of the story will reveal that the latter was the case.

Camp Notes —July 13, 1941

> *Daylight came and Doc tried to get Elzo Smith to go to the peak and go down into the shaft with him. No one else but Elzo Smith was permitted to go in, but Elzo was waiting for the officers to come for Doc and Elzo did not go with him.*

> ~

That same day, Horzmann wrote that daylight found the camp in a confused state. Elzo was waiting for Sheriff Tony Trujillo and a U.S. Marshal named Sam Frasonn to come for Doc, but for what reason is unknown. Perhaps it was thought that it stemmed from striking Harold. Horzmann continued:

> *Tony Trujillo, the Alamo Sheriff, and U.S. Deputy Marshal Sam Frasonn from Roswell arrived at camp. Miss Kelly and Prince Hilliard came to camp too. Elzo Smith and I told the officers about Doc's abusive ways. Smith and Turner were prepared to swear out a warrant, but the officers had brought none. Doc's bags were packed and he was ready to go to the U.S. pen. Working on his own, Smith was ready to get out. Turner said Doc had taken the $1,570 and bought travelers checks and paid bills, got groceries for $32.50, lumber bill $115 for instruments, but Elzo said it was $90. Tony Trujillo gave Doc 10 days to produce evidence the cave was there and the gold was in it. I weighed pros and cons of the story, but I did not believe it was a hoax. But why delay opening of the cave? Doc promised to get another engineer. I showed Pat Patterson my credentials and my description of Bloody Hands. Patterson* said that I knew too much. – Tom wrote, "The same one I knew."*

> *At Bloody Hands there was what appeared to be an altar in front of a cave that had been filled in. There were small hands like those of a child, a square with an "x" in it that was supposed to be Geronimo's insignia. There were interlaced Ms and Ws and the Sun Face overlooking at the canyon to the southeast. Further to the left and on down into the small canyon are other caves and other camping grounds where the teepees evidently stood with the rocks around their bases. But those caves were too small for bodies.*

> ~

---

* What Horzmann meant about Patterson claiming *she knew too much* is unknown; there can be a number of explanations. However, Patterson likely said it.

Horzmann's comment that *"those caves were too small for bodies"* could have been a reference to the Lorius/Heberer couples' burial place, but who knows. Also, there are no documents that Doc ever allowed *any* federal agent to enter the excavated shaft to examine the treasure, nor is there any record of the Treasury Department ordering Doc to open the cave for an inspection. According to Horzmann, Sheriff Trujillo gave Doc a deadline to prove that a treasure did in fact exist. It is therefore possible that Barman and Robinson had filed some complaint against Doc, saying that he was a fraud and there was no treasure, but Trujillo would not have had jurisdiction; Alamo was one hundred miles away. It is more logical to assume that a local sheriff would have been involved.

The position can also be taken that Elzo Smith and Merle Horzmann justified their actions, when they brought the law against Doc, on the basis that Doc had been abusive. If a U.S. Deputy Marshal and an out-of-county sheriff had come to arrest Doc for whatever reason, there was a jurisdictional question, not withstanding any criminal charges for abusive behavior, which could have been Doc's worst nightmare had he not been struck with a rock first. There is no mention of a civil complaint against Doc regarding Barman and Robinson. Besides, attorneys Newell and Scoggin were the legal representatives for Doc's company; if there were a civil issue pending with Barman and Robinson, they would have handled it, not a far away sheriff and a deputy U.S. Marshal. Basically, there is not enough information to draw a conclusion of any value from Horzmann's notes[105] regarding the presence of the sheriff and the U.S. Marshal. More:

> *Then in the afternoon George Turner returned. Then Elzo Smith, Bill Boone Davis, and I went to the peak. Doc had found a crack in solid rock about 27 feet long from end to end and it was pinched out at both ends. It was about 3' wide. The bottom was earth and rock that Doc had tracked over, but there were no indications of any opening. The drop was about 30' from where the opening was which we could only get into on the windlass rope. The floor of the cave appeared to pinch out under a 14-inch drop at the east end. Rock and dirt filled that in.*
>
> *It was there the 'day* opening' was supposed to be that led into a tunnel, which went to the big cave. It was supposed to have measured 20 feet down to the lower tunnel. Indications were there, but not proven. Doc said the 4 [gold] bars and the lariat rope were as he and Tony Carriaga had left them four years ago. Doc said the attorney had advised him not to touch them, but to leave them until federal agents had inspected them. We couldn't see† them from where we were. Elzo finished measurements on the shaft. We returned to camp.* —Merle Horzmann

~

---

* The day opening was a spot inside Victorio Peak where light came in from the outside letting in daylight.

† Horzmann was not down far enough in the newly excavated shaft to witness the day opening.

Additionally, and according to Horzmann's earlier camp notes, Doc claimed that investors Fred Barman and Lester L. Robinson of California had failed to reopen the cavern and had therefore *forfeited their contract.* However, at the *first* meeting of the Cheyenne Mining Company on June 14 that year, it appears that Barman and Robinson were present, or someone had represented them, probably Elzo B. Smith. Nothing was mentioned in Horzmann's notes whether or not Doc was still arguing that Barman and Robinson remained in violation of their agreement to reopen the cave during the agreed time period spelled out in the January 10 contract.

Eleven days later, on June 25 a special meeting of the Cheyenne Mining Company was held in the law office of J. Benson Newell in Las Cruces. During the meeting, Elzo B. Smith submitted a notice on behalf of Barman and Robinson that they had completed the construction work and shoring and that the mine was ready for inspection. The notice also said that, "should entrance to the treasure be gained as a result of the work completed, that the division of shares were to proceed based on the signed agreements of January 30, 1941." There was no objection noted by Horzmann that sustained Doc's earlier contention that Barman and Robinson had not fulfilled the January 30 agreement. It was later brought out that Doc had agreed to an extension of the contract.

The following day, June 26, Doc burst into anger when he learned that Horzmann was secretly conveying information to Barman and Robinson; Doc was the president of the company, but she opted to involve herself in matters without permission and she had also provided notes to Scoggin. The following day, June 27, Horzmann went to see Sheriff Trujillo, but he was not there. By then, Horzmann had learned that Claude Fincher told Doc that she had given her diary to Scoggin. Horzmann's secret activities naturally ran against the grain with Doc whenever he discovered her disloyalties.

Then, eight days later, she wrote that everyone had seen the papers she had given to Scoggin and the next day, which was Sunday, July 6, they all headed to camp. Sunday was the last day that O.G. Turner and Roscoe Parr had to "put up their $3,500 to complete their part of opening the shaft." According to Horzmann's notes, Barman and Robinson had until Monday night, the next day, to get it finished. Either Turner or Parr was helping to finance Barman and Robinson's excavation costs, or they were standing by to take over when and if Barman and Robinson did not finish clearing the shaft by Monday night. The entanglement Horzmann presented was consistent with what she wrote earlier. The Barman-Robinson issue was a matter for Doc's lawyers.

Work continued on the shaft through the next week, as did the financial wrangling between Turner/Parr and Barman/Robinson. Work had been temporarily suspended on Sunday July 12th. Elzo Smith called Robinson for money they had previously agreed to furnish by June 14, which had long passed. Barman and Robinson were out and Doc took over the excavation. It was that final excavation that led to the discovery of the *Day Opening*. The *Day Opening* mentioned by Horzmann leans toward the possibility that Doc had excavated the shaft to a point where he was finally able to intersect the lower portion of the original route that led to the caverns and the treasure. It can be taken from Horzmann's notes that reentry was made by excavating down to a 3-foot wide crack in the solid wall about 27 feet long and as Horzmann put, "it was pinched out at both ends."

The floor of this new area was earth and rock that Horzmann said Doc had "tracked over," but there was no evidence of any opening. When Doc excavated the east end of the floor, he uncovered a 14-inch drop that had been filled by the rock and dirt. It was through this opening that Doc had found what was described as the *Day Opening*. Why it was given that name is not clear, perhaps because the opening might have allowed light to enter the area during the daylight hours. One such opening was also found about fifty years later during Terry Delonas' excavation efforts; it was a room they called *Starlight*. One of the team members in the 1990s recovery effort, entered the room, he looked up and saw a bright star that was visible through a small hole in the roof of the room.

Camp Notes —July 14, 1941[106]

The Breeches and Pat Patterson had to leave, also Frank the cook. Doc told me the opening was under all that loosed dirt and rocks. One time he said it was under the place where the drop was, and this time he said it was right at the bottom as you dropped down

and that the dirt had to be mucked out. He said the opening was just large enough for a small person to get into. There would be 20 feet of rock and dirt, and seven steps made of boulders down to the floor of the tunnel. The second time he said that it was in the middle of the opening, and the first time to the east end. Which was right?

Doc, Joe, and Frank left the peak. Claude Fincher* had a key to the shaft. He and his wife, Letha, Babe, Bill Davis and I were the only ones there. Letha and Bill dug in the dirt and rocks. There was no sign of the opening. Roscoe Parr and two others arrived, one supposedly an attorney. Joe Andregg's father arrived, too. One of the strangers warned Joe[†] that he knew too much. —Merle Horzmann

~

---

* Claude Fincher at the top shaft; taken in 1941.
[†] The warning was directed to Joe's father that his son "knew to much." Young Joe was also known as *Sonny*.

The person who said that Joe "knew too much" was right; whenever Doc moved gold from the cave, young Andregg accompanied him. Joe made an "x" on a government topo map in every place that he and Doc hid treasure from the main caverns. Those records are still in the possession of the Noss family.

Camp Notes —July 17, 1941[107]

Jack Bruton came to the basin today to meet up with Roy Henderson, the new ranch owner at the peak. He told us that Doc had been in Las Cruces and he was drunk and officers were trailing him. He told us that Doc had a thousand dollars worth of Travelers Checks on him and he was heading to camp.

I discovered Ted Farnsworth's Mexico address. He supposedly had a gold mine there. While we were talking, Bruton said that Robinson of Barman and Robinson was some kind of relative to Ted Farnsworth. Bruton also said to our surprise that he thought Ted and Letha were nearly engaged.

Henderson showed up with pipe to run water from the spring to the tank at the corral. Claude and Joe arrived and said they found Doc and took him to Alamo. Doc told them he would never open the hole unless Turner and Parr raised the $1,570 they agreed on. Some of it was raised, $250 and $800. — Horzmann

Camp Notes —July 18, 1941[108]

On July 18th, it was decided that all women in the camp were to retire and give the men the free reign of the camp surroundings to facilitate work and lessen expenses and responsibility. — Merle Horzmann

The Turner boys went back to work. I went to Las Cruces and got the papers from Judge Scoggin. Doc met up with Babe and Letha, who would go back to Alamo the next day. Doc stayed in Alamo for several days, allowing the boys to work on the opening. — Merle Horzmann[109]

Camp Notes —July 21, 1941

Another passage in Horzmann's camp notes[110] read:

We learned that Jack Bruton's lease was cancelled on the 640 acres of Section 16 but his lease was due to run until 1942. Roy L. Henderson was out of Tularosa and had acquired his lease to 1945. Then it was to be extended to 1950. —Merle Horzmann

~

The Henderson ranch sat at the foot of Victorio Peak. From time to time, Doc had given Henderson money to improve his ranch and ranch house. Doc liked Henderson, and Henderson knew why Doc was able to be so charitable; he knew Doc's money came from the gold inside Victorio Peak. Doc never asked to be paid back and only Ova knew about Doc helping Roy Henderson. Henderson was another victim of the Army, as well as hundreds of other ranchers who were swept aside when their lands were seized. Even though Doc had helped Henderson with his ranch, over time a sense of uneasiness grew between them, for what reason is not known.

Camp Notes —August 5, 1941

On August 5, 1941, Merle Horzmann wrote a two-page letter[111] to Santa Fe's Bureau of Ethnology, the study of the origin, distribution and behavior of humans. It was a winding and somewhat disjointed letter that concerned her evaluation of the Hembrillo Basin and her personal, forensic investigation on the early inhabitants of the area. The first paragraph:

> *In the past few months, I have had occasion to examine a locality in which there are a few caves from which old Indian pottery had been removed, but the caves are very small, and apparently occupied by some pygmy tribe.*

~

The remainder of Horzmann's letter was basically informative and coherent, in fact well written. However, her theory that pygmy tribes had inhabited the area of the Hembrillo Basin might well be a case of her imagination walking away with her common sense.

Camp Notes —August 16, 1941

Her attempts to build a case against Doc continued. On August 16, Horzmann wrote to Prince Hilliard in Hot Springs, claiming that funds Noss had received from investors for the Cheyenne Mining Company and other investors outside the group, namely "money gotten from people in other states" was fraudulent, in her opinion. But there apparently *was* a hearing by authorities to look into charges concerning Doc striking Ova's son. Horzmann's August 16 letter[112] to Hilliard: (underlining inserted)

> *Was sorry not to be able to keep my promise, but we had a very bad storm out here, and the dips were flooded so I could not get through, and besides that [I] was advised by the attorneys not to appear unless summoned with the type of evidence I have. It was not that I did not want to do so, as I am willing to do anything I can to assist in your work. There is evidently something back of it that I do not know about, and decided they must know best. I am quite anxious to know what was done, and any other information pertinent to the case. The question has been asked me several times if I knew of any letters Doc might have written concerning his project, and the only ones I know of are those sent to Barman and Robinson, but have not mentioned it in my answers to them. If I understand correctly, money gotten from people in other states on anything of that kind, where proof can be had, constitutes a Federal case. This is just my own surmise, however.*
>
> *Will appreciate hearing from you, and I am quite sure that if I could talk to you about it, I could enlighten you considerably concerning my position.*
>
> *—Merle Horzmann*

~

Once again Horzmann is using her official capacity as secretary of Doc's company to gather information and forward it to outside authorities. She is also keeping close ties with attorneys who were working a case against Doc, presumably for striking Ova's son.

Camp Notes —August 19, 1941

Another example of how Horzmann attempted to snare Doc came in a letter she wrote to Mr. J. Victor Bate at 545 Fifth Avenue in New York City. In her letter, Horzmann explained her reasons for not attending Doc's preliminary hearing on charges against him for striking Ova's son. The incident happened on July 10, when Doc told Ova he was going to divorce her and said he wanted Letha and Harold out of his life. Harold responded by hitting Doc with a rock. Reference was also made in her letter to some unidentified attorney's letter to her insisting she attend the preliminary hearing on August 15, 1941, whose advice she questioned. Horzmann's legal adviser told her not to go. Portions of Merle Horzmann's letter[113] to Victor Bate:

> Your letter of August 13 received. I was very glad to get it, and will tell you that at the time I wrote you, it looked as if the case might be prosecuted, but there has been nothing done that I know of positively at this time.
>
> My reason for thinking it was a letter I received from an attorney asking me to be at a preliminary hearing that was to have been held on the 15th of this month. Somehow, I questioned the authenticity of it, and consulted with a legal advisor, who told me positively not to go unless summoned through the legal process.
>
> You are right again about the possibilities of the people you referred to. I accidentally let it slip that I could identify the Mr., and that they had been in our home several times, etc., and from then on it seemed a fear permeated the general atmosphere, and since coming home, discovered that that was one of the best clues they had had. It would also include the people from El Paso, if it were according to the information I received from a party on the investigation end of it in Albuquerque [possibly the Secret Service]. Yet, that too should be checked more thoroughly.
>
> Since writing you, I feel as if the letter I received was a ruse to get me to bring legal documents and evidence in my possession at this time to get it out of my hands so I wouldn't use it if called on. Another party familiar with it was to have written me Monday, and I still have not heard from him, as to just what the idea was with this attorney, if it was really the attorney who wrote it.
>
> Have also found out that the stuff is out there in that area, but that he is making a grand racket of it and they are swallowing it hook, line and sinker, just like I did at first. But the authorities know of this possibility and it seems they can do nothing about it until they can prove one essential point, the W.F.* scheme, which they can do, I am sure, if they want to.
>
> I can't say positively that it is not there, nor do I feel he is going to be successful in taking it out. But I did find out that Billy the Kid still lives, and I have seen him. He is said to know just where the gold is, and goes out there whenever he needs funds and

---

* This might be a reference to Wire Fraud.

helps himself. But just to make certain, a friend of mine here is going with me to make the positive identification of Billy. If this should be true, it also will ring a little jingle. But like you, I have to be shown.   —Merle Horzmann

~

Horzmann's claim to have seen Billy the Kid (also known as Brushy Bill) is a chorus that is sung to this day, namely that he was not killed by Sheriff Pat Garrett and lived until the mid-1950s, a tale that most historians discount as fiction. Whether or not she had seen him is immaterial to the subject matter of this book, but one thing is certain: Mesilla, where Billy the Kid was jailed, Pat Garrett's home in Las Cruces, his ranch in the Tularosa Basin, the place where Garret was murdered, and Victorio Peak, are all eggs in the same geographic basket. However, Horzmann's belief that Indian Pygmy tribes had inhabited the small caves she encountered in the Hembrillo Canyon, and that she had seen Billy the Kid do little to establish much confidence in the legitimacy of her information gathering and her writings; some of the time her writings are lucid and informative, while other times they are not.

Camp Notes —August 19, 1941

Lampros' letter[114] to Horzmann of August 19:

Just a few lines to let you know of how everything stands. In Hot Springs I met Mr. P.C. Hilliard and I had a long conference with him. In the first place, he withdrew the bond he had for Dr. Noss and forced Noss to put up cash bond. Second, he put new charges against Noss for hitting the boy in the head with the gun. Third, he put charges against Noss on my account. They postponed the case until September 15. I told him to write to you and to give you all the necessary details. So you can be prepared for that date. Thence I proceeded to Socorro. I went to the District Attorney's Office and I met with J.C. Enloe and had a nice conference with him and I left all the necessary proofs that I had with me and I told him to write to you and to explain to you about everything. This is all at present. I will write to you from Phoenix about what day I will be in Lordsburg. It looks like that everything is going OK. I remain with best wishes.

—B.D. Lampros

~

It was Lampros and Elzo Smith who visited the Victorio Peak site in 1941 and examined the gold bars Doc had shown them. Lampros had also taken a bar to Hawley & Hawley and found it assayed high in gold; Doc's drinking habits surfaced only months after Lampros first came to the Hembrillo Basin. Three years after Doc was murdered, Lampros signed an affidavit; even then he hoped "to see the complete excavation of this cave and the great treasure to come to reality." So the animosity Lampros was conveying in his letter to Horzmann stemmed from Doc's behavior, not that he thought Doc was fraudulent in claiming he had found a treasure. The treasure's existence would eventually be documented, but in August of 1941, there were other matters that needed to be resolved, Doc's temper and abusiveness when he drank.

Lampros and Doc had been friends since 1937, and what Lampros meant when he mentioned "necessary proofs" he had left with Enloe is unclear, but it could have been a record of Doc's actions when he drank. Once again, trouble was looming on the horizon for Doc Noss.

Soon Horzmann, fulfilling her role as a self-admitted spy of "the government," would take on the task of putting Doc's head on the chopping block in the Lorius/Heberer murders that followed their strange disappearance on May 19, 1935. She would pursue her unfounded belief that Doc was responsible for the murders; she would develop theories and convey flimsy and self-serving information to the authorities unwinding her thoughts and beliefs, hoping to pin the murders on Doc.

Camp Notes —August 20, 1941

In pursuing her agenda against Doc, Horzmann wrote to the Chief of Police* "Butter" Pyle in Du Quoin, Illinois, about the disappearance of the two couples. Assuming that Doc Noss was involved, she began her own personal investigation hoping to implicate him. However, Horzmann's letter, in which she admitted having a personal "business connection with Mr. Lorius." is particularly interesting; no other person connected with Noss had *any* connection at all with the families, only Horzmann and her husband. Time would show that no charges were ever leveled against Noss for the disappearances, either by local, state or federal authorities, only suspicions they had acquired from Horzmann's homespun investigation, prying and finger pointing. It can be construed that she was looking to make a buck for her efforts. "Butter" Pyle's letter:[115] (underlining inserted)

> *In the last few days, I have gotten a most startling clue to the disappearance of the Lorius and Heberer families, but at the time it all happened, I was in Illinois, and had no idea whatsoever of ever having anything to do with the solution to this situation, and while I was interested because of business connections with Mr. Lorius, did not take particular notice of certain details that are now essential to determine whether there is any foundation to the story.*
>
> *Would you be so kind as to answer the questions, which I shall tabulate on a separate sheet of paper if it is within your power to do so? <u>The party who is supposed to have been instrumental in a major way in this case is cited for a preliminary hearing on another charge on the 15th of September</u>. I was asked to appear on the 15th of August as a witness but was detained and not summoned and was advised not to go otherwise, and the case was postponed.*
>
> *Meantime, it is just possible that with your information, I can complete an investigation to such a point that I will know what to do about it when the time comes. There should*

---

* The Du Quoin Chief of Police at the time the St. Louis couples disappeared was "Butter" Pyle.

be no publicity whatsoever on it at this time, not until I have had a chance to look into it properly. I think some of the state authorities here may take it up, but until I have something more to go on, do not feel inclined to make my purpose known.

~

Merle Horzmann had viewed herself as an archeologist and an anthropologist, and now a criminal investigator, even though her experience was limited to having recently signed up for a mail order correspondence course on criminal investigation. More:

I might explain that it is only recently that I began to take up the study of Scientific Investigation with the I.S.A.S., Chicago, and my file number is 3549-G. But whatever I do at this time is entirely on my own and I am not being financed by anyone, other than my regular allowance from home, which makes progress pretty slow, but if I can help to solve this, I shall feel repaid almost in full measure. The information had come to me voluntarily, and for no apparent reason, except that I am from E. St. Louis, and being a common topic that would concern E. St. Louis people, have seemed to have that confidence more or less automatically, by way of general conversation. It may not be good policy to even mention it to any of the family, as it may be a blind lead, but I would like to have a picture of the car they drove. I mean the Heberers, if there was one. Thank you for any information you can furnish me.   —Merle Horzmann*

~

Jeff S. Moore of Steins, New Mexico sent an undated letter to State Police Chief Tom Summers on August 29 regarding "the Noss case." The salutation read: "Friend Tom." The letter establishes that Horzmann's letter of August 20, together with Moore's supposed interest in the case was an effort to convince Chief Summers to act on Horzmann's behalf regarding her earlier request to Butter Pyle. The possibility cannot be dismissed that Horzmann, who obviously knew Moore (she had a copy of his letter to Tom Summers), had prompted Moore to urge Tom Summers to supply her with police file information (a photo of the Lorius car), but also an expense account, as well, something she had hinted when she wrote to Pyle. Moore wrote:[116]

I personally know that the bearer, Mrs. Merle Horzmann has some very potent evidence and that she is capable and in a position to render you some very valuable assistance, and I suggest that you provide her with an expense account and give her a free hand for a few weeks. I am certain she can and will crack this thing in a pleasing and surprising manner.

—Jeff S. Moore

Camp Notes —August 30, 1941

It was during August that Horzmann began making suggestions that Doc might have had knowledge of the Lorius-Heberer murders. Although she had not yet made a direct accusation, her remarks were beginning to take a foothold in her writings to Captain Roy Vermillion of the New Mexico State Police. Her letter to him on August 30, 1941 mentioned an August 28 meeting with

Vermillion at her home in Lordsburg regarding a Mr. Gibson, which prompted her to project the notion Doc knew that certain murders had taken place. From Horzmann's August 30 letter:

> *When you were here on the 28ᵗʰ inquiring about Mr. Gibson, I could not place the name or the circumstance. I was talking to Mr. Holt today and he reminded me of the case, and I was thinking of another person of the same name.*
>
> *However, Gibson was not in the same party you asked about, but a few days later I heard a little story that might be worth checking. You may take it for what it is worth, even though it is rather hazy in my mind.*
>
> *It seems that there is a group of men in or near Hot Springs who are contending for the things* we were talking about in the mountains, and between the two factions, there has apparently sprung up a sort of feud. They call themselves the Guerrilla Gang. The story is, that one of the gang was responsible for the killings, but there was no mention of which one, that I can recall. You might try to get their alibis, since it will do no harm. Those I remember were Bob Ward [Buster Ward] and Willie Douthit. There are others in it, but I am unable to recall their names, and for all I know they may be perfectly respectable citizens. If I remember correctly, the "Dr." [Doc Noss] said there was some enmity between them and Mr. G. [Johnny Gordon Sr.] and he [Doc Noss] advanced the idea that it [the Heberer and Lorius murders] could be traced in that direction [meaning in the direction of individuals in the Guerrilla Gang].*
>
> *That same evening, another story was told [presumably by Doc Noss] of how a person named 'Bill Williams' was lured into a cave in the Caballos, and his skeleton is still there. That [murder] was hung on one of the two men [Ward or Douthit]. Due to some lurid things he [Doc Noss] told me, I paid very little attention to them, but when I think them over, there might be another side to the question.*

~

There was a lot more to it; someone in *addition* to Bill Williams and the St. Louis couples was also murdered to protect the gold in the small stash cave Ward and Douthit had in the Caballo Mountains. The Noss files contain more than three hundred video and audio recordings of individuals who throughout the years had or claimed to have had direct knowledge of matters related to the Victorio Peak treasure trove *and* the Caballo Mountain treasures and other matters; Willie Douthit was one such person.

In one video interview conducted by members of the 1990s' ONFP expedition crew, Douthit talked about a man named Willie Stromm, describing him as a "little bitty guy" that didn't weigh over eighty pounds. Ward and Douthit had moved gold bars from one of their larger finds and hid them inside their stash cave not far from the Gordon cabin. The cave is accessed through an opening at ground level; Stromm found the entrance, crawled in and removed some of the

---

* The reference to the "things" was the large gold cache in the Caballo Mountains found by Willie Douthit.

gold. Today, the entrance to the Ward-Douthit gold stash cave can be found by walking east up Hackberry Draw. As one approaches the site, the sand-filled draw widens and a formidable rock formation appears on the right. Originally, the ground level opening was small, barely wide enough to enter easily. However, over the years people who knew the story of the cave have excavated it in hopes of finding gold. It is the general belief in the area that people in addition to Stromm were murdered here; lower photo taken inside of the cave.

This writer learned the actual account of what happened to Willie Stromm from a confidential source, a man who learned about Stromm's murder from a well-informed person named Sonny Mitchell, a man who grew up around Ward and Douthit. Mitchell was present in the Caballo Mountains at a time when Ward and Douthit were removing gold from an accumulation* room they discovered higher up in the Caballo Mountains. It was by pure luck that Mitchell happened to be standing at a spot that overlooked the small stash cave that Ward and Douthit were using to hide a number of gold bars they had

---

* Treasure accumulation rooms were usually caves (big and small) where Spanish miners stored gold bars they had melted and cast in crude forms called dory bars.

brought there for safekeeping. It was then that Mitchell saw Stromm coming out of the cave carrying a half-bar of gold. Even though Stromm was a man in his early twenties, he had the body of a young boy, being dwarf-like in appearance. Because of the weight of gold, Stromm removed only part of a bar, which he had most likely cut in half inside the cave. After observing Stromm's activities, Mitchell found Douthit and told him what he had seen. That same night Douthit and Ward caught up with Stromm at a place called the Caballo Bar (or the Caballo Café) and confronted him about stealing their gold, which Stromm denied. As a warning, Ward and Douthit threatened him. The following day, Ward and Douthit hid out near their stash cave and waited to see if Stromm came back for more of their gold. Sure enough, they caught Stromm removing some. Here are Douthit's words taken in from 1990s' video interview concerning Willie Stromm. In part:

We grabbed him and said what are you doin' messin' around with our gold? He said, 'I'll just take a little. This is all I'll take.' You're damn right that's all you'll take. The only thing I know to do to silence ya' forever and keep ya' outta there, is to kill ya. Ol' Buster said, 'That's right, let's kill him.' We argued who was gonna do it. Ol' Willie was just scared to death. So, we finally decided I would deliver the blow. So, I turned him around and said, you run, and if you run fast enough, we won't kill ya. I said, Buster what the hell should we do? If we leave the son-of-a-bitch alive, he'll come up in here and he'll steal us blind, so what are we gonna do?' Buster said, 'Well all I know to do is just kill the little bastard.' I said, well, all right, Willie, take off. Then I leveled down on him and I aimed to kill the little bastard. What else could you do? So he was runnin' and I aimed to shoot him in the back of the head and I missed him. My gun was a little off, or I was, and I just shot the tip of his ear off. The concussion knocked him out, ya know. So we just drug him off to the side of the road and let the buzzards have him. Ya' know, Buster and I had taken a lot of crap from people and we were gettin' mean. So he woke up after we left and took off.

~

Douthit claimed that he only wounded Stromm, hitting his ear, which knocked him out. Douthit also claimed Stromm returned to the area thirty years later, but when he learned that he had also returned to the Caballo Mountains, Stromm left again. Douthit said, "He woke up after we left and took off." Whether Stromm had lived to tell the true story, we'll never know. Did Douthit actually kill Stromm as he and Ward had intended? The consensus, among those who knew Douthit, is that Stromm died that day.

More from Horzmann's August 30 letter:

Just whether this would mean anything to you or not, I do not know, but when I talked to Mr. Holt, and he explained who the party was, this flashed through my mind and he suggested I write you.

Another thought that comes to my mind when I asked you if he was supposed to have been in the Rodeo that night, the "Dr." substituted in one ride, and his horse is supposed to have fallen on him across his stomach. On Sunday, all day, he was very ill, and for several days his knee was so sore he could scarcely walk. Nobody in our crowd saw him ride, and the man he was supposed to have substituted for was said to be lying over a truck too drunk to ride, and this was done to save his entry. But none of us attended the Rodeo, so it really went over our heads.

I hope if you get ready to work on this case in the mountains [the Heberer and Lorius murders] you will let me make a few little suggestions that would simplify it very much, I believe, and get the agony over with very shortly in a nice way, without stirring up too much dust.

~

The more haunting tales of the region were the murders said to have been committed in the Caballo Mountains and the unanswered questions and rumors that surfaced about those who were suspects in the killings. These were the tales of the Caballo Mountains: tales of murder, betrayal and gold, the driving force that permeated every lurid story. Horzmann would continue to perpetuate her own investigation of the Lorius-Heberer murders and do what she could to make Doc a suspect. More of Horzmann's letter[117] to Captain Roy Vermillion: (underlining inserted)

This L.C. Montgomery I mentioned, is said to have stolen some of the gold bars and taken them either to Texas or to California, and is said to have gone into the cave with Doc and saw the bullion stacked up, double-ricked and the other things that were mentioned.

Another point that could be checked is correspondence with Barman and Robinson, Room 200, Metropolitan Bldg, Los Angeles. Information I have is that they conduct a loan agency for the purpose of assisting mining ventures and the lifting of hidden treasures, etc., and they have a belt and some other articles, so Doc says, which I presume they are holding for security. Monty is supposed to have dynamited the cave shut to prevent others from finding it, then pulled a gun on Doc and left with the gold bars, something like $9,994, if I got my notes right. This amount corresponds to the amount Doc has spent since November.

I am fully aware that if this preliminary hearing does not have strength enough, it will affect the investors who have invested heavily in it with a great deal of force. And even if it does, and it is proven there is nothing in the cave as he presents, there is nothing that can be done to get them their money back. But his statement had been that he could get into that hole in five hours. The question is: Why hasn't he done it? He told us about it in May.

You asked for pictures of the bar. Mr. Holt has them. Letha has others.

It would not be wise for me to talk to this Loeffler, since [someone] here made a statement that I was working on that particular case, and that they had better leave me alone. Don't know where he got his information unless through a conversation he overheard in Hurley* one night with Sam Matson. But he is also a friend of Bill's.

Mrs. N. [Ova] is the one who solicited the aid of B&R† of Los Angeles.

One party advanced the idea that they thought they had gotten rid of the old group and started getting another group into it, in order to raise more money. Don't know how authentic that is. This information came from Las Cruces.

Until these points are checked up on, to me, they are only hearsay or surmises, but which will no doubt have considerable bearing.

Can only depend on what you find out as to its authenticity, which I had hoped to be able to get myself, but circumstances have not permitted."   —Merle Horzmann

P.S. Might add that other information I received was, that Dr. M. [Miller] has been going to that location for the last 9 years, and has "[discovered] quite a few things."

~

What the relationship was between the underlined sentences above and the sentence before it is not clear. Also, Horzmann's mention of the preliminary hearing that was set for August 15 dealt with Doc's physical attack charges for striking Harold with the butt end of his revolver. But the larger question arises about "another entrance" in addition to the well-known top entrance; an entrance that Horzmann said Doc had claimed he could "get into the hole in five hours."

The only known entrance was the ancient top shaft, the natural air ventilation shaft that Doc entered time after time to get to the treasure rooms. Horzmann also claimed in her letter to Vermillion that in May Doc said it would take only a "few days" to get at the treasure. Others have always discussed this issue over the years, but mostly amongst the Noss family members who later learned the night before Doc was slain that by his own words there *was* another entrance—an easy passageway that Horzmann seems to confirm in her letter.

---

* *Hurley* is a small town located between Lordsburg and Hatch, New Mexico.
† *B&R* is Barman and Robinson.

Chapter 15

Horzmann: a One-Woman Lynch Mob, Doc Sees Bodies in Douthit's Cave

Even though Doc was sitting on a vast fortune, and from time to time he was provided with funds to keep his recovery efforts going, he was always scrambling for cash. Whether there were more cave-in problems with the shaft is unknown, but whatever work was done in the shaft was expensive and Doc was reaching out for help. An example of his money problems were spelled out in a letter Doc wrote to Wesley White, one of his friends, the Sheriff in Sonora, Texas.

Camp Notes —September 1, 1941

Doc's letter[118] to White, in part:

> *James and I have just come from the mines where we had a bad cave-in. I need 2' x 12' timbers. We are working 12-hour days. Lawyer Ben Newell has my case for the 16th. I need $200 to beat the case. The $1,000 we have for camp goes only for mining. I need $600 for lawyer Newell and the timbers. I will sign a note or mortgage or sign Mrs. White a percent. We are getting talc and copper claims in shape for sale. I wish you could be here for the trial. You could see how I have fought to do the right thing, to be honest. I need the money for 30-60 days. The day we break through, Leo O'Connell will be on the road to you. Hoping everyone is healthy, also Nellie.**
> —Doc

Camp Notes —September 8, 1941

September brought more of the same—another letter by Merle Horzmann aimed at doing in Doc. Horzmann noted that she had "just received a letter from one of the parties in this Noss case, saying P. C. Hilliard was going with the prosecution on the 15th of the month and insisted that I testify." She was talking about the upcoming trial on criminal charges brought against Doc for striking Harold. More would develop on that issue, but it appears that people were lining up to testify against Doc, witnesses such as Horzmann who would later be called in an investigation aimed at proving Doc's treasure was a scam and that investors were victimized in the process.

Then Horzmann's attention once more swung back to the Lorius-Heberer killings, which had comprised most of her letter to Roy Vermillion. In the letter she recalled when the Lorius-Heberer couples left East St. Louis in Lorius' 1929 Nash sedan. It was on this day that Horzmann made a concerted effort to put Doc on the front burner as *her* prime suspect for the killings that took

---

* Oscar Nellie, thus the Nellie Mines

201

place a little more than six years earlier. The remainder of her September 8, 1941 letter[119] is presented here:

> Since I cannot get to Albuquerque myself, would it be possible for you to arrange an interview with William (Bill) Loeffler of Albuquerque, and get a statement from him with regard to the night that Ova asked him to take her home to the east side of town, the party said he thought it was after she and the Dr. had quarreled. That must have been on or around the 20th of May 1932 [the date they were last heard from was May 22, 1935], whatever year it was the Lorius party disappeared. She is supposed to have become panicky and screamed out about the Dr. 'leaving those people out there in that hole', and then she went to Loeffler and asked him if he would take her home, and on the way, she told him about it. Please be very careful not to disclose the source of the information, as his wife told it to me, and they are also very good friends of Loeffler, and several things would be spoiled if they knew.
>
> This happened after they were seen together in the Sturges Hotel and the four left following the Noss car and were not seen after that. I could be wrong, and so could they who told me, but it is one of the things that will have to be verified. If they had wrecked their car just outside Albuquerque, as it is generally believed, the Noss car could have taken them the rest of the way. But not being able to check up on it and review the case after I got home from the camp, dates and incidents relative to it are not at all clear, and this information came to me so spontaneously, that I have been more than mystified and anxious to check it. The reason I believe there may be something to it, is because I happened to mention the E. St. Louis people one time, and from then on the work was stalled from time to time rather exasperatingly, and unnecessarily, we thought.
>
> If it is possible to get this story, and it proves anything, I will be a little more willing to present my side of the story to the court, and have my report ready if they want it, but there is still checking to do on it, and I am not in a position to get the necessary information.
>
> Another point that should be checked is concerning the frequent visits of Ted Farnsworth. This is relative to the question as to whether he could have smuggled gold. I think that address is the Campbell Hotel in El Paso; and his car license number is Texas, 1941, 413-743. His native home is, according to Letha, Colonia, Garolia, Chihuahua, Casas Grandes, Mexico, where he and his father have a gold mine, and the samples I saw were exactly like some I had that were given to me from not far from there by another party entirely disinterested, and the geology of the country where the shaft is being sunk gives no indication of such ore being found any way similar to it. I have retained the specimens.

~

Horzmann's name does not appear on the bottom of this letter, so it is possible there was a second page, and there was no trace of the letter in the NMSP file, but it takes little imagination to see that Horzmann was straining to make a case against Doc for the four murders by telling Vermillion what Doc had told Ova about seeing bodies in Willie Douthit's cave and what had transpired between Doc and Ova after he told her. But what was significant about her letter was that she said, "If they had wrecked their car just outside Albuquerque, as it is generally believed, the Noss car could have taken them the rest of the way"—the rest of the way to where?

Nowhere in the *Albuquerque Tribune* article was it mentioned that Lorius had wrecked his 1929 Nash sedan near Albuquerque, or anywhere else for that matter. However, it was later established that the "charred remains of some luggage, a thermos bottle, and a medicine bottle" belonging to the couples were found on the "edge of an arroyo on Albuquerque's east mesa, north of the present State Fairgrounds" by the Fullingim brothers, which *was* printed in the Albuquerque Tribune shortly after the four people disappeared.

However, in a statement given to Officer B.E. Lucas of the New Mexico State Police on October 28, 1953, C.P. Newkirk claimed that Clarence A. Palmer "drove the car to a point east of Albuquerque where he burned the luggage. He was afraid he might get caught in the mountains east of Albuquerque, so he headed back south on U.S. 85." Newkirk also said in his statement that, "Somewhere north of Hot Springs he [Clarence Palmer] wrecked the car slightly and drove on to El Paso and spent the night."

The same newspaper article said that along the way, Sullivan had been spotted when "passers-by helped him on two separate occasions after he had driven off the highway" leaving the impression that Sullivan and Palmer might have been one and the same. Horzmann's reference to a "wrecked car" could have been a fragment of her recollection of what appeared in the *Albuquerque Tribune* article

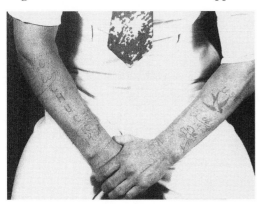

and was used in her letter to Vermillion to put Doc in the picture. A man who was seen by the passers-by showed up in El Paso at a "small hotel" where he registered under the name of James Sullivan and used Lorius' Shrine credentials as identification. The article also said that the "Lorius' car was found in Dallas, Texas, abandoned there by a man who was described as having a heavily tattooed left arm and who had also left a string of Lorius' Travelers Checks from El Paso to Dallas, which the man had forged." However, none of this points to Doc Noss, in any way. The photograph shown here is from the New Mexico State Police cold case files[120] and is evidence that a man whose arms were heavily tattooed was questioned, yet there is no indication that he was a viable possible suspect. So, was the man shown here Clarence A. Palmer? If it was, did Palmer give the name of James Sullivan when he checked into the hotel in El Paso?

It is doubtful that Ova had set out to harm Doc by consulting with others on something that Doc had said to her about the murders. Ova's comment to Bill Loeffler about Doc "leaving those people in the hole" stemmed out of Doc's argument with Willie Douthit and/or Buster Ward. According to what Ova explained to Terry, Doc was extremely angry after he had seen several bodies in what is believed to have been Douthit and Ward's treasure cave; according to Terry, there is supposed to be a letter written by Letha that describes Doc having walked inside the cave and seen bodies. After an argument with Douthit and Ward, Doc returned home to Hot Springs very angry over what he had seen. There is no record of Doc ever contacting the police, nor has the letter been found.

Horzmann reached back six years on her mental blackboard and recalled what had transpired then. Every so often she was supportive of Doc, but overall she wanted him out of the picture. Doc and Ova were in a struggle to raise the massive treasure at Victorio Peak, and it is unlikely Doc would have jeopardized his treasure trove quest. Horzmann had implied that members of the Guerrilla Gang were involved in the killings, and named Willie Douthit and others as members of the gang.

Camp Notes —September 12, 1941

The following letter was sent to J. Victor Bate in Chandler, Oklahoma. Her letter reveals that she was a racist who manipulated and distorted unfolding events to suit her behavior, all the while counseling and corresponding with her husband. Her letter[121] to Victor Bate: (underlining inserted)

> Your letter of the 6th received, and I am just now getting this case lined up to where I can see daylight. The preliminary is to be held this next Monday, the 15th. The Attorneys have written me repeatedly to be there, but owing to the dual situation, will only go if they send officers for me, and the information I have. But you might watch the papers around that time for the developments. It will likely come before the Federal Grand Jury after this Prelim.
>
> I shall follow your advice in both instances very closely, and if I am in touch with the party I think it is, I shall make every effort to verify the identity. But the person who told me is acquainted with him personally. I refer to Billy the Kid.
>
> Well, we are about to see the end of an Indian's pipe dream, I think. He is supposed to be Tom Starr. Wish I could get some data on the Starr family. His sister, Belle Starr, was hung, and her head was jerked off in the process, I understand, and his father, another Tom Starr, was killed, or hung. He was an outlaw, also. But the State Police said they had fingerprinted Tom Starr, and that there is nothing to that story. But there are times when Doc Noss calls himself Tom Starr, and I have a photograph of the door on which that name is burned on by a carbide light flame, together with all the old Indian symbols used in identifying places and things, hieroglyphics in other words.
>
> I think in the libraries of some of the Oklahoma towns, and especially around Oklahoma City, there would be found historical data concerning them. His mother was

also an outlaw, but just how, I cannot remember the story. They were supposed to be Cheyenne, and he claims to be 3/4 Indian.

I found another interesting character here, which I may have told you of, a Sam Bass. I think he is an illegitimate son of the old Sam Bass, who was killed in 1878, and he was born at that time, or rather, in November, after Sam Bass was killed in June or July. Can always go back and pick that one up, but thought you might like to meet him some day if you get back out this way. I want to see him again and take down some notes on some of his stories. He is a very alert man, and full of the old Saint Nick, himself.

I saw Mr. Holt a little while ago, but he was very busy, so I didn't talk much to him except to tell him of the DA's letter and what I answered. Best regards to Mrs. Bate, and tell her I hope when you get out this way again I can get better acquainted with her, and see what we can do about her condition. I am very sympathetic with illness.

—Merle Horzmann

~

Little is *certain* about Doc's true lineage. Although Doc claimed that his father was Tom Starr, he never claimed *he* was Tom Starr, or that he openly took the name; it was merely a childhood sentiment, an image he carried with him throughout his life. Horzmann was wrong in her portrayal of Doc as it related to Tom Starr.

Camp Notes —September 12, 1941

More of Horzmann's betrayal of Doc is evidenced by her confession that she kept a diary to use against him, which she discussed in her September 12[122] letter to James Enloe, Assistant District Attorney in Socorro, New Mexico: (underlining inserted)

Your letter at hand, and in regard to the Noss case, will say I would be glad to assist you in any way I can, have enlightened Mr. Vermillion and Mr. Eagleton on some of the things which I felt might possibly have some bearing.

The reason I did not go into more details with them about it, was because I did not know just what they wanted, or why, and being very late at night when they came, was tired and really unprepared to talk the matter over properly. It is quite difficult to know just whom to trust, and while I know there was certain information that should be looked into, I could not do it for lack of funds and was glad to give part of it to them. They will no doubt let you know what they found out about it.

Mr. Hilliard wanted me to appear in Socorro at the preliminary on Monday. I answered that I would try to be there, but I do not have the traveling funds at this time, and have no income, other than that received from home, which is very negligible at this time, owing to the strenuous obligations Mr. Horzmann has to meet there.

Another reason for my reticence is due to the fact that I have been entrusted with certain legal documents of the Cheyenne Mining Company, of which Mr. Noss is the head, and they elected me Secretary. Unless these documents are ordered by the usual legal process, it would be violating the trust reposed in me at that time, and <u>would likely jeopardize any future confidence I might wish to obtain.</u>

In the matter of reviewing incidents during the time I was at camp with them, <u>I have</u> *<u>kept a diary from which I have compiled a story up to the 18th of July</u>. After returning home, I received some very startling information, which I had not thought of previously in connection with it, which will probably account for his delay in opening the shaft, if there is such a thing. But unless they have checked up on it, I would not know about it until they were ready to tell me. This information is in the form of a supplementary brief, besides some historical data, which I have attempted to check with the Bureau of Ethnology and Anthropology.*

My reason for keeping the diary was because we were to have publicity rights, if there is such a thing, and I did not want to be found without the necessary data. But when things began to take on a different color, I began using it to further investigations in a manner I thought fitting to the case, and to protect myself in case of an inquiry.

If this data, or any part of it is necessary for you to have Monday, I shall be glad to give it to any officer you care to send for it, and if necessary, go with them. But you will understand the position it places me in if I voluntarily give it up. I fully understand that this matter should be expedited at an early date, however, and am willing to do what I can. I am enclosing a copy of this letter to Mr. Hilliard.   —Merle Horzmann

~

Horzmann said that it was "difficult to know just whom to trust" and it was apparent that she was once again looking to be paid for the information she was willing to provide, at least for the expenses she incurred in obtaining the information and for future expenses. Similarly, on August 20, 1941, she wrote to Du Quoin Chief of Police "Butter" Pyle and told him that her time was her own and was not "being financed by anyone." On August 29, 1941, her friend Jeff Moore wrote to New Mexico State Police Chief Tom Summers and asked him to provide her with an expense account. She then dangled documents of the Cheyenne Mining Company under District Attorney Enloe's nose that were "entrusted" to her as the company's elected secretary, company information that she had been required to properly record and administer. She reminded Enloe that unless the company documents were "ordered by the usual legal process" it would "likely jeopardize any future confidence" in her if she turned them over voluntarily.

As District Attorney, Enloe knew that if he needed the Cheyenne Mining Company records he had the power of subpoena. When it was evident that a newspaper or magazine deal was not coming together, Horzmann offered her diary, but with the same precautions and fears she had if she gave it up "voluntarily." But by December 5, Horzmann's conscience waned and she volunteered her information to Chief Tom Summers. It is not known if her file included minutes of the company meetings.

Camp Notes —September 12, 1941

This letter to Prince C. Hilliard of Hot Springs refers to Horzmann's letter[123] to Enloe, one of her more venomous letters concerning Doc and Ova:

Just received a letter from Mr. James C. Enloe, in which the following is set forth: 'I have talked with Lampros and certainly would appreciate any assistance you might be to us in the matter of M.E. Noss, which has been referred to the federal authorities due to the fact the transactions involved are said to have taken place in several states. Both Mr. Lampros and Mr. Hilliard feel that you are very competent and that you are in possession of data, which will be invaluable in the thorough investigation of the matter, for which I am grateful. We would certainly appreciate any assistance you would be willing to give to the federal authorities investigating the matter…J.C.E.

I am enclosing a copy of my answers and I feel that you will appreciate the position I am placed in this respect, and will fully understand why I have had to be very careful of all I did, and use extreme caution.

Not only this, but should things become involved in such a way, I realize that my life would be more or less in danger, owing to the treacherous tendencies of both of them, [meaning Ova and Doc] should I volunteer information, evidence contained in either my notes or the documents they have entrusted with me. Yet, on the other hand, I know the case must come to a head, and there is no better time than now.

My son is leaving the meeting after the 16th for St. Louis, which will leave us entirely alone out there, and except for this case and some other things, which I believe I explained in my last letter, I would return with him.

However, I shall be willing to abide by my letter to Mr. Enloe, as I have been advised strenuously not to do otherwise. This should reach you and Mr. Enloe in time to advise me by wire or otherwise what to do, but you did not say what time the case was to be tried in Socorro.   —Merle Horzmann

Camp Notes —September 22, 1941

One of Horzmann's more cryptic letters was sent to Vermillion on September 22, 1941. It dealt with a variety of issues: secret visitors, the Archaeological Department in Washington, D.C, the Guerrilla Gang and Eppie Montoya. In fact, Horzmann sent *two* letters to Vermillion that day. The first, which was not finished or signed, appeared to be an overture to the second letter. Her first letter[124] to Vermillion in its entirety:

At 11:45 the 14th, visitors arrived, giving me quite a bit of information which seemed to me to answer one question you asked me while you were here. After that, I got a line-up on some more that linked with other things.

This afternoon, I had another visitor, who enlightened me some more, and corroborated to some extent my thought on the other, but I do not believe it is the wisest thing to write it.

However, there are some questions I will note here, which I should like very much to know the answers to, and may have some more bearing.

Statement was made that the Archaeological Department in Washington had assumed control of that area known as the Hembrillo Basin. Did they? To counter that question, the A. D. [Archaeological Department] at one time assumed control of the region in

the Caballos [Caballo Mountains]. Could that sign* have been removed and used in H. B. [Hembrillo Basin]?

Statement also made that [the] Gorilla Gang [or Guerrilla†] had jumped two of the claims and had moved into the adjoining canyon and that they had entered the camp grounds with malicious intent. Gave names of this in it, including those mentioned in a previous communication.

To answer your question concerning the condition across the border, the answer would seem to be yes. But the monkey was put on the other fellow's back. See Eppie Montoya.

Visitors will return at any time after 26th. Have had my telephone‡ reinstated and should you be in this neighborhood, might be best to call me and if I have anyone here, I can meet you elsewhere, or give you the cue in case the ones here you need to listen to. In that case, I could have the north window open where you can hear the entire conversation.

—(Horzmann's name not indicated)

~

From her second and signed letter[125] on the same day, which is repetitive:

As per your request, to let you know if I learned anything new; at 11:45 the same night you were here [I] had visitors from out of town. It is best for me not to write about it, since following that, other things developed, also.

Have had my telephone reinstalled, since my son went to St. Louis to take the Hup back to his dad and will be gone three weeks from last Wednesday. Number is 195, in case you are in the neighborhood.

Expect some more definite information after the 26th, when they will return. Write or wire [me]. Had another visitor this afternoon, who verified some points.

Hope you had success in "getting your woman" in L.A.   —M. Horzmann

~

Her letters of the 22nd leaves no question that Horzmann had developed a working relationship with New Mexico State Police Captain Vermillion, but what elements they were working on is difficult to ferret out from her letters. Although, one particular matter does stand out, which is the question asked if the "sign" was moved and used in the H. B. (Hembrillo Basin). Any sign left behind, by those who left it as a marker indicator, would have been specific to the place where and how it was intended to be used, i.e., Guerrilla geographic starting point, direction in which to go, gold or silver to be found here, or a number of other indications. A marker in one location moved to another location would have been useless.

---

* The sign Horzmann mentioned is probably a reference to the Cross Rock, which according to Doc was an additional indicator for the Victorio Peak treasure.
† Gorilla indicates a large ape. Guerrilla refers to a rebel, which was probably Horzmann's intent.
‡ The reference to her phone being reinstated was in Lordsburg, obviously not Victorio Peak.

Camp Notes — September 24, 1941

Two days later, she wrote to the San Carlos Indian Agency. Her letter:[126]

> *For the past few months I have been compiling some historical data in the area just back of the White Sands in the San Andres Mountains, and I am told you have a woman on the Reservation whose first name is Asa, and she lives near White Tail who lived at one time in these mountains.*
>
> *Could you give me any information concerning her, and if she is there, could she be interviewed? I could not find any place on the map by this name, and would naturally require instructions as to how to reach her if it is possible, and if it is off the main highway.*
>
> *It is presumed that she is a daughter of Chihuahua, the old Indian Chief, and has had some conversation with Mrs. M.E. Noss of Alamogordo. I have checked with the State College here about that region, and they know very little about it, but encouraged us to try to see Asa.*
>
> *Am enclosing a stamped addressed envelope for your reply, and will appreciate any information you may be able to give me. In case Asa is not the one, there may be someone else who would know of the old rock house used as a stage depot and a fort that is on top of a hill to the northwest about a mile. It is one of the old retreats of Victorio, and Nana visited there during his raid after Victorio's death.*   —Merle Horzmann

~

There were two buildings in close proximity to each other: the Rock House and an old fort, often referred to as the Rock Fort, which was situated at a higher elevation and in a northeasterly direction away from the Rock House, which it overlooked. Both of these structures were built in a similar manner and the large stones that made up the walls of both structures were gathered from the immediate area.

According to Terry, Ova Noss had a long conversation with Asa, but when that took place and what Ova learned from her remains unknown. The only information Terry got was that Ova was interested in learning about the area where the two structures stood. Authors Henry James* and Karl Laumbach have written about these structures, but information concerning their intended use is limited and there seems to be no historical records that the Rock Fort, or for that matter, the Rock House used by Doc and Ova Noss, were ever used as a stage depot as Horzmann had implied in her letter.

That same day, Horzmann wrote to the "Archaeological Department" in Washington. Here is a brief passage from her letter:[127]

> *...I was advised that your department had taken over that area and that no one would be admitted without a written permit from you. Circumstances have caused me to question the authenticity of this information, but if such is the case, would it be possible for me to secure your permission?*   *— Merle Horzmann*

~

Camp Notes —October 9, 1941

Doc's trial date was set for Tuesday, October 14, in Socorro County. Horzmann was making arrangements to attend, but in the meantime she wrote to Socorro County District Attorney James C. Enloe, Prince Hilliard and Captain Roy Vermillion concerning her traveling arrangements and time schedules. From her letter[128] to Enloe:

> *Am leaving sometime Monday morning en route to Santa Fe, and would like very much to see you as soon as I get to Socorro. Expect to see P. C. Hilliard on the way up, also.*
> *—Merle Horzmann*

~

* Not the famed Henry James.

From her letter[129] to Hilliard:

Will stop off in Hot Springs and would like to talk over some things with you before going on.   —Merle Horzmann

~

Another interesting letter by Horzmann was the one sent to Vermillion that day concerning a planned flight to Washington, D.C. An attorney who represented Doc had made arrangements for them to meet with President Roosevelt concerning the treasure trove matter. What had always been rumored as a possibility is once more confirmed in her letter[130] to Vermillion: (underlining inserted)

Expect to leave Lordsburg Monday morning shortly after 8 en route to Santa Fe. Will stop in Deming, Hatch and Hot Springs where I expect to see P.C. Hilliard and Mrs. Lulu Fincher, and there is a case in court in Socorro against M.E. Noss at 9 Tuesday, which I expect to attend. Before going to it, will try to see Mr. Enloe.

I will stop in Albuquerque for a few hours or probably until Wednesday morning and on in to Santa Fe. By the time I get there, I may have some more light on the subject with regard to possibilities relative to your last call here, but feel it quite necessary to discuss a few points with Mr. Enloe before going any further.

I might suggest that you question Neal Graham in Las Cruces. I do not know who he is, but his plane flew over the camp quite low one Sunday afternoon that I know of, and it was about the 25th of May when I saw it. Next day the "hero" [a sarcastic reference to Doc] of my story went out and dug up a specimen gold bar to show some people who

arrived to look over the prospects. It was that week that the trip to Washington was planned, but never pursued. Neal Graham was supposed to have been the pilot to take Doc and his attorney there.

The cave was supposed to have been ready by the 26ᵗʰ or 27ᵗʰ of September. The permit expires the first week in November for excavation, unless he expects to get another from the new owner, Henderson.*

Will discuss these things more fully with you when I get there and find out what I want to know en route. My family is getting very anxious for me to come home, and I would like to get this over with before I leave, since these old people are without help on it, but are so confident in it, and I have not discussed the adverse possibilities with them for fear of creating undue disturbance.

It is just possible that I will find it expedient to go on in to Las Cruces to pick up some information there, which will necessarily take a little more time, but will call you when I arrive in Santa Fe, or stop at the office.   *—Merle Horzmann*

~

According to records in the Socorro County Court House, Doc had been charged with the offense of *insulting another while armed,* which stemmed from his striking Ova's son, Harold. Doc had been charged on September 12ᵗʰ and was arraigned three days later and submitted a plea of not guilty; James C. Enloe was the prosecuting attorney. But it didn't work out for Enloe or Horzmann that day—Doc was found not guilty. He returned to camp the following day and resumed his activities at Victorio Peak. The inspection inside the cave entrance was complete, and the men were hard at work with the excavation efforts.

Camp Notes —November 3, 1941

A little more than two weeks had gone by since Doc's jury trial in Socorro. His exoneration must have had its effect on Horzmann; in fact she was never called to testify in the trial. Had Noss been found guilty and a prison sentence been imposed, Horzmann would have had a free hand at things in camp. In the future handling of the Cheyenne Mining Company, with Horzmann as secretary of the company and her husband being her mentor and collaborator, they would have stood a better chance of getting their hands on some of the coveted treasure. In spite of her hopes being dashed when Doc was found not guilty, Horzmann continued with her efforts to link Doc to the disappearances of the Heberer and Lorius couples. Doc's not guilty verdict might explain the most bizarre letter[131] Horzmann ever wrote. It was sent to Vermillion:

In the June issue of the Finger Print and Identification Magazine from Chicago, there is a picture and the finger prints of Enrico Sapietri, alias Enrico Sapietre, San Pietro, Charles Delmont Adrian, Alfred Hector Donadio, etc., whose age was 36 in 1937,

---

* Roy L. and Alice G. Henderson, seen here, were the new owners of the ranch below Victorio Peak.

which would check with my information, height 5'11-1/2"; weight 200, hair course wavy brown; eyes BLUE, complexion fair; neat dresser, occupation, engraver; nativity, claims Milan, Italy. Middle finger left hand stiff and cannot be bent at joints. The U.S. Secret Service and the Treasury Department want the man for counterfeit notes.

~

She continued with more of the same kind of talk, convoluted and disjointed conjecture without any reasonable foundation, especially her suggestion to Vermillion that Doc, in order to change his appearance, might have changed the color of his eyes.

If you have not already done so, it might be wise to compare the fingerprints of M.E. Noss with these. His age is the same, and I have heard Noss say that in 1937 he weighed 200 pounds, and it may also account for his reason for never doing any work in which he would have to use his fingers. I have also seen him dress so he looked just like this picture does, and I <u>understand there is a way to change the color of the eyes</u>, and at that time he could have had wavy hair, though now it is straight, but coarse, and he keeps it dyed. Naturally, it would be gray and brown, more heavily streaked at the temple I believe on the right side.

~

Horzmann's inference was that Doc and Enrico Sapietri, AKA: San Pietro, Charles Delmont Adrian and Alfred Hector Donadio, were one and the same. Doc Noss was from Oklahoma, not Milan, Italy. He had mostly Cheyenne blood, his hair was black and straight and his eyes were very dark brown.

The other day, O. G. Turner stopped in to see me on his way home from California, and we discussed the case a little, and I asked him where Doc got that sword with the engraving on the back of it. He said he didn't know, but he was quite sure he didn't get it out of the cave, and he guessed he put the engraving on it himself. A sugar bowl and a copper cup that were supposed to have been found in the cave were also engraved, and the sugar bowl was too newly engraved to have been underground.

~

He was neither an engraver nor a counterfeiter. Horzmann claimed at times that Doc's operation was a racket, yet from time to time her letters authenticated the treasure. Examination of the articles mentioned above have been closely examined by experts who have authenticated their originality. Expert engravers did the engraving on the articles, not Doc Noss, as Horzmann suggested was the case from her conversation with Turner. She continued with her forensic analysis: (underlining inserted)

I have been urged many times to ask you to check this set of prints and the picture. Doc could have had an operation to loosen the joints in his left middle finger, and that may account for his not doing anything where he would have to use his fingers for.

I could be all wrong, but sometimes it pays to follow a hunch, even if it seems a little far-fetched. While in Santa Fe, I got another important address—the one I thought was in Albuquerque. That has been better than three weeks, however, and it may not be any good now. Kept thinking you would be through here and I could tell you about it, but have about decided you would work it out differently, which is all right, too. Also, the man that drove my car for me is well acquainted and said he would tell you about how this case got started in the first place. (He said this 'racket').

—*Merle Horzmann*

Camp Notes —November 4, 1941

If there was ever any doubt that Horzmann intended to hang the murders of the Lorius-Heberer couples on Doc, her letter[132] of November 4, 1941 to the United States Secret Service at the Treasury Department in Washington, D.C. stands as proof. Horzmann reached out once more to convince the Secret Service that Doc Noss was Enrico Sapietre. Horzmann wrote:

In the June issue of Finger Print and Identification Magazine, Chicago, a picture and fingerprints of Enrico Sapietre, alias Enrico Sampietro, etc., appears.

While the description as given does not fit, I have reason to believe that they should be compared with those of M.E. Noss. Little circumstances that have come to my attention may have some bearing on the two descriptions, but I have not had an opportunity to compare the prints. Noss' identification is rather obscure to his acquaintances, but I have seen him dressed so he looked extremely like Sapietri.

Would appreciate knowing what you find out about it.   —Merle Horzmann

Camp Notes —November 7, 1941

Here, B.B. Ownby writes to Chief Summers concerning a handgun Doc had borrowed from him. Although it plays no role in the drama, it is interesting to read:[133]

On June 25, 1941, Dr. M.E. Noss came to my house and in the course of the conversation asked to see my revolver, which I showed him. It was quite late, around midnight. He asked to borrow it and insisted on it until he finally took it with him. Up to now, he has not returned it.

In checking over the case, as you no doubt are, [as I have learned] through some of your men, would there be any way to get this gun? It was the only protection we had in the house, and I am not in a position to purchase another one.

It was a .41 on a .45 frame, pearl handle with a bull's head on one side and plain on the other, nickel-plated, and in good shape.

If this gun can be gotten somehow, I would be glad if you would send it back to me as soon as possible.   —B. B. Ownby

Camp Notes —November 15, 1941

Chief Tom Summers wrote to Merle Horzmann concerning a file she had sent to him on Doc. Once again Horzmann stoked the coals by persuading Chief Summers to take an interest in the matter; it seemed to never end. The issue of Enrico Sapietri surfaced again. Chief Tom Summers wrote:[134]

Your file regarding Doc Noss has been received, and may prove of great value in the case. We have an investigator on the case and he has hopes of being able to assist the Department of Justice in taking the Doctor out of circulation.

Sorry to say we were unable to identify Noss as Enrico Sapietri. The fingerprints of the two subjects are not the same. It is hoped we might recover Mr. Ownby's gun. In the event there should develop anything of interest in the case, you will be promptly advised.

— *Chief Tom Summers*

Camp Notes —November 27, 1941

Doc called a special meeting of shareholders of the Cheyenne Mining Company at the Rock House. Horzmann received her notice and wrote[135] to Tom Summers. Here she was called upon in her official capacity as an officer of Doc's company to attend a meeting. Rather than attend and report her official findings later, she asks Chief Summers what she should do about attending the company meeting:

We are in receipt of a letter from Noss today, wanting us to be at the camp on the morning of December 4, by 9 o'clock and to bring our contracts, bedding and eats, for the purpose of knowing and understanding some things of interest, etc. He says he had two officers* working with him at camp, and that this is to be a general meeting of everyone having an interest in the mines.

Knowing the conditions out there, and Mr. Holt's age, and the fact that we will have to sleep outside or in tents, with what information you have by this time, would it be advisable for us to go? I mean are they far enough along?

By his wanting us to bring our contracts, he must have something up his sleeve. Besides that, he wants Mr. Holt to bring the letter he received from L.L. Robinson. Why? Has Robinson started proceedings?

I should like to know what to do before I start out with Mr. Holt, or anyone else. He said for us to notify Bramble B. Ownby [B. Bramble Ownby], also, but it is out of the question for us to try to take him out there. I would appreciate an immediate answer, as there are other things for me to do here before I can leave at this time.

—*Merle Horzmann*

~

Doc's reasons for calling the meeting appear to be reasonable, yet Horzmann's comments about Doc having "something else up his sleeve" was just another slam. Even worse, matters had escalated to the boiling point because of Horzmann; the New Mexico State Police, and perhaps the Department of Justice, were looking over Doc's shoulder regarding his business.

November 29, 1941

A letter[136] sent to Doc by the U.S. Department of the Interior indicated that Doc had written to Washington on November 26, 1941 to make application for

---

* The reference to "two officers" was two law enforcement officers, local sheriffs.

a permit to excavate Indian ruins in the Hembrillo Canyon. The reply came on November 29, 1941, by U.S. Department of the Interior Chief Clerk Lloyd Dolson, who advised that "permits for the examination of ruins" were only granted to "reputable museums, universities, colleges or other recognized scientific or educational institutions upon proper application." The Department of the Interior would eventually follow up with a second response.

Camp Notes —December 2, 1941

Chief Summers' letter[137] of December 2, 1941, to Horzmann:

> *Your letter of November 27th in hand and contents noted. I am very sorry indeed that this letter reached my office too late for me to be of any assistance at this time, but hope that you people will make this trip and find out just what this is all about. Also received copy of the letter to Colonel Holt at Alamogordo, New Mexico, written by Dr. M.E. Noss, which is very interesting. I will send Capt. Vermillion to Lordsburg at the earliest possible moment.*
>
> *Thanking you for your interest in this case and also for your cooperation, and assuring you of ours, we beg to remain.*   *—Chief Tom Summers*

~

Whatever information Horzmann had given the New Mexico State Police was important enough for Chief Summers to believe she was a viable asset.

Camp Notes —December 4, 1941

Just three days before the attack on Pearl Harbor, the second and final organizational meeting of the Cheyenne Mining Company was held. In spite of all the concerns put forth by Horzmann in her letter to Chief Summers, the meeting was heavily attended, but without Ownby, who was quite elderly.

Horzmann took the minutes as Doc called the special meeting to order at 10:45 am. Present were: Doc, Ova, Letha, Col. Willard Holt, Herman Horzmann (Carl and Merle's son), W.V. Martin, C.A. Cunningham, H.L. Liner, P.B. Griffin, Roscoe W. Parr, Warren Ware, Frank Vigil, (D.S.) [Deputy Sheriff], W.A. Stepp, Dale Pepper, Ernest Gatlin, Claude and Lulu Fincher, C.F. Garth, Dan and Mrs. Louden, Ben Galloway, and Mart Gilmore.

Doc discussed the progress of the work and said that they were down 264 feet in the shaft and that it was going to take money, time, and labor to get the shaft open, but he thought within 2 weeks it would be finished and ready to open if it was provided. They needed 6,000-7,000 feet of lumber to finish timbering to comply with the mining regulations. Doc told the gathering that he had the cooperation of the state and federal governments and a deputy sheriff on the grounds.

Doc told everyone that he had the opportunity to sell some mining claims and that the men who were interested were expected to arrive Sunday, others on Wednesday and Thursday (December 10 and 11). Since it was too expensive to go back and forth to town, he requested that someone be appointed to help on the outside. Doc suggested that if they had a representative in town to take care of the details from there, it would leave him in camp to oversee the work. Louden said he could furnish lumber for the timbering of the shaft for the required distance at a cost of $75 or $80.

Loose overhanging boulders were considered to be unsafe, so Galloway suggested that two men be allowed to go down to see what was needed. Doc said you could enter at your own risk, but he had been advised by the state mine inspector and he wouldn't be responsible if someone entered at their own risk. Doc also said that the hole was never measured until Saturday night, but he would take some safety precautions. Holt said if we could sell some of the claims, he thought it should be done. There was a $22,000 offer for one of them.

There was a motion to have officers authorize the sale of property of lead, silver and gold, on the basis of $1,000 cash and over-riding royalty of 1/8. Gilmore had prospects for another deal, but it would not interfere with the cave. A question about the different bombing areas the military had selected was also raised. From the minutes of the meeting:

> *The question came up as to the bombing field. The answer was that the area was not protected by the U.S. Department of Archaeology and was exempt from the bombing area, which included Sections 8, 9, 10, 12, 13, 14 and 15 in township 16 south, Range 3 East to the south of the Hembrillo Canyon.*

> ~

To provide the immediate financing needed, Doc offered 1% of his interest, which was matched by Ben Galloway and Ova. On July 12th, after Elzo Smith had timbered 28' down, he made an injurious report that the shaft pinched out and nothing was there. He had received $1,650 in cash, and tools and instruments that should have been left on the property, the meaning of which is not clear.

The property where Victorio Peak was located had been turned over to the U.S. Department of the Interior. Representatives had been on the property and soldiers from Fort Bliss made nine trips to examine the location. Notices were posted on November 26, 1941, to this effect.

Debts were listed as $487.45 and postdated checks were issued for $137.45 to J.B. Oliver for camp supplies, $150 for K.C. "Casey" Jones for the deputy salary, and $100 for Frank Vigil for deputy salary; both are at the rate of $100 per month. It was estimated it would take $600, after which it would require only two weeks to open the cave and no more than three weeks at most, but a system would be necessary to get it open.

"It was pointed out" that the 5.22% originally owned by Jack Bruton was out, including 1% owned by Ermile Smith, 1% owned by Elzo D. Smith *and* the 33.3% owned by Barman and Robinson. From the minutes:[138]

> *Also since all parties were notified of the meeting on this date, December 4, 1941, at the Rock House, that only those present would be admitted to the opening of the cave*

and that the officers [the two deputies hired by Doc] would meet them at the entrance to Hembrillo Basin.

There were other offers to purchase property; one being $35,000 for talc claim, $32,000 on the silver claim, $150,000 for the treasure cave, which was flatly refused. The state was to receive 10% of the amount of the find, and the Federal Government is to receive 12% of the amount of the find. Dr. Noss said he had no more authority to move anything than anyone else. There were only two paid men on the ground, and they were Mr. Frank Vigil, Deputy Sheriff and Casey Jones.

Application was made to the Department of the Interior for 8 men to work inside cave: C. Fincher, Dale Pepper, Fred Baker, C.F. Garth, Ernest Gatlin, Roscoe W. Parr, and Dr. M.E. Noss. This arrangement did not jeopardize the interest of the others. Newell and Scoggin, attorneys of Las Cruces, are required to do all of the legal work. It is estimated that the tunnel is 2700 feet long. There are 50 feet already timbered and from 110 to 125 feet more to go, but they encountered difficulties.

Ben Galloway was appointed business agent, to be assisted by Roscoe W. Parr and Mrs. Noss to handle sales on mines.

By the authority of Dr. and Mrs. M.E. Noss, Colonel Willard E. Holt has exclusive publicity rights.

The value of 2% interest was set at $2,000.

Roscoe Parr was appointed as executive secretary, Claude Fincher construction manager, and Dan Louden as assistant construction manager. After a few more minor points were discussed, the meeting was adjourned.   —Merle Horzmann, Secretary

Camp Notes —December 5, 1941

The next day, Horzmann sent another letter[139] to Chief Summers telling him that Colonel Holt, her son Herman, and herself entered camp the previous day and the first thing they saw was a human skeleton that had been dug up in a canyon near the corral, which had been "piled in a box." Beside it was a big rock with a cross on it, which Horzmann said was claimed to be a marker for the treasure. There was another rock that was claimed to be the headstone where the skeleton was found, which Horzmann described as a Masonic emblem:

> *It had what looked like a Masonic emblem marked on it with pencil and painted over with a coating of what looked to me like a very thin paint in which the lime had eaten through a little, just enough to take the gloss off.*

~

Horzmann wrote that Officer Frank Vigil was there and that he had stayed at the camp that night. She said they were told to keep quiet about the skeleton. She also described an old pair of hobnail shoes with the skeleton, which had been unearthed innocently during Doc's absence from the camp. More from her letter:

> *It has created a very great wonder in my mind as to the probability of other things linking up with the skeleton. Doc was very nervous, and explained it away with some other matter entirely. I am not sufficiently familiar with anthropology to be sure that the*

skeleton was as old as it was claimed to be, but it came from a place that must be pretty damp, since it is near a spring.

~

Until Horzmann wrote to Tom Summers on December 5, it was not known that there was *another* spy in camp—Vigil, the person Doc hired to guard the site. Considering Horzmann's prior actions, it is not difficult to believe that she might have recruited him. From her letter:

> *I don't know whether the officer who was on the grounds, Frank Vigil, has made a report to you by this time or not, but he was staying out last night.*
>
> *This matter was not to be given out to outsiders, but there were some 22 people on the ground, who saw it [the skeleton], and I have their names if it is necessary to produce them later, all good citizens…*

~

Horzmann, the spy in the mist, who had written to District Attorney Enloe on September 12, was now providing Captain Summers with the minutes of the December 4 meeting of the Cheyenne Mining Company. More from her December 5 letter:

> *I have the minutes of the meeting, which I am to write up and send them, together with the minutes of the previous meeting. Would you want me to send you a copy of them, too? Let me know if you want any of this other information yourself or if I should wait for Captain Vermillion.*   —Merle Horzman

Camp Notes —December 6, 1941[140]

> *He [Doc] called a meeting at the Rock House in Hembrillo Basin on December 6th to discuss further exploration and the prospects to sell some of the mining claims involved in a contract drawn up on June 14, 1941 for the original group, members who were to share pro rata in the proceeds of all mines and minerals. A skeleton was exhibited of a human body, together with the Cross Rock, which was apparently the one described in the waybill, and the skeleton coincided with historical data found in the library. More financing was undertaken. On 7 December came Pearl Harbor, which stopped much of the activities there and took some of the boys into the Army.*
>
> —Merle Horzmann

~

The United States was at war.

Chapter 16

Work at Camp Abates, More Proof of the Treasure

E xcavation work on the top entrance shaft inside Victorio Peak began to wind down immediately after the Japanese attack on Pearl Harbor. Now, able-bodied men were leaving camp to fight in the war.*

Camp Notes —December 15, 17, 1941

Horzmann wrote[141] to Chief Summers:

> *Your letter came last Friday, just at the time Dr. Noss was here. Mr. Vermillion has never arrived, and there is little more I can say about it, now that I have written. However, the Department of the Interior instructed him [Doc] to apply to the Smithsonian Institute for the permits for removal of such things as they may find there, and the skeleton was replaced after a severe grilling by investigators that someone had reported to.*
>
> *While waiting for the Smithsonian, however, they are going to work on the Old Spanish Mine. There had been an article about it in the El Paso Times this morning and it is possible they will be able to sell ore to raise the rest of the funds needed. That is the plan now I think.*

---

* Rear left to right: Mac Turner, O.G. Turner (Mac's father), Roscoe Parr, J.W. Parr (Roscoe's father), and Joe "Sonny" Andregg - Front left to right: Ova Noss, *Buster*, Doc Noss, *Tick* and Bill Lampros.

Should other irregularities occur, I shall be in a position to know, and will let you know, but I see no reason for Mr. Vermillion being taken from something he may be needed worse on at this time.   —Horzmann

~

Two days later, on December 17, Horzmann made another camp note[142] entry.

Pearl Harbor stopped much of the activities and took some of the boys into the Army. Ernest Gatlin's father-in-law was Roscoe Parr, whose partner was O.G. Turner. Turner's sons, Mack and George worked for an interest in the mining company, which was headquartered at the rock house.

Claude Fincher and wife lived in a small house nearby and cooked meals. At first, a lot of assessment work was done under Doc's supervision. Then work began to slow down. At night, Doc told stories about finding the cave and sleeping in one, guarding it and not knowing what to do. Once a hunter came up and Doc got excited and told the man about it, and then wished he hadn't.

Ben Galloway came in from Friona about that time, as others had, such as Parr and Turner. Although Doc was often skeptical of other people who showed up, and a lot of time was lost because of it, things began to look promising and there was progress made.

Doc would get drunk, or pretend to be drunk, and there were long waits for him to get ready to work. Lots of trips made to Alamogordo. Babe and Letha were mostly staying in Alamogordo. We slept in tents for 6-8 months, grueling nights and days. Doc was nervous and played with his guns. We were not allowed to leave camp and were escorted to the digging and back and we weren't allowed to congregate or get together and talk. We found cans in the mouth of the cave and signs of inhabitants before us. Later, Doc had confidence in me and told me of the contents. I worked with Sonny [Joe] Andregg, and a young Spanish man, a good friend. He had gone down with Doc and helped carry out bars. He mysteriously disappeared. The rumor was that Doc got rid of him. After a year, I made a trip home; Doc and Babe went with me to spend the night in Muleshoe. When we started back, Doc gave me $100 and asked me to make a check out to Roscoe Parr for him to have cash. I came home when the Army closed us down.   —Horzmann

~

The "Spanish man" Horzmann referred to was Jose Seraphin Sedillo, whom Doc hired to help him remove bars before the top entrance collapsed. Ova and Doc were very uncomfortable with Sedillo and didn't trust him. It wasn't long until they let him go. Horzmann's twist on the matter was that his absence was "mysterious" and that she relied on rumors that Doc *got rid of him;* an inference can be made that Doc killed him or had him killed. After Doc was murdered, Sedillo reappeared and came looking for work. Ova hired him for a short time to help locate the alternate entrance to the caverns, but he became a problem. Eventually Sedillo left camp and made his way to Anthony, New Mexico, to pick cotton.

That same day, December 17, 1941, Doc received a second letter from the U.S. Department of the Interior advising him that his request was referred to the Bureau of Indian Affairs. Apparently, Doc had used Box 329, Alamogordo, New Mexico, as his return address. The letter, one of three similar letters found in the Noss files, was an attempt by Doc to approach the matter concerning removal of artifacts in a proper fashion. The reply came from Under Secretary John Wimfrey. His December 17 letter:[143]

> *Acknowledgment is made of your letter of December 12, and I am referring the matter to John Collier, Commissioner of the Bureau of Indian Affairs. You will undoubtedly hear from the Commissioner direct within the near future.*
>
> —*Under Secretary John Wimfrey*

~

Doc was eventually instructed to apply to the Smithsonian Institution for the permits. However, no document has been found in the Noss files concerning the matter.

Camp Notes —December 19-23, 1941

Once again there is mention of Doc moving treasure from inside the mountain to hiding places in the Hembrillo Basin. The only place he could have taken the treasure from was the treasure rooms, which raises the same question—had he used the upper shaft or did he have an alternate entrance known only to him? Horzmann wrote:[144]

> *Doc moved some items from inside the peak and hid everything in a canyon* several miles away. Doc made reference to an Old Spanish map that originated in the Convent of St. Augustin in 1861, a map described by Pedro Navares. It described the directions from El Paso and how the treasure was buried and the signs to look for: crockery, clothing, packsaddles and tools, jars of fine jewelry, mule loads of bar silver, and gold. The map also referred to a treasure hidden in the springs where copper can be cut with an axe and it made reference to an old cabin. There would be figures and pictures cut in the logs. Three peaks were described in the legend: 'homes of Geronimo, Victorio, and Nana.' Doc Noss named them in that manner. ...A Chihuahua Indian, named Asa, is living on the San Carlos reservation. Ova met her.*

~

Asa said at one time that's where the stagecoach trail went through, referring to the Hembrillo Springs Canyon that crossed through the arroyo where the Bloody Hands wall is located, no more than one hundred feet from the canyon road, or trail. Dave Twitchell, a person with considerable knowledge of this period, often referred to Asa and said that Ova had met her. More of Horzmann's letter:

---

* The site was thought to be Lost Man Canyon, which is located several miles from the Rock House.

Fifty years ago a Mexican in California gave a Dr. McCullough of Bakersfield, a map to the San Andres treasure. McCullough gave it to B.B. Ownby age 84 of Lordsburg an old Territorial Ranger and Deputy U.S. Marshal. Through Ownby, O.G. Turner and J.W. Parr became interested. The three men hunted for it.

There is a large rock that stands on edge, smoothed off on both sides like an altar. Doc said it was a worship place. Behind it there appears to be a cave that is filled up. Above it is a group of Indian paintings: a sun face, a square with an X in it, four small hands, and others symbols. Doc claims Geronimo left the square with an X and that it was made with human blood. From the face of Sun God there is a pig face at Bloody Hands.

Doc pointed to another cave in a direct line up the canyon that joins the main one on the east. The mouth of this cave is square. He walked to it, climbed over the trail around the mountainside and stood in it. It makes a sharp turn a few feet inside but becomes small.

~

One of the many photographs in the Noss collection is a small color photo of the "cross rock." Another photo shows Doc standing in the mouth of a "square" cave opening near the Rock House; the photo was taken at the same time that Horzmann referred to it in her notes. However, it is the following entry that sheds more light on how the discovery of the treasure came about, confirming that Doc had entered the treasure rooms from the top of Victorio Peak. The crudely written entry lends additional information in support of Doc's original account of the discovery. More:

Beneath the Fort, a little to the west, there is another cave, sealed with Indian cement, a mixture of animal blood and clay. It is under the rim of a long mountain, but it is difficult to ascend. But once there, a trail winds around it that is easy to manage. On the outside of the entrance is a rock with "George Manning" carved on it indicating May 14, 1939. Since 1932 Claude Fincher was Doc's companion. For nine years they searched together. In 1937, Doc and Seraphin Sedillo found a marker that verified the map. Doc followed the interpretations on maps and the symbols and was led to the top of a high peak with a hole. Opening led straight down 54 feet to where it led into a tunnel. 2700' from beginning of main tunnel they came to cave with stalactites and where a freight train could go 60 mph on the floor of it, being so smooth and straight. They came to a yawning cavity. They dropped a rock into it and didn't hear it hit bottom. Also there was a waist deep river they waded across to the other side where there was a cross tunnel that led to smaller caves and rooms on either side. In the last room skeletons, gold, a gold vein, chests, clothing, saddles, beds, antiques, crowns, candelabra, gold gong, a sword marked 1463, and a fan. Tony Carriaga, Seraphin Sedillo, Doc with his dog, Buster along, removed 80 or 86 bars of gold. Ova said Doc was frightened each time he came out and she feared for his sanity. Doc said there was a round hole that sun shined through at high noon. Ownby's document is almost the same as the one Doc has. It could be the same document Ownby took to S.E. Montgomery to continue his search. Ownby obtained another copy. To the left of a spring covered with trees and rock and dirt and then upon removing them are timbers [these were the descriptions given on the Pedro Navares waybill]. But in the spring there is much wealth under the water. The spring is to the left of peak where the cave is and water flows. Doc said they had recovered 11 silver bars from it. Letha and Ova helped pump it out, with Claude Fincher and Frank Wicks or Elzo Smith. Supposedly silver and gold about 7 feet down.   —Horzmann

~

The person who was with Doc on several occasions when he made his first search of Victorio Peak was Tony Carriaga, *not* Seraphin Sedillo. It is obvious that Horzmann was referencing the "Confessions of Pedro Navares" as she wrote. In viewing Victorio Peak from the Rock House, the spring Horzmann mentioned would be in a southerly direction on the floor of the basin between Victorio Peak and Geronimo Peak, known as the saddle. She identified the spring as being "to the left of the Peak where the water flows." Water once flowed through that arroyo, and might still during heavy rains. She also wrote that upon removing the debris to the left of the spring "there are timbers," meaning the timbers became visible. Were these the same timbers, or *long logs* that Doc said he saw deep inside the caverns? Was this the hidden ox cart entrance so often mentioned?

Camp Notes — Thursday, April 2, 1942
Ova's notes,[145] abridged: (underlining inserted)

Doc wanted all of Merle Horzmann's papers. Doc had learned that the FBI was checking on her for mail fraud on <u>some oil deal she and Carl had put together</u>. Doc had questioned her on the matter, but she denied everything, but in the corporate minutes on page 84, she admitted involvement. In her notes, Horzmann said that Ownby reported to federal authorities on what was happening with Doc's operation, although there was no mention of what she was referring to. Also, Horzmann was supposed to have lost Mrs. Ownby's camera and Mr. Holt's gun and wound up paying Mrs. Ownby $25.00. Herman Horzmann, Merle's son, thought that Ownby and the Nosses were too friendly. His comment was said with meanness, confirming that the apples don't fall far from the tree.   —Babe

~

There must have been some dissension concerning Doc's demand for Horzmann's papers. Although Carl Horzmann's letter to Merle is only dated as *Saturday Morning*, he was responding to a letter he had received from her. She could have written to him the same day Doc had demanded her papers, which was on Thursday, April 2. Per Carl Horzmann's letter[146] of Saturday morning: (underlining inserted)

Dear Merle: Just got your letter from Las Cruces. Don't let anybody scare you, because you have not done anything against the law and all this stuff of getting the FBI on your neck <u>because of the oil lease deal</u> is just a lot of boloney. You have a perfect right to go ahead and sell leases on a proposition of this kind, and it is not against the law to solicit business of this kind, unless it would be the sale of unlisted securities, which however, was

not the case, as oil leases are not securities, and as some of the parties involved are citizens of New Mexico, the question of interstate does not even enter into the matter. I think the whole damned outfit is trying to throw a scare into you, but don't let it bother you. The question of hoarding gold does not apply to you, because you certainly did not hoard any, and Dr. Noss would be the only one that could be accused of that because of the 83 bars, which he removed and of which he actually had possession. All the rest of you do not come in on that deal, because you may have known this through hearsay, but not to your own knowledge, because none of you have seen the 83 bars. Just keep a stiff upper lip and paddle your canoe the way you have been doing, straight to the front and down the river, and no one can touch you.

I think that Mr. Holt will understand that you did not try to do anything underhanded. As a matter of fact, I believe that the government, when it does come in, will uphold all your actions in the matter and you do not have to be afraid. Am sending you a blank check to use in case you need it badly. Sent you a check for 3$ yesterday – maybe you can get along, but I do want you to get your stuff as soon as possible. Keep me informed.

—CW   [Carl W. Horzmann]

~

Colonel Holt, one of Horzmann's closest allies, is seen here in possession of one of Doc's gold bars, one of many he had cut in half.

Camp Notes —April 3, 1942

Horzmann talked to Garnett R. Burks, Doc's new attorney. Burks asked Horzmann if she knew whether Doc and Ova had ever mentioned a Doctor Wells. Horzmann asked Doc and he told her, yes. He said he was with the School of Mines and that he had domestic and financial troubles and had killed himself. Horzmann's abridged notes:[147]

> *Doc was diligent about his assessment work and signed the location claim on his sites. Assessment was also completed on: Cheyenne Mine No. 1 (road, cabin and tunnel), Lost Star No. 1 (repairing shaft, repairing tunnels and road work to mine), and Cheyenne Victorio No. 1 (one shaft 85' deep 6'x6'), and Cheyenne Mine No. 2 (lead mines – work on roads to shaft and claims).*   *—Horzmann*

Camp Notes —June 10, 1942

Six months passed before there was any additional activity related to Barman & Robinson. During that time it is difficult to determine what was going on at the Peak to understand why they once again became involved in the project. A good deal of work that was completed in the top shaft, work that was necessary to gain access to the treasure, was performed in two stages; the first stage was done by B&R and the second stage by Doc Noss and his crew at Doc's expense.

The problems attached to the excavation of the Peak, as it related to Barman & Robinson, began in 1941 when a group was formed under Doc's guidance to raise the necessary capital to do the top shaft* shoring work; Barman & Robinson was the contractor selected by an agreement dated January 30, 1941. B&R's efforts began three and a half months later after the weather improved and continued from May 12 to July 12, 1941. When the January 30 agreement was struck, B&R's reward was to come only when they completed the work as specified, provided the shaft construction and timbering work met the standards of New Mexico Bureau of Mines' regulations *and* they reached the required depth to access the passageway. Doc had consistently held to his claim that the route leading to the treasure rooms was 2,750 feet[†] long and could be accessed from deep beneath Victorio Peak. Had B&R continued with their excavation and shoring activity and reached the required depth, they were to receive 33⅓ percent of the money realized from the sale of the treasure.

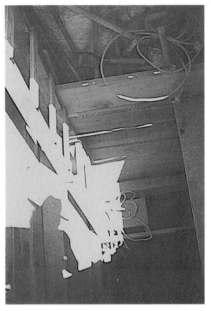

The problems began when B&R stopped excavating at the forty-eight foot level. As a result, a special meeting of the Cheyenne Mining Company was held on June 25, 1941 in the office of J. Benson Newell in Las Cruces. At the meeting, it was brought to light that B&R had sent a letter to Doc and Ova claiming they had fulfilled the terms of the January 30, 1941 agreement, namely that the entrance to the mine was timbered and was ready for inspection and that once the treasure was found the division of the proceeds from the treasure was to be honored per the terms of the January agreement. The question raised by Doc and his attorneys was whether or not Barman and Robinson had performed as agreed.

To make matters worse, Doc had discovered that Merle Horzmann was secretly conveying company information to Fred Barman and Lester Robinson and that she had been involved in doing so with attorney Scoggin without

---

* Shadow of Doc Noss examining the newly constructed shoring by Barman & Robinson.

† From the center of the top shaft on Victorio Peak to the highest point on Geronimo Peak is about 3,000 feet. Doc maintained that a passageway measuring 2,750 joined the two peaks from deep underground.

Doc's knowledge. The proof of her secret involvement with B&R came on July 5, 1941 in a letter she wrote, saying, "I wrote to Judge Scoggin. Everyone had seen my papers."

Out of nowhere, Sheriff Trujillo from Alamo, a small town in the Cibola National Forest one hundred miles away, became involved in the dispute. Additionally, U.S. Deputy Marshal Sam Frasonn arrived at Victorio Peak because of problems Horzmann and Elzo Smith unnecessarily became involved with over B&R's charges that Doc's treasure claim was a fraud. Trujillo, clearly out of his jurisdiction, gave Doc a deadline to prove that a treasure did in fact exist when the purpose of B&R's involvement was to gain access to the treasure. The incident was another case where Horzmann caused problems for Doc that would not have existed otherwise. Her interference also raised the question in Doc and Ova's minds whether or not B&R had filed a criminal complaint for fraud, claiming there was a treasure to be found when none existed. Even though some individuals made charges that Doc was guilty of fraud during the various attempts to reopen the top shaft, no evidence has been found in this investigation that would prove such accusations were true, and no official complaints that should have been filed were ever found. In fact, for years many individuals worked for Doc on an hourly basis to do the same work that Barman and Robinson were doing. In their case, when the treasure was lifted, they stood a chance of becoming wealthy people. Barman and Robinson owned a loan agency in Los Angeles and were involved in other mining ventures with the hope of uncovering hidden treasure, so they were well aware of the issues involving the Victorio Peak treasure.

By November 27, Horzmann again immersed herself in more secret activity related to B&R that served only to worsen the problem when she wrote to New Mexico State Police Chief Tom Summers. In her letter, she revealed that Doc had called a meeting for December 4 for everyone who had an interest in the mine and wrote, in part:

> ...He wants Mr. Holt to bring the letter he received from L. L. Robinson. Why? Has Robinson started proceedings?

~

The December 4 meeting was heavily attended and it was made clear by Doc that Barman and Robinson's 33⅓% financial interests in the Cheyenne Mining Company related to the recovery of the treasure was no longer valid, in other words, they were to get nothing because they failed to complete the work as agreed.

Then, on June 10, 1942, Doc wrote[148] to L.L. Robinson concerning the treasure and the work to be done. In Doc's letter, which had obviously been written by either attorney Newell or Scoggin, were four affidavits signed by Claude C. Fincher, B.D. Lampros, Ova, and Doc, all of whom held the opinion that:

All existing contracts between us are cancelled by mutual consent and a new contract be drawn. If you are to have the contract prepared and send them to us for inspection, we will be glad to execute them if we find them to be in order.

~

From the contents of Doc's letter it can be casually accepted that he and Robinson had agreed to agree on certain matters related to the past work done by Robinson and what needed to be completed, and that they had agreed to move forward again; there was no mention of any lawsuit by Robinson. The following seems to clarify the differences between them, which was spelled out in the June 10 letter:

We have discussed in detail three points or matters we would want covered in such proposed new contract:

a. *The engineer selected to complete the work shall be acceptable to a majority of all five of us.*

b. *In view of the fact that you agreed to open the treasure under the original contract, but quit at the forty-eight foot level, and in view of the fact that we four have sunk the hole an additional one hundred thirty-five feet to the main cave entrance at our own expense, we do not feel that the additional five hundred dollars and the furnishing of the engineer's services should entitle you to more than seventeen percent interest of the amount realized from the venture.*

c. *With reference to the handling of the money, we suggest that the five hundred dollars be deposited in the bank either at Lordsburg or Las Cruces, New Mexico, and expended by checks drawn by a secretary and a treasurer, such to sign all checks, and said secretary and said treasurer to be selected by a majority vote of we five.*

We are just about ready to go into the main entrance in order that the Government Inspector may go in and inspect the workings.

Please wire your answer at your earliest possible convenience and follow by letter with any further details. Kindly note address below.   —Dr. M.E. Noss

~

In June, what appears to be a supplemental letter[149] to the June 10 letter recapitulating the itemized requirements was sent to Robinson by Doc: (underlining inserted)

I have enclosed above affidavit and statement showing amount necessary to complete the project. Expect you to furnish funds and engineer to complete it, in an amount less than $500. <u>All existing contracts between us were cancelled by mutual consent.</u> New contract is needed. Engineer must be acceptable to majority of all five. You quit at the 48' level. We four sunk the hole down an additional 135' at our expense. Additional now requested entitles you to only 17%. The $500 in the bank was to be expended by a secretary and a treasurer to be elected by a majority of five. We are ready to go in the main entrance so the government inspectors can go in.   —Doc

~

No documents were found that said Robinson and Doc had gone beyond what was written above. It appears that the matter had been settled to that extent.

Camp Notes —July 4, 1942[150]

The onset of military involvement in the Tularosa Basin was extending over to the Hembrillo Basin and affecting the excavation work at Victorio Peak. More notes:

> The road from Tularosa was closed when the government took over the area for a bombing range. No other ingress was available except through Rincon by foot or horseback over the pass. A petition was drawn up requesting county commissioners of Socorro County to put in a road. This was granted, and Sierra Talc Company used it to haul talc over to ship to New York, from claims east of Victorio Peak. Passenger cars could not get into basin.   —Merle Horzmann

~

Doc and Ova went to the treasure site whenever they could, but the trip in from Rincon was time-consuming on horseback. When they drove in, they would load up enough supplies to stay for weeks. They camped at the Rock House, drew water from a nearby spring, and shot wild game for their meat supply. Occasionally, someone in the old crew would wander into camp, wondering what was happening with the excavation in the shaft. Horzmann would arrive and stay for short periods.

Chapter 17

V-2 Rockets at Peenemunde

On July 6, 1942, two days after the military had closed the road from the Tularosa Basin into the Hembrillo Basin, and only six months after the bombing of Pearl Harbor, a special Nazi weapon was test-launched from Peenemunde in Nazi-controlled Europe—the V-2 rocket. Compared to today's standards in rocket technology, the V-2 was crude and unsophisticated: it lacked the reliable guidance system, range and massive destructive power of modern weaponry.

Regardless, it turned the heads of military leaders in the Allied Forces, especially in the United States and Russia: it was the first test of a potential practical design of an intercontinental ballistic missile—technically, the first ICBM. Development of the missile program was carried out under the direction of Wernher von Braun and his team of scientists under *Projekt Amerika*. The Nazis' development and research facility was located at Peenemunde, situated on an island base in the Baltic Sea. There were more than two thousand Project America rockets, some of which were named *Washington, D.C.*, *Philadelphia*, and *New York*, but time ran out for Germany in developing a rocket that could reach the United States. Allied forces quickly destroyed most of the Nazi launch sites, killing the threat. However, thousands of V-2 missiles fell on England, France, and Belgium. It took only three years for the United States and Russia* to connect the dots—rockets armed with nuclear warheads.

In October of 1942 a third test rocket flew 170 miles. Soon afterwards Hitler's V-2 rockets rolled from an underground assembly line in great numbers.

Germany's missile manufacturing, supplies, and materials site was at Nordhausen, the assembly and distribution plant for the dreaded V-2. Slave laborers from nearby concentration camps worked in the Nordhausen tunnels until

---

* The Soviets had an ICBM by 1958, but the U.S. soon closed the "missile gap" and never looked back. Photo credit to Lars Aronsson commons.wikimedia.org.

they died of starvation or disease. In less than four years, the entire advanced German missile technology would arrive at the White Sands Proving Ground in New Mexico; the rumor that Nazi gold had been secreted in the missile shipment persists to this day.

America was at war and they needed a large standing army. All over the United States men were enlisting, and if they weren't enlisting, they were being drafted. Things were no different in Hot Springs, New Mexico; on July 30, 1942, Doc's notification to register and to appear for physical examination for military service arrived.[151] He was directed to report to Dr. A.C. White in Hot Springs at 1:00 p.m. on Monday, August 3, 1942. In spite of the chance of being drafted into service, Doc continued with the assessment work requirements at Victorio Peak and proof of labor notices of intention to hold the claims were filed. As a result, state engineers came to the Peak on several occasions to check the mining properties with a view to leasing the claims, but nothing ever came of it.

Soon after the Army's arrival in the Tularosa Basin, the entire area was registered with the Department of the Interior. Notices were posted against removal of anything that might be valuable as historical artifacts. During this period, Doc drifted in and out of the Victorio Peak area to keep an eye on the treasure entrances, but he was being watched closely. It wasn't long after the Army settled in its new headquarters that the federal government fostered the opinion that the treasure alleged to have been found by Doc Noss, if it did exist, was subject to public domain, an opinion that was patently false; the discovery had already been made and the treasure trove laws came into play when it was discovered by Doc and Ova Noss.

The problem was that the treasure was found on state-owned land, which the Army was now leasing from New Mexico. But the federal government nevertheless had its eye on Doc's gold. To protect the treasure and their interest in the claim site, Doc and Ova obtained permits from the State Land Office for prospecting and mining rights, which had to be applied for and approved by that office. Doc filed his applications with John E. Miles, now the Commissioner of Public Lands. Miles was Governor of New Mexico from 1938 to 1942, but after his term ended he became commissioner and served from 1944 to 1948. Miles was Governor of New Mexico when the U.S. Army took control of the Tularosa Basin in 1945. Before that time, the basin was used primarily as an artillery range, but not the entire basin or the mountain ranges that surrounded it.

Chapter 18

Tribulations of Doc and Ova Noss

Because of the urgency for materials and raw supplies needed to support the war effort, Congress legislated measures to speed up the normal production of materials such as fluorspar and copper that were being mined in New Mexico. Assessment work was a process that allowed the State Land Office to inspect the progress of companies mining ore on state-owned land. Without having assessment work responsibilities, mining could proceed at a faster pace. So on May 3, 1943, Congress suspended assessment work on mining operations. Even though it was not required, assessment work was kept up at Victorio Peak and the proofs of labor and *Notices of Intention to Hold* were filed with the New Mexico Land Office in Santa Fe.

Horzmann wrote[152] about the activity of the Cheyenne Mining Company:

> *Only the assessment work was kept up and Proofs of Labor filed, and Notices of Intention to hold. Engineers went in from time to time to check on the mining properties with a view to leasing, but nothing ever came of it. The area was registered with the Department of the Interior, and notices were posted against removal of anything that might be valuable of historical evidence. It was at that time thought to be on Public Domain, but the discovery was made that the cave was on State Land. This changed the aspect of it, and to protect the interests there had to be permits obtained from the State Land Office for prospecting. Dr. Noss filed his statement with John E. Miles, State Land Commissioner.*   —Merle Horzmann, Acting Secretary

~

Doc was eager to proceed with mining his copper claims and urged Ova's daughter, Letha, to join them in New Mexico; after the entrance shaft collapsed in 1939 Letha went back to Oklahoma. Months later, she moved to California to work at an aircraft assembly plant. Doc and Ova wanted Letha to return to Hot Springs to be with them. Doc's letter to Letha was sent on the letterhead of Cheyenne Mining Co., Box 708, Hot Springs, New Mexico. Doc's letter[153] of May 25, 1943: (underlining inserted)

> *I just received your letter and was indeed glad to hear from you, and about the mines, I have a couple of copper claims now at High Rolls, east of Alamogordo in the mountains. It sure is nice up there. I had the government engineer out there and he left Saturday the 22ⁿᵈ. I'm getting a twenty thousand dollar loan on it and I am sure the loan will go through. I'm starting operations again in the Hembrillo Basin. Claude Fincher and a crew of men are working there, now.*
>
> *Letha, why don't you come home, at least we have plenty to eat, and what we want to eat. I'll see that you make it [out here]. I could tell you all about my moves if I could*

talk to you. Don't worry, Doc is damn sure in the race and I believe I am going to win, too. The government agents are wanting my copper and lead. Now is the time to make it if there ever was on earth.

About the cave, Letha, I cannot tell when I will be able to finish it up. I guess you know that old Ownby at Lordsburg had me arrested and I have been under bond for several months. He cannot win, but you know things like that hold up the deal for us all. Benson Newell at Las Cruces is my attorney. He told me Saturday he was going to have the District Attorney throw it out for they had no evidence against me. Believe me, Hot Springs sure is a dead hole. Babe and myself are going fishing tomorrow morning to pass some time away.

Letha, come on home, you can do better here than you can ever hope to there. You worry and work hard and I know you can do better here when we start operations at High Rolls. You can take over the commissary and mess hall. I'll see you make plenty of money. Expect to feed 30 men 3 times a day at $.75 for each meal. It will be under the O.P.A.* and you certainly can do good. Babe would like to have you here. She is by herself most of the time. I have to be away taking care of business in the mines. How is Wesley [Letha's son]? Fine I hope. Tell him hello for me. Be sure and bring him with you. It takes too much of your time and money out there [California] to get by. Well, Letha, think it over and pack up and come on. We will be in production by June 15 anyway and get in on it with me. I'll see that you do good. Write soon and tell me how you are and what you are doing and when you will be here with us.   —Doc

~

Few had ever known that Doc had requested assistance from the federal government to help him open the collapsed shaft at the top of Victorio Peak to gain access to the treasure. Up until this investigation, even Noss family members were unaware he had solicited such help, but it was true. In spite of his distrust of government, Doc exposed himself to his worst fear that the government would eventually close in and steal the treasure, or bar him legally as a legitimate finder under the treasure trove laws. Four months had gone by since Doc had written to Letha concerning his hopes to begin mining copper in High Rolls, however, nothing had developed.

September 16, 1943

Gustave Voelzel, Regional Technical Adviser, Mining Division, War Production Board (WPB) of El Paso, wrote[154] to Doc on September 16, 1943, concerning his request for assistance. From Voelzel's letter:

I talked to Mr. S.A. Colwell Monday morning about surveying the shaft and working on Soledad Mountain [Victorio Peak].

---

* Office of Price Administration - During WWII, food rationing was instituted nationwide in the spring of 1942. Mining companies were allowed a certain price per meal for their workers.

He said he would get in touch with you and would probably be able to do this work in a couple of weeks. One of his helpers is supposed to return shortly and then he may be able to arrange time to do this job.   —*Gustave W. Voelzel*

~

Unfortunately, no other documents were found in the Noss files related to Doc's request for assistance, or whether or not the WPB had followed through as it had indicated it would. Chances are the WPB lost interest in the Victorio Peak treasure recovery effort. With no help or response from the government, and now with his loan proposal not being approved, Doc began to pick up on his old habits, but with increased intensity. Per the FBI: On February 2, 1944, Doc was in El Paso, drunk.

Camp Notes —March 1944

Interest in the happenings at Victorio Peak still caught the attention of a number of publications: newspapers, magazines, and especially treasure magazines. In the March issue of *Desert Magazine*, an article appeared entitled, "Go Where the Gold Lies Buried." Merle Horzmann wrote[155] about the article:

This was an account of the legend of the Lost Padre Mine, and fitting in with much of the description Dr. Noss had given of the cave, it aroused further interest and renewed effort. Historical records were further searched in the libraries for data that might have more bearing on it.   —*Merle Horzmann*

~

But the spirit and excitement of the excavation for the treasure inside Victorio Peak had slowly died off. Even with the short boost of interest by the article, the few workers that remained at the Victorio Peak campsite had lost their drive. Though Doc and Ova visited the operation often and stayed there weeks on end, things were different now: the men no longer gathered outside the Rock House for orders from Doc to start the workday, the hustle and bustle of cars with workers coming to work their shift had stopped, and trucks coming in and out of the basin with materials and supplies had ceased altogether. For the first time since Doc and Ova began their quest to bring the entire treasure to the surface, they found themselves alone and unable to carry out the workload required to raise the treasure. Also, and unbeknownst to them, something else was happening, something that was seemingly unconnected and remote from the operation at Victorio Peak had already taken root, something that in the years to come would prove that the treasure Doc and Ova Noss had discovered inside Victorio Peak was real, undeniable, and massive.

On March 7, 1944, a man named Lloyd Gorman Tucker entered the U.S. Army at Fort Sill, Oklahoma. His separation papers[156] listed him as *"in continual service"* for one year, two months, and three days. Nearly three decades later, during the Thanksgiving Day weekend in 1973, Tucker would play a crucial role in the theft of 36.5 tons of gold bullion and precious antiquities from the Noss treasure trove, a mere fraction of the entire treasure. Tucker was not alone when the theft took place; he had a great deal of help, including the assistance of the military at White Sands Missile Range, and a sitting President.

Information concerning Lloyd Tucker came directly from Tucker's wife, Betty. She and Lloyd were born in 1922; Lloyd was Betty's third husband and Betty was Lloyd's fourth wife. They were thirty-seven years old when they married in 1959 and were married thirty-one years until Lloyd's death in 1990. Betty never remarried. Here are excerpts from a series of recorded interviews in 2004:

> *John Clarence: You said he served in WWII.*
> *Betty Tucker: Yes.*
> *John Clarence: Do you know what his rank was?*
> *Betty Tucker: It varied from sergeant back down to nothing.*
> *John Clarence: Do you know where he served in Europe during WWII?*
> *Betty Tucker: Not exactly. I know that his ship dropped in England and I don't really know the sequence of the countries that he was shipped to. He was always in a special unit; there were only about six men in his unit. A glider flew them behind the lines or they would have to parachute in. Once he got in he had to get out at his own risk because there was no escape out.*
> *John Clarence: Was he a Ranger?*
> *Betty Tucker: I don't know, he never said.*
> *John Clarence: Did he ever tell you if he was with the OSS or Army Intelligence?*
> *Betty Tucker: He never mentioned it, just CIA.*
> *John Clarence: It wouldn't have been the CIA then.*
> *Betty Tucker: Probably not, but that's what he told me and that's all I knew; it was before I knew him, but he always maintained that he was CIA.*
> *John Clarence: And that's how he said it; he was CIA?*
> *Betty Tucker: Yes.*
> *John Clarence: Can you please explain to me in a little more detail how this came about and under what conditions he told you this?*
> *Betty Tucker: It was just conversation. When something came up he mentioned it, more than once, many times.*
> *John Clarence: How did he say it?*
> *Betty Tucker: Well, ah, his training; don't ask me any questions and it's for your safety that you don't know anything I'm doing or have been doing. He said because if anybody ever picks you up and quizzes you, you have no information to give them. If I gave you a bunch of stories or information, your life would be in danger.*
> *John Clarence: So his job when he was in the military was secret?*
> *Betty Tucker: Yes, always behind the lines. They thought he was German because of the name Gorman (Lloyd Gorman Tucker), which was Irish, not German. He stood and watched Hitler speak many times in the vast crowds. They would blow up bridges and they would do whatever they had to do to get out when they could.*

~

The Office of Strategic Services (OSS) was formed on June 13, 1942 by an order from President Roosevelt, mainly for the purpose of collecting and analyzing critical military information for the Joint Chiefs of Staff. The OSS was a loosely fitted intelligence-gathering operation attached to the British Secret Intelligence Service and Special Operations Executive which was connected to the Department of State, the U.S. Treasury, Navy, and the War Department (now the Department of Defense). Shortly after the war ended in the Pacific theater, President Truman signed an Executive Order dividing the OSS between the War Department and the Department of State. The CIA came to life when the National Security Act of 1947 established it as this country's first peacetime intelligence agency.

John Clarence: Do you know what generals he served under?

Betty Tucker: No.

John Clarence: Did he ever have any direct encounter with any Nazi forces?

Betty Tucker: I wouldn't have any idea, other than he and his group had found these Nazis hiding in a cave; there were just a few of them. Lloyd said we have to bring them back as captives because the war was still going on fast and furious. The other men got real tired of sharing practically no food or water and they wanted to kill them. Lloyd said, 'No, we're going to do what we came here to do and we're going to take them back.' It so happened that years later he [Lloyd] went into the bank with their [Lloyd and his associates] gold deal, I guess, because that's what they dealt in, and the president of the bank recognized Lloyd and he recognized him as the officer whose life Lloyd had saved.

John Clarence: Was it a Frankfurt bank?

Betty Tucker: It was either in Frankfurt or Hamburg; he was in both places.

John Clarence: How long after the war was that?

Betty Tucker: It was long after that when he was in private business again, the gold business. When he went into that bank they recognized each other.

John Clarence: What languages did Lloyd speak?

Betty Tucker: A little bit of a lot of them.

John Clarence: Could he speak and understand German?

Betty Tucker: To some extent: French, Spanish, German, Italian, many languages.

John Clarence: Was he trained in those languages?

Betty Tucker: He never elaborated.

John Clarence: You said Lloyd came into possession of German bearer bonds.

Betty Tucker: Yeah, there must have been a whole bunch of them, but all I saw was a couple, about three or four that he had in his hand. He was supposed to try to sell them, and I don't know whether there was no market or there was fear in the market at that time, and so he didn't deal with the thing. He kept a couple of the bonds and I don't know whatever happened to them.

John Clarence: Did this occur sometime after WWII while he was in business?

Betty Tucker: Yeah, while he was in business. I can't remember the dates.

~

April 1944

The workforce at Victorio Peak campsite was gone. Per Merle Horzmann's notes:[157]

In April, Bramble B. Ownby* died, leaving his widow, Anna, now 91 years old, blind, and unable to walk, living in the old folk's home in Lordsburg.

—Merle Horzmann

~

By now, the men who normally came and went from the Hembrillo Basin had wandered off to places unknown: some had left to serve in the military, others were too old to work the shaft inside Victorio Peak, while others simply lost interest. Some of the workers had died, such as B. Bramble Ownby, a one-time

friend and shareholder in Doc's Cheyenne Mining Company. Ownby was a former Deputy U.S. Marshal, an 1883 Territorial Ranger, an Indian War veteran, and a well-known National Judge Advocate.

Wednesday, May 24, 1944

Doc sent a telegram to Ova at her apartment in Clovis on May 24. He was somewhere in Texas trying to raise cash by selling gold bars from Victorio Peak he had stashed in the Hembrillo Basin; it was in Texas that he eventually met a man named Charley Ryan, a man who would play a dark role in Doc's life.

Even though he had not given up, Doc was approaching the time when he would make a decision on how and when he would reengage his efforts at Victorio Peak; whatever decision he made, though, it would require a good deal of working capital to keep the digging operation going: material and supplies, legal expenses, living and emergency expenses, gasoline, and transportation costs. The telegram[158] dealt with closing a gold sale deal. Roscoe Parr was with him this time:

I couldn't close the deal at Las Cruces. I just talked with the doctor here. I will close our deal today. I guess I am fine, only tired. Roscoe Parr is with me. I'll wire you tomorrow.

—Dr. Noss

~

Sunday, May 28, 1944

The notations on the back of a Western Union Telegram, which were made by Ova, tell a story that has never been told, one that was unknown by most

---

* Ownby's headstone in the Lordsburg cemetery reveals that his true name was Bradley Bramble Ownby.

members of the Noss family. The notations direct attention to Doc's obvious activities in selling off gold bars and his famed drinking binges. According to family members, he had a habit of selling gold and celebrating afterward, sometimes for periods long after the transaction. Doc was still in Texas on Thursday the 25th, but he was jailed on Friday in Farwell, a small rough-and-tumble border town ten miles east of Clovis, New Mexico. He had beaten up a cop and was held for two hours. He left Texas that night and drove to Albuquerque and stayed all night and into the night of the next day. He then drove to Hot Springs, arriving at the Hot Springs Hotel at 9 a.m. on Sunday, May 28. Ova's notations[159] read in part:

> *Doc came home May 28 Sunday at 10 o'clock a.m. drinking bad. He had $2,245 on him. Said he was jailed for beating up a cop at Farwell, Texas. He got to the Hot Springs Hotel close on to 9 a.m. and never came home until ten o'clock and was drinking bad. He stayed drunk until he left on the bus for California via Albuquerque. He said he might take a plane for Palo Alto, California or take the El Capitan train.*

~

From Monday May 29 until Friday June 2 Doc was traveling. On Saturday June 3 he finally arrived home. More of Ova's notations:

> *This is one o'clock Saturday and no word from him yet—he just came in Saturday 3 June, drinking.*

~

On June 6, three days after Doc arrived, the invasion of the European mainland by the Allied Forces commenced on the shores of Normandy in France.
July 1944
Doc exhibited all the signs of being an alcoholic and, to add to his miseries, most of the men he knew and trusted to do the work on Victorio Peak worksite were gone; except for Ova, who maintained a vigil there. If there ever was a man who was lost in his own backyard, it was Doc Noss: disappointment faced him at Victorio Peak and most of the close friendships and associations were vanishing. Instead of reasoning his way through his difficulties, he chose to drink. Doc was at sea. Horzmann wrote:[160]

> *In July, Dr. Noss again got into legal difficulties and narrowly escaped a prison sentence for impersonating a Federal Officer, but he was acquitted.*

~

Terry shared what he knew about this period in Doc's life:

> *There wasn't much Babe didn't tell about the troubles Doc got himself into. One thing that stands out in my mind were the vague references about Doc being deputized as a Federal Marshal, which according to Babe was true, but we never understood for sure what that was all about, but it has been common knowledge in our family that for a short period of time Doc was actually deputized as a Federal Marshal, but no one can*

explain why he was made one or what his mission was or what he was to do. I think this Federal Marshal thing happened around 1946, or maybe before then. We also know that he was discharged from that, from being a Marshal, but he somehow kept his badge and identification papers and continued to identify himself as one, which wound up causing him more problems than you could imagine. So, the only thing I can say is that the whole matter over Doc being a Federal Marshal will always be a mystery.

~

Doc had the ability to slip in and out of problems he created. He had been arrested many times, but soon afterward he was released after paying a small fine, or, in some instances, the charges were dismissed. The question is why? Federal authorities were certainly keeping an eye on his comings and goings. Is it possible that Treasury and Secret Service agents were interested enough in Doc's gold that his actions were usually dismissed at the request of federal authorities? Until the time came that either Doc successfully raised the treasure or was caught with a substantial number of gold bars that the Secret Service could trace back to the caverns of Victorio Peak, he was left alone. Government officials knew they were up against the treasure trove laws and Ova would not go quietly if they attempted to steal it, if they could get to it; there were too many eyes and Ova didn't hesitate to stand up for her rights and for Doc's.

Apart from the drinking, the brawling, and a marked propensity to drop out of sight at a moment's notice, Doc had an array of more positive attributes: he spoke five languages, he had a quick and clever wit about him and a remarkable sense of humor. There were many tales that Ova passed on to Terry Delonas; some were tragic, but many were comical stories that led straight to Doc's deep-rooted dry humor. On the south side of Las Cruces lies a small mountain, called "A Mountain" where an extremely large "A" was painted on rocks placed there by students from New Mexico State University, NMSU, "A" meaning—the "Aggies." Doc, Ova and Letha were driving back to camp from El Paso one day when Ova looked at the mountain and asked Doc what the "A" meant. Ova and Letha were also from Oklahoma. Doc responded seriously, "Why, it was put up there for you Okies. When you learn that, they're going to put up a 'B,' though I don't expect we'll be seeing that for a long time."

Letha confirmed his sense of humor and and further explained the domestic scene. Letha:

> *Doc had a dry humor and he loved to fish and hunt, and he was a good marksman, too. Doc liked steaks, and ham and eggs, stuff like that, and he ate Mexican food, too; he liked Mexican food a lot. Sometimes they'd put a cooler in the car and put some cheese or something in it to nibble on and they'd head down the road and stop to see the sights. Mama just loved that; she and Doc always took time to go for a Sunday drive. I can remember that Doc and Mama would go to dances with Dorothy and me; they'd sit with their crowd and we'd sit with ours.*

~

Then something strange and unexpected happened—Doc slipped out of sight and was not seen at Hot Springs or at Victorio Peak. In fact, for months, his exact whereabouts were a mystery to the Secret Service and the FBI. The stress of the operation at the Peak had gotten the better of him; Doc simply pulled away from the foundation of his life, his soul mate, Ova, who always remembered what they had shared together during the difficult times of the discovery and the grueling efforts to raise the treasure. He was gone—but not completely; from time to time he contacted Ova, letting her know where he was and what he was doing to make ends meet. Before he left, Doc left her with a sizable sum of cash, enough to last for years. But he could no longer stay in the area; Secret Service and FBI agents were constantly tracking him, so he couldn't chance moving any more gold bars. He took several small bars with him for an emergency, but only enough to exchange small pieces of gold to trade for cash when it became necessary.

There was little he could do at the Peak; because of the war in Europe, the operation there was all but abandoned. With the exception of Ova going there on a weekly basis to make sure no one was attempting to reach the treasure, traffic in and out of the basin by civilians was limited to those with cattle and ranching operations, and crucial mining ventures essential to the war effort. Military patrols in the general area of the Hembrillo Basin were now commonplace, so it was no place for Doc and his relentless efforts to move the hundreds of gold bars he had removed from the treasure rooms and bury them in other places nearby; there were too many eyes watching him. So, Doc wandered, somewhat aimlessly at times. He maintained his usual interest over what was going on at the Peak, but he was seldom with Ova—in fact rarely. There would be weeks she didn't see or hear from him, then months, then a year or more. When he settled in one place for a spell, he would give Ova an address where she could write him letters. Then word came from Attorney Melvin Rueckhaus that Doc was in Del Rio, Texas, depressed and all but defeated. He had taken a job as a radio personality. Rueckhaus' July 7, 1976 letter,[161] in part:

> *Doc became involved with Doctor Brinkley in Del Rio, Texas, and had set up a business of selling astrology readings through radio advertising. He stated that he was doing well under the stage name of The Great Kareem. During the war years, I heard from Noss irregularly and only saw him on one occasion, we went to Chihuahua, Mexico, together to handle a problem of some confiscated property of his acquired during the Del Rio days. Doc had taken to selling fractional interests in his treasure venture and also appeared to be doing well selling certificates. Visits thereafter were infrequent and largely social. I did not see him again until sometime shortly before his death, when he discussed with me what problems he was anticipating with Parr and Ryan.*
>
> —*Melvin D. Rueckhaus*

~

Del Rio, Texas is a small border town near the Rio Grande and Mexico. Two hundred and eighteen miles southeast of Del Rio is the town of Alice, Texas where Doc met a businessman named Charley Ryan. They soon became personally acquainted after Doc showed him a few gold bars. In time, Doc, Charley Ryan and Roscoe Parr would return to New Mexico and the Hembrillo Basin. Before they arrived, Doc would get an annulment of his marriage to Ova, remarry, and enter into an agreement with Ryan to fly gold into Mexico from Victorio Peak. Alice, Texas was the end of the line for Ova and Doc; disaster was looming, but Ova never knew it until it was too late.

July 9, 1944

Realizing the future threat of missile warfare, the War Department* in Washington began a site selection process for its own testing range facility. The goal was to find an ideal site for the firing and retrieval of missiles in a complete guided missile warfare scenario. By July 9, 1944, a suitable location had been found in the Tularosa Basin in New Mexico and the White Sands Proving Ground came into being.

The U.S. Army had closed all roads leading to the San Andres Mountains eighteen months earlier; getting in and out of the Hembrillo Basin was now time consuming and difficult. In Germany, the V-2 rocket program had been in deployment since early 1940 and reached peak production by February 1945. The Germans produced 3,000 rockets[†] in a struggle to meet Hitler's production target of 3,600 rockets in one year. The source of the V-2s came from an underground production facility at Nordhausen, a secluded location containing 900,000 square-feet of assembly and production area. The plant was comprised of two mile and a quarter parallel tunnels 500 feet apart cut inside a solid rock mountain. The main rocket assembly line started at one end of the first tunnel. From there, missiles moved along on rails and were finished and tested when they reached the opposite end of the tunnel where they were made ready for delivery to various launching sites in Germany. The total length of the entire tunnel-web was 18 miles.

The American Army beat the Russians to the vast inventory and successfully moved most of it out of Stalin's reach. Several months later, Hitler's coveted weapon system, including nearly every V-1 and V-2 rocket, support equipment, supplies and materials, and the range testing equipment was on its way to White Sands Proving Ground in New Mexico.

August 23, 1944

Soon afterwards, Doc wrote to Ova and gave her his new address. The same day she received Doc's letter, she sent him the following two-page letter;[162] Doc's address did not appear on Ova's letter:

---

* From the "Status and Future of White Sands Missile Range, Report of a Blue Ribbon Panel," Chapter II, 1. (a)."
† The summary in this paragraph was taken from the official website of White Sands Missile Range.

Hello Sugar: How's my darling? I wrote you yesterday, but will write a few lines today. How is your business? Mine is rotten. Mrs. Ashley said several people came to my house, but that was Saturday evening and again Sunday some came.

I seen Mr. Parr [the elder] and had a long talk with him. He said he would try and see you Saturday and make plans with you to bring you and Roscoe to Hot Springs anytime. Mrs. Fincher told Mr. Parr yesterday that she blamed me for not taking the toe of my shoe to that no good woman-chasing Jack Rawlings. But get a letter out to Claude right away telling him to copy in his own writing just how Jack Rawlings tried to make a play at me. Also as to the threats Jack made against you and Roscoe and where he was going to send you.

Mrs. Boren hasn't showed up yet. I talked to Hogue and he hasn't heard anything and don't believe there will be any trial. All of the following was in town last night: Judge Fowler, Claren Waggoner, and Sheriff Murray. They were with Pete Kinney, Jennie Martin and Mr. Wyatt, the man that leased from Winnie Ritch. I seen them all in the Victory Café and talked to them a while. I never learned just what their mission here was.

Claren insisted I join them, and I did and ate some pie and had a cup of coffee. They all asked where you were. I told them I didn't know and asked why. Then Claren said, 'Mrs. Noss that man Doc is his own worst enemy. No one wants to see him in trouble. I sure like him and do wish he would try and stay in a middle-aged man's place and cut out this drug store tough guy stuff. He's too smart to try to keep pulling this kid stuff at his age.' Then Murray spoke up and said. 'It's just lowering him Mrs. Noss and isn't he embarrassed when he gets sober and sees the fool things he tried to pull like stopping those people on the highway.' I said sure he is embarrassed and I don't know for sure he done it. Then Claren said, 'Oh yes he did,' and laughed. I called Murray to one side and asked if he heard the FBI say, 'I was a battle ax and that Doc would get along all right if it weren't for me.' He said, 'I did not and I was with the FBI when he asked Mrs. Mason or Allen or LaRue as to just who she was and what part she played in this deal of Doc's.' He said, 'Mrs. Mason showed the FBI man some letters he read pertaining to some mining and said she wasn't interested in any of Doc Noss' life or mining, but not one word about you, Mrs. Noss.' Well, they're still in town today so there must be a few court trials or something. Write real soon, Sugar, and be good. Bye, Darling. With love   *—Babe*

~

Sometime around May 1944, Rawlings had certain business dealing with Doc, which he admitted to in a letter[163] dated November 1, 1952. Apparently there were bad feelings between Rawlings and him, and according to Ova's letter, Rawlings had "made a play" on her while Doc was away. For the next fourteen months he ceased all contact with everyone connected to the operation at Victorio Peak *and* the Cheyenne Mining Company, including Ova.

September 8, 1944

On September 8, 1944, a little more than one year after Adolph Hitler began full production of the V-2 rocket, England became the target of his special weapon when the first V-2 hit Cheswick, a small London borough. The weapon the Nazis had developed was no longer a secret and the devastating power of Hitler's new and deadly combat weapons were in constant flight.

October 16, 1944

On the above date, Doc surfaced in Santa Fe where he was accused of impersonating a federal officer. He pleaded not guilty in District Court of impersonating a federal officer and for wrongly detaining A.D. Baracat of Amarillo, Texas. He was acquitted. The FBI gave Ova the information.

February 3, 1945

Doc was arrested in Camden, Arkansas and charged with violation of the National Stolen Property Act. There was no evidence to support the charges and the case was closed sixteen months later in June of 1946. Such reports were placed in government files and later in time used by his enemies, the military and the Treasury. It was always the opinion of the Noss family that many of Doc's problems, other than those that were alcohol-related, were a result of Merle Horzmann providing information to the authorities to get Doc out of the way.

March/April 1945

By March 1945, the Army had eased up on restrictions of traffic coming in and out of the Hembrillo Basin. Ova had better access now, using the western rim of the basin, cutting new roads, and repairing the existing ones. For a brief period in March and April, Doc, along with Roscoe Parr and Ova, finished the assessment work on Victorio Peak, repaired the shaft and cut new roads on the sides of the Peak. Assessment work was also completed on Cheyenne Star No. 1. Then Doc disappeared again and wasn't seen or heard from for more than four months.

Chapter 19

Nazi Gold and the United States Army

On Friday, April 6, 1945, while Hitler's Army was in retreat, some of General Patton's troops uncovered a large cache of gold and other valuable Nazi loot in a salt mine located at Merkers, Germany. In spite of efforts by the military and Army intelligence to keep a lid on the discovery, word about the Merkers treasure leaked out and the hoard was shipped to Frankfurt—but some of it did not arrive there.

In his book,* *A Soldier's Story*, General Omar Bradley said, "We flew in a line of low-flying cubs to the village of Merkers where three days before the 90th Division had stumbled into an underground cache containing the Reich's last gold reserves. The hiding place was discovered accidentally one evening when an MP (Military Policeman) accosted two women on the street shortly after curfew. They explained they had gone to fetch a midwife. To check their story the MP went along. As they walked past the entrance to a salt mine, one of the women gestured and said, 'That's where the bullion is hidden.' The following day the cache was uncovered." Bradley described the cache: (540)

In addition to $100,000,000 in gold bullion, the MPs found three billion Reichsmarks. Another $2,000,000 in American greenbacks together with lesser quantities of British, Norwegian, and French currency had been stacked in those dry salt chambers 2,100 feet below the ground.

~

Another book† entitled, *Nazi Gold: The Merkers Mine Treasure,* by Greg Bradsher gives a precise account of the discovery. Bradsher wrote that, on the evening of March 22, 1945, Patton's Third Army crossed the Rhine, "drove into the heart of Germany" and "cut into the future Soviet Zone." Bradsher said, "Just before noon on April 4, the village of Merkers fell to the Third Battalion of the 358th Infantry Regiment, Ninetieth Infantry Division, Third Army [Patton's Army]." That day and the following day, locals, "who had been interrogated by the Counter Intelligence Corps (CIC) personnel…mentioned a recent movement of German Reichsbank gold from Berlin" to a potassium mine at Merkers, the Kaiseroda mine. In a more detailed account concerning the two women, Bradsher wrote that the following morning, two MPs, who stood guard at the road entering the town of Keiselbach from Merkers, stopped and

---

A Soldier's Story by Omar N. Bradley, Henry Holt and Company 1951 p. 540.
† *Nazi Gold: The Merkers Mine Treasure* by Greg Bradsher - U.S. National Archives & Records Administration.

questioned the women, both "French displaced persons." They were taken to the "XII Corps Provost Marshal Office" where they were questioned and then taken back to Merkers where they showed the driver the Kaiseroda mine and said that it had been used by the Germans to store "the German gold reserve and valuable artworks." The loot was brought there weeks earlier by German forces. Locals were used to help unload and store the treasure inside the mine. Bradsher also wrote:

> *In order to examine the contents, some of the seals on the bags were broken, and a partial inventory was made. The inventory indicated that there were 8,198 bars of gold bullion; 55 boxes of grated gold bullion; hundreds of bags of gold items; over 1,300 bags of gold Reichsmarks, British gold pounds and French gold francs; 711 bags of American twenty-dollar gold pieces; hundreds of bags of gold and silver coins; hundreds of bags of foreign money; 9 bags of valuable coins; 2,380 bags and 1,300 boxes of Reichsmarks (2.75 billion Reichsmarks); 20 silver bars; 40 bags containing silver bars; 63 boxes and 55 bags of silver plate; 1 bag containing six platinum bars; and 110 bags from various countries.*

April 12, 1945

At 10:30 a.m. Generals Eisenhower, Bradley and Patton, and Colonel Bernard D. Bernstein entered the Merkers mine site to inspect* the treasure. Bradsher wrote:

> *Later, Patton would write that he saw 'a number of suitcases filled with jewelry, such as silver and gold cigarette cases, wristwatch cases, spoons, forks, vases, gold-filled teeth, false teeth, etc.' acquired by 'bandit methods.'*

> *Bernstein informed the generals that some of the treasure had come from victims in the concentration camps.*
>
> ~
>
> (541) Bradley[†] wrote, *"When news of the gold trove reached LUCKY, Patton had ordered a censorship stop on the discovery."* It was now under American military control and questions over what should be done about the find soared and

---

* Eisenhower, Bradley and Patton inspecting Nazi loot: chests of gold teeth, bags of cash and paintings.
† O. Bradley, ***op. cit.***, p. 541.

proposals varied. Bradley asked, "What would you do with all that money?" Patton said, "The Third Army was divided into two schools on the issue." One view was that the gold be cut into LUCKY medallions, "one for every sonuvabitch in the Third Army." The other view was that the "Third Army hide the loot until peacetime when Congress again cracked down on military appropriations. Then, whenever funds got particularly tight, the army could dig down into its *cave* for more money to spend on new weapons." Eisenhower, looking at Bradley and laughing said, "He's always got an answer."

On that day President Roosevelt died.

April 14, 1945

The Merkers discovery was handled with a reasonable degree of security. Ladislas Farago described in his book, *The Last Days of Patton,* how the Merkers loot was handled and transported to Frankfurt. Farago wrote: (47,48)

> *The moving began at 9:00 a.m. April 14. In 20 hours, the gold, currency, and a few cases of art were loaded on 30 ten-ton trucks, each with a 10% overload. Down in the mine, jeeps and trailers hauled the treasure from the vault to the shaft where the loaded trailers were put aboard lifts and brought to the surface.*
>
> *At the surface an officer registered each bag or item on a load slip. Then an officer and an enlisted man checked the load slip to verify that each item from the vault was loaded on a truck. Another officer recorded the name and serial number of each driver, assistant driver, and guard.*
>
> *The convoy left Merkers April 15 for the 85-mile drive to Frankfurt. It was escorted by five rifle platoons, two machine gun platoons, ten multiple-mount anti-aircraft vehicles, a flock of Piper Cubs and a fighter squadron for air cover.*
>
> *In the early afternoon of that same Sunday, the convoy arrived in Frankfurt, and the trucks were unloaded—the job lasted the rest of the day and the whole night. Each item was checked against the load list and was checked again as it was taken into the bank. Two infantry companies cordoned off the area. Although rumors floated around for some time afterward that one of the trucks had disappeared on the way to Frankfurt, the Army insisted that the 30 trucks that began the journey also ended it exactly as planned and scheduled.*
>
> *The gold remained in the Reichsbank vault in Frankfurt under Army control until January 24, 1946, when responsibility for it passed to the International Reparation*

---

*The Last Days of Patton by Ladislas Farago, McGraw-Hill, 1981.

Agency. It returned the gold on a pro-rated basis to the various governments from which the Nazis had looted part of it and which therefore had legitimate claims.

~

But a large cache of gold bullion at Mittenwald had already been looted when the Allies found where it had been located, causing a great deal of speculation about the fate of the treasure. The account of the Mittenwald loot in Farago's book started with Hitler's approval to move the loot to "safe places" under supervision. The gold associated with the Mittenwald gold came from another trove and was referred to as *Allgeier's gold* (126), named after U.S. Army Major Richard G. Allgeier who learned of the gold from one of his lieutenants, Jack Murphy (115). A captain in Allgeier's command, "Captain Neubauer asked Allgeier to assign a detail and a truck to bring in the gold. Allgeier sent forty men under three officers to return to the treasure trove" (116). The Allgeier's gold cache "never made it to the Reichsbank in Frankfurt." According to Farago, the officials who were in charge of the Mittenwald gold "were the two Reichsbank officials captured at Merkers, Albert Thoms and Emil Johann Rudolf Puhl, the senior vice-president of the Reichsbank, who had responsibility for the whole treasure trove" (119-120).

Prior to the Merkers' discovery, Phul had sent the entire Mittenwald trove to the "secluded monastery of St. Nicholas near Mittenwald on the Austrian border" and secreted it in "a huge cave in Einsiedel Mountains where the Nazis previously had kept some stolen treasures of the Roman Catholic Church" (121).

Farago wrote that the Guinness Book of World Records had listed the Mittenwald loot as "the greatest robbery on record" of the Reichsbank's reserves committed "by a combine of U.S. military personnel and Germans." The loot was to have consisted of 728 gold bars valued then at $9,878,400 and six sacks, which contained $404,840 in American currency. It was stolen from a cache hidden near Einsiedel, Bavaria on June 7, 1945. Farago had concluded that the treasure's existence was proven beyond the shadow of a doubt since the fact that it "had vanished from Mittenwald had been established from evidence that the Army had come to regard as reliable." Farago also wrote:

> *More than 300 investigators were assigned to the case. The Army clammed up only when nothing was found - not enough hard evidence, that is, that would have closed the case. To this day, the Pentagon denies categorically that anything resembling the robbery mentioned in Guinness had ever really occurred, or that any part of the German gold or Nazi treasure, which the Americans had succeeded in finding, is unaccounted for. (123)*

~

A source in Farago's book, British writer Frederick Nolan, said, "the *Einsiedel* treasure was partially plundered by a combination of U.S. Military Government personnel and German civilians." Nolan said "if the gold was stolen by U.S. officers in association with German civilians, it is conceivable that Patton would have known them, and once an investigation started, it was possibly only a matter of time before he made the connection in his own mind." Farago concluded that, "By hovering over the secret, it seemed, Patton signed his own death warrant. Others marked him for death as the man who blocked their way to the treasure. One way or another, Patton was doomed by the Mittenwald gold." Farago also wrote in his book that, "The evidence is now conclusive that the gold had no connection with General Patton's end and that he had nothing to do with its disappearance" (126).

> *In spite of the Pentagon's denials, it is a common belief that some of the missing Nazi gold from World War II was connected to Victorio Peak, or other hiding places at White Sands Proving Ground in New Mexico. There were other rumors as well. General George Patton died in Germany and some thought he was murdered for standing in the way of other high-ranking U.S. Army officers whose plan it was to ship or airlift stolen gold out of Germany to the United States shortly after WWII. Then there was the question as to why General Omar Bradley chose to live out the remaining years of his life in a private wing of a hospital in El Paso, Texas, a short drive from White Sands Missile Range. Although Bradley's presence in El Paso could easily have been a mere coincidence, the charge that high-ranking military officers and select civilians at White Sands Missile Range were involved in the theft of gold bullion from the Noss treasure within or around Victorio Peak, and that the Central Intelligence Agency was involved persisted. Later, charges that were leveled by a United States Congressman would be denied. The formal denials were set out in an Army-sponsored inquiry* held at White Sands Missile Range, a little-known and uninvestigated fact that is briefly discussed in Chapter 22.*

April 30, 1945

Hitler committed suicide on April 30 at his bunker in Berlin, followed by Germany's surrender seven days later. On May 7, the Allied Army claimed victory in Europe. On or about May 10, Lloyd Tucker arrived in the Rhineland in Central Europe.[164] His arrival there was within days of the time when the Hungarian gold train theft took place. The incident did not escape public scrutiny: the *Las Cruces Sun-News* carried this AP story on October 15, 1999:

> *U.S. officials allowed Nazi loot from a train out of Hungary to be sold, taken by American generals or turned over to Austria instead of returned to the Jews...a presidential commission concluded Thursday. Some valuable items seized from the Hungarian gold train nine days after the May 7, 1945 Allied victory in Europe, were put up for auction in New York, and less valuable goods were sold in the U.S. Army Exchange....*

~

---

*The March 5, 1974 inquiry is revealed in great detail in book two of *The Gold House— The Lies, The Thefts.*

Appropriation of Nazi loot by U.S. forces took place "at the highest levels," the report said. Five American generals "took valuables from the gold train to furnish their residences and offices."

The loot included 1,100 paintings, which were turned over to Austria and never officially accounted for, and a suitcase full of gold dust that disappeared... Some items were stolen from U. S. military warehouses...

~

The opportunity to seize German Nazi loot in 1945 appears to have been wide-open. Many U.S. soldiers slipped small amounts of German gold into their pockets. But then there were incidents when U.S. soldiers removed "larger loads" at various times, the article said. In all cases, the motivating element was the voracious lust for gold, power and money—the rhyme of the eons. Roman poet Virgil said, "O cursed lust for gold, to what dost thou not drive the hearts of men."

After WWII, Lloyd Tucker became a successful real estate broker, land developer, gold courier, an expert in the mining and processing of gold, and was known to be associated with organized crime. But it was his connection to the White House and the CIA that enabled him to take government officials into the caverns at Victorio Peak to observe and inspect the Noss treasure. In time, Tucker became a treasure hunter and, with his financial connections, he often visited Ireland and England. During many long stays in those countries he developed a business relationship with a London gold broker named Simon John Ashley Smith. Tucker and his colleagues referred to Smith as "Silent John."

June 1945

In the summer of 1945, Leland Howard was sent to Frankfurt, Germany to help assess and inventory the Nazi gold hoard. Howard's seven-page report was named the "Howard Report." As acting Director of the Mint and Chief of the Bureau of Silver and Gold Operations, he became actively involved with activities at Victorio Peak in the 1960s and had correspondence with Paul Ignatius, Secretary of the Army, regarding gold at WSMR.

It has also been a repeated rumor that twenty-nine officers of General George Patton's staff in 1945 requested and were given transfers to White Sands Proving Ground and other nearby military installations after WWII. These individuals are difficult to sort, and the number of upper-level military officers who actually went there is equally difficult to determine, but the chance that some of the Nazi gold had made its way to the White Sands area and bases nearby is possible in light of: 1) there is undeniable proof U.S. Army personnel had taken a leading and major role in stealing Nazi gold, 2) high-ranking Army officers had the facilities, manpower, opportunity, transportation and removal capability, and excellent storage places once the gold came to the White Sands Proving Ground, and 3) most importantly, those who were involved had a strong motive—the staggering financial opportunity the gold provided.

Chapter 20

The United States Army and the Tularosa Basin—White Sands

The summer of 1945 was one of change and uncertainty in the Tularosa Basin. On July 9, 1945, six months after the War Department* had selected the site, the White Sands Proving Ground was created, an annex of the Ballistic Research Laboratory (BRL) in Aberdeen, Maryland. The San Andres Mountain Range was its western border, where the Hembrillo Basin and Victorio Peak were located. The Tularosa Basin was now the Army's new missile testing installation. Large tracts of land were being taken for the testing of ordnance and delivery systems and many of the ranchers, including those in the Hembrillo Basin, were paid for the withdrawal of their grazing lands, while fee simple[†] lands and trust lands were essentially condemned on a short-term basis. The government had begun leasing various lands from ranchers pursuant to *lease and suspension agreements,* with the stipulation that the lands would eventually be returned to the ranchers. One such tract was the Henderson ranch, which encompassed Victorio Peak.

Army Lieutenant Colonel Harold R. Turner[‡] became the White Sands Proving Ground's first commander, arriving in Las Cruces on June 14, 1945, two days prior to the nuclear test explosion at Trinity Site. Turner is claimed to have said:

I had arrived in Las Cruces, NM, two days before the explosion. When the

---

* "Status and Future of White Sands Missile Range," Chapter II, page II-I, a. "The Range Operations Function"
† Fee simple land, the most common form of real estate, provides the most complete ownership, other than *allodial* title land, which cannot be taken by any procedure of law.
‡ www.wsmr-history.org/Commanders.htm

bomb went off, I was asleep in the Amador Hotel* in Las Cruces. The first I knew of it was on reading the morning paper although it was on the property I was supposed to command.

~

Turner's mission was to prepare a new facility for rocket testing. The rockets to be tested had already arrived inside 300 railroad cars that were strung from Las Cruces and north to sidings for miles, a huge inventory of captured German V-2 missiles, parts, and testing components. When Turner stepped on the sands of the Tularosa Basin, which he called "that place in the desert," there was nothing there: no buildings, no permanent water source or transportation facilities—Turner was starting from scratch. It is Lieutenant Colonel Harold R. Turner, later *Colonel* Turner, who can be credited with jump-starting a desert wilderness into what is now the large, modern, military installation we know today as White Sands Missile Range. It was also Turner who selected the site for White Sands' operational headquarters beneath the Organ Mountains at the San Andres Pass. Turner's efforts earned him the Legion of Merit, and rightfully so. Many V-2 rockets were launched while he was still in command at White Sands.

~

Monday, 5:29:45 a.m. Mountain Time, July 16, 1945

It had been unusually hot that summer. Ova had planned to spend the entire week at camp. She had left Hot Springs early that day, so she would arrive there by first light. She hadn't seen Doc since late April when he, Claude Fincher and Roscoe Parr had been at camp doing road and assessment work, but Doc was on her mind. She hoped they could work things out, but he disappeared again as he had before.

Ova had suffered emotionally from his actions, leaving her the way he had, but rarely did she let her anguish show. "One thing was certain though," Terry said when he talked about Ova, "The entire episode of the discovery, losing access to the caverns, and the endless task of raising money and avoiding the Secret Service had taken its toll on her, not to mention what Doc went through." Terry's account of what Ova told him:

> *Doc was on the front line of all that activity and he never told us a lot. But one thing he said that I never forgot was that the government had no right to the treasure, not a penny. He told me he had it all checked out and found that they were running a bluff. Doc stood up to them, he wasn't afraid of no man, especially the military, but the Treasury and the Secret Service boys were another matter. Doc said they could have caught him red-handed lots of times, but they didn't, they just took the gold. Some of them got rich doing that, too. Doc said they never intended to jail him for anything related to the gold,*

---

* The old Amador Hotel in Las Cruces still standing today.

that was their way of telling him he was right. Doc said the treasure was ours to keep. What really bothered Doc was the danger it put me and Letha and my boys in. Doc knew when they had the opportunity and when the Army was ready, they would kill us all and make it look like an accident. They can do that; believe what I say. The FBI, the Army and the Secret Service take the law into their own hands and dispense it so it comes out to what they want things to be like. Doc told me they did it to his people before he was born and they intend to keep doing it. Doc was an Indian and I was married to him. That was our problem, Terry. If our name was Rockefeller or Roosevelt, we'd still be polishing those gold bars.

~

The following is the account of that morning as told by Terry Delonas; the story is condensed and presented here in reconstructed dialogue:

Ova had crested the western rim of the basin. There was a pickup stopped in the middle of the road. Ova pulled up beside it and got out. Doc was waiting there for her.

"Strange seeing you here," Ova said.

"I figured you'd be out here today, so I waited for you."

"Well, you were right."

"This is all the further either of us are going. The Army is up to something. Some Army boys in a Jeep stopped me here and said not to come down in the basin. They went on ahead somewhere. Something's going on, but I don't know what."

Ova was about to respond when suddenly night became day. Startled, Doc grabbed Ova and turned her away from the light. When the light subsided they watched a brilliant ball of fire turn to amber. Soon they felt the heat from it; then shortly after that it went dark. Whatever it was, they thought it was over, but suddenly an enormous explosion followed, as if dynamite had been set off nearby. Ova trembled. Doc held her tightly, astonished by what they had just witnessed.*

---

* The credit for this photo belongs to Jack W. Aeby. Many publications that have used the photo owe it to an Army or Los Alamos National Labs photo, but that is invalid; Aeby was a civilian employee on the Manhattan Project; he "took the photo with his own camera and film."

"That was the Army's doings. What are we up against, Doc?"

Doc said nothing at first. They waited and watched with astonishment as a mushroom cloud began to form. Then darkness returned.

"You better get out of here," he told her and walked her to the car. "I'm going to go down the road a piece. I got some bars buried halfway down the ridge." Doc reached down inside his boot and pulled out a roll of money, one thousand dollars in fifty-dollar bills. "Here," he said and walked to his pickup and drove away. That's all he said to her. They would not see each other again for some time.

~

Victorio Peak was on the opposite side of the San Andres Mountain Range, fifty-three miles away from the blast. There were no additional nuclear detonations conducted at Trinity Site. Trinity was the *only* prewar site used by the military for nuclear testing. Other numerous sites used after WWII were in Nevada, Bikini and Eniwetak Atolls, and more at the Johnston and Christmas Island sites, also one or two in the south Atlantic.

Chapter 21

The Nazi Invasion of New Mexico
Doc Divorces Ova and Consults the Army to Help Raise the Treasure

Under a "Top Secret" program, the Joint Chiefs of Staff in July 1945 approved the import of 350 Nazi scientists* and technicians who had developed the V-2 program. O.S.S. intelligence officers, Allen Dulles and William Clark, approved a program dubbed *Operation Paperclip*, the last of three such secret operations conducted by Army Intelligence, the final step that brought a vast number of Nazi scientists, war criminals, and other dark elements of Hitler's dredges to America. William Donovan was then head of the O.S.S. in Europe, while Allen Dulles headed up the operation in Switzerland.

Operation Paperclip Crew

The spoils of World War II: Gehlen's Abwehr Spy Group, a wide array of Nazi spies, double agents and intelligence operatives that were forged from a furnace of evil fired by Hitler's quest for world domination were headed to America. They arrived here at the order of FBI head J. Edgar Hoover and were in time injected directly into the American mainstream. In his book,[†] *Called to*

---

* Nazi scientists began arriving at White Sands Proving Ground on November 17, 1945 three months after the German V-2 rockets had arrived there. Twenty in the group remained at White Sands; others went to Fort Bliss. Wernher von Braun is in the front row, seventh from the right.

† B. Gritz. *Called to Serve* (Lazarus Publishing Company 1991).

Serve, Colonel Bo Gritz, who was the former head of U.S. Army Special Forces for Latin America, wrote:

> *General Reinhard Gehlen, Hitler's chief intelligence officer against the Soviet Union, had struck a deal with the 'Americans' (called Operation Sunrise) that was not, for obvious reasons, released to establishment media. The principal negotiators were Allen Dulles and William Casey of the OSS, Sir William Stephenson for the British, and SS General Karl Wolff, head of the Gestapo in Italy and former chief of Heinrich Himmler's personal staff. Wolff was spared from hanging at Nuremberg after killing 'at least' 300,000 Jews at the Treblinka Camp. (561-562)*

~

In addition to Gehlen's Spy Group, a plan to bring German missile scientists onto American soil was also developed by the O.S.S. With the assistance of General Walter Dornberger and Nazi scientist Wernher von Braun, Operation Sunrise developed into Operation Overcast. Then the operation was dubbed Project Paperclip*. As a result of those early covert operations, von Braun and many other Nazi V-2 scientists, engineers, and researchers arrived with their families; many were taken to White Sands Proving Ground to further develop the U.S. missile program. Although many of the Nazi scientists were assigned to other locations in New Mexico, much of this activity took place at Fort Bliss, which is land-connected to the entire southern border of White Sands over a wide operational area.

During the early days of the Cold War, Gehlen had infiltrated the Soviet intelligence organization and formed an alliance with Dulles, which eventually became the Central Intelligence Agency, which over time became a vigorous foreign intelligence-gathering bureau. The National Security Agency (NSA) was formed from the central part of Germany's Nazi SS intelligence officers. As mentioned, those beginning elements of the CIA and NSA bureaus entered the United States under the cover of those three separate early spook operations: Operation Sunrise, Overcast, and Paperclip. The dark cloud that had once formed over Europe in 1933 drifted steadily westward and settled over the Tularosa Basin, its ominous shadow cast over the Organ Mountains, north across the San Andres Mountains onto the Jornada del Muerto, renewing that area's legend of death and violence. America was preparing itself for a new era—global nuclear domination.

August 6, 1945

The second test of the atomic bomb occurred on August 6, 1945. A B-29, named the "Enola Gay" released the bomb[†] over Hiroshima, Japan. Three days later, the third atomic bomb exploded over Nagasaki. Both cities were completely destroyed, but the destruction of the atomic bombs dropped on

---

*www.wsmr.army.mil/wsmr: Key in (White Sands Missile Range – The Paperclip Crew)
[†] Smithsonian magazine, "The Bomb." *p.* 96

those cities paled in comparison to the destruction that had already taken place across Japan. Fire bombings by low-flying B-29 bombers had devastated cities throughout Japan. Robert McNamara,* former Secretary of Defense, said the United States, under the direction of General Curtis Lemay, had "won the war by waging brutal, relentless and unyielding attacks on Japan, fire bombing and scorching the earth as Sherman had in the American Civil War."

Some of the components and material brought to White Sands included 215 combustion chambers, 180 sets of propellant tanks, 90 tail units, 100 sets of graphite jet vanes, and 200 turbo pumps—and treasures from Europe. What once belonged to Adolph Hitler, namely his vast collection of V-1 and V-2 rocket components and assemblies, was now the property of the United States military. Most of Hitler's missile program had been loaded aboard ships for a long voyage from Europe across the Atlantic Ocean to the Port of New Orleans. There the military's precious cargo was unloaded into three hundred railroad cars for the last leg of the journey. Slowly the trains gained speed and headed west across wet and humid Louisiana, then through more arid country across Texas, and finally entering the hot, dry desert of New Mexico. Last stop: White Sands Proving Ground east of Las Cruces. Hitler's entire missile weapon system arrived there safely and without a hitch.

Mid-August 1945

A *Las Cruces Sun-News* article[165] published on September 28, 2001 read, in part:

> In mid-August 1945, 300 railroad freight cars carrying German V-2 rocket components captured in Europe, arrived in New Mexico. The Santa Fe Railroad slotted 10 cars per day in Las Cruces for unloading and transport by U.S. Military and German personnel to the Proving Ground. Every railroad siding from El Paso, Texas to Belen, New Mexico, a distance of 210 miles, was full of railroad cars. The Army hired every flatbed truck in Doña Ana County to move the material. The task was completed in 20 days.

October 26, 1945

Through rumors coming from different sources, it was eventually assumed that Doc had succeeded in obtaining a divorce, but Ova's claim was that she was never notified of any legal proceeding in the course of such action. Regardless, the fact remained that Doc was gone, and only suspicions, innuendos and rumors persisted month after month, but they were not rumors, nor was there ever a divorce. By early fall, Doc was granted a Decree[166] of Annulment† (No. 7451) in Pulaski Chancery Court in Pulaski County, Little Rock, Arkansas. But

---

* From the film, *The Fog of War* featuring former Secretary of Defense Robert Mc-Namara

† A judicial decree in such a case declares that something was defective in the marriage.

Doc did not appear in court; his attorney, O.W. Pete Wiggins, represented him in his absence. A portion of the decree read:

> *And it appearing that due service of process by publication of warning order against defendant for time prescribed by law, issued on the complaint herein, has been made in this cause; that an attorney to defend for the non-resident defendant has been appointed more than thirty days since and has filed his report herein; and this action having been reached upon the call of the calendar is submitted to the court for its consideration and judgment upon the complaint, plaintiff's affidavit of defendant's non-military service, and the depositions of the plaintiff and of R.E. Bondurant and Charles L. Clover taken on behalf of plaintiff.*
>
> *The court, being well and sufficiently advised as to all matters of fact and law arising herein and the premises being fully seen, doth order, and judge and decree that the bonds of matrimony subsisting between the plaintiff, Milton E. Noss, and the defendant, Ova M. Noss, be, and the same are hereby annulled, set aside and shall forever be held for naught.*
>
> *That all property not disposed of at the commencement of this action, which either party hereto obtained from or through the other during the marriage hereby annulled, and in consideration or by reason thereof, be restored to them respectfully.*

~

After Doc's death, Ova maintained for the rest of her life that she had no knowledge of why or how Doc had been granted a divorce; even when Doc and Ova discussed it after the fact, nothing was revealed, only that he had been granted an annulment in Arkansas. Not only was it a mystery to Ova, the entire family was equally puzzled. It was not until Ova died that the following document surfaced when Letha discovered it among Ova's personal belongings. It shows that five days after the Decree of Annulment was granted, the Pulaski Chancery Court entered this "AGREEMENT"[167] into the official record in the same case number, which reads as followed: (underlining inserted)

AGREEMENT

> *It is agreed by and between O. W. Pete Wiggins, Solicitor for the plaintiff, and <u>John L. Sullivan, Attorney Ad Litem* for the defendant</u>, that the deposition of the plaintiff's witness may be taken upon written interrogatories and cross-interrogatories.*
>
> *All formality in the taking and transcribing of said depositions is hereby waived by the attorney ad litem for defendant, and all exceptions for irrelevancy, immateriality, and incompetency may be taken at or before the submission of said testimony to the court for its consideration upon the trial of the issues in this cause.*

---

* Latin (lit. "for the case") for the purposes of a particular case; in law "an *administrator ad litem* is a person that is appointed by a court to represent the interests of a decedent's estate in a case." Source – James E. Clapp, Random House "Webster's Dictionary of the Law," 2000

Dated this 31st. day of October 1945.
(SIGNED) —O. W. Pete Wiggins, Solicitor for the Plaintiff
(SIGNED) — John L. Sullivan, Counsel for Defendant

~

The questions to be asked are: who was Doc's witness and why did Doc's attorney waive the deposition? Ova did not know these details at the time, but in an effort to protect the interests of everyone involved with the Cheyenne Mining Company, those who were legally connected to the company were called to a meeting at the Buena Vista Hotel in Hot Springs at Ova's direction. The reason for the meeting was clear and justified; by November 1945 solid evidence was in hand that Doc had remarried. Perhaps the information came from Roscoe Parr, but no matter how the information reached Ova, she was duty-bound to protect everyone's interest in the company, and, apart from Doc, she held the highest percentage of interest in the company and therefore called for the meeting to discuss or resolve the relevant issues related to Doc's unexplained absence. Horzmann wrote[168] about the meeting: (underlining inserted)

Camp Notes —November 1, 1945

A meeting was called at the Buena Vista Hotel, Hot Springs in November for the purpose of organization and to form a corporation. Dr. Noss had been gone all year and the information as to his whereabouts was unavailable. Mr. A.G. Bohrnsted proposed to draw up the necessary corporation papers, but in checking the titles, found them badly in need of clarification. At the expense of Mrs. Noss and Mr. Bohrnsted, titles were redeemed and proper papers filed to take care of the situation and to protect the interests of the group. Roscoe Parr was notified of these steps, with good faith and confidence, and so were the other members of the group. <u>But before the papers could be executed, Dr. Noss suddenly appeared and he and Roscoe caused a cancellation.</u>

More than $200.00 had been spent in this effort. The intention was to form a holding company, and then give an Operating Contract to some good, reliable construction company to work the mines and market the ore. About this same time, Dr. Noss obtained a divorce from Mrs. Ova Noss, a transcript of which proceeding is on file, and he remarried.

—Acting Secretary Merle Horzmann

~

Doc returned periodically to the Hembrillo Basin, but he made no effort to meet with Ova. On one of his returns in 1946, he took one or more persons from the Army Corps of Engineers to the Peak asking for their advice on how to open the blockage. As much as Doc hated the military, it came as a surprise to Ova when she learned that he had consulted military personnel. During this time period, Ova was not always at camp, but when she was, the Peak was a half-mile away; Doc could have come and gone without her knowing it. However, nothing came of it and Doc was still facing the dilemma of removing the debris.

January 29, 1946

According to a letter[169] by Commissioner of Public Lands John E. Miles dated January 29, 1946, Doc had previously applied for a prospecting permit in Santa Fe. In his letter he advised Doc that a field representative would inspect the property, which was the usual procedure. Commissioner Miles then notified[170] the field man to check the application "and see if anything has been done in the way of prospecting or developing, and whether or not any ore has been shipped from the land." The field representative for the Land Office in Santa Fe, Gordon E. Herkenhoff, did a cursory review of the records pertaining to Victorio Peak, and, on February 12, 1946, he submitted the following report:[171] In part:

> *I checked records in the courthouse to ascertain the names of locators of the claims. It was found that five mining claims, named the Big Fault Nos., 1 through 5 were recorded 5-4-41 in book 120 pages 416-417 from a location made 3-30-41. The locators were Lester D. Robinson, Elzo D. Smith and Frank R. Wicks.*

Herkenhoff met Doc that afternoon in Hot Springs and spent the rest of the day interviewing him on "the history of the claims." Herkenhoff learned that the reason Doc had secured the claims to "the property" was that it was supposed to be the site of the "lost mine of Padre LaRue." When writing his report, Herkenhoff quoted the official reference to the lost mine in the State Bureau of Mines and Mineral Resources publications Bulletin No. 11, page 188 "Ore Deposits of the Organ Mountains." More of Gordon Herkenhoff's report:

> *It is said that in the late years of the Spanish occupation of New Mexico, a priest named LaRue, stationed at a hacienda in Chihuahua, was told by a dying friend of placers and a fabulously rich gold bearing lode in the mountains two days journey north of Paso del Norte. When drought brought a famine to the community of peons in his charge at the hacienda, Father LaRue* persuaded them to migrate northward with him, the Organ Mountains being his goal. Arriving here, the priest recognized landmarks, which had been described to him, and, sending his men out to search, succeeded in finding the rich deposits. The colony settled at Spirit Springs and here the gold was concentrated in arrastres, and some of the gold was smelted in vassos or adobe furnaces.*
>
> *The mine is supposed to have been located in a deep canyon west or southwest of the springs. The long silence of the priest led the authorities of the Church in the City of Mexico to send an expedition to his former place of labor; finding this deserted, they traced him to the Organ Mountains. Learning from his guards that the expedition was approaching, LaRue gave orders that the mine was to be covered up and the gold hidden. When the expedition arrived, he refused to divulge the secret of the whereabouts of the mine and gold, asserting that they belonged to this people and not to the church. By night*

---

* An account of LaRue's mine is covered in book two of *The Gold House—The Lies, The Thefts.*

a soldier who was attached to the expedition murdered him and afterwards some of the colonists were tortured, but the secret was never told. The mine is supposed to have been covered up with debris from the mountains. Several people have claimed they have found it. Col. A. J. Fountain is said to have discovered it shortly before his mysterious disappearance. A goat herder named Tirso Aguire, well known in the mountains about twenty years ago, was supposed to be a descendent of one of the original miners. But none of the claims has been substantiated, and the search for the lost mine continues. It should be added that, although several of the supposed localities were investigated during mapping of the Organ range, neither rich gold mineralization nor mine was found.

~

The report stated that Doc claimed he "found the mine in 1941" but that in 1941 the collapse of the top entrance shaft sealed the entrance. Herkenhoff also claimed that Doc said that he was "inducted into the armed forces and nothing further has been done to gain entrance to the mine." Further on in the report Herkenhoff said that Doc had entered the shaft, but was unable to go further than "the timbered section." Once again, the mention of a 2,700-foot tunnel led to the main treasure, where a large group of people had lived for many years. The report also mentioned the treasure, according to Doc's estimate, was then worth $22,000,000.00. However, according to the report, because of the lack of "proof of labor" or "intent to hold," the status of the claims was open and there were no subsequent recordings by Doc. After five years of continuous operation at the claim site, it *appeared* that it was open for someone to take over.

Whether Victorio Peak was the site of the Lost Mine of Padre LaRue or not will always remain a question. Regardless, the date of discovery of the Victorio Peak treasure was always 1937, *not* 1941, as Herkenhoff reported. In the first place, there was no "timbered section" in the top shaft until *after* Doc explored the 2,700-foot passageway, found the treasure and began bringing gold bars and other treasure items to the surface. Furthermore, Doc began shoring the top shaft *after* the initial discovery to make it safer and easier to enter and exit. It was in the fall of 1939 that a dynamite charge was set off to dislodge a large obstruction, which caused the shaft to collapse *below* the shoring. After the collapse, contrary to Herkenhoff's report, Doc and Ova continued with the assessment work requirements at Victorio Peak. In fact, on May 3, 1943, Congress suspended assessment work on mining operations. Even though Congress had suspended assessment work, proofs of labor and notices of *Intention to Hold* were filed with the New Mexico Land Office in Santa Fe. Herkenhoff wrote, "Before it could be reopened, he was inducted into the armed forces and nothing further has been done to gain entrance to the mine." Doc was *never* "inducted into the armed forces" as Herkenhoff reported. The facts are that on July 30, 1942, Doc received notification to register for military service and he was required to report to Dr. A.C. White in Hot Springs on Monday,

August 3, 1942 for a physical examination. Doc *never* served in the armed forces. Herkenhoff's report on these matters was flawed.

~

Doc wanted a mining lease, and he told Herkenhoff that if it was granted, "that it be made to Dr. Noss, his wife Ova M. Noss and Willard E. Holt of Lordsburg." Why he did what he did on that day, considering there was an annulment, is unknown. The report indicated that there were eleven other individuals who had expressed an interest in the claim. More from his report:

> There was also mentioned the name of an Indian, a Greek, a movie star [Burt Lancaster], Ethel DuPont, and officials of Metro Goldwyn Mayer, and many others whom Dr. Noss claims have forfeited any rights or interest in the claims.
> —Gordon E. Herkenhoff

~

The investigation into the lives of Doc and Ova Noss and the Victorio Peak treasure has led this writer to believe that many individuals were drawn to the story of the treasure. Some were Hollywood figures, others were attorneys, and others just plainly sought the treasure. Another possibility for Herkenhoff reporting that Doc claimed he was inducted into the service was that Doc intentionally lied or presented a stroke of fantasy, not unlike other cases where he said he was someone he was not, or when he was drunk. Such claims did him harm and damaged his credibility. However, this writer's opinion is that Herkenhoff carelessly or deliberately slanted his report so it cast negatively on Doc's reputation. The exact same report is found in two different locations: in the Land Office records in Santa Fe and in a July 3, 1961 letter to the Secret Service; it was one of the documents that was in possession of the Army at White Sands Missile Range and was received in discovery after a lawsuit was filed. The New Mexico State Land Office had sent Herkenhoff to do an investigation and report his findings on the Noss claim site at Victorio Peak, but there were other developments that were *not* recorded in the Land Office records.

~

Later, Merle Horzmann went to the Las Cruces Courthouse* and examined Book 20, pp 313-315, recorded April 16, 1941. She thought the claims were invalid, as there is no record of proof of labor. Her opinion was that if a lease were to be granted in favor of Doc, Ova, and Willard Holt of Lordsburg, Doc would have to relocate and record it. Also of interest were Lester Robinson of Los Angeles and Elzo Smith, and Frank Wicks, two associates of Robinson. There were others mentioned in the Land Office: Mr. Mullins of New Mexico, Mr. Barber of Albuquerque, Mr. Ponder of Albuquerque, James and Joe Weldon of Sonora,

---

* Claims such as this were filed with the Bureau of Land Management field office in Las Cruces *and* at Santa Fe. The BLM also required such records be recorded with the clerk of courts in the appropriate county.

Texas, Mr. Johnson of Hatch, Clarion Wagoner of Socorro, and others who Doc said had no claim, including Barman and Robinson. A search of the records[172] in the Doña Ana County Courthouse in Las Cruces was conducted by this writer to confirm the names indicated in Herkenhoff's report. They were accurate.

In a File Memo[173] dated August 21, 1973 by Land Office Counsel William Jordan, he noted that R.L. Coker of Los Alamitos, California, came to his office that day and "brought with him originals of Agreements between his father and Doc Noss and one between Coker and Doc Noss." Coker claimed that he and "two brothers, Joe and Jim Whitten helped Doc dig and search in and around Victorio Peak" *and* the Caballo Mountains. Coker was under the impression that Doc had buried some "30 bars somewhere around Lordsburg," which was the hometown of Buster Ward. Coker described Doc as "quite a character and an adventurer, but that he was getting quite touchy along towards the last and feared for his life." He also claimed that on May 30, 1946, he and Doc struck an agreement[174] for $10.00 that if he found any "hidden treasure, mines or minerals on state lease lands and patented lands owned by Jack Bruton in the San Andres Mountains" that he would receive a percentage of the find. This, of course, did not include the Victorio Peak treasure, which had been discovered by Doc and Ova in 1937.

Herkenhoff had more of an interest in the Noss claim than just his report— he was willing to invest if he could see the gold. Later Doc showed him two bars of fake gold, fearing that Herkenhoff was a plant and would take the bars. Doc didn't trust *anyone* from the Land Office at this point, but he did grant Herkenhoff a stake in the treasure, but under what conditions and for how much is not known. Above all matters one thing was certain; there was never an end to the accounts and stories involving Doc Noss. They continued into infinity.

Also, on February 14, Commissioner Miles wrote[175] to Doc and informed him that his lode mining locations were not valid, meaning that their exact site locations had to be better defined and the information returned to the Land Office. Miles advised Doc that Herkenhoff would instruct him on the proper procedure on getting and recording the locations. Therefore on February 15, 1946, Doc and Ova Noss, together with Willard Holt, filed[176] the following Notice of Lode Mining Location applications:

Noss No 1 witnessed by Jack Bruton and R.W. Parr. Situated at NW corner of claim S 49 degrees 36' E of NW corner of Section 16 – [Filed February 20, Book 138, pgs. 301-2, Socorro County and also at the Land Office];

Noss No. 2 witnessed by Jack Bruton and R.W. Parr, situated at NW corner of claim 73 degrees 16 E, 2335.8' from NE corner Section 16; west end joins east end of Noss No. 1. [Filed February 20, Book 138, page 302, in Socorro County and the Land Office];

Noss No. 3 witnessed by Jack Bruton, R.W. Parr, situated on the NW corner of Section 16. West end of claim joins east end of "Noss No. 2." [Filed

February 20, Book 138, pages 302 and 303 in Socorro County and also at the Land Office];

Noss No. 4 witnessed by Jack Bruton, R.W. Parr, situated on the NW corner of claim S 81degrees 43 E, 5290.7' from NW corner of Section 16. West end joins east end of Noss No. 3. Filed February 19, 1946, [Book 20, page 627, Doña Ana County; he also filed at the Land Office in Santa Fe].

March 1, 1946

On March 1, 1946, Commissioner Miles granted an application[177] to Doc, Ova and W. Holt, No. L-2140 and permit Number M-2140 for all four claims, being charged $1.00 each. Doc had ninety days to prospect all claim sites, but it was expressed that no minerals could be shipped from the premises until information was acquired by the Land Office regarding the minerals. Grazing leases had to be protected, and the shafts had to be covered. Doc was permitted to apply for a lease if he performed prospecting development of at least ten feet in the shaft, tunnel, or open cuts that show indications of minerals of sufficient value to warrant further development. The State of New Mexico reserved the right to lease *surface* land and the permit holders had the right of ingress. All could be cancelled for failure to comply after thirty days' notice. If minerals were discovered, permit holders could file application for a mining lease.

~

Another interesting event involved attorney Melvin Rueckhaus. In his letter[178] of July 7, 1976, he wrote that he had accompanied Noss to the Land Office in Santa Fe "to get some sort of a state lease on a piece of mining property." It was there that Rueckhaus became acquainted with a person by the name of Mrs. Cave. Rueckhaus wrote, "In connection with this endeavor, Noss took me to the Peak, which he described as being the location of his find." Later, Mrs. Cave told Rueckhaus that she had gone down and entered the cave at Victorio Peak, but that the powdered guano (bat dung) was so strong that it made her violently ill and she had to leave. Rueckhaus said, "Mrs. Cave described a gold sword, which Doc Noss had shown her during one of these visits."

May 29, 1946

Doc kept busy. He wrote[179] to Commissioner of Public Lands John E. Miles on May 29 concerning his prospector permits in the Hembrillo Basin. He was concerned with the difficulties in obtaining men and materials and told Miles they were "slow in starting the work at the property." However, he told him that the "shaft has been collared and timbered" to "20 ft. deep by tonight." From the description of the work, it is apparent that Doc was not referring to the shaft at Victorio Peak; that shaft was far deeper than 20 feet. The following week, on June 3, Commissioner Miles acknowledged[180] Doc's letter and enclosed an application to be completed and returned to the Land Office for consideration.

June 16, 1946

During the spring and early summer months of 1946, Doc continued his assessment work on his claims. He also surveyed possible sites to stake state lease mining claims in the Hembrillo Basin; one such claim, which was situated in both Socorro and Doña Ana counties, had been filed with the Land Office by Doc years earlier, but the prospector permits had expired. Now, Doc and B.D. Lampros were interested in renewing the permits and converting them into permanent state mining leases. On June 16, field examiner Herkenhoff wrote[181] to Commissioner Miles telling him that Doc's prospector permits had expired on June 1, 1946. In an effort to help Doc, B.D. Lampros paid the $100 application fee, but Lampros didn't have the necessary information for the application. From Herkenhoff's letter to Commissioner Miles, in part:

> *"Mr. B.D. Lampros, 234 East Jefferson St., Phoenix, Arizona, one of Dr. Noss' associates handed me $100.00 to cover the state lease application for four claims. Also, I was requested to prepare the application for the lease. I have assisted Dr. Noss with a little engineering at his claims, but I have not the necessary information to make the application for the lease."*   —Herkenhoff

June 26, 1946

Commissioner Miles followed up and wrote[182] to Doc on June 26 saying that Herkenhoff had received the $100 from Lampros for the lease application on four mining claims. He also told Doc that he had been "receiving some confusing and disquieting information" in his office regarding Doc's operation. For that reason, the Commissioner rejected Doc's application until such time that Doc made an appointment with him to discuss the matter at his office in Santa Fe. Doc's application fee was refunded, but the reason for the rejection was not known.

Last of the Camp Notes —July 12, 1946 [183]

> *"Doc sat over maps night after night telling Gordon [Herkenhoff] things that Gordon made notes on, things Doc had never told me. Gordon sat there and took notes. Herkenhoff suggested a shaft at a place he thought would go into the tunnel. This work was abandoned when Herkenhoff had to return to his own duties at the Land Office. Herkenhoff made a geological report that was marked confidential."*   — Babe

February 2, 1947

Less than a year had gone by since Ova had seen Doc. The last time they were together was when she and Doc had filed on several mining locations at the Land Office in Santa Fe a year earlier. Friends would report to her when and where they had seen him, but there was no effort on Doc's part to return to camp to see Ova. But then on February 2, 1947, it appears that they *had* been together, at least from the implication of two cash receipts[184] signed by Doc on the above date. The receipts read:

Received from Ova M. Noss, forty-five dollars and no Cts. Borrowed in cash for expense of mining equipment for Cheyenne mine. $45.00

—Dr. M.E. Noss and associates

Received from Ova M. Noss seventy dollars and sixty cents used as expenses in securing claims and titles to mining property in Socorro Co.   —Dr. M.E. Noss and associates

~

The receipts indicate that she had financed some of the mining operations for the Cheyenne mine and a mining property in Socorro County.

February 13, 1947

Then Doc slipped away again and those individuals who had an interest in the treasure became restless, even Lampros. Signing off as "Coffee Man," Lampros wrote to Seraphin Sedillo on February 13. In part:

I saw Ova yesterday and I lined everything up. Write to Ova. She wants to take you to Santa Fe to get the permit to open the cave. Ova Noss is the founder and it belongs to her. Now is the time to act. I saw engineer Gordon in Socorro and he wants to see Ova. He is ready to open the cave now.

—Coffee Man, El Fidel Hotel, Santa Fe, New Mexico.

July/August 4, 1947

During the summer of 1947, Ova, Letha, and Dorothy visited the Rock House campsite periodically. It had been two years since the war in Europe had ended, but laborers were still difficult to find and few from the regular crews ever returned to Victorio Peak to seek work.

It was in July 1947 that James Hirst became the Secret Service agent in Albuquerque where he remained for about two years until shortly after Doc was murdered. Although Hirst is mentioned several times, his involvement in  Victorio Peak activity concerning the Secret Service is somewhat blurred; he remained behind the scenes during the Noss treasure trove controversy and little was heard from him. A month after Hirst arrived in Albuquerque, Colonel Turner left White Sands Proving Ground and Brigadier General Philip Blackmore (shown here) took over the command there; that happened on August 4.

It was not until August 8, 1947, six months after Doc had borrowed money for the mining and filing expenses, that Ova learned he was married to Violet L. Boles. Regardless of the conditions under which Doc borrowed the money or Ova's agreement to give it to him, she went to her grave contending that she had never been notified that Doc was granted a divorce, or, in the actual legal sense, an annulment. Research shows that George W. Scott, Justice of the Peace in Pulaski County, Arkansas, had performed the marriage; Doc gave his age as forty-two, but he was actually in his mid-fifties; Violet was thirty-six. He gave his address as General Delivery, Mountain Home in Baxter County, Arkansas. After they were married, Doc and Violet moved to Corpus Christi, Texas. In his absence, he allowed the claims covering the site of Victorio Peak to come within days of expiring.

The news of Doc's marriage came as a shock and it was only because of her children and close friends she was able to cope. When news came that Doc had remarried, help rushed to her side from those who believed in her and in the project at Victorio Peak.

September 6 - 9, 1948

It had been nearly three years since Ova called the meeting at the Buena Vista Hotel to tie off some of the loose ends caused by Doc's absence, an honest attempt to protect the interests of those who were legitimately involved with the Cheyenne Mining Company and the operation at Victorio Peak. Ova's persistence to keep business matters flowing smoothly continued; on September 6, 1948, she wrote[185] to Ernest Gatlin, and other members of the Cheyenne Mining Company to advise them of her intention to hold *another* meeting; this time it would be a reorganizational meeting where they would elect new officers and discuss business matters of vital importance. It wasn't two weeks later that Doc came to the Hembrillo Basin with Claude Fincher, not unlike he had done on November 1, 1945 after the meeting at the Buena Vista Hotel. Even though Doc was back temporarily, he and Ova had still not crossed paths. But during his short stay, he and Claude Fincher began relocating some of the same mine sites that Ova and Doc had filed claims on previously. Wisely, Ova kept busy sorting out the problems caused by Doc's absence by working regularly with Mrs. Minnie Cave in the Minerals Division at the Land Office in Santa Fe on claims she had renewed and filed in her own name. As a result of that continued effort, on September 9, Ova wrote[186] to Gatlin again and advised him that her permit and lease for Victorio Peak had been drawn up and that she was waiting for Commissioner Miles to sign the papers; Ova was gaining a foothold on important matters that affected the Victorio Peak treasure site. She worked long and hard to protect her interest in the claim site, surrounded herself with other individuals to accelerate efforts to lift the treasure, and paid close attention to important details, all without Doc's involvement.

September 14, 1948

In a two-page letter[187] signed by Merle Horzmann on September 14, 1948, which appears to have been written by Attorney Ben Newell, many factors related to Ova's activities were covered. But one paragraph stood out from the others, a compliment attesting to Ova's intrepid effort to stabilize business matters and activities that would eventually connect to efforts aimed at raising the treasure. Horzmann (by Newell) wrote, in part:

> *Frankly, I am very well impressed with the proposition you have at this time. However, I would like to see just how the 10% they are asking would work out on paper in relation to the rest of the [current] interest holders' percentage, and according to Judge Fowler and Mr. Wagner's figures. I feel that it would mean that this amount would be deducted from the net proceeds taken from the property upon which they would take a contract, regardless of whether it proved to be the main claim [the Victorio Peak treasure site], or any of the others they might work.*

~

Specifics of Ova's ideas were covered, particularly the percentages being considered with the new individuals interested in working the claim sites in relationship to the previous interests of others that remained intact. More of the letter: (underlining inserted)

> *This 10%, however, or other percentage they would agree upon, would necessarily come out before anything else was divided. Since no one holds as much as a ten percent interest, I wonder if that is not a little high. Other offers we have had, if you remember, were from 3% to 5%. But let us take this properly into consideration. If this is not done now, this area is likely to become a bombing range, or taken into the bombing range, and we would have difficulty in obtaining permits to work this later on. By you going ahead, getting it taken care of now, in cooperation with myself and whoever you select that can work in harmony with you to get things through on a congenial basis, and a satisfactory one, I believe you will find that in the end, those who have caused so much friction in the past will feel that you did exactly the right thing.*
>
> *However, if they are to get ten percent, they will have the major portion of whatever is removed from the property. At the same time, if it proves to be the thing Dr. Noss has described, <u>it is to be a permanent thing from which we will all derive royalties for the rest of our lives under the original percentage under the Noss contract.</u>*

Once again here is proof that Newell had a vested financial interest in the gold from Victorio Peak, as did Attorney Scoggin. More interesting aspects of the letter:

> *Another thing is the possibility of changing the County Line. This may or may not have an effect upon this property, but if it does, all these papers will have to be filed in whichever county takes over this area. This will not necessarily have to be done right away, but [it will] on the filing of the next papers. It will be in the same category as Grant and Hidalgo [Counties], with the papers being filed originally in Grant, and still remaining in Grant, and we have to go to Silver City to look up the records prior to this division.*
>
> *For my part, and for the good of others who may not understand the legal aspects of this case as we do, the time is right for this to be carried through, while there is a dormant condition existing among those who have held back on allowing outsiders [to] come in who could do these things, either with their ability, finance, or their efforts, and there would be less entanglements at this time. Anything coming up in the future should*

be coped with at the time it comes up, and not allow any one person in the minority at this time sway you from what you feel is right. Will leave that up to your judgment, as far as it is possible, though at times, it had appeared that perhaps I did things you would not understand about and take the wrong viewpoint. That is natural. But no one is hurt except to the extent that that has been justified.

~

It is probable that Merle Horzmann *and* Ben Newell got together and devised the letter, which Horzmann re-typed; Carl might have been present when the letter was drafted. In Chapter 11, Carl wrote in an affidavit that he *"became acquainted with Dr. Noss personally in 1941 at the office of Attorney Newell in Las Cruces, N.M., where* [he] *helped organize the now defunct Cheyenne Mining Co."* Carl Horzmann's connection to Newell's office is clear. Horzmann said in his affidavit, *"Dr. Noss wanted me to represent him in all future dealings with the government since he claimed I was the only honest man he had run across in years."* In six months, those words, *"I was the only honest man he had run across,"* would become part of the transcript in the trial of Charley Ryan, the man who shot and killed Doc Noss. Then too, there is the question of the hypocrisy of the letter itself, one ripe with complimentary words and warm praises directed at Ova for her efforts in formulating the new business ideas to restructure the Cheyenne Mining Company. Then contrary to those platitudes were the times when Merle was equally unkind and disloyal to Ova. In Doc's case, Horzmann went to extremes.

Merle Horzmann's activities as a spy for the New Mexico State Police, the Secret Service and other law enforcement entities demonstrated a duality of her personality that had played out from 1941, seven years of scheming against the Nosses while she and Carl counted the potential rewards of their actions. Evidence of the Horzmann's plot to include themselves in the profits from the treasure appeared in Chapter 12 when Merle wrote to Carl saying, *"My share* (which was about $32.5 million in 1941), *will be somewhere about 1/8 or more, provided I can do my part."* She also told Carl, *"You better not tell anybody there I am in on Government Affairs."* On May 7 she wrote to Carl and referred to Doc and Ova as *"the chief and his wife"* and Doc as *"the Indian."* In another letter on that day she told Carl confidentially, *"I believe if I prove this case,"* which meant pinning the Lorius-Heberer murders on Doc, *"it will put me tops with even the FBI."* She also claimed in a letter she wrote to her husband on May 15, 1941 that, *"I have become Secret Service Operator, 3549-G. This is my first assignment."* Three months and five days later, on August 20, 1941, she wrote to Chief of Police "Butter" Pyle in Du Quoin, Illinois, and told him, *"I began to take up the study of Scientific Investigation with the I.S.A.S., Chicago, and my file number is 3549-G."* It seems that she had taken a correspondence course and used her file number as a ruse to allow her husband to think that she was being embraced by the Secret Service.

~

Unfamiliar names appeared in the letter as individuals who had acquired an interest in the development of the treasure site, or at least had expressed such an interest, names such as: Rowland, Shull, and Coucher. The following paragraph of the Horzmann/Newell letter is, in its entirety, a reference to Doc Noss. Even though it references *people, their, and they*, it is attributable to Doc's actions; Roscoe Parr could be targeted as well. Parr might well have been a deflection used to say things that might otherwise have offended Ova. Regardless, the letter's content can be attributed to there being more than one person present while the letter was drafted, all of whom likely took part in constructing certain portions of it. The next to the last paragraph of the Horzmann's September 14 letter:

> *One more thing: Just because we do not know where Doc is, is no sign that this cannot be put on a legal status. His interest will be protected in the end, and properly. No one wants to cut him out, and no one should be greedy enough not to see that he gets it. He can be found if it is necessary, I know, but as I mentioned, there are people who do not know what is good for them, and try to be like spoiled babies. We have no need for them in a clear-cut business transaction, and their interests should be cared for just as if they were our children, and they will.*
>
> *I trust you to work these matters out to complete satisfaction, and I have let it be known that I may have to be out of town next Saturday, also, so if there is any chance for me to get there and you need me, I will gladly go, provided we can accomplish our purpose, or enough of it to count and you do not call in all the outside options that have no bearing on the present case. The past is gone, and the future is the thing that has to be looked into NOW.*   *—As ever, Merle*

September 16, 1948

In spite of what was being done by Carl and Merle Horzmann to control Ova and steer her thoughts and activities, Ova proceeded religiously on a course that protected the treasure and those who had a legal interest in it. A response to her request for permits to continue on with the work at the treasure site came on September 16. Under the signature of Commissioner Miles, Minnie Cave, now a good friend to Ova, wrote[188] and told her that the permits were prepared, but also advised her that there were only four claim sites and not five. Ova wrote[189] back on September 20 and corrected the matter. By now, Ova had arranged the financing ($10,000) to begin the work needed to open the top entrance; men were ready to start work on the shaft by September 29 and she hoped to have it opened by November 1.

As if there were not enough problems, on September 23, Minnie Cave wrote[190] again, informing Ova that there was some "confusion" related to the claims and that the commissioner was away, but that she would see him soon for his signature. But when Commissioner Miles returned on October 1, he wrote[191] to Ova advising her that he refused to issue prospecting and leases on Section 16 "until such time when a more thorough investigation can be made by" his "office of this location and its mineral possibilities." Victorio Peak was located in Section 16. Miles also copied M.E. Noss & Associates, Claude Fincher, L.G. Rowland, J.A. Shull, and W.A. Coucher on his letter to Ova. Since the permits had elapsed, Doc and others lined up to get the prospecting permits.

Matters improved, however, and, on October 8, E.C. Anderson, under a directive from Commissioner Miles, ordered an examination of the area where Ova had requested prospecting permits. Days later, a geologist and field engineer named Donn Clippinger made an inspection at the site. His report was finished three days later.

October 13, 1948

From assays taken from samples of diorite, Clippinger claimed there was a high probability of gold content at Victorio Peak. Clippinger's October 13 report[192] stated in part:

> *The extensive mineralization in the district, the lead, copper, silver and gold ore found in small pockets along the diorite dike that bisects Victoria [Victorio] Peak, definitely points to the probability of a highly mineralized zone as reported, in spite of the fact that it is not shown by indications on the hill [Victorio Peak].*

~

The Clippinger report was as much a recital of the historic background of Victorio Peak, the legend of the treasure, Doc Noss and the potential of Padre LaRue's campsite being within a close distance to the Peak as it was a geological report. Clippinger wrote:

> *The only present indication of early habitation found near the caverns is the remains of an ancient Indian camp. Below in the canyon, about 1,500 feet northwest of the peak, Indian sherds, metates, and manos* may still be found. The inhabitants of this camp might have been the party brought by the early Spanish padre to work the mine.*

~

The report seemed extensive in that regard and revealed certain other geological characteristics that supported Doc's repeated claims of an ancient mine operation in the caverns below Victorio Peak. Clippinger's description of the area is covered in the "Location" section of the report where he describes fissures that had been "part of an underground water source, resulting in the formation of caverns in the surrounding limestone."

The report also said, "The evidence shown by action of water upon the limestone, the travertine deposited on the walls of the main fracture, as well as on other smaller fractures northwest of it, and a sink-hole on the northwest slope of the hill, verify conclusively the existence of the caverns that are reputed to occur there."

---

*A sherd is a fragment of pottery. A *mentate* is a mealing stone, such as in *mortar and pestle*, used for pulverizing grain and seeds; a stone *manos* (plural for *hand*) being the pestle.

It also mentioned that Doc had "described mine workings, the remnants of a small underground Spanish smelter comprised of two five-foot bull hide bellows, vassos*, ingot molds, and mountain mahogany that had been used as fuel. The fact that both mining and smelting operations were carried on in the seclusion of the cavern gives some credence to the following description of a particular lost mine, the tale of which is related by Dunham." The passage by Dunham in Clippinger's report was the story of Padre LaRue, a short but excellent account of a real person. The official New Mexico account of LaRue's mine was *supposed* to be somewhere in the Organ Mountains, although it was never found. In the "Possibilities" part of his report, Clippinger wrote:

> *Disregarding all folklore and fable, the existence of an ore body exposed in Victoria [Victorio] Peak by the caverns along the contact between the limestone and diorite, is not only possible, but also highly probable. Samples taken of the diorite itself that were exposed on Victorio Peak assayed a trace of gold.*

~

Clippinger also mentioned the cause of Doc's reference to a *bad odor* in many of the chambers where he had to walk knee-deep through a fluffy brown material, "which had an unpleasant odor, irritated his eyes and nostrils and caused his legs to itch and break out." It was guano, *bat dung.* Clippinger reported that the value of the guano alone would be a profitable venture in itself. He closed his report by saying, "These proposed claims are certainly worthy of further investigation." Letha knew about this condition and she gave an account of it. Letha:

> *There were awful fumes in there. Doc would tuck his pants legs in his boots and wrap material around the outside and tie it off. But that stuff would get inside and make little blisters all over his feet and legs. Doc said that it was very fine dust and there was about four inches of it that he'd be walking in. This dust would get in his face and he had to put a handkerchief over his mouth so he could breathe.*

~

When Doc had returned to Corpus Christi, Texas, he was broke. Needing work, he drove to Alice, Texas, where he met up with Charley Ryan and began to work for his company, The Ryan Tool Company. It wasn't long afterwards that Doc and Roscoe Parr drove to Santa Fe and learned that Ova had been given a permit, which included Victorio Peak. The stew in the pot was beginning to simmer.

In addition to Donn Clippinger's report of October 13, E.C. Anderson, Director of the

---

* A vasso is a primitive adobe furnace.

Bureau of Mines, visited Victorio Peak on November 19 and reported back to Commissioner Miles. Anderson's November 30, 1948 letter:[193]

> *I visited Victorio Peak on November 19th with McKinlay and Clippinger. There was no mineralization of possible importance found on state land in the immediate vicinity. I didn't go below the timbered shaft. The weight I dropped indicated a depth of 117' and soft loose material at the bottom. Then 600' to the south of the shaft, at the lower level, is a second shaft approximately 20' deep in shale bed, which is not timbered. There is a platform and windlass in place there. Probably work was done with it over the past five years. I don't recommend a prospector's permit, but it is okay for a treasure permit if allowed legally. If the permit is issued, the Bureau is willing to see that the request is carried out.*   *—E.C. Anderson*

January 1949

The Christmas holiday season came and went, and by January 1949, Ova had received the permit from the Land Office to do the sorely needed work at Victorio Peak. With renewed hope she returned to the Rock House campsite with a new handpicked crew to reopen the top shaft. Now, with Ova in charge, activities that were once handled by Doc were underway.

It was also on a cold winter day that January when to everyone's surprise Doc pulled into the campsite with Charley Ryan. When Doc arrived it was plain to see that work was continuing without him and since permit applications had already been filed, approved and issued by the Land Office in Ova's name, there was little Doc could do about the matter. To be certain of this, Doc, Roscoe Parr, and Charley Ryan came to see Minnie Cave shortly after Ova had acquired her new permit. Ova then requested a letter from Mrs. Cave showing that the property was open in January and that Doc's original claim was no longer valid. Mrs. Cave assured her there was no way anyone could have taken it from her after January 1949.

Here is an account concerning an interesting event that resulted in Ova filing the claim permit at Victorio Peak in her own name, as told by Terry Delonas:

> *The first mining claim of record we found was in 1942. From that time on until Doc's death, they had to renew their claim; I think every year. I know that they always did that; one of them did for sure. Then, when Doc was away during part of 1948 and 1949 my grandmother found out quite by accident that their claim was up for renewal. Just when the claim was about to expire she happened to be selling insurance door-to-door. She discovered this when she called on a man in Hot Springs who said he wanted to buy some insurance from her. He gave the reason that the old Noss claim out there on Victorio Peak was expiring at midnight the next day. He told her that he intended to get the claim for himself and he'd better get some insurance. So, surprisingly, she wrote him a policy, and I don't know how she kept him from knowing that she was Ova Noss at the time, but she did.*

~

Letha gave the following account of the same event as told to her by Ova, but with a more detailed breakdown of the circumstances. In part:

> *Mama was selling insurance door-to-door in Hot Springs. She went to this guy's door and told him she was selling insurance. He said to her, 'Well, ya know, I'm going out and jump Doc Noss' claim tomorrow, so maybe I ought get some of that insurance.' He laughed, ya know. He didn't know who she was and Mama had no idea the claim was going to expire. Mama told him, 'Then you better get some insurance, a lot of insurance and you better get double indemnity, too.' She asked him when he was going to do this and he told her he was going out to Santa Fe the next day. Mama told him she'd get the policy ready for him and get back to him. Then she came a dashin' home and went and got the necessary claim papers ready and put them where they belonged in the monuments out there at Victorio Peak and then she dashed out to Santa Fe and got them filed in her name to save the claim.*
>
> *About three or four days later, this man came over to Mama's house and he said, 'Are you Mrs. Noss?' And she said, 'Yeah.' And he said, 'You're that insurance lady.' Mama said, 'Yeah.' He said, 'Why, you beat me to it.' Mama said, 'I'm sure glad you told me. I thought we had another week or two.' And that was that.*
>
> *We learned right after she had refiled the claim out there that Parr had gone up to Santa Fe with Doc and Ryan and when they had found out that Mama had already filed the claim, Parr came over to Hot Springs. I was there when he came to the house. He told Mama that Doc wanted to see her. Mama told him, 'If Doc wants to see me he can let me know. I wouldn't take your word for nothin'. Parr said, 'Well, I'm letting you know now.' She told him she wasn't goin' with him and then told him to get out and he left.*

~

Knowing that Ova had taken the proper steps to secure the claim site, Doc and Ryan began filing on all open claims around the ones covered under Ova's permitted claim area. Then, in anticipation of selling gold bars that Doc had stashed at different places, Doc, Charley Ryan, and Roscoe Parr journeyed into Old Mexico where Ryan made arrangements for the sale of the gold; there were 110 bars that were to be recovered and converted into cash. The plan was to hire a pilot and fly the gold out in an airplane capable of taking off with the entire load, about 4,000 pounds in all. The pilot would then fly the gold, Ryan, and Doc south across the border from an airstrip that Ryan and his crew had cleared on a ranch owned by Jack Bruton, which was a short drive from the Hembrillo Basin.

After the arrangements were made, the three men and their wives returned to New Mexico and rented houses in Hatch: Ryan and his wife and one or two of his men rented a small house located at 459 Jefferson Street. Doc and Violet took a small bungalow on Canal Street on the east side of town. Parr stayed close by at a motel somewhere in Hatch. The plan was to remain at these locations until the gold transaction was completed. Ryan's people would drive back to Texas and rendezvous with Doc, Ryan, and the gold.

After the group returned to Hatch and settled in, they drove to Victorio Peak only to find a group of disgruntled people waiting for them; Ova, her son Marvin, Seraphin Sedillo, and Sedillo's wife all watched closely with keen eyes and suspicious minds. According to Ova's writings* on July 15, 1951 concerning the issue of Doc and Ryan's workers, everyone at the camp was rightfully suspicious of them: Roscoe Parr, Charley Ryan, Buck Harris, Jack Lawrence, and others, including Doc, all of whom were "working on lead and silver claims surrounding Ova's state land permits." Everyone, especially Ova, was afraid that Doc and Ryan were carrying bullion out of the basin on every trip, namely the eighty-six bars that Ova and Doc had brought out of Victorio Peak early in the discovery. Ova wrote: "They had a small mattress in the bed of Ryan's truck going and comin' every trip."

The exact day-to-day details of what transpired after Ryan's group and Doc arrived in the Hembrillo Basin were never recorded, but, according to Terry Delonas' account of what Ova had told him, she and Doc were able to resolve the issue concerning the permits that covered the treasure site, but *not* the matter of Doc leaving her and marrying the Boles woman—that was still on the front burner to be resolved at a later date. Up until this point in time it had been the interpretation from the records at the Land Office in Santa Fe, combined with Roscoe Parr's statements to Doc, Ova had beaten Doc out of his share of the treasure. But that was not the case, as Doc would soon learn. Letha and Dorothy spoke about the key events that took place during a recording session taken in 1972. In part:

> _Letha_: *A few days went by, but I can't remember how many days it was, but this is when Marvin got involved. Marvin had been in the service and he went up there to the Victorio Peak worksite when Doc and his crew came up. So when Marvin seen Doc comin' he stepped out with his gun and stopped him at gunpoint. He didn't know it was Doc because he hadn't seen him for years and we didn't tell Marvin all of the details, you see. So Marvin sees him and says, 'Doc, is that you?' Doc said, 'Yeah, it's me.' Marvin said, 'Why in the world did you come here?' Well, Doc wasn't sayin' too much. He kind of felt we had all turned against him.*
>
> _Dorothy_: *Well, in a way we had because he just disappeared and left Babe with all of the responsibilities and all.*
>
> _Letha_: *But Doc was told that Mama had beaten him out of his percentage; that's what Parr told him, ya' see. So Marvin told Doc that Mama planned to be up tomorrow.*
>
> _Dorothy_: *Babe wasn't there that day.*
>
> _Letha_: *Well, when she came up the next day, Doc went over to her and they sat down under a tree. Doc said, 'I see you jumped my claims and you ended up with all the treasure.' And she said, 'Doc, what are you talkin' about?' He said, 'Well you got the claim in your name.' She said, 'Yeah, I got it in my name, but you weren't here and I didn't know*

---

* O. Noss, **op. cit.**, p2.

what to do, Doc. I still have your percentage; your half is reserved for you. I found out by accident that the claim was going to expire so I refiled the claims. I just didn't want some stranger going in there and getting it. You still got it.' Doc said, 'Babe, did you do that?' She said, 'I sure did. We found it together and I wasn't going to beat you out of it.' And Doc said, 'But Parr told me that you had grabbed it all and you were going to keep it all. That's what was at the Land Office.' She said, 'Doc, I had no intentions whatsoever of taking your half, but I heard that you were living with some gal and that you were dealing me out, too.' Doc said, 'And I thought you and your family was going to take over; Marvin's out here now and you have a gang out here workin'.'

Dorothy: She told Doc, 'Come up to the mine and I'll show you what we've got done, but I reserved that for you and I had no intention of beating you out of your share.'

Letha: So they went up to the mine and he seen the road, and he said, 'My God, how'd you get that road up there?' She told him that she had Jack Woods bring his bulldozer in and she promised him a share of the gold to do the work.' Doc said, 'Babe, this road is as good as a highway. When I left it was nothin' more than an old cow path.' Doc told her, 'Well, Babe, I found out one thing; you've proven to me you could do this, but why didn't you do this when I was around?' Mama just told him, 'Doc, you were always taking care of the business, not me.'

Dorothy: After Doc and Mama talked he knew that Parr had convinced Doc that Babe took over rights to the mine operation and the treasure.

Letha: And when she told him to come on and let's work and get this done together, Doc knew for sure that Mama never intended to hurt him. Doc told her then, 'Babe, we'll get together and finish that last seventy-four feet and we'll open this thing up.' He told Mama to keep Jack Woods doing the bulldozing work because he had this gold hid out there at the peak and that he had a big thing comin' up and there would be enough money to open up the cavern.

Dorothy: So Parr at this point was completely out of the deal because Doc knew by what Babe told him that Parr was out to make trouble.

Letha: Ya' see, Marvin was there when this happened with Doc and Mama. And Marvin walked over to Ryan's men because they were sittin' around watchin' everything. Well, they saw Doc and Mama talkin' and when Doc laughed and hugged Mama. Well right then, ya' see, Parr's plans went down the drain. The problem, though, was Doc had already been back to the peak a day or two and he had shown Ryan where he put those gold bars, but Doc hadn't seen through Ryan, yet, what he was up to and what he had planned for Doc. Ryan had this big airplane comin' in and they were working on a landing strip out there on Bruton's ranch and they made it look like they were drilling for water out there when all along they were clearin' this airstrip.

~

In spite of suspicions voiced by Ova that Ryan and Doc were removing gold from the Victorio Peak area under a mattress in the bed of Ryan's truck, there has never been any evidence that Doc had removed any of the eighty-six bars mentioned above; that particular cache remains hidden in a canyon in the

Hembrillo Basin on the White Sands Missile Range to this day. The value of that cache is estimated to be worth more than $40 million.

Joe "Sonny" Andregg* had helped Doc move the eighty-six bars in June of 1941. Sonny had told Jack Bruton about it and was warned by Bruton that there "could be trouble over having the knowledge of it." It wasn't simply a matter of eighty-six bars that Andregg had helped Doc move; there were many other sites, at least fourteen of them. He talked about his activities with Doc on August 13, 1973 and wrote a short letter[194] to explain that there were many sites, more than fourteen, where he and Doc had hid gold bars that he and Ova had removed from inside Victorio Peak. The fol-

lowing letter was written after Andregg helped Letha and Ova identify each site, which he marked on a map. Andregg's letter:

I, Joe A. Andregg, have marked this map in several places where Doc Noss and I worked. I saw gold bars at these locations. I would help him uncover his caches, then I would go stand watch and he would move it, why I don't know.

We loaded a heavy box in Doc's pickup truck. He unloaded them somewhere [exact location deleted] near Alamogordo. Again, I stood watch while he unloaded it. I believe he had at least 10 different caches in the San Andres [Mountains]. I don't believe any man would go to that much trouble for a bunch of brass bars. I know of one occasion in El Paso when he left me in a hotel. When he returned he had a book of Traveler's Checks worth $1,700. I have seen at least 40 bars in one cache.

— Joe Andregg

~

Ova rarely knew where Doc had taken the gold he had removed from the caverns, only that he had taken it to various places for safekeeping. There are a number of such caches that Joe marked on a map—fourteen sites in all. Many

---

* This photo of Sonny was taken at the Rock House the last year he worked for Doc. He and Doc had at least 14 gold bar stash sites within a five mile radius of Victorio Peak, all of which Sonny marked on a topographic map.

of those sites have never been visited since Doc and Sonny Andregg hid them. The map on which Andregg marked each site is an official geodetic survey map (topomap) of the San Andres Mountain Range; each site is within close proximity of Victorio Peak.

Then there was the matter of the one hundred ten gold bars Doc and Ryan were planning to fly to Mexico. It included one cache of fifty-one bars Doc had secreted near the goat shed* shown below, a site that was known to Ryan, a cache of gold bars that was about to cause a lethal situation.

Apart from all the problems that came when Doc arrived at Victorio Peak with Charley Ryan, he had taken time to consider what Ova had told him about her reasons for filing the claim papers, and, in doing so, he realized that he had not only misread his assessment of the situation, but he had also hurt Ova deeply by leaving her. He also gave thought to his association with Ryan and Roscoe Parr, namely the fact that he had no reason to continue on with them after he completed his end of the deal. It wasn't long before Doc told Ova about his relationship with Ryan and the arrangements they had worked out to fly 110 bars into Mexico.

In Ova's March 1974 deposition,[†] the issue of the fifty-one bars was covered:

> *Q. Now, in 1949, when Doc was going to sell those fifty-one bars, who was he going to sell them to?*

---

* The goat shed (the long dark structure center right) is seen in respect to the Henderson ranch as taken from the slope of Victorio Peak. The insert photo shows a view of Victorio Peak from the Henderson ranch.
† N. Deposition, ***op. cit.***, pp. 108-111

A. To Ryan Tool Company in Alice, Texas. Charlie Ryan.

Q. Was any work done by Doc and you to prepare for the transaction?

A. Oh, yes, yes.

Q. What did he have to do?

A. He had to make an airstrip. It's still visible out there.

Q. Who constructed this strip?

A. Doc and the men who had the plane. They hired a construction man.

Q. They went out and got a bulldozer to clear a landing strip?

A. Yes.

Q. Where is this landing strip?

A. It was a mile and a half from this saddle [between Victorio Peak and Geronimo Peak].

Q. And why did they have to build a strip?

A. They were going to fly this gold out.

Q. How long a strip was this, as you remember it?

A. I guess a quarter of a mile. It was quite a distance, and pretty wide.

Q. You said Doc was going to sell these bars to the Ryan Tool Company.

A. It was his last effort. He said, 'I'm going to sell it.'

Q. At about the time, there was an airplane crash, wasn't there?

A. Yes.

~

According to Terry, Ova told him that Doc had apologized and that he wanted to get back together, but he needed a day to work things out with Ryan and after he settled with him, Doc wanted to get back on the job and raise the treasure, feeling confident that they would be able to get it out. In addition, Doc had acknowledged the fact that Ova had saved the day by acquiring new permits to protect the treasure.

January 10, 1949

Since the permit by the Land Office was specifically issued to recover treasure trove, which had been recommended by E.C. Anderson in his November 30, 1948 letter,[195] Guy Shepard, the newly elected Commissioner of Public Lands, seen here, wrote to Ova on January 10 advising her "that in case anything is discovered" she was to notify his office "before anything is removed." Ova had the ear of the Land Office in Santa Fe; they were cooperating as much as possible, even in the light of the fact that the Army was slowly but steadily laying claim to the lands that encompassed Victorio Peak and areas beyond.

In the interim, work continued on the landing strip for the plane that would take some of the Victorio Peak gold across the border into Mexico. Also, during January, Ryan filed prospecting claims in the Hembrillo Basin in addition to the ones filed jointly by Doc and him. In all, Ryan had filed[196] ten separate claims.

There were six men on Ryan's lead mining crew working on the slope of Geronimo Peak across from Victorio Peak. Willard L. Blake, who worked for Ryan, was an unemployed truck driver who lived in Hatch and had actually been hired by Doc Noss to work at the lead mine operation for Ryan. Doc was Blake's boss at the mine site, but Blake took orders from Ryan as well. Ryan and his crew worked only during the day. But Doc made night trips into the basin that aroused the suspicion of Charley Ryan and Roscoe Parr—especially Ryan. The trips were necessary to gather the 110 bars he had agreed to hand over to Ryan for the sale in Mexico. It wasn't long afterward that Doc had finally managed to gather up the bars to close his deal with Ryan, which *included* the fifty-one bars at the goat shed. After Ryan paid him for his share of the profit, Doc agreed to give half to Ova. Where the remaining complement of bars came from is unknown, except for one cache of twenty bars, which Doc dug up at a windmill near Rincon on the night of March 4 or early morning on the next day when he was murdered. Other men who were working under Ryan's direction were: Jack Lawrence, Allan Ray, Pedro "Pete" Nunez, and Charley and Buck Harris.

January 26, 1949

Horzmann continued to manipulate Ova, attempting to steer her in a direction that best suited her own purposes. In a letter[197] to Ova on January 26, Horzmann spelled out a cryptic approach to something she had scribbled on her mental blackboard, something she was unwilling to share with Ova, something she "*would have to be certain of first before* [she] *could discuss it*" with her. Horzmann's con-like move was again typical of the manner in which she wormed her way into matters that did not concern her. From Horzmann's January 26 letter, in part: (underlining inserted)

> *I felt confident that Doc and Roscoe would do just as you said they did, but I believe that regardless of the argument, you will be wisest to just sit tight, say very little, and go right ahead with your own plans. It is your one and only chance, and no good can come having too many fingers in the pie. Have just been wondering if those people came back that promised to do it – <u>Rollins</u> or the Dr., you did not say. If not I have an idea, but do not know how workable it might be. It is something I would have to be certain of before I discuss it, but will not do anything about it until I see you and see what the score is there. Then, maybe I couldn't do anything about [it], but may know about it by noon tomorrow.*
>
> —*Merle*

~

There is no reference in the files to a man named "Rollins," nor was any information available to know what "it" meant.

February 18, 1949

By now, and to his regret, Doc had shown Ryan where he had hid the fifty-one bars, which was about half of the agreed deal. Ryan had promised to pay Doc in advance for his end of the profits before they loaded the plane. When

Doc reminded Ryan of his promise, Ryan reneged and said no. Upset with Ryan and suspicious of his true intent, Doc held to his side of the agreement to deliver all of the gold to the airstrip, but only if he was paid as agreed. Even in the face of Ryan's broken promise, Doc held to his end of the bargain, hoping Ryan would reconsider and pay up—but it would never happen. There was an understanding between Ova and Doc that they would get back to the task at hand, namely to do everything possible to raise the treasure. In addition, they had discussed Ryan's refusal to pay Doc his percentage up front; either he paid half of the profits now—or it was no deal. Doc said he would take care of the matter *before* he was to deliver the gold on March 5, which was less than two weeks away. Ova's 1975 deposition* focused in on that particular event:

> *Q. Did Doc have a conversation with you concerning an intention to move some of the gold?*
> *A. Yes.*
> *Q. Did you and Doc make a decision that you would not go through with the deal with Ryan?*
> *A. Yes.*
> *Q. What was the decision based upon?*
> *A. Doc was going to move it because it didn't bring him any money.*
> *Q. Did something in the transaction with Ryan fall through?*
> *A. Yes.*
> *Q. Did Doc move the gold that he had brought out to sell?*
> *A. Yes.*
> *Q. And was Ryan told?*
> *A. No.*
> *Q. Do you know where he moved it?*
> *A. No.*
> *Q. Did he tell you where he had moved it?*
> *A. I didn't see him. He was dead.*
> *Q. When was it that you and Doc decided not to go through with the deal?*
> *A. It was about two days before this [the plane crash].*
> *Q. But, Ryan had not done what he was supposed to do?*
> *A. He never brought any money. He was going to pay Doc at the other end.*
> *Q. Was Ryan going to take the gold and pay him after he transacted it?*

---

* N. Deposition, ***op. cit.***, pp. 12-14

A. Yes.
Q. And you folks were not going to go along with that?
A. Well, sure. No money, no gold.

~

That was not the end of it; things were only beginning to heat up. Doc told Ova earlier that he would take care of the matter concerning the fifty-one bars at the goat shed—which he did. He dug them up and hid them at several different locations. But the only person who profited from those stashes of gold was a cowboy, a part-time rodeo performer who was passing through Hatch on the night of March 4—his name was Tony Jolley.

Chapter 22

March 5, 1949 - The Day Doc was Murdered

Although it is not known for certain who wrote the following letter of February 19, 1949, the general language of the letter and the fact that Ryan was charged $100 for *corporation expense,* suggests the sender was an attorney. Ben Newell was Doc's attorney regarding the Victorio Peak treasure, and the subject matter of the letter[198] was treasure trove issues, written in response to a legal question raised by Charley F. Ryan. The most likely explanation was that Doc introduced Ryan to Newell. It read:

> *Dear Mr. Ryan: Regarding treasure trove, New Mexico has no statute on this matter, hence the State acquires no title to any portion of such treasure and the finder becomes the owner, subject to title of the true owner. It must be concealed underground—lost by reason of being buried and the owner having died or passed out of existence. Such treasure is usually defined as gold or silver bullion. Should such treasure be found, it could then be determined by proper action in a court whether the real owner could be found and if not then the title becomes perfected in the finder. Certainly a method of determining this could be evolved in a proper court proceeding--otherwise title could never become perfected. That is a bridge that we could cross when we get to it, but not before. Hope this serves your question. PS You may send a check for $100 on corporation expense with signed paper. (No signature)*

~

The author of the letter had a clear understanding of the law regarding treasure trove, which lends to the notion that Ryan had asked for a legal opinion on the matter, a sort of *what if* scenario—what if someone found such a treasure; what would one have to do to claim it legally? There are no warnings in the letter concerning the perils involved with possessing gold, let alone being caught while in the process of smuggling it out of the country. What Ryan's motives might have been for getting a legal opinion on the matter, beyond what the letter actually says, is not known. What *is* known, however, is that Ben Newell was Ryan's defense attorney for the murder of Doc Noss.

~

Jack Woods was twenty-two when he met Ova Noss, but he was eighty years old when he was interviewed in 2007. Jack was a congenial and friendly man who recalled with great clarity the events of March 4 and 5, 1949. Jack and his wife, Elaine, were living in the small community of Caballo, New Mexico, and they had lived there since they left Gallup in 1989.

Jack was born in Clayton, New Mexico, in the shadow of Rabbit Ear Mountain on the edge of the Seneca and Kiowa National Grasslands situated in the northeast corner of New Mexico. But Jack wasn't raised there; he was raised in the small town of Gallup on the opposite side of the state, the same town where Doc had sold gold bars and other valuables. He would have been a young boy of about ten or twelve when Doc first started doing business there. Evidenced by the young age at which Jack Woods started his own business, he proved to be an industrious man; by the time he was twenty-two, he had his own earth-moving equipment including a D7 Caterpillar dozer.

Marvin Beckwith and his wife, Henrietta, also lived in Gallup at the time. It was Marvin who had introduced Jack to Ova. Jack described her as a feisty woman, a go-getter who knew how to stand on her own feet and bargained plainly for what she wanted to accomplish. Knowing that Jack was an excavation contractor, Ova told him that she needed some roadwork done at Victorio Peak, so, in order to determine the scope of the work, Jack agreed to drive out to the Hembrillo Basin so he could determine the extent of the work. At the time, Ova had some financial assistance from a man who lived in Michigan, a physician by the name of Dr. Keucher Monroe. The three of them met in Hatch and together they drove to Victorio Peak in Monroe's 1938 Hudson Terraplane sedan, a rugged, stable car able to make the journey.

In his recorded interview, Jack said, "On the return trip out of the basin, Monroe stopped the car to allow the engine to cool down. It was then that Ova reached into her purse and said, 'I want to show you something, Jack.' She pulled out a small gold bar and handed it to me; it looked like a *Baby Ruth* candy bar. It was soft enough to cut with my knife, so I removed a sliver from the bottom of it and gave the bar back to her. Ova said that it came from Victorio Peak." Shortly afterward, Jack had the sliver examined by an El Paso jeweler who told him that it was pure gold; there was no longer any question in Jack Woods' mind that Ova had access to a lot of gold from inside Victorio Peak. "I think the treasure was a big one," he told me. Jack claimed that Dr. Monroe had also shown him a gold bar that he had received from Ova. "It was rough and dark, about 9 inches x 2 inches that weighed twelve pounds or so." Jack went on to explain how he finally became so familiar with Victorio Peak, but it was a tragic story. In part:

> It was in February of 1949 that Ova and I came to an agreement and outlined a time schedule for the completion of the road and made financial arrangements. The scope of the work included dozing new routes in and out from the western rim of the basin all the way to the top of Victorio Peak and making repairs to the existing road where it was necessary.

> ~

Jack was also required to excavate for another opening into the caverns. As compensation for the work, Jack said, "I took a small percentage of the treasure when and if we recovered it."

It was during the first few days in February of 1949 that Jack hauled his equipment from Gallup and unloaded his dozer ten miles west from the rim of the basin and began working on the road. A month later he had not only cleared a good road from the western rim all the way to the base of the Peak; he had also excavated a drivable road to a point near the top of the Peak as he agreed. It was then that he began excavating on the sides of the mountain in search of another opening that would hopefully lead to the caverns below. Although he didn't know it at the time, Jack had uncovered an entrance to such a passageway, but it was months later that Ova discovered it and called him and told him that he had uncovered something, a small opening into what she and Letha thought was a cavern.

On the day that Doc was murdered, Woods was putting the finishing touches on the road, which was now in excellent condition for travel. He had also improved the road leading from the campsite at the Rock House to the Peak. That same day Jack was operating his dozer close to where Doc had set up a small camp near the silver and lead mining operation that Doc and Ryan were working. Woods said, "Doc drove up in a Jeep with Charley Ryan" and claimed that the two men seemed to get along. He knew Ryan had money and that he owned vehicles and equipment and that he saw Doc and Ryan "quite often going in and out of the basin where they were working their claims nearby." Jack told me that from all the stories he had heard about Doc Noss that he expected him to be about ten feet tall, but he wasn't, only a man of average height and weight, but friendly and quick-witted.

Jack also said he knew that Ova had secured the needed permits to work at Victorio Peak and that there had been a rift between her and Doc over her filing the claims; he did not know the details, but he told me that when he was at Ova's campsite near the Rock House one day he saw Doc and Ova talking for quite a while, and from what Woods could determine, there seemed to be some hard feelings between them. But what Jack did not know was that they had come to terms and agreed to work together.

That day, Jack's bulldozer was sitting idle on a road near the base of Victorio Peak waiting for parts. Letha was in Hot Springs working as a waitress. She gave

her account of what she knew about the sequence of events that involved a young man named Curtis Noble and Letha's brother, Marvin. Here is her account of that day, Friday, March 4, 1949, in part:

> *I was waitressin' at this café in Hot Springs, and this fella came in and he said his name was Curtis Noble. He told me that his brother was running a bulldozer out at your place, and he meant out there at Victorio Peak. He told me that he had been in Alaska for three years and that he wanted to see him, Curtis. I told him I didn't know how in the world I'd get him out there, but I told him to go over and see Mama, and I gave him her address. And then by coincidence, Marvin walks in to the café, he'd come down from Gallup, and they both went to Mama's house. So Marvin decided he'd go up to Victorio Peak and see if they could fly over and see the old trail that was supposed to lead right into the side of the peak. So they left and I didn't think much about it and when my shift ended I went home to Mama's house there in Hot Springs.*

~The Plane Crash~

It was in the predawn hours of Friday, March 4, 1949 that Doc arrived at Victorio Peak in hopes that he would have the opportunity to move the fifty-one* bars Ryan had already seen, part of the 110 bars that were to be flown across the border. The plane that would fly Doc's gold to Mexico was thought to be a privately owned surplus DC-3 from WWII, and it was scheduled to land sometime late Saturday, arrangements that were initially made by Doc and with the complete knowledge of Ryan. The DC-3 had a range of 1,000 miles and it could easily handle the estimated 4,000 pounds of gold. The gold had to be taken to the edge of the airstrip and made ready for a quick withdrawal. It is also believed that the five men working for Ryan would be used at the last minute to help move the gold, but only if Doc and Ryan needed help. Once the gold was in Mexico and the money was in hand from the sale, the plan was to close down the operation on Ryan's claims in the Hembrillo Basin on the basis that there was little or no profit in the silver and lead mining operation, which was simply a front for the real reason that Ryan was there with Doc. The runway was finished, but the problem about the money had not abated; unless Ryan came up with the cash for half of Doc's profits, the gold would not be loaded onto the plane. So, to keep from losing out completely, Doc had to move the gold—he had no choice.

Jack Woods, the *Cat Skinner*, as Ova called him, arrived at Victorio Peak early Friday morning. Soon other men from Ryan's work force entered the basin: Willard Blake, Ollan Brown, Pedro "Pete" Nunez, and brothers, William E. and Denver L. Brizendine all arrived at Ryan and Doc's lead mine operation together in Ryan's Jeep. Across the way, Jack was on his bulldozer working on the road

---

* Over the years, the contention has always been that there were fifty-three bars, not fifty-one as Ova claimed.

leading to the top of Victorio Peak when he suddenly developed a mechanical problem with his dozer* and had to shutdown. Jack wasted no time and left for El Paso to get parts so he could do the necessary repair work on his machine. While he was gone, Doc was off doing something with Ryan's men, hoping for a chance to move the gold. But it was too risky; he had to wait until the cover of night.

While Jack was on his way back from El Paso with parts for his bulldozer and had just entered the road coming in from the west that led to the Hembrillo Basin, a good forty-minute drive, a small light plane flew into the area between Victorio Peak and Geronimo Peak. Jack told me he knew why the small plane flew into the basin that morning and said that Clay Noble, Curtis Noble's brother, was working for him at the Peak: helping with the roadwork, occasionally operating the dozer, and maintaining it as well. While Jack was in El Paso, Clay was getting the dozer ready so they could begin making repairs as soon as he returned. Jack said, "Clay and his wife Gloria didn't know that Curtis was back in the country until two days before when they had run into him in Hot Springs. From there they brought him out to the camp at Victorio Peak." Woods told me that Clay and Gloria, who was Jack's sister, were staying in a small *turtle back* trailer while Clay was also helping them with the road work. "Elaine and I gave Clay and Gloria the trailer for them to use while they were out at the peak."

Jack said that the day before the plane crash, Clay gave Curtis his car to use with the understanding that he would be back in a day or two. "Curtis drove Clay's car to Hot Springs where he met up with Marvin Beckwith and decided they would fly out to Victorio Peak and drop a note telling Clay that *Daech*, Curtis Noble's nickname, was going to bring Clay's car back the following day, Saturday, March 5." Jack said, "The boys rented a plane there at the airport in Hot Springs, a small, light plane, a J-3 Piper Cub[†] and together they flew toward the peak."

Jack was on his way back from El Paso and was still a good distance away, moving across the basin toward the Peak just about the same time that Curtis and Marvin's plane

---

* O. Noss, **op. cit.**, p3.
[†] J-3 Piper Cub similar to one flown by Curtis Noble - Compliments of Edward T. Herlihy, Sandpoint, Idaho.

flew over. Below, Doc watched as it soared over the arroyo between the peaks, a plane much smaller than the DC-3 that would arrive the next day. Curtis spotted Jack's small trailer below, throttled back on the engine and began his descent into the arroyo. As they soared closer to the ground, Marvin slid the window back and dropped the note Curtis had prepared. Suddenly the plane dipped a wing, and to the horror of those who were watching, they crashed on a large flat rock in the arroyo; the plane had hit a pocket of dead air and Curtis could not recover from his descent.

Doc was less than a hundred yards away when it happened and ran to the crash* site. When he got there, fuel was pouring out of the ruptured tank; Curtis was unconscious leaning against the instrument panel and Marvin was struggling to free himself from the wreckage. Doc reached in and pulled Marvin out and then carried him to a safe distance away from the plane. Then Marvin groaned, "Doc, get Curtis out." Doc returned to the plane and managed to get Curtis loose from his seatbelt and then carried him to where Marvin was and placed him gently on the ground beside him. He gave Marvin a quick look: his leg, right arm and shoulder were badly cut, his face was bruised and lacerated and he was in great pain. "I've gotta' get you two outta here," Doc said as he cradled Marvin in his arms. He turned and carried him to Ryan's pickup truck and laid him gently on a mattress in the bed of the truck. Some of Ryan's men rushed to the scene as well and helped carry Curtis' limp body to the truck. Doc quickly got in behind the wheel. By then, Gloria, who was staying in the small trailer at the base of the Peak, ran up to the truck and got in beside Doc. Clay climbed into the back of the truck with his brother and Marvin. Doc then sped off across the basin and headed for Hatch.

---

* Claude Fincher standing at the crash site the day after the accident. Original cockpit is inset.

As Doc's truck approached the western rim of the basin, Jack Woods was heading back from El Paso on the same road heading toward them from the west. It was then that Jack spotted Ryan's pickup truck speeding toward him. Not knowing the circumstances, he came to a halt at the side of the road. Doc closed the gap and skidded to a stop beside Jack's car and told him what happened. Jack explained the moment:

> *I could see Curtis and Marvin in the back of the pickup on a mattress. Gloria got in the car with me. I told Doc we would drive ahead of him and notify the doctor in Hatch that they were coming in. Doc was right behind me all the way to town. We got to the doctor and a few seconds later, Doc pulled in. We could see that Marvin was alive, but the doctor said that Curtis was dead. The doctor then gave Marvin some first aid while an ambulance was called to take him to Beaumont Hospital in El Paso.*

~

Soon the ambulance arrived, and they loaded Marvin inside. Doc started to get in the ambulance to go along, but Marvin was conscious then and told Doc, "No, I want Jack to go with me." Doc, knowing Marvin's discontent with him over leaving his mother, withdrew. Just before Jack got into the ambulance with Marvin, Doc pulled him aside. Now, with the death of Curtis Noble and the serious injury of Marvin Beckwith, Doc had reached a point of surrender, a point where he could no longer justify keeping his biggest secret—an alternate entrance that led to the Victorio Peak treasure, a passageway that Ova and the Noss family members were certain existed, a secret entrance that Doc knew about, but for how long no one knew. Doc looked at Woods and said, "I'm going to divorce Charley Ryan. Get with me as soon as you come back and I'll show you how to get into that place." To this very day, Jack Woods holds to the belief that Doc was referring to a hidden entrance that led to the treasure below Victorio Peak.

In her 1975 deposition, Ova said she was in Hot Springs with Letha when the plane crashed. "Doc couldn't find me and he called the police to run me down. I pulled up to a stop sign and I said, 'Now, what have I done?'" The policeman spotted Ova in her car and pulled her over, then told her about the plane crash and that someone had been killed. According to Ova, the policeman said, "'Doc's trying to get a hold of you, it's desperate.'" Ova said, "Thinking Marvin was dead, I ran to the beauty shop where Letha was. She was under the dryer. I ran in and told her that Marvin was killed. She came out of there with all them things on her head. She ran down the street so crazy. We went home to go to El Paso."

Sometime after Marvin was taken away in the ambulance, Doc was finally able to speak to Ova on the phone.* He called her at her home from Valley Auto Company.

---

* O. Noss, **op. cit.**, p3.

Doc called me in Hot Springs and told me where to get him in Hatch, which was the Valley Auto Company, and he went into details about the plane crash, gave me his phone number and said, 'If you need me, you can call me at this phone, but I am filling up my truck now and going out on the range to move fifty-one bars of bullion to the Graham ranch that I and Ryan were going to smuggle into Old Mexico, but I have changed my mind by the Noble boy losing his life,' and he said, 'I never wanted anyone to lose his life.' My daughter, Letha and I begged him to leave the bullion lay there until we found out how Marvin was and Doc said, 'No this is my best time, because I can't get out from under Ryan's nose and he'll think I have gone to El Paso to see Marvin, if he misses the truck.'

~

But before the night was over, Doc would discover another reason to move the gold, *besides* Noble's death and Marvin's injuries.

From what Ova said in her writings, Doc told her to meet him in Hatch, which is about forty miles away, less than an hour's drive from Hot Springs. Ova also said in her deposition that she and Letha were "too shook" to drive and that a man named Bill Rusk drove them to Hatch. If Doc, Ova, and Letha had driven to Hatch within a reasonable time after Ova talked to Doc, they would have arrived at Valley Auto Company close to noon. Assuming that Ova and Letha drove to the Beaumont Hospital in El Paso after meeting up with Doc, which they had, Doc had at least another five or six hours of daylight, ample time to find someone to help him move the gold.

Another portion of Ova Noss' March 4, 1975, deposition* also provides additional information on what happened *after* Marvin Beckwith was taken to El Paso. Whether the conversation between Ova and Doc was over the phone or they talked in person is not known. Ova gave an account to Attorney David Daar of what she and Doc talked about sometime that afternoon:

Q. Did Doc go with you to the hospital on that occasion?
A. No.
Q. Where did he go?

~

There was more reference to Doc telling Ova that he needed to move the gold. Ova told Daar that Doc said, "I'm going to go move the gold tonight, because all of the publicity is on Marvin and you down there, I'm going to slip out there and move the gold." Daar asked Ova if she had agreed with him about moving the gold that night. She told Daar, "I didn't blame him. I sure wouldn't let anyone come and take it and pay at the other end. If they aren't big enough to come and buy it, let them stay at home." (118)

Q. That's what you said at the time?
A. Yes.
Q. So, as far as you know, Doc went off to move the gold?

---

* N. Deposition, ***op. cit.***, pp. (117).

A. He did, I know. I have proof of that.
Q. He went off to move gold, and you went on to see Marvin at the hospital?
A. Yes.

~

From what Ova said in that part of the deposition, it leans to the probability that Ova and Doc had met in Hatch, he went his way and she went to El Paso from there.

~Doc Solicits Help to Move One Ton of Gold~

In addition to the plane crash, Curtis Noble's death, and Marvin's serious injuries, another problem was looming; Doc wasn't able to move the gold bars Ryan had seen without someone in Ryan's work crew seeing him do it, especially Jack Lawrence. The goat shed was in plain sight across the road from Victorio Peak; Doc couldn't do *anything* without being seen. But Ryan knew nothing about the location of the balance of gold bars needed to make up the 110 bars for the flight, totaling *about* two tons gold, so those bars were safe. But Doc was smart enough to know that Ryan was keeping a close eye on him. He had pushed Ryan hard to come up with the money he had promised to pay him in advance for his share of the gold profits. Had everything gone as originally planned, Doc's share would have been close to $250,000.00—a lot of money in 1949. Now, beginning to suspect that Ryan had lied about the money or he intended to beat him out of his share of the profits—or both—Doc and Ova had made up their minds not to chance losing out altogether. Doc would have to move the gold to a safe spot where Ryan could not find it; time was running out and Doc had to act quickly.

Because it was so difficult to handle that much gold alone, especially in the dark, Doc called someone he could trust to help him move and rebury the bars. The first person he thought of was Leo O'Connell, an old and trustworthy friend. Doc had met Leo in Belmont, Arizona in 1942 and had told him about the treasure. In fact, shortly after meeting Leo, Doc invited him to come to the Rock House. There, Leo was shown a place where Doc had buried fifty-three gold bars. Doc placed the call to Leo from Hatch shortly after they took Marvin to the hospital in the ambulance, but his friend was not at home. Doc talked to Leo's wife, Luella, who told him that Leo wasn't expected home until early Saturday morning, but said she would give him the message the minute he arrived. Twenty-four years later, Leo O'Connell sent a letter[199] to Ova explaining what he knew about that frightful night. From Leo O'Connell's August 13, 1973 letter, in part:

> *I was with Doc at various times when he picked up gold he had hid at different places. I have seen different sizes and shaped bars. Some was molded with Wells Fargo's name. Doc showed me an old spring where he had 53 bars cached and I saw them. This is the gold Doc wanted me to help move [the] night before he was killed. He told my wife the*

Renegades had double-crossed him and he needed help. I went down as soon as I got his message, but Doc was dead when I got there.

—Leo O'Connell (written by his wife Luella O'Connell)

~

The letter contained a map Leo drew revealing the locations of two caches Doc had shown him: one having two bars, which was near the Rock House, and the other containing fifty-three bars buried near Henderson's goat shed. O'Connell's letter was explicit about the fifty-three bars he had seen, but his little map indicated fifty-six bars at Henderson's goat shed, an obvious error when Leo drew the map.

At a time when things were moving along as planned with Ryan and antici-pating that Ryan would come up with the money as he had agreed, Doc moved thirty-seven *additional* bars from other hiding places and dumped them on top of the bars that were already buried at the goat shed, a fact not known to either Ryan or Ova. What was once known to Leo O'Connell as the fifty-three bar site, now contained ninety bars, part of the one hundred-ten bars that Doc intended to give to Ryan to take to Old Mexico, nearly all of the bars Doc had had agreed to put up for the sale.

When Doc and Ryan had first made their appearance at Ryan's silver and lead operation, Ova, as well as the others who were camping at the Rock House, including Merle Horzmann, suspected that Doc was moving gold bars out of the basin in the back of Ryan's truck under the mattress* they had seen there. Contrary to everyone's suspicions, Doc was not moving any gold bars out of the basin at that time, he was merely gathering bars from various smaller caches he had developed over the years. But now matters had changed abruptly and Doc was in trouble; unless he could find someone else who was willing to help him, someone who knew nothing about his gold ventures, he stood the chance of losing the gold.

~

Willard L. Blake, a truck driver from Hatch, had worked for a man in town named Ray Morgan. A week earlier, Doc had hired Blake to work the silver and lead mines across from Victorio Peak. Blake was both foreman and timekeeper at the worksite. After work on Friday, he left the basin and drove to Hatch in Ryan's Jeep. Ollan Brown, Pedro "Pete" Nunez and the Brizendine brothers were in the Jeep with him and they arrived together at Ryan's house late that afternoon to pick up their paychecks. That morning Blake had left his personal car at Ryan's house; he had broken a spring coming in from the mine on Thursday night and his car was not drivable, so he used Ryan's Jeep to take the men to the work site Friday morning. Eleven weeks after Doc was murdered, and during Ryan's murder trial, Blake testified about the Friday when he used Ryan's Jeep.

---

* O. Noss, ***op. cit.***, p2.

Blake told the jury he was working in the San Andres Mountains east of Hatch, about a forty-mile drive from Ryan's house. After work on Friday, Doc asked Blake about the spring on his car and if it could be driven home. Blake told him that he was afraid to, and Doc said, "Go ahead and take the Jeep." Blake asked

Doc if "anything would be said about it" and Doc said that he didn't think so. After getting the okay from Doc, Blake drove the four men home from Ryan's house in the Jeep. After Blake dropped everyone off, he drove to Valley Auto Company in Hatch, gassed up, and then drove home. Blake said that in the beginning, when work first started at the mine, they all drove to Doc's house* on Canal Street, only a few blocks from Ryan's house. But, shortly after, that routine changed and they all met at Ryan's house and left for work from there. In the court trial, Blake admitted running into Doc at Valley Motor Company at eight o'clock Friday night.

The following is an excerpt from the direct examination of Willard L. Blake by District Attorney T. K. Campbell in the Ryan murder trial before the Honorable W.T. Scoggin Jr. in May 1949. Attorneys Melvin Rueckhaus and Paul Watkins were Special Prosecutors; District Attorney Campbell examined his witness, Willard L. Blake, who told Campbell that he drove to Ryan's house after work on Friday evening, March 4:

> *Q. Mr. Ryan asked you when the Jeep was gassed up the night before?*
> *A. Yes.*
> *Q. What did you tell him?*
> *A. It was gassed up at the Valley Auto Company.*
> *Q. Didn't he ask what time it was?*
> *A. He asked what time it was.*
> *Q. And Doc tried to butt in and answer?*
> *A. Yes.*
> *Q. Did you ever tell him what time it was?*
> *A. I didn't tell him what time it was because I didn't know.*
> *Q. Could you tell what time it was?*
> *A. It was about eight o'clock, I imagine.*
> *Q. You came in from the mine and you wanted to take the boys home?*

---

* Doc's rented house on Canal Street in Hatch, New Mexico.

A. I took the others home before I gassed up.

Q. Wasn't Doc at the station with the pickup when you gassed up?

A. Yes.

Q. Did he gas up the pickup also?

A. Yes.

~Tony Jolley's Arrival in Hatch~

One of the key individuals in the saga surrounding the murder of Doc Noss was a cowboy named Tony Jolley, who claimed in a video interview that he "knew Doc very vaguely." He went on to say that he had first met Doc "in Albuquerque" and "in Silver City." From Jolley's interview:

> *I was not well acquainted with him, but I knew who he was. I thought of him then as a cautious man; he never bulled ahead, he was rather quiet and friendly. What I knew of Doc then, I liked.*

~

Tony had been down in Texas, somewhere around Dallas. He was on his way home and stopped for the evening in Hatch:

> *It wasn't a room; they had separate cabins. I got one of these cabins for the night. There's not much to do, sittin' around a cabin in the evening. At that time there was no television. I thought, well, I'll go up town and gas up and if I wake up early I can be on the road. Sometimes in those little towns the service stations don't open up early in the morning; they're kind of independent. I drove up to the service station and while the fellow was puttin' in the gas I went to the restroom.*

~

When Tony got back to his car from the restroom, he had a surprise waiting for him; Doc Noss had pulled up in Charley Ryan's pickup truck, which meant that Blake had pulled in just about the same time. Jolley explained what happened next:

> *As he got out of the pickup, we exchanged hellos and he said, 'Say, I know you,' and we talked very briefly. He asked me where I was staying and I told him. I paid for my gas and went back down to the cabin.*

~

From the time that Doc had run into Tony Jolley at Valley Motor Company until he arrived at the cabin where Jolley was staying for the night, about an hour had elapsed, maybe less. It was then, sometime near dark on Friday evening, that Doc finally learned the truth that confirmed his suspicions that Ryan was not on the up-and-up. The account of how Doc found out about Ryan's plan to double-cross became common knowledge among Noss family members. Doc had told Ova the night before he was killed that he had managed to sneak up to the side of Ryan's house and listen beneath the window and overheard Ryan and his wife talking. He heard Ryan say that once he had the gold on the

plane he was going to escort the gold to the buyer, one of the men* was going
to shut down the operation, pay the men their earned wages and pick up the
cash in Old Mexico. Doc was never going to hear from Ryan after that. The
short version was that Ryan planned to fly the gold across the border and leave
Doc holding the bag.

Doc was running out of time; the DC-3 would arrive just before the sunset
on Saturday. Torches were lined up to mark the runway, and a large windsock
was standing by that could be raised at a moment's notice. The gold was supposed to be stacked and waiting alongside the airstrip for a quick load onto the
plane. Doc had already ruled out any chance of Leo O'Connell being of any
help to him that night. Then he recalled his conversation with Tony Jolley. It
was worth a try; Doc headed for the cabin where he knew Tony was staying for
the night. From Jolley's video interview:

> *Just shortly after dark is when he came to the cabin and he asked me if I would help
> him do something. He said, 'I've got something I need to do and need some help and I
> wondered if you'd help me.' I told him, 'Sure.' You don't want to sit around waitin' to
> get sleepy, so I was more than happy to go.*

~

Jolley got into Ryan's pickup truck with Doc and they headed for Rincon.
They had driven quite a long way when Doc pulled up to a windmill where
there was a horse corral:

> *He just drove up there and we got out. He took a shovel and gave me one and then,
> with the headlights on, he said, 'Let's dig right here.' And we started digging. Then
> about the next thing I know, we rolled a bar of gold out of the ground and I got a
> little curious, because I knew gold when I seen it and I mentioned this to him and I said
> 'Doc, that's gold,' and he said, 'Yes.' I said, 'What's goin' on?' He said, 'Well there's
> a fellow that's coming tomorrow that's going to fly in here and he was supposed to take
> this gold and sell it and split with me and I got word that he's going to sell it and keep
> right on going with the money. I've got to put it where he can't find it.' And he says, 'I
> need you to help me.' And I said, 'Fine.' And we dug twenty bars of gold out of the
> ground right there and put them in his pickup and then we went on down and up into
> some low hills.*

~

Jolley described the trip that followed the unearthing of the twenty gold
bars at the windmill. He said they came on down to a switchback road, down
into the Hembrillo Basin, traveled past a house and then turned off that road
to the left:

> *From there, Doc drove out onto a flat place and we reburied those bars of gold. Then
> we came back past the house by the peak and went around to the left and up a little hill,*

---

* Most likely Jack Lawrence.

came around there and there was like a prospector's hole there, and here's where a big
pile of these bars were. It turned out to be ninety more. I got pretty curious then, too. I
asked Doc where they came from and he told me out of that peak there.

~

The "prospector's hole" Jolley referred to was on the right side of the road
on top of a low ridge. It was about five feet deep. It was then that Tony Jolley
expressed some concern, concern that he had gotten himself into a "peculiar
predicament."

~Jack Woods returns from El Paso ~

While Doc and Tony Jolley were in the Hembrillo Basin moving the gold,
Jack Woods arrived back in Hatch from El Paso in the ambulance. It was
about one o'clock a.m. on Saturday. It had been a rough day for everyone:
Clay's brother was laying on a slab somewhere in Hatch, Marvin was seriously injured and undergoing emergency surgery in El Paso, Jack's dozer was
busted, and to make matters even worse, Jack was informed that his wife and
his father had been told by the New Mexico State Police that it was Jack who
was flying the plane and was killed in the crash; Jack was also an experienced
pilot. Consequently, Jack had hoped to intercept Elaine and his father as
they passed through Hatch. When he arrived in town, he got a motel room;
luckily, he could look right down Route 85 from the motel and see any car
coming into town. "There was a street light there," Jack said. "I sat on the
wall next to that motel and watched and waited for my father's car to come
by, a green Pontiac, so I knew what kind of car to look for. Pretty soon this
green Pontiac came by. There was much less traffic in those days, so I jumped
up in front of them and stopped the car. It was my father and my wife and
Marvin Beckwith's wife, Henrietta."

They told Jack that about sixty miles out of Gallup, Jack's father, Howard,
and Elaine stopped at a service station to fill up and were told by the station
owner, a friend of Howard's, that Jack was *not* the pilot; it had been Curtis and
that Jack was alive. It was a joyous reunion and a sad one at the same time.
Howard was exhausted, drained from the thought of losing his son, so Jack and
Elaine insisted he remain in Hatch at the motel room they had rented. Jack and
his wife then drove Henrietta to El Paso in the Pontiac so she could be with
Marvin. A short while afterwards, Jack and Elaine headed back to the motel in
Hatch where they could finally get some sleep. It had been Jack Woods' third
trip to El Paso in less than twelve hours.

~

Matters in the Hembrillo Basin became intense. Tony was a stranger to the
region and no one knew he was with Doc in the middle of the desert, digging
up and reburying gold bars. He paused for a second and looked around to get
a bearing on his location, but it was useless. Jolley continued:

I noticed I could see no city lights. I started to orient myself a little bit, and I knew we were in a basin, and I asked him, where are we, what place is this? He said, 'This is a place called Soledad.'

~

That meant little to Tony Jolley, and he continued to explain what he considered to be a growing dilemma. More:

We loaded fifty of those bars and came back around and went back past the house out in approximately the same area we came in. It was a flat area off to the left. That's when the headlights picked up that rock structure. I asked Doc what that was and he told me it was an Old Spanish fort that the Spaniards built to fight the Indians. We stopped and got out and I went over to it and looked at it a little bit. Then we came back and he said the ground is too hard to dig, which it was. He said, 'Let's just put ten in a bunch—just ten in a bunch.' I noticed that he would always orient himself where he was putting these bars and he would take a piece of paper out of his pocket and get in the headlights and he would do something and I figured he was orienting himself.

After we would put ten in a bunch, he would move to another place and he would always break a little limb off a juniper tree and he would brush over where we had shoveled. We barely buried those fifty and we went back up where the others were and we loaded the other forty, and they were heavy and he had a good load in the pickup, a heavy load.

~

Jolley and Doc drove south for a while and came to a house that set off to the right. Doc stopped the pickup and walked toward it. Jolley said they went inside where Doc had stashed a kerosene lamp, which he lit. In the corner of the room there was a table where Doc had stored some soda crackers and some cans of Vienna sausage:

We ate two cans of these little Vienna sausages that he opened up. Right to the side of the cabin there's a hill that comes down that's flat and kinda comes down to the point about where the cabin is and we went up on top of there and he took his flashlight with him. He looked around up there and then he started digging. I carried ten of those bars up that hill.

~

Jolley claimed that nine of the bars were just alike, but one was square. "Then Doc said, 'Ah, this is not a good place. We don't want to put any more here. Let's leave.'" They left that site with the other thirty bars and headed back up the road beyond the cabin, up the switchback* to a place where there was a crossroad. "When we got to the crossroad, Doc turned to the right and went down that road, I suppose two miles, three miles, something like that." It wasn't long until the headlights picked up another house. According to Jolley, Doc didn't go to the house; he cut to the left across the meadow in front of it and continued on to another road intersection, which he turned onto.

---

* The crossroad Jolley referred to was later known as "Hell Site" during Operation Goldfinder in 1977.

By now, Jack and Elaine had arrived back in Hatch. According to Jack Woods' interview and the account of what took place that night, it was about 3:00 a.m. Saturday morning when they arrived there; Gloria and Clay had already taken a room in the same motel after Curtis' body was taken to another facility. Jack and Elaine finally had a chance to rest. But such was not the case with Doc and Tony Jolley; they were still hard at work digging up and burying Doc's gold.

But as the night wore on, Tony became more and more concerned with his exposure and vulnerability; he was alone in the desert hiding a fortune in gold with a man he barely knew. Jolley described his location, and his precarious position, by what he was able to see; on one side of the road there were mountains and on the other side was a flat grassy place. "Doc stopped and we got out and proceeded, I suppose, fifty yards off that road or so and he started digging some more holes.* I packed the gold over to those holes." It was then that Tony claimed he became very nervous about Doc:

> *He was acting very strange for some reason and I got a very uneasy feeling about him and I realized that I was in a situation that I shouldn't be in. By accident, I got in this situation and I realized that nobody knew where I was. I was the only man who knew where the gold was and I got very uneasy.*

~

When Doc finally covered up the last ten bars, Tony said, "I broke a branch off a dead juniper tree and I confronted him." I said, "I know you got a gun in the glove compartment 'cause I seen it when you got the flashlight out. And I have a feeling you're going to leave me here. For some reason I have that feeling." Jolley warned Doc, "If you reach for that gun, or you make any quick movement on me, I'll splatter your brains out with this stick." And Jolley meant it:

> *He never answered me, he never said he wasn't going to do it; he never said anything— which made me feel even more uneasy. Right there we just distrusted each other; you could see both of us were changed.*

~

They returned to the pickup and threw the shovels in the back. Tony kept the club by his side as they started back down the road. "We didn't go very far until there was a wire fence with a gate. Doc told me, 'Get out and open the gate.' I told him, no; if I get out and open the gate you might shoot me in the back. I said we'd *both* get out and open the gate. So we both got out and opened the gate and we both got back in the pickup. We drove through and we both got out, and we shut the gate and we both got back in the pickup."

It was over. Doc finally headed back to Hatch.

> *But he never spoke to me and I never said nothin' to him either. I noticed he would look at me sideways from the corner of his eye. He did it quite often. We just drove on*

---

* This was the thirty-bar site. A team of ONFP investigators was able to locate the exact spot Tony Jolley had referred to in his video interview.

back to town. When he left me out at the motel, I told him, 'Doc, I don't care what you're doing out there. That don't belong to me and I'm going on about my business and I'm not telling anybody. Whatever you do that's your business.' He acknowledged that and I went in and went to bed.

~Early Saturday Morning in Hatch~

More from Ova's deposition* of March 24, 1975: (119)

Q. The trial was based on a complaint against Ryan for killing Doc. Correct?

A. Yes. He was responsible. Yes.

Q. Doc died of a gunshot wound, as I understand it?

A. Yes.

Q. Where was he killed?

A. He was killed at Ryan's house. Ryan saw him at the filling station and told him to come over. He wanted to talk to him.

~

Doc had not been home all night, and when morning came, problems arrived with it. It was getting close to the time when the men would be showing up at Ryan's house to start the new workday. Doc also had to replace the gas he had used in Ryan's truck, but it was too early and the filling station, Valley Motor Company, was not open, so he drove home. It was Saturday March 5, 1949—the last day of Doc's life.

According to Ova's writings[†] of July 1951, she made another notation and said, "But Ryan drove clear to where they had the fifty-one bars buried and found it dug up. When Doc drove up,[‡] Ryan caught him and asked him where he had been all night. Doc said, 'Down to see Marvin,' thinking it would cover up [his activities that night]. Ryan says, 'You're a liar; I've been out there to where we had the gold buried and you've dug it up.'"

Ova could only have gotten that kind of information from Doc himself. The fact that Ryan had driven to where Doc had the fifty-one bars buried meant that Doc had called Ova after he had returned from moving and reburying the bars, though he never mentioned Jolley to her, or for that matter that he had help from anyone with the work.

When he left Jolley's cabin, it is unlikely that Doc drove to Ryan's house after he had moved the gold, certainly not at that hour in the morning; he probably went home to get some sleep while Ryan was out in the desert looking for him, wondering where he had moved the gold bars he had shown him earlier. If Doc was at the Graham ranch, which Ova said he was, it was unlikely that Ryan would have seen the headlights on the pickup truck. The Hembrillo Basin is huge, and, by the time that Ryan and Lawrence discovered that Doc had

---

* N. Deposition, ***op. cit.***, pp. (as indicated).

† O. Noss, ***op. cit.***, p 3.

‡ Meaning at Valley Motor Company.

moved the bars, Doc and Tony Jolley were burying the remaining forty bars, a task which would have taken hours to complete. The chance of Doc and Ryan crossing paths in the Hembrillo Basin that night was highly unlikely, they were at least fourteen miles apart—two ships passing in the night.

Ryan's only chance of getting his hands on the gold was to catch up with Doc in Hatch, hoping he had some or all of the 110 bars in the back of the pickup truck. So, he left the basin, drove to Doc's house, and waited for him to arrive. When Doc and Tony finished moving and reburying the bars, they drove to Hatch where Doc dropped Tony off at his cabin. Jolley said, "It was about morning when we got there." It was sometime around 6:00 o'clock on Saturday morning. According to Ova's statement in her deposition, "Doc come into town the next morning at 7:00 o'clock and was filling up with gas. Ryan was a-waiting for him. Ryan seen him at the filling station and told him to come over; he wanted Doc to talk to him."

Considering all of the facts that eventually came to light before, during and certainly after the trial, the sequence of events that unfolded from the time Doc got back from the desert until he and Ryan finally connected most likely occurred in the following manner: Doc had not yet arrived at his house on Canal Street from the desert, so Ryan left there and drove to his own house, which was closer to the middle of town; he had to be there when Blake and the other men checked in before they headed out for the mine worksite. In the meantime, Doc finally arrived home on Canal Street, just missing Ryan. Doc either called Ova from his house or went directly to Valley Motor Company to get gas and called her from there. He told her about the events that morning, the same way he had the day before when he called her from there to tell her he was removing the gold so Ryan wouldn't get it. After Blake and the work crew left for the Hembrillo Basin to work the mine, Ryan left his house in an attempt to find Doc. He probably went to Doc's house first. Not finding him there, he left for Valley Motor Company. When Ryan pulled in, Doc was still inside talking to Ova on the telephone, and, when he walked outside, Ryan and Lawrence were waiting for him.

Ryan tried to corner Doc into admitting that he was out in the desert moving the bars and asked him where he was all night. Doc responded by telling Ryan he was in El Paso with Marvin. It was then that Ryan called Doc a liar and admitted that he and Lawrence drove out to the site and found the bars were gone. After he and Doc had quarreled about the gold bars not being at the site, Ryan walked across the street to a hardware store to check on some hardhats he had ordered that were supposed to have arrived. Ryan then went to the drugstore next to the hardware store and called his banker. While Ryan was across the street, Doc went back inside Valley Auto Company and called Ova and told her what had just happened. He then hung up and walked outside and walked over to where Lawrence was waiting for him. It was then that Ryan came back across the street and ordered Doc and Lawrence to go out to the Hembrillo Basin and tell the men to come to Hatch and get their pay. Doc and Lawrence drove there together to advise the men and immediately returned to Hatch. With this scenario of the sequence of events, all of which later came to the surface during the trial, plus what Tony Jolley had attested to in his recorded interview and what Ova had said in her writings and under oath during her 1975 deposition, all of the pieces came together. Ryan would later testify at his trial that he and Lawrence were at Valley Motor Company with Doc that morning, they talked, Ryan went across the street to check on some hard hats, and also made a call to Alice, Texas, to his banker friend. It was then that Ryan instructed Doc and Lawrence to drive to the mine site to tell the men to come back to Hatch and pick up their pay envelopes.

Testimony given later at the trial revealed that before noon on Saturday, Doc and Jack Lawrence came to the lead mine where Ryan's men were working and told them to close down the operation until their hardhats arrived, which was supposed to be on Monday. It was Saturday, payday and the workers were told to go to Ryan's house to get their paychecks. Before the men left the Hembrillo Basin, Doc and Lawrence left for Hatch, stopped at Valley Motor Company again to fill up but were told by the station attendant that Ryan had stopped doing business there and they could not get any more gas. Upon hearing that, Doc and Lawrence headed for Ryan's house. When they got there, trouble was waiting for Doc. An argument ensued, tempers flared, threats were made, because there was no gold for Ryan to take to Old Mexico. By now, Blake and the other workers arrived at Ryan's house from the Hembrillo Basin. There were three other cars parked in front of the house when Blake pulled in: a red pickup with a sign on the door that read Ryan Tool Company, Alice, Texas, which Doc had been using since he arrived in Hatch with Ryan and the others, Blake's car, which was a 1940 blue Ford sedan, and behind it, a Buick sedan that belonged to Charley Ryan. Blake stopped the Jeep, got out and walked up to the house; the other men stayed in the Jeep. When Blake got to the house, Charley Ryan, Doc Noss, and Buck Harris came out. The following is testimony from the trial. Blake was under direct-examination by one of the prosecuting attorneys:

> *Q. Noss, Ryan and Buck Harris came out?*
> *A. Yes.*
> *Q. Do you recall the order they came out?*
> *A. Charley Ryan was first, Noss behind him, then Buck Harris.*
> *Q. Where were you standing?*
> *A. I was on the walk that goes from the street straight to the back door.*
> *Q. When you walked up what was the first thing said and by whom?*
> *A. Charley Ryan asked me about the Jeep.*
> *Q. Relate as near as you can his exact words.*

~

Blake explained that he handed the time book to Buck Harris, who took it inside. Ryan then asked him who gave him permission to use the Jeep and what time did he come back with it, meaning on Friday evening. He told the prosecutor that Doc had told him he could use it, but Blake didn't know what time it was when he got back with the men Friday evening. Doc was about to tell Ryan what time Blake came in when Ryan suddenly pulled a gun. Minutes later, Doc was dead.

~

Ryan's murder trial began on May 25, 1949, in the District Court of the Third Judicial District in Doña Ana County in Las Cruces. Although the line of questioning by J. Benson Newell occurred months after Doc's murder, it suggests that there might have been some concern on Newell's part that the matter of gold would come up in the trial as the reason for the argument in Ryan's house, a strong motive for Ryan killing Doc. Whether or not Blake and Doc had seen each other at the gas pumps at Valley Auto Company had nothing to do with the reason for Ryan killing him.

Within days after the trial, Ova Noss visited Newell's office in Las Cruces to ask him to sign an affidavit that he had seen one or more of Doc's gold bars, because she knew he had. He did not give her such an affidavit then, but about three years later, when Ova returned to his office with Letha, Newell did provide them with the following signed, notarized statement[200] dated December 12, 1952. Newell's affidavit:

> *To Whom It May Concern: Somewhere in the late 1930s I became acquainted with Dr. M.E. Noss and subsequent to that time I had done legal work for him in the preparation of various contracts relative to the Hembrillo Basin and his applications for leasing of the property for the purpose of exploring the Cave where he claimed to have found buried treasure, mostly gold bullion; sometime approximately between January and June 1941, he visited my office in Las Cruces, N.M. with a small bar of metal about 3" wide and about 3" to 4" thick and about 5" long; very heavy, had two drill holes in it, dark in color; it was not left and I do not know of my own knowledge what the metal was, nor did I see any assay of this bar to my knowledge.*   —*J.B. Newell*

~

It was then that Ova and Letha learned some startling information concerning the trial and a bribe offer made by Charley Ryan. According to Ova, Newell told her during the visit to his office that Ryan had offered a three-way split of fifty-three gold bars; a third for himself, a third for Newell, and a third for Judge Scoggin—provided he was acquitted. What Ryan didn't tell Newell and Scoggin was that he had already gone to the place where Doc showed him the bars and discovered they were gone. Ryan was lying to his attorney *and* Scoggin knowing he would not be able to deliver on his bribe. Newell never admitted in writing about Ryan's bribe offer.

Ollan Brown lived in Hatch. By trade he was a lineman, but on the day of the trial, he told the jury that he worked for the Porter Lumber Company, and on the day Doc was killed he was sitting in the Jeep in front of Ryan's house. When he was working for Ryan, he was hired to do "some dynamiting for him" and had worked for him for approximately a week. He gave the identical set of circumstances that Blake had given: he saw Ryan, Noss and Buck Harris come out of the house, that Blake had given the time sheets to Buck Harris, that Ryan pulled his gun and pointed it at Doc's back and led him back in the house. He then heard the window break, saw Doc run from the house, saw Ryan come after him and shoot at Doc. Brown said that he heard Mrs. Ryan say, "Shoot that son-of-a-bitch," and that he heard Ryan say, "Get up from there, you son-of-a-bitch." He also heard and saw Ryan fire a second time, after which Brown said, "We got out of there and run like hell."

Pedro "Pete" Nunez, who was nineteen years old at the time, also testified. Nunez also lived in Hatch and gave a nearly identical account of the story given by Brown and Blake. William Edward Brizendine's account was a mirror image of the testimonies given by the others. William's brother, Denver Brizendine, also gave a nearly identical version as well and added that he saw a man [Jack Woods] doing some work about a mile away, and that he had seen a Caterpillar and a house trailer at Victorio Peak.

~ Jack Woods and Tony Jolley's Accounts Match ~

When Jack Woods woke up that day, it was approaching one o'clock in the afternoon. He had slept much longer than he had intended; the events of the preceding day and his early morning arrival from El Paso to Hatch had taken its toll. He was also without transportation; Clay had borrowed his car and had driven it to Hot Springs with a friend to pick up his own car at the airport that Clay had left there.

Shortly after Jack woke up, he walked down Main Street to a small diner and ate a late breakfast. From his video interview:

I finished eating and started to walk toward Charley Ryan's house to see if I could find Doc; after what he had told me the previous day, that he would show me how to get into the caverns, I was anxious to speak with him. While I was walking down the street and was getting near Ryan's house I heard shots coming from that direction.

~

Jack picked up the pace and when he turned the corner he could see Ryan's house and he had also found Doc—lying with his head against the bumper of Charley Ryan's pickup truck. "I saw Ryan standing on the porch. Then suddenly people began showing up from everywhere." Jack stood there for a minute when suddenly the local police arrived, ordering people to clear the area as they took command of the crime scene. There was nothing to do but stand and watch. Rather than do that, Jack turned around and walked away, shocked by what he had seen. "I didn't need to see anymore so I left and walked back to the motel where Clay knew to meet me. It wasn't long before Clay returned with my car and I told him that Doc had been shot and was dead. I also told him what Doc told me [about the other entrance] when I was at the ambulance with him."

~

Tony Jolley concluded the description of his first and last hours with Doc while they were together in the late night hours of Friday, March 4, and the early morning hours of the next day just before Ryan murdered Doc:

When I went to sleep that night, it was about morning when we got there, we had worked all night. I imagine it was mid-day before I ever woke up. I went up town to eat some breakfast. A man came in the café and told the waitresses that somebody had shot Doc Noss and killed him. How it happened I don't know. The thing that went through my mind was, when did it happen; did it happen right after he left me? The thought went through my mind that I might have been the last man to see him alive and I might have a hell of a lot of explaining to do. I decided the best thing to do was to head up the road and mind my own business. That's what I done.

I wasn't looking for anything. The things that happened put me in the right spot. I look back now and see why he came to me. I was a man passing through and he barely knew me, he knew I was moving on and I wasn't someone who lived in the area; someone who lived in the area would have been a problem for him, so I can see why he came to my cabin because I'm going out of the country and I didn't live there. It was a good move on his part.

~

Tony Jolley had seen and handled a lot of Doc's gold that night. But that wasn't the end of the story; he returned to New Mexico in 1961 and made his fortune. Tony had had a financial loss about that time, so in an effort to recoup his losses he decided to go back to the Hembrillo Basin and try to find some of the gold bars that he and Doc had buried in the desert that night.

> *I never forgot that incident; it was fresh on my mind all those years. But when I went back, I thought I could go right in there and get it, but it wasn't that easy; the first time I went there I could see I wasn't going to find any without a metal detector. So I went back home, I got a metal detector, a backpack, a sleeping bag, and some food and water and headed back.*

~

Tony spent a good deal of time searching every spot he could remember where he and Doc had buried the gold bars. More of his interview:

> *I was about to give up when finally the thing buzzed. I found the ten bars Doc and I buried up on that hill. I dug them up and brought them out. I assayed them and I know what it assayed at and I disposed of ten bars of gold. They were not bars of brass or copper. I had them very thoroughly assayed by a mining company and I knew exactly what they were and they brought money—they brought money! Doc had a terrific amount of gold—a terrific amount. I got a very little part of it. I got ten of those gold bars back. I disposed of the bars and got quite a lot of money for them.*

~

In the end it was Jolley's reward for helping Doc, an ironic sort of compensation that reflected the incredible events of that strange and chilling night in the nearly barren landscape of a rugged stretch of unforgiving desert. Tony knew that he had moved a fortune in gold around that night to help Doc. He knew it was gold then and knew it was gold when the assays came back on the ten bars he was fortunate enough to recover years later. In spite of Tony's good fortune, he found it difficult to dispose of them. "At that time it was illegal to have gold. You just cannot go down and find someone to buy a bar of gold on every corner. I found out it was *really* tough." Tony hid those bars at his home for more than a year. But in the end, it worked out in his favor. "I had a very good friend who was a project manager of a large mining company." Tony went to his friend and "over a long period of time" was able to get the cash he wanted for Doc's gold bars.

> *I am not going to tell you his name. I promised not to. We devised a plan where we could dispose of the gold and turn it into money; we did it, we covered our tracks very well and I'm not going to uncover them.*   —Tony Jolley

~

There was another unresolved matter; the day after Doc was murdered, Roscoe Parr told Ova that he had gone over to the house on Canal Street where Doc and Violet had been living. While he was there he saw a photo of Doc in Violet's bedroom. After learning this, Ova went to the local sheriff and told him

that she might have some trouble retrieving a photo of Doc, a photo that belonged to her and then she related the story presented to her by Roscoe Parr. Shortly afterwards, a deputy sheriff accompanied her to Canal Street. Ova followed the deputy into the house and then to the bedroom where the photo was
located. Violet stood in the doorway in an attempt to keep Ova from entering the bedroom, but Ova simply pushed her aside and walked over to the dresser and retrieved the framed photo* of Doc. She also saw some of Doc's clothes in the room. In a recorded interview, Letha revealed more of the event as it happened that day. In part:

> *Mama went and got Doc's clothes and threw them down the stairway and then Violet started to grab the picture back. Mama just gave her a push and knocked her across the bed. She turned around to the deputy sheriff and said, 'See, I told you I might have some trouble retrieving this.' Then she told Violet that was just a hand-pat. Then she said, 'I'm going give you a whippin' every time I see ya' and I'm gonna make it a point to see ya' once a day.'*

~

What was also interesting about the interview was that Letha had confirmed that Doc was in contact with Ova the entire time he was gone. It was also learned that Violet had had two other husbands; one was an engineer and another man who was said to have a lot of money. The aftermath of Doc's murder and the trial of Charley Ryan followed.

---

* Ova Noss holds the same photo of Doc that she retrieved from the house on Canal Street.

Chapter 23

The Days after Doc's Murder

The *Albuquerque Journal* Sunday edition was one of many newspapers throughout New Mexico that carried the story[201] of the killing:

> HATCH, March 5 (AP)—M.E. Noss of Hatch was shot to death today. Charley Ryan surrendered voluntarily to Doña Ana County officers. Sheriff A.L. Apodaca received the following account of the shooting: 'Noss, labor foreman for Ryan's mining company, and Ryan engaged in a loud argument over their business matters about 3 p.m. Noss hit Ryan and knocked him into a window. Then Noss ran out of the house toward a pickup truck owned by the mining company. Just as he reached the truck, two shots were fired. One of the bullets hit Noss in the right cheek just below the eye and lodged at the base of the brain below Noss' left ear. No charges have been filed.'

~

Another account of the shooting appeared in *The Hatch Reporter*. Although the article was written five days after the shooting, the account fills in some of the on-scene happenings that were not in the official Sheriff's report,[202] in part:

> After the shooting, Ryan turned to Mr. Lawrence, telling him to get the sheriff. He was taken to the Hatch jail very peacefully.
>
> Booze Mitchell and Paul Mabry notified Happy Apodaca* [the town Sheriff] in Las Cruces, who drove immediately to the scene of the shooting and took charge of the proceedings. Judge Clear was called and a coroner's jury was held at the scene immediately after examination of the body of Noss. The body was taken to Las Cruces. Upon his removal from the city jail Ryan immediately asked about his wife who has been ill. Benson Newell, who is a prominent lawyer of Las Cruces, is representing him. A preliminary trial will be held Thursday of this week in the Doña Ana courthouse at 9 a.m. and Ryan will enter a plea of not guilty.

~

The Doña Ana County Sheriff's report[203] indicated that Apodaca arrived at the site of the shooting at 2:30 p.m., which varies from the time indicated in *The Albuquerque Journal* story, where he met Deputies Sandman and Mabry. An

---

* When this 1940 photo was taken Apodaca was with the N.M. State Police. In 1949 he was elected Sheriff of Doña Ana County. Photo provided by New Mexico State University Library Archives and Special Collections.

investigation was started on the murder, pictures were taken and witnesses who were present at the murder scene when the shooting occurred were interviewed. Shortly afterwards, Charley Ryan was fingerprinted, his gun was taken by Roy Sandman and he was formally charged with first-degree murder. Information about Doc's murder reached Washington, D.C. and the FBI became involved in the case from the first day. The FBI report[204] identified Ryan as being "39 years old, ruddy complexion, 5'11" inches tall, brown eyes, weight 175 pounds, brown hair and slender build." According to the report, Ryan was born in Kentucky on July 24, 1907.

Apodaca's report indicated that Ryan was taken before Justice of the Peace A.J. Robertson on Thursday, March 10. Since it was a case of first-degree murder, Ryan was held over for trial without bail. The Federal Bureau of Investigation noted the case on their records as "information taken from the Sheriff's Office." A preliminary hearing was held that day in the Doña Ana Court House and prominent county lawyer J. Benson Newell was there to represent Ryan, who pled not guilty.

The following day, Jack Woods visited Ryan in jail. Although he was not allowed to see him, the following letter[205] was delivered to him:

> *Mr. Ryan, We came to see you but the sheriff refused to let us talk to you. If there is any way we can help you let us know and we will be more than glad to do so. If you need evidence as to Doc Noss' character, I believe we can find plenty. Mr. Ryan, is there anything we should know?? If so, your wife or the other two men can find us around Hatch. I am sorry it turned out this way. If we can be of any help, let us hear from you*
>
> .   *— Mr. & Mrs. Clay Noble, Jack Woods*
>
> ~

The reason for Woods' letter is not known, but he and the Nobles could have been trying to learn something from Ryan regarding what Doc had told him [Woods] about a secret entrance to the treasure while Marvin was being loaded into the ambulance after the plane crash. Since Woods was working for Ova and was doing roadwork with the goal of opening an entrance to the interior of the Peak, it seems to be a logical assumption, or better yet, a reasonable conclusion; one sentence in the letter (*Mr. Ryan, is there anything we should know??*) supports such a conclusion. It is also possible that Jack and Ova had their heads together on the letter because neither Woods nor Ryan could gain access to the Peak without Ova's approval. Woods might have already told Ova about the conversation he had with Doc at the ambulance, which again leaves the distinct possibility that Ova and Woods were together on the letter. The fact that a copy of Woods' letter was found among Ova's personal property supports such a theory.

March 6, 1949

The day after Doc was murdered, Merle Horzmann wrote to Victor Bate. It was her first letter to him in eight years. She had sent two other letters to him in 1941 that involved Doc's preliminary hearing and matters concerning her role in The Cheyenne Mining Company. Horzmann's letter[206] was somewhat benign, wherein she explained current events to Mr. Bate, but she expressed no sympathy for Ova's loss, nor did she express sorrow for Doc being killed, which was not inconsistent with her mindset regarding them. From her letter of March 6:

> *And so the story goes into another great chapter! I do not know if the Associated Press has published the account of a crash in the San Andres Mountains, resulting in the death of Curtis Noble, and seriously injuring Marvin Beckwith, but the El Paso papers had it Saturday morning, and now, today, Sunday, they have another story giving the account of the shooting of M.E. Noss, in Hatch, by Charley Ryan, of the Ryan Tool Company.*
>
> *I just talked to Mrs. Noss Thursday night, and she said they were within 200 feet of the top of the mountain with the bulldozer, ready to tunnel in, and that they intended to go out this morning. I did not get in until about 8:30 last night, and since this has all happened, they took Marvin, who is Mrs. Noss' son, to an El Paso hospital, and I have not seen any of them to get more of the details than the accounts in the papers, except that the notes they were dropping were information about parts they needed for repairs to the machinery, also looking for an old ox trail more visible by air than afoot.*
>
> *My mail will come here to General Delivery, and since I have not been to the post office when the G.D. window was open, I do not know if there is anything there from you or not, but will go early in the morning.*
>
> *So far, there has been no cause to publicize the opening of the cave, or the attempt. This will not necessarily hamper it, except temporarily, while all this other is going on. Mr. Noble was a relative of the bulldozer operator, and she and her husband were on the ground when the plane crashed. Am sending you clippings of it, in case you did not notice it.*
>
> *When I got in last night there was nothing available except Cozy-Corner Apartment, No. 2. It is well located for me, and I suppose I will keep it while I am here. Will advise you when it is time to pick up the rest of the story, as it will get plenty interesting from now on, and I am here now to pick up the loose ends.* —Merle Horzmann
>
> ~

Shortly after Ryan was jailed the FBI confiscated Doc's files and personal belongings; under what authority they had to do so is unknown. It didn't take long for Ova to react to the FBI's actions, nor did it take long for her and Violet Noss to lock horns as to which one had the right to continue with the search for the treasure and to whom Doc's personal effects belonged. Ova's treasure trove permit to excavate at the Victorio Peak site was approved prior to Doc's murder and was continually in effect. Since the FBI had possession of many of Doc's items that were important to Ova, the matter over who would get Doc's personal effects was up for grabs. As strange as the facts that surrounded the death of Doc Noss were, so too was the petition[207] filed in Doña Ana Probate Court on Tuesday, March 8, 1949, by Merle Horzmann for appointment as

Administratrix of Doc's estate (Estate Case No. 1668). Two days after Doc's death, Horzmann secured the required $1,000.00 bond and posted it with her application. Probate Judge Samaniego F. Chavez granted her petition the same day. When questioned, Horzmann told reporters Tony Thein and Laurence Mc-Swain of the *Santa Fe New Mexican* newspaper that "Ova Noss was the only heir to the fabulous estate and Ova had asked her to act as administrator." Although Ova knew Horzmann to be disloyal and contemptuous to her and Doc, the rationale to use her to administer Doc's estate was overcome by events: publically, Horzmann was the least controversial in the matter regarding the filing of the petition because of her status as secretary of the Cheyenne Mining Company, a factual and legal status granted to her by Doc. Conversely, Ova's claim that the divorce granted to Doc was not legal, that she was still technically and legally married to him, and that she and Doc were the sole owners and joint finders of the treasure, were matters that could have only been settled through a court action. Therefore, Horzmann filed for the appointment, which was decided upon, carried out, and approved.

March 9, 1949

On Wednesday, March 9, the day after Horzmann filed the inventory, she wrote[208] to Violet L. (Yancey) Noss and requested the return of specific items that belonged to Doc and/or the Cheyenne Mining Company. The letter asked for the "peaceable delivery of all documents, jewelry, trinkets, suitcases and their contents, regardless of where they came from, and all money or anything whatsoever belonging to him at the time of his death, as may have come to the Cheyenne Mining Company under an original agreement entered into in Las Cruces on June 14, 1941." Horzmann told the Santa Fe reporters that in her letter she said, "These items are valuable only to those to whom they belong," and "we have no intention to harm you in the least, but rather, to maintain harmony and confidence in you and you in us. I am sure you prefer it that way. It will be most helpful to yourself if you comply with this request."

The following day, Thursday, March 10, Jack Woods was out at the Peak repairing his bulldozer hoping to finish work by the next day and Charley Ryan was out on bail; after he had shot and killed Doc, he was confined to jail for only 5 days. *The Hatch Reporter* article of March 10 read:

> *Due to the fine defense of J. Benson Newell, Charley Ryan is out on $25,000.00 bond, which was posted at once. Bound over to District Supreme Court, the date to be announced later.*

~

It was reported that Ben Newell, who would eventually defend Ryan in his murder trial, was in some way responsible for putting up Ryan's bail. What was more surprising was that the murder was a capital offense and Ryan was an out-of-state defendant, which under normal circumstances should have made Ryan a flight risk. In spite of this, Ryan got out. Josephine and William

C. Newell, individuals who were related to Ben Newell, put up security for the bond. More questions arise—what was the incentive for William and Josephine Newell to post security for Ryan's bond? And how did Ben Newell justify his representing Ryan when he possessed information and documents regarding Doc's business and personal affairs for a percentage of the profits of The Cheyenne Mining Company? Newell had a rich history with Doc that went back to 1939 when he had filed a complaint as Doc's attorney against a New Mexico State Patrolman who had stolen a gold bar from Doc's car in Hatch. Hidalgo County Attorney Melvin Rueckhaus had sworn in an affidavit that he had assisted Newell at Newell's office in doing the paperwork for Doc's mining company. Even though Rueckhaus had done legal work for Doc with Newell, he was appointed Special Prosecutor in the trial against Ryan.

Also on Thursday, March 10, a newspaper[209] headline: "Details Of Murder Are Told," appeared in the *Las Cruces Citizen*. Although it was a bit sensationalized, the article was a fair account of Doc's murder, in part:

> *The preliminary hearing of Charley Ryan on the charge of murdering an employee at Hatch last Saturday was still in progress before a small audience in the district courtroom here at 11:15 today. Ryan is charged with blasting out the life of M.E. Noss, about 40. The shooting, which occurred within a few blocks of the Hatch Baptist Church, was related in detail at the hearing with the testimony of witnesses. 'The murder followed an argument over time and labor details, according to testimony.'*

~

To kill someone over a payroll dispute is hard to imagine, but Ryan was also angry that Doc had given Willard Blake permission to use his Jeep and he was equally concerned about the time frame in which Blake and Doc gassed up at the Valley Auto Company, not to mention the fact that the fifty-three gold bars Ryan knew about were gone. In any case, there was little cause to shoot an unarmed man while he was running away. There was more to the story as would come out in Ryan's murder trial. New Mexico had not become a state until 1912, and one of the reasons was because of the lawlessness in the territory; the last Indian battle was fought in New Mexico that same year. In the 1940s, New Mexico was not on the cutting edge of human rights and consequently many of the difficulties Doc and Ova had when they were together were a residual of the government's long history of violent treatment of the American Indian and its territorial expansion policies. When Ova was on her own, the difficulties she had with the United States Army and government officials related to the treasure continued for decades.

In the late 1940s, life in Hatch was a clip from the film, *The Life and Times of Judge Roy Bean,* in which the titular character dispensed a special kind of justice, "The Law West of the Pecos." Hatch is west of the Pecos River. So, to paint a clearer picture of life in that small adobe village in 1949, a special public notice appeared in *The Hatch Reporter* on March 10 that provides a clear window into the past:

> *All dogs caught without licenses will be shot on sight.*   —*Mayor Black*

~

Life in Hatch was different in those days, compared to now: a two-pound box of crackers was 49¢, a pound of fresh ground coffee was 53¢, beets 5¢ a bunch, three pounds of uncolored Oleo margarine went for 87¢, a pound of fresh sirloin steak cost 69¢, and you could buy a brand new Ford four-door sedan for much less than what a new car depreciates today when you drive it off the dealer's lot; a new Dodge "job-rated" 2-ton truck cost less than two thousand dollars.

Towns along the Rio Grande still had not yet emerged from the days when the law of the land was the short end of a rope and branding irons were still a cattleman's best friend. In Hatch, not unlike other towns along the Rio Grande in the 40s, you could still ride into town to the blacksmith on horseback and pack a six-shooter on your hip. And if you had a mind to, you could shoot an unarmed man in the head and get away with it, if there was enough money involved and if the man you shot was part Cheyenne Indian like Doc Noss, which was true in both cases.

In 1941, corruption in Las Cruces was rampant; the tainted trail ran from the Mexican border town of El Paso, north to Las Cruces all the way to New Mexico's capital in Santa Fe. One of the most corrupt politicians along the trail was Judge William T. Scoggin Jr., a former district attorney whose base of operation was Las Cruces. So, if a local bought-and-paid-for judge, say, Judge William T. Scoggin, Jr., who owned one half of a 3% interest in Doc's gold venture at Victorio Peak, decided he wanted to preside over the trial of Doc's killer—no one was going to stop him; *his* protection came from Santa Fe where Chicago crime syndicate bosses such as Meyer Lansky and "Bugsy" Siegel had a firm grip on gambling casinos and prostitution throughout New Mexico. In Santa Fe, high-ranking politicians were paid handsomely to turn their backs. Crime-oriented individuals with their hands out for some of the payoff money, like Scoggin, played into the hands of the syndicate. Or, if a Las Cruces attorney, say, J. Benson Newell, who also owned one half of a 3% interest in the same mining operation venture as the judge had, wanted to be the defense attorney for the man who murdered Doc Noss over a near-million dollar gold smuggling operation into Old Mexico—*no problemo!*

Ten days after Merle Horzmann wrote to Violet Yancey, Carl Horzmann wrote[210] to Merle from St. Louis: From his March 15, 1949 letter: (underlining inserted)

> *I certainly was surprised to hear you have been appointed Administrator of the Estate of Doc Noss, and I am just wondering what that job will lead you into. You know*

the old proverb, 'Where angels fear to tread------.' Nevertheless, the last time I talked to Doc, he said he had divorced Babe and that he had married an Indian woman in Arkansas. Now the question that Babe brings up, she had given him $50 just before the divorce was granted, would not invalidate the divorce, as such, unless there had been some intimate relations.

As you say, it is a mess and I think a much bigger mess than you had anticipated. Doc also told me that he has a sister still living and she is on an Indian Reservation in Oklahoma. Of course, he claims that he was a full-blooded Cheyenne Indian, but I believe that the Cheyenne and the Choctaw are all on one reservation, and you undoubtedly will be able to find out just where they are. Doc did not get his citizenship papers until 1938 after he left the Reservation, and established himself as non-dependent of the Government.

As far as everybody else is concerned, I believe that it is a good thing that Doc was killed because he certainly would have done some killing himself before this whole mess would be settled. If I am not mistaken, you will be entitled to a fee amounting to 5% of the monies handled plus, of course, your expenses while you are Administrator of the Estate, but it will mean, of course, that you will have to be in New Mexico for another year or until the whole matter is out of the way.

I still believe that Ryan will get away with a fine since Doc's reputation as to temper and ferocity was the worst ever. I don't know what Roscoe Parr and Violet Mason-Noss can do to keep the cave from being opened as the FBI are on ground now. Anyway, since you are taking care of the interest of Mr. Holt and Ownby both, and Doctor Noss is dead, and three should be a charm, maybe nobody else will get killed from now on and everything will come out all right.

I am feeling all right, but we have had a rather unexpected snowstorm that did not last long but made the weather rather cold.

Keep your chin up and don't lead too much with it, and watch out for 'Babe.' Trust her as far as you can throw a bull by the tail. I had to pay $35.00 additional income taxes.   *—Carl*

~

Two things in Horzmann's letter deserve comment. Violet Yancey was mentioned as Violet Mason-Noss, so he must have known something about her. Perhaps she had been married before and her maiden name was Violet Mason. Also unknown is why Horzmann felt so strongly about Ryan's fate and that Doc was better off dead. Believing that "it was a good thing Doc was killed" says that Carl Horzmann* put little value on a man's life, and in Doc's case as being worthless. To a limited degree, Doc

*Photo of Carl Horzmann

and Ova entrusted Merle Horzmann with handling the company's records as secretary; she was also given a share of the treasure with no outlay of money, all while Merle Horzmann was an admitted spy and her husband was a collaborator in the same enterprise. Letha gave an account of her feelings toward Merle and Carl Horzmann. In part:

> *Doc never did like Merle. She got in with Parr, who was a brownnoser, and she also buddied up with Mama; she was trying to get everything she could out of Mama. I was completely fooled with Merle Horzmann. I didn't think she would do what she did. When I started reading those letters I was dumbfounded. Horzmann and Parr were as thick as thieves and they thought that if they could get Doc thrown in jail, they could go in and steal some of his stuff. She even made copies of the letters she wrote. When Doc died, Mama and I went to Lordsburg. Carl was there. Merle was sick and that's why she came to the desert. We told him we would like the stuff pertaining to the treasure and he handed us a great big box full. There were letters in there from both of them and Carl didn't know they were in there.*

March 18, 1949

Thirteen days after Doc's murder, Merle Horzmann wrote to J. Victor Bate, claiming that federal authorities had seized some of Doc's gold and were hot on the trail of finding more. Horzmann's letter[211] in part: (underlining inserted)

> *The FBI has taken over the investigation of this proposition out here. Some of the bullion has been recovered and is in their hands. There is already several thousand dollars worth of it in the U.S. Treasury, pending the finale. We are going out Sunday and that may be THE DAY. However, we are not going to say until it is a proven fact. However, I am authorized by Probate Court to take care of Doc's estate, whatever there might be, and outside of that, probably nothing, but that will not be hay. There is absolutely no telling what can come from the cave, if anything, and the way it stands now, the FBI will confiscate everything in it, and make the proper audit of everything and its value, before it's distributed. The boys out there are still working and tomorrow we have data that will be proof of the effort, we think. Two or three of the boys [FBI or the Secret Service agents] will be in from Albuquerque, including one of the State Engineers.*
>
> *I operated the C. of C. in Lordsburg as Secretary-Manager from May first last year until November when I left and went to Deming, just about the time activities started again on this business in the San Andres. I can go back there any time and get a job if I want it, but I also have a 40-acre subdivision, which I hope to develop as soon as this is over, or sell it out.*
>
> *Now, as to what they expect to find in the cave, I understand it is ricks of gold bullion that will amount to a fabulous amount, jewels, clothing, old relics, church relics, royal crown with the jewels intact, and no one knows what else. The bulldozer is being used to find the entrance to the tunnel where it was hauled in by oxcarts, and pack loads. There is also a shaft in the very top of the mountain that is also said to connect with*

the tunnel below, and in which I have been down into 84 feet. The Government retains the gold, and the other things will either be placed in a museum or distributed among the interest-holders. We do not know just what they will decide to do about that until they have it. It will then be made into a state or national monument—the area in which this is located. Roads have been built into it, over which they can haul it, if it is to be removed from the ground. As it is, it is rather difficult to get to, but the Government is behind it now, and it must be done.

I have the story of it, together with the history of it as far as I know, in topics you have suggested. But I do not believe it will turn out to be fraud. There is too much evidence otherwise, according to the Chief FBI, of Albuquerque. This is all written up in my diary, and in the research material I gathered that same year and part of the following year, of 1941-1942. Since then, things have been added, and I think the next chapter will be the best of all.

Perhaps this gives you a better idea of what I am working towards. If not, let me hear from you again, and you can either reach me at Box 93, Hot Springs, or c/o Herndon Hotel, Las Cruces.   *—M. Horzmann*

April 9, 1949

Acting as the Administratrix of Doc's estate, Horzmann filed an inventory[212] of his estate in the Probate Court of Doña Dona on April 9. Under the heading of "Real Property" she listed "Small interest in two mining claims, 'Noss No. 7 and 8, Doña Ana County, N.M. and Noss No. 5 and 6 in Socorro County." Under "Personal Property" she listed: (underlining inserted)

One metal steamer trunk containing papers, documents, books, maps, and other miscellaneous items held by [the] United States Government, [and a] Secret Service agent [in] Albuquerque for investigation; one metal strong box containing documents, papers, and miscellaneous items, also being held by U.S. Government, S.S. Agent, Albuquerque. Supposedly three bars of metal believed to be held by the U.S. Mint in Denver, said to have been receipted for to M.E. Noss, in the amount of approximately, $90,000.00 since 1940 or 1941.

Supposedly, fifty-one (51) bars of metal of undetermined value or content, believed to be in possession of the U.S. Government Agent in Albuquerque, together with the above named bars, pending investigation and evaluation.

Two bars of metal, presumably in Del Rio, Texas, at the Val Verde National Bank, value unknown.

One bar of metal, said to be in Grand Junction, Colorado, or Colorado Springs, Colorado, probably now in the hands of United States Government. One suitcase not found, presumed to contain legal documents, metal bars, gems, and ore samples, trinkets, and other miscellaneous items—this may have been a metal strongbox having two padlocks. These and other items are presumed to be in possession of R.W. Parr or Mrs. Violet Noss, now of Friona, Texas. This may also be in the hands of U.S. Secret Service Department. Other information is unavailable.

One 'Cross Rock', now in the hands of Charley Ryan, Alice Texas, valuable for historical exhibit.

One .38 Caliber gun, Smith &Wesson, being held in the Sheriff's Office entered as an exhibit at the preliminary hearing of Charley Ryan and being further held for exhibit in the pending trial, May 1949 term of Court.

Two bars of metal presumably in a bank in Phoenix, Arizona, with F.M. Goldstein having knowledge of it since 1938 or 1939.

Due to circumstances of cause of death of said MILTON ERNEST NOSS, the United States Government, Secret Service Department, seized all personal property for the purpose of investigation, James W. Hirst, Albuquerque, N.M., Agent.

—Merle Horzmann, Administratrix

~

After Doc's death, Ova Noss was on her own, taking up the fight and standing her ground against the lawlessness brought by the U.S. Army and others to steal the treasure she and Doc had discovered. Later another person would emerge, an FBI agent who played an important and cooperative role in covering up the military's crimes related to the theft of gold from the Noss treasure trove. The cover-up took place a little more than three months after the theft during a special inquiry held at the White Sands Missile Range on March 5, 1974, twenty-five years to the day after Doc was murdered. The FBI agent's connection to the Noss treasure in 1974 involved his corrupt investigation of the theft of thirty-seven tons of gold by the military and other individuals. Names such as White Sands Missile Range Commander Major General Arthur H. Sweeney, State of New Mexico Attorney General David Norvell, a convicted gunrunner named Fred Drolte, a gold smelting plant owner by the name of Kenneth Meadows, a London gold broker named Simon Ashley Smith, an organized crime-connected CIA operative named Lloyd Tucker, a Washington, D.C. attorney named David T. Austern, United States President Richard M. Nixon and FBI Special Agent Herb Greathouse, an agent who gave a fraudulent FBI presentation at the inquiry, would emerge. Other Greathouse reports, preceding and subsequent to the inquiry, were fraudulent as well, obvious cover-ups to hide the activities of individuals involved in the theft.

April 10, 1949

A newspaper article in the *Santa Fe New Mexican* by Art Morgan appeared on April 10. Morgan wrote in a way that more than suggests he was given access to FBI files; "FBI record notes" was the term he used. He also was given access to records from the State Penitentiary in Santa Fe. For these reasons, Morgan's entire article is quoted:

Identification of the late Dr. Milton Ernest Noss as an ex-convict today dampened nationwide interest in a treasure hunt in southern New Mexico, which he set off. His FBI record notes that he has operated in the Confidence racket, old gold brick and gold mine swindle and buried treasure swindle. The quest he left behind is being carried on by Mrs. Ova Noss, his former wife, in Hembrillo Canyon of northern Doña Ana County.

Noss, who was recently shot and killed at Hatch, claimed to have discovered a golden treasure and a mine there. He told of bars of gold bullion stacked like cordwood and a rich vein of ore. He said a cave-in prevented his removing the ore. Warden Howell Gage disclosed today that a Dr. M.E. Noss had done time in the State Penitentiary here. He was sent up from Roswell in 1935, having been committed to from six to nine months for 'insulting while armed.'

Gage said the prisoner was a foot doctor. Dist. Atty. T.K. Campbell at Las Cruces said the slain man was a foot doctor. State Land Commissioner Guy Shepard, when shown a penitentiary photograph of the Noss, who had done time, identified him as Mrs. Noss' former husband. The thing that indicates Mrs. Noss may be deluded is an FBI report in the Noss jacket on file at the state pen. It contains the notation: 'Operated confidence racket, old gold brick and gold mine swindle and buried treasure swindle.' The foundation of this comment was not given.

The FBI report also shows that the convict was arrested at Wellington, Tex., in 1934, charged with theft and practicing medicine without a license and jumped bond. Then he was arrested in Albuquerque in 1944, charged with impersonating a federal officer (the disposition of the case was not shown.) The 'Doc' Noss, who claimed to have discovered an enormously valuable mine in Hembrillo Canyon, was slain March 5 at Hatch. Charley Ryan of Alice, Tex., an associate in the treasure quest, is awaiting trial charged with the shooting.

The late Doc Noss made his claim of discovery to Gordon Herkenhoff, Santa Fe engineer, in 1946. At the time, Herkenhoff was checking up for the Land Office on claims in the Hembrillo district taken out by Doc Noss, Mrs. Noss and the late Willard Holt of Las Cruces. Doc told Herkenhoff he thought he had found the lost Padre LaRue mine of legendary lore. However, the state Bureau of Mines places it about 35 miles to the south.

On Jan. 10 this year, Mrs. Noss, in the meantime divorced, got prospector's permits for several claims in the same section. The permits held by her, Doc, and Holt had long ago expired. Mrs. Noss now has a force of men working in search of the treasure Doc described. She was reported Friday to be on the verge of breaking through the cave-in, which Doc said had deprived him of fabulous wealth. A strong wind was blowing out of the cave entrance to the mine. This was taken to mean that the barrier had been penetrated. Paul A.F. Walter, retired president of the First National Bank, and other residents said that Doc and his wife had once resided here several years ago for a short time.

~

By providing news agencies with such information (supported and unsupported charges and claims), the FBI was able to maintain the position that Doc Noss was a hardened criminal. Doc's various arrests have been revealed throughout this book, but turning over flimsy accusations and information for public view was a trademark of the local FBI; the criminal justice system from

Santa Fe to the Texas border at El Paso was corrupt. It can be argued from the tone and the extent of information in Morgan's article that Doc Noss was a target, but the one fact the article did *not* mention was that the Federal Bureau of Investigation knew where he was at all times. If he had "jumped bail" in Wellington, Texas, he could have and should have been arrested and returned to Texas, but he wasn't. Making charges of "confidence racket" and "gold mine swindle" public were the FBI's tools of the trade under J. Edgar Hoover; the law was what Hoover wanted it to be. Consider this: Hoover was a racist, a blackmailer, an extortionist, and in being such, he was a racketeer and confidence man in his own right, a prime target under the Rico Act today:

> *When a government agent engages in extortion 'under color of official right,' he is essentially using the governmental powers entrusted to him to gain personal or illegitimate rewards.*   —*Rico Act*

~

Hoover, as the Director of the Federal Bureau of Investigation, targeted innocent individuals randomly and maintained secret files on their lives without approval and did so for decades at great expense to the American taxpayer. He took these illegally acquired records and used them for his own personal gain to advance himself and assure his highly ranked position from one administration to the next, and he was feared because of what he knew. Under normal application of the law he should have been indicted, convicted and sent to prison on every count, which would have kept him behind bars for his entire life. What is perhaps the greatest indignity played against the American people is that his name is boldly engraved on a Federal building in Washington, D.C.— *"J. Edgar Hoover Building, FBI Headquarters."*

April 25, 1949

A little more than two weeks later, on April 25, Violet Noss petitioned the court and asked that Horzmann's appointment "as administrator be set aside." Violet had contended that she was "reliably informed" that there was a will. She had charged that, "Miss Horzmann had no opportunity to know or be advised if there was a will in the two days between Noss' death and her petition." She also said she, not Mrs. Ova Noss, was the widow and she had never been contacted [concerning Horzmann's petition] and that she took Horzmann's letter as an "an implied threat to the effect" by giving her an opportunity "to escape the fate which befell her late husband."

~ Jack Woods Returns to Victorio Peak ~

After things settled down, Jack went about finishing the repairs to the final drive on his bulldozer; he had the necessary parts to complete the repairs and Clay Noble was helping him with the work. "Then these guys showed up to help with the dozer," Jack* said. "They came clear from Santa Fe to lend a hand. I guess they heard about what was going on concerning the death of Doc Noss and curiosity brought them out to the Peak. I think they were hoping they'd get a chance to get a close look at Victorio Peak more than helping me fix my dozer." After that a Secret Service agent came to the Peak to talk to Jack. His name was Jim Hirst.

Jack Woods' comments about Hirst:

> *I was down at the peak a few days after Doc was killed. Hirst talked to me for a while and asked me to stop at his office in Albuquerque on my way back to Gallup. I stopped there like he asked on my way home and was asked what I knew about Victorio Peak. I agreed to provide him the answers to a few questions, providing he answered a few of my questions.*
>
> ~

At his office in Albuquerque, Hirst showed Jack a small metal box containing a piece of metal that appeared to be melted and looked like a leaf, but it was not gold. It also contained trinkets and some letters. Jack was told that the Secret Service had been after Doc for gold peddling for years. Hirst said, "It had to come from some place." Jack was told that the Secret Service knew Doc had gold. He then left Hirst's office and returned to Gallup. Doc's estate inventory included a metal box taken by them, which was later denied by the Secret Service. Hirst was transferred to Los Angeles in July 1949.

Although the following event occurred at a much later date, Jack Woods and Tony Jolley finally got to meet each other in 1977 during the thirteen-day siege on Victorio Peak, dubbed *Operation Gold Finder*. In a videotaped interview, Tony told Jack that he had run into Doc at a service station in Hatch in March 1949, and that Doc had asked him to help him move some gold around. The conversation was a confirmation of the events the night before Doc was murdered. Tony said, "They went out to the Peak and dug up bars from two different places and reburied them at various places in the Hembrillo Basin. Doc put ten bars behind the Rock House and I later found them and eventually bought a ranch with the money from the sale of the bars." Jack said Tony was an old rodeo hand and he liked him.

What is interesting about the story is that while Charley Ryan was still in jail, Jack Woods returned to the Hembrillo Basin to work on the road at Victorio Peak. He was also ready to begin exploring for a cave entrance to the inside by

---

* Jack Woods is second from right (head and shoulders showing).

using his bulldozer to scrape away the mountainside. "I was doing some work on the road, when Jack Lawrence, Charley Ryan's right-hand-man showed up and hired me to scrape the surface for gold bars that were buried shallow east of the Rock House. I scraped an area about twenty-five feet by seventy feet. I made some passes, but never turned anything up. Lawrence didn't say much and went on his way." By telling Jack Woods where to excavate, Lawrence had admitted that he knew the prior location of the fifty-one bars.

Jack Woods' letter to Charley Ryan must have had its effect; Lawrence either was given the information about the fifty-one bar site by Ryan from jail, or Lawrence knew its location in his own right. If that was the case, then he surely knew about the intended flight to smuggle nearly one million dollars of Doc's gold into Mexico.

Later, after the May trial, when Ryan was back on the street, Ova went to Benson Newell's office. While she was there, she alleged that Newell had told her Ryan had propositioned him and Judge Scoggin with gold bars from the fifty-one bar site, the only cache known to Ryan. Perhaps Ryan thought that he had missed seeing the bars that night. After he was in jail, he sent Lawrence out to find them with the assistance of Jack Wood's dozer. Since they were not found, and if the bribe offer had been agreed upon, then Ryan obviously did not tell Scoggin or Newell that he was unable to find them.

About a month after Jack Woods had left the Peak, Ova and Letha called him and said that they had found an opening between some large boulders he had moved when he was there trying to find another entrance into the caverns. He drove into Hot Springs and met Ova and Letha. From there they went to Hatch, bought candles and batteries and left for Victorio Peak. He found that he had loosened a rock and below it was a small cavern. A sixteen-year old boy and Woods went in. They went down about twenty feet and disappeared for about two hours and found another opening, which he could not go through. They threw a stone down into it and never heard it hit. Letha called it the snake pit. "I was the first person in there. There were no markings or footprints, not even from an animal." Not able to go any further, Woods left for Gallup and did not return until years later.

The death of Doc Noss did not go away quietly; the general consensus was that Ryan deliberately killed him with motive, malice, and forethought. Specific issues that never came to light in the trial kept Ryan from going to prison. Had Newell been faced with the true issues of the events that transpired the night before Doc was shot, Newell would have been put in an uncomfortable position, especially if he had first-hand knowledge of Ryan having a motive for killing Doc, which he did. Four years and one week after Doc Noss' death, a letter[213] surfaced that told why Doc was murdered: (underlining inserted)

On Feb. 12, 1953, I accompanied Mrs. Ova M. Noss and her daughter Mrs. Letha Berato [Guthrie], on a trip to visit Jack Bruton who resides on a ranch east of Rincon,

New Mexico. While discussing other matters, the conversation got around to the reason for her husband's being killed in the town of Hatch, New Mexico, March 5, 1949, by a man by the name of Ryan, who was connected with Doc Noss, husband of Mrs. Ova M. Noss, in mining operations in that area.

I inquired as to the cause of the killing. Mr. Bruton then stated that, 'it was no doubt about it. It was because Mr. Noss had removed the bars of gold, which belonged to Mr. Noss, but had been hidden in a certain location, known to only Doc himself, Mr. Ryan and a man by the name of Jack Lawrence.'

<u>The reason he was killed, as related to Mr. Bruton by the other surviving member, Jack Lawrence, was that Doc Noss refused to disclose to Mr. Ryan where he had hidden the gold bars the night before.</u> Mr. Noss in some manner had found reason to believe that Mr. Ryan was going to double cross him and once the gold had been placed on an airplane, which was supposed to be furnished by Mr. Ryan for a share of the gold and which Mr. Ryan was supposed to negotiate a sale for the benefit of both on a percentage deal, he would see no more of Mr. Ryan or the gold.

Mr. Ryan had pulled a gun on Doc Noss and brought him to a house [the house Ryan was renting] on the outskirts of Hatch. While Doc was sitting at a table in this house, he suddenly shoved the table into Ryan knocking him through a window. In the commotion, he ran through the door getting as far as the front of his pickup truck, when he was struck in the head by a bullet from the gun fired by Mr. Ryan, killing him instantly.   —*Gordon A. Bjornson*

~

Bruton, Doc, and Ova were more than casual acquaintances: 1) Bruton owned a ranch south of Victorio Peak, 2) at one time he had a 5.22% interest in the Cheyenne Mining Company, 3) Bruton and Doc had common friends such as Roy Henderson, 4) Bruton attended many of Doc's mining company meetings, 5) Bruton also knew that Judge Scoggin and Benson Newell were attorneys for the company, 6) he was vocal in many matters concerning the treasure, and 7) he had warned Joe Andregg in 1941 that his [Andregg's] knowledge of the location of the gold that had been moved could lead to trouble for "having the knowledge of it."

But what is important is that, according to the letter, Jack Lawrence told Bruton that Doc was murdered because he refused to tell Ryan where he had taken the gold. Whether or not Lawrence told Bruton the truth of the matter before or after the trial is unknown, but what Lawrence admitted to fit hand-in-glove with the events that occurred that fateful night in March 1949, events that never came to light during the trial.

Chapter 24

Prelude to the Murder Trial of Charley Ryan

One month after Doc Noss was killed, Albuquerque Secret Service Agent James Hirst said that he was in possession of fake bars from Noss' personal belongings, which they held in custody immediately after his death. One of the fake bars was shown to the Cheyenne Mining Company partners and Gordon E. Herkenhoff. Herkenhoff's February 12, 1946 confidential report had been part of the official Land Office records in Santa Fe for three years; copies of it had been widely circulated, and the report did not deny Doc's contention that a treasure existed.

As much as the Treasury and the Secret Service wished otherwise, fake gold bars and the existence of a treasure trove had nothing to do with each other. Noss had used fake bars when he was concerned with his safety, or when he felt he was going to be double-crossed, which was a common event over the years. But Doc's biggest concern was that the government would take the treasure and use some point of law to justify their actions, or they would eventually drive Ova and him off the treasure site and steal it. His encounter with the Denver Mint was proof enough to him that corruption in high government places was his biggest enemy. So, was Hirst's release of this information aimed at advancing the government's argument that no treasure existed?

Although Doc had possessed gold bars and had conducted gold transactions regularly for nearly a decade, there has never been any record of an official statement by the FBI or the Secret Service that he was involved with or had been charged with fraud related to the treasure site itself, or possession of gold bars, a *supposed* violation of the Gold Reserve Act of 1934. From all appearances, Hirst's comments about Noss' fake bars was water thrown on the flames that arose with the death and the notoriety associated with Doc's murder, flames that in the years past were dry kindling primed to ignite.

As the activities of the military, the FBI, and the Secret Service unfolded over the following decades, it is clear that Hirst's motive was to dampen any suggestion that Doc Noss had ever found any treasure. And then there was Leland Howard of the U.S. Mint, a man who worked in the shadows directing the activities of the Army at White Sands, the FBI, and the Secret Service, a man of influence and power, power given to him at the highest level of government. The Noss treasure was real, and it had been molded into an element of national concern.

April 18, 1949

A letter[214] from Carl W. Horzmann to Merle refers to the exact time period and instance when Doc returned to the Hembrillo Basin. It also reveals some interesting thoughts on the matter of Doc and Ova's situation. Horzmann's April 18 letter, in part:

> *I just can't get that Hot Springs business quite clear in my mind. According to the papers, Babe got a permit from the State to go after the cave, and Doc, somewhat later, tried to get another permit to do the same thing. She got the backing financially and otherwise to go ahead and he finally managed to get into the deal by getting a job from Ryan.*

~

Since Carl Horzmann didn't have the complete facts relative to the situation, his bewilderment was understandable. Ova had no intentions of ever harming Doc or taking his share of the treasure. As proof of her sincerity, she restored his interest by allowing him to excavate the shaft for a full half share. This fact was a family matter and was never made public. Horzmann continued: (underlining inserted)

> *Now then, you say that there is an entirely new setup under which the old gang is out, but definitely. If Babe is divorced from Doc and stays divorced, then she and her new crowd are on a new venture, with which Doc has nothing to do except as a hired employee. If, however, she gets the divorce set aside at this later date, then he or his estate will be entitled to one half of the income, and naturally the old gang will then be in a position to tie up his portion through lawsuits under the grubstake laws, etc., and it might be years before any distribution could take place. So what would be the advantage of having the divorce set aside? These are just ramblings of mine and may be all wrong because I don't know too much about the whole setup and for a matter of fact, don't want to know too much.*
>
> *The opening of the cave will be distinctively news and as such, neither Babe [nor] you will get paid for giving out information, to which the public is entitled. However, there are a lot of little details that you don't need to make public at this time, which later could be woven into a story and then sold for the price you mentioned. But at the present time, you will still have to give some news to the reporters and keep them on <u>our</u> good side, because with all the ramifications in the particular case, you may need the help of the papers one of these days.*
>
> *Here's hoping they open the darned thing pretty soon and find everything the way it should be. I still think it is of the greatest importance that all the money paid into the Perlite deal should be paid back first before the rest get anything, because I still have no great confidence in the deposit.* —*CW*

May 20, 1949

On May 20, 1949, Penitentiary of New Mexico Warden Howell Gage wrote[215] to Attorney J. Benson Newell and enclosed a "certified copy of commitment" providing Newell with documentation of Noss' prison confinement records related to his guilty plea of the Ann's Place incident fourteen years earlier in Roswell. In part:

Enclosed herewith you will find the certified copy of commitment of the above-mentioned subject. You requested this commitment in your letter of the 17th.

—*Howell Gage, Warden*

~

When Ryan's trial began, the State District Attorney, T.K. Campbell, had appointed attorneys Melvin D. Rueckhaus and Paul F. Watkins as special prosecutors in the state's case against Ryan. And still there was the potential problem of the legality of the marriage between Doc and Violet Boles and Ova's rights as Doc's true widow. The concern over the marriage being a serious legal issue led to Rueckhaus and Watkins' motion in Probate Court on April 26, 1949, in reference to Violet M. Noss. The motion read:

That she, as the widow of Milton E. Noss, Deceased, fears mishandling of this estate might result in dissipation of assets of great value as well as assets which might lead to assets of great value and therefore makes this request as provided by Chapter 33 – 502 New Mexico Statutes Annotated, 1941 Compilation, for notice of all and any proceedings were to be mailed to her Attorneys, Rueckhaus and Watkins, 113 West Central Avenue, Albuquerque, New Mexico.   —*RUECKHAUS & WATKINS*

~

Essentially, Rueckhaus and Watkins had asked the court to set aside Merle Horzmann's appointment as Administratrix of Doc Noss' estate. Violet feared her assets were in jeopardy and requested notice of all proceedings. The issue of *"assets, which might lead to assets of great value"* referred to treasure maps, which Ova Noss knew about. Ova had at least a half-interest in the treasure as a discoverer, including maps, which were part of the treasure, or other locations. She also held an interest in The Cheyenne Mining Company. Complications over *who* was entitled to *what* loomed. Two days after Doc's death, Horzmann had presented a petition to the court contending that Doc had no will. But Violet explained to the court that there *was* a will. Violet Noss claimed that Horzmann had intentionally misrepresented the facts when she indicated a low bond on an estate of fabulous proportion. Also, it was claimed that Horzmann had not taken custody of the items of inventory nor had she given such inventory to the widow of authority. Violet's attorneys had charged that Horzmann was only using the court as a means for her to take control of matters related to the treasure after Doc's death.

So as it stacked up, the judge was Doc's attorney and business partner, the defense attorney was Doc's attorney and business partner, the prosecuting attorney had also worked on Doc's business dealings, and he was the attorney for Violet Boles. Where did that leave Ova Noss? Who knows? If it appears that preemptive legal maneuvering and jostling for position were complicating matters before Ryan's trial began, it's because they were. By the time Ryan's murder trial had started there was more in-house fighting, questionable business and personal and legal relationships and obvious conflicts of interest than there were split hoofs in the Chicago stockyards.

Not surprisingly, it was also heavily rumored that jurors had been bribed to find Ryan innocent; statements were also being raised as to how much each received for their cooperation. The long line of witnesses for the defense, mostly "character witnesses," were each asked the same questions and responded almost robotically with the same answers about Doc's potential for violence, but there was little mention of Ryan's obvious display of *actual* violence when he shot and killed Doc. Many of the questions asked and answers given would not be allowed in today's courtroom, objections were rarely heard and testimonies were full of contradictions that triggered protests yelled out by Ova and family members which only served to interrupt the process. Many of the witnesses who were friends of Doc's and whom he had employed and trusted were appearing as witnesses for the defense.

And, to make matters worse, across the hallway from Scoggin's courtroom was yet another trial of great public interest, which ran concurrently with the Ryan murder trial. Cricket Coogler was a young, attractive prostitute who had had sexual relationships with prominent political figures and other well-known individuals. People were moving back and forth from one courtroom to the other so as not to miss out on the trial activity; it was a two-ring circus. A young FBI agent by the name of Herbert Greathouse was involved in the Coogler case. Remember his name.

Chapter 25

The Defense for Charley Ryan

I t was May 25, 1949, the first day of Ryan's murder trial at the Doña Ana County Court House in Las Cruces. Las Cruces was still a small western desert town suffering growing pains since its arrival into the 20th Century. It was part of an area that had been colonized by Juan de Oñate in 1598. After the town was founded in 1849, it blossomed rich in history from its famous Sheriff Pat Garrett to its infamous outlaw Billy the Kid and scores of other familiar and historical names in-between. The town grew rapidly, soon to become a thriving desert community. But to think that political corruption had not infiltrated Las Cruces when Scoggin was judge, you'd be wrong. Scoggin and certain town, county and state officials were picked to be the designated criminals. Others who attempted to jump on board to make a fast buck were pursued, arrested, prosecuted and jailed. That's the way it worked.

DOÑA ANA CO. COURT HOUSE   LAS CRUCES N. MEX.

Author Peter R. Sandman was a native of Las Cruces and twice an award winning sports columnist. His father was Doña Ana County Deputy Sheriff Roy Sandman, who had investigated the Cricket Coogler murder and Doc Noss' murder as well. Sandman wrote, "By the summer of 1946, Brooklyn gangster* Benjamin 'Bugsy' Siegel, helped by Chicago and Cleveland mobsters, moved in on the west coast wire services that notified gamblers across the country about

---

* P. Sandman, "Murder Near The Crosses," (Barbed Wire Publishing, 2006) p. 4

horseracing results and netted the National Crime Syndicate…millions a year." Because of Siegel's close association with gangster Albert Anastasia, he is credited with having a role in establishing Murder, Inc.; he was also the recipient of much of the syndicate's money. In New Mexico, Siegel turned his attention to Santa Fe where he aligned himself with politicians who supported his gambling operations. Sandman wrote: "Individuals like Moe Dalitz, Edwin Rogers, Butts Lowenstein, and Frank Ardovino were quick to capitalize on Siegel's idea. To this day, people remember Siegel in Santa Fe. In 2002, a Las Cruces resident said, 'my parents were teenagers in Santa Fe. My dad recalls that when Bugsy Siegel was in town, word got out and everybody would be mentioning it.'" With Siegel in Santa Fe and the wire services, gambling, and prostitution rackets in full swing there, corruption drifted south to Las Cruces—one more place the crime syndicate could make a fast, illegal buck.

No one was exempt from the temptations that organized crime provided; if you were a political bigshot and you needed someone to attend to your sexual appetite, Las Cruces was a good destination. According to Sandman's research, New Mexico House Representative Joseph Manuel Montoya,* who owned Western Freight Trucking, was no exception when it came to making an illegal buck "by 'fudging' bills of lading for U.S. Army[†] personnel transfers from various bases in New Mexico to other parts of the country." Sandman also wrote, "One of Montoya's men in Las Cruces was the sheriff and former state policeman, Alfonso Luchini Apodaca, who was also fond of women and money. He was a ruthless person whose sheepish smile earned him the nickname 'Happy.'" What went poorly for Apodaca was the death of a young woman, a prostitute by the name of Ovida "Cricket" Coogler. "From the day that Cricket Coogler's body was found, rumors flew around Las Cruces and Santa Fe that Apodaca had killed her."

Montoya rubbed shoulders with a man who was corrupt and ruthless——Apodaca. In 2008, award-winning writer Paula Moore[‡] wrote about Apodaca in her book, *Cricket in the Web*. She wrote that Apodaca's law enforcement career began in 1942 when he "became a state policeman and immediately made himself conspicuous." Her in-depth investigation revealed that FBI archives referred to Apodaca's NMSP personal file where the records showed that he was given a leave of absence in 1942 because of an "accumulation of

---

*Lt. Governor Joseph Montoya, 1947-1948 New Mexico Blue Book.
† *Ibid.,* p. 6.
‡ P. Moore, *Cricket in the Web,* (University of New Mexico, 2008) pp. 16,17, 18.

complaints." One incident accounted for the results of a "political argument" Apodaca had with Dan Williams, who was reported to be the "president of the college's board of regents and head of the highway department in Doña Ana County." Even though Williams' jaw was broken and he lost one of his eyes in the argument, Apodaca was reinstated early the following year. In 1949 he ran for and was elected Sheriff of Doña Ana County and was seen by newspaper reporter Alice Gruver "handing out pint bottles of whiskey to voters" at the polls on Election Day.

After Apodaca was elected, he "fixed" problems including drunk driving and even worse offenses and subsequently expected citywide favors in return. He "created" problems as well; when a family member or a friend was "crossed," Apodaca was "relentless in ensuing payback." During his term of office there was "about one violent death a month." Russell Allen Soper was a hotel operator in nearby Hatch. He was also a "member of the county grand jury that held hearings on the handling of the Coogler case." Soper had also "confirmed on tape that" Apodaca's office "was a semi-headquarters for politicians, a place where favors were expedited." One of Apodaca's deputies in the Coogler investigation was Roy Sandman, the father of author Peter R. Sandman. Moore reported that Deputy Sandman "abruptly resigned his deputy position in June 1949." His resignation stemmed from his "initial two months" investigation of Coogler's murder, because according to FBI investigators, "Sandman's hands were tied by Apodaca throughout the investigation of the Coogler case and Sandman never could conduct the investigation as he wished."

When gambling arrived, it was necessary to secure protection for operations in New Mexico from the highest political level downward to every political subdivision throughout the state. For Doña Ana County, the payoffs were "divided in three ways: one payment went directly to Doña Ana County Sheriff Apodaca; another to District Judge W. T. Scoggin Jr.; the third to the Democratic Central Committee in Santa Fe. This payment was handled by State Corporation Commission Chairman Dan Sedillo, who distributed it to local politicians and to the governor's campaign funds."

The small towns made out very well in the arrangement, and so did District Judge William T. Scoggin. "FBI* files show that in 1949 Judge Scoggin purchased a brand new Oldsmobile sedan with his share of the Alamogordo payoffs." Scoggin's role in

---

*Sandman, *op. cit.*, pp. 6-8.

maintaining the casino establishments was fundamentally simple. "The FBI*
also noted that whenever a gambling raid was planned in southern New Mexico,
Judge Scoggin was the only man notified. It was his responsibility to inform
Sheriff Apodaca, who carried out the raid. Scoggin was the tip-off man. Once
the unsuccessful raid was over, the equipment was moved back and business
resumed. However, there were times when circumstances dictated the destruc-
tion† of seized gambling equipment to demonstrate to the general public that
crime doesn't pay; this gesture by the gambling syndicate in Las Cruces was
simply good public relations.

"The FBI had long known of Scoggin's and Apodaca's‡ involvement and their records reflect that while
Scoggin was the local district attorney, big money interests who offered to finance his campaigns approached
him. He accepted the money. When the judgeship
opened, it was decided that Scoggin was worth more in
this capacity so they assisted monetarily in getting him
elected. Scoggin was then able to protect any of the 'boys'
who got into trouble. The seat of his authority, however,
still lay in the capitol building in Santa Fe." When the trials
in the murders of Doc Noss and Cricket Coogler began,
Scoggin was at the top of his game, criminally.

~

Attorney Newell began his defense of Charley Ryan by telling the jury that
he intended to prove that Doc had bounced a personal check in the amount
of $150 in Corpus Christi and that Ryan, his employer at the time, went there
and paid that amount to get Doc released§ from jail. According to Newell's
comments to the jury, it turned out that Doc had written the check before a
business associate of his had a chance to deposit cash into Doc's account at the
Bishop Bank. Newell explained that Ryan had to put more money into Doc's
account since other checks had come in.

He said that Doc owned a dilapidated truck and that Ryan had purchased
a new truck for him and that Doc's job was to go out and "bring tools in and
repair them." Newell also contended that Doc "would visit with" Mr. and Mrs.
Ryan and tell them he had valuable lead claims in New Mexico that had been
neglected and he needed to get back to "take care of them." Ryan agreed to
come to New Mexico where he supposedly filed some fifteen lead claims, some
of which Doc also claimed contained uranium. It was here that Newell began
to introduce elements he felt would support Ryan's innocence. Newell claimed

---

* *Ibid.*, p. 9.
† Public demonstration of gambling equipment being destroyed in Las Cruces.
‡ The flipside of Doña Ana County Sheriff "Happy" Apodaca.
§ "Trial Transcript" (State of New Mexico vs. Charley Ryan), pp. 89-240.

Doc had told Ryan, "These people up there are dangerous. This is very valuable property I have and we have to be armed." He continued on with an account of how Doc left his gun with his second wife and how Ryan finally went to the Sheriff's office in Socorro County and got a permit. He claimed that Ryan never carried a gun in Hatch, only when he went to the mountains to work. Newell also told the jury that Ryan went to the School of Mines in Socorro and solicited a Mr. Walters to come and survey the claim site in the Hembrillo Basin. Later, after Ryan shot and killed Doc, Walters showed up, inspected the sites, deemed them worthless from a commercial standpoint, and said they contained only half the amount of lead necessary to make a profit and no uranium.

Where Ryan took Walters to take the samples for the assays was not introduced by Newell, only Ryan's account of what Walters had told him about the physical characteristics of the sites. Newell pressed the point in his presentation that Doc was quarrelsome and dangerous. He described specific acts of violence on the part of Noss in every community he was in and said he was a habitual gun-toter.

Newell finally got to the day of the killing. He told the jury that Ryan was going back to Texas and he wanted the men to come to Hatch for their paychecks, which they did, and that Noss also came to Ryan's house where Mr. and Mrs. Ryan, Jack Lawrence and Buck Harris, two of Ryan's employees, were living. Newell said that Doc told Ryan he wasn't going to go back to Texas and that he wanted $350 from Ryan so he could take some gold to El Paso and have it *rerun* so he could take it to Arizona and dispose of it. Ryan refused and went out to ask Blake about the Jeep and learned that Doc and Blake had been to the filling station at eleven o'clock (that Friday night) and the Jeep had not been returned. Ryan's reason for being away all night was that he and Lawrence, feeling something had happened to the boys, made a ninety-mile trip looking for them.

As stated earlier, on Friday night, Doc had told Blake he could take the Jeep home with him. Newell said that Ryan had also been to the filling station paying the bills. On Saturday, when Doc came out of the house, Ryan, armed with his pistol, told Doc to go back in the house and "we will discuss the matter." Ryan went back in the house and Doc was supposed to have said to Ryan that if he didn't give him the $350 he was going to kill him. Ryan's alleged response was, "I don't care. I don't want to have anything to do with an illegitimate deal of that kind." Newell then said that Ryan gave the gun to Jack Lawrence, took his position by the window and told Doc he wouldn't let him have the money. It was then that Doc hit Ryan and ran out and said, "I will kill every one of you sons-of-bitches." Ryan grabbed the gun from Lawrence and "went out and fired one shot to try to stop him" and then another shot "that resulted fatally." This was Newell's case—Ryan was acting in self-defense when he shot Doc who was running away. Newell then examined the five character witnesses:

W.B. Billingsley, Baptist Minister – Alice, Texas

Newell's first witness was W. B. Billingsley, a Baptist minister who said that Ryan had a very good reputation, which was the extent of his testimony. Under cross-examination by Special Prosecutor Watkins, Billingsley admitted that in the last two years of the four years he had known Ryan, he and his wife never visited Ryan and his wife together at Ryan's home, nor did the Ryans ever visit them. He had no business dealings with Ryan and he had flown from Texas for the trial. That was the extent of Reverend Billingsley's testimony under cross-examination.

J.L. Carlisle, Banker – Alice, Texas

The second witness was J.L. Carlisle, a banker who had known Ryan four years and had business dealings with him through his bank. He referred to Ryan as a "peaceable and law-abiding citizen with a good reputation." Under cross-examination, Carlisle said the bank had loaned Ryan $25,000, but admitted that he had never been a partner in any business dealing with him. When asked if he had bought any interest in a treasure "in which Mr. Ryan was involved," he denied it. He said that he came to the trial with friends. That was the extent of Carlisle's testimony.

Claude L. Tolson, Contractor – Alice, Texas

The third witness was Claude L. Tolson, an oil rig contractor who had business dealings with Ryan and claimed that Ryan had a good reputation in the community and spoke of Ryan's truthfulness and veracity. Under cross-examination, Watkins asked Tolson if he came without a subpoena, to which he answered, "Absolutely."

L.M. York, Oil Driller – Houston, Texas

The fourth witness was L.M. York, an oil driller who knew Ryan for fifteen years before Ryan left Houston and went to Alice. He said Ryan had a good reputation and spoke of his truthfulness and veracity. He said he flew to the trial in his own plane. Under cross-examination, York said he didn't know much about Ryan for the last five years and that he came to the trial voluntarily.

J.T. Hines, Oil Field Welder – Alice, Texas

The fifth witness was J.T. Hines, a welder whose work was mainly in the oil fields. He said he had known Ryan for five years. He claimed Ryan's general reputation was that he was a peaceable and law-abiding citizen and spoke of Ryan's truthfulness and veracity. Under cross-examination Hines claimed he only knew Ryan through business dealing and that he "thought quite a bit of him" and that his wife and Ryan's wife were friendly. He admitted that he drove to the trial with Mr. Carlisle and had come there voluntarily without subpoena. Hines was the last character witness who testified on Ryan's behalf. The court recessed until the next day.

The following morning the jury was seated and Newell asked Judge Scoggin to allow as evidence a "certified copy of commitment to the State Penitentiary of M.E. Noss, 1935." Watkins was quick to object and told Scoggin the jury should be excused, but it was too late. They had heard Newell's request. Newell's courtroom trickery had begun. Scoggin agreed and claimed there was no foundation for such evidence; it seemed to be a planned event cooked between Newell and Scoggin. Newell said, "Exception. We further offer in evidence a certified copy of a plea of guilty in Chaves County." Again, Watkins objected. Scoggin finally "retired" the jury, but the jury heard all of Newell's comments. After the jury withdrew, Newell moved to have the documents marked as Defendant's Exhibits 1 and 2. Watkins objected again. Scoggin sustained. Then, strangely, while the jury was still out of the courtroom, Newell called another witness to the stand to testify. Scoggin allowed him to be sworn in and Newell proceeded to examine the witness before the court without the jury present.

Claron E. Waggoner, District Attorney – New Mexico

The sixth witness for the defense was Claron E. Waggoner, District Attorney for the Seventh Judicial District for Socorro, Sierra, Torrance and Catron Counties, New Mexico. Waggoner stated that he was familiar with the general reputation of Doc "M.E." Noss as to his general reputation as being a peaceable and law-abiding citizen and that it was "bad." When asked by Newell if he were "acquainted with the reputation of Doc Noss in those counties as to truth and veracity" Waggoner said, "It was bad." Watkins objected, saying, "I don't know the purpose of cross-examining this testimony; the jury is not here." Watkins asked that Waggoner's testimony be stricken. Watkins said, "There has been no foundation laid to question this man as to the truth and veracity of this man [meaning Noss]." Scoggin sustained and called the jury in. Newell said, "Exception." After the jury was seated, Newell told Scoggin he wanted the record to show the "Court's ruling that the Defendant is compelled to take the witness stand and testify to any previous testimony regarding the general reputation of the deceased, or any specific acts of violence upon his part." Watkins said, "We object to the use of the word 'compel.' If a man has to abide by the law he is not compelled."

Newell countered, "I am asking if I am required to put Mr. Ryan on before that testimony is admissible."

Scoggin replied, "The very fundamental principle [is] that you can prove the bad character of the deceased."

Newell asked, "Then I must put on Mr. Ryan?"

Scoggin answered, "That's right."

Newell told Scoggin, "Then we except to that ruling."

The trial of Charley Ryan had become a fetid event. It would seem that in light of Judge Scoggin's alleged bad character, which according to Sandman was known to the FBI, and Scoggin's own opinion that proving the "bad character" of an individual was a "fundamental principle" in a first step in establishing a justification for shooting someone, it then follows that anyone in the jury box could have stood up and shot Scoggin* and would have been acquitted.

The one person who stood the best chance of keeping Ryan out of the penitentiary was Ryan. Even though Newell postured by taking exception to Scoggin's ruling to put Ryan on the stand, Newell in fact wanted Ryan to take the stand. His entire defense strategy was built around Doc's questionable character; the sole reason Newell called Waggoner to the stand in the first place. With Ryan on the stand, it presented an opportunity to get other elements of Doc's poor reputation on the record as well. In preparation for Ryan's testimony, Newell had gathered a wide range of not-so-good-to-hear comments, key words, sentences and accusations for Ryan to say to the jury, a variety of things to present regarding Doc's reputation, things Ryan would not have known unless coached, pumped, and primed well in advance of Newell putting him on the stand. So, all Ryan and Lawrence had to do was remember their lines. The only thing Scoggin had to do was overrule as many of the prosecuting attorney's objections as possible, which he did. The only thing Newell had to do was keep his fingers crossed that his client remembered his lines. The only thing Ryan had to do was lie, effectively.

Charley F. Ryan, Machine Shop Owner – Alice, Texas

The seventh witness was Charley Ryan. He owned and ran a machine shop that primarily served the oil field industry in Alice, Texas, "all my life, about twenty-five years," he said. Ryan said he became acquainted with Doc Noss after Doc had answered an "ad in the paper for a truck driver field man. He answered the ad and we hired him the latter part of November, 1948." Ryan told the jury that Mr. Shell, his bookkeeper, hired Doc in his absence and he had been working there for a few days before Ryan came back to the shop. He said that Doc's job was to go out in the oil fields, pick up customers' work, bring it back to his shop for repairs, and then return it to the customers.

According to Ryan, Doc had told Shell that he had a truck suitable for the work, but Ryan found out that it wasn't. Doc then claimed he had the money to buy a new truck, but later told Ryan he didn't. Ryan said that Doc had asked him to loan him the money for the truck, but Ryan said, "I couldn't do that." Afterward, Ryan decided to buy the truck and said, "He could pay me back at

* Photo provided by New Mexico State University Library Archives and Special Collections.

$100 a month, which we had done quite often." Ryan said they went to Corpus Christi to look for a truck. While on that trip, Doc told Ryan about a Mr. Smith who owed him money. So Ryan drove to the Bishop Bank in Bishop, Texas. After talking to the bank president, Mr. Buck, he found out that Doc had told him the truth; Buck verified Smith owed Doc $760 and that Smith "had agreed to mail a check to the bank to deposit in Doc's account, which he hadn't."

Ryan said they left the bank and went to look at some trucks when a police officer drove up and asked, "Who is driving this Dodge truck?" The car salesman pointed to Noss. The policeman walked over and told Doc he was under arrest. Ryan soon learned the charges against Doc were "for giving worthless checks." At Doc's request, Ryan went to the jail to learn the amount of the checks, met District Attorney Martin there and was told the bond was $500. They brought Doc down from the jail, and Doc told Martin the checks would not exceed $85. Ryan gave Martin a check for $150, then Martin called Buck at the bank and they discussed the matter.

While Doc was still behind bars, Ryan said that he had learned there were two more checks of $50 each to a man in McAllen, Texas. Ryan told the man to "run the checks through" and then called Buck and told him to honor them. Doc returned to work at Ryan's machine shop. However, the day that Ryan and Doc were leaving for New Mexico, Doc came to Ryan with a note "on the Bishop Bank for $289." The note was for "checks Mr. Buck had been holding." Buck signed the note, which Ryan said was never paid. In the end, Ryan had covered $235 in checks and a note Doc had signed at Bishop Bank for $289, both against the $760 that Smith had owned him. When Doc and Ryan returned to Alice, Ryan said that he had told Doc he couldn't work for him and "give hot checks or get drunk or not pay his bills" because it wouldn't be tolerated. Ryan said, "He in turn began complimenting my business and said how well people spoke of me." I said, "Yes, it's like owning a gold mine if you can't sell the gold [whatever that meant is unknown]. That's the way the gold and the lead claims came in," Ryan said. It was then that Noss began telling Ryan about the treasure.

One night Doc received a call from Roscoe Parr who told him that his "former wife" was obtaining "a permit on the mountain where the treasure was supposed to be." Noss told Ryan that he had to go to Santa Fe, and although Ryan was suffering from a sprained ankle, Doc wanted Ryan to go with him. He finally did, but by then Mrs. Noss had already been given a permit. Ryan said, "We stayed around for a couple of days, talked to the Attorney General and the Assistant Attorney General. I told them the only reason that I was there was that I felt sorry for the man." Doc told him that people had stolen from him and had lied to him and that Ryan "was the only honest man he had ever found." Ryan was supposed to have told the Attorney General that he had a business that required his full-time attention and that he didn't want to get connected to the treasure.

Ryan explained that Doc talked more about the lead and silver claims and also about a "cross rock" he had to get out of New Mexico. It was then that Ryan admitted that he had taken four men with him on the trip and had stayed four weeks "during bad weather" to help Doc find the cross rock. He explained the cross rock was of a certain size, "about so long with a square on it" and that Noss had claimed it was very valuable. Then Ryan said, "While we was here, we checked
the records and claimed a mining permit on the lead and silver claim." In fact, and according to Newell himself, Ryan had filed "some 15 lead claims" but he never mentioned any silver claims being filed by Ryan, only lead claims.

After they had secured the mining permits, they returned to Alice. Upon their arrival there, Ryan told Noss he would give him $1,000 and he could bring the pickup to New Mexico, that he didn't "want to fool with it" and that Noss could pay him back for the truck. Ryan admitted though, that Noss, Buck Harris, and Jack Lawrence, who were his good friends, went to New Mexico with Ryan and his wife. Ryan went along to see what equipment was needed, intending "to go back to his business." However, the other men talked him into staying, which he did for four weeks, all the while looking for a rock with a cross on it, which Ryan admitted to the jury was the *reason* for going to New Mexico. Then, while Ryan was in New Mexico, he had assays completed on the lead ore samples taken from the claim sites, which were marked as Defendant's Exhibit 3. The assays showed 6 to 8 percent lead, but according to Ryan, Noss told him, "When you get down a little deeper it will be a whole lot better."

They continued cleaning out the mine and on the last week, which was the fourth week, Ryan's wife got sick and Ryan said, "I wouldn't go out on the job." Ryan claimed that Noss said, "They will kill you when they find out you are the man putting up the money to operate this." Ryan said, "After I got a chance to talk to a few nice people here, I began to find out what kind of a man he was" and told his wife about it. Ryan said, "The next day I didn't go to the mine." The next day was Wednesday. When Noss came to Ryan and said he wanted to go to Douglas, Arizona, that he knew someone who would "put in a $50,000 mill to take care of the ore." Ryan sent Jack Lawrence along to "listen to the conversation." Noss and Lawrence came back from Douglas after they had talked to Mr. Hawley (of Hawley & Hawley), but according to Ryan, Noss didn't discuss the Douglas trip until the "day of the murder." Ryan also testified that Doc told him that it wasn't safe "to come up here and start operating those mines without being well protected," so Ryan purchased a pistol "at the Alice Hardware in Alice, Texas" before he left for New Mexico.

Ryan said he bought an M-scope machine, an instrument used to locate water lines. "Any steel or silver under the ground, you can locate it with this machine," he said. He also bought a $45 compass and a pair of field glasses. Ryan said that Doc wanted the glasses to see people up on the mountain "who wanted to shoot him" so he could see them first. Ryan admitted that he had contacted Newell to have corporation papers drawn up, "due to the fact" that he "had business in Texas" and "didn't want to have a partnership business in New Mexico." While under direct examination, and while talking directly to Newell, Ryan said, "That is when I first met you--when you drew up the corporation papers for me." Newell said, "You and he [Doc] came to my office and you say I prepared the initial papers for you?" Ryan said, "Yes."

If there was ever a protective comment, that was it; had anyone known about the letter Newell sent to Ryan concerning treasure trove, it could easily be covered as incidental to the real reason for Newell writing to Ryan—the $100 charge for Newell setting up Ryan's corporation. Ryan then talked about Mr. Walters, Dean of the Socorro School of Mines and how he learned "quite a bit of information of the mining business." Ryan also told the jury that he had never carried a gun before but had obtained a "special deputy sheriff's commission in Socorro County to carry a pistol," which also required a $500 bond and therefore was referred to Assistant District Attorney Enloe, one of Merle Horzmann's confederates against Doc. Enloe referred him to the local druggist, a man of the Masonic Order like Ryan, who took Ryan down to meet Mr. Walters at the mining school where Walters signed the bond, took him to his home, and according to Ryan he was shown "letters people had written him dated back to 1939 where Noss had swindled people in New Mexico."

Scoggin said, "I believe this is hearsay."

Newell said, "Eliminate that. Don't say what the letters showed" and instructed Ryan how to phrase the answer, while the jury listened intently. Then Ryan claimed that he told Walters that he had invested $5,000 in the mining venture, and Walters told him he would come there for $200 and tell him "whether he had anything or not." After Ryan murdered Doc, and while Ryan was still in jail, Walters sent him a card saying he could come down. Ryan then called Walters and told him what had happened. Ryan didn't see Walters "for approximately a week after this happened."

Ryan also told the jury that Doc had been to the mining school in Socorro, had learned a lot of information and had displayed his knowledge and "had a name for all those rocks and told me the claims we had was worth $87.50 a ton." Ryan then told a story of a man named Grover who had jumped Doc's claim and that Doc and some men had beat Grover up because Doc had a buyer for the site in the amount of $50,000.

Newell got into the issue of who was working for Ryan in his lead mining venture. Ryan claimed there were a total of five men working for him during the same time the former Mrs. Noss was "working on this mountain (Victorio Peak)." Ryan said he "had to go by the side of it" to get to his claims. He said that he had met Mrs. Noss "ten days" before he killed Doc and that Doc had told him about Ova, saying, "Well, she was about the worst person I ever heard of, how mean she was and that a bunch of thieves worked over there on this cave. Don't dare speak to them, they would kill you on sight." He then told the jury that Doc shot a hawk that was sitting on a bush "63 steps away."

Ryan said they went to El Paso where he bought Doc a handgun and a .30-06 rifle and then he told the jury that when Doc wasn't carrying the pistol, it was in the "glove compartment of his truck." He then went into a convoluted story about how nice Doc was until he got to New Mexico, that Doc had no respect for Ryan's position, that Doc agreed to work for nothing and that he would eat jackrabbits, that an attorney in El Paso said to Doc in Ryan's presence, "The only thing is I can't see how you are out of the penitentiary today" and that "when the government got hold of him they would send him to the penitentiary for selling these 130 shares." Ryan said that Doc claimed he knew "where we can sell $50,000 worth of stock on these lead claims tomorrow." Ryan said, "Fine. We have to have some money to operate." Then Ryan claimed that Doc wouldn't use it to operate and that they would take $25,000 each. Could it be possible that Newell had a file full of papers and documents related to Doc's private life and his business transactions so that Ryan knew what figures to give to the court during his testimony?

Ryan then admitted the mine sites were not visited by Walters until April 12, 1949, more than a month after he had killed Noss. He claimed Walters said, "They wasn't worth five cents." He also claimed that Doc told him "there was five people he had killed in his time. That went on for several days and my wife was sick and nervous." Ryan said, "Doc, please don't come in my house anymore saying there is going to be a killing." Ryan also said, "He wanted to go to Hot Springs and kill Claude Fincher." Ryan told him, "Go ahead, but don't take one of my guns to kill him."

In a letter to her husband on May 14, 1941, Merle Horzmann had written that Doc "threatened a killing before morning." Horzmann's connection to the government, her connection to Newell and Scoggin as Secretary of the Cheyenne Mining Company and her admitting that she gave a copy of her records to the New Mexico State Police might suggest that she also made sure that Newell knew about Doc's comment, a similar comment made by Ryan at trial. Ryan also condoned Doc killing Claude Fincher, as long as he didn't use *his* gun.

Ryan's testimony became more intense. He claimed he was riding in the truck with Doc when Doc said, "There never was a more cold-blooded killer that ever walked the face of the earth than I am. I would just as soon kill you as say good morning to you." Ryan asked Doc, "Why would you want to kill me? I don't like to talk about these things. I have loaned you a lot of money and helped you out and I don't appreciate a man sitting around telling me he would kill me or other people."

Ryan claimed that on the same day that he shot Noss, that Noss told him about a "conversation" he had with Mr. Hawley in Douglas "with respect to selling him $220,000 worth of gold Doc claimed he had hidden out there somewhere." According to Ryan, Doc's conversation with Hawley had taken place two days earlier. Ryan also claimed Noss said that, "Mr. Hawley told him, 'I almost went to the penitentiary over that last bullion I bought from you and I'm not going to buy anymore unless you have it rerun.'" According to Ryan, Doc said Mr. Hawley referred him to a man in El Paso and that Jack Lawrence and Doc went there, but the man had to check with Hawley, which he did, and then the El Paso man agreed to rerun Doc's gold for $500, which Doc got down to $350. Ryan said, "That's what he wanted me to give him the $350 for. He was supposed to take the gold to El Paso on Saturday night. The man was going to rerun it Saturday night and Sunday while there wasn't anybody there but himself. Noss was to pick it up Sunday and be in Douglas, Arizona on Monday." Ryan claimed that he told Doc he didn't want any part of the gold business since he had been informed by Walters that having more than two ounces of "gold in your possession at any time was illegal."

Chapter 26
Analysis of the Trial Transcript

R yan talked about the night before he killed Doc. He said that Lawrence had told him that Doc came in late from the mine Friday night because Doc shot an antelope and "detoured around by Hot Springs." Ryan said, "My wife and I got in my car and drove about twenty or twenty-five miles, and on the way back I met Jack Lawrence in the pickup." Ryan said, "What is the matter?" Then Ryan said that Lawrence "related the story about the antelope and said that they had to come back through Hot Springs and they had gotten stuck and had trouble getting through there. They did not get in until late." The question is—who were *they*? Lawrence said *they* detoured around Hot Springs, got stuck, and as a result *they* were late. So who was with Doc? It could not have been Ryan's work crew because the work crew's time was accounted for after 8:00 Friday night; according to Blake and the gas station attendant Doc was in Ryan's truck when he pulled in to fill up at about 8:00 Friday night and Blake had already dropped the crew off at their homes. Tony Jolley had already pulled in and went to the men's room and when he came out to his vehicle, Doc was at the pumps. That was when Doc and Tony Jolley had their conversation. Therefore, Newell had no idea that Doc *and* Tony Jolley were moving gold around Friday night, and neither did Ryan for that matter. As it turned out, Tony Jolley was an invisible witness to Doc's whereabouts from Friday night until early morning on Saturday. Jolley said, "It was about morning when we got there," meaning that it was dawn when they got back to Hatch. Ova also confirmed the time in her deposition and said, "Doc come into town the next morning at 7:00 o'clock and was filling up with gas. Ryan was a-waiting for him. Ryan seen him at the filling station and told him to come over; he wanted Doc to talk to him." So, the antelope story was a constructed lie and was used simply because no one on the defense team for Charley Ryan could account for Doc's time after 8:00 Friday night and had no knowledge that Doc had a witness for his activities from 8:00 Friday night until close to dawn on Saturday morning. Was the antelope story developed by Ryan and Lawrence without Newell's knowledge, or was Newell part of the conspiracy for Ryan to lie under oath? If that were the case, then Newell had knowingly allowed his client to commit perjury.

Stranger yet was that Newell allowed Ryan to ramble on and on with disjointed and difficult-to-understand testimony that lacked any focus or direction. Newell rarely stepped in and asked Ryan specific questions that he could answer systematically and with purpose. Instead, Ryan talked endlessly in chopped up sentences devoid of any flow of thought, purpose, or continuity. Attorney Watkins would often object and Scoggin would usually overrule his objection.

Ryan's testimony became even more convoluted: there was no reference made when Ryan was talking about a.m. or p.m., or to whom he was referring when he explained certain matters.

Then Ryan continued with his fabricated story: "We sat around there waiting for them to come in. I go downtown and walked around and couldn't see the Jeep. I drove over to Noss' house and his pickup wasn't there." One minute, Ryan had claimed Lawrence talked to *them* on the way back from Hot Springs. But according to Ryan's new story, he didn't find his Jeep or Doc's recently purchased truck at Doc's house. Ryan claimed to be concerned about the men. So he and Lawrence drove out toward Victorio Peak. Ryan told the jury, "Around 9:00 o'clock, Jack Lawrence and I got in my car; Mrs. Noss had had the road graded, so we could drive down to Mr. Baird's. I drove down there and Mrs. Baird came to the door and I asked her if she had seen my Jeep come out. She said, 'Yes, it come out at 5:00 or 5:30 [p.m.].' We knew that everything was alright." The only road that had been improved was the road that came in from the western rim into the Hembrillo Basin to Victorio Peak, which had recently been rebuilt by Jack Woods for Ova; the road from Rincon came into the basin from the south, while the road Ryan and Lawrence were on came in from the west, and he claimed that he was driving his *car* when he and Lawrence made that particular trip. The Baird story accounted for Ryan and Lawrence's time between 9:00 p.m. Friday night and when they returned from Baird's ranch and got back to Hatch. Had they just gone to the Baird ranch and returned directly to Hatch it would have taken about an hour. The exact location of the Baird ranch is unknown, but if Ryan and Lawrence came in over the improved road, the only ranches before they got to the rim were west of the rim. So the Baird ranch trip and the subsequent return to Hatch would have been about 1.5 hours. By their own admission they were away from Hatch for 3.5 hours. The antelope story and Ryan's trip to the desert because of his concern for his work crew established a rationale for Ryan and Doc to be in the desert that night, something that the jury knew nothing about—fifty-one gold bars.

Tony Jolley's presence in Hatch that weekend lifted the veil on the lies Ryan had told the jury, lies that fogged the mirror about everything Ryan and Lawrence told the jury about Doc, including the real reason Ryan came to New Mexico and why he murdered Doc Noss—Ryan had gold fever and good judgment no longer ruled the day.

Ryan had been adamant that he had no interest in any matter involving gold, and he made a point of it to the jury. However, contrary to what Ryan told the jurors, exactly two weeks before he shot and killed Doc, he indeed had a very *strong* interest in gold, and a very specific one. He had received a letter[216] from an attorney dated February 19, 1949. The letter was the perfect definition of the treasure trove laws, how it applied to the finder, what was necessary to claim any gold bullion found as a lost treasure and the legal process required to perfect title to the finder. But who wrote the letter? Whoever it was had sent Ryan a bill for $100: "PS You may send a check for $100 on corporation expenses with signed paper," the letter instructed. Ryan had gone to Newell on Doc's recommendation for the purpose of setting up a corporation; it was Doc who introduced Newell to Ryan, so there is little question remaining that Newell had in fact written the letter to Ryan concerning treasure trove. Ryan was far from home, he had been in town for only two weeks, he was a stranger to most everyone, and he had told Doc he wanted to start a corporation for the purpose of his business dealings with him. So Doc arranged for Ryan to meet Attorney Newell. The unsigned letter to Ryan about treasure trove read, *"It must be concealed underground—lost by reason of being buried and the owner having died or passed out of existence."* It also read, *"Certainly a method of determining this could be evolved in a proper court proceeding--otherwise title could never become perfected. That is a bridge that we could cross when we get to it, but not before."* Newell was Doc's legal advisor as well as a shareholder in the Cheyenne Mining Company, and so was William Scoggin. If anyone in the courtroom was up on the law concerning treasure trove claims, it was Newell and Scoggin because they were involved with Doc's treasure trove at Victorio Peak.

According to Ryan, though, Doc did not want to have his name on any corporate papers. Probably so, Doc already was corporately involved with other people who were associated with the Cheyenne Mining Company, in fact, with many individuals. In contrast to Ryan's inconsistent ramblings to the jury, he was lucid enough to tell the jury that Doc didn't want his name on any "corporate papers." This was a confession after the murder; if anyone knew Doc would have been in conflict with interest holders in the Cheyenne Mining Company if he dealt with another party regarding Victorio Peak gold, it was Newell and Scoggin. Newell was protecting himself and Scoggin, and it seems he had coached Ryan accordingly.

Whatever Ryan's motives were for seeking a legal opinion on treasure trove matters from Newell beyond what the letter actually said is not known, but one cannot avoid the feeling that his actions and that of Newell were suspicious at best. Ryan had a growing knowledge of gold and since he was on trial for Doc's murder there were two things he had to do: convince the jury he feared Doc was going to kill him, and make it seem he had no interest in acquiring any of Doc's gold; both avenues were approached vigorously by him. In the Douglas, Arizona/Hawley & Hawley matter, Ryan claimed that he explained to Doc that he didn't want any part of the gold business since he had been informed by Walters that having more than two ounces of "gold in your possession at any time was illegal." Ryan lied to the jury on many occasions and more lies would come.

What the jury did not know while Ryan was testifying about his lack of interest in Doc's gold, was that, while Ryan was still in jail, he instructed Lawrence to

approach Jack Woods to uncover the fifty-one bars Ryan had seen. Woods said, *"Jack Lawrence, Ryan's right-hand man, showed up and hired me to scrape* the surface for the gold bars buried east of the Rock House. I scraped an area about twenty-five feet by seventy feet. I made some passes, but never turned anything up. Lawrence didn't say much and went on his way."* So Ryan knew where Doc had buried the fifty-one gold bars.

Ryan testified that after he called J.L. Carlisle, his banker in Texas, he walked out of the drugstore across from Valley Motor Company where Doc and Jack Lawrence were waiting. Ryan said, "When I went outside, Noss asked me for the $350." I said, 'No, I'm not going to give you any money for that (meaning the money the El Paso man agreed on to rerun Doc's gold). That was our under-standing.' I said, 'You go out to the mine and tell the boys the hats didn't come in and for the boys to come in and come by my house for their checks. They went out.' Then Ryan went back across the street to Valley Motor Company. He said, "I went over to the filling station. I went by and paid some bills and

---

* Goat shed area that Woods scraped with his Caterpillar dozer (insert) is still visible today on GoogleEarth.

told those people we were going to discontinue operations and not to charge anything else to C.F. Ryan….That was the only station in town I had made such arrangements with."

Blake said that the time he and Doc were together at Valley Motors Friday night was about at 8:00, a 45-minute difference from what the gas station attendant had told Ryan, an acceptable margin since Blake was merely guessing when pressured by Ryan to give him a specific time on Saturday afternoon. What is interesting about the timing, which the service station attendant verified, is that when Tony Jolley drove up to the gas station, Doc wasn't at the pumps, but he was there *after* Jolley came out of the men's room. If the attendant was correct about what he told Ryan, namely that his Jeep and truck were the last two cars to come in, it meant that Jolley left *before* Doc pulled away, then Blake pulled in for gas. Then he said to the jury, "Well, that was a long ways from 11:00 o'clock." Ryan was referring back to his contention that Doc told him he had filled up at 11:00 and that he had seen Doc's truck parked in front of his house on Canal Street an hour and a half later at 12:30 a.m. Saturday morning, which in each case was a lie—Doc was in the desert with Tony Jolley; Ryan had lost track of what he had already told the jury.

Ryan continued, "So I also gave him instructions not to let anyone have any gasoline." He added, "When Jack Lawrence and Doc Noss came back from the mine, they went in this station to fill up with gasoline. The boy told him he couldn't put any gas in the truck unless I was there. Doc wanted to know why and the station attendant said, 'Mr. Ryan came by and told us not to charge anything else to him.'"

Based on Ryan's testimony, Doc and Lawrence drove over to Ryan's house from the filling station. Ryan said, "They came on to the house and we was sitting there discussing that and he (Doc) wanted to know the reason for it. I said, 'Doc, we have spent all the money I am going to spend up here. I have paid all the accounts and we are going back to Texas. I have called Mr. Carlisle and told him when we will be there, and we are going to leave today.' He said, 'What about the $350?' I said, 'I am not going to give you the $350. I have found out what kind of a man you are and I don't care to associate with you in any way, shape or form.' He said, 'I'm not going back to Texas, and that truck is not going back.' I said, 'Yes, the truck is going back, I don't care about you.' He said, 'Give me the $350 or I will kill you.' I said, 'You might kill me, but I am not going to give it to you.' Ryan said that at about that time, Mr. Blake drove up with the other boys in the Jeep. Blake came to the door and handed me the time book. I asked Mr. Harris to figure up the time so my wife could sign the checks. I wanted to talk to Blake. I asked Blake what time he filled up with gas Friday night. About that time, Noss came out the door. I was on the step. Noss stepped off of it. Doc said, 'God damn it, I told you what time we filled up, it was 11:00 o'clock.' I said, 'I didn't ask you what time you filled up.' Blake never did answer me, Noss started to the truck. The gun was on the drain board in the kitchen when I came in, I picked it up and stuck it in my pocket. I didn't want to leave it on the drain board or go out in the yard when Noss had threatened to kill me. Noss started walking towards the truck and I said, 'Doc, don't go to the truck.' He didn't stop. I kind of jumped sideways and got between him and the truck. That is when I put my hand in my pocket and took the pistol out. I said, 'You go in the house until we get our business straightened out.' He went in the house; I never did get to talk to Blake. We walked in the house. Noss was at one end of the table. I was standing with my back to the window. Lawrence was in the kitchen and I handed the gun to him as we went in." When Ryan got inside he told Noss he was not going to give him the money. Ryan said, "I have had all of the dealings with you I want to have, I am going to send and get the Deputy Sheriff and arrest you and I am going to send you to the penitentiary; you are nothing but a liar, a swindler and a thief."

Ryan claimed he was going to have Doc arrested for being a liar, a swindler and a thief. If his inference was that he had been lied to, swindled and robbed because Doc's estimate of the value of the lead claims were only half of what he said they were, he would have had a difficult time putting Doc in jail on that account, and Newell understood that to be true. He would have been better off having Doc arrested for threatening to kill him in front of witnesses, which according to Ryan, Doc had done on more than one occasion, or having him arrested for wanting to murder Claude Fincher, which Ryan also said happened in front of witnesses. Ryan also told the jury that, while they were still in Texas, Doc "began complimenting my business and said how well people spoke of me." Being the good businessman that Ryan had purported himself to be, he could have proceeded more cautiously and exercised a degree of due diligence without leaving his Texas business in jeopardy. Rather than do that, he plunged headlong into a new venture when he could have easily called the Land Office in Santa Fe and asked them for recommendations on how to have the lead claims assayed, thus determining their value in advance of making any investment decision.

Instead, Ryan left his business behind him, which he claimed "required his fulltime attention," visited with the New Mexico Attorney General and Assistant Attorney General and assured them that he didn't want to become "connected to" the treasure, and told them he came to New Mexico because he "felt sorry" for Doc. In an effort to make Doc feel better about himself, Ryan then returned to Texas, packed up his wife, his car, his Jeep, two friends, whom he referred to as associates, Doc and the new truck Ryan had bought for him, and headed for New Mexico after he admitted he had no idea about the mining business. Worse yet, he had already been to Santa Fe with Doc and failed to complete any due diligence then or have Doc checked out for his peaceable and law-abiding citizenship, his good reputation, truthfulness and veracity. Even more remarkable was that this all took place *after* Ryan bailed Doc out of jail, paid $289 for bad checks on Doc's behalf to his banker friend at the Bishop Bank, and then warned Doc that he couldn't work for him and "give hot checks or get drunk or not pay his bills because it wouldn't be tolerated."

When Ryan's entourage rolled into Hatch, all of course suffering from lead-fever, Doc got busy and handpicked five men in town to work at the lead mine. If the truth were known, Doc more than likely covered his end of the deal in Alice with one or more gold bars and collateralized the truck Ryan bought for him, and maybe he financed some of the expenses associated with the venture—maybe all of it; Ryan later admitted seeing "one of Doc's gold bars while he was still in Alice, Texas." What greater lure and incentive could there have been for Ryan to make such an expedition to New Mexico with men he referred to as business associates and a banker back in Texas who had a keen interest in what Ryan was doing financially? Was it a pot at the end of the rainbow filled with gold, or a pot filled with lead? Newell and Ryan cut and pasted a story together in advance in order to win at trial, knowing full well that nobody was going to be able to refute or contradict *anything* Ryan said regarding conversations he had with Doc.

Ryan was in trouble because he had murdered someone. He had to do something about his obvious lack of business prowess in the mining game he staged with Doc to cover the true intentions of coming to Victorio Peak—flying one ton of gold into Mexico for big profits. To avoid looking totally stupid and to allay suspicion as to why he had not been more prudent in his lead-mining venture, Ryan did his due diligence *after* he shot Doc, *after* he was released from jail on a capital murder case, *after* hiring Doc's business associate, Ben Newell, to defend him for killing his new business partner, Doc Noss.

Who had more information than J. Benson Newell did about Doc Noss? In addition to Newell, who was it that had lied, connived and cajoled to have Doc blamed for *five* other murders he never committed or was even suspected of committing? Who had possession of a laundry list of names and incidents that if all were poured on the courtroom floor would be enough to crush Doc and set Ryan free? There was only one person who could do that, someone directly associated with Newell, Scoggin, and Doc in an official capacity—the Executive Secretary of the Cheyenne Mining Company, the same person who on September 12, 1941, vowed in writing: "We are about to see the end of an Indian's pipe dream." That person was Merle Horzmann.

Ryan's testimony as to what happened inside his house grew more descriptive. He related comments Doc had made, comments heard only by those who had much to lose if Ryan went to prison, especially Ryan's wife and business associates. Ryan claimed that Noss ran out the door and said, "I will kill every one of you sons-of-bitches." Ryan told the jury, "My wife was present and Jack Lawrence was present." He said, "When I started out, I grabbed the gun from

Lawrence and went out and fired at him once and hollered to him to stop. He made no attempt to stop as he was starting around the truck to get to the glove compartment of the truck where I knew the pistol was. I fired the second shot and that is when he fell on the bumper."

Ryan told Newell, "He had threatened to kill me. I was afraid of him. He had already hit me in the house. He is quite a bit bigger than I am. He bragged about how many people he had killed. I didn't want to kill him, but I was trying to protect my family, my home life, my associates."

~

Jack Lawrence was the last person to testify. Lawrence was from Alice, Texas, and had known Ryan professionally and personally for five years and Ryan had employed him at his tool business in Alice for the last two years. It was on Ryan's second trip to New Mexico that Lawrence went with him on the mining venture. Lawrence testified that they had stayed in New Mexico for a month, and while he was there Ryan said that Doc had to make a trip to Douglas, Arizona, to see the assay firm of Hawley & Hawley to connect with Mr. Hawley who was willing to invest $50,000 in a mill to process Ryan's lead ore at the mining operation. Lawrence said that Ryan instructed him to tag along to "listen in on the discussion" between Hawley and Doc. Lawrence told the jury that he went to the meeting but very little was discussed; in fact, Lawrence said nothing about what he had heard in the discussion.

Lawrence then testified that on the day of the shooting he and Doc had driven out to the mine in the morning to inform the men to come to Hatch for their pay. Lawrence and Doc returned to Hatch and arrived there between 12:00 and 12:30 p.m. and drove directly to the filling station at Valley Motor Company, and then drove from there down Main Street toward Ryan's house. While on Main Street, Lawrence said that Doc told him to put his [Doc's] pistol in the glove compartment, which Lawrence claimed he did before they got to Ryan's house. When they arrived, Lawrence said that he could see that "Mrs. Ryan was lying down" and "Buck Harris was in the dining room figuring up" the paychecks, which Mrs. Ryan would then have to sign. It was then that Lawrence said that Doc wanted Ryan to give him the $350, but Ryan told Doc he wouldn't give it to him. Lawrence said, "Doc told Ryan he was going to get the money or he had to kill him and that if he didn't get the money he would be knocked out of $220,000." Lawrence's comment concerning Buck Harris being "in the dining room figuring up" the paychecks failed to explain how Buck Harris could have been "figuring up" anything without the time book that Willard Blake had not yet handed over to Ryan.

There were a lot of loose ends Newell used to defend Ryan, and what made Ryan's lies light up like a road flare on a foggy night was Tony Jolley, who remained an unknown quantity. Had he surfaced, and had it come out in court that Ryan and Noss were in fact partners in such a transaction, a strong motive would have been established for Ryan to kill Doc, not to mention Ryan's link with Newell, the same attorney who had advised him on matters of handling a gold treasure trove and the legal course to follow to perfect title to the gold.

The investigation into the murder of Doc Noss was not difficult to understand, nor was the plan to have Ryan and Lawrence lie by using valuable information most likely supplied to the defense team by Horzmann; once Tony Jolley's interview surfaced, looking back, it was plain to see when and why Ryan and Lawrence had lied, how often, and for what reasons. Had it not been for Jolley's taped interview, it would have been difficult to prove that Ryan or Lawrence had lied at the trial at all, but with Jolley's statement there was no reason to think that Ryan and Noss were not partners in a huge gold smuggling endeavor. The testimonies of Willard Blake, Ollan Brown, Pedro Nunez, and the Brizendine brothers alone were not enough to put Ryan in prison; those testimonies would have been weighed against Ryan's, Lawrence's, and Harris' testimonies, and even Mrs. Ryan's testimony had it become necessary to put her on the stand to testify—it would have been a standoff.

The counter balance in the trial was Newell's defense strategy: paint a picture of Noss the jury would accept as the truth, a picture that proved Ryan had every reason to suspect and fear that Doc was going to kill him had he been able to get to the truck and retrieve his handgun from the glove compartment. Without Tony Jolley's and Jack Woods' testimonies to prove that Ryan and Lawrence knew about the location of the fifty-one gold bars and that Ryan and Noss were in fact together on a huge gold deal, the prosecution had an uphill battle to keep Noss' reputation from being a formidable tool to prove Ryan was not acting in self-defense, had motive for killing him, and had not acted prudently in his business dealing with him in the lead mining project.

In any given trial, especially a murder trial, it is difficult to determine what any juror is thinking, especially in Ryan's case, a man who was an outsider, had no friends in the area and was involved with Doc Noss, who all the locals knew was involved with a gold treasure at Victorio Peak; the talk of gold travels fast, especially in a small town like Hatch, New Mexico. The notoriety that had attached itself to Doc and Ova Noss and their gold treasure trove at Victorio Peak was well known, *especially* in Hatch. It was common knowledge that Ova and her small work force were still laboring in the Hembrillo Basin to open the shaft that led to the treasure. Suddenly Doc Noss is back on the scene, he and his new wife take up residency on Canal Street, the gossip starts, strangers arrive and take up residency closer to the center of town, Doc hires five men, locals who become information sources, five men who have a dozen friends and relatives, they begin to talk, the word gets out—*Doc Noss is after the treasure*, the news travels faster, picking up speed, men shuffle back and forth from Victorio Peak, something is happening there, day after day the men come and go from the Peak. One of the local gathering spots in town, Valley Auto Company, is tending to the needs of Ryan's vehicles, now word had spread throughout the entire community, all of Hatch is waiting for the good news—lead.

From the start, J. Benson Newell saw the benefits of being Ryan's defense attorney; he knew all about Doc Noss, Ova Noss and the gold treasure inside Victorio Peak and the treasure trove laws that wrapped around the entire matter— and he had a personal financial interest in it, as did Scoggin. Newell and Scoggin attended to any and all of the legal matters for the Cheyenne Mining Company. Newell and Scoggin were in a win-win position: they would each learn a lot of information about the gold transaction Ryan and Doc had going on between them and Newell would get paid for his efforts to defend Ryan in the process; whether or not Ryan went to the New Mexico State Penitentiary or went back to Alice, Texas was irrelevant. The trick was to keep the shades pulled down on the jury until the end, hopefully to spring Ryan on the murder charge.

No matter how they painted the picture, Ryan could easily have been seen as a treasure hunter, a seeker of gold, and Doc Noss, the most celebrated treasure hunter the Southwest had ever known, was his partner. Newell had a lot of ground to travel and a lot of tracks to hide. Considering those obstacles, Newell needed something more convincing than the testimonies of those who had attested to Doc's sub-par reputation. Newell knew Ryan was the vessel to deliver the evangel of Doc's bad reputation; someone who could persuasively explain why, how, and under what circumstances Ryan came to New Mexico, the best and only person to convince the jury he was not the bad guy; therefore, Newell was compelled to put him on the stand. That meant Newell had to overhaul the motivating truth that he was working with Doc Noss on a gold treasure deal.

Ryan's testimony had to systematically track every element involving his association with Noss from the time he met him in Alice, Texas, up to and including the moment Ryan shot and killed him. The facts of the case that demanded overhauling were: 1) the payment of bad checks on Doc's behalf, 2) having seen one of Doc's gold bars while he was still in Alice, Texas, 3) buying a new truck for a man Ryan knew bounced checks, didn't pay his bills, and had a drinking problem, 4) the fact that he had made two trips to New Mexico to check Land Office records in Santa Fe, 5) the reason Ryan admitted he checked the prospecting claims of Section 16 where the treasure was located, 6) why Ryan left his thriving business behind him without pursuing a course of due diligence in a venture he admitted he knew nothing about, 7) why he drove to New Mexico with the hope of fame and fortune in a lead-mining expedition with a man he knew from the onset was a treasure hunter, 8) doing business with a man who was arrested while Ryan was buying him a new truck, 9) doing business with a man Ryan admitted had lied to him, yet continued with him in an expensive and risky business enterprise, 10) explaining away his rationale for sending Lawrence to Douglas, Arizona to look over Doc's shoulder and listen to the conversation he had with Mr. Hawley, 11) explaining why Lawrence and Doc went to El Paso to get a price on what it would cost to "rerun" the $220,000 in gold Ryan had revealed he knew about, and to explain why Ryan had such knowledge of the smelting costs and the pick up and delivery schedule for the gold that was to be taken to Hawley in Douglas, and finally, 12) explaining away the total lack of any information born out of Lawrence's trip to Douglas, Arizona to investigate the $50,000 mill, which Hawley was going to invest in to process Ryan's lead ore.

More important than all of those things together, Newell had to convince an entire town that Doc Noss and Charley F. Ryan were not after gold—and that they were only interested in *lead*. Ryan and Lawrence had to deliver a seamless and believable story to counteract all of these events in such a way that the jury would suck it up. That, and combined with the witnesses against Doc's character, Newell hoped to be victorious. To do all of this, Ryan and Lawrence had to lie endlessly in order to keep Ryan out of prison for murder and Lawrence from being Ryan's cellmate for committing perjury. Their safety net was that Doc's reputation preceded him, and whatever Ryan was able to get on the record that dealt with Doc's alleged threats to kill him could be casually linked to his claim of self-defense in the eyes of the jury.

To be a good liar one must have a good memory. To be an excellent liar one must have an excellent memory, and there was a lot of lying to do. Ryan murdered Doc Noss in cold blood, and it might have been premeditated as well. Ryan lied to the jury concerning the many factors involved with his relationship with Doc—and so did Jack Lawrence; they were on a roll and the plan was slowly unfolding. Ryan told the jury that he sent Doc on a business trip to Douglas to transact a $50,000 deal for a mill to handle the ore at the lead mine he was working near Victorio Peak, and for whatever reason, Ryan sent Lawrence with him to *listen in*. On the Tuesday before he killed Doc, Ryan didn't go to the mine; he said he stayed home because Mrs. Ryan was ill. According to Ryan's testimony, Doc came to him the following day and said he wanted to go to Douglas, Arizona, that he knew someone who would "put in a $50,000 mill to take care of the ore." Ryan testified that's when he sent Jack Lawrence along to "listen to the conversation." Lawrence and Doc came back from Hawley & Hawley on Thursday, but Ryan said he didn't talk to Doc about the trip until the "day of the murder."

Here's where Ryan's bad memory kicked in. According to Ryan's own testimony, he said that on the day he killed Doc, which was Saturday, Ryan talked with Doc not long before he killed him. Ryan said, "After Doc had come back from Arizona" he told him about his "conversation with Mr. Hawley in Douglas" with "respect to selling him $220,000 worth of gold he claimed he had *hidden out there somewhere*." The next logical question to ask is what happened to the $50,000 Mr. Hawley was going to put up for the mill to process Ryan's lead ore? It was another lie by Ryan, which Lawrence inadvertently exposed. That is why Newell objected to Prosecutor Watkins' question to Lawrence. Watkins asked Lawrence, "Can you tell me, or tell the jury, what connection this $350.00 has to do with Blake's story about the Jeep?"

> *NEWELL: If the Court pleases, I don't think that question is proper.*
> *WATKINS: What's wrong with it?*
> *NEWELL: That's for the jury to decide.*
> *WATKINS: The witness was stating what he heard.*

~

Scoggin had allowed just about everything Newell asked the witnesses to go on the record, even the testimony from Newell's own witness when the jury wasn't even in the courtroom. Scoggin, by now, was at sea with all of the lies being told.

> *THE COURT: Go ahead. Answer.*

~

One can imagine how Newell might have cringed; he objected because Pandora's box might have been opened and if the prosecution honed in on how Lawrence responded, it could have spelled trouble. Watkins and Lawrence's Q. & A. follow:

> *A. Well, he [Doc] wanted to run hot gold with it.*
> *Q. What did that have to do with the $350?*
> *A. It takes money to do something with it [the gold].*
> *Q. What was the $350 to be used for?*
> *A. To be given to the man in the mint - smelter - or whatever it is.*

~

Unfortunately, and for whatever reason, Watkins didn't take his line of questioning any further and turned to the issue of the handguns. Regardless, nothing was ever mentioned by Lawrence about the $50,000 mill to process the lead, simply because the trip to Douglas had nothing to do with lead; it had everything to do with gold. Lawrence had only made it worse because Ryan had already said, "After Noss had come back from Arizona" he told him about his "conversation with Mr. Hawley in Douglas" with "respect to selling him *$220,000 worth of gold he claimed he had hidden out there somewhere.*"

Because of Lawrence's and Ryan's poor memories and Newell's poor coaching, Ryan revealed that he knew that Doc had gold "hidden out there somewhere." It meant that he and Lawrence were lying and knew the location of the fifty-one bar cache and that Doc had moved the bars. It was the only reason Ryan and Lawrence went to the desert Friday night, and it was the sole reason that while Ryan was still in jail he sent Lawrence to Jack Woods to bull-doze the exact area where Doc had shown them he had hidden the fifty-one bars. The only problem was that much to Jack Woods' surprise, he was never called as a witness; had that happened, Newell's house of cards would have tumbled, not to mention what would have happened if Tony Jolley walked into the courtroom—but Woods wasn't and Jolley didn't.

Jack Lawrence's testimony contrasted greatly with everything Ryan and he swore to as fact. Lawrence said, "So Blake and them came up [on or close to the porch] and Mr. Ryan went outside to talk to Blake." Lawrence claimed he was in the kitchen standing by the refrigerator and that he "heard Ryan ask Blake what time he got in and what time he filled up. Ryan wanted to know where the Jeep was all night." Lawrence then claimed, "We made a trip out to that canyon to find it. We didn't know but what maybe they were out there stuck or something."

The following is Lawrence's testimony covering the time when Ryan killed Doc: Lawrence said Ryan went outside to talk to Blake and asked him what time he got in and he heard Doc say, "God damn it, I told you what time they gassed up." That is when, according to Lawrence, Ryan said, "Go back into the house." Lawrence said that Doc came in first and Ryan came in, "then gave me the gun" and Doc and Ryan went into the living room. Lawrence claimed he was at the kitchen door to the living room and that he had "a clear view of both men in the dining room." Lawrence said, "I heard part of what they said" and that Doc insisted on getting the money, and Ryan told him "we're going home, you lied to us, cheated us out of everything we've got and we're going home."

Things began to heat up. Lawrence claimed Ryan said, "I am going to send Jack after the law and I am going to send you to the penitentiary." It was then Lawrence said that Doc struck Ryan causing him to fall "into the window." From the trial transcript:

> *Q. Then what did Doc do?*
> *A. He ran out of the house and he said, "I will kill every son-of-a-bitching one of you."*
> *Q. What happened when Doc ran out?*
> *A. Mr. Ryan grabbed the gun out of my hand and went out on the porch and said, "Doc don't go to that truck."*
> *Q. What did Doc do?*
> *A. He kept running.*
> *CROSS EXAMINATION OF JACK LAWRENCE BY MR. WATKINS*
> *Q. You heard Doc Noss say, "I will kill every one of you sons-of-bitches"?*
> *A. Yes.*
> *Q. Then [he] ran out by you?*
> *A. He came by me.*
> *Q. Did you do anything to stop him when he came by you?*
> *A. No, sir.*
> *Q. Did you consider you were included in the threat?*

A. Yes, sir.

Q. You didn't point the gun at him?

A. No, sir.

Q. You just stood there?

A. I suppose I did.

Q. And watched him go out the door.

A. Yes, sir.

Q. And go toward that pickup?

A. That's right.

Q. Did you know where he was going?

A. Sure, I knew where he was going.

Q. You didn't try to stop him?

A. Well, I was scared, wouldn't you have been?

Q. You were scared?

A. Sure I was.

Q. Now, I believe you said just like that (and you snapped your fingers) the whole thing took place.

A. That's right.

Q. I believe you testified on your direct that Mrs. Ryan was in one of the bedrooms on the bed.

A. I don't know, she was feeling bad, and I'm sure she was lying down when we got to the house.

Q. How soon after Noss and Ryan passed by did Mrs. Ryan pass by you?

A. Well, it wasn't too long.

Q. He [Ryan] ran outside too?

A. Yes.

Q. You were still standing in front of the refrigerator?

A. I caught Mrs. Ryan as she came out the door.

Q. Did you go outside with her, or did she go outside alone?

A. Yes, sir, we both went outside.

Q. On the stoop or on the ground?

A. I was out there. Then when Mrs. Ryan came out I heard her hollering.

Q. You were outside?

A. On the porch.

Q. When she came out she didn't say anything?

A. No, sir.

Q. Didn't open her mouth?

A. Only said not to shoot.

Q. There is something new. She said not to shoot him?

A. She said, "Don't shoot."

Q. Are you sure she didn't say, "Shoot him again?"

A. She did not.

Q. Or "Shoot the son-of-a-bitch again?"
A. She did not.
Q. Just the one phrase, "Don't shoot?"
A. Yes.

~

Lawrence continued with his description of the shooting. He said that Ryan fired one shot and claimed that Ryan said, "Doc, don't go to that truck." He then claimed that, "Doc kept running."

Q. Did Ryan say, "Get out from under there, you son-of-a-bitch?"
A. He didn't say it. He said, "Get up."
Q. After the second shot?
A. Two shots had been fired.
Q. Noss was already lying across the bumper when he said that?
A. Now, I don't know. I had a hold of his wife at that time.

~

Lawrence said, "Then Ryan shot Doc. I then heard Mrs. Ryan scream. Doc was dead."

Q. You didn't go to the pickup for the gun before the shooting?
A. I sure didn't.
Q. You knew it was there?
A. I knew it was there.
Q. Were you afraid to do that?
A. Well, yes and no. I didn't want to go out and get the gun.
Q. Why didn't you want to go out and get the gun?
A. I didn't have no right to go get the gun.

~

Lawrence told Watkins that while everyone was still in the house, he became afraid after Doc "started out there," but he was not afraid before that. After Doc "knocked Charley down" and ran outside, Lawrence said he "knew he was going for the gun." While this was happening, which according to Lawrence happened at the snap of a finger, he was still holding Ryan's gun and Doc was unarmed and bolted out the door.

Q. At that point you became afraid he might be going for the gun?
A. I knew he was going for the gun.
Q. But you did nothing to stop him?
A. No, sir.

~

The following is an accurate breakdown and comparison of the lopsided testimonies presented by Ryan to the jury and Lawrence's presentation to the jury of his recollection of the same events compared to that of five solid eye-witnesses who had a front row seat from Ryan's Jeep. They had been sitting there watching the events unfold from the moment Blake pulled up in front of

Ryan's house* until the lead started flying, five men who testified to everything they heard and saw up to and including the moment Doc was dead. These were Ryan and Doc's workers, people who had no vested interest in the affairs of Noss, Ryan, Lawrence, Harris or Ryan's wife; they were only interested in being paid for the work they had done during the week and nothing else. None of them were from Texas, none of them were associated with Ryan prior to his coming to Hatch, and none of them had any financial interest in the lead mining operation. They were laborers from Hatch that Doc had hired for Ryan to work at the lead mine site: Willard Blake, Ollan Brown, Pedro "Pete" Nunez, and the Brizendine brothers.

Blake said he stopped the Jeep in front of Ryan's house and got out while the other men remained in the Jeep. He walked toward the house on the walkway that led from the street straight to the front door. When he got to the house, Charley Ryan, Doc Noss, and Buck Harris stepped outside onto the front porch in that order. It was then that Blake handed the time book to Harris and he took it inside. Ryan asked Blake about the Jeep and who gave him permission to use it. Blake told Ryan that he used the Jeep due to a broken spring in his car. Ryan then asked him where the Jeep was that night and what time was it when he gassed up Friday night. Blake told him that he was at the Valley Auto Company, later saying under cross-examination he had *guessed* that it was about 8:00 that night when he gassed up. Ryan then asked Blake what time he came back with it on Friday night. Blake said that he didn't tell Ryan the time because he didn't know what time it was when he got back. Blake said that Doc tried to butt in and answer and was about to tell Ryan when Ryan suddenly removed a hand gun from his pocket, pulled the hammer back and pointed it directly at Noss' back. Ryan then ordered Doc "to get in the house." Blake said that he stepped back and Ryan "marched him in the house." Then Ryan followed Doc inside, still pointing the gun at him. He heard them "arguing and talking very loud," but he claimed that he could not detect what was being said. Blake said he stood there for a few minutes and then returned to the Jeep and stood beside it and that he could see Ryan by the dining room window and that he had a white shirt on and a gray pair of pants and that Ryan's back was against the window. He "had not been at the Jeep

---

* Ryan's rented house at 459 Jefferson Street in Hatch, New Mexico. Years later, the front porch was enclosed and an addition was made to the kitchen and the living room.

but a few minutes when he heard the window go out" and that it was Ryan going against the window that broke it out. About the same time he heard the window break, he saw Noss running out of the house and Ryan came running out behind Doc. Ryan's wife came running out next, followed by Buck Harris and *then* Jack Lawrence. When he saw Ryan, he "was armed with the .38 caliber revolver." It was at this point that Blake said the first shot was fired at Doc while he was fleeing and that Ryan had shot at Doc when Ryan got to the corner of the porch stoop. Blake said he was not watching Doc at that instant and was watching Ryan. After the first shot, Ryan stepped on the ground and hollered, "Come out from under there, you son-of-a-bitch." Then Ryan's wife hollered, "Shoot that son-of-a-bitch." Blake said he was standing at the Jeep when Ryan fired the second shot. He said, "Ollan, Pete and me and the two Brizendines ran west, afraid Ryan might shoot us next." He ended his testimony by saying, "He saw no other firearm other than the one used by Ryan."

Ollan Brown said that Blake handed the time book to Jack Lawrence and then Lawrence and Harris went inside. Except for that variation, his testimony was identical to that of Blake's, the main points being that he saw Ryan pull a gun from his pocket, point at Doc's back, and lead Doc back into the house. He heard the window break out in the "little dining room" and then saw Doc run from the house and Ryan run out after him. Mrs. Ryan came out next. Ryan stepped out on the stoop and shot at Doc. He then heard Ryan say, "Get up from there, you son-of-a-bitch." After the first shot he heard Mrs. Ryan say, "Shoot that son-of-a-bitch again." Ryan was out in the yard when he fired the second shot at Doc. Then Brown said, "We got out of there and run like hell." Pedro "Pete" Nunez gave a nearly identical account of the story given by Brown and Blake. William and Edward Brizendine's accounts were a mirror image of the others' testimonies as well.

The major conflicts in Ryan's testimony were:

1) He claimed Doc said, "I told you what time we filled up, it was 11:00 o'clock." None of the five witnesses ever heard such a statement.

2) Ryan said that Blake never answered him. Blake testified that he told Ryan he didn't know what time it was when he got back, that he used the Jeep due to a broken spring in his car and that he gassed up at the Valley Auto Company and later under cross-examination said he guessed it to be at 8:00 p.m.

3) Ryan said that during the conversation on the porch, Noss started "walking towards the truck" and Ryan said, "Doc, don't go to the truck." The five independent witnesses said everything happened on the porch and none of them testified that Ryan made such a statement.

4) Then Ryan testified that Doc "didn't stop, he kept walking" and that he "kind of jumped sideways and got between him and the truck." None of the five independent witnesses testified that ever happened.

5) Ryan said that is when "I put my hand in my pocket and took the pistol out." The five independent witnesses said Ryan pulled the gun on Doc while he was on the porch.

6) Ryan testified that Doc ran out the door and said, "I will kill every one of you sons-of-bitches." None of the five independent witnesses said they heard Doc say anything.

7) Ryan admitted that he said, "Get up from there you son-of-a-bitch," but claimed he made that comment after he had fired the second shot. All five witnesses said that comment by Ryan was made *between* the first and second shot.

8) On one occasion during his testimony Ryan said he wasn't paying any attention to his wife, meaning he hadn't heard her say anything. Later in testimony Ryan was asked, "You don't recall anyone telling you to shoot him again?" Ryan responded, "No, sir, I don't. I won't say my wife didn't say that. I didn't hear it, and I wouldn't blame her if she did say it." Yet, all five witnesses heard Mrs. Ryan holler, "Shoot that son-of-a-bitch."

Major conflicts were also created by Jack Lawrence related to his testimony regarding what was said by whom when Ryan shot and killed Doc.

9) When asked if Mrs. Ryan said anything when she came out, Lawrence said she didn't say anything, only "Don't shoot." However, all five witnesses heard Mrs. Ryan holler, "Shoot that son-of-a-bitch."

10) When Lawrence was asked during the course of the shooting if he had heard Ryan say, "Get up from under there, you son-of-a-bitch," Lawrence said, "He didn't say it, he said, 'Get up.'" Even Ryan told the jury he *had* made that comment. Ryan claimed he said, "Get up from there, you son-of-a-bitch." All five witnesses heard Ryan say, "Get up from there you, son-of-a-bitch."

11) Lawrence testified that Ryan had made the same comment after the *second* shot. All five witnesses said the comment was made after the *first* shot.

Newell never called Mrs. Ryan or Buck Harris to testify. Then, after Ryan knew that he had shot and killed Doc, among the last things he said under cross-examination were characteristic of the illogical, weak and unpersuasive testimony:

Q. Then you said, "Get up from there."
A. Yes, sir.
Q. You had already fired both shots?
A. Yes, sir, when I fired the last shot is when he fell. I never shot a gun before in my life. I was lucky to hit him, but I think it was an act of God.

~

All of the witnesses gave identical accounts of what they saw, while Ryan and Lawrence's testimonies were nothing less than a scattering of lies, lies poorly thought out, most likely told to the jury with Newell's knowledge and consent. Newell had dealt directly with Ryan prior to the murder, had filed corporation papers on his behalf, and he was probably the attorney who advised Ryan legally concerning treasure trove requirements to gain clear title. Again, the complete letter[217]:

> *Dear Mr. Ryan:*
>
> *Regarding "treasure trove" New Mexico has no statute on this matter—hence the State acquires no title to any portion of such treasure and the finder becomes the owner, subject to title of the "true owner". It must be concealed under ground—lost by reason of being buried and the owner having died or passed out of existence. Such treasure is usually defined as gold or silver bullion. Should such treasure be found it could then be determined by proper action in a court whether the real owner could be found and if not the title become[s] perfected in the finder. Certainly a method of determining this could be evolved in a proper court proceeding, --otherwise title could never become perfected. That is a bridge that we could cross when we get to it but not before.*
>
> *Hope this serves your question.*
>
> *Sincerely,*
>
> *PS You may send a check for $100 on corporation expense with signed paper.*

~

Ryan and Scoggin were in bed with Doc Noss and the treasure when they acted as Doc's legal representatives, especially when they had filed the corporation papers for The Cheyenne Mining Company, Doc's company, to which Newell admitted in his affidavit[218] as to his involvement, not to mention the fact they would share 3% of the proceeds when and if the treasure was lifted.

Many of the criminal attorneys and state and local law enforcement officers had testified in great detail how often Doc carried a gun, how proficient and accurate he was at using one, that he had threatened to kill people on many occasions, that he was a bad guy, that he was arrested for acts of violence associated with being drunk and abusive while armed and was imprisoned because of the gun-waving incident in Roswell, New Mexico. But not *once* was Doc Noss ever accused of or arrested for shooting anyone. On the other hand, Ryan, who said he "never shot a gun before in his life," killed Doc Noss on his first outing. It seemed the jurors had stopped listening. After the state concluded its case, the jury was instructed on verdict choices which were first-degree murder with life imprisonment, second-degree murder, manslaughter, or not guilty and then were dismissed to decide Ryan's fate. They returned a verdict of not guilty—justifiable homicide.

Ova said, "While I was selling insurance I ran into several valley farmers who told me that they had been asked what they would take [money wise] to sit on the jury. Those people, not only one but also four or five, told the same story of being asked to sit on the jury. Ryan got a verdict of killing in self-defense, but Doc had no gun, and was running away."

July 13, 1949

The early summer months were difficult for Ova; she had to open the shaft that led to the treasure and do it alone and by July, many of the workers who had stayed behind after Doc's murder slowly drifted away from the camp. Even those people who had helped Ova financially with the needed excavation work had left. Ova Noss was alone, depressed and unable to do the work on her own, so she returned to Hot Springs and took a job as a waitress at the Elite Café in town until she could work things out. And if her problems were not enough, Donn Clippinger, Mining Engineer, wrote[219] to E.C. Anderson, Director of New Mexico's Bureau of Mines and Mineral Resources on July 13, 1949:

> *On July 7, as instructed, I visited Hot Springs and Victoria Peak in Hembrillo Canyon to determine the progress being made in the search for the 'Noss treasure caverns.'*
>
> *In Hot Springs I talked with Jim Shull who, together with Dr. William Coucher and Mr. Mosley, had been financing and working on the project. Mr. Shull reported that they have abandoned the search completely. They have decided that there are no caverns on the property, merely fissures that do not form large rooms as had been described to them. They followed up several of the stories that had been told to them by Mrs. Ova Noss and found that none of the tales could be substantiated. Shull and his associates concluded that there is no truth in the whole story of the treasure, caverns or mine and cancelled their contract early in June.*
>
> *Mrs. Noss is now working as waitress at the Elite Café in Hot Springs. Since being deserted by her other partners, she has had some exploring done on the peak by a couple of young men living in Hot Springs. According to her reports, she has had five men 'working' on the property and two most of the time. When we visited Victoria Peak we found that no one had been on the property for several days (since the previous rain) and that very little excavation work, if any, has been done in the past month. The fissures that had been cleaned out were of no great extent or depth.*
>
> *Personally, I am fully convinced that the entire Noss tale is a complete fabrication.*
>
> *—Donn Clippinger, Mining Engineer*

~

On August 1, E.C. Anderson wrote[220] to State Land Commissioner, Guy Shepard, and recommended no extension of Ova's "present lease be considered." Commissioner Shepard, who became sympathetic with Ova's troubles at the treasure site, extended the lease in spite of Anderson's recommendation.

Ova Noss was a prisoner in her own dilemma and Ryan was free. On October 8, 1949, he went to Sheriff "Happy" Apodaca, and retrieved his six-shooter.[221] By November, and in the face of her hardships, Ova Noss applied to the State Land Office for a mining permit at Victorio Peak, but it was not granted.

November 15, 1949

Merle Horzmann was having her own problems. On November 15, 1949, she wrote a letter[222] (jointly) to E. Forest Sanders, R.C. Garland, and Mrs. Beatrice

Mitchell-Gossett. It is not clear who these people were, but they could have been attorneys. In her letter, Horzmann complained that a man named B.J. Ward had stolen a manuscript from her personal files and *"took it to your offices,"* an indication that Sanders, Garland & Mitchell-Gossett was a law firm. Horzmann wrote: (underlining inserted)

> *Sometime between July 26 and August 10, 1949, B.J. Ward took a manuscript out of my files, and admitted it, without my knowledge and consent, with the view of having it investigated by the Doña Ana County Grand Jury. This contains better than 83 pages, and is titled "The Great San Andres Treasure. ...<u>There were Supplementary sections of it containing history and notes and possibilities.</u>"*

> ～

Horzmann contended that the manuscript belonged to "an estate" and urged to have it returned to her, and wrote that the people "whose names were mentioned [in the manuscript] were the real owners," but that she in particular was also an owner of the manuscript and that its removal from her files was "with malicious intent." Then she explained the issue of the manuscript belonging to an estate:

> *It also belongs partially to the estate of M.E. Noss, deceased, as per records in Doña Ana Probate Court, but it does not yet appear on the Inventory due to its incompleteness. It is however a record of the case, and has nothing to do with anything B.J. Ward may be interested in whatsoever. He took it unlawfully, and further delay in its return is not desirable, and I am sure no one else would want it.*   —Merle Horzmann

> ～

Apparently Ward felt that a grand jury needed to look at what he had found in Horzmann's papers to the extent that he stole them from her for that purpose. Was Ward convinced that what he had seen in Horzmann's records was sufficient enough to convene a grand jury, but for what reason? Doc was dead and Ryan was acquitted.

The summer had come and gone and Ova Noss was alone with a lot on her mind to contemplate in the New Year, 1950, and, apart from Horzmann's self-generated dilemma over the stolen manuscript, other matters began to develop, matters of which Horzmann and Ova were unaware. The subject matter was gold, not the gold Ova and Doc had discovered, but another kind of gold with a different provenance—Nazi Gold. As in Horzmann's case, someone else had stolen something, too. A 1950 report written by Bavarian State Police Chief Michael Freiherr von Godin revealed that "advancing Americans" had found gold that had been seized by the Nazis and took "possession" of it shortly before WWII ended in Europe. Then the gold suddenly disappeared. Later a German newspaper cited the report and claimed that the "GIs Swiped Nazi Gold."

Chapter 27

Events after the Verdict

A slight glimmer of hope arrived with the new year when more information surfaced that could potentially validate the truth about the Victorio Peak treasure. On December 28, 1949, a man named Lloyd Waterhouse met with an old friend, Attorney J.O. Ehlinger, in Houston, Texas, concerning a matter that related to gold bars that Doc had left in a bank there. In the course of following up on their meeting, Ehlinger wrote to Waterhouse to confirm the substance of their conversation. His January 9, 1950 letter,[223] in part:

> It is my understanding three (3) bars of gold and one (1) solid gold statue was brought from New Mexico to a bank in Texas by Mr. Noss, and that this bank had agreed to lend him some money on this, but at the last minute refused to lend him the money or return these articles to him.
>
> It is my opinion, if proof of the above matter can be had, that these items or the value thereof can be recovered from the bank.　　　　　—Ehlinger

~

Less than two weeks later Waterhouse wrote to Ova and provided more information about the gold. Waterhouse's letter,[224] in part:

> …I asked him [Ehlinger] what the chances were to recover the gold or the value of same that you and Doc had left in a bank in Texas and he told me that he was sure that he could and I had him write me a letter so that I could show you, so I am enclosing it in this letter.

~

Ova had told the family, and specifically Letha and Terry, that Doc had removed a solid gold statue of the Virgin Mary from inside Victorio Peak. Ova and Doc had delivered the statue and three large bars of gold to a banker in Laredo, Texas or El Paso, the exact bank that held the items has been lost in time, but there were also two bars of gold in Del Rio, Texas at the Val Verde National Bank. The balance of Ehlinger's letter dealt with another matter and another individual who had expressed an interest in a business proposition with Ova concerning the possibility of opening the shaft. Although the man's name is not mentioned in Waterhouse's letter, his name was Duc d'Atri, Prince D'Aragon. When the scent of gold was in the air, anyone from a pauper to a prince advanced himself or herself to get in on the action. More from Waterhouse's letter:

> I wrote you on December 16 and mentioned to you that if you cared to and would send me that name and address of the man that had a proposition here in Texas (Houston) that required eight hundred dollars to handle, that I would check into it for

you and ourselves and see if it had any merit to it, and if it did would try to work out a satisfactory deal for you and ourselves.

And will appreciate it very much if you will drop us a few lines and let us know if the deal that we discussed is like we left it so that we can arrange our business to get there as soon as it is possible for us to.   *—Lloyd Waterhouse.*

March 6, 1950

One of the individuals who arrived at the Peak was Seraphin Sedillo, claiming he had valuable information. Another person, a man of means, claimed he was interested in developing a business deal with Ova. From the writings* of Ova Noss—abridged:

One year and one day after the death of Doc Noss, Seraphin Sedillo appeared at my house and said he knew all about going into the cave. It so happened that Bill Lampros was in town. Bill and I talked it over and decided to grubstake him and send him out. He was four days getting out there, got lost and couldn't find the canyon. I went out there on the fifth day and he had just gotten in there the night before, so I called my sons in and hired another fellow to go out and help him. We all came to the opinion in the matter of two weeks that Seraphin didn't know as much about it as we did.

Harold Mounce from Santa Fe came down. On the third week that he was out there, Seraphin told me that Mounce told him that I did not have anything in there; that the finder was the owner, and that I was going to be beaten out of it. So I refused to work with him or tell him anything more. We had a meeting in Santa Fe; following that, Merle had a recording machine and took Harold Mounce's testimony and his recording said that he was convinced that the Mexican did not know anything. I told him the story of the Mexican and he cussed him out.

While Seraphin was still staying out there, another party by the name of Duke d'Atri, Prince d'Aragon, from Texas came out. He was considering opening it up. The place looked deserted and we drove up on the hill in my car and Seraphin came up the west side on horseback, pulled a 30-30 rifle on us and tried to run us off of the hill. Seraphin slapped himself on the chest and said, 'Doc Noss is dead. I'm the big shot now.' I out-talked him on the gun by telling him to get his things ready and let's go to town and get drunk, knowing that he would rather get drunk than anything else. He got drunk and we never took him back out to the mine. When cotton-picking time came no one was financing Seraphin, so he went down by Anthony to pick cotton.

I made a deal with Raymond Robinson in the meantime. The Mexican heard of it some way or other and drove into the basin with wagon and team. Then the Mexican and his wife camped at the rock house and talked himself into a job working for Robinson, gave him stories as to how he had helped Doc Noss explore. He had never been down any further than the second room, he said he stood there when Doc Noss brought back three bars of gold bullion and helped him carry them out. After he got Robinson believing he was on the wrong foot dealing with me, Robinson pulled out without ever notifying me.

      —Babe

* O. Noss, **op. cit.**, pp.1, 2.

March 30, 1950

By now, Letha had remarried; she was now Letha Kipper. It was Letha who generated Duc d'Atri's* interest in the treasure. On March 30, he wrote[225] to her in Hot Springs:

> *Dear Madam: I have been in contact with Mr. Lloyd Waterhouse of Burnet, who came to see me in order to make a project for financing the exploration of the mine, which your father seemed to have discovered ever since 1937. From what I gather, I can see that your mother, Mrs. Ova Noss has the lease and the mining permit.*
>
> *I would be very much obliged to you and your mother, if by return Air Mail you would let me know in which standing you are in this business with Mr. Waterhouse, in other words: Do you have any agreement with him? In case you have an agreement, is it for the exploration or search on the mine? Are you protected with regard to your right on the lease and the mining permit?*
>
> *I wished you would be frank with me, because I have to consider the possibility or not of advancing capital for this business, but for the moment I do not see anything positive in it besides what had been told me by Mr. Waterhouse. The sooner you answer my letter the better it will be for the sake of the business. I want you to understand, that being asked to finance a business, it is only natural that I come right to the source to request information. It is for this reason that I request you to keep this letter confidential between yourself, your mother and myself.*
>
> *Thanking you in advance for your reply, I am sincerely yours.   — Duke d'Atri*

~

Whether or not Letha had a business connection to the Duke in unknown, but judging from his letterhead it seems that Prince D'Aragon (the Duke) was actually Prince Ludovic Pignatelli of Aragon, grandson of Count Alfred Gaston De La Rochefoucauld, one of the most respected members of the noble aristocrats in Paris, as reported in an article[226] by *The New York Times* on July 4, 1912. Rochefoucauld's wife was the former Mattie Mitchell,† who was the daughter of the United States Senator from Oregon, John H. Mitchell. The headline from the same article read: 'Spanish Nobleman, Who Courted Miss Mary Duke, Shoots Himself in Paris." The account, which was transmitted over the "Marconi Transatlantic Wireless Telegraph" on July 3, told that Prince Ludovic was suffering from a near fatal case of moonstruckitis. The article read, in part:

> *According to the usually well-informed Excelsior, the Prince Ludovic Pignatelli-d'Aragon, a grandson of Count Gaston De La Rochefoucauld and well known in Paris society, attempted to kill himself in his apartment in the Avenue Kléber last evening.*

~

The story was that Ludovic had shot himself in the chest, but the bullet struck a rib and exited his back. His attempt at suicide resulted from a love

---

* "Duc" is the Spanish for "Duke." D'Atri used "Duke" at the bottom of his letter.
† Her true name was Marie Elizabeth Mitchell; her nickname was *Mattie*.

affair gone wrong because of religious differences. According to another *New York Times* article[227] published decades later on May 4, 1941, Ludovic was sent to prison for attempting to extort $500,000 from his cousin, whose wife was Henrietta Hartford, whose family controlled the Great Atlantic and Pacific Tea Company, the A&P food stores.

After his release from prison, Ludovic became interested in treasure hunting and built an estate in Houston, Texas. It was shortly after Doc was killed that Letha began receiving telegrams from Ludovic, claiming that he became aware of the Victorio Peak treasure from news articles in Europe and that he had discovered records in Spain that confirmed the treasure and its location. For months, Ludovic sent telegrams to Letha. Then, on March 30, 1950, he finally wrote to her about his meeting with Lloyd Waterhouse. There were also phone calls from D'Atri [Ludovic] to Letha in Hot Springs; one such call[228] came on April 9, 1950. Although D'Atri had visited the Peak in March that year, no one in the Noss family ever conducted any business with him.

April 4, 1950

In spite of the difficulties Ova was experiencing at the claim site, activities began to pick up. Merle Horzmann's letter[229] to Mrs. Florence J. Parr of Hereford, Texas, gives a hint of the new stir at camp since Doc's death. Her letter, in part:

> *Ova asked me to write to you concerning the Indian with Doc at the time of discovery. He showed up with willingness to cooperate in getting into the cave and has told us verification of the story. Seraphin and his wife and the rest of the new group are here now trying to get far enough down to gain access to the main entrance. All are putting in $50 minimum to keep camp going and buy timbers and equipment. Since you were in on the old deal you might like to establish the same percentage as before. This is a new set up. We are choosing those who maintained confidence in the discovery. Notify Ernest Gatlin. He is also sincere. Ova Noss has spent a considerable amount of money to reestablish her rights over some of*

> *the former group that tried to get the permit over her head. Doc's old group is practically out except those who have stayed with us after his death. No one is part of the present set-up unless they shoulder responsibility. It appears that within the next two weeks we should finish the work.*
>
> —*Merle Horzmann*

April 5, 1950

Another letter[230] went out the following day to Jack Woods. Horzmann's letter:

> *Dear Jack: Mrs. Noss asked me to write you and tell you that the boys are out at the camp with Seraphin* and his wife, as Bill Lampros had no doubt told you. Harold*

---

* Seraphin had worked for Doc and Ova at Victorio Peak in the past.

Beckwith and Harold Mounce and two boys he brought out—one is his son—and one of Letha's boys, are working under Seraphin's direction. They seem very much encouraged and expect to have some favorable news in here by Friday, but they will be in need of supplies by then and some more lumber. They took out $70.00 worth, which is charged back to us.

We have notified all we could reach and they have tried all week to reach you by phone, but now is the time for us to all do something we can while Seraphin is here and in the notion to help with it. We are trying to put in a minimum of $50 from those who are unable to work out there and can do so to keep up their percentage of interest, as it is a new set-up under Babe's prior right to it to keep others from going over her head. We can't let her down, though we may all be busy with home affairs, but I believe it is important to push now if ever. This time there is to be very little, if any, publicity on it until we have something to show for it, but with this change of the name of Hot Springs to Truth or Consequences and the publicity it is getting, we have made some new contacts for later on when we need it. Let her know by return mail or wire what you want to do to protect your interests, as they could get through by Friday and then it will be too late.

—*Merle Horzmann*

~

In 1950, during an NBC radio game show called "Truth or Consequences," its host, Ralph Edwards, told his listening audience that he would broadcast his program from the town that agreed to rename their town "Truth or Consequences." In Hot Springs, New Mexico, 81 percent of the townspeople voted "yes" to change the name of its town; Hot Springs was about to lose its historical identity.

Ova Noss wrote[231] the following on the reverse side of Horzmann's letter:

Dear Friend Jack, I've read Merle's letter to you. I also instructed Bill Lampros to talk to you personally & explain all to you. He should have been to your place by now. Come or wire me if you are interested, at once. —*Bye, Mrs. Noss*

May 1, 1950

The mysteries and entanglements never stopped. The letter[232] opened with:

This is a preliminary to proceedings expressed in the letter, necessary because of the close proximity to the opening of the cave, which is due to happen at any time, and due also to the fact that another party has leased the surface rights from the bank in Hatch as a residence, and it covers a part of the ground claimed by the mining company [a reference to the Cheyenne Mining Company], and the mining claims are on State Land on which permits are existing now for the exploration and prospecting together with sworn statements from the discoverer and co-discoverer of the treasure presumed from their story to be contained in it.

~

This was the opening paragraph of a May 1 letter sent to a Mr. Payne by Horzmann. It has never been discovered who Mr. Payne was, nor has it ever been determined whom the "other party" was that Merle Horzmann referred. More perplexing was the mention of "sworn statements from the discoverer and co-discoverer of the treasure" filed with those claims. Doc was dead, so his and Ova's sworn statements must have been filed prior to March 5, 1949. The next paragraph was equally mysterious:

> *The party who examined the underground workings found it nearer than he expected and has advised definite procedure in this matter to protect us. We could also put in a clause that this property is being opened up under the supervision of the State and Federal Authorities. The State Land Commissioner, the School of Mines, and the U.S. Treasury, with Jim Hirst, as the Special Agent* for the UST, or it could be better to leave out specific names.*

~

Horzmann had the inside track on what was going on behind the scenes, but the question that remains is how much of it was shared with Ova Noss. Secret Service Agent Jim Hirst would soon begin to play a significant role in the happenings at Victorio Peak, and he would also surface years later when he escorted two individuals to the Treasury Department in Washington regarding the treasure. Even later on he would escort another person to visit with President Lyndon Johnson, also to discuss the size and value of the Noss treasure trove. More from the May 1 letter:

> *The story has already been publicized all over the U. S., and no need of going into further details about it, but so long as everything is legitimate now we are unconcerned about any new person coming into it. However, funds will be necessary to do the preliminary work to establish validity of the interests held in the original agreement, some of which have lapsed, died, or stated disinterest.*
>
> *If there is anything for me to sign on the Perlite† deal, I can do it after 1 [o'clock], or run down between times if necessary.*   —M. Horzmann

May 31, 1950

Having developed matters to a workable stage, and with full intentions of continuing the excavation at Victorio Peak, Ova called for a meeting of the members of M.E. Noss Associates. The heading on the May 31, 1950, letter[233] read, in part, "To all members of M.E. Noss Associates." Horzmann wrote to every member of the Cheyenne Mining group informing them that it was "necessary that we meet again and reorganize" in "order to function properly" stating that the need to do so was "relative to the original agreement drawn up on June 14, 1941, and the sub-agreements made after that." She stressed the urgency of having the meeting as "imperative circumstances arising since January 1, 1950."

---

* Jim Hirst was a Secret Service Agent for the United States Treasury.
† Perlite is a volcanic glass with high water content. It is useful because it's light in weight after it is processed.

The letter called for members or their proxies to attend a meeting scheduled for June 19 at 10:00 a.m. in the office of Judge A.L. Zinn in Santa Fe.

The agenda for the meeting was as follows: 1) reorganization of the "Original Group members" to continue the exploitation of the project as might be determined in the meeting; 2) exploitations at Victorio Peak were "detrimental to the welfare of the group" and their interests; 3) the need to protect the "valid interest holders" in the group; 4) the need for members to assist with expenses; 5) qualified members to be selected to handle emergency matters; 6) the possible selection of a Secretary-Treasurer.

Since the nature of the meeting was to address the "imperative circumstances" that had arisen since January 1, 1950, it can only be speculated that one or more issues were to be addressed. After Doc was murdered, and definitely after the trial of Charley Ryan, hundreds of treasure hunters invaded the Hembrillo Basin in search of the one hundred-and-ten gold bars that Doc had buried. Ova's knowledge that the gold had not been recovered and the specific mention that there were bars to be found spread like wildfire.

Now, even though Army range riders were patrolling the basin, amateur treasure hunters found their way to the treasure site. The summer months of 1950 were not uneventful, and there was much to be done. Even though there were overwhelming circumstances that were pressing down on Ova, the treasure had to be lifted.

~

Although it was never totally documented in the Noss records, there was a possibility that harm could come to the treasure, or *had* come to it. While attending Baylor University, an individual named Irving Bush Jr. met a building contractor, Travis Carroll, who introduced Bush, Jr. and Bush, Sr. to Lloyd Waterhouse. The Bushes had invested $12,000 in Waterhouse's mining operations near Mason, Texas. Waterhouse said shortly afterward that $2,000 of that money went to New Mexico to "dynamite a ventilation shaft to a treasure trove." Whether or not there was some connection between Waterhouse and engineer

S.E. Montgomery eleven years earlier when Montgomery destroyed the top shaft entrance at Victorio Peak and exactly when the issues between the Bushes and Waterhouse took place is unknown. Regardless, later in the year, Waterhouse played a financial role in the new effort to gain access to the treasure and entered into an agreement with Ova. However the terms of that agreement are unknown; no documents were found in the Noss

records that spelled out their arrangement. What is known, though, is that Waterhouse agreed to finance the work with arrangements he had made through Merrick Construction Company, which was owned by a Mr. Hardy Merrick. His construction work would not involve the top shaft; it would involve work at a new site, which has become known officially as the Lower Noss Shaft, as compared to the original opening at the top of Victorio Peak that eventually became known as the Upper Noss Shaft.

The Lower Noss Shaft was conceived and implemented by Ova. Because there was so much difficulty associated with the original top entrance and the debris that blocked it, Ova's plan was to start much lower on the Peak and begin digging another parallel shaft far below the top entrance with hopes of intercepting the top shaft as the excavation progressed downward. The lower shaft went through a series of development stages, trial and error, before it proved to be a safer and more viable way of finding Doc's original passageway that led to the treasure.

The excavation began with a small work crew, which included Ova. Although the work progressed steadily, they needed a method of disposing of the debris, so a windlass was constructed and positioned over the new shaft. As the shaft grew deeper, shoring walls were built from heavy plank and timbers. The process required that each bucket had to be filled by hand, cranked up to the surface, and then carried a distance away from the shaft entrance. To overcome this disadvantage, Ova devised a pivoting crane that permitted the loaded buckets to be cranked to the top and then swung out and away from the opening that created a debris pile, which could be easily managed. During the excavation, Ova worked* as long and as hard as any man. She is seen here

coming up from the shaft after she had filled a bucket; someone on the surface had cranked it up so it could be dumped.

During the time period that preceded Merrick's work efforts, Ova was the driving force that kept the work moving forward at the Peak. The excavation methods she developed worked well, and she often labored from early morning until dark, and, even though there were other people there to help her, she insisted on doing her share of the work.

---

* Ova climbing out of Lower Noss Shaft

Even though the Lower Noss shaft was a logical place for the new shoring work to begin there was another problem; Violet Yancey's possible interference at the claim site. Less than a year after Doc was murdered, widow Violet Noss married Roy Yancey in Sandoval County, New Mexico, and became Violet Lena Mason Noss Yancey. Another reason for the urgency was that, on January 12, 1950, Brigadier General George G. Eddy took command of White Sands and there was fear that the Army would bring pressure on Ova to vacate the Victorio Peak treasure site.

BRIG. GEN. G.G. EDDY

June 19, 1950

As planned, the meeting took place on June 19 at Judge Zinn's office in Santa Fe at the El Fidel Hotel. A report[234] by Merle Horzmann recapped the events of the meeting and the activity that had taken place through the following weeks. One of the matters discussed was the issue concerning the Army; the government had filed condemnation proceedings against the State to take over the section containing Victorio Peak. As a result of the action by the government, "nothing could be decided until the following Monday when Guy Shepard was in his office, but he could not confer with us until Tuesday." At the meeting Judge Zinn had recommended that the group incorporate. The last paragraph of the June 19 letter was a blind notation to Jack Woods. It read:

> *It was my understanding that Babe and Mr. Waterhouse were to call you on the 28th or 29th. After that, she was going on to Clovis over the 4th, and Mr. Waterhouse was going to spend the 4th in Louisiana before going ahead. His report to us was that there was more work to be done than Jimmy Lampros could do alone, or had the money to do with others. But Guy [Commissioner Guy Shepard] put thumbs down on a corporation. We are protected, however, by the amount of work already done and the time and money spent, and Guy's word that no one else can get any permit over her [Ova's] head, and the work could go ahead. If you have not already been contacted, you will be. —M.H.*

~

On Tuesday, June 27, Horzmann and Ova met with Commissioner Shepard; Waterhouse arrived unexpectedly and expressed a willingness to put up the money as long as he was assured continued access to the treasure site over concerns that someone other than Ova would get a permit and have priority to the site. Shepard said he could give no assurances since "no one else could have priority except the government." He advised to hold off on incorporating, since it would involve the sale of stock and that his office could not guarantee anything until the issue of condemnation was settled, which was indefinite.

Because of the 4th of July holiday, little could be done, so Horzmann advised Waterhouse and the Merrick Construction Company* that she would have more information and would advise accordingly. In the addendum to her report she had "Guy's word that no one else can get any permit over Ova's head, and that the work could go ahead." With an agreement set between Ova and Waterhouse and on the word of Commissioner Guy Shepard, Merrick, the contractor[†] from Abilene, Texas, began the work to gain access to the treasure rooms by opening the collapsed shaft down to where the original old ladder was located. The crew began working on July 2, 1950.

Judge Wallace from Del Rio, Texas, was also financially involved in the business arrangement with Merrick, and as far as the hands-on work was involved, Ova Noss was always there, too, pitching in during any excavation work that was done.[‡]

A third person, a less visible one, was Benjamin P. Farris. Recorded conversations between Farris and a colonel at White Sands Proving Ground would soon emerge and clear the air on Farris' involvement with Ova and Victorio Peak, and that of Judge Wallace's financial involvement. The colonel's name was John G. Shinkle.

Circa August 1, 1950

In the eye of the storm, Horzmann was pushing for publication of a manuscript on the Victorio Peak story with all its ramifications, implications and the events connected to the Noss treasure trove as they unwound. Only eight months and three weeks earlier, she had written to Sanders, Garland and Mitchell-Gossett concerning the theft of a manuscript that she admitted belonged to "the people whose names are mentioned in it" as the "real owners" of the manuscript and that she in particular was also an owner. It can be safely assumed that Letha Guthrie, Dorothy Delonas and Ova Noss were the other three people Horzmann referred to as the "real owners" notwithstanding any interest the estate of Doc Noss might have held and how *that* played out.

---

* Merle Horzmann, Ed Goldman (Merrick's job foreman), Hardy Merrick (Merrick Construction Company).

[†] O. Noss, *op. cit.*, p 2.

[‡] Ed Goldman, Merle Horzmann and Ova.

Everyone seemed to mesh, and with the hope that the treasure would soon be raised, Merrick's crew* and his family would often pose for photographs. Then, on or about August 1, 1950, Horzmann received a letter from Eldon B. Howard, a letter that lifts the fog on some of the mystery surrounding her November 15, 1949 letter to E. Forest Sanders, R.C. Garland, and Mrs. Beatrice Mitchell-Gossett. The August 1 letter from Howard contained the elements of a deal wherein it appears that he had purchased certain interests in Horzmann's manuscript, but was it entirely hers to sell? According to her November 15, 1949 letter, it was only partially hers. So was it a percentage of the manuscript rights she was selling? What appears to be more in line with what was written in the letter, Horzmann was selling off some of the 1% interest she was given by Doc and Ova in April 1941 for her secretarial services for the Cheyenne Mining Company. One month later, on May 31, 1941 (Chapter 12), Merle was telling Carl to calculate the return on her 1% interest, telling Carl to "*take these figures and work them out. 152 x 53 x 2 x 10,000 - 1 % ratio of 120 =? But don't tell anyone about it.*" A week later, Carl wrote back and told Merle, "*The total of the figures you sent me was $165,120,000.00 and 1% of the amount would be $1,651,200.00 or a return of over 100,000 per dollar invested.*" But Merle hadn't invested *anything*; Doc and Ova gave her the one percentage interest; she didn't pay for it. The first paragraph of Howard's letter:[235]

> *Please find enclosed two assignments of your interest, which will need to be recorded and two personal checks to you in the amount of $100.00 for a one tenth (1 / 10) percent interest and one for $50.00 for a one twentieth (1 / 20) percent interest, which will need to be recorded and acknowledged before being valid.*

---

* Horzmann, Hardy Merrick's son, Ova Noss, Mrs. Osborn (friend of the Merrick's), Jackie Goldman, Ed Goldman, unknown, unknown, Mrs. Merrick, Hardy Merrick, person behind Mrs. Merrick is unknown.

Then came the mention of the manuscript:

I'm still interested in the story about the mine, and I would like very much to read the manuscript you had in your office the day I was in Lordsburg. If you could see your way possible, I would appreciate you sending it to me for reading, register with return receipt. Inasmuch as the story is copyrighted, you would not have to worry, or if you'd rather send it under contract that would be all right with me. Please let me know what you think about it. I know that the manuscript holds more information than I have before gathered or heard about, and probably is more authentic.

Eldon Howard was either a literary agent, someone who worked for a publishing company, or possibly a publicist; from the letters between Horzmann and him, it is hard to pinpoint their *exact* relationship and business dealings. One thing is certain, though; Howard had listened long enough to Horzmann to feel confident in spending a few dollars with the hope of getting rich. Meanwhile, work* progressed steadily at the treasure site.

August 8, 1950

A week later, Horzmann wrote[236] to Howard and mentioned the manuscript:

Just arrived back in Lordsburg at 11 this morning. I had too many around me in Hot Springs to write more than I did, and after thinking it over, I just put both checks through the Hot Springs bank.

~

That Horzmann was in Hot Springs when she wrote to Howard is an indication that she was living close to Ova; she did not move from Hot Springs to Clovis, New Mexico, until 1952. Perhaps Horzmann was staying at the Cozy-Corner Apartments where she had stayed shortly after Doc was killed. There is no information available that explains why Horzmann limited what she wrote to Howard that day, only that she was reluctant to write more because she had "too many around [her]." The next three paragraphs dealt with procedure, the manner in which Horzmann was going to manage her writing: editing, rewrites, form, etc. Then she moved on to more interesting matters:

My week past in Hot Springs has been quite mixed with experiences, and we found some of the stuff talked about, but we cannot mention gold bullion in connection with

---

* Hardy Merrick's son standing beside Ed Goldman, sitting on truck bed – others unknown.

anything sent through the mail, unless it is in fact a story in the making. If you have access to an attorney there, please check with him, because this is vital in going ahead with it from the idea I had.

~

Although somewhat cryptic in general, the letter leaves little doubt that Horzmann was talking about Ova and her finding some of Doc's gold bars, which she describes as "gold bullion." She continued:

At the present time, all we have is Doc's story, but we have strong indications that he was not wrong. It still remains to be proven, and this may be done in the very near future if nothing disastrous happens to prevent it. With the find of this, it is likely.

~

Doc had apparently helped with structuring the story, as Horzmann felt certain that the eventual lifting of the treasure would prove he was telling the truth and "that he was not wrong." Doc's story could have been his description of what he did to locate it while he was exploring the caverns inside the Peak before the collapse, *and* his description of what he saw in the caverns as well as the makeup of the treasure. Next Horzmann explains more about B.J. Ward and the grand jury issue. More from her letter:

I might tell you that one copy of it was stolen and I found out who it was. It was a man who was at one time quite close to Doc, and wanted in on the deal, but he was such a character that Doc would not have him around, but he got into my house and took the story. Admitted he did it, to present to the Grand Jury for investigation. After a great deal of torture and agony on my part, and my having to use all the strategy I could muster, I finally got it back just a couple of weeks ago. Fortunately, it went into hands that knew me and the effort I have put in to carry on with the rest of it, and he was told in no uncertain terms to be sure that it went no further than himself until he gave it back to me. Out of the clear sky, he handed it back when I went to get him to sign a legal document necessary to clear a cloud he had put on my property (another part of the story full of action and concern).

~

The next three paragraphs were interesting, but they dealt primarily with some of the material she wanted to include in the manuscript, uneventful matters. However, the following paragraph was quite revealing as to Horzmann's connection to Secret Service agents from the Treasury Department.

These are some of the reasons I would not like to send the story out. It is true, but the Special Agent from the Treasury Department has advised against it, so long as it deals with the element I mentioned before. That, too, is the reason I mentioned in my letter it would be best for you to stop at my office long enough for me to go into the more intimate things related to it. I could tell you so much more that one book would not be enough to contain it if all were told, but it is all interesting – to me, at least. And I know it is to those who have spent money in it in any way, hoping to get it back with large dividends.

~

The rest of the letter was long but it did not contain any earth-moving information. Horzmann closed her letter by writing:

> *My application to the Copyright office covers the "Compilation of all data relating to the San Andres Treasure…*   *—Merle Horzmann*

~

Although it is not known whom Horzmann was writing to, or when the following letter was written, it is placed here because it deals with the size of the Noss treasure trove and mentions an element concerning Colonel Holt not previously known. Only the second page of Horzmann's handwritten letter[237] was found: (underlined by Horzmann)

> *Maybe my dream will come true; have almost lost hope, but not quite. If we can just get in for this little bit, it will be worth more than anything I know of. It [the Noss treasure trove] is one of the largest in the <u>world</u>. So don't forget what it will mean to be in on it because there will be world publicity whenever the story can be released, but I might tell you, too, that Holt controls the AP, too, in New Mexico.*   *—Merle*

October 8, 1950

While the work* progressed at the site to open the top shaft, the cool, pleasant months in the desert had passed and the much cooler winter months were slowly edging in. It was on October 8, 1950 that Ova opened mail box 93 at the Post Office on Main Street in Hot Springs and retrieved a letter sent to her by Isabella G. Lemons, the wife of Cecil Lemons of Sonora, Texas. The letter contained information that involved a gold bar being held by a person named Wesley White, who also lived in Sonora. Merle Horzmann was with Ova when she opened the letter and claimed that Isabella was her [Horzmann's] assistant. Why Horzmann's assistant had sent the letter to Ova is unknown; regardless, the following day, October 9, Horzmann signed an affidavit[238] swearing to the

---

* Left to right: Ed and Jackie Goldman, Merle Horzmann, "Mr. Ryan" and Ova. The man in the Jeep is thought to be Ryan's broher, William, who came to see Ova after the trial. Notation on back of photo read: "Mr. Ryan"

contents of the letter and gave it to Ova for her records. From Horzmann's affidavit, in part:

> *Hope you have good luck at the Cave. C. (Cecil)said his mother and Dad told him Wesley White still has that Bar of Bullion, right at his house in Sonora; they saw it themselves. Cecil said he sure would like to have a talk with Wesley, and perhaps get some help on the proposition, but you know more about it than I do.*

~

The reason Wesley White had a gold bar in his possession was explained in the previously mentioned letter written by Doc on September 1, 1941; Doc had asked his friend, White, the Sheriff for Sonora County, to loan him expense money. Excerpt from Doc's September 1, 1941 letter:

> *Lawyer Ben Newell has my case for the 16th. I need $200 to beat the case. The $1,000 we have for camp goes only for mining. I need $600 for lawyer Newell and the timbers.*
> *I wish you could be here for the trial. I need the money for 30-60 days. The day we break through, Leo O'Connell will be on the road to you.*   —Doc

~

Doc had kept his promise to repay White and gave him a gold bar in payment of the loan; he had settled his debt with his friend Sheriff White with a bar of gold from the treasure trove. However, the connection between Ova and Isabella Lemons is unknown, but one thing remained certain—there was gold inside of Victorio Peak, many, many tons of it.

Even though it was extremely cold that November, Ova and her son Harold* roamed the hills in and around Victorio Peak relocating the claim sites that Doc had filed. Together they found the corners of claim sites "Victorio" Nos. 1 through 5 and Geronimo No. 2 and refiled those claims during the first week of December in Doña Ana County.

By January 1951, while Merrick's crew was working diligently to open the top entrance, the United States Government requested and received surface rights from New Mexico for the purpose of expanding missile testing in the major area of the Tularosa Basin, an expanse known today as the White Sands Missile Range. The 1951 expansion of the range included the Hembrillo Basin *and* Victorio Peak. It was then that Ova Noss received

---

* Harold Beckwith, Ova's son, seen here at the top entrance of Victorio Peak.

notification that Victorio Peak was under Army lease. Knowing full well that certain parties in the military had their eyes on the treasure, Ova ignored any suggestion of having to leave her claim site and continued forward with Merrick's team to clear the collapsed entrance shaft that led to the treasure.

A major adversary to Ova and her right of claim to the Victorio Peak treasure had already entered the picture; his name was John G. Shinkle. Shinkle began his military career as a cadet at the U.S. Military Academy at West Point and graduated with a commission in Field Artillery in 1933. His first assignment was at the Presidio of Monterey, then to Hawaii where he served in the Army Ordnance Corps and continued in that capacity for the remainder of his military career. Shinkle made two separate appearances at White Sands: first in January 1951 as a colonel when he served as the Director of Technical Operations under range commander Brigadier General George Eddy, and a second appearance nine years later in June 1960 as a brigadier general and range commander at White Sands.

March 14, 1951

Sometime between Colonel Shinkle's arrival at White Sands in January 1951 and March of that year, he became directly acquainted with Ova Noss, Victorio Peak, and a man named Ben P. Farris. Farris was one of Ova's business partners whose responsibility was to coordinate with Shinkle so that excavation could continue at the treasure site, a job and work team headed by Hardy Merrick and financed partly by Judge Wallace.

Farris had called Shinkle to inquire on tentative arrangements for the work team to continue, but Shinkle was not interested in dealing with anyone other than Ova Noss. The telephone conversation between Shinkle and *Farris was transcribed and was thought to have taken place on March 14, 1951; the first page was missing when it was turned over as a discovery document. However, the balance of the conversation was "certified" by Army Major Lloyd T. Purvin as a "true copy" of the conversation. This was the first of many conversations that occurred where the Army at White Sands began recording without advising the other party. The question now surfaces as to why the Defense Department thought it was necessary to record private conversations[239] between military officers at White Sands and civilians such as Farris regarding the Noss treasure. From the conversation, in part:

> SHINKLE: *As far as that deal goes, I would like to work with one person and that is the principal on it. Apparently, Mrs. Noss is the principal, is that correct?*
> PHARIS: *Yes, she is.*
>
> ~

Shinkle made it a point that he was not going to allow anyone on the site but Ova; she had visited Shinkle the day before Farris had called him and she was given permission to "visit" the claim site at Victorio Peak to make an inspection

---

* Farris' name was spelled incorrectly in the Army transcription as 'PHARIS'

the coming weekend, but with the firm understanding that she would do no excavation work. Enter H. Karl Shadel of the Army Corp of Engineers,* a man who would gradually enter the drama and play a significant role in providing Shinkle, who was then with the Army Ordnance Corps, as was General Eddy, with anything he needed to keep the treasure under the Army's control.

> *SHINKLE: You see, I have no particular interest in this thing because it's her business entirely, but I would like to take all the business and tie it up in one batch rather than to deal individually with you and with her and whomever or whatever interests she may have. Now, just for your information, that land has been withdrawn from any prospecting.*
>
> *PHARIS: Yes. I learned that from Karl Shadel in Albuquerque. I have gone into that quite thoroughly. I'm trying to answer your question but to save time I have all the particulars in a letter from Karl Shadel. The last paragraph I'll read to you from his letter, it says:*
>
> *'You are advised that your requirements to the area would continue for only a short period of time. In view of this, it is suggested that a pass arrangement be entered into with military authorities at White Sands Proving Ground which might meet with your requirements.'*
>
> *And I told Mr. Shadel this, I thought we could complete this work in 30 days and not to exceed 45, and he thought it could be arranged. And I made a trip up there at quite some expense and I am working with Mrs. Noss. I don't know how she feels about it but she…so there is quite a bit of straddling the fence, I'll say, or whatever you want to call it with this one and that one and we have a contract and we want to do it right and fair and be right with everybody.*
>
> *SHINKLE: Yes. My particular stand on this thing is going to be this…that to a limited extent, I'll allow access for observation, that is, for inspection, which I have already done but I am not going to allow access for improvement of the property and things of that sort.*
>
> *PHARIS: Under a visiting permit, you wouldn't allow anybody in there for 30 days?*
>
> *SHINKLE: That's correct. I haven't had my legal people on this yet, but I shall do it. I would rather instead of making any deal with you I would rather make it with the principal in the affair, which to my understanding now is Mrs. Noss.*

~

It had been two years since Doc was murdered; according to what Shinkle said to Farris, he was reconciled to the fact that Ova Noss was "the principal in the affair," falling just short of telling Farris that she had the sole legal interest in the treasure trove claim. The conversation went back and forth with Farris trying to convince Shinkle to allow further excavation at the site, but Shinkle would not budge.

---

* H. K. (Karl) Shadel's official title was Chief, Real Estate Division; he operated out of Albuquerque. He was involved in matters concerning Victorio Peak for many years.

PHARIS: Would it do us any good for us to meet you and show you these contracts like Judge Wallace's of Del Rio as he is one of the principals in the affair because he is definitely required to do this work. He had put a lot of money into it.

SHINKLE: I don't know the legal angle of it, who is the principal and who isn't but I don't want to tell three or four people who are interested in the thing a different story.

PHARIS: We want to be right and clear with everybody, including her definitely. We just don't want to waste our time and money and maybe it is all a hoax but we are willing to see. And if we could make an arrangement with you and if you think it would do any good to come see you we will.

SHINKLE: Right now, there is no permission for access to that land for any other purpose other than these two days to inspect. Now, I think that you ought to get all of your interested parties together and if you have some other proposition and present it to me as a single piece and then I can make a decision or refer it to the proper place for decision after I have the single piece of work to be done.

Shinkle's proposition was fragmented and unclear, but he had no intention of allowing Farris to come on the range to complete the excavation work.

PHARIS: I will do that and I won't take up any more of your time and you say you haven't met Karl Shadel of Albuquerque?

SHINKLE: No, but I suspect he is in the District Engineer's office…who handles the legal matters as far as land tenure.

PHARIS: Yes, that's right and he is quite familiar with the whole thing and, of course, so is General Eddy, because they were in there under a permit last year. According to the Land Commissioner in Santa Fe and Mr. Shadel, I don't think there can be a new lease entered into on account of the government taking over that ground.

SHINKLE: I, myself, am not a land lawyer, so I don't know.

PHARIS: I will talk this over with the attorney in Del Rio and we will try and contact you later.

SHINKLE: Fine, Mr. Pharis.

PHARIS: Thank you a lot.

~

Shinkle signed the recorded conversation, but regardless of his temperament to allow Ova to inspect her claim site, she was earmarked; she would soon be banned from Victorio Peak, yet other miners and ranchers were permitted to come and go periodically for various reasons, and without harassment or interference.

With a renewed sense of purpose and hope, albeit a temporary one, the efforts by Ova Noss and her family at Victorio Peak continued. In the spring of 1951, Ova's family returned to the Peak to work and explore areas where Doc had hidden gold bars over the years.

Many Noss family members came to the Rock House on a regular basis trying their hand at finding some of the gold bars they knew Doc had buried;

it had become a temporary distraction from the time when they would have to face the inevitable reality of being forced to abandon the treasure site because of the Army's increasing presence at White Sands Proving Ground.

Harold's brother, Marvin Beckwith, and Harold's wife, Betty, are seen here spending some time in the Hembrillo Canyon with a metal detector hoping to strike it rich by finding one of Doc's gold bar stashes.

The clock was ticking for the Noss family and the priceless treasure that remained hidden beneath Victorio Peak.

Chapter 28

Ova Evicted from Her Claim Site and More Proof of the Treasure

It was a brisk, windy March afternoon in 1951 when the United States Army evicted Ova from Victorio Peak. Ova and Seraphin Sedillo and his wife were physically removed under Public Land Order No. 703. The Army told her she could return to the Peak when there was a lull in missile testing operations—in about 300 days. However, she came back to continue the work on periodic thirty-day passes or she sneaked in whenever she could to inspect her claim. But on her first visit back to the Hembrillo Basin and the Rock House, which had been the scene of many anxious moments during her life with Doc, she found that the Army had not released the horses from the corral as they had promised they would. She discovered the corral gate was closed, the water pipes were pulled up and the horses, four of them—were dead.
One of the horses belonged to Letha, a stallion* that Doc had given her before he left for Texas. The four horses seen here are the ones that died. Three of

---

* Letha's horse shown here with Doc holding gold bar - Buster was usually by Doc's side when he was at camp.

383

the horses that died are seen here being tended by Ova; they belonged to her and were kept at camp.

Letha gave an account of the incident during one of her audio recording sessions. In part:

> *We went back in there and found those horses all bloated up—beautiful horses; they couldn't get out. We found them dead and the house [the Rock House] all shot up. They promised her [Ova] they would let her back in, but we never got in again after that, but we snuck on a couple times. Nobody saw us; we got on and off real quick.*

~

When the 1951 eviction took place, Ova and Merrick's crew were working hard to clear the shaft. Once again, Letha gave an account of the events when the Army gained surface rights to use the land and began evicting the miners and the cattlemen. In part:

> *They were practically at the bottom of it [the top entrance shaft]; that's why Mama was so mad. They had dug down and found Doc's name and a sign that he had put on the wall. That's when the Army extended the boundary and grabbed that little spot [the Victorio Peak site]. They figured Mama was getting too close to it and they wanted it. I'll tell you a thing they did to the ranchers…the Army was very cruel. Instead of allowing the ranchers in so they could go and sell their cattle, they told the ranchers they had to get all of their cattle off [their leased ranges]. They made a big thing of it in the papers—all cattle must be off the White Sands Range by such a date. Well, the cattle buyers were setting back and the ranchers only got fifty-percent on their cattle [meaning half their true value].*

~

Shortly after Ova was evicted, and saddened at what she had seen, she made her way to the top of the Peak and discovered the Army had padlocked the upper and lower shafts. Ova talked to Terry about the incident. He related the conversation. In part:

> *Babe told me that at that moment she felt so detached from everything. She sat on the edge of the small bed in the rock house and cried. It was as though none of it had really happened, but it had. She said she could still hear Doc's voice giving instructions to the men who would gather out in front of the rock house each morning to get the work schedule for the day. 'They were a good bunch of boys,' she told me. 'But some weren't, though.' Babe and I laughed as I watched a few tears come to her eyes. I never saw her cry before. She was always so strong and brave, always proud of what she and Doc had accomplished, staying alive and keeping the dream going. 'It's not over, Terry,' she said. 'When I'm gone, I want you to keep it going for Doc and me. I don't ever want to think he died in vain. You know as much about this whole thing as I do. You and Letha know it all.'*

~

July 24, 1951

When she received the following July 24 letter[240] from Judge Wallace, her friend and financial contributor to the work being done by Hardy Merrick, she knew that he was unaware that she had been removed from the Victorio Peak claim site. Mr. Merrick and his crew had performed well, lasting bonds of friendship were made, and, had they been able to continue, perhaps Mr. Merrick and everyone associated with his efforts would have had the honor of telling the world they located the passageway that led to the main caverns and the treasure itself. Now, with Ova's eviction those hopes would have to be set aside. Judge Wallace wrote:

> *I am enclosing herewith copies of several agreements executed by Mr. Merrick, myself, and others in connection with the lease there, which copies I apparently failed to leave with you and Mrs. Horzmann. I believe with these copies, and the copies I gave you on the other transactions, will be complete.*
>
> *I am mailing this to you today, although I expect to be at Hatch on Thursday of this week, unless in the meantime I am called to meet you and Mr. Merrick at Santa Fe. I expect to leave here early Wednesday morning for Roswell, and can be reached at M.C. Trent's residence, phone 3227-J.*
>
> *Trusting everything is still going smoothly and in accordance with expectations, I am yours very truly* — W.P. Wallace

~

It is most likely Ova had responded promptly to Judge Wallace about the unfortunate work stoppage; however, no account of any written communication was ever found. Since Mr. Wallace had provided Ova with a phone number where he could be reached, she might have called him to explain the situation.

July 31, 1951

Ova had resigned herself to the fact that her longstanding ability to come and go from the treasure site had been terminated, but she still grasped the hopeful thought that she would someday be able to return to complete her work. It is apparent from the following letter that she had a friendly relationship with a White Sands Proving Ground officer, Lt. Col. Paul H. Scordas. Ova wrote[241] to him on July 31, 1951:

> *We are this day vacating the premises known as the Roy Henderson property, Section 16, Township 16, Range 3 East, and are enclosing the passes.*
>
> *On behalf of the entire group, we extend sincere appreciation for the courteous manner in which you have all handled our cause, and we regret very much that we could not have had more time in which to complete our project. We are looking forward to the time, however, when we return and go ahead again.* —Ova M. Noss

~

The letter was evidence that the Nosses and their associates had passes to come and go from the range ever since her eviction in March. But it didn't seem to settle well with General Eddy that she had received passes to go in. Even though Ova had turned the passes over to Lt. Col. Scordas and thanked him, Eddy chose to rub salt in an open wound and wrote to Ova on August

24, 1951 to confirm what was beyond the obvious. What was odd, knowing
that Doc was long dead, Eddy addressed his letter[242] to Doc _Nass_—not Ova.
He also copied R.B. Yancey, Violet's new husband:

> *Dear Dr. Nass,*
>
> *I have taken up the matter of your claims and desire to remove ore above ground with
> the Land Office of the Army Engineers. They have been very prompt in investigating
> your claims and request for entrance thereon.*
>
> *The records, as furnished to me, indicate that you were issued a Prospector's Permit
> by the State of New Mexico and further that the State cancelled the permit. Therefore,
> any ore on the surface should have been removed during the tenure of your permit. It
> cannot be removed now since it has reverted to the State.*
>
> *With respect to all of your mining claims on Big Faults Nos. 1 through 5, and your
> claim of patented land SE4 SW4, Section 9, the Department of Interior advises that
> these claims are not valid.*
>
> *In view of the foregoing, this office cannot authorize further access to these claims and
> further work under your cancelled Prospector's Permit.*

~

Although Section 9 was not the area where Victorio Peak was located,
Eddy's comment of removing "ore above ground" stemmed from the fact that
the military had only surface rights granted to them by the State of New Mexico.
Likewise, any notion that there was any hope of claiming ore that was on the
surface of the ground was meaningless and unimportant to Ova's core efforts of
uncovering the treasure. Doc had been dead for two years and five months when
Eddy wrote the letter, and there is no reason to believe that he was not fully aware
of the circumstances. It is difficult to believe that, with all of the commotion
concerning Ova's work at the Peak, and just three weeks earlier she had written a
sincere and courteous letter to Lt. Col. Scordas informing him that she was "va-
cating the premises" and had surrendered her passes, Eddy didn't make an effort
to address his letter properly. It is equally difficult to give Eddy the benefit of
the doubt that he was unaware Doc had been killed in March 1949. Additionally,
the records at the Land Office in Santa Fe show that the permits in question that
involved Doc Noss had expired March 1, 1946 and that Ova had been granted a
permit by Guy Shepard, the newly elected Commissioner of Public Lands. On
January 10, 1949, Shepard issued her a permit to recover the treasure at Victorio
Peak, which had been recommended by E.C. Anderson to the former commissioner on November 30, 1948. The treasure recovery permit expired on August
10, 1949, which was the date the federal government took exclusive possession
of the surface rights by condemnation proceedings in federal court.

By 1952, White Sands Proving Ground was expanded and the Army's order
to deny Ova access to her claim at Victorio Peak was strictly enforced. After
constant requests to enter the basin to inspect her claim site, General Eddy
finally allowed her occasional weekend visits, but it was a rarity. Although access

to the Peak was greatly restricted, Ova tried valiantly to get back to the Peak to continue the needed work to open the route to the lower caverns. Other people she knew, like Ben Farris, who believed in the existence of the treasure, helped her behind the scenes.

August 15, 1952

After consulting with Ova on the matter, Farris wrote to the Denver Mint on her behalf requesting information on the gold deposit made by Doc. Farris also requested information on the discovery of buried treasure. In July 1939, Ova wrote to the Mint and asked the same questions. Her request was forwarded to Washington, D.C. and eventually Leland Howard replied one hundred and ten days later in the form of a convoluted secondhand oral message, an aggravating and uncalled-for stunt. It was clear then that Howard had taken an adversarial position on providing information related to the Noss treasure. When Farris wrote to the Denver Mint, his letter was likewise forwarded to Washington, D.C. where once again Leland Howard replied personally as the Acting Director of the Mint. This time Howard's response came in a timely manner. Leland Howard's letter[243] (underlining inserted)

> *Dear Mr. Farris: Your letter of July 23, 1952, addressed to the United States Mint at Denver, Colorado, has been referred to me for attention.*
>
> *In reply to your inquiry regarding buried treasure, you are advised that any gold which is found in this country by any person <u>should</u> be reported promptly to the Treasury Department, stating the circumstances under which found, in order that specific instructions may be given as to the disposition of the gold and the tax aspects relating thereto.*
>
> *Regarding your request for information concerning possible deposits of gold by one Doc Noss, pursuant to a <u>rule</u> published in the Federal Register on December 24, 1943, Code of Federal Regulations, Title 31, Chapter 1, Section 92.29 (b), information as to deposits of gold and silver made by specific depositors may be furnished to a person properly and directly concerned, upon the furnishing of a <u>court order</u> therefore entered in pending litigation, or in lieu thereof with the written consent of the depositor.*
>
> *If the wife of Doc Noss, who you state is deceased, wishes to address an inquiry to the Director of the Mint, setting forth the information which she desires, the Bureau would be prepared to <u>consider</u> such request. Unless she had written to this office, however, it would not be advisable for her to make the trip to the United States Mint at Denver, Colorado, as they are not permitted to give out such information without authority from this office.*   —*Leland Howard*

~

The reason Howard gave for not giving Farris any information about any gold deposited by Doc Noss at the Denver Mint, was that a *rule* in the Federal Register stated that such a request was required to be submitted by a person who was "properly and directly concerned." It meant that Farris needed to obtain a court order.

Rules in the Federal Register are not laws per se, but they have the force of law. They are supposedly accurate interpretations of the laws enacted by Congress; the drafting of federal regulations is known as the "rulemaking" process. The Constitution of the United States provides Congress the authority to make laws to govern our country. When Congress enacts a specific law that properly and legally addresses an economic or social problem, the appropriate regulatory agency establishes specific rules and regulations to oversee and enforce the law as Congress had intended. This process gives federal regulations the legal teeth to enforce those enacted laws. If these rules and regulations are interpreted correctly within the framework and the intent of the legislation, when finalized, they should contain no ambiguous language or words that would subvert the intent of the law or its meaning. This would entail writing regulations with proper and effective words and phrases such as: *you shall, it shall, they shall, the law requires, according to the strict provisions of the intended legislation,* etc. On the other hand, the regulations dare not include such words or phrases such as: *well, we're not sure about that yet, it might be a good idea, or if we decide otherwise, it sounds like a good idea…but, maybe, perhaps, or the word—should, instead of shall!*

The issue here is Howard's repeated failure to act in a professional and civil-minded manner in handling a request for public information. But it was not just Howard's response letter to Ben Farris concerning the "court order" that is at issue; it was Farris' question about "buried treasure." Ova asked for the same information when she wrote to Howard in 1939, but he deliberately gave her the run-around. Instead of sending a similar letter to Ova concerning questions she asked about treasure trove in her July 10, 1939 request, Howard ordered the Chief of the Secret Service, Frank J. Wilson, to assign an agent to provide her with an *oral* message, a process that took nearly four months to reach her. Why didn't Howard provide Ova the same information in a formal letter as he did with Farris?

On November 3, 1939, agent Hargett reported[244] that, "per the request of Mr. Leland Howard" he had delivered the following message—not to Ova, as instructed by Frank Wilson, but to her son, Harold Beckwith: (underlining inserted)

> *Per the request of Mr. Leland Howard, Acting Director of the Mint, I delivered the following oral message to Harold Beckwith, son of Mrs. M.E. Noss, that he might deliver same to his mother, in view of the absence of his mother from her home 'that finding of any gold in this country by any person <u>should</u> be reported promptly to the Treasury Department, together with a statement as to the circumstances under which it was found.' —Hargett*

~

The intentional misuse of words, or any other abuse construed to make someone think that a regulation or statute prohibits one thing or another when it is does not, is improper, especially to the extent that Howard did when he refused to answer Ova in writing; Howard couldn't have been more ambiguous.

Considering the meaningless and costly effort in delivering a vague oral message, one can conclude that such an effort was Leland Howard's intended purpose from the onset. And, since Howard had historically handled the Noss file personally, it demonstrates how important it was for the government to contain potential problems that could arise regarding the Victorio Peak treasure and the Nosses' legal claim to it. Howard's letter to Ben Farris, who was obviously acting on behalf of Ova Noss, also mentioned Farris' request for information concerning the deposit of gold bars made by Doc Noss, which Farris could not access without a court order. Even if Ova made the same inquiry, she could not access the information through the Denver Mint; Howard wrote *"they are not permitted to give out such information without authority from this office."* Beyond that, Howard said, *"…The Bureau would be prepared to consider such request."* It was a matter of public information; Howard was compelled to give Ova the information—not consider it.

August 27, 1952

Another note[245] written by Ova on August 27, 1952 was simply to remind herself to "get a copy of the letter Farris and Greer wrote to the Denver Mint inquiring if M.E. Noss had ever left any gold there." The next part of the notation is interesting: *Answer came from U.S. Mint delivery December 16, 1944.*

It can be interpreted to mean that the Denver Mint wrote to Farris and Greer telling them the delivery date of the gold Doc and Ova brought to the Denver Mint was December 16, 1944. At the end of the notation, she reminded herself to secure the letter Leland Howard sent to Farris on August 15, 1952, which she had done:

> *Also get copy of the letter mailed to Ben P. Farris, Cisco, Texas, from Washington.*
> *— Signed, Ova M. Noss, 2020 Gidding Street, Clovis, New Mexico*

September 12, 1952

There was never any question in Ova's mind that Doc had deposited gold bars at the Mint; she was present when Doc and Claude Fincher took the bars inside and delivered them to the Mint assay office. The only question about the deposit was the *date* when it took place. Even during Ova's 1975 deposition, she was unsure; but she and Letha were certain that the transaction had taken place. In 1975 Ova told her attorney, David Daar, that when Doc and Claude Fincher came back to the car, Doc said, "They were going to confiscate the gold" and he was accused of stealing the gold in Mexico. Ova said that instead of confiscating the gold, they gave Doc a "hold certificate"* for $97,000.

Leo O'Connell was always ready and willing to assist Ova. O'Connell wrote[246] to her on September 12, 1952 concerning his efforts to learn more about Doc and Ova's Denver Mint deposit. His letter, in part:

---

* Ova and Letha used the terms "Hold Certificate" and "Receipt" synonymously.

...Two men, Lawyer Wallace and Mr. J.L. Greer are up to something tricky...the birds also said they had checked the Denver Mint and positively found out there was ninety-seven thousand there that Doc left there in 1943. It seems to me that was the date he took it there. God, I've heard Doc tell it so often then. Those birds told me not to tell you what they had found out. Come see us so we can talk.   —Leo

~

Had Judge Wallace and J.L. Greer been successful in finding proof that Doc had turned over gold bars to the Denver Mint? The reason for O'Connell's concern that Wallace and Greer were "up to something tricky" is unknown, however their relationship to each other was their involvement in the efforts to recover the Victorio Peak treasure, which was spelled out eighteen months earlier (March 14, 1951) in a transcribed recorded phone conversation between Farris and Colonel John G. Shinkle at White Sands:

> *PHARIS (sic): Would it do us any good for us to meet you and show you these contracts like Judge Wallace's of Del Rio as he is one of the principals in the affair because he is definitely required to do this work. He had put a lot of money into it.*

September 26, 1952

Ova's popularity in the political side of issues surrounding the Noss treasure trove was not solid. In fact, the mere mention of Ova's name caused some politicians who were in a position to help her to shy away, if not to oppose her and to work against her. Some formed secret coalitions that allegedly involved top government officials; such as Commissioner of Public Lands Johnny Walker, who was said to have promised to "cancel" Ova's permits or "lease" at Victorio Peak and give it to someone of his choosing. Consequently, Ova allowed others to act on her behalf, such as D.C. Scott of Ponca City, Oklahoma. In the early 1930s, Ova lived in Ponca City and perhaps had known Mr. Scott from having lived there. Six months later, on March 27, 1953, another one of Ova's friends, Mr. Herb Lipps, would prove to be loyal. Lipps' name surfaced sooner in the chronology of events when Commissioner Shepard wrote to him in Enid, Oklahoma. A Mr. Bohanan is also mentioned in Shepard's letter, and it sounds as though Bohanan was also connected to the treasure recovery efforts. From Commissioner Shepard's letter[247] to Mr. Lipps on September 6:

> *Mr. Bohanan will be in next week, at which time I will issue a mining permit in Socorro and Doña Ana Counties. The Permit will be in the name of D.C. Scott of Ponca City, Oklahoma. Mr. Bohanan in now in Chicago and told me yesterday, by telephone, that he would see me on Monday or Tuesday.*   —Guy Shepard

~

October 20, 1952

Still pursuing the issue of the gold bars left at the Denver Mint by Doc and Claude Fincher, Ova gained official assistance on October 20, 1952, from Commissioner Shepard, who wrote to the U.S. Mint in Washington, D.C. regarding the gold bars Doc had delivered to the Denver Mint. One month later, on November 21, the Director of the Mint, Nellie Tayloe Ross, responded in a way that was typical of how the Treasury Department misled or used misinformation when anyone inquired about the Noss treasure, in this case New Mexico's Commissioner of Public Lands. Here is Ross' entire letter[248] to Mr. Shepard: (underlining inserted)

> *Dear Mr. Shepard: "This is in reference to your letter of October 20, 1952, pertaining to a deposit of gold purported to have been delivered to the Mint at Denver, in 1944 by Dr. M.E. Noss of Hot Springs, New Mexico. <u>It is a fact that a bar of metal was received by the Mint at San Francisco in 1939 from an individual which upon melting was found to contain such a small amount of value that the Mint charges for melting and assaying the deposit exceeded the gold and silver value. This bar, through investigation, was traced back to Dr. M.E. Noss, now deceased.</u>*
>
> *The files of the Bureau of the Mint contain several investigative reports concerning the activities of Dr. Noss, and his widow, Mrs. M.E. Noss who have appeared to have originated various gold schemes involving an alleged gold hoard, although to our knowledge they have never actually produced any gold.*
>
> *On the basis of information available, it appears that a number of persons in recent years have been victimized by investing in non-existent gold hoards. The foregoing is supplied for your official use, on a confidential basis.* —Nellie Ross

~

If the criminal activities Ross alleged were true, why hadn't the Department of Justice filed criminal charges against the Nosses? The San Francisco Mint reference was a much larger deal than Ross implied in her letter because it was a deflection that involved Poor Ussher and it had nothing to do with Doc depositing gold on his own behalf at the Denver Mint. The claim by Ross that Doc and Ova were involved in "various gold schemes" and that people were "victimized by investing in non-existent gold hoards" were all criminal acts considered to be 'bunco" games—prosecutable under racketeering statues. Why weren't they prosecuted, and why did Ross insist that her comments remain confidential? Furthermore, why did Secret Service Agent Carl L. Eliason of the Los Angeles, California office close the file on the Ussher case in December 1939, which Ross referred to in the underlined portion of her letter? The reason is not difficult to figure out: the government was committed to a course of cloaking the Noss treasure in any manner it could, in this case Ross was used as a bureaucratic weapon to further an illegal scheme against the Nosses. The process would continue for another six decades and it would extend to other members of the Noss family who struggled relentlessly to gain access to the Noss treasure.

Unfounded allegations were often used to discredit the Nosses, which might explain why Ross wanted Commissioner Shepard to keep her remarks on a confidential basis. Such unfounded allegations were constantly introduced, copied and recycled among various departments of government at the federal *and* state levels, as indicated by Ross' letter to Shepard, and they were regularly shared with the Department of the Army. The process was simple, subtle and effective in its approach, a whispering campaign of character assassination often chiseled out of thin air from vague and ill-placed comments or false accusations. This process and intent of disseminating misleading disinformation within the branches of government reflected the corruptness of certain people who held influential positions, people such as Ross and Howard, and once such letters and memos took flight and got into the system, they were repeated, embellished, and further distorted, both verbally and in additional letters and memos. Some of these protagonists in the Noss smear campaign were highly ranked officers at White Sands Proving Ground and other officers of equally high rank in later years when the range became known as the White Sands Missile Range.

Leland Howard, who often wore Nellie's bonnet as the Acting Director of the Mint, was one of the more prominent and secretive of the protagonists. Ross, a Democratic political appointee, served Roosevelt during his entire presidency and after *he* died, she served under President Harry Truman. When Dwight D. Eisenhower became President, Ross was replaced immediately, even though she had served as Director of the Mint for twenty years. Leland Howard was never *officially* the director of the Mint; he served as acting director *and* chief of the Bureau of Domestic Gold and Silver Operations at various times. Unlike most senior officials of the time in the Treasury Department, he survived six administrations. From those indications it appears that Howard was the one making the critical decisions related to gold, especially in later years, in the 1960s when the *real* trouble began at White Sands Missile Range.

At the end of WWII, Howard was sent to Frankfurt, Germany to make an accounting of the Nazi Gold—Ross wasn't. The importance of the U.S. Treasury's appearance at the Reichsbank in Frankfurt cannot be overemphasized in its historical context, especially as it related to the presence of Nazi gold in the possession of the U.S. Army. Since Howard's objective was to assess and inventory the Nazi gold stored at the Reichsbank, gold that was eventually turned over to the Inter-Allied Reparation Agency, it is not unreasonable to assume that General Eisenhower, or one of Eisenhower's immediate staff, had communicated one-on-one with Howard while he was in Frankfurt. Howard's trip to Germany was an important political junket and it was Leland Howard who was sent, not Nellie Ross. Howard's seven-page report became known as the "Howard Report"—not the Ross report. It suggested that Ross was political window dressing, a puppet to Leland Howard who held the *real* power at the U.S. Mint. Later Howard's direct involvement in the promotion and solicitation of alleged misconduct and criminal activity that led to a "top secret" operation by the Army at Victorio Peak is heavily documented in book two. It is plain to see that Ross had lied to Guy Shepard: she knew the facts about the gold content in the bar given to Eliason at the San Francisco Mint in 1939, she had

Secret Service Agent Carl L. Eliason's report to Leland Howard, and she also had Ussher's Lewis and Walker assay report. However, none of this information was mentioned in her letter to Commissioner Shepard. Ross also avoided answering the core question Shepard had asked regarding Doc's deposit of gold bars in the Denver Mint. None of the important issues that related to Shepard's question was addressed, only the lies Ross chose to forward on behalf of the U.S. Government.

After Ross responded to Commissioner Shepard, Ova drove to Denver and visited the Mint where she and Doc had been given a receipt, or *hold certificate*, as she had claimed in her deposition. Soon afterward the Superintendent of the Denver Mint wrote[249] to Ross:

> *My dear Madam Director: Mrs. Ova Noss, 2020 Gidding Street, Clovis, New Mexico, widow of Dr. M.E. Noss, was in this office today, inquiring if Dr. Noss had made any deposits of gold bars at this Mint from November 1937 to March 15, 1949, or if any shipment of gold bars had been confiscated. Our records in the deposit weight room show no deposits received from Dr. Noss. We will appreciate it if you will please answer this inquiry.*   *—Superintendent (Poor Signature)*

October 28, 1952

After Ova Noss was forbidden access to the Peak, her attorney, Harry Harris of Ft. Worth, Texas, contacted General Eddy by telephone on October 28, 1952. His call was based on rumors of theft from Ova's claim site. Eddy's memorandum for the record was a transcribed telephone recording of the phone call between them. Major Lloyd Purvin, Ordnance Corps and Assistant Executive Officer, attested to the document. Brigadier General G. G. Eddy initialed the transcript:[250] (underlining inserted)

> *EDDY: State of New Mexico had relinquished to the Federal Government all rights pertaining to mining claims, grazing rights, et cetera. All of the land and mining claims are under the exclusive use of the United States Army. There is no legal paper of any kind that Mrs. Noss has, which grants her permission to go in there. She had no mining claim, she has no prospector's permit, and, in other words, she has no legal basis for requesting permission to enter the area to the mine.*
> *HARRIS: <u>They gave me a photo static copy of a permit that they had from the State of New Mexico dated September 19, 1952.</u>*
> *EDDY: Yes, but <u>that must have been issued through error because the state no longer has the authority to issue those because they have relinquished those rights to the Federal Government.</u> So the paper is not legal. <u>I don't think that she ever had a legal document from either the State or the Federal Government.</u>*

From page 4:

> *HARRIS: Well, Mrs. Noss asked me to check into it. I told them as a courtesy to them that I would call you.*

EDDY: Mr. Harris, doesn't common sense tell you that if there were millions of dollars of gold lying around in a hole that the federal government had claim to, that they would go get it?
HARRIS: Well, I think that anyone who had claim to it should go get it, if it is actually there.
EDDY: People have been prospecting for that for years, Mr. Harris.
HARRIS: Do you think it is there?
EDDY: I doubt it very much.

~

The U.S. Army at White Sands had a policy of recording telephone conversations and transcribing them. These transcriptions, and other documents, were provided by an unknown source at White Sands Missile Range in the 1990s during the discovery period in a lawsuit against the government. The individual was referred to as the "Document Fairy," not unlike "Deep Throat" in the Nixon era.

In the years ahead, many such conversations were revealed, conversations that dealt with the Central Intelligence Agency, Leland Howard at the U.S. Mint, the Secret Service and United States Attorney General Robert Kennedy. These transcripts involved highly sensitive conversations that peeled back the true facts on the Army's "top secret" and illegal excavation of Victorio Peak *and* the removal of large portions of the Noss treasure trove. A few of the transcriptions included a U.S. Representative from Levelland, Texas who was the chairman of the Arms Appropriation Committee. But those documents were merely the tip of the iceberg when compared to others that prove parties in the government stole from the Noss treasure.

Eddy knew, or should have known, that the condemnation proceedings were still in the process of litigation and it would be months before the federal government had any say over who did or did not go onto the areas in question on the range, especially Victorio Peak in Section 16 where Ova had valid permits to stay on her claim site. Eddy was simply strong-arming Harris, as he had Ova Noss.

Additionally, for one to accept Eddy's view that there was no substance to the existence of a treasure trove at Victorio Peak is to accept the notion that the Treasury Department and the Secret Service were not in the information loop with the executive office and the Defense Department, and most certainly the FBI. The entire time that Doc was selling gold from Victorio Peak he was being watched and followed by the Secret Service. Seven years earlier, Noss had already made contact with President Roosevelt to come to terms on an agreement concerning the treasure, but, because of prevailing circumstances, Doc never kept the appointment. Parties in the government knew the treasure was there—and they wanted it! Events would eventually unfold that proved the military at White Sands Missile Range and others illegally removed tons of gold from the Noss treasure.

August 27, 1952

Commissioner Guy Shepard wrote one of the more important letters ever written by any Commissioner of Public Lands. Commanding General Eddy had challenged Ova and Doc Noss' prior prospecting and lode claims to Section 16 *and* Victorio Peak when he said, "I don't think that she ever had a legal document from either the State or the Federal Government." Harris took the message to Ova, who in turn contacted Commissioner Shepard, who then wrote[251] to General Eddy on August 27, 1952 rebuffing his comments:

> *To Who It May Concern: This is to say that Mrs. Ova M. Noss is the only Mrs. Noss who had had any contact with the State Land Office during my administration and the records of this office disclose.*
>
> *That upon expiration of Prospecting Permits Nos. 2137-38-39-40, in the name of M.E. Noss, Mrs. Ova Noss and Willard E. Holt dated March 1, 1946, Mrs. Ova M. Noss was granted permits Nos. M-2723-25-26-27, M-2771-2-3-4, dated January 10, 1949 when the same expired. Since that date the United States of America, by Condemnation Proceedings No. 394 in Federal Court for the District of New Mexico had taken exclusive possession of this area—Section 16, Township 16 South, Range 3 East. This office may grant no permits, except by authorization of United States authorities.*
>
> *Our records do not disclose any rights to any other Mrs. Noss who may have purported to be the wife of the late Dr. M.E. Noss by a subsequent marriage.*
>
> *—Guy Shepard, Commissioner of Public Lands*

Eddy's foundation that the Noss family had no right to any treasure was based on his homespun notion that the Nosses never had *any* claim, and it could only have meant mining claim, prospector's permits, lode claims or treasure trove permit issued by the Land Office. He was dead wrong and he probably knew it while he spoke to Harris. But there was far more to the legal issue that came into play later; a huge error was committed during the condemnation that fell in Ova Noss' favor. It will be discussed later when it becomes an issue again. But even if Eddy *was* correct, he was receiving poor counsel; the issues raised over Doc and Ova Noss finding the treasure trove as opposed to whether or not they had a mining claim or prospector's permit, or any other claim, were completely separate issues and Eddy most likely knew it when he talked to Harris. His further hypothetical supposition that "if there were millions of dollars of gold lying around in a hole that the federal government had claim to, that they would go get it" meant two things: Eddy arbitrarily claimed that if the gold hoard existed, it belonged to the government and if the gold was there the government would go get it—which they eventually did, committing a string of serious crimes in the process.

In spite of Eddy's legal theory as to Ova Noss' rights, claims, and permits covering Victorio Peak and other Noss claim sites, Commissioner Guy Shepard went forward on September 29, 1952 and issued a prospector's permit[252] to D.C. Scott of Ponca City, Oklahoma for a payment of $8.00 on Ova's behalf for Section 16, T-16S, R-3E, claim sites 1-2-3-4-5-6-7-8. That record, combined with a complete survey and inventory[253] of all claims filed and given since May 29, 1939, indicate a rich history of properly recorded filing over the years. Also a letter dated December 1961 by Attorney Robert Martin confirmed that Ova had properly refiled her claim on September 29, 1952. Even though D.C. Scott had filed it on Ova's behalf, her claim was extended for three more years, until October 29, 1955, but Eddy chose to lie.

~

Although she was on the outside looking in, Ova stayed the course and protected her right to the treasure by establishing documentation that superseded others *before* the military came to Tularosa Basin and *after* they removed her from her claim site, a chain of unbroken events and documentation that she aggressively pursued. The records on file in various counties in New Mexico and in the Land Office at Santa Fe indicate a long and continuous practice by Doc and Ova Noss of filing the appropriate claims for Victorio Peak and other sites they were working. The records of these filings, which were secured by Ova Noss Family Partnership (ONFP) in later years, clearly indicate that was the case.

With the history established before Eddy came on the scene, combined with the activities of the military when aggressive moves were taken to extract the gold from Victorio Peak under Leland Howard's initiative, it is a casual assumption that Brigadier General George G. Eddy had been totally briefed before his arrival at White Sands Proving Ground on the status of the Noss mining claims and the treasure trove at Victorio Peak.

November 13, 1952

If there was one letter[254] that best explains the trials of Doc and Ova Noss, it is one that was sent to Secretary of Defense Robert A. Lovett on November 13, 1952 by a man named Gordon Bjornson of Wahpeton, North Dakota, a close friend and business associate of Ova Noss. The four-page letter included affidavits from B.D. Lampros, C.D. Patterson, Don Breech, Eppie Montoya, Edgar F. Foreman and Leo D. O'Connell, a copy of a State Permit, and seven pictures. It chronicled the lives of Doc and Ova Noss as it related to their painful efforts to remove the ancient treasure from its resting place.

Bjornson's plan was a two-pronged approach; he enlisted the help of Senator Young of North Dakota, who also sent a letter[255] directly to Secretary Lovett, both letters hitting the secretary's desk simultaneously. Naive and unaware, Bjornson's battle was lost before it began. In spite of his sincere intentions and his businesslike approach to the task, he was on a political treadmill, going nowhere.

November 19, 1952

The next stop in the hapless journey occurred on November 19, when a Washington-based politico, Mr. Harry D. Van Kuran, who, by the contents of the letter, was obviously knowledgeable on the Victorio Peak issue, called Major C. Wentz, Ordnance Corps at White Sands Proving Ground. From the synopsis[256] of the recorded call:

> *(Telephone call from Mr. Van Kuran, Washington, D.C.):*
>
> 1. *A telephone call was received by Mr. Karsch from Washington, D.C. at approximately 0920 hours this date which was referred to the undersigned.*
>
> 2. *Mr. Van Kuran asked if the undersigned was familiar with the Victoria [sic] Mine, which is located on the WSPG Range. This is the Noss claim. The undersigned told Mr. Van Kuran that he was familiar and had been to the mine several times and knew the location.*
>
> 3. *Mr. Van Kuran asked where this mine was located in respect to the Headquarters Building of WSPG. He was told that it was approximately 40 miles North and 5 miles west of the Headquarters Building of WSPG and that it was 5 miles inside the Range boundary.*
>
> 4. *Mr. Van Kuran asked if there was any other correspondence on this property and he was told that there was that Senator Anderson (U.S. Senator Clinton Anderson), New Mexico had written to General Eddy requesting that personnel be permitted to go to the mine and that General Eddy refused this for safety as well as security reasons. Mr. Van Kuran asked if it was in an impact area and he was told it was.*
>
> 5. *Mr. Van Kuran stated that a Senator Jorgenson (?) from North Dakota had written Sec. Lovett about his property and that he (Mr. Van Kuran) was going to prepare an answer for Sec. Lovett to the Senator.*
>
> —*Major William C. Wentz, Ordnance Corps*
> ~

The requests by Senators Young and Anderson were on a journey that also went nowhere, a paper chase that continued beyond December 13th when Senator Anderson wrote[257] to General Eddy somewhat confused over the fact that the State of New Mexico still had the authority to issue prospector's permits on land under exclusive use by the Federal Government.

Before Bjornson became involved, Ova had been physically removed from her claim site by the military, but later, and because of her unrelenting stubbornness, she had been permitted from time to time to inspect her claim, but that was it—nothing more. It served the Army's purposes more than it benefited Ova Noss; it kept her pacified, busy at times, but most importantly they knew where she was, what she was concentrating on, and where they needed to look for the treasure when the time came. Bjornson was there to get something done, but his efforts were destined to fail; hidden and lurking behind the scenes were people who knew of the treasure's existence, powerful officials who had their own designs on the Noss treasure trove.

The best efforts ever put forth to recover the treasure were done at the hands of Ova and Doc Noss, efforts necessarily funded by the small amount of gold that Doc removed for such purposes, to sustain them and those who worked with them on the recovery efforts. Money was also raised through agreements with certain individuals who had an earnest interest in the treasure and who had the funds to invest. Gold does strange things to people who wish to take it dishonestly and tales of the lure of gold and how it affects certain people fill the shelves of libraries and homes around the world. Powerful, greedy individuals within the United States Government were no exception. For the modern Army, it started in the battlefields of Europe and found its way to Victorio Peak after the defeat of Hitler.

The issues over the Noss claim at Victorio Peak had bounced back and forth between Washington, D.C. and New Mexico time and again from the day the news of the discovery became public, but the number of individuals who involved themselves in a positive manner was greatly exceeded in number by individuals who chose to steal it. One of the good guys at the state level in New Mexico was Oscar Jordan, but he had not yet arrived on the scene; he would not arrive until the summer of 1953 as General Counsel for the New Mexico State Land Office. Oscar Jordan was sympathetic to and was the "point of contact" between the Nosses and the various New Mexico State Land Commissioners throughout the years until the fall of 1982 when he left the Land Office.

A lot was happening at Victorio Peak when Nellie Ross wrote to Commissioner Shepard on November 21, 1952; affidavits were flooding the Land Office that the Noss treasure was real. The Secretary of Defense and Robert A. Lovett had also received information on matters related to Victorio Peak. Oscar Jordan would say later, "The only reason the Land Office did not renew them [the Noss mining permits] or convert them to 1955-type leases when requested by the Nosses was because the Army had condemned the right of the state to do so."

When Nellie Ross wrote to Commissioner Shepard, the Nosses had prospecting and mining permits for Victorio Peak and areas surrounding it—and that was a problem for Leland Howard. The Army at White Sands wanted Ova Noss and her family out of the way. Powerful interests wanted to go in and remove the massive gold treasure trove, which was later confirmed as a fact in the years ahead. The war between these interests and Ova Noss and her family was only beginning. Two decades later, Leland Howard would use the same disinformation tactic Nellie Tayloe Ross had used with Guy Shepard to gain illegal access to the interior of Victorio Peak when more than one billion dollars worth of gold bars was stolen by these interests in a single extraction, but it was only a grain of sand in a bucket as to what was stored deeper inside the mountain.

November 24, 1952

The issue of allowing Ova Noss to return to her claim site had a weighted value depending on who was making the suggestions. On November 24, 1952, the first of several internal letters began to emerge. Lt. Colonel Russell J. Baldwin, Deputy Executive Officer, Ordnance Corps, U.S. Army wrote[258] to G4* concerning Senator Young's request. The letter consisted of some of the history of Victorio Peak, more detail on the operation of the White Sands Proving Ground and a concern regarding safety and interference with the military's firing schedules.

At face value, these concerns were certainly legitimate ones. Baldwin said in his letter that, "the corps obviously cannot look with favor upon entry into the range area of any persons not essential to the intensive technical program." Baldwin then offered up a caveat and qualified his remarks:

> *However, if the Department of the Army determines that good public relations and potential advantage to the Government dictates the granting of a permit under these circumstances, the Chief of Ordnance will not impose objection thereto providing timing and control measures are compatible with mission objectives of the Proving Ground.*

> ~

According to Baldwin, Eddy's issues were not critical as long as the Army's mission objectives were not impeded. However, Baldwin did not run White Sands—Eddy did, who was set on a course not in accordance with Baldwin's suggestions.

Baldwin then recommended that any permit granted "be issued by the Department of the Army rather than the Ordnance Corps or the Commanding General at White Sands Proving Ground, and that the Department of the Army assume responsibility for the inclusion of terms protecting the Government...."

In paragraph five, Baldwin suggested that matters concerning the entry should be worked out "between the *permittee* and the Commanding General with the understanding that the operational mission in all cases must take precedence."

Then the matter of treasure came up. Apparently, Baldwin was well versed on the matter and the problems the Army had with Ova Noss, her claim, and the early history of the treasure trove as it involved Doc Noss. Baldwin concluded by saying:

> *It is noted for the record that since recovery of treasure is a factor, a legal opinion will be required of the Judge Advocate General. It is understood that granting of a permit will be considered after submission through this office to your office of a plan mutually agreeable to by the Commanding General and the proposed permittee.*   —*Baldwin*

> ~

The letter set the boundaries for such a permit to be issued. Baldwin's letter was perhaps the most honest and cooperative recommendation the military would ever make concerning the Noss treasure.

---

* Supply and logistics.

November 26, 1952

On the heels of Baldwin's comments came another glimmer of hope from the Chief, Legislative & Liaison Division, T.A. Young, that on the surface there appeared to be a chance that Bjornson, who was acting for Ova, *might* get a permit. His letter[259] dated November 26, 1952, indicated, "…it is desired that a proposed permit to Mr. Gordon Bjornson and Associates, including the Noss interests, be prepared and submitted through the Judge Advocate General (JAG), Chief of Ordnance and Chief Legislative Liaison, in turn, to G4 for decision."

November 28, 1952

Then came the bad news from Senator Anderson who wrote[260] to Ova on November 28 concerning her request to reenter the White Sands Proving Ground:

> *I have received from General Eddy a letter advising me that he cannot grant your request to have access to the claim you purported to own near the White Sands Proving Ground. General Eddy tells me that he had communicated this information to your lawyer, and I notice that a copy of his letter to me was sent to Mr. Jess R. Nelson, who is representing you.*
>
> *The contents of the memorandum which he enclosed has been designated 'Restricted Security Information' and I am, therefore, not able to forward it to you.*
>
> *—Clinton Anderson*

~

In spite of Anderson's thoughts concerning the recovery of the treasure and his notion that a JAG attorney's opinion was needed, his aspirations to develop a plan so that Ova Noss could return to the treasure site was an exercise in futility. The Department of the Army had apparently gotten to Anderson and gave him a new balloon to float—*restricted security information,* which meant anything the military wanted it to mean. What restricted security information? Ova Noss knew more about those hills than Eddy could have learned in his lifetime. There was never any restricted secret military plan for the Hembrillo Basin that would have fallen under the mantle of strict secrecy, except the treasure itself; eventually it would become a "top secret" military operation, but the area itself was in no-man's land, a parched desert basin that was on the fringe of the range's testing area. If there were ever any strict security issues for the Hembrillo Basin, they had nothing to do with military operations, except to steal the treasure, which they did.

If Senator Anderson was looking for a way out of helping Ova with her problem, the *Restricted Security Information* dodge was the best card he could deal. The more likely scenario was that Anderson was told more about the true end game the military had in store for the Noss treasure, more than he cared to share with Ova; it wouldn't be the first time it would happen. Later Representative George Mahon of Levelland, Texas was given "top secret" information that dealt with the Army's agenda concerning the treasure during another Army-recorded conversation. The Commanding General at that time was John G. Shinkle, but all future illegal activity by the government and the U.S. Army, and the treasure, began under the command of Brigadier General Eddy.

December 2, 1952

As early as December 2, 1952, and in spite of the newly installed military objectives at White Sands Proving Ground, Ova Noss had a valid State Prospector's Permit for Victorio Peak in Section 16. On that day Commissioner Shepard wrote[261] to Brigadier General Eddy asking him to establish a "co-use" agreement with Ova, permitting her to operate her State Prospector's Permit.

December 3, 1952

The next day, Ova asked Senator Chavez for help for the second time. He wrote[262] to General Eddy on her behalf. At the same time, Ova asked Senator Anderson for more help, not knowing that her letter to him was crossing in the mail with his *Restricted Security Information* message. In the face of all adversity the New Mexico Land office said that Ova had the legal right to remain on her claim site until the end of her permit, but the Army refused to allow her entrance. In defiance of Eddy's orders, Ova periodically slipped onto the range to inspect and protect her personal property. Her concern was that when she was not there the Army would try to get at the treasure.

December 4, 1952

The following day, the fog began to lift concerning the government's legal interest in the treasure. A December 4 letter[263] by JAG Chief (Lands Division) Lieutenant Colonel Byrnes Bentley relative to Bjornson's November 26 request for "permission to excavate a cave in Mt. Victoria" was examined by Bentley. He wrote: (underlining inserted)

> *This office concurs in the legal aspects of the action recommended in comment No. 2, dated November 26, 1952, relative to an application by Mr. Gordon Bjornson and Associates for permission to excavate a cave on Mt. Victoria within the White Sands Proving Ground, New Mexico, for the purpose of recovering treasure trove. Pending taking the action recommended, no opinion is expressed by this office as to the interests, <u>if any</u>, the United States might have in the property.*

~

The government knew precisely what its interests were in the *use* of the land, but Bentley's "*property*" reference was the Noss treasure, which is *personal* property. He also went on record strongly suggesting that the "United States" had no interest at all.

Another paradoxical issue in 1952 related to Ova not being allowed to go to and from her claim site was evident by virtue of certain lease agreements issued to farmers and ranchers by the federal government due to condemnation. As previously mentioned in Chapter 19, the government leased various lands from ranchers and farmers in the form of *lease and suspension agreements* that stipulated their lands would eventually be returned a foolish dream. The government kept the land. However, the ranchers and farmers *were* permitted to go to and from their ranches under the provisions that during tests that might endanger them, they were required to leave; they were then paid money for the time they were required to be away. In contrast, Ova Noss was totally banned from returning to her claim. One of the ranches where a lease and suspension agreement was issued was the Henderson ranch, which lay at the foot of Victorio Peak.

December 9, 1952

Five days later, H. O'Neill, Assistant Chief, Real Estate Management and Disposal Division at White Sands Proving Ground, wrote to the Division Engineer in Dallas, Texas, concerning the Victorio Peak problem. The letterhead[264] was entitled AIR MAIL IMMEDIATE ACTION. The subject was "Authorization to permit excavation in Mt. Victoria, New Mexico." O'Neill's December 9 letter, in part:

> *...Concerning an application by Mr. Gordon Bjornson, Wahpeton, North Dakota, for permission to complete an excavation on Mt. Victoria within the White Sands Proving Ground, New Mexico, is referred for the furnishing of the following information: a) In whom title to subject property is vested. b) In the event the property is leased from the state of New Mexico, the matter should be coordinated with appropriate agencies of the State in regard to the present permit No. M-3901-2-3-4-5-6-7-8 dated September 29, 1952, granted by the Office of the Commissioner of Public Lands, Santa Fe, New Mexico, To D.C. Scott, Ponca City, Okalahoma to prospect for lode minerals, as indicated in paragraph 4 of Comment no. 2. c) Any conditions to be incorporated in the license from the United States to the State's permittee should be coordinated with the Commanding General, White Sands Proving Ground, as indicated in paragraphs 4 and 5 of Comment No. 1, from Chief of Ordnance.*   — H. O'Neill
>
> ~

The letter was merely a response to the earlier request by Gordon Bjornson on Ova's behalf, which had been requested back in September. It becomes obvious that such a request was appropriate and needed only to be "coordinated" and approved by Eddy, which he refused to do. O'Neill was apparently not in the official party line concerning the treasure. The fog thickened.

December 12, 1952

Less than two weeks before Christmas, and during the midst of the turmoil in their efforts to return to Victorio Peak, Ova and Letha went to see Benson Newell and asked him for an affidavit concerning a gold bar Doc had shown him, an incident he had mentioned to her in an earlier interview when he claimed that he had actually held one of Doc's gold bars. Without hesitation, Newell signed an affidavit[265] and gave it to Ova. The affidavit described the bar as:

> *...a small bar of metal about 3 inches wide and about 3 inches to 4 inches thick and about 5 inches long.*   —J. B. Newell
>
> ~

Newell said the bar was very heavy and that there were two holes already drilled in it when he had it in his possession. The murder trial of Charley Ryan was more than three years in the past and perhaps Newell felt safe under the shelter of time gone by in giving an affidavit to Ova that he had in fact held a bar that was given to him by Doc, although Newell did not say or claim he had knowledge that the bar was gold.

December 16, 1952

By December 16, it had finally been decided—almost finally decided. Colonel Charles H. McNutt, District Engineer, wrote a somewhat lengthy letter[266] outlining to division engineers in Dallas, Texas his view on the ongoing issue of Ova getting permission to go to the Peak. Here are parts of McNutt's December 16 letter:

> *Section 16, township 16 South, Range 3 East, on which the so-called Victoria Peak is located, is six miles [5.26 miles] within the project by direct line from the westerly boundary of the Proving Ground. However, six hours' travel time round-trip by vehicle would be required in using the property for the investigations described. Permits to enter, therefore, of short duration, would not be of much benefit to the investigators.*
>
> *The Army, Navy and Air Force are represented in the mission objectives of the Proving Ground, and the presence of persons inside the military area cannot be permitted without jeopardizing the security required in the conduct of these activities. Therefore, the Commanding General, White Sands Proving Ground, cannot approve the granting of the subject permit or license.*
>
> *The District Engineer has also received numerous contacts from persons at various locations interested in this matter. The present views of the Commanding General, as above indicated, are fully concurred in.*   —McNutt
>
> ~

An even heavier fog settled over the hopes of Ova getting back onto the Peak. One would assume that the answer to Ova's request was a resounding— No! But it was not a *final* no, not yet.

December 17, 1952

More things surfaced. Karl Shadel had contacted the Commissioner of the Land Office, Guy Shepard, to learn the status of Ova's permit and found that "such had been renewed and extended to March 29, 1953." Shadel's letter of December 17 to the commanding general talks about a similar matter, that of a missing photo* taken by Ova Noss. Shadel wrote[267] in part:

> *There is also lacking from the enclosures certain photographs taken by the applicant of excavation activities previously conducted at the site of the buried treasure. Prints of these, of course, are not available to furnish for your files.*   —Shadel

---

* A matter that has infuriated the Noss family was the theft of a significant number of items from the Land Office file boxes. One of the missing records was a group of photos of the treasure inside Victorio Peak.

December 18, 1952

Ova reached out for help in getting a true mining *lease* on the Noss treasure trove claim site in lieu of her current mining *permit*. On December 18, she once again reached out to Senator Clinton Anderson. He wrote[268] back to her concerning his efforts:

> *In accordance with your request, I have today written the Commissioner of Public Lands asking him to consider your request of transfer from permit to lease.*
> —*Clinton P. Anderson*

December 19, 1952

Three days went by. Colonel Herbert E. Tumin, CE Executive Officer, wrote[269] to the Army's Washington, D.C. real estate division. The AIR MAIL memorandum, in part:

> *…Since the Commanding General, White Sands Proving Ground, is so firm in his opinion that granting of subject permission would seriously interfere with the military program and as he is in a far better position than anyone else to judge the effect granting of the permission would have on security requirements and military operations, this office recommends that favorable consideration not be given the request of Mr. Bjornson at this time.*
> —*Tumin*

December 23, 1952

General Eddy got back into the controversy and wrote to Senator Clinton Anderson. Eddy's December 23 letter:[270]

> *Dear Senator Anderson:*
>
> *I shall try to answer your query of 13 December, although it is rather complicated so far as the Noss case is concerned. As far as I can find out, and for some reason undetermined, the prospector's permit, which the State issued to Mrs. Noss is the only one issued by the State on land under exclusive use by the Federal Government in the State of New Mexico.*
>
> *It is my belief that the whole matter is pretty well under control and about to be straightened out. By stipulation of the State of New Mexico, the Secretary of Defense submitted to the Federal Courts the necessary papers to suspend or transfer to the Federal Government all State's rights pertaining to minerals on the land comprising White Sands Proving Ground. This includes the old Alamogordo Range and consists of approximately 4,000 square miles in the Tularosa Basin.*
>
> *As soon as this Court Order, which I have been told is issued in the District of Columbia, is received by the State of New Mexico, this whole Noss matter will be cleared up. Meanwhile other federal laws and rights of the Federal Government are in force and are sufficient to protect the interest of the Government since Judge Hatch ruled in favor of the Government in the Case of Trespassing by Colwell vs. Fort Bliss. I take this opportunity to wish you a Merry Christmas and a Happy New Year.*
> —*G.G. Eddy, Brigadier General, USA, Commanding*

~

Anderson's request letter to General Eddy was not in the Noss files, but even if he had taken the time to write back to Eddy or even called him to ask why ranchers and farmers could go onto the range under a lease and suspension agreement, while Ova Noss was banned from her claim site on the same range location for similar purposes, it would have answered many questions, but he did not. A more serious question arises when one considers Anderson's November 28 letter to Ova wherein he told her that he could not reveal the rationale for Eddy's denial because the memorandum contained "Restricted Security Information."

December 26, 1952

Anderson wrote[271] to Ova Noss on December 26:

> *The enclosed letter from General Eddy regarding your prospector's permit will be self-explanatory.*   —*Clinton P. Anderson*

~

The only response from Anderson came to Ova on November 28, stating that Eddy would not grant her request to her claim site she "purported to own near the White Sands Proving Ground." If Ova owned *anything,* it was the mining permit granted by Guy Shepard on September 6 through D. C. Scott on her behalf, *and* her personal property, which was the treasure trove. Anderson wrote to Ova on November 28, fifteen days *prior* to his December 13 letter mentioned in Eddy's December 23 letter. The question is: how could Anderson tell Ova that she couldn't go to her claim site for reasons he could not explain because the information he allegedly received from Eddy was designated 'Restricted Security Information'? According to the dates, Anderson was providing Ova with information he didn't receive from Eddy until fifteen days *later.* Was there another letter? The discrepancy leads one to think that the November 28 and December 23 letters from Anderson were not credible, in that he knew more about the situation than he was willing to pass on to Ova. If so, where was Anderson's loyalty? Was it with the Army or his constituent, Ova Noss? And what was behind the 'Restricted Security Information' issue Anderson posed? Someone was lying, or being secretive about something.

December 31, 1952

Even under pressure *not* to go against the Federal Government, Guy Shepard extended Ova's permit for thirty days until April 29, 1953. Ova had a good working relationship with people at the New Mexico State Land Office, especially Minnie Cave, who understood and identified with her problems and her struggle to recover the treasure. On behalf of Commissioner Shepard, Minnie Cave wrote[272] to Ova on December 31:

> *Dear Mrs. Noss: Your letter was received yesterday and it came to me from the Commissioner's office this morning with the notation 'Give her a 30 day extension', so this is all I can do. The Commissioner is gone and will not be back in the office. Mr.*

Walker comes in Friday and I am not at all sure that I will be retained. The chief clerk will sign the extension; there will be no doubt about that, this notation will be placed on your permit 'Extended to April 29, 1953 by order of the Commissioner of Public Lands.'

Hoping you will have the cooperation of the new administration and my very best wishes to you all for a Happy New Year.

—GUY SHEPARD, COMMISSIONER, By M. M. Cave

Chapter 29

A Motive for Doc's Murder, Interest in Victorio Peak Increases

On Tuesday January 20, 1953, Dwight D. Eisenhower was sworn in as President of the United States and gave his first inaugural address. Three months later, he removed Nellie Tayloe Ross, a political appointee, as Director of the Mint, but Leland Howard was not touched. Was it because of Howard's performance and reporting of the Nazi gold caches uncovered in Germany and/or the gold inside Victorio Peak? That same month, E.S. "Johnny" Walker, seen here, was sworn in as the new Commissioner of Public Lands for the State of New Mexico at Santa Fe.

March 27, 1953

An interesting letter was written and signed by Herb Lipps and David F. Berggren on March 27 regarding a meeting they had on March 17; the letter is presented here in its entirety. However, Mr. Lipps, who signed the letter with Mr. Berggren, wrote several lines in the third person. The letter[273] reads as follows: (underline by writer)

> *To Mrs. Ova Noss: Mr. Lipps received a call from Mr. Yancey on March 16, 1953 at Midland, Texas, to come to a meeting, that it was very important. Mr. Lipps, in turn called Dave Berggren to accompany him. They went to Midland on March 17th and attended a meeting at Judge Hazel's office. Those present were: Judge Hazel, Mr. Yancey, Mr. Roscoe W. Parr, Mr. Herb Lipps and Mr. Dave Berggren. They talked for a long time on oil and finally Mr. Berggren said, 'Why were we called to this meeting?' The conversation hadn't progressed very far before Mr. <u>Parr bluntly stated that he had</u> <u>orders to tell Mr. Lipps to stay out of this mine, to forget about it, that bullets had been</u> <u>flying and would be flying again. Mr. Parr also stated that 'you know many people have</u> <u>been killed over gold' following up the foregoing statement.</u>*
>
> *The next question came from Judge Hazel to Mr. Lipps. 'Mr. Lipps, do you represent Mrs. Noss?' No answer. Mr. Berggren stated, 'Of course, you represent Mrs. Noss.' Later on in the conversation, Judge Hazel again asked Mr. Lipps the question. 'Would you go with us if we secured the lease on this mine?' Mr. Lipps stated he would go with anyone who is successful in opening up this mine and that he would finance the project. After Mr. Parr's threat, Mr. Lipps seemed quite subdued and seemed to be very scared and nervous after this gangster-type of intimidation.*

Mr. Parr and Judge Hazel stated that Johnny Walker, the present State Land Commissioner, would cancel the lease now held by Mrs. Noss and give same to them and that they in turn were promised a permanent permit from the government to go and open this mine. Mr. Berggren stated that there was no need in continuing this meeting and that he was very happy to obtain this information. This is the sum and substance of the meeting at Judge Hazel's office on March 17, 1953.

After Mr. Lipps and Mr. Berggren left and were on their way back to Enid in Mr. Lipps' automobile, Mr. Lipps said to Mr. Berggren that he would be afraid to open the mine for fear of being murdered and that he was not about to lose his life over any gold mine.   *—Lipps, Berggren*

~

Ova Noss did not have a *lease* on the land inclusive of Victorio Peak; she held a *mining permit* or at least a permit to remove treasure in Socorro and Doña Ana Counties approved and issued by former Commissioner Guy Shepard under the name of D.C. Scott, who was acting on Ova's behalf. But the newly elected Commissioner of Public Lands, Johnny Walker, was now the boss at the Land Office in Santa Fe, and if the circumstances related to Ova's claim in the Lipps/Berggren letter were factual, Walker's intent was to play ball with the highest bidder, which excluded Ova Noss. The letter clearly indicated that Parr and Judge Hazel claimed that Walker intended to use the power of his office to circumvent Ova's access and right to possess the treasure once it was uncovered and, in turn, to extend special privilege to other individuals who had less rights than Ova. If Parr and Hazel were correct and were informed by Walker that he intended to follow such a course, then Walker's plan was corrupt whether he executed it or not. Walker's benefit in the scheme, if there was one, is unknown. The question is: why would he become involved in such a plot unless he had something to gain? Meetings such as the one mentioned in the Lipps/Berggren letter didn't suddenly appear out of the blue. In this case, the meeting had all of the appearances that Johnny Walker and a sitting judge had conspired to use their political positions to push Ova off the Peak and take the treasure without any benefit going to her.

If the allegations made in the Lipps/Berggren letter were accurate, then the meeting sprung from a decision made earlier, a decision that involved Mr. Walker. If, in fact, that was the course of events, it was a conspiracy to prevent Ova from securing what belonged to her. Walker's actions in the manner he handled the Noss treasure issue in the coming years gave weight to the possibility that the plan described in the Lipps/Berggren letter by Judge Hazel and Roscoe Parr had strong roots.

More reason to believe that the Midland, Texas, meeting happened as reported by Lipps and Berggren came in a letter[274] written to Ova Noss by a Mr. L.A. Cook on April 3, 1953, only two weeks and three days after the alleged March 17 meeting. What was convincing about Cook's letter was the date when he knew about the pending meeting, which was on March 1st, two weeks and two days *before* the meeting actually occurred. Cook's complete letter:

> *About March 1st, I stopped at a tourist court, the Cozy Corner Tourist Court, at Portales, New Mexico seeing about a mining deal with the manager of the court. There was a message for me to see Mr. Roscoe W. Parr at Friona, Texas as he had some valuable information to give me. Not knowing what the man had on his mind, I drove over to see him. They were eating dinner when I arrived. Mr. Parr said he had to go to the field, so for me to lock up the car and go with him. We drove about five miles out to an elevator* and parked and talked all afternoon. Mr. Parr turned the conversation to the Noss treasure saying that he was the only living finder left. He said that he was looking for the treasure through the historical way and Doc Noss through the Indian way when they met in the basin and through this meeting they continued to hunt for the mine until they located it.*
>
> *In the conversation that day, Mr. Parr asked me if I would like to get the permit on that property. My reply was NO as that was for Mrs. Noss or Mr. Lipps to have. He said he could get it, that he had a Federal Judge that was an old buddy of his and that he would help him get the permit.*
>
> *I related my visit with Mr. Parr to Mr. Lipps and later on, I've been told Mr. Lipps was called to Midland, Texas for a conference with Mr. Parr and others.*
>
> *Mrs. Noss, I am writing this letter to clear myself of causing any disturbance in assisting you in opening up this mine and that I am with you 100%. I would appreciate very much hearing from you in regards to this matter.   —L.A. Cook*

~

If anyone knew that Ova Noss was the co-finder of the Victorio Peak treasure trove, it was Roscoe Parr. Doc and Ova shared the discovery, not Parr, as future events will prove to be the case; Parr was the consummate opportunist. Two decades later, on July 6, 1973, Richard Nixon received a letter from Parr's attorney who reeled off the Noss treasure story in generally good detail, a letter that also mentioned John Dean, Bob Haldeman, Todd Hullin, *and* F. Lee Bailey. The letter said that Parr was "closely associated with Doc Noss when he was active at Victorio Peak." Not once during the Nixon letter-writing event did Parr ever claim to be the co-discoverer of the treasure, nor did he know how to locate it. The letter was written two weeks after John Dean volunteered information to the Senate Watergate Committee Chairman, Sam Ervin, about a luncheon meeting between Bob Haldeman, John Ehrlichman, John Mitchell, and Dean involving F. Lee Bailey's clients and "an enormous amount" of White Sands gold. This entire account is covered in great detail in Book Two of *The Gold House—The Lies, The Thefts.* Parr never claimed in his 1973 letter to Nixon that he discovered the treasure trove with Doc Noss.

---

* Most likely a grain elevator.

Another document[275] that attributes the discovery of the Victorio Peak treasure trove to Doc Noss was signed on June 10, 1942; Doc and Ova Noss, Claude Fincher and B.D. Lampros signed it. It read:

> *Dr. M.E. Noss, Claude C. Fincher, B.D. Lampros and Mrs. M.E. Noss, being by me duly sworn, upon their oaths, each for himself or herself, as the case may be, dispose and say: that Dr. M.E. Noss, of the town of Hot Springs, State of New Mexico, did, on the 7th day of November, 1937, discover a lost treasure or treasure trove located in El Hembrillo Canyon in the San Andres Mountains in the County of Socorro, State of New Mexico; affiants further depose and say that affiants were the original partners in the venture for the location of such treasure trove.*
> —*Notary Public in and for the Hidalgo County, State of New Mexico*
>
> ~

For what reason the affidavit was signed on that day is unknown, but what *is* known is that in all the years that Parr knew Doc Noss, he never claimed that he was a co-discoverer of the treasure. Only after Doc was dead did Parr surface, claiming he was "the only living finder left," a lie he pursued knowing that Ova was the only living co-discoverer.

~

For nearly eight months all was quiet regarding matters related to Victorio Peak and the Noss treasure site—but that soon changed. In a hand-written letter[276] dated November 29 to Minnie Cave at the Land Office, Ova told her that Roscoe Parr and Roy Yancey were "causing more trouble." Ova had learned that Violet Yancey and her husband, Roy were telling people in Wichita Falls, Texas they were given a permit to work at the treasure site and made additional claims that the property was theirs. And then there was the commander at White Sands Proving Ground that Ova Noss was forced to deal with; she was not through with Brigadier General Eddy, and she fully intended to pay him a visit. She had seen and experienced the worst situations from the time she and Doc had discovered the Victorio Peak treasure; Eddy's gold stars and rough demeanor meant little to her. Sometime during 1953, Ova and Letha met with Eddy in his office at White Sands Proving Ground. Eddy announced to them that he was "going to dig it up himself." He ordered Ova and her family "to stay off the base," and if they returned they would be shot on sight. Hanging on the wall behind General Eddy's desk was a framed topographical map of Victorio Peak. The "Noss mine" was marked boldly on the map.

From the end of summer to December there was little activity at Victorio Peak. Six weeks before Christmas, Ova and Letha drove Letha's son, Dan, to Ponca City to see him off; he had joined the Navy.

January 21, 1954

It was a new year: 1953 had come and gone, and the help that Ova received from Minnie Cave continued; Minnie was not replaced when Walker took over. She wrote[277] to Ova on January 21, 1954. From her letter:

Just got the permit at 1:30 today (Thursday). It is ready to go and hope you get it in time for the weekend. Registered mail is always late in getting distributed, also late in getting from the Post Office to this office. Good luck.   —M. M. Cave

~

From January 1954 until the end of the summer that year, Violet Yancey and her husband, Roy, were busy in the Hembrillo Basin making their presence known to Ova and members of her family, but they steered clear of Ova, knowing her intense dislike for them. They came and went, off and on, walking the hills and locating old sites from maps Violet Yancey had in her possession when Doc died.

But Violet and Roy Yancey were not the only ones looking for gold. In the years immediately after Doc's murder a myriad of trespassers infiltrated the Hembrillo Basin searching for the gold that Doc had stashed away. One such person was a man named Fred Drolte, who, according to revelations in later years, had located the alternate entrance to the caverns, the entrance Doc had referred to when he last talked with Jack Woods the day Marvin was injured and Curtis Noble was killed in the plane crash. There were other sites where gold was hidden, small, individual caches in and around the Bloody Hands wall-art cliffs and in a number of canyons and arroyos that came from Victorio Peak.

It is most likely that Drolte discovered the alternate entrance through earnest searching and from the knowledge he gleaned from Doc's maps that were in Violet Yancey's possession before Doc was killed. Drolte's knowledge of an alternate entrance and other places where Doc had stashed gold over the years, such as the Bloody Hands site in the Hembrillo Canyon, led to the theft of 36.5 tons of gold and artifacts from the Noss treasure. Warehouse receipts, personal interviews and a number of FBI documents prove that the theft occurred. Another source of information concerning the theft came from a civilian Army intelligence employee who was involved in the investigation.

Another letter from Roscoe Parr on March 3, 1954 to General Eddy speaks for itself. Subject – "*Alleged gold cache by the late Dr. M.E. Noss.*" The entire letter:

First, I think I should let you know about myself. Attached you will please find seventeen character references, letters from people who know me, some of whom I have been doing business with many years and some who have known me since childhood. After carefully reading what each has to say, I wish you would check on each of these people. I also wish you would please check with the United States Secret Service, P. O. Box 472, Albuquerque, New Mexico, Robert B. Wells, Special Agent in Charge. He is familiar with my past activities, present position and future intentions.

~

The name Wells surfaced once again, but this time he had a first name and middle initial. In Chapter 12, Terry Delonas said that a Secret Service agent named "*Walsh or Wells*" was present at Doc's funeral asking questions. Terry's

Aunt Letha also mentioned a Secret Service agent by the same name* and referred to him as being one of the agents assigned to protect Eleanor Roosevelt after FDR died. Also in Chapter 12, another reference to a person named Wells was brought out in the letter written by Melvin Rueckhaus on July 7, 1976, wherein he said that after Doc was killed he was approached by *"a Civil Service man by the name of Wells."* Rueckhaus claimed when Wells presented a bar to him it *"did not resemble the bars"* shown to him by Doc. Wells told Rueckhaus that the bar in his possession *"did not contain gold."* Rueckhaus did not recall whether Wells told him the source of the bar. The question that arises is whether the two names of Walsh and Wells were the same person or if they were two separate individuals.

Enter Vincent Palamara. Palamara, shown here, is a Duquesne University graduate with a degree in sociology, a man who has gained a worldwide reputation of being "the Secret Service expert," a credential he was given in 2003 by the History Channel. Perhaps one of the reasons he has gained so much positive recognition for his extensive work can be found in the fact that the House Select Committee on Assassinations during its investigation of President Kennedy's murder conducted forty-six interviews of Secret Service agents while Palamara  conducted over seventy interviews, not including a number of White House aides and many family members of deceased Secret Service agents. He has also interviewed many witnesses connected to Parkland and Bethesda Hospitals where President Kennedy was examined after he was killed.

During the course of his research, he wrote two books on JFK's assassination: *Survivor's Guilt: The Secret Service & The Failure To Protect The President,* and *JFK: The Medical Evidence Reference.* In addition to being mentioned in scores of books on John F. Kennedy's murder, Palamara's work was given greater attention when noted author Philip Melanson in his book, *Murder in Dealey Plaza, The Secret Service: The Hidden History Of An Enigmatic Agency* dedicated two entire chapters to Palamara and his work. Palamara's work is currently a part of the National Archives, Harvard University, the Assassination Archives and Research Center, the Dallas Public Library, and the John F. Kennedy Presidential Library.

Hoping to resolve the question concerning *Walsh* and/or *Wells,* and wanting to learn if a Secret Service agent assigned to Eleanor Roosevelt had in fact shadowed Doc during his days at Victorio Peak, and more specifically had questioned people who attended Doc's funeral, Mr. Palamara was contacted in an email message. He responded and a recorded phone interview was arranged. Mr. Palamara's comments, in part:

---

* It was not clarified whether Letha had referred to the agent as Walsh or Wells.

The good news is that there were not a whole lot of agents back then. Frank Wilson was the Secret Service Chief, a high-powered Secret Service agent during most of the FDR era; in fact, he was the Treasury agent who was responsible for Al Capone's fate.

~

In an email Palamara wrote: (underlining inserted)

As for Eleanor Roosevelt, who refused formal Secret Service protection, she did receive somewhat discrete protection. Top candidates for your "Wells, Walsh," "W" is: Harry Welsh, based out of the NY field office, my number one candidate of the two. Albert Whitaker was the SAIC of the NY field office from the 1940s to the 1970s. Luckily, the Secret Service was very small back then—only thirty-seven agents on the White House detail at the start of WWII and less than three hundred overall; [it's] easy to pin down the 'Ws' (we can rule out Chief Frank J. Wilson.)

~

Whitaker's name was not close to Wells or Walsh and Palamara ruled out Frank J. Wilson and, likewise, Agent Whitaker, so it looked like Harry Welsh was the most likely "candidate," per Mr. Palamara. It also would appear that Agent Wells' involvement with Doc Noss only stemmed from activities he directed from the Albuquerque office and that he was not responsible to protect Mrs. Roosevelt as an agent on the White House detail.

The Noss gold-connection to the White House was mentioned in Chapter 15 in a letter written on October 9, 1941 by Merle Horzmann to Captain Roy Vermillion concerning a planned flight to Washington, an attorney who represented Doc arranged the trip. They were to attend a meeting with President Roosevelt to discuss the Noss treasure. From Horzmann's letter, in part: *"It was that week that the trip to Washington was planned, but never pursued. Neal Graham was supposed to have been the pilot to take Doc and his attorney there.*

More from Parr's March 3, 1954 letter:

I am also quite certain you would get a prompt reply from any inquiry to Mr. Everett M. Grantham, 409 First National Bank Building, Albuquerque, New Mexico. He has known of me since before going to Washington, D. C., and later while he was the U.S. Attorney at Albuquerque circumstances brought us closer.

~

It is worth mentioning here that a tenant in the First National Bank Building in Albuquerque (a warehouse leasing company) played a role two decades later when it stored tons of gold that was stolen from the Noss treasure. Many of the steel barrels that held the stolen gold were assigned to the First National Bank at Albuquerque. There was far more to the Noss/Washington gold connection than was contained in Parr's March 3, 1954 letter. A quote from a letter written by Mr. Parr's attorney to Richard Nixon on July 6, 1973, had a more poignant odor:

Mr. Parr was contacted about January of 1972 by a man representing that he had connections to the top of the federal government, and Mr. Parr would get no permit to make explorations so long as Mr. Nixon was President. Mr. Parr* was asked to assist in obtaining the treasure for this man and his group.

~

The balance of Parr's 1954 letter to General Eddy:

This part of the country has been my home over thirty-five years now, the last thirty here at Friona.

Now, after working toward, with and on the above-mentioned subject for better than twenty years, I would really appreciate an opportunity to prove or disprove same. Therefore, I would like to come and discuss same with you. I might be able to give you a correct rough idea what it is all about in an hour or so.

An appointment at your convenience will be appreciated.   —R.W. Parr

~

In addition to Parr's admitted alleged collaboration with Secret Service SAIC Robert B. Wells in Albuquerque, his letter to General Eddy was equally interesting. Of the seventeen character references Parr provided to General Eddy, nine were people with business concerns, five were personal references, two were banking executives, and one came from the President of the Eastern New Mexico University, Mr. Floyd D. Golden.

What is particularly interesting is that Mr. Golden's name had surfaced at such an early date in the timeline of events concerning the Victorio Peak treasure. It was in 1974 that Golden was an invited guest at an Army inquiry held at White Sands Missile Range on March 5 that year. The need for the inquiry stemmed from a request by the Chairman of the House Appropriations Committee, Representative George Mahon. The purpose of the inquiry was to squelch rumors that a theft of gold from the Noss treasure was imminent because "efforts [were] underway to remove it." Major General Foster[†] at the Pentagon spelled out the urgency for the inquiry in a written order to Major General Arthur Sweeney, Commanding General of White Sands Missile Range at the time. Members of the party who attended the inquiry included, but were not limited to the following: "Mr. Bland West, Deputy Army General Counsel, GS-16; Mr. Gordon Hobbs, Office of the Assistant Secretary of the Army GS-15; Mr. David Norvell, Attorney General, State of New Mexico, and Dr. Floyd

---

* Photo taken in Portales, New Mexico – L/R: O.G. Turner, Roscoe Parr, Letha, and a Mr. Pondete, Pat Patterson.

[†] Disclaimer: Possibly U.S. Army Major General Hugh F. Foster, Jr.

Golden, former president, Eastern New Mexico University." The people General Foster mentioned in his order were referred to as members of "Mr. West's party." Apart from the Parr-Golden connection, another connection in relationship to one of the attendees at the Army inquiry also deserves mentioning—New Mexico Attorney General David Norvell and his direct and personal relationship with convicted gunrunner, Fred Drolte. A transcribed phone conversation* between the two men peels back the veil on the common interests they shared in the Victorio Peak gold and other matters.

However, in spite of all of the pomp, protocol, and posturing, the military's inquiry could hardly be called one, but rather a call to circle the wagons, a poorly orchestrated whitewash, commonly known as a cover-up, to mask the factual events that preceded the inquiry. In March 1974, President Nixon was embroiled with Watergate problems *and* the Noss gold—36.5 tons of it. According to General Foster, gold from the Noss treasure was *about* to be stolen when in fact it had already been stolen and military personnel at White Sands were heavily involved—and so was Nixon, thus the need for the military to distance itself from their Commander-in-Chief, thus the need for the inquiry, thus the need to have an audience at White Sands Missile Range's March 5, 1974 dog-and-pony show to witness the event. Fact—the Army at White Sands Missile Range had investigated itself and it was clear that Mr. Golden's good name and professional status were used to make White Sands' laundry appear whiter than it really was.

In response to Roscoe Parr's March 3, 1954, request for an audience with General Eddy, he received four letters from the Army: March 10, March 13, April 7, and April 23, 1954. According to the following response letter of April 7 from Colonel Homer D. Thomas, Parr had also written letters on April 6 and April 14, and he had already visited White Sands headquarters *and* Washington, D.C. a year earlier.

From Thomas' letter:

> *Reference is made to your letter of 6 April replying to mine of 13 March.*
>
> *Since the time of your visit about a year ago, several discussions have been made in reference to the so-called "Lost Padre Mine" or "Noss Gold Cache".*
>
> *At least one of these discussions was made at the Washington level, and they have all been uniform in denying any and all access to the area.*
>
> *In view of the increased activity on the range and the stringent safety and security requirements under which we operate, there will be no access granted to the subject area for any purpose either now or in the foreseeable future.*
>
> *It was with the above in mind, and to spare you the time and expense of a trip, that I denied your earlier request for a visit. However, if you still wish to come here for a personal discussion, you are perfectly welcome to do so. —Colonel Homer D. Thomas*

~

---

*The document was received from the White Sands Missile Range during the discovery period stemming from a lawsuit filed by Terry Delonas' ONFP organization.

The response to Parr's April 14 letter also came from Colonel Thomas:

This is in response to your letter of 14 April 1954,

General Eddy is absent from the Post temporarily, however, if you desire to visit White Sands Proving Ground, I shall be glad to see you. Please understand that the conference will, in all likelihood, not result in a reconsideration of this Command's decision not to permit access to the range, for the reason set forth in my letter of 10 March 1954.

If you decide to come to the Post, please let me know the hour and date you intend to be here and I will arrange a conference.   *—Colonel Homer D. Thomas*

~

Roscoe Parr's persistence was evident, but the question that remains is what information did Parr reveal to individuals at White Sands and in Washington? If Parr had attended conferences in Washington at the Pentagon, he would have been asked questions about Doc, Ova, and Ova's family members and if he had ever seen gold that was taken from Victorio Peak. In light of the Army's tactics and their activity in later years, it apparently had certain information regarding the contents of the treasure and where and how to access it.

Even while Ova Noss was considering every possible means to regain access to the treasure and while Roscoe Parr was keeping company with the military without her knowledge, the military was laying plans to once and for all remove Ova from her claim site. By August 1, 1954, Major General William L. Bell took command of White Sands Proving Ground; General Eddy, one of Ova's archenemies, was gone.

July 23, 1955

Up until July 23, 1955, Ova continued the quest to clear the entrance at Victorio Peak, but on that day the military ordered her to shut down her operation. Even though Ova's claim was still valid, she was forcibly ejected from the Hembrillo Basin without due process of law. Ova Noss was no longer allowed to maintain a presence on her long-standing legitimate claim; the eviction occurred months before her legal claim had expired on October 29, 1955. Ova spent the rest of her life battling to continue her excavation, but she never surrendered to the demands of the Army. Now the pariah of the Hembrillo Basin, Ova wrote to Minnie Cave for another extension on October 23, 1955. She told Mrs. Cave that if rancher Roy Henderson did not renew his permit, she wanted it. Although her eviction did not affect her rights to the treasure under the treasure trove law, the situation left the door wide open for someone to move in and take possession of her claim.

February 1, 1956

On August 1, 1956, Brigadier General Waldo E. Laidlaw became the 5th Commander at White Sands. Still persistent to work on her claim, Ova was permanently banned from entering the Hembrillo Basin; the Army had condemned and taken full control and jurisdiction over all the state's right, title, and interest in and to the minerals under a lease arrangement by Civil Action 946, United States District Court. Ova's last permit had expired. According to an August 22, 1956, letter[278] from Attorney William O.

"Oscar" Jordan at the State Land Office, if she wanted to continue her search for the treasure, she was compelled to make her case with the United States Government.

June 4, 1957

Nearly one year had passed. To achieve her goal of getting back on the Peak, Ova drove to the New Mexico State Land Office on June 4, 1957, and met with Oscar Jordan. To help clarify her true past history of legal and proper activity on Victorio Peak as it related to the claims and permits, Jordan wrote a memorandum[279] to Snyder H. Downs at the Land Office and requested certified copies of her claim. Ova learned from Jordan's letter that Doc had "staked and filed four claims" in Section 16 and he had "filed location notices and proof of work done, etc. in Socorro County prior to July 1941, apparently thinking the section to be public domain." As a result, he never filed notices with the Land Office until about 1946. The Army's condemnation complaint (C.A.946), which asked for lease and "exclusive possession, pending a determination of the rights of the defendants," was filed on October 4, 1945. Therefore, Doc was *not* listed in the Land Office's *track book* because his name was not on the Land Office records until 1946, a year *after* the condemnation. Jordan's letter indicated that the records at the Land Office didn't show any judgments until 1950 when a "stipulation and consent was filed" on December 31, 1952, which "extended the government's lease from July 1950 through 1951, extendable annually until 1970." Permits were issued to Doc in 1946. After he was murdered in 1949, the permits were extended from time to time to Ova Noss until 1955. After the condemnation complaint was filed in 1945, the allowance for permitting Ova at her claim site was a co-use agreement; therefore, the permits granted to Ova Noss were valid. Terry Delonas had an accurate recollection of Doc and Ova's claim permits, knowledge he gained over the years from his close relationship with Ova and from what he learned by an intense investigation of the records at the Land Office in Santa Fe in the 1990s.

As I recalled, she continued to renew the claim every year up until 1952. By then, the Land Office could no longer accept her money for the fees required to continue the claim because the military had the surface rights to the land where Victorio Peak was located. They told her that her claim was still good, but because the Army owned the surface rights, they could no longer give her access and so there was no point in her renewing the claim. Babe was stubborn and she was determined not to jeopardize any rights she had in her claim, so she just kept sending them checks or she would deliver them in person. In fact I went along with her a couple of times when she delivered the checks. She just wanted there to be a record that she had offered to pay her claim fee so it wasn't uncommon for her to deliver them in person, and she also kept a record of the checks the Land Office sent back to her.

~

But the issues connected to the acquisition of state land by the federal government were complex ones; there existed innumerable questions regarding the land rights of the State of New Mexico, including the question of the source of acquisition of the land by the state. However, if New Mexico had acquired its territorial land from a Mexican or Spanish land grant, it is possible then that New Mexico land never became the public domain of the United States. The land and *any* mining laws would be under the control of and subject only to New Mexico state law and the federal government would have no say in the matter, an issue that should be researched by historians.

Commissioner of Public Lands Alex J. Armijo defined the military's interest in the land it occupied in a letter[280] sent to Deputy General Counsel, Military and Civil Affairs Bland West on July 9, 1974. Armijo claimed that the Army's condemnation complaint asked for a long-term lease and exclusive possession of the land for military purposes. The complaint was filed on October 4, 1945 and land included Section 16 where Victorio Peak is located. The lease was granted, but it would expire on July 1, 1970. Then, under civil action No. 8527, the United States Government acquired an exclusive leasehold interest in the land solely for military purposes for one year with an option to extend the lease year to year until July 1, 1980. Under this agreement, the State of New Mexico still owned the land and the minerals in the ground; consequently, the Army was prohibited from using or mining such minerals during the term of the lease. With such an agreement in place, the public could not enter onto the land without approval from the State Land Office *and* the U.S. Government.

Chapter 30

Recollections of the Life and Times of Doc and Ova—and the Treasure

When it came to the government's persistence in keeping Ova Noss from returning to her claim site at Victorio Peak, one might think it premature to address the issues of the case beyond those specific events, events that took place prior to the time when certain individuals, including those within the government, began exploiting the treasure in the 1960s. But, there had to be a beginning to this story as it concerned the actual thefts, and there was. It began when the treasure was discovered by Doc and Ova and continued when World War II erupted in Europe, and it was greatly amplified when the war ended and German missile technology came to White Sands Proving Ground. These events were ongoing and they played out while Doc was alive and during the time that he and Ova worked together in efforts to raise the treasure. The fate of the treasure was sealed when "the bomb" was tested at Trinity site and was later dropped on Japan. The U.S. had the German-made missiles and a new proposed payload—nukes. Technological development of a nuclear warhead came at a great price, and it began at White Sands. It was this conflation of events that fused the elements of the gold at Victorio Peak to the real story of its fate; the Victorio Peak story is timeless in that regard. It led to criminal interloping by individuals within the military and other parties upon civilian rights and it never stopped. So, it matters greatly to establish now that it was not a spurious thing or an isolated event when the generals at White Sands moved rapidly and without legal authority or precedence on the Noss treasure, especially after Doc was murdered and Ova was on her own. It is in that regard and context—the timing, the history, the facts and the action by the government—that welds the 1940s to the present day and the time in between.

After more than five years of studying hundreds of government letters, memos and documents and private writings recovered from the Noss collection, nearly 50,000 documents in all, and after reviewing all of the interviews this writer conducted, and those conducted by the Ova Noss Family Partnership, a picture began to emerge. It was a picture that had been lost in time during a scramble to survive, a story that had been concealed in unseen pages of letters and notes that Ova and Letha had written, and certainly in the iniquitous writings of Merle Horzmann and other, kinder individuals who swore to the accuracy of Doc and Ova's claim that a vast treasure existed. With those resources and after long talks with Terry Delonas, who had the clearest and broadest knowledge of the lives of Ova and Doc Noss, the true story finally emerged from the fog.

Doc's strange departure from Victorio Peak, his divorce from Ova, whether legal or not, and then his marriage to Violet Mason Boles, were bewildering, something that had been discussed time and again by Noss family members, especially by Letha, who probably understood Doc as much as anyone. She told Terry, "The stress Doc had experienced over the years trying to get the treasure out and trying to keep the government from taking it had taken its toll on him." Ova wrote,* "Doc would go on these hellish drunks because he couldn't reach his goal. I remember him saying, 'It makes me so mad to know what I've got, risking my life to get the stuff down there, to know what's down there, and can't do a thing about it. A fellow can stand just so much.'"

It was well known in the family that, when Doc drank to escape his mental state, there were times when he became unmanageable and was prone to go *fist to cuffs*† in an instant. Outside of his family, Doc trusted few people, especially government people, not the working stiffs, but the higher-ups, the ones that cause the real trouble. "Doc told Letha and me that the federal government had designs of their own, moving in and taking over, and stealing the treasure. They never put Doc in jail for selling the gold, and he never was arrested for possessing it," Ova told Terry. "They knew Doc was selling it. They just couldn't catch him at it. Them government fellows got some of it, took it, kept it, and made money on our toil and labor. Them boys took for themselves, because you never seen any of it show up in court, and they were not about to admit that it was there either. They just stuck it in their pockets. That was the deal, take what they could get, and they were better at lying than they were at stealing." Terry said that Doc had told Ova and Letha his concern about working with the politicians in Washington, the Secret Service, or the FBI agents in the area. He said, "If I bring them government boys down there to take a look see themselves, I'll never come out of those caverns alive and they'd take care of the rest of you, too. Don't think they wouldn't."

Ova told Terry about all the times she and Doc had "festered" over the problems they had through the years. "Doc took gold to the Mint in Denver. They gave him a receipt for ninety-seven thousand and asked him where the rest of it was. But Doc read into what they were up to and got out of there with just the receipt. It was like that with some of the assayers, too. Doc took gold ore to get assayed and to sell. There were some assayers Doc wouldn't deal with." In one of Ova's writings‡ she said that one of them told Doc, "you got a beautiful story, but if you will go show me the stuff, I will let you have the money." Doc said, "I won't need your money then."

---

* O. Noss, ***op. cit.***, p 9.
† The term *Fist-to-cuffs, fist-a-cuffs,* and *fisticuffs* have been used since the 1600s; it meant fistfights that ended with handcuffs on the wrists of those who chose to fight.
‡ O. Noss, ***op. cit.***, p 8.

During the times spent with Terry, Ova told him that she could hardly blame Doc for his feelings, meaning the way he thought about the government:

Doc was a Cheyenne Indian, and he knew how the government boys worked, and they worked us over real good, especially Doc. I learned that he would melt a few chunks of gold he took from the vein or from some small pieces of bars with a torch and let it fall onto the ground in a puddle of water. He was making nuggets. Sometimes he'd make a bar or two from a few molds he made and sell them.

~

From what Ova told him, Doc could do *anything*. But they made him out to be a thief and a con man. He was no thief; he just wouldn't go by their rules. "They made the law to come out to what they wanted it to be," she told Terry. He told me Ova knew Doc had found a big vein of gold beneath Victorio Peak. "Doc took an axe down, never brought it back up either. But he brought back chunks of gold he whacked out of the vein. When funds got low, Doc and Bill Lampros would head for Gallup or Texas, somewhere just over the border from Clovis and sell it. I got notes on the day that Doc got stalled in Texas. The day he got tossed in jail for beating up some policeman. He finally came home drunk and with a fist full of money. Sometimes he would go to Old Mexico, too."

Terry told me that Ova would often talk about the Denver trip: "Doc took the gold bars to the Mint in Denver. He tried it their way." Terry said that Ova later wrote to the Denver Mint after Doc was murdered and told them she wanted information about how to handle gold bullion. "We were looking for the treasure from a map we had. That's what I told them in writing. I wanted to know the exact law about the way we had to deal with handling the gold bars if we were to start unloading the caves. I wanted it in writing. But I never heard back from them for a long time. Then Marvin got word. They sent some federal man around, telling Marvin something about how to do it, how to handle the treasure with the Mint. He wasn't clear on the matter when he told me," she told Terry.

"That's the way they did it with us. It was always secret-like. Nothing was proper or straight up with them. I came to dislike them folks in ways you can't imagine, especially the Army; them boys considered us the enemy and they had the whole Defense people backing them up. I knew things were stacking up for Doc. It all affected him. He suffered more than anyone of us did."

Most of the money they had came from selling the gold bars, small pieces and some nuggets, some natural, some that Doc had made. But trading in gold became too dangerous. Except for the final days before he was murdered, when he and Ryan made the airstrip south of the Peak, Doc went for broke and decided to sell off enough gold so they'd be set for life and could afford to play the waiting game and fight the Army and the Washington politicians for what belonged to them.

——

With the accounts Terry told about their lives together, and from records and accounts Ova had recorded of her years with Doc Noss, a tragic story unfolded. One account Terry told me about happened a few days before Doc was murdered when Doc and Ova came face-to-face in the desert. Ova had been driving across the basin headed toward the Rock House camp when she spotted Doc in the distance coming toward her in Ryan's truck. They slowed down and stopped their vehicles in the middle of the road facing each other nearly bumper-to-bumper. Doc sat in the truck for a minute and looked ahead at Ova, then cut his engine and got out of the truck. Ova had already gotten out of her car and she was standing beside it. Doc's head was down, like he had been defeated. She'd never seen him like that, Terry told me; Ova said, "Doc always walked tall, his shoulder back and head up, the way he always carried himself." In her writings, Ova explained Doc's demeanor and appearance:* "Doc was always neat and he was always well dressed, a natural orator† and a good conversationalist." From all indications, Doc was a man's man, someone who had the guts to come face to face with anyone who crossed him. Ova wrote, "I saw him so mad at that cop [the patrolman who shot his tomcat and took the gold bars from his car] that time. Doc said, 'Why don't you fine me? Why don't you fine me?' The fellow just kept on talking and Doc went up and slapped him and said 'Now maybe that'll put some spunk into you.' When Doc set out to do some serious drinking, no one knew what he would do next, but when he was sober he was a more conservative and genuinely likeable person."

Terry talked about the times Ova and Doc shared; a story that stuck in my mind was when they went to a restaurant in Juarez. Ova told Terry that she recalled it as she watched Doc walk back to the truck. He turned for a second and looked back at her, and then kept going. She recalled her thoughts about that particular time and wrote‡ about it:

> We used to go to a restaurant somewhere in El Paso or Juarez. Things weren't goin' good about then. We went out to eat so we could talk some things over. I remembered that day well. Doc was at his best. There was a little Mexican shoeshine boy there, a real cute little boy. You just wanted to hug him when you saw him. He used to shine Doc's shoes while he was eating, and Doc would always give the lad a nice tip. Doc used to take other women there, but this time I was there, and the little Mexican boy was puzzled. Finally he said to Doc, 'Is she your wife?' And Doc said, 'Well, I'll tell you son, she's my wife, but we're not on very good terms these days.'
>
> Another time we went into this same restaurant, and this cute Mexican boy was there that day. Doc saw him. He said, 'You make good money, boy, how about you setting

---

* O. Noss, *op. cit.*, p8.
† Doc spoke five languages: English, Spanish, Cheyenne, several dialects of Apache, and Yaqui.
‡ O. Noss, *op. cit.*, p9.

us up for dinner?' The boy looked sort of sheepish, and finally said he didn't have any money. So Doc says, 'Well, I'll tell you what. If you're broke, I'll set us up this time.' So Doc ordered the dinner and the little Mexican boy ate with us.

~

When Doc came up to the side of the car Ova wasn't going to talk first, so she waited. She knew he kept things from her throughout their years together, but knew also that he never deliberately set out to hurt her. There were times when he'd get so drunk he'd say words he wouldn't have said sober. But she always stood her ground and let him have it on the jaw, literally. Doc would laugh and walk away, but he was always sorry after he did the things he did when he was drinking. And there were times when it was difficult for Ova and her children to forget those moments. He was a proud Cheyenne, but even though he was right about most of the ways he handled matters, his pride caused him more problems than the whiskey he drank.

Doc spoke up first and the whole story came out. It wasn't pleasant for Ova to hear it, but she knew he was being honest; that day he told her what she believed to be the truth. He said that Roscoe Parr and Charley Ryan had come from the same geographical pocket in Texas, and during the turbulent days that existed between Doc and Ova, Parr came up with an idea to separate them thinking Ova could be more easily handled from a distance. It all started when Doc decided to get away from Victorio Peak and wound up in Del Rio, Texas where he took the name of the Great Kareem and sold astrology readings on the radio, talking back and forth to the crackpots that called in. Doc had hit the bottom.

Doc told her something that made sense, the truth about what had happened. He said that Parr and Ryan had a plan, the purpose of which was to steer him away from Ova. The scheme was to hook Doc up with another woman; that person was Violet Boles. It was a likely story, knowing how Parr worked. Letha and Ova had little time for him, or for Merle Horzmann for that matter. Parr was a manipulator and Merle was a spy in the midst of them all. It took time for Doc and Ova to find out the truth; Horzmann was good with words that threw them off time after time. She was working with the FBI, the New Mexico State Patrol and Secret Service agents from the Treasury Department and she had done her best to hang the Lorius-Heberer murders on Doc, but even according to Chief Summers, she was off on the wrong foot. It was known in the family that Ova and Roscoe Parr hated each other, and that he was always there with Horzmann, trying to divide and conquer. After Doc let the claims lapse, Ova filed the claims with the Land Office in her own name to secure the treasure site at Victorio Peak.

Regardless, the intrigue and the cumulative effect of what had happened in their lives caused Doc to leave and split away from what he held to be most important in his life: Ova and the Victorio Peak treasure they had discovered.

In the shadow of his weakness, and under the influence of others, he deserted Ova—and his dream. His return to the Hembrillo Basin with Parr and Ryan drew bitterness and resentment from Ova and her children, but in the end it proved to be the hope of a new beginning. Doc made her no promises that day when they met on the road, only his apologies and the hope of forgiveness. They parted with assurances that they would talk again soon. That day came when he and Ova sat under a tree and discussed future plans. Doc told her, "Babe, I'm going to be back with you right away. I didn't know you could do this much work. You've done more in three months than I've done in two years." There was far more to the conversation, but they had reconciled their differences. Doc returned to his truck and backed up to the side of the road and allowed Ova to pass. It was the last time she saw Doc before he was killed.

~

At the end of 1957, the front page of every newspaper in the world carried the report—Russia had beaten the United States into space by successfully launching and orbiting an instrument the world came to know as Sputnik. The race for space was on and eventually the facilities at White Sands would be utilized to advance America's *new* manifest destiny—beat the Russians to the moon. By 1958, White Sands Proving Ground became officially known as the White Sands Missile Range, but U.S. space initiatives were still not officially on the agenda at White Sands; their mission was the development of offensive and defensive missile weaponry. The heartbeat of the newly named facility was the Technical Staff Office of the Range Operations Directorate, the organization that ran the missile range. For more than a decade the range had been testing missiles at the facility. Over the next four years, the Athena Program would take up much of the activity; about one-hundred-and-fifty missiles were fired from Utah and flew successfully, hitting designated impact areas located at White Sands.

Many of the weapon systems developed there were tested at the component level for environmental and nuclear effects for government and non-government systems. When the range was operating on a *bulk-funding** basis, the Defense Department provided additional funds for unique instrumentation needed to support the Athena Program. One of the challenges facing the testing facilities was to determine where to locate new instrumentation coming into White Sands to optimize the support of all the projects ongoing at that time. In addition to missile flight operations and testing, a series of tests that simulated the bomb blast effects from nuclear detonation was conducted over a number of years on the northern part of the range.

~

---

* In the 1970s the White Sands Missile Range received one bulk amount funding, one pot of money, as it was called, general funds the commander was permitted to use for anything that was done on the range.

The year 1958 was a signature year for another series of new names and new faces, especially concerning the Noss treasure trove, names with military designations: Rice, Gorman, and Gasiewicz, the new self-proclaimed "Heirs" to the Noss treasure. Among these new "Heirs" were two other men with military designations, U.S. Air Force Captain Leonard V. Fiege and Airman 1ˢᵗ Class Thomas Berlett. USA TODAY wrote about Berlett on September 1, 1992, and it had *everything* to do with what happened in 1958.

The article by reporter Kevin Johnson read, in part:

> *Berlett carved his initials in a gold brick and placed it atop a 6-foot-high pile of gold bars, lighted a stick of dynamite to blow up the entrance to the cave and then walked out in 1958.*

~

A polygraph examination,[281] administered by James McNevin, was authorized by the District Commander, OSI District 17 and was "conducted from 1320 to 1435 hours on September 5, 1961, at Holloman AFB, New Mexico." The 17ᵗʰ OSI* District is situated at Kirtland Air Force Base in Albuquerque, New Mexico. McNevin was a "Lie Detector Examiner" from the 17ᵗʰ Office of Special Investigations (OSI) at Kirtland AFB.

The polygraph examinations undergone by Leonard Vernon Fiege and Thomas Berlett produced identical results. Fiege's examination, in part:

> *Did you find bricks in a cave in the San Andres Mountains in November? Yes.*
> *Is your statement concerning the finding of the bricks completely true? Yes.*
> *Did Berlett also see these bricks in the cave? Yes.*

~

McNevin concluded that Fiege was telling the truth. The military refused to utter the word *gold*; it consistently referred to the gold bullion inside Victorio Peak as bricks, or bars, or bars of metal, or alleged gold.

~

On the homefront that year, other names and new developments entered into the American mainstream: the first video game was invented by William Higginbotham; for Eddie Fisher, Liz Taylor was in and Debbie Reynolds was out. Three American singers were born: Madonna Ciccone, Prince Rogers Nelson and Michael Jackson. Because of political issues, Russian novelist Boris Pasternak refused the Nobel Prize for *Doctor Zhivago* and a 17-year-old Brazilian became an international soccer hero. His name was Pelé, known to his countrymen as "Pérola Negra"—the Black Pearl. That same year molecular biologist Rosalind Franklin died; but she had taken "the most beautiful X-ray photographs of any substance ever taken"—the DNA structure.

---

* The Air Force Office of Special Investigations (AFOSI) was instituted August 1, 1948, and since then has been its major field operating agency. AFOSI headquarters is at Andrews Air Force Base in Maryland.

Endnotes

INTRODUCTORY NOTE
1. Article: *The Albuquerque Tribune* (AP) March 12, 2005

PREFACE
2. Document: "Prediction of Pedro Navares, Convent of San Augustine, City of Mexico in November 1839"

CHAPTER 2: *Doc, Ova and Others*
3. Census: Dewey County, Taloga, Oklahoma District No. 1 School Census Year ending June 30, 1913
4. Transcript: Undated Transcript of recorded conversation

CHAPTER 3: *People of the Caballo Mountains*
5. Obituary Notice: Chicago, Illinois Newspaper Obituary of May 31, 1973
6. Newspaper Article: *The El Paso Herald* by I. A. Cardwell Thursday Evening, November 19, 1929
7. Letter: From Your Loving Kids to father of Buster Ward dated June 25, 1933
8. Article: *The El Paso Herald*, Thursday Evening, May 8, 1930

CHAPTER 4: *Roosevelt, the Gold Standard, the GRA, the Depression, and Leland Howard*
9. Document: U.S. Department of the Treasury, "Directors of the United States Mint: 1792 – Present"
10. Telegram: Western Union Telegram from Dr. Noss to Mrs. Ova Beckwith October 5, 1933
11. Marriage License: Beckham County, Oklahoma Certificate of Marriage October 18, 1933

CHAPTER 5: *Trouble in the Caballo Mountains*
12. Article: *The Albuquerque Tribune* by Howard Byron May 16, 1974
13. Letter: M. Horzmann to Mr. Joe Roach, Chief of Police, Santa Fe, New Mexico March 20, 1951
14. Letter: J. P. Roach, Acting Chief, New Mexico State Police to Miss Merle Horzmann March 21, 1951
15. Letter: M. Horzmann to Mr. Roy Vermillion [Captain NMSP], Santa Fe, New Mexico September 8, 1941
16. Report: Officer B. E. Lewis, NMSP, Albuquerque Re: "Lorius Case" November 4, 1953

CHAPTER 6: *Gold in the Caballo Mountains and Bodies in a Cave*
17. Transcript: Undated Transcript of recorded conversation
18. Letter: Tom Summers, Chief NMSP to Sgt. Amos Leach NMSP August 6, 1941
19. Transcript: Undated Transcript of recorded conversation
20. Letter: Josie Butler to Joe Edwards: January 22, 1973

CHAPTER 7: *Imprisoned, Paroled, and Pardoned*
21. Official form: New Mexico State Penitentiary Description of Convict No. 8372, M.E. Noss
22. Letter: District Judge James B. McGhee to Hon. Clyde E. Tingley, Governor August 6, 1935

52. Letter: Melvin D. Rueckhaus to (EUI) regarding his association with Doc Noss July 7, 1976
53. Letter: Melvin D. Rueckhaus to (EUI) concerning connection with Doc Noss December 16, 1987
54. Manuscript: Page 105 from *The Doc Noss Ill-Fated Gold At Victorio Peak* by Guthrie-Delonas
55. Letter: Xanthus (Kit) Carson to Norman Scott concerning Victorio Peak matter May 1, 1973
56. Letter: Attorney Leonard Pickering to Kit Carson regarding billing costs re Victorio Peak July 31, 1973
57. Letter: Xanthus (Kit) Carson to Norman Scott re: invoice related to Victorio Peak matter August 2, 1973
58. Letter: Norman Scott to Xanthus Carson concerning invoice sent August 6, 1973
59. Manuscript: Page 106 from *The Doc Noss Ill-Fated Gold At Victorio Peak* by Guthrie-Delonas
60. Letter: Carl W. Horzmann "TO WHOM IT MAY CONCERN" letter related to Doc Noss' gold bar -- dated December 13, 1952
61. Affidavit: Sworn statements of B.D. Lampros and Letha B. Berato [Guthrie] regarding U.S. Mint, undated
62. Letter: Superintendent Denver Mint to Ella Binion August 17, 1961
63. Letter: Acting Director of the Mint Leland Howard to Miss Ella Binion August 29, 1961
64. Agreement: Mining Agreement between Dr. M.E. Noss and Rebecca Taggart October 21, 1939
65. Letter: Agent Emmet B. Hargett to Chief, U.S. Secret Service Frank J. Wilson November 3, 1939
66. Camp Note: Merle Horzmann, acting Secretary January 1940
67. Letter: Charles E. Ussher to Director of the Mint Nellie Tayloe Ross January 25, 1940
68. Letter: Writings of Doc Noss; account of closing a cave entrance on the Peak undated
69. Agreement: Between Dr. M.E. and Ova Noss, Claude Fincher and S. E. Montgomery January 30, 1941

CHAPTER 13: *Horzmann's Big Payday and Mr. Montoya, the Spy Sent by Federal Marshals*
70. Affidavit: Sworn statement of Ted Farnsworth December 12, 1952
71. Camp Note: Merle Horzmann, acting Secretary January 1941
72. Camp Note: Merle Horzmann to Carl Horzmann April 2, 1941
73. Letter: Merle Horzmann to Carl Horzmann May 7, 1941
74. Camp Note: Merle Horzmann to Carl Horzmann May 7, 1941 (second letter)
75. Letter: Merle Horzmann to Carl Horzmann May 14, 1941
76. Camp Note: Merle Horzmann to Carl Horzmann May 15, 1941
77. Letter: Bramble B. Ownby to Merle Horzmann May 19, 1941
78. Camp Note: Merle Horzmann May 21, 1941
79. Camp Note: Merle Horzmann May 28, 1941
80. Affidavit: Sworn statement of Eppie Montoya October 19, 1952
81. Camp Note: Merle Horzmann May 31, 1941
82. Camp Note: Merle Horzmann June 6, 1941
83. Letter: Carl Horzmann to Merle Horzmann June 6, 1941
84. Camp Note: Memorandum Merle Horzmann June 7, 1941
85. Camp Note: Ova Noss (Babe) June 7, 1941
86. Camp Note: Ova Noss (Babe) June 9, 1941

87. Camp Note: Merle Horzmann June 13, 1941
88. Minutes: Merle Horzmann Office of J. Benson Newell, Mesa June 14, 1941
89. Document: 7th Judicial District, Socorro County, Case 4794-Crim. State of New Mexico vs. M.E. Noss

CHAPTER 14: *More Camp Notes, Murder, Bodies, and Who Done It*

90. Minutes: Merle Horzmann San Andres Mountains, Hembrillo Basin June 23, 25, 1941
91. Camp Note: Ova Noss (Babe) June 26, 1941
92. Camp Note: Merle Horzmann June 30, 1941
93. Camp Note: Merle Horzmann June 27, 1941
94. Affidavit: Sworn statement of C. D. Patterson October 27, 1952
95. Affidavit: Sworn statement of Don Breech October 27, 1952
96. Affidavit: Sworn statement of Edgar F. Foreman October 27, 1952
97. Affidavit: Sworn statement of Leo D. O'Connell October 19, 1952
98. Affidavit: Sworn statement of B.D. Lampros October 19, 1952
99. Camp Note: Merle Horzmann July 5, 1941
100. Camp Note: Merle Horzmann July 6, 1941
101. Camp Note: Merle Horzmann July 7, 1941
102. Camp Note: Merle Horzmann July 8, 10 1941
103. Camp Note: Merle Horzmann July 10, 1941
104. Camp Note: Merle Horzmann July 12, 1941
105. Camp Note: Merle Horzmann July 13, 1941
106. Camp Note: Merle Horzmann July 14, 1941
107. Camp Note: Merle Horzmann July 17, 1941
108. Minutes: Merle Horzmann San Andres Mountains, Hembrillo Basin July 18, 1941
109. Camp Note: Merle Horzmann July 18, 1941
110. Camp Note: Merle Horzmann July 21, 1941
111. Camp Note: Merle Horzmann August 5, 1941
112. Camp Note: Merle Horzmann August 16, 1941
113. Camp Note: Merle Horzmann to J. Victor Bate August 19, 1941
114. Letter: B.D. Lampros to Merle Horzmann August 19, 1941
115. Letter: Merle Horzmann to DuQuoin, Illinois Chief of Police "Butter" Pyle August 20, 1941
116. Letter: Jeff S. Moore to New Mexico State Police Chief Tom Summers August 29, 1941
117. Camp Note: Merle Horzmann to New Mexico State Police Captain Roy Vermillion August 30, 1941

CHAPTER 15: *Horzmann: a One-Woman Lynch Mob, Doc sees Bodies in Douthit's Cave*

118. Letter: Doc Noss to Sonora County Sheriff Wesley White September 1, 1941
119. Camp Note: Merle Horzmann to New Mexico State Police Captain Roy Vermillion September 8, 1941
120. Document: Photo, New Mexico State Police files, tattooed man
121. Camp Note: Merle Horzmann to Mr. J. Victor Bate September 12, 1941
122. Camp Note: Merle Horzmann to Socorro County District Attorney James C. Enloe September 12, 1941
123. Camp Note: Merle Horzmann to Prince C. Hilliard September 12, 1941
124. Camp Note: Merle Horzmann to New Mexico State Police Captain Roy Vermillion September 22, 1941
125. Camp Note: Merle Horzmann to New Mexico State Police Captain Roy Vermillion September 22, 1941
126. Camp Note: Merle Horzmann to San Carlos Indian Agency September 24, 1941

127. Camp Note: Merle Horzmann to Archaeological Department, Washington, D.C. September 24, 1941
128. Camp Note: Merle Horzmann to Socorro County District Attorney James C. Enloe October 9, 1941
129. Camp Note: Merle Horzmann to Prince C. Hilliard October 9, 1941
130. Camp Note: Merle Horzmann to New Mexico State Police Captain Roy Vermillion October 9, 1941
131. Camp Note: Merle Horzmann to New Mexico State Police Captain Roy Vermillion November 3, 1941
132. Camp Note: Merle Horzmann to the U. S. Secret Service of the Treasury Department November 4, 1941
133. Camp Note: B. [Bramble] Ownby to New Mexico State Police Chief Tom Summers November 7, 1941
134. Letter: New Mexico State Police Chief Tom Summers to Merle Horzmann November 15, 1941
135. Camp Note: Merle Horzmann to New Mexico State Police Chief Tom Summers November 27, 1941
136. Letter: Chief Clerk Lloyd Dolson U.S. Department of the Interior, Washington, D. C. November 29, 1941
137. Letter: New Mexico State Police Chief Tom Summers to Merle Horzmann December 2, 1941
138. Special Meeting: Merle Horzmann, San Andres Mountain, Hembrillo Basin December 4, 1941
139. Camp Note: Merle Horzmann to New Mexico State Police Chief Tom Summers December 5, 1941
140. Camp Note: Merle Horzmann, acting Secretary December 6, 1941

CHAPTER 16: *Work at Camp Abates, More Proof of the Treasure*
141. Camp Note: Merle Horzmann to New Mexico State Police Chief Tom Summers December 15, 1941
142. Camp Note: Merle Horzmann December 17, 1941
143. Letter: Under Secretary U.S. Department of the Interior John Wimfrey December 17, 1941
144. Camp Note: Merle Horzmann December 19-23, 1941
145. Camp Note: Ova Noss (Babe) April 2, 1942
146. Letter: Carl Horzmann to Merle Horzmann dated "Saturday morning"
147. Camp Note: Merle Horzmann April 3, 1942
148. Letter: Dr. M.E. Noss to Mr. L. L. Robinson June 10, 1942
149. Camp Note: Doc Noss to L. L. Robinson June 1942
150. Camp Note: Merle Horzmann, acting Secretary July 4, 1942

CHAPTER 17: *V-2 Rockets at Peenemunde*
151. Selective Service: Notice to Appear for Physical Examination for Dr. Milton Ernest Noss July 30, 1942

CHAPTER 18: *Tribulations of Doc and Ova Noss*
152. Camp Note: Merle Horzmann, acting Secretary May 1943
153. Letter: Dr. M. Noss to Letha Beckwith May 25, 1943
154. Letter: War Production Board Gustave W. Voelzel to Dr. M.E. Noss September 16, 1943
155. Camp Note: Merle Horzmann, acting Secretary March 1944
156. Document: U.S. Army Discharge and Separation paper for Lloyd G. Tucker
157. Camp Note: Merle Horzmann, acting Secretary April 1944
158. Telegram: Western Union Dr. Noss to Ova M. Noss May 24, 1944

188. Letter: Minnie Cave (by John E. Miles, Commissioner) to Ova M. Noss September 16, 1948
189. Letter: Ova M. Noss to Mrs. Minnie Cave September 20, 1948
190. Letter: Minnie Cave (by John E. Miles, Commissioner) to Ova M. Noss September 23, 1948
191. Letter: Minnie Cave (by John E. Miles, Commissioner) to Ova M. Noss October 1, 1948
192. Report: New Mexico Bureau of Mines and Mineral Resources by Don M. Clippinger October 13, 1948
193. Letter: Director, Bureau of Mines Anderson to Commissioner Miles November 30, 1948
194. Letter: Joseph A. Andregg to Ova Noss August 13, 1973
195. Letter: Commissioner of Public Lands Guy Shepard to Ova M. Noss January 10, 1949
196. Official Document: Claim location notice - M.E. Noss, J.M. Lawrence and C.F. Ryan February 18, 1949
197. Letter: Merle Horzmann to Ova (Babe) Noss January 26, 1949

CHAPTER 22 *March 5, 1949 - The Day Doc was Murdered*
198. Letter: Unknown to Mr. C. F. Ryan February 19, 1949
199. Letter: Leo D. O'Connell to Ova Noss August 13, 1973
200. Affidavit: Sworn statement of J. B. [Benson] Newell December 12, 1952

CHAPTER 23: *The Days after Doc's Murder*
201. Article: *The Albuquerque Journal* March 6, 1949
202. Article: *The Hatch Reporter* March 10, 1949
203. Report: Doña Ana County Sheriff Case Report by A. L. Apodaca
204. Report: Federal Bureau of Investigation, Department of Justice, Washington March 5, 1949
205. Letter: Mr. & Mrs. Clay Noble, Jack Woods to Mr. Ryan undated (circa March 11, 1949)
206. Letter: Merle Horzmann to Mr. J. Victor Bate March 6, 1949
207. Document: Doña Ana County Probate Court Record Case 1168 March 8, 1949
208. Letter: Merle Horzmann to Mrs. Violet L. Noss March 9, 1949
209. Article: *Las Cruces Citizen* March 10, 1949
210. Letter: Carl Horzmann to Merle Horzmann March 15, 1949
211. Letter: M. Horzmann to Mr. J.V. Bate March 18, 1949
212. Document: Doña Ana County Probate Court Record Case 1168 April 9, 1949
213. Letter: Gordon A. Bjornson (open letter) dated February 15, 1953

CHAPTER 24: *Prelude to the Murder Trial of Charley Ryan*
214. Letter: Carl W. Horzmann to Merle Horzmann April 18, 1949
215. Letter: Howell Gage, Warden, The Penitentiary of New Mexico to J. Benson Newell May 20, 1949

CHAPTER 26: *Analysis of the Trial Transcript*
216. Letter: Unknown to C. F. Ryan February 19, 1949
217. Letter: Unknown to C. F. Ryan February 19, 1949
218. Affidavit: Sworn statement of J. B. [Benson] Newell December 12, 1952
219. Letter: Donn M. Clippinger to E. C. Anderson July 13, 1949
220. Letter: E. C. Anderson to Mr. Guy Shepard August 1, 1949
221. Document: Receipt for six-shooter taken by Roy Sandman and owned by C. F. Ryan October 8, 1949

258. Letter: Russell J. Baldwin to G4 [Supply and Logistics] November 24, 1952
259. Letter: T. A. Young to G4 November 26, 1952
260. Letter: Senator Clinton P. Anderson to Mrs. M.E. Noss November 28, 1952
261. Letter: Guy Shepard to G. G. Eddy December 2, 1952
262. Letter: Senator Dennis Chavez to G. G. Eddy December 3, 1952
263. Letter: JAG Chief Lieutenant Colonel Byrnes Bentley to Corp of Engineers December 4, 1952
264. Letter: H. O'Neill, Real Estate Management and Disposal Div. to Division Engineer December 9, 1952
265. Affidavit: Sworn statement of J. B. [Benson] Newell December 12, 1952
266. Letter: Colonel Charles H. McNutt to Dallas Division Engineers December 16, 1952
267. Letter: H. Karl Shadel to Commanding General White Sands Proving Ground December 17, 1952
268. Letter: Senator Clinton P. Anderson to Ova M. Noss December 18, 1952
269. Letter: Colonel Herbert E. Tumin to Army Real Estate Division, Washington December 19, 1952
270. Letter: General George G. Eddy to Senator Clinton Anderson December 23, 1952
271. Letter: Senator Clinton P. Anderson to Ova M. Noss December 26, 1952
272. Letter: Commissioner Guy Shepard to Mrs. Ova M. Noss December 31, 1952

CHAPTER 29: *A Motive for Doc's Murder, Interest in Victorio Peak Increases*

273. Letter: Herb Lipps and David F. Berggren to Mrs. Ova Noss March 27, 1953
274. Letter: L. A. Cook to Ova Noss April 3, 1953
275. Agreement: Treasure Trove Affidavit, M.E. & Ova Noss, Claude Fincher, B.D. Lampros November 7, 1939
276. Letter: Ova Noss to Minnie Cave November 29, 1953
277. Letter: Minnie M. Cave to Mrs. Ova Noss January 21, 1954
278. Letter: Commissioner of Public Lands E. S. Walker to Mrs. Ova M. Noss August 22, 1956
279. Memorandum: Land Office Counsel William O. Jordan to Snyder Downs June 4, 1957
280. Letter: Commissioner Alex Armijo, General Counsel Department of the Army July 9, 1974

CHAPTER 30: *Recollections of the Life and Times of Doc and Ova—and the Treasure*

281. Document: Lie Detector Examination of USAF Captain Leonard V. Fiege on September 13, 1961

Index